HUMAN DEVELOPMENT IN
POPULORUM PROGRESSIO

HUMAN DEVELOPMENT IN *POPULORUM PROGRESSIO*:

CHALLENGING UGANDA'S DEVELOPMENT CLAIMS

Peter Debo

To order additional copies of this book, contact:
Xlibris Corporation
1-888-795-4274
www.Xlibris.com
Orders@Xlibris.com
47553

CONTENTS

Acknowledgments.. xiii
Abbreviations xvii
General Introduction... 1

Chapter One
Foundations for Understanding Integral Human Development in
Populorum Progressio: The Tradition that Impacted Paul VI's Life
and Thoughts 11
   I.   Introduction 11
   II. The Biography of Giovanni Battista Montini (Paul VI)............... 14
       A. Childhood, Educational, and Vocational Developments
          (1897—May 29, 1920) 15
       B. From Brescia to Rome/Vatican 1920-1953........................... 18
       C. From Vatican (Rome) to Milan, 1954-1963 20
       D. The Return from Milan to Vatican (Rome), 1963-1978........ 24
       E. People who influenced Paul VI 25
          1. Parental and Family Influence................................. 25
          2. Andrea Trebeschi 26
          3. Francesco Galloni 27
          4. Giulio Bevilaqua... 28
          5. Paolo Caresana.. 30
          6. Jean Guitton 30
          7. Karl Adam 31
          8. Jacques Maritain 33
          9. Henri de Lubac... 33
   III. The Encyclical, Conciliar and Pastoral Tradition preceding
       Populorum Progressio... 34
       A. *Rerum Novarum*: On the Condition of Labor (1891)—
          Pope Leo XIII... 34
       B. *Quadragessimo Anno*: Forty Years Later, On the
          Reconstruction of Social Order (1931)—Pius XI 41

C. *Mater et Magistra*: Christianity and Social Progress (1961)— Pope John XXIII 45

D. *Pacem in Terris*: Peace on Earth (1963)—Pope John XXIII 48

E. The Second Vatican Council (1962-1965): Two Significant Documents—GS and DH 51

    1. *Gaudium et Spes*: Pastoral Constitution on the Church in the Modern World (1965) 52

    2. *Dignitatis Humanae*: Declaration on Religious Freedom (December 7, 1965).. 57

IV. The Influence Of Louis Joseph Lebret In *Populorum Progressio*..... 59

A. Louis Joseph Lebret and Paul VI.. 60

B. Development and *The Last Revolution*, 1960/ 1965.............. 63

C. The Influence of Louis Joseph Lebret on *Populorum Progressio* 68

V. Significant Pontifical Documents During Paul VI's Pontificate..... 72

A. *Humanae Vitae:* On the Regulation of Birth (1968) 72

B. *Octogesima Adveniens*: A Call to Action (On the Eightieth Anniversary of *Rerum Novarum*—1971)............................ 81

C. *Justitia in Mundo*: Justice in the World (Synod of Bishops, Rome, 1971) 84

D. *Evangelii Nuntiandi*: Evangelization in the Modern World (1975—Paul VI) 87

VI. Conclusion 91

Chapter Two
The Doctrine of *Populorum Progressio* 93

I. Introduction 93

II. The Crux of the Problem: The Fundamental Issues 96

A. Socioeconomic and Political Conditions............................. 98

    1. Poverty and Avarice... 100

    2. Inequality and Injustice 101

    3. Culture.. 102

    4. Population Explosion... 104

    5. Nationalism and Racism.. 105

B. A Misconstrued Notion of Development............................. 107

C. Causes of the Problems... 109

    1. The Evil Legacy of Colonialism 109

    2. The Current Neocolonialism 111

    3. Trade and Power Imbalance 112

III. Paul VI's Response: General Considerations................................ 114
    A. Historical Church Involvement and Contribution.............. 114
    B. Development in Solidarity... 116
        1. Aid to the Weak... 120
        2. Equity in Trade relations................................. 123
        3. Universal Charity... 125
    C. The Invaluable Significance of Culture............................ 127
    D. The Primary Significance of Education 130
    E. A Credible Notion of Human Development 134
    F. Means and Models of Change: Violent Revolution or
       Passive Resistance 143
        1. Means of Change: Five Principal Suggestions.............. 143
        2. Models of Change: Consensus and Confrontational
          Models.. 145
    G. Agents of Change.. 152
IV. Paul VI's Response to the Outstanding Problems 155
    A. The Right to Private Ownership of Property 155
    B. Two Consequential Virtues: Charity and Justice with
       Peace as Consequence... 161
        1. Charity... 161
        2. Justice.. 164
        3. Peace.. 168
    C. Three Contextual Principles: Subsidiarity, Option for the
       Poor, and Affirmative Action 172
        1. Subsidiarity.. 172
        2. Preferential Option for the Poor 175
        3. Affirmative Action 177
    D. Two Significant Social Principles: Common Good and
       Solidarity... 179
        1. Common Good.. 179
        2. Solidarity 183
    E. Necessary Conditions: Association and Participation.......... 186
        1. Association 187
        2. Participation/Involvement 187
V. Conclusion 189

Chapter Three
Populorum Progressio and an Anthropology for Integral
Human Development... 192

I. Introduction 192
II. Contending Notions of the Human Person................................ 194
    A. Development of the Notion of the Human Person 195
    B. The Communitarian View of Person 204
    C. The Individualist/Liberal View of the Human Person.......... 208
III. Human Dignity.. 212
    A. Meaning and Origin.. 212
    B. Universality and Equality of Human Dignity 219
    C. Importance of the Vision of Universality and Equality of
       Human Dignity.. 224
IV. Human Rights: The Individualist and Communitarian
    Notions... 227
    A. Individualist Notion of Rights: The Euro-American
       Model 228
    B. Communitarian Notion of Rights: The African and the
       Third World Model.. 236
    C. The Universality and Equality of Rights 240
V. The Anthropology of *Populorum Progressio*............................... 243
    A. The Human Person 243
    B. Human Dignity in *Populorum Progressio* 245
    C. Human Rights in *Populorum Progressio* 251
VI. Reconciliation of Notions: The Need for an Inclusive Vision 253
    A. Impediments to Reconciliation of the Concepts 253
    B. Reconciling Notions: The Roman Catholic Tradition.......... 258
       1. Human Dignity: The Fundamental Solution 259
       2. Prudence in the Priority of Individual or Community.... 262
       3. A Right Concept of Human Freedom 272
       4. Common Language as a Solution 274
       5. A Synthesis and Conclusion...................................... 275
    C. The Importance of Reconciliation of Notions 279
VII. The Ultimate Principle: Its Relation to Other Development
    Factors 281
    A. Human Dignity: The Ultimate Principle for Integral
       Human Development... 281
    B. The Relationship between Human Dignity and Other
       Development Factors... 283
VIII. Conclusion 286

Chapter Four
Integral Human Development in *Populorum Progressio*:

Challenging Uganda's Development Claims.................................289
  I.   Introduction 289
  II.   Problem Statement: A *Precis* of the Uganda Context.................294
  III. Challenging Uganda's Development Claims: The Choice
        between Confrontation and Mutual Respect.........................306
        A. The Anthropological Challenge: The Challenge of
            Mutual Respect 307
        B. Universal and National Charity: The Challenge of
            Authentic Love...319
        C. Universal Destiny of Natural Resources: The Challenge
            of Private Ownership.....................................324
        D. Subsidiarity: The Challenge to Promote Initiatives.............331
        E. Common Good: The Challenge of the Requisite
            Conditions for Development...............................337
        F. Justice and Equality: The Challenge of Equality and
            Fairness in Social Diversity..............................341
        G. Preferential Option for the Poor: The Choice between
            Priority and Self-Interest................................352
        H. Affirmative Action: The Challenge of Genuine
            Government Intervention..................................358
        I. Solidarity: The Challenge of Nonfragmented or
            Segmented Solidarity.....................................362
        J. Peace: The Most Delicate Challenge to Uganda..................371
        K. Association: The Challenge of Laissez-Faire or Restricted
            Association 379
        L. Participation or Involvement: The Challenge of Ethnic
            and Cultural Diversity....................................382
        M. Education: The Challenge of Universal, Integral, and
            Relevant Education 391
  IV.   Some Recommendations......................................399
        A. Integral Education.......................................399
        B. Practical Political Democracy 407
            1. Tolerance 408
            2. Impartial Democracy 409
            3. A Federal Political System for Uganda....................414

      4. Affirmative Action Policies.. 417

      5. Healthy Church-State Relationship............................... 418

    C. Balanced Socioeconomic and Political Policies.................... 421

      1. Selfless Interests and Relevant Development
        Innovations... 421

      2. Active Participation or Involvement of the Exploited
        and Oppressed 423

      3. Strong and Heroic Leadership....................................... 425

      4. Innovations that Aim Higher.. 427

      5. Population Policies.. 429

      6. Uganda's International Reputation................................. 437

    D. Relevant and Sound Religious Policies.............................. 441

      1. Interdenominational Cooperative Action...................... 441

      2. Leadership Formation and Promotion 442

      3. Effective Basic Religious Communities: Relevant
        Ongoing Catechesis 445

      4. Family and Parental Involvement and Participation 446

V. Conclusion 448

General Conclusion.. 453

Bibliography.. 461

To my deceased parents—Henrico Adroa Jalawere, my father (RIP, May 27, 1991), and Julia Drateru Ajikoa, my mother (RIP, October 3, 2005)—who treasured my life, dignity, and rights and nurtured me; to Fr. Lawrence Dema Govule, PhD, and Fr. Mario Ajiga, MA of the Diocese of Arua, who both died in a tragic motor accident the day I left Arua for studies in the United States, and to all people and institutions that care for and respect the human person, human life, human dignity, and human rights and render committed service for the promotion of all.

ACKNOWLEDGMENTS

I acknowledge my gratitude and thanks to all those to whom I am deeply indebted in various ways. I cannot mention all by name, but I sincerely recognize the significance of all their contributions. First, I acknowledge my deepest gratitude to my parents—my late father Henrico Adroa Jalawere and my late mother Julia Drateru Ajikoa—and my family members who worked hard to raise and educate me. I will not forget your support to me since childhood, and I cannot reciprocate it adequately.

Rt. Rev. Frederick Drandua, STL, Bishop of the Diocese of Arua, I sincerely appreciate and thank you for allowing me to use the opportunity to do graduate studies at Duquesne University, an institution whose lofty resoucefulness I will never forget. I appreciate your continued invaluable support and cooperation that helped me to accomplish this project.

I thank the congregation of the Spiritans and the previous and the current dean of McAnulty College and Graduate School of Liberal Arts—Dr. Constance D. Ramirez and Dr. Francesco C. Cesareo. Also, the theology department chairs whose administration and care I went through—Dr. James P. Hanigan; Fr. Sean P. Kealy, CSSp, professor of sacred scriptures; Dr. Michael Slusser; and Dr. George S. Worgul Jr., as well as the entire faculty of the Department of Theology and Duquesne University administration at all the different levels for their contributions which made this achievement possible. This accomplishment would be in vain without your financial, advisory, moral, social, academic, and spiritual support.

The generous support and contribution of my academic advisors/ directors—Dr. James P. Hanigan; Fr. Sean P. Kealy, CSSp, professor of scripture; Dr. Aaron Marckler; Dr. Anne M. Clifford, CSJ; and Dr. Maureen O'Brien—all shaped my thoughts. I am grateful for the diligent and in-depth input of the entire faculty (current, retired, and deceased) of the theology department (from fall 1996 to fall 2006), without which the shape of this work would be different and this achievement would be in vain.

I acknowledge my gratitude to Most Rev. Donald Wuerl, DD, STD, who is the predecessor of the current bishop of the Diocese of Pittsburgh, and his administrative team for generously offering residence for me in the Diocese of Pittsburgh during my graduate studies at Duquesne University. Fr. John Rushofsky, thanks for mediation regarding my residence in the parish.

I cannot express adequately my appreciation to Word of God Parish community. I sincerely thank Fr. Francis Drabiska, MS Ed, pastor of Word of God Parish, for generously hosting me for being understanding and respecting my schedule as priest-student. I acknowledge and appreciate the love and friendliness of the priests I lived with in residence at Word of God Parish—Fr. Charles T. Geiselhart, Fr. Paul D. Cwynar, Fr. Paul Henne (RIP), Fr. Dam Nguyen, Fr. Alvin Gutierrez, Fr. Kevin McKnight, and Fr. Michael McDermott. I thank the Sisters of Charity at Word of God and Seton Hill for their gracious support. I am deeply indebted to the entire parish staff—including Ann Soltis, Mary Lou Furman, Karen Flynn, Sarah Adams, and Theresa Trojanowski—the Word of God school administration, Sr. Mary Victor Powers, the faculty, students and parents, and the entire community of Word of God Parish for their generosity, encouragement, care, and support. I thank members of all the parish associations or organizations whose love and concern I experienced while in residence at Word of God Parish. I could not have had a better time, community, and a more conducive academic atmosphere in a parish pastoral context than what you provided for ten years.

I acknowledge my very sincere appreciation of the work of Dr. James P. Hanigan, the director of this work and, in a singular way, an architect of the work for his sense of direction and his prudent, profound, and wise guidance, which helped bring this work to completion. Dr. Hanigan, your understanding, dedication, encouragements, caring ways, and support were invaluable contributions to my continued efforts to complete this work. I am deeply grateful and thankful to you for your patience.

I thank all the members of my dissertation committee. Your commitment to read the work in moments when other students needed your attention and advice is sincerely recognized and appreciated. Your care was handy and invaluable to my success. I sincerely thank you for your services: Dr. James P. Bailey and Dr. William M. Wright VI. Your generosity with your precious times cannot be appreciated enough.

Fr. Lawrence Hoppe, PhD, your concern and love for me and your interest and commitment to the cause of this work, always hosting me in your parish as I prepared for impending examinations and academic endeavors since the time I started my graduate studies at Duquesne in 1996 is memorial. I appreciate your critical reading of the work, you corrections, suggestions, and moral and material support, which contributed to the shape of the work. I will live to remember your consistent interest in my academic pursuits.

Dr. Roberta Zolkoski, Fr. James W. Garvey, Mr. Richard Bernardo, Kathryn Galligan, and Mrs. Patricia Boyd, all of you never minded when I submitted to you many pages to read in a short time, even when your schedules were extremely tight. I am grateful, and I thank you for your generosity with your time and your critical reading. I appreciate your corrections and thought-provoking suggestions. I cannot adequately appreciate your support and contributions to my academic and general life in the course of my studies in United States, but know that I sincerely do.

I acknowledge my gratitude to the following people, who supported me through their pieces of advice, academic resources, moral and spiritual support, and in many other ways just before and during my studies at Duquesne: Fr. Festo Adrabo, CSSp; Fr. Geoffrey Odama (RIP); Fr. John Munduni Ochatre (RIP); Fr. Carmen D'Amico; Fr. Joseph Luisi; Fr. Albert T. Dalfovo, MCCJ, PhD; Fr. Peter Kanyandago, PhD; Sr. Theresa Wambui, LSOSF, PhD; Fr. Ruffino Ezama, MCCJ; Fr. Frank Siler; Fr. Lawrence Gowon Kenyi; Sr. Mary Victor Powers; Linda and Mark Fialkovich; Michael Francis Burke and Karen Goldbach; the Boyd-Haibach family; Michael George and Peggy Evans Matthysse; Mrs. Diane M. Sasso; Mr. Matthew Boyer; Jim and Mary Ann Macek family; Mr. Jake Blazina; Mr. Harry Skrocki; Ms. Joyce L. Viola, Michael and Mary Folan; Sr. Jane Catherine H. Ajiambo, LSOSF; Ann Soltis; Joseph Markowski; Mary Lou Furman; Maritha Wodjak; the priests, religious, and the laity from Uganda with whom we lived in Pittsburgh and/or studied at Duquesne in particular; and African laity, priests, and religious I encountered in the United States, especially in Duquesne University or Pittsburgh. Your support and encouragements made my difficult times easier than they would have been. I thank the priests, religious, and laity of the Diocese of Arua who encouraged me from across wide stretches of land and sea. When I shared with you my frustrations and discouragements in the course of my studies, your encouragement and advice helped me to continue.

Many other people supported me but have not been mentioned by name. I appreciate all that they contributed to my well-being in the course of my studies at Duquesne University. All of you have been God's gifts to help me achieve the plans of a God to whom I am most grateful for you and for all.

ABBREVIATIONS

AAS	*Acta Apostolica Sedis*
Acts	Acts of the Apostles
AD	*Anno Domini* (in the year of the Lord)
AFER	African Ecclesial Review
AMECEA	Association of Member Episcopal Conferences of Eastern Africa
AMSRIU	Association of Major Superiors of Religious Institutes in Uganda
Apr	April
BCCs	Basic Christian Communities
Ca	*circa*, around, approximately
Cand	Candidate
Cf/Cfr	*Confer* (compare)
Col	Colossians
Co	Company

Cor	Corinthians
COU	Church of Uganda
CRE	Christian Religious Education
CUCR	*Circolo Universitario Cattolico Romano* (Club for Roman Catholic University Students, at the University of Rome).
CSSp	*Congregatio Sancti Spiritus* (Congregation of the Holy Spirit)
DC	District of Columbia
DD	Doctor of Divinity
Dec	December
DH	*Diginitatis Humanae* (Vatican II Declaration on Religious Freedom)
DRC	Democratic Republic of Congo (Former Belgian Congo or Former Zaire)
Dr	Doctor
Ed	Edited by or Editor
Eds	Editors
Eg/eg	For example
EN	*Evangelii Nuntiandi* (Evangelization of Peoples)
Enccyl	Encyclical
Eph	Ephesians
Et al	*Et allii* (Latin), and others

Etc	*et cetera* (Latin), and so forth
FAO	Food and Agricultural Organization
Ff/ff	and the following
FUCI	*Federazione Universitaria Cattolica Italiana* (Federation of Catholic University Students of Italy)
Gal	Galatians
Gen/Gn	Genesis
GS	*Gaudium et Spes* (Second Vatican Council Constitution on the Church in the Modern World)
HIV/AIDS	*Humanae Immuno Virus*/Acquired Immune Deficiency Syndrome
HSMF	Holy Spirit Mobile Forces
HV	*Humanae Vitae* (On Human Life/On the Regulation of Birth)
Ibid	*Ibidem,* In the same place (in the same work just cited or immediately preceding)
ICJ	International Court of Justice
ICPD	International Conference on Population and Development
IDP	Internally Displaced People/Persons
IMF	International Monetary Fund
Inc	Incorporation
ISAP	International Society of African Philosophy

Lect	Lecture
Lk	Gospel According to Luke
LRA	Lord's Resistance Army
LSOSF	Little Sisters of Saint Francis
MA	Master of Arts (degree)
MCCJ	Missionarii Comboniani Cordis Jesus (Missionaries of Comboni of the Heart of Jesus)
MPM	Master of Pastoral Ministry (an academic degee)
MSEd	Master of Science in Education
Mt	Gospel According to Matthew
NFP	Natural Family Planning
NGO(s)	Nongovernmental Organization(s)
No/no	Number
NRM	National Resistance Movement
NT	New Testament
OA	*Octogessima Adveniens,* A Call to action (Pope Paul VI's Pastoral Letter On the Eightieth Anniversary of *Rerum Novarum*)
OP	Order of Preachers
OT	Old Testament
P/p	page

par/para	Paragraph
passim	Here and there
PhD	Doctor of Philosophy
PP	Pope
Pp	pages
PTC	Primary Teachers' College
QA	*Quadragesimo Anno,* Forty Years Later, (Pope Pius XI's Encyclical letter On the Reconstruction of Social Order)
Rev	Reverend
RIP	Rest in Peace
RPF R	wandandese Patriotic Front
Rt	Right
SAPINA	Society for African Philosophy in North America
SCCs	Small Christian Communities
sic	so, thus (suggesting something is erroneous)
STL	Sacred Theology Licentiate
STD	Sacred Theology Doctor
Trans	Translated by/translator
UNATU	Uganda National Teachers' Union
UN United	Nations

UNESCO	United Nations Educational Scientific Cultural Organization
UNLA	Uganda National Liberation Army
UPDF	Uganda People's Defence Forces
US(A)	United States (of America)
USAID	United States Agency for International Development
(U)Shs	Uganda Shillings
Viz.	videlicet (videre licet), namely
Vol/vols	Volume/volumes
/	or

GENERAL INTRODUCTION

Paul VI introduced the issue of true human development by way of reaffirming the notion of *integral human development* initially used by Louis Joseph Lebret. Human development is a crucial and perennial notion many people have questioned and attempted to redefine in the course of human history. In his 2006 Lenten message, apparently reechoing Paul VI's teaching in the encyclical *Populorum Progressio* about authentic human development, Benedict XVI referred to the question of development as a debatable issue.[1] Similarly, Mark Leopold alludes to development and describes the notion of development as being often "vague and contested."[2]

This work is a study of *Populorum Progressio*, Paul VI's ground-breaking Catholic social encyclical about the development of peoples to which Benedict was alluding in the 2006 Lenten message. The work treats especially Paul VI's doctrine of integral human development, the requisite principles, virtues, and conditions to achieve such a development and an application of the teaching and the suggestions of the document to the context of Uganda. It is an attempt to espouse and question the development claims of Uganda. This will be realized in the attempts to apply the teaching of the document in the context of Uganda, but the study can help one to interpret other contexts too. The work is in no way exhaustive of the understanding of the doctrine and application of *Populorum Progressio*. It is an attempt to provoke further

[1]   Benedictus PP. XVI, "Jesus at the sight of the crowds was moved with pity" (Mt. 9:36). message of Pope Benedict XVI for Lent 2006 in *Arua Diocese Bulletin*, no. 69 (Arua: Arua Diocese Communication Department, March 2006), 1.

[2]   Mark Leopold, *Inside West Nile: Violence, History and Representation on an African Frontier* (James Currey: Oxford, 2005), 147.

reflection on the document and the possibilities for its application in other developmental contexts.

Paul VI's encyclical *Populorum Progressio* was written just two years before he visited Uganda in 1969, which was the first visit of a Roman Catholic pontiff to Uganda and the first papal visit to Africa. A critical reading of the encyclical and a careful relating of its doctrine to the situation in Uganda, before that visit and since then, would suggest that in *Populorum Progressio* Paul VI was only directly addressing the problems of Uganda when he wrote the encyclical. However, this is not the case because from the history of his international travels and visits he was never in Uganda before he wrote the encyclical. His direct intention was to address world problems of human development in general, but the very problems he addressed were and are still obvious in Uganda. The work reverses the scope of Paul VI's teaching. While Paul VI dealt with the international development issues, this work attempts to limit the development issues on national level, notwithstanding the fact that there is inevitable mutual exchange and relationship between the two levels—national and international.

Reflecting on some of Uganda's problems, Anna Mary Kayonga made the following intriguing and comprehensive statement about Uganda:

> It is paradoxical that Uganda, the "Pearl of Africa", so richly endowed with an abundance of natural resources: in terms of favourable climate, fertile soil; in terms of human resources; as well as in traditional and Christian values, should have such a large number of poor people. The factors that have reduced many Ugandans to destitution, are the series of incompetent, corrupt governments, and civil wars, especially since independence in 1962.[3]

The above statement almost summarizes the situation, the problems, and the needs of Uganda. It is true even of the Uganda of today. Despite their struggles to develop their country and the claims that the country—so much blessed by natural resources and good climate—is developing, Ugandans face development problems. The country is rich in many ways. Uganda lies astride the equator, about 2 degrees south and 4 degrees north of the equator, and

---

[3]   Anna Mary Kayonga, "The Church's Role in the Care of Orphans and Destitutes," in *Church Contribution to Integral Development*, eds. Joseph Therese Agbasiere and Boniface K. Zabajungu (Eldoret, Kenya: AMECEA Gaba Publications, 1989), 215-216.

stretches "about 400 miles from north to south" and "about 350 miles from east to west," covering an area of about "91,134 square miles, of which 16,386 square miles is open water and swamp," rising from 2,000 feet in the north to 4,000 feet in the southwest above sea level, currently with a population of about 27.7 million people.[4]

Generally, it is agreed that after its independence in 1962 "until 1971, the Ugandan economy enjoyed a fairly robust growth."[5] The conditions of people were at least tolerable if not good. When Idi Amin came to power in 1971, the situations changed. Development was hampered by many factors—exodus of experts from Uganda, the collapse of the parastatal sector, corruption, incompetence and maladministration, and ravages caused by war.[6] After the collapse of the Amin regime, international bodies such as the IMF financially supported the Obote II regime, which soon slipped into mistakes similar to what prevailed during Amin's reign. The relapse retarded development and prompted rebel insurgencies that terminated Obote II regime and four other short-lived regimes.[7] The IMF and Western financial institutions and organizations resumed support after Yoweri K. Museveni took over power in 1986. According to Ayittey, "by African standards, Uganda has performed well and President Museveni has made credible, serious and continued efforts at reform."[8] It is true that comparatively speaking, after learning from some of the past mistakes of Uganda's presidents, Museveni has done better than his predecessors. Suggestively, he raised the level of Uganda's development. However, in this work, the developmental contributions of all Uganda's

---

[4]   International Bank for Reconstruction and Development, *The First Five Year-Development Plan, 1961/62-1965/66* (Entebbe, Uganda: Uganda Government, 1961), 1. Also see The International Bank for Reconstruction and Development, *The Economic Development of Uganda* (Baltimore: John Hopkins Press, 1962), 5. Also see Tom McKnight, ed., *Graphica: The Complete Illustrated Atlas of the World* (New York: Barnes and Noble Books, 2004), 366. Also see *Oxford World Encyclopedic World Atlas*, 6th ed. (New York: Oxford University Press Inc., 2002), 222. Also see Kakaire A. Kirunda, "Population Growth May Fail Development Goals," in *Daily Monitor* (Kampala, Uganda), September 21, 2006.

[5]   George B. N. Ayittey, *Africa Unchained: The Blue Print for Africa's Future* (New York: Palgrave Macmillan, 2005), 204.

[6]   Ibid., 205.

[7]   Ibid., 206.

[8]   Ibid., 207.

different governments since its independence will be questioned by the doctrine of *Populorum Progressio*.

Human development has consistently been a crucial issue in history. Its notion has constantly been contentious, a matter of differences of opinions because diverse views and fundamental principles of human development have been propounded, some of which are appealing and others not. Historically, to implement the various views has practically proven to be difficult or impossible in various countries, including Uganda. Everywhere there are problems related to the understanding of human development.

With the help of the insights of Louis Joseph Lebret, the protagonist of the doctrine of authentic human development and personal critical reflections, Paul VI developed a more comprehensive notion of human development. He termed integral human development—a holistic development of individuals and all peoples. However, the application of this notion is fraught with difficulties. This raises the question: Why has it been and why is it still difficult to implement Paul VI's teaching about integral human development? This is one of the central questions to which this work attempts to suggest answers. Therefore, it is important to examine the theme of integral human development advocated by Paul VI in *Populorum Progressio* and to apply it to a specific context such as that of Uganda where development claims are questionable in light of the teaching of the document.

The encyclical is related to other Catholic social teachings about human development, but it is different from them, especially those that preceded it because its notion of human development and social justice is broader than what earlier documents advocate. Many authors refer to it as the Magna Carta of Catholic Church's teaching on human development. This means *Populorum Progressio* is a great charter, a fundamental document of the Catholic Church's teaching about human development even though it is not the first Catholic document to deal with this issue. *Rerum Novarum* of Pope Leo XIII (1891), *Quadragessimo Anno* of Pope Pius XI (1931), *Mater et Magistra* of Pope John XXIII (1961), *Pacem in Terris* of Pope John XXIII (1963), and *Gaudium et Spes* of the Second Vatican Council (1965) treated some of the same issues Paul VI grappled with in *Populorum Progressio*, but they were more limited than what Paul VI advocated. The document is representative of a remarkable advancement in the Catholic Church's teaching about human development, although its advance and novelty is a conceptual one.[9] This means Paul VI

---

9   Donal Dorr, *Option for the Poor: A Hundred Years of Catholic Social Teaching* (New York: Orbis Books, 1992), 180.

never articulated or suggested a framework and model for achieving what he called integral human development.

The notion of human development conceived by Paul VI as presented in *Populorum Progressio* is a major contribution, relevant for the time he wrote it and for the world and time after the encyclical was promulgated. This is suggested by the Pontiff's notion of human development and social justice and his treatise of diverse issues related to the question of development. He gave a more comprehensive definition of human development than ever before in any Catholic social teaching on development, and viewed justice both nationally and globally.[10] All human development-related Catholic social doctrine preceding *Populorum Progressio* gravitates toward the doctrine of the document, and those that succeeded it, such as *Sollicitudo Rei Socialis*, emanated from the document.[11]

This study affirms that Paul VI's vision of human development is directed to the development of the human person and the practical application of theological anthropology and other theological principles. It is not as *utopian* as some critics of Paul VI claim, because the ultimate purpose of Christ and of theology is integral salvation.[12] The human development advocated by Paul VI is, in fact, the one reiterated by Benedict XVI, the salvation of body and soul—material or social and internal salvation.[13] It is development at the service of people. Paul VI himself also emphatically affirmed this. Theology's goal is the perfection of human life, vision of God, and the ultimate union with God, using resources God has made available to people. He further said the following:

> Added to this is the fact that the noble harmony of this human
> nature, which each one by his own effort and awareness of his duty

---

[10]   David J. O'Brien and Thomas A. Shannon, eds., *Catholic Social Thought: The Documentary Heritage* (Maryknoll New York: Orbis Books,1992), 238. Also see Dorr, 184.

[11]   John Paul II (Pope), *Sollicitudo Rei Socialis, on Social Concerns,* (Rome, 1987), 2-4. Also see O'Brien and Shannon, 396 and Donal Dorr "Solidarity and Integral Human Development" in *The Logic of Solidarity: Commentaries on John Paul II's Encyclical on Social Concerns,* eds. Gregory Baum and Robert Ellsberg (Maryknoll, New York: Orbis Books, 1989), 3-4,143-144.

[12]   Benedictus PP.XVI, "Jesus at the sight of the crowds was moved with pity" (Mt. 9:36), message of Pope Benedict XVI for Lent 2006 in *Arua Diocese Bulletin,* no. 69 (Arua: Arua Diocese Communication Department, March 2006), 2.

[13]   Ibid., 1.

brings to ever greater perfection, is destined for a higher dignity.
Ingrafted in Christ, the giver of life, man receives a new dimension
of life and attains to a *humanism* as it is called which transcends
his nature and confers on him the greatest fullness of life to which
the perfecting of man looks as to its final goal.[14]

This work centers the doctrine of *Populorum Progressio* on a more emphatic
theological anthropology than Paul VI employed. It emphasizes the value of
human life, the human person, human dignity and rights. In the *Proposition
on the Dignity and Rights of the Human Person*, the International Theological
Commission underscores the gravity of theological anthropology by affirming
that "it is not possible for the Church to omit preaching the dignity and rights
of the human person."[15] Anthropology contributes greatly to the practice of
theological knowledge, especially to a relevant development education of the
masses. Consequently, this study will attempt to advance the understanding,
acknowledgment and appreciation, and the practical application of the
teaching of *Populorum Progressio* based on the human person, human dignity,
and human rights. Therefore, a relevant and compelling anthropology is
crucial.

The study will attempt to, specifically, make an application of the
doctrine of *Populorum Progressio* to Uganda's development claims. The
work attempts to show how Paul VI's doctrine in the document challenges
Uganda's development claims and how it could best be applied in the context
of Uganda. The significance of the study should be seen in light of Paul VI's
comprehensive teaching about integral human development. It surpasses
most, if not all, teachings on human development. He consistently taught
that integral human development addresses the problem of both material
and spiritual poverty. This teaching is relevant for all people. Therefore, the
treatise is relevant to and significant for the situation in Uganda. People in
other contexts can also learn from it and use it for reflection about their own
development.

Denis Goulet, one of the renowned development ethicists, explicitly states
that the United Nations' documents, development plans, and manifestos talk

---

14   Paul VI (Pope), *Populorum Progressio, on the Development of Peoples* (Washington
      DC: United States Catholic Conference, 1967), 16, 8.

15   International Theological Commission, *Propositions on the Dignity and Rights of
      the Human Person* (Washington DC: United States Conference, 1986), 1.1.0.

about or deal with better life, greater equity in the distribution of wealth, and the need to assure social improvement of all. He elaborates on this idea: "Here is a clear proof of the existence of a 'demand' for development ethics."[16] Such concerns outside ecclesial circles, such as of the United Nations, underscore the importance of the question of human development and indicate how enduring, all embracing and efficacious the teaching of *Populorum Progressio* has been and continues to be.

The work will attempt to establish the foundation for all other principles for integral human development. The understanding of the human person, human dignity, and human rights is a significant question that touches all people at the core elements of their being, and they constitute this foundation. Paul VI argued that the centrality of the human person demands that in our vision of the world the human person must always be at the center.[17] For the human person to be the purpose and center of every activity, education is necessary. Consequently, the study will advocate that a careful education about integral human development based on the value of human life, the human person, human dignity and rights could make a significant difference in efforts to promote human development. The understanding of the human person and human dignity are crucial for a change of attitude. It is through this understanding that human dignity can be acknowledged as an inalienable (God-given) element of the human person.[18] This enables people to see the sense of mutual claims they make. It also helps people to rethink the ways of working for human development. They may also be helped to adjust their conception of human development and their action plans and procedures for human development. This way, human development becomes an activity that challenges and transforms people's thinking and practical life. Education of all categories of people about their rights, duties, human ability, and moral or ethical responsibility to alleviate and treat maladies that confront individuals and society promotes individual and human community.

The study is intended to help educate believers or members of religious communities, and understanding people that theology and ministry are directed toward the protection, promotion, and enhancement of human life,

---

[16]   Denis Goulet, *A New Moral Order: Studies in Development Ethics and Liberation Theology* (Maryknoll, New York: Orbis Books, 1974), 15.

[17]   Giovanni, Cardinal Battista Montini (Paul VI), *The Christian in the Material World* (Baltimore: Helicon Press, 1963), 47.

[18]   Reichmann, 213.

human person, human dignity, and human rights. The duo are directed to the salvation of the entire person and all people. As people can be self-destructive or invite suffering and degradation upon themselves and others, they are also able to reconstruct and develop themselves and others. Theology and ministry facilitate this process. The International Theological Commission succinctly summarized the significance of such and similar assertions when it stated that

> This duty and right of God's people to proclaim and defend actively the dignity of the human person is particularly urgent today because of the simultaneous appearance of two challenging factors: On one hand, there is a deep crisis as to the nature of human and Christian values. On the other, the modern conscience is profoundly sensitive to injustices perpetrated against human beings.[19]

The treatise on *Populorum Progressio* is significant in the general context of Christian teaching. This assertion is implied in the preceding paragraphs in terms of the relation of the document to other church social teachings. *Populorum Progressio* is foundational in this regard and a resource to seek out when questions regarding development are raised. The long-standing Catholic tradition and teaching about love as the fundamental and the ultimate commandment, the dignity of the human person, ownership of property, justice, peace, and the confrontation of suffering are related to the question of development. This study attempts to deal with these and similar issues.

The efforts to elaborate, develop, and apply Paul VI's notion of and principles for integral human development are not in vain, at least, from a Christian or theological point of view. Even outside this context there are conflicts, socioeconomic and political differences, imbalances, injustices, and violations against the human person, and there is global suffering including that found in Uganda.

This study offers some insights for reflection in the endeavor to resolve some of the problems in Uganda; and to make some recommendations to alleviate such problems. The work reiterates Catholic social teaching and human rights tradition and, in particular, suggests some ways to confront the renewed challenges presented by *Populorum Progressio* and other Catholic social documents dealing with human development.

---

[19]   International Theological Commission, 1.1.0.

The work is divided into four chapters. Chapter one deals with the foundations for understanding integral human development. It espouses the influences behind Paul VI's vision of human development: childhood experiences; key personalities behind his vision; his personal, professional and international experiences; and the encyclical, conciliar, and pastoral tradition that preceded the document. All of these affected him, his profession, and vision of human development. The chapter is vital because it shows the forces that influenced Paul VI's trend of thoughts and shaped his notion of true human development. It shows the implicit and gradual development of the notion of the human person, dignity, rights, and other related notions, which culminated in his view of integral human development. The chapter outlines and explains the notion of human development and ownership of property in response to human need and suffering. It includes the teaching of the *Magisterium*, papal encyclicals, pastoral letters, and reflections of some theologians.

Chapter two treats the interpretation and understanding of Paul VI's teaching in *Populorum Progressio*. It outlines and explains the main issues treated by Paul VI in the document and states how Paul VI attempted to resolve these issues. The chapter reiterates Paul VI's vision of true development, which is precisely his acknowledgement of the vision of Louis Joseph Lebret, one of the drafters of *Populorum Progressio*, who advocated the notion and nature of true development as being integral—the development of the entire person and of all people in a similar fashion. It suggests the necessary development principles that can, at least, be inferred from a general reading of *Populorum Progressio* and explains the requisite principles for integral human development.

The thrust of chapter three is the anthropology for integral human development. It underscores the understanding and emphasis of the human person, human dignity, and human rights as forces that compound the significance of Paul VI's teaching on integral human development. These will be treated as the most fundamental principles running through all other principles in the document. One principle is stated and emphasized as the most outstanding and fundamental—namely, *human dignity*. Consequently, in the work, I have argued that an anthropology for integral human development as advocated in *Populorum Progressio* is an imperative. The anthropology presented in this chapter facilitates the acknowledgment of the need for integral human development and the implementation of *all other principles* for integral human development. All other principles stated or implied in *Populorum Progressio* are necessary for human development, but human dignity is de facto the basic principle to be understood, acknowledged, and underscored.

Notwithstanding the fact that much has already been written about Uganda's religious, cultural, socioeconomic, and political history, chapter four delves into a general outline of the problems in Uganda without a detailed presentation of Uganda's situation and the historical factors that impacted development in Uganda. The chapter attempts to make an application of the teaching of *Populorum Progressio* to the Ugandan context and to demonstrate how it challenges the status quo in Uganda. This chapter will also try to show the implications of the teaching of the document and to make some recommendations to Uganda.

CHAPTER ONE

Foundations for Understanding Integral Human Development in *Populorum Progressio*: The Tradition that Impacted Paul VI's Life and Thoughts

I. INTRODUCTION

The phenomenon of human development, historically, is initiated by human activity and directed to the human person and the human community. It is also consequent to the prevalent events. Chapter one explains the foundations for understanding the notion of integral human development as presented by Paul VI in *Populorum Progressio* written in 1967. The principal thesis of this chapter is that a thorough comprehension of *Populorum Progressio* requires an understanding of the *Sitz im-leben* of the author and factors that influenced his thoughts, orientations, aspirations, and personality. The origin of the doctrine of *Populorum Progressio* is *Rerum Novarum: On the Condition of Labor* written by Pope Leo XIII in 1891, but other successive social encyclicals and church documents also influenced its teachings. *Rerum Novarum* is fundamental because it was the first Catholic social encyclical, which radically influenced other ecclesiastical social documents. Commentators on Catholic social thought are explicit on this issue. Peter Riga says of Pope Paul VI in relation to *Populorum Progressio*:

> His encyclical continues the clear teaching of his predecessors, from
> Leo XIII to John XXIII, in the matter of social justice, that man

has been called by God to live in a total fashion: socially, politically, culturally, economically, morally, and spiritually.[20]

Paul VI himself relates *Populorum Progressio* to preceding encyclicals such as *Rerum Novarum, Quadragessimo Anno, Mater et Magistra, Pacem in Terris,* and Pope Pius XII's radio addresses.[21] Pope John Paul II is explicit about such a relationship in his statement that "the encyclical *Populorum Progressio* follows directly in the line of the Encyclical *Rerum Novarum,* which deals with the condition of the workers."[22]

The document is evidently related to *Gaudium et Spes, The Constitution on the Church in the Modern World,* which expanded the range of the social question to all human relations.[23] We shall trace the evolution of Catholic social doctrine about human development beginning with *Rerum Novarum,* notwithstanding the fact that other documents prior to that document and period, including early Christian teachings, touched upon the issues of human development in various ways.[24] The rationale behind this genesis is that *Rerum Novarum* made the initial modern breakthrough in the question of integral human development with which *Populorum Progressio,* the Magna Carta of Catholic social teaching on human development, fundamentally deals.[25] The documents on Catholic social teaching advocate care for both the

---

[20]   Peter J. Riga, *The Church of the Poor: A Commentary on Paul VI's Encyclical on the Development of Peoples* (Techny, Illinois: Divine Word Publications, 1968), 5.

[21]   Paul VI (Pope), *Populorum Progressio: On the Development of Peoples* (Washington DC: United States Catholic Conference, 1967), 2,2. Also *see Populorum Progressio,* 9, 4 and 23-24,10-11. Also see John J. Kelley, *Freedom in the Church: A Documented History of the Principle of Subsidiary Function* (Dayton Ohio: Peter Li, Inc., 2000), 13.

[22]   John Paul II (Pope), *Sollicitudo Rei Socialis: On the Social Concerns* (Boston: Pauline Books and Media, 1987), 8, 14. The document makes reference to Leo XIII's *Rerum Novarum,* which primarily dealt with the condition of workers.

[23]   *Populorum Progressio,* 3, 2 and 4, 2-4.

[24]   Charles Avila, *Ownership: Early Christian Teaching* (Maryknoll, New York: Orbis Books, 1983), 102-103.

[25]   Mary Snyder Hembrow, "Development" in *The New Dictionary of Catholic Social Thought,* ed. Judith A. Dwyer (Collegeville, Minnesota: Liturgical Press, 1994), 280. Also see William Murphy, "*Rerum Novarum*" in *A Century of Catholic Social Thought: Essays on 'Rerum Novarum' and Nine Other Key Documents,* ed. George

material and spiritual dimensions of the human person, hence, underscoring the significance of integral human development based on the dignity of the human person. This means that all documents on Catholic social teaching are founded on the principle of *imago Dei,* that is, the principle of the dignity of the human person created in the image of God, whether this is explicitly stated or just implied.[26] Therefore, it is appropriate and necessary to start this treatise about integral human development with the examination, analysis, and understanding of the *corpus* of Catholic social literature related to human development.

Catholic social teaching is a compendium of works covering a diversity of areas dealing with issues affecting the human person. This work will treat themes that deal only with integral human development: development, justice, common good, subsidiarity, human dignity and human rights, preferential option for the poor, women and feminism, affirmative action, ownership of property, participation, and peace. The most central of these issues is that of the human person: human dignity and human rights. The significance of the human person, rights, and dignity cannot be emphasized enough because a relevant political, social, economic, and religious system is one that provides goods and services essential to a life of human dignity.[27]

This chapter will treat different documents in relation to development principles presented in *Populorum Progressio.* The principles feature in Paul VI's biography, his prepontifical and pontifical writings, and the documents that impacted his trend of thought in *Populorum Progressio* such as Leo XIII's *Rerum Novarum*. The study of Paul VI's biography and these documents helps in the grasping of his personality and what influenced him to write *Populorum Progressio* in the way he did.

The chapter presents the gradual development of the notion of human development in Catholic social teaching preceding and immediately after *Populorum Progressio*. It explains the development of ideas such as the human person, human dignity, human rights, ownership of property, and the response

---

Weigel and Robert Royal (Washington DC: The Ethics and Public Policy Center, 1991), 1.

26 David Hollenbach, *Claims in Conflict: Retrieving and Renewing the Catholic Human Rights Tradition,* (New York: Paulist Press, 1979), 108ff.

27 Avila, 43 and 154. Also see Stephen Everson, ed. *Cambridge Texts in the History of Political Thoughts Aristotle, The Politics* (Cambridge: Cambridge University Press, 1988), xvi.

to human need and suffering. This chapter includes a biography of Paul VI, the social teaching of the *Magisterium* in papal encyclicals and pastoral letters, and reflections of some theologians. Its principal purpose is to demonstrate the centrality of the notion of the human person in articulating the question of development.

The chapter is divided into four sections. The first deals with the life of Paul VI. The second addresses the encyclical, conciliar, and pastoral tradition, which preceded *Populorum Progressio*. The third is about the influence of Louis Joseph Lebret on the document. The fourth section treats significant papal doctrines and statements during the pontificate of Paul VI.

II. The Biography of Giovanni Battista Montini (Paul VI)

Social interactions and circumstances at a particular period influence and shape individuals' thoughts and responses to the phenomena of life though they do so differently. A thorough understanding of *Populorum Progressio* depends on an understanding of the influences that affected the author. In the case of Paul VI, there was no logical pattern of life. Peter Hebblethwaite notes this about him:

> Ordained priest without having been a seminarian he was made archbishop of the most prestigious diocese of Italy without having being a parish priest, and his name was put forward as a candidate for the papacy in 1958 though he was not even a cardinal. His election as pope in 1963 was the single "logical" event in his life.[28]

It was the circumstances of Paul VI's upbringing and life that influenced the course of these events. Many other contemporary forces helped shape the life of Paul VI (Giovannni Battista Montini) and made him an important personality in the life of the church and society in general. He personally experienced them as he grew up and interacted with the world in which he lived. According to Hebblethwaite, Giovanni Battista Montini "had first-hand knowledge of Modernism, Futurism, Facism, Nazism, Communism, Thirdworldism, Feminism, Ecology—all the movements that shook and

---

[28]   Peter Hebbelthwaite, *Paul VI: The First Modern Pope* (New York: Paulist Press, 1993), 13.

shaped the century now closing [20th century]."[29] All these phenomena impacted Paul VI's thoughts, life, and actions.

A. Childhood, Educational, and Vocational Developments (1897—May 29, 1920)

Pope Paul VI, christened Giovanni Battista Enrico Antonio Maria Montini, the second of three sons, was born on September 26, 1897, at Concesio, Brescia, in Lombardy, in northern Italy, of Giorgio Montini and Guiditta Alghisi, a family initially of lesser nobility that rose to higher status.[30] Giovanni Battista Montini was born to a wealthy family of ancient and respected elites, professionals, and intellectuals of a profoundly Catholic background, which eventually emerged as upper class nobility. His father, Giorgio Montini, "was a principal editorial writer and reporter"[31] though he was actually a professional lawyer. Clancy had this to say of Giorgio's influence on his son:

> He had profound influence on young Giovanni Battista. The latter's gifts as an organizer, his involvement in social questions, his charity, his intense interest in art and philosophy, his love of writing, his commitment to all the aspects of modern life—these were to come to him from his father, as in his home he received the most modern educations [sic] free from narrowness and provincial flavor which characterized so many homes in those years before the First World War.[32]

The above claim alludes to elements Paul VI would later articulate in *Populorum Progressio*: charity and participation, involvement, the diverse social questions and open-mindedness, which would be expressed in his idea of integral human development. Charity or generosity to the poor and

---

[29] Ibid., 1.

[30] Alden Hatch, *Pope Paul VI* (New York: Random House, 1966), 12-13. Also see Hebbelthwaite, 17-18; William E. Barrett, *Shepherd of Mankind: A Biography of Pope Paul VI* (Garden City, New York: Doubleday and Company, 1964), 45; John G. Clancy, *Apostle for Our Time: Pope Paul VI* (New York: P.J.Kennedy and Sons, 1963), 2.

[31] Hatch, 15.

[32] Clancy, 7.

interest in public affairs were also qualities that Giovanni Battista's mother, Guiditta, exhibited, and so his qualities were partly a blend of the qualities of both parents.[33] This is the trend of life Giovanni Battista Montini would follow most of his life.

Battista Montini had two brothers and no sisters, yet he grew in the company of three experienced women—his mother, paternal grandmother, and an unmarried aunt—who probably helped to shape his attitude towards women. Hebblethwaite suggests such influence on him and says that "from his student days in 1919 he welcomed women at conferences, and was always on the lookout for talented women to serve the Church in what today would be called 'ministry.'"[34]

Battista Montini's early educational life was surrounded by a diversity of experiences. He was not very outgoing in the early years of his childhood and school. Initially, he "was only completely at ease in the insulated serenity of his family circle."[35] However, this phenomenon eventually changed. As he grew he became more open and less shy.

Giovanni Battista Montini was raised in a unique environment, compared to other places in Italy, because the region was rich and fertile, industrially wealthy, a reconciliation of diversities, which produced a macrocosm and a "political barometer of Italy."[36] His family closely associated with advocates and lovers of modernism and people who looked forward to the day of active involvement and contribution of Catholics to the socioeconomic and political life of Italy and to an age of harmonious working of science and religion. The home of his parents had more influence on his personality than the school environment. It was very hospitable, open to all calibers of people—clerics, lawyers, politicians, and writers—and the family discipline was strict yet carefully moderated, and it was comprised of various aspects of life including practices that were spiritual, religious, traditional, and cultural.[37]

Battistta Montini was a frail and sickly child but intelligent. He received his early education from the Jesuits of Brescia, his home place.[38] In 1903, at

---

[33]   Ibid., 8.

[34]   Hebbelthwaite, 5-6. Paul VI personally assigned prominent positions to women in different capacities.

[35]   Hatch, 16.

[36]   Hebbelthwaite, 21.

[37]   Ibid., 22-26.

[38]   Clancy, 11-12. Also see Hatch, 17.

the age of six, Giovanni Battista Montini started school at the Jesuit school, *Collegio Cesare Arici,* where he studied until 1914.[39]

In 1914, in accordance with the decision of his parents, Giovanni Battista Montini had to "leave the Jesuit College of Arici, for health reasons, and finish his education privately, taking exams at the state high school, *Arnaldo da Brescia.*"[40] He completed his studies at the Jesuit Institute of *Liceo Arnaldo da Brescia* at the age of nineteen. It was during this same year that he disclosed his intention to become a priest, though this was not "a surprise but neither was it inevitable" for as a child he never thought of being a priest and his grandmother, Francesca, wanted him to serve the secular world.[41] By making this decision, Battista Montini departed from his family's traditional vocations of medicine, law, and public service. Initially, his dreams were patriotic but were frustrated by his poor health despite his efforts to improve it through vacation and rest.[42] When he wanted to join the Italian military to defend his country in 1916, he was found unfit and denied that service to which he felt he was called, necessitating him to make another choice of vocation.[43] In the same year (1916), he entered the Seminary of Brescia though, in fact, he was dispensed from living in the seminary because of his poor health, and he lived and studied at home to train to become a Catholic priest. As a seminarian, his father involved him in some extra projects. Giorgio Montini scheduled Giovanni Battista's life and involved him to work in his *Cucine Economiche,* a kind of soup kitchen for the poor where Giovanni Battista served people with humility, charity, friendliness and listened to their problems and treated them humanely.[44]

In 1917, together with Andrea Trebeschi, Giovanni Battista Montini founded a student magazine called *La Fionda.* As editor of the paper, he exhibited great organizational abilities and skills and made numerous contributions since he was an intelligent student, often at the top of the class.[45] Clancy's study of Battista Montini's life shows that he followed the regular curriculum of the seminary but privately pursued his own agenda.

---

[39]   Barrett, 52. Also see Hebbelthwaite, 22; Clancy, 11; and Hatch, 17.

[40]   Hebbelthwaite, 29. Also see Clancy, 18.

[41]   Hebbelthwaite, 29-30.

[42]   Ibid., 39.

[43]   Barrett, 69-70. Also see Hebbelthwaite, 43.

[44]   Hebbelthwaite, 44.

[45]   Hatch, 25. Also see Hebbelthwaite, 46-47.

> While at the seminary he studied the usual courses in Philosophy
> and Theology and church history and Scripture, at home he
> continued to grow in knowledge of political and social forces
> shaping the world . . . . There was always a balance in the forces
> that shaped Giovanni Battista intellectually.[46]

Battista Montini manifested a global and comprehensive outlook of life and the general human situation. This, partially, explains why he thought integrally and wrote *Populorum Progressio* the way he did. According to Barrett, "Battista Montini was in tune with the thinking of his time, politically and philosophically, through his active role in the discussion groups of Brescia."[47] but from what Clancy states, it is correct to say that part of his knowledge, experience, and standing depended on his private readings, interests, encounters with the friends of his family and the input of his family members. All these shaped him and contributed to his attainment of the goal to the priesthood and of his entire career. He was ordained a priest on November 21, 1920, by Bishop Gaggia.[48]

B. From Brescia to Rome/Vatican 1920-1953

After ordination, Battista Montini's plan was to get involved in pastoral work and to experience the actual life of the people. However, on November 10, 1920, because his bishop wanted him to pursue further studies, he entered the Lombardy Seminary and enrolled for courses at the Gregorian University and the University of Rome.[49] He pursued advanced studies at these universities and at the *Accademia dei Nobili Ecclesiastici*, the Academy of the Noble Ecclesiastics, which he entered during the fall of the year 1922.[50]

Battista Montini was soon to leave Rome for a sojourn outside Italy. "In May 1923, Don Battista went to Warsaw, Poland, to act as secretary to the Apostolic Nuncio, Archbishop Lorenzo Lauri and his assistant Monsignor

---

[46]   Clancy, 21.

[47]   Barrett, 63.

[48]   Hatch, 25. Also see Barrett, 73-74. There are conflicting dates of Paul VI's priestly ordination.

[49]   Barrett, 74.

[50]   Hatch, 31. Also see Barrett, 85; and Hebbelthwaite, 58. There are conflicting dates in this case.

Carlo Chiarlo."[51] Later in 1924, he was appointed assistant chaplain for CUCR—the *Circolo Universitario Catholico Romano*—"a club for Roman Catholic students, at the University of Rome" and according to Hatch, he was made "an assistant chaplain of the University of Rome Branch of the Federation of Italian Catholic University students generally known as FUCI."[52] Eventually, Pius XI appointed him to be the national moderator of FUCI (Federazione Universitaria Cattolica Italiana). Although he and FUCI suffered humiliation from the Facists of Italy, he never abandoned the course of helping young Catholics as their chaplain and moderator.

From 1932 until 1933, Battista Montini was a member of the Vatican Department of State, "diplomatic arm of the Holy See," and he also conducted classes in *Accademia dei Nobili Ecclesiastici*.[53] Shortly thereafter, he was promoted to higher positions. In 1936, he became papal undersecretary of state, where he served in moments of crisis and turmoil as one of the central Vatican figures in the struggles against external and domestic forces, especially during the peak activities of the Nazis and communists and during the holocaust and the world wars.[54]

Due to his administrative and leadership abilities, Battista Montini earned important positions in the Vatican. In 1937, Monsignor Montini was summoned to the office of "Secretary of State and named *Sostituto* of the Secretariat of the State" (Substitute for Ordinary Affairs).[55] From 1944 until 1954, he acted as secretary of state for Pius XII. When working in the Vatican, he founded a service for prisoners of war, employed radio as an aggressive means to communicate, established a resettlement for those displaced and taken to concentration camps, showed mercy to refugees, offered hope and assistance to many such people including Jews who lived in fear in the Europe of 1942.[56]

In the post-World War II years, Battista Montini was deeply interested and involved in works of charity and peace. He founded and supported organizations that worked towards helping the poor, weak, and dispossessed

---

[51]　Barrett, 85. Also see Hebbelthwaite, 69; and Hatch, 33. Conflicting dates and descriptions of office held by Giovanni Battista Montini.

[52]　Hatch, 37. Also see Barret, 91, and Hebbelthwaite, 79.

[53]　Barrett, 130-131.

[54]　Ibid., 142, 144-145.

[55]　Clancy, 49. Also see Hatch, 57.

[56]　Ibid., 53.

and worked hard for peace and tried to promote a deeper understanding of the meaning of peace.[57] He was entrusted with the responsibility of preparing for the Holy Year in 1950. He articulated a notion of authentic peace, which became one of the requisite conditions for integral human development in his encyclical *Populorum Progressio*, in the way he had previously articulated it in 1949. This claim is supported by Clancy, according to whom Battista Montini emphasized the notion and vitality of peace in the following words:

> The world had come to think of peace, he said, as merely a cessation of battle, a failure to resist. Not this, not the abandonment of principle, not the desire to enjoy life and the compromise making this possible, and certainly not the enforced peace of totalitarian regimes—none of these was peace.[58]

Prior to *Populorum Progressio*, in 1963, John XXIII wrote *Pacem in Terris*, which promoted the notion of peace based on the dignity of the human person. This was not a surprise because Battista Montini was a contributor to the draft of *Pacem in Terris*. He is even said to be the thinking behind this encyclical of John XXIII.[59] Peace is founded on shared human dignity, and human dignity is shared because of the common origin of humanity. Peace can be attained if human dignity is valued, and development is possible only because human dignity is valued. For this reason, the issue of peace was crucial to Battista Montini's agendum of integral human development in *Populorum Progressio*. This explains why Paul VI considered development and peace as synonyms and called development "the new name for peace."[60]

C. From Vatican (Rome) to Milan, 1954-1963

On November 3, 1954, Monsignor Montini was appointed archbishop of Milan, consecrated on December 12 of the same year and assumed the most challenging assignment in the whole of Italy.[61] It was challenging

---

57   Hatch, 89. Also see Clancy, 72-73.
58   Clancy, 74.
59   Barett, 265. Montini was also blamed for being communist because of his articulation of the notion of peace. Also see Clancy, 230.
60   *Populorum Progressio*, 77, 32; 83, 34; 84,34-35; 87, 35.
61   Hatch, 102, 104 and 110-111. Also see Clancy, 80 and 88; and Barrett, 235.

because of the contextual diversity in which he worked. The situation was one of industrial growth, enlightenment, ultramontane, modern civilization, affluence, soullessness, neurosis, and despair.[62] The diverse challenges he encountered partly explain why he wrote an encyclical that made the notion of integral human development central although his biographies do not make explicit statements to that effect. This is further manifested in his approach to conflicts. He did not like conflicts. He preferred persuasion, conversion, and peacefully winning people to his side.[63] He sought peace and persuaded people through the translation of Christian social principles into reality, maintenance of the dignity of people, and labor and provision of hope and vision.[64] The dignity of the human person and integral human development are at the center of the questions he attempted to articulate in *Populorum Progressio*. The fact that Battista Montini's theme of integral human development was emphatically projected in his life before his pontificate is attested to by what Clancy recounts him, saying,

> I should like to see the workers given every assistance—social, professional, religious. I should like them to realize not only the wrong done them by forcing on them the materialistic view of life, but that our own spiritual view of life has far more respect for them as persons and recognizes in them the boundless treasure of a soul that thinks and prays and believes. I should like to see technical schools helping them to realize that there can be a vocation, a redemptive value, a religious dignity in human work.[65]

Such expression of attachment to the workers explains why Battista Montini is sometimes called the Archbishop of workers.[66] In his attempts to meet the needs of workers, one can notice his holistic approach to their problems. Battista Montini looked at development from both material and spiritual points of view. He later developed this vision of true human development

---

[62] Clancy, 93-94.

[63] Hatch, 87.

[64] Clancy, 97-98.

[65] Ibid., 102-103.

[66] Granfield, "Paul VI, Pope" in *New Catholic Encyclopedia*, 2nd ed., vol. 11 (Washington DC: The Catholic University of America, 2003), 28. Also see Hatch, 102ff.

in *Populorum Progressio,* a view which Clancy affirms, acknowledging with Battista Montini that the two dimensions of the human person have to grow in a balanced manner to affirm that the person is truly developed.[67]

Battista Montini's emphasis on the religious dignity of work is related to the private ownership of property, which he upholds in a qualified way. According to him, ownership of private property should be disinterested, just, and enhancing to the human condition.[68] The questions of human dignity, private ownership of property, justice, and human rights, which eventually featured in *Populorum Progressio,* are here anticipated.

Giovanni Battista Montini had genuine concern for people, caring about both material and spiritual dimensions of the human person. As an archbishop, Montini reorganized diocesan structures, revitalized social action and newspapers and magazines, inspired and encouraged priests to be involved in spiritual and social acts of charity and to guide the populace in moments of crisis. He established an archdiocesan office of charity and built inexpensive churches all over the Archdiocese of Milan to care for the needs of the growing population, and he established an institute for priests to study sociology and economics to help them explain the social doctrine besides explaining dogma.[69] A comprehensive vision of life and undertakings for development reinforced Battista Montini's advocacy for integral human development.

In 1957, Battista Montini initiated an integral mission, one of his most powerful pastoral initiatives, in the Archdiocese of Milan, that aimed at reaching out to different categories of people in the community. The project also involved the expertise of people from different walks of life. It was directed to hospitals, clinics, homes of the sick and the elderly, women and men, and schools as a priority because education is the means of transforming people's life.[70] Hatch says of this mission that

> Montini's most spectacular offensive in his battle against the forces of atheism was the Mission of Milan . . . starting on November 4, 1957 and lasting for three weeks.[71]

---

[67] *Populorum Progressio,* 14, 7. Also see Clancy, 105.
[68] Clancy, 103.
[69] Ibid., 108-112. Also see Hatch, 110-111. Also see barret, 257-258.
[70] Ibid., 116-117 and 124.
[71] Hatch, 114-115.

This mission revealed the mind and intentions of a man who wanted no person and no aspect of human life to be excluded in the struggle for development. This was Battista Montini's outlook from an international or a global point of view. He further demonstrated this when, in 1957, he founded "the Overseas College especially for Catholic students from underdeveloped countries, and Indians, Africans, South Americans, Syrians and Indonesians were among those granted the opportunity for free education" in the college.[72] Here again, it is apparent that the future pope had a keen interest in the development of all people and this was later reflected in *Populorum Progressio*. The development he advocated was of the whole person. Here we notice a man who tries to strike a balance between faith and material social action and ensures that the two are integrated. For Battista Montini, when social action is being promoted, traditional Christian teaching should not be compromised or overlooked because both are essential for an integrated growth of the human person. Hatch confirms this when he states, "But for all his progressive ideas Montini was firm in preserving the deposit."[73]

On December 18, 1958, Battista Montini was named a cardinal. As cardinal, he was enthusiastic and instrumental in the preparation for the Second Vatican Council and particularly emphasized the importance of the dialogue of Christianity with the modern world.[74] Alden Hatch says,

> Montini's enthusiasm for the council stemmed from his ardent wish to bring the Church into harmony with the Kingdom of the Modern World without losing any significant traditions . . . the Cardinal Archbishop of Milan was the first member of the Sacred College to publicly hail the Pope's move toward the renewal of the Church.[75]

On January 25, 1959, when Pope John XXIII announced to the College of Cardinals his intention to convene an Ecumenical Council, the news was not well received by a majority of the Cardinals, but it was good news for Montini. This partially explains his contributions during the Second Vatican Council, especially in drafting *Gaudium et Spes*. It also helps us to understand why and how the document influenced Paul VI's thoughts in

---

[72] Clancy, 126.
[73] Hatch, 111.
[74] Clancy, 144-145; 147; 149-151 and 202. Also see Hatch, 119.
[75] Hatch, 119-120.

his own encyclical, *Populorum Progressio*. Finally, Battista Montini's interest in seeing the church placed in the modern context demonstrates the legacy of his contacts with personalities like his father Giorgio, Andrea Trebeschi, Paolo Caresana, Giulio Bevilaqua, Giovanni Maria Longinotti, Jean Guitton, Jacques Maritain, Fornari, and Henri de Lubac who all looked forward to dialogue between the church and modernism or at least seeing the church placed in a context where dialogue could be fostered.

The preparation of the Second Vatican Council would also provide him with an opportunity to encounter people who had views similar to his. He would particularly meet the French Dominican priest, Louis Joseph Lebret, whose vision of life was similar to his own, and who eventually helped him to draft *Populorum Progressio* when he was pope.

D. The Return from Milan to Vatican (Rome), 1963-1978

On June 21, 1963, after John XXIII died, Battista Montini was elected to succeed him as pope, and he returned to Rome. He took the name Paul VI and emphasized the significance of dialogue between Christianity and the modern world.[76] Due to his travels and diverse experience, he viewed life and the world comprehensively. He was conscious that the world consists of "the common man in a diversity of races, beliefs, national and cultural backgrounds," and he was comprehensively sensitive to the diverse forces affecting the world of his time, thus making him a "global thinker."[77] His mind was already reflected in the words of the 1963 encyclical, *Pacem in Terris,* of John XXIII whose writing he influenced. According to Clancy, Paul VI had the following to say,

> One cannot overlook the fact that even though human beings differ from one another by virtue of their ethnic peculiarities, they all possess certain essential common elements and are inclined by nature to meet each other in the world of spiritual values, whose progressive assimilation opens to them the possibility of perfection without limits. They have the right and duty therefore to live in communion with one another.[78]

---

[76] Hatch, 147. Also see Barrett, 271 and Clancy, 202.

[77] Clancy, 206-207and 230. Also see Hatch, 122-123, 196, 205-214, 166-187 and 233ff.

[78] Clancy, 230.

These words forecast Paul VI's mind in *Populorum Progressio* where he shows that integral development—its necessity and possibility—are based on the common origin and the shared human dignity of all people. Though he did not elaborate, he advanced the dignity and rights of the human person as core principles and foundation stones for peace, justice, and development. As one who lived in times of political, social, and economic turmoil, Paul VI was sensitive to peace. Having contributed to the preparation of the 1950 Holy Year, which had the intention of elucidating the idea of peace, and being a contributor to the drafting of John XXIII's *Pacem in Terris*, he had already pushed forward some of the peace agenda he intended to perpetuate. Hatch describes Paul VI's concern for peace:

> The pope's overriding preoccupation beyond, even the work of the Council was World peace, and in speech after speech, in allocutions and informal talks, he emphasized his intense concern.[79]

Chronologically, since Pope John XXIII died in 1963 and Giovanni Battista Montini was elected pope the same year, he bridged the First Vatican Council (1870) and the Second Vatican Council (1962-1965). He brought the Second Vatican Council to completion in 1965 and implemented the deliberations and the acts of the council up to his death in1978. It can be suggested that what he implemented after the Second Vatican Council was not novelty to him because it was a doctrine to which he contributed.

E. People who influenced Paul VI

The personality of Paul VI was a blend of personalities of some of the people of the society and time in which he lived, especially those with whom he interacted and who shaped his life from childhood to adulthood. The main concern of this part of the work is just to treat some of the significant people who are in this category.

1. PARENTAL AND FAMILY INFLUENCE

Paul VI was aware of the influence of his parents on his life. According to him, his father Giorgio's influence was that of courage because he "did not

---

[79]   Hatch, 189.

know fear" but knew how to "be a witness"; and his mother Guiditta's influence was one of "the sense of recollection of the interior life, of meditation that is of prayer, of prayer that is meditation . . . . All her life was a gift."[80] However, the personality of Giorgio was more dominant in Paul VI than that of Guiditta.

This is not to deny the influence of his mother upon him because spiritually Guiditta influenced him significantly. This just shows that each of the parents influenced him differently. Paul VI's personality and life were, therefore, partly a reflection of a blend of the character and life of his parents and partly his own making and the influence of other people.

2. Andrea Trebeschi

There was an enduring relationship between Paul VI and Andrea Trebeschi. Paul VI first met Trebeschi at the age of six at Cesare Arici, but they did not become friends until eleven years later.[81] On November 30, 1914, he disclosed to Trebeschi his intention to become a priest when they met on St. Andrew's day, and Trebeschi encouraged him to carry out his plan.[82] Trebeschi became one of Battista's closest friends as a youth and also a source of encouragement and mutual support especially because they shared similar views of life and the world.

The two, however, at times were separated from each other by life's demands. Nonetheless, they were able to work together whenever they had the opportunity. This is how they founded a student newspaper.[83] After the winter of 1917, when Trebeschi was back from Bologna after pursuit of studies in law, the two "began to plan a student magazine called *La Fionda* (The Sling) which had its first issue on 15th June 1918."[84] The magazine was launched "with the aid of other young crusaders, designed to forward the aims of the Society of Saints Faustina and Giovita," founded by his father, and "to combat current evils and serve the cause of Christian democracy."[85]

Battista Montini and Trebeschi shared the same confessor, Caresana, who saw the "faith-potential of their friendship."[86] Their common relationship with

---

[80]   Hebbelthwaite, 28.

[81]   Ibid., 22.

[82]   Ibid., 29.

[83]   Clancy, 22.

[84]   Hebbelthwaite, 46-47.

[85]   Barrett, 61. Also see Clancy, 22.

[86]   Hebbelthwaite, 32.

Caresana consolidated their friendship. Even if factors of life separated them, they kept communicating with each other in letters for "Battista knew the need of love, took the risk of love, was compassionate and deeply vulnerable. Friendship pulled him out of himself."[87]

Trebeschi was an example, comfort, and encouragement to Battista in moments of "darkness and doubt."[88] The relationship between Trebeschi and Battista Montini continued even though they embraced different vocations. Trebeschi's article in the magazine *La Fionda* contributed to the issue of September 5, 1925, which articulated and related his Polish experience to the wider world, namely to "concepts such as people, nation, nationality, country (*patria*), state, government, patriotism" significantly impacted Battista Montini.[89] According to Hebbelthwaite, the influence of Trebeschi on Battista Montini is evident because

> Montini defended patriotism as a fundamental Christian virtue, the concrete expression of "love of one's neighbor." It can be corrupted or go horribly wrong, but patriotism as neighborly love is the right place to start. He actually calls it *"fraternal solidarity."* Naturally he expects Polish patriotism to take Christian shape.[90]

This quotation affirms elements striking to and influential upon Paul VI. They were also eventually reflected in his vision of life. It also shows his wish for the integration of specific cultural practices with Christian values. This vision of life was probably facilitated by Paul VI's short life in the Secretariat of the Nunciature in Warsaw, Poland, and his encounters with people of different cultural backgrounds.

3. FRANCESCO GALLONI

Francesco Galloni was a priest appointed to Concesio in August 1915. Shortly after his appointment, he became an adopted member of the Montini family and influenced Battista Montini. He had many plans of which contact with the youth of the outlying areas was impressive to Battista Montini, but

---

[87] Ibid., 33.

[88] Ibid., 50.

[89] Ibid., 76.

[90] Ibid. Here Hebbelthwaite quotes Fappani-Molinari, *Montini Giovane*, p. 406 and *Familiari*, p. 224.

Galloni impressed Battista most because he "was among other things an authority in Alessandro Manzoni, the nineteenth century Italian novelist," and his works, and finally he was a young priest, barely older than Giovanni Battista himself, and he "was zealous, cultivated and pious."[91] Consequently, Giovanni Battista adopted Galloni as a priest model and a senior brother.

In May 1915, Italy was at war with Austria, all Italians were called to fight and there was "no clerical exemption" in the military service. Consequently, Galloni, Battista's new friend, enlisted to go and fight; but before his departure, Battista requested to have a retreat with Galloni at Camaldonese hermitage at San Genesio in the Brianza mountains, and they were joined by Caresana who was also the spiritual mentor of Galloni.[92] However, on reaching the Hermitage they got a cold reception. The two priests could stay with the monks, but Giovanni Battista was denied accommodation because he was a layman though he was eventually given a "woodshed" to sleep in as instructed by the superior of the monks.[93] This was a learning experience for Giovanni Battista. He learned to be receptive to all people and not to alienate and discriminate against anybody. He has no personal and explicit statement to this effect, but this can be deduced from his life and writings.

Although Galloni went to the barracks and the two were separated from each other during the war, Battista kept communicating with him, and he was in the battle field with Galloni in spirit, implying that one factor that united Battista and Galloni was their patriotic attitudes.[94] This also explains how caring and concerned Giovanni Battista was and how intimate they were, not only as friends but also spiritually.

4. Giulio Bevilaqua

Giulio Bevilaqua was an Oratorian priest, born in Verona in the year 1881, appointed to work in La Pace in Brescia. He was a compulsive and unconventional person who "disliked learning which was not backed up by experience."[95] According to Bevilaqua, knowledge should be founded on

---

[91]   Ibid., 36-37.
[92]   Barrett, 69. Also see Hebbelthwaite, 38.
[93]   Hebbelthwaite, 39.
[94]   Ibid.
[95]   Ibid., 26.

practical life experience and lead to a practical living. This explains why he was able to see the link between the church's social teaching and liturgy.

Bevilaqua was at first Paul VI's roommate and later his confessor even after Giovanni Battista became pope. This explains why Paul VI is said to have owed Bevilaqua so much wisdom and spiritual inspiration and why Bevilaqua was later made Cardinal by Paul VI when he was pope.[96] Giovanni Battista was close to Bevilaqua who constantly extended his cultural and intellectual horizons and taught Giovanni Battista to look for the signs of the Holy Spirit in the Modern World.[97] This eventually played into Giovanni Battista's interest in other cultures and his enthusiasm for traveling to other lands beyond Italy. To Giovanni Battista, Bevilaqua was and remained a source of support, encouragement and counsel, and a "master and friend" as Paul VI (Giovanni Battista) himself later said when making Bevilaqua a cardinal in 1965.[98]

Bevilaqua guided Battista in his reading of some of the literature of that time, but he left Brescia on February 5, 1917, to serve as an army chaplain though soon thereafter he was taken prisoner. However, Bevilaqua had already helped Battista to become aware that

> reading was not a self-indulgent retreat into an aesthetic ivory tower but a way of listening to the contemporary world . . . . Reading was the first stage towards what would become dialogue. Later he would present Bevilaqua himself in the figure of *"modern man,"* the modern thinker, with all the energy, the weariness, the doubts, the struggles, the discouragements, and the hopes that the philosophical, scientific, religious and social crises have caused in the exhausted soul of modern man.[99]

Bevilaqua taught Battista Montini to read for a purpose, not just as a hobby. In other words, Battista Montini's mentor taught him to use what he read to interpret real life situations confronting people in the current world and

---

96   Clancy, 41. Also see Hatch, 153.
97   Granfield, 27. Also see Hebbelthwaite, 26.
98   Hebbelthwaite, 26.
99   Hebbelthwaite, 46. Here Hebbelthwaite is quoting *Notiziario*, 3, 9.

to act to change the status quo if this was necessary. In their relation, Bevilaqua was not just a friend; he was also an advisor to Battista Montini.[100]

5. PAOLO CARESANA

Paolo Caresana, from Pavia province, was a calm diocesan priest who worked among "the oppressed rice-growers of his province, whose cause he defended, and later joined the Oratorians in 1912, and became the confessor and spiritual director of Battista Montini and remained so for life."[101] He was a confessor to both Battista and his friend Trebeschi, and he asked Battista Montini to help him in his various pastoral ministries. During the war, Caresana employed Battista Montini as his unofficial and unpaid secretary.[102] It is, however, not easy to measure fully how much influence he had on Battista Montini because their relationship was a spiritual and confidential one, but they had a long relationship.

Battista Montini met Caresana for the first time during a retreat in 1915 through his friend Galloni who was also the spiritual son of Caresana.[103] Caresana was Bevilaqua's oratorian colleague who helped Battista Montini through 1917. He frequented the Montini family because he helped out in their parish church of San Giovanni. Battista Montini considered his fatherhood as "my seminary."[104] The relationship between Giovanni Battista and Caresana was motivated by the similarities in the attitudes of the two. Like Bevilaqua, Battista Montini was attracted to Caresana partly because they both liked the cycling sports. However, their relationship went deeper than sports to real issues affecting life, both spiritually and materially.

6. JEAN GUITTON

Jean Guitton's intellectual qualities influenced Giovanni Battista. Guitton was a French philosopher to whom Paul VI was partially attracted because he was French. Paul VI had a great admiration for and attachment to "the

---

[100]   Clancy Hebbelthwaite, 99.

[101]   Hebbelthwaite, 26.

[102]   Ibid., 26-27 and 32. Hebbelthwaite is quoting *Familiari*, 66.

[103]   Ibid., 38.

[104]   Ibid., 46. Hebbelthwaite is quoting *Familiari*, xx here.

French Dominicans and Jesuits who were Montini's masters."[105] Paul VI and Guitton first met in 1950, and Paul VI was probably attracted to Guitton because "Guitton, member of the *Academie Francaise* was every inch a French intellectual capable of transmitting the most banal observations by brilliance of his style."[106] It was Guitton's intellectual qualities that Giovanni Battista wanted to and did emulate in his own life.

The two had several intellectual exchanges. Guitton always sent Giovanni Battista Montini his new publications, and their enduring relationship, which started in 1950, involved a lot of dialogues initiated the same year.[107] These dialogues ultimately proved useful for and exerted influence on Giovanni Battista.

Giovanni Battista Montini's encounter with Guitton was helpful to him in his analysis of situations. It was partly because he looked at life in the light of Guitton's vision that he was able to recognize "the experience of modernity"[108] during his sojourn in Paris when the duo partially discussed the use of intellectual abilities in articulating issues correctly and to arrive at mutual consensus about issues. From such exercises, Giovanni Battista Montini seemed to have learned to be more open, to learn from others, to be more objective, and to look at things more critically than ever before.

7. KARL ADAM

Karl Adam was another influential person upon Giovanni Battista. He was a leading German Catholic theologian and a reformist Tubingen University professor who "represented the best of Catholic thinking at that time."[109] Karl Adam was one of the people who greatly contributed to Catholic *aggiornamento* even if this was not immediately recognized and acknowledged publicly. One of Adam's influences upon Battista Montini was through the latter's reading of Adam's book, *The Essence of Catholicism,* which imprinted

---

[105] Ibid., 9.

[106] Ibid., 10.

[107] Clancy, 132. To understand the nature of the dialogues between Jean Guitton and Paul VI and the extent of the influence of Jean Guitton on Paul VI, read Jean Guitton, *The Pope Speaks: Dialogues of Paul VI with Jean Guitton,* Trans. Anne and Christopher Fremantle (New York: Meredith Press,1968), 5ff.

[108] Hebbelthwaite, 86 and 236-237.

[109] Ibid., 89 and 95.

an indelible influence on Giovanni Battista Montini's ecclesiological thoughts. The final chapter of the work, titled "Catholicism in Its Actuality," made a radical change from the idealistic view of Christianity and Catholicism to the actuality of Catholicism, which addressed practical and relevant issues like the place of sin in the church, and from the "contrast between the 'essence' of the Church and its existential reality Adam deduced that the Church was in need of constant reform."[110] The works were attractive to Giovanni Battista Montini because he was interested in the transformation of the life of people when necessary. *The Spirit of Catholicism,* in particular, captured his attention because it implied a reform project although this was a very controversial issue at that time.[111]

Robert Anthony Krieg says that "according to Adam, Catholicism embraces all that is truly human. It is an affirmation of all values wherever they may be, in heaven or on earth."[112] Here Adam gives a holistic or integral view of the church, which Paul VI would accept with ease. The influence of Adam's writings was significant to Battista Montini because he lived and worked in a confused world where he wanted to provide a "theology for committed lay people, giving them a sense of spiritual direction," and "the Church to which he introduced students was in need of reform."[113] The ideas of Adam were useful to Battista Montini when the Second Vatican Council was convoked, and there was a felt need to read and analyze the signs of the times to address the needs of the world of that time.[114] At this juncture, it is correct to suggest that during the Second Vatican Council the ideas in Adam's writings influenced Battista Montini's (Paul VI's) contributions in the drafting

---

[110] Ibid.

[111] Ibid., 95.

[112] Robert Anthony Krieg, *Karl Adam: Catholicism in German Culture* (Notre Dame: University of Notre Dame Press, 1992), 36. Here Krieg quotes *Karl Adam: The Spirit of Catholicism.* Trans. J. McCann (New York: Macmillan, 1929), 9.

[113] Hebbelthwaite, 95.

[114] Flannery Austin, ed. "*Gaudium et Spes*: Pastoral Constitution on the Church in the Modern World" in *Vatican Council II: The Conciliar and Post Conciliar Documents* (Leonminister, Herefords, England: Costello Publishing Company, 1981), 5, 906-907. Also see Lorentzen Lois Ann, "*Gaudium et Spes*" in *The New Dictionary of Catholic Social Thought.* Ed. Judith A. Dwyer (Collegeville, Minnesota: Liturgical Press, 1994), 407.

and deliberations of *Gaudium et Spes*, which addressed ordinary life issues and placed the church in dialogue with the modern world.

8. JACQUES MARITAIN

Jacques Maritain was a French philosopher. He wrote a work entitled *La Primaute du Spirituel*. Through this work and other works, he had a great influence on Italian Catholics. This influence was partly facilitated by the translations Battista Montini made in 1928 and 1934.[115] When studying French, Battista Montini met Maritain at the Institute Catholique or some other place in France and encountered other outstanding Frenchmen of different backgrounds during this time.

Maritain influenced Giovanni Battista Montini who eventually translated and introduced Maritain's *Three Reformers* to Italian readers.[116] These were Martin Luther, Rene Descartes, and Jean Jacques Rousseau whose works together resulted in the French Revolution and a modern world. Battista Montini's attraction to Maritain was possibly because in him Battista found somebody with his own type of attitude, an attitude positive toward reforms. It was the knowledge from the writings of Maritain and other people that was ultimately attractive to the young students.[117]

9. HENRI DE LUBAC

Henri de Lubac's life and writings impacted Battista Montini. He was influenced by what he knew and read about Henri de Lubac and some of his writings.[118] Battista Montini's reading of Henri de Lubac's *Meditation on the Church* had an impact on his vision of the church, especially "the doctrine on collegiality in Chapter 3 of *Lumen Gentium*."[119] Many of the ideas of Henri de Lubac in this book found their way into *Lumen Gentium*, and some of these were the ideas of the centrality of Mary in the church and ecclesiology, the mysterious nature of the church, and the sacramental character of the church, instead of viewing the church as a perfect society contesting the "infiltration

---

[115] Granfield, 27.
[116] Clancy, 132. Also see Hebbelthwaite, 83 and 96; Granfield, 27.
[117] Ibid., 35.
[118] Ibid., 132.
[119] Hebbelthwaite, 393.

of the modern world."[120] Such ideas were assimilated by Giovanni Battista who used them during the Second Vatican Council and his pontificate. The ideas found their way into the thoughts of Giovanni Battista Montini because he favored a dialogue between the church and the modern world. This was reflected in *Gaudium et Spes,* which influenced Paul VI's writing of *Populorum Progressio* tremendously.

In conclusion, we can say that Giovanni Battista's various encounters and experiences with different people were ultimately all important in various moments of his life. These experiences shaped his philosophy of life. His selfless love and compassion, deep and caring sensitivity and concern, determination, easy, diversified and ongoing relationships with people of all colors and religions, openness to criticisms, his integral vision of life and approach to issues, and his well-developed talents were consequent to his diverse encounters and experiences.[121] It was due to such diversity of experience that Paul VI was able to conceive of an *aggiornamento*, a reform of the church, as one of the aims of the Second Vatican Council, and he "was able to affirm the value of the world without diminishing the uniqueness of the Church" or "to balance tradition and reform without compromising either."[122]

III. The Encyclical, Conciliar and Pastoral Tradition preceding *Populorum Progressio*

A. *Rerum Novarum*: On the Condition of Labor (1891)— Pope Leo XIII

Rerum Novarum marks the foundation of modern Catholic social teaching. According to Donal Dorr, the document was a breakthrough and major solution to the social question and the first church document to initiate vigorous attempts to resolve social problems—a "solid foundation on which the later encyclicals and other Church documents could build."[123] Barret confirms this assertion by acknowledging that *Rerum Novarum* was

---

120 Granfield, 29. Also see Hebbelthwaite, 393.
121 Hatch, 122-123 and 195-196. Also see Hebbelthwaite, 1;33;166ff; 180-187; 205-214 and 233ff; Clancy, 8-8; 53-54;66 and76; Barret, 81-82 and 100.
122 Granfield, 33.
123 Donal Dorr, *Option for the Poor: A Hundred Years of Catholic Social Teaching* (New York: Orbis Books, 1992), 14.

one of the world's great social documents, a high point of Christian thinking on the condition of the laboring classes and on the relationship between employer and employed.[124]

The document addressed specific questions about the changes in industry, physical sciences and labor, disparities between the rich and the poor, and increased self-reliance of workers and moral degeneration which influenced the course of economic activities.[125] The document was the brainchild of Leo XIII, the protagonist of the framework of modern Catholic social teaching. However, this does not mean that the problems addressed in *Rerum Novarum* were not previously addressed. In fact, Christian social workers and social movements created before 1891 were already dealing with social problems. Schafer notes that:

> The social encyclical *Rerum Novarum* of 1891 confirmed the beginnings of the solution to the "social question" which had taken shape within the German Catholicism of the nineteenth century and had been arrived at through disputes and class struggles in society and the church.[126]

This contention is affirmed by David O'Brien and Thomas Shannon who think that "in *Rerum Novarum*, written in 1891, Leo attempted to persuade Catholics to concentrate less on politics and more on the "social question."[127] The place of the document in Catholic social thought is certain. According to Peter J. Henriot and others,

---

[124] Barrett, 55.

[125] Richard Rousseau, *Human Dignity and the Common Good: The Great Papal Social Encyclicals from Leo XIII to John Paul II* (Westport, Connecticut: Greenwood Press, 2002), 11. Also see Dorr, 15.

[126] Michael Schafers, "*Rerum Novarum*: The Result of Christian Social Movements. "From Below" in *Concilium, Rerum Novarum: A Hundred Years of Catholic Social Teaching*. Ed. John Coleman and Gregory Baum, (London: SCM Press, 1991), 14.

[127] David J. O'Brien and Thomas A. Shannon, eds., *Catholic Social Thought: The Documentary Heritage* (Maryknoll, New York: Orbis Books, 2001), 12-13. Also see Dorr, 15.

because of the principles which he set forth to guide in the formation of a just society, this document has become known as the *Magna carta* for a humane economic and social order.[128]

In *Rerum Novarum*, Leo XIII attempted to resolve a wide range of issues that affected human society before and at the time it was written and even later. Leo XIII's teaching about living wages was empathetic and "put the Church squarely on the side of the workers in the struggle for recognition of trade unions."[129] This resonates with the alternative English title of the document, "On the Condition of Labor" and confirms the view that the new things *Rerum Novarum* fundamentally dealt with was the question of the condition of workers.[130] Leo XIII articulated the recurrent contemporary socioeconomic and political problems in society; critiqued the socialist solutions to the problems; laid out the role of the church in society; outlined and explicated the rights and duties of workers and employees; treated the question of just and legitimate ownership and the just use of money, the duties and the responsibilities of the state, and its limits of intervention for the common good, the importance of the just wage; and finally he "laid a solid foundation for the concept of social justice"[131] and the workers' right of association. The document was a reaction to both socialism and capitalism. It dealt with the pitfalls of the opposed socioeconomic and political systems and ideologies. The document's response was relevant not only for the time and circumstances which it was addressing, but also for the situations that prevailed later and today.

In addressing major issues such as the "care for the poor, rights of workers and employers, return to Christian morals and the role of public authority,"[132] *Rerum Novarum* placed the social question in the hands of individuals,

---

128 Peter J. Henriot et al., eds, *Catholic Social Teaching: Our Best Kept Secret* (Maryknoll, New York: Orbis Books, 1988), 7. Also see Dorr, 13-16.

129 Williams, 8-9.

130 Michael Walsh and Brian Davies, eds., *Proclaiming Justice and Peace: Papal Documents from Rerum Novarum through Centessimus Annus*, rev. and exp. ed. (Mystic, Connecticut: Twenty-Third Publication, 1994), 15.

131 Dorr, 15-16; 19; 28 and 57. Also see Leo XII, *Rerum Novarum: On the Condition of Labor* (Washington DC: National Catholic Welfare Conference, 1891), 2, 5; 29,13-14; 34,15-16; Rousseau, 3-4; and O'Brien and Shanon, 13.

132 Henriot et al, 27.

institutions, groups, and society. Leo XIII introduced the question of the equality of people who are distinct from other creatures and do not have the honor that people hold. People are the highest perfection of animal nature. Human persons have to live in mutual esteem and love because of their equality. This implies that everybody has a duty, role, and responsibility to fulfill. This advocacy was founded on Leo XIII's contention that all people are created equal, have a common destiny, and have a right to a share of nature's resources on the basis of sharing a common origin—God.[133] The equality Leo advocated was the equality of human dignity.

Another question Leo XIII addressed was that of capital and labor. He was particularly concerned about wages paid to people for their work and advocated that it should help promote their livelihood.[134] Just as he made a distinction between human persons and the rest of creation below the human person, recognizing human dignity as an important characteristic of the human person, Leo XIII advocated for the rights of workers. He in no way advocated that capital and labor are on equal footing. They are both important factors of production, but labor must be given precedence over capital. This is clear in his argument about the equality and dignity of persons. Consequently, he contended that the employer, who is the capital owner, may not value himself or capital more than a fellow human being who constitutes labor because all people are created equal in dignity, and all need the basic necessities to live a dignified life.

Leo XIII was aware that some degree of inequality among people is undeniable. Naturally, people may be unequal in talents even if God has endowed them with the same dignity.[135] This is a pragmatic contention because it is indubitable that individual differences exist on the basis of personality, character, talents, and the ability to perform. It is impossible to get the same achievements from all people because of their variable traits.

Leo XIII spoke strongly against socialism, acknowledged the legitimacy of ownership of private property, which is also for the benefit of other people. He contended, in accordance with divine design, that other people should have a share of the private property of an individual. The right is presented here as a natural right. This contention was in line with the Early Fathers

---

[133] *Rerum Novarum*, 11,7-8; 12,8 and 38, 17-18.

[134] *Rerum Novarum*, 3, 5-6; 9, 7 and 81, 35-36.

[135] *Rerum Novarum*, 26,12-13. Also see Henriot et al, 28.

of the Church, and W. E. von Ketteler's understanding of the use of natural resources that

> in the Christian view human beings have "only a God-given right to use the goods of the earth in the order that is prescribed by him, with the intent that all human beings should receive their necessary bodily needs from the fruit of the earth."[136]

The consistent argument about the ownership and the use of private resources is that natural resources have a universal destiny—they are for the use of all people. The right is conversely presented as a natural right to use the goods of nature.

Von Ketteler was acknowledging that divine design, according to Christianity, is that people are entitled to use natural resources as God willed so that all people receive the material needs for their survival. This right is, however, limited by moments when there is a dire need and the person who worked to earn ownership of the property has met personal basic and crucial needs. Therefore, this right is not absolute because natural resources are destined for the good of all people; they "all have basically the same and equal claim to the wealth producing resources of nature."[137] Schafers aptly summarizes the whole argument of von Ketteler in these words:

> Nevertheless, the right to property was not an absolute right since God created nature to nourish all human beings, and this purpose must be achieved. Therefore, each individual must again make the fruits of his property a common good in order as far as in him lies to contribute to the achievement of this determination. Here Christian love of neighbor is enjoined for the poor.[138]

This is a view Paul VI later promoted in *Populorum Progressio* where he argued that in the event that an estate becomes counterproductive to the common good, public prosperity would demand that it be expropriated

---

[136] Schafers, 8. Schafers is quoting W. E. von Ketteler, *Samtliche Werke und Briefe*, ed. E. Iserloh, I.1, Mainz, 1977, 18,19. Also see Dorr, 17-18.

[137] Avila, 71 and 79.

[138] Schafers, 8. The original source Schafers is quoting is von Ketteler, 30.

and put to a better use.[139] Paul VI advocated that resources should be used appropriately and adequately. It is right to conclude that like *Rerum Novarum*, *Populorum Progressio* restrained the limit of private ownership by referring to the needs of other people, but Paul VI was more vigorous in limiting the right to private ownership of property than Leo XIII.

According to Leo XIII, society has a crucial responsibility to care for individuals in the society. Its purpose and duty is to allow, facilitate, and promote the common good as its ultimate end.[140] This means authority has the responsibility to serve the entire community. The contention suggests the significance of the principle of subsidiarity. If individuals and small groups are not capable of meeting their needs, the civil authorities have the obligation to intervene to help them to meet their needs. It also demonstrates that the wealth of a nation is the fruit of the labor of its working class.[141] Civil society should, therefore, be envisioned as owned by all its members.

This viewpoint is what Paul VI later advanced more vigorously, and it has a significant implication in the way ownership of wealth or property is understood. On account of the fact that labor is crucial for the wealth of a nation and individuals, people have the right to own private property. However, private ownership must be limited because of the social responsibility of each member of the society. Property should also serve the common good and provide for other individuals' needs.

Leo XIII's argument had a dual foundation. First, the workers' right to private ownership of property is grounded in the fact that they have earned what they claim to be theirs by working. Since they have worked for what they rightly claim, they have the right to dispose of it as they judge fitting. Second, the right of other individuals to claim the same property is founded on the fact that nature's resources were not specifically predetermined for an individual but for the good of all creation. This is the gist of his theological argument here. However, Leo XIII cautioned "that the just ownership of money is distinct from the just use of money."[142] This according to him is a significant teaching of the church, which has been handed down in the church's tradition and ought to be observed. It is a caution that governs the

---

[139]   *Populorum Progressio*, 24, 11.
[140]   *Rerum Novarum*, 71, 30. Also see Henriot et al, 28.
[141]   Henriot et al, 28. Also see *Rerum Novarum*, 51,22-23.
[142]   *Rerum Novarum*, 35,16. Also see Henriot et al, 28.

use of wealth despite the right to own wealth. It suggests a responsible use of wealth.

Just ownership and use of property points to the relational character of ownership and disposition of property. This also means that there is a social dimension of both personal property and the human person because people share common traits. These need to be cared for by all. Similarly, the dignity of every individual and his rights need to be protected by all. According to Curran,

> the beginning of modern Catholic social teaching insisted on what might be called today a relational anthropology that avoided the opposite extremes of individualism and collectivism.[143]

Curran's claim is crucial for an understanding, appreciation and application of the notion of human dignity, human rights, and the human person, and ultimately the notion of integral human development because development cannot be complete unless it is inclusive. This claim, therefore, typifies integral human development advocated by Paul VI. It provides a relevant foundation for Paul VI's teaching on integral human development because Paul VI is concerned about the development and the good of all. It is here that the relational concept of a person and the phenomenon of integral human development challenge the disregard for a relational anthropology and, above all, for a theological anthropology. The Aristotelian dictum that "man is a social being," not a being in isolation, should be esteemed as relevant and significant in facilitating our vision of socioeconomic and political issues too.[144] The underlying reason here is that a human person is always part and parcel of the human family.

In sum, the contents of *Rerum Novarum* were as follows: advocacy for a movement to develop social conscience and a demand for state intervention in the social question, freedom of association for workers, ownership of

---

143 Charles E. Curran, *Catholic Social Teaching, 1891-Present: A Historical, Theological and Ethical Analysis* (Washington DC: Georgetown University Press, 2002), 9.

144 Stephen Everson, ed. *Cambridge Texts in the History of Political Thought: Aristotle, The Politics*, (Cambridge: Cambridge University Press, 1988), 4, 1253a-30, 1252b-30, 1538-3, and xvii-viii. Also see James P. Hanigan, *As I Have Loved You: The Challenge of Christian Ethics* (New York and Mahwah: Paulist Press, 1986), 76-77; Curran, 3.

property, a response to socialism and capitalism, and the role of the Church in social questions.[145] The document outlined and dealt with the following significant questions and principles for human development: the principle of *imago Dei* or human dignity based on the human origin from God, a principle which implies human equality, the questions of common good, option for the poor, human rights in general and particularly the right of the workers, the universal destiny of the goods of nature and the right to private ownership of property, responsible participation and involvement, and the mutual claims and duties or obligations of workers and employers. Finally, the document articulated the role of affirmative action, understood here as aggressive government intervention to redress injustices against the disadvantaged because it spelt out the role of the state or public authority in the enhancement of the human condition.

B. *Quadragessimo Anno*: Forty Years Later, On the Reconstruction of Social Order (1931)—Pius XI

Pius XI's *Quadragessimo Anno,* written in 1931, was an updating of *Rerum Novarum.* At the time it was written, the world faced the effects of the destruction of the First World War, the Great Depression, socioeconomic and political turmoil and anarchy, opposing political economies and social ideologies, systematic socialism and capitalism, which compounded conflicts and crises. Pius XI responded to help resolve some of these problems.

In *Quadragessimo Anno*, Pius XI continued Leo XIII's intervention in the social question and "reaffirmed the right and the duty of the Church to address social issues."[146] According to him, the church cannot afford to remain indifferent to the problems of people for whose good it was instituted. The document dealt with the recurring problems of the Industrial Revolution exacerbated by the great depression at the end of 1920s and its impact on workers.[147] Similarly, Henriot and others contend that the document was written at a time of "severe world wide economic depression" to address "the issue of social justice and" to call "for the reconstruction of social order"[148]

---

[145] Schafers, 14.

[146] Henriot et al, 8.

[147] Curran, 10.

[148] Henriot, 7-8. Also see Dorr, 76; Pius XI, *Quadragesimo Anno: On Reconstructing the Social Order,* (Chicago Illinois: Outline Press, 1931), 88, 49-50.

in accordance with what Leo XIII taught in *Rerum Novarum*. These views support the idea that in *Quadragessimo Anno* Pius XI perpetuated the doctrine of *Rerum Novarum* about the

> defense of workers and their rights-calling for some state intervention, the qualified right to private property, which also retains its social dimension, and the condemnation of the extremes of socialism and capitalistic individualism.[149]

Human dignity, human rights, solidarity, and social justice, which Pius XI vigorously introduced into Catholic social teaching, were the bases of his "response to the extremes of totalitarianism and capitalism," which affected people's way of conceiving the ownership of property.[150] By advocating and emphasizing that there should be "social responsibilities of private property and the rights of working people to a job to a just wage and to organize to claim their rights,"[151] Pius XI lent his support for what Leo XIII taught in *Rerum Novarum* forty years earlier. Pius XI also reinforced the issue of a life-supporting wage initially introduced by Leo XIII in *Rerum Novarum*. He demanded that remuneration should be adequate to meet the needs of the workers, their families, and dependents. Alegria says of a just wage that "it should be sufficient reward to cover the human needs of the worker and his family."[152]

As the title of the document suggests, Pius XI contended forty years after *Rerum Novarum* that the social order needed to be reconstructed. This endeavor should include "the positive role of governments in promoting the economic good of all people in society."[153] He suggested that it was the role of both individual members of the state and civil authorities to contribute

---

[149]   Curran, 10. Also see Maria Jose Diez-Alegria, "Ownership and Labor: The Development of Papal Teaching" in *Concilium, Rerum Novarum: A Hundred Years of Catholic Social Teaching*, ed. John Coleman and Gregory Baum, (London: SCM Press, 1991), 19; Dorr, 75; *Quadragesimo Anno*, 10, 13-14: 17-20,19-21; 59,39-40 and 112, 61: Walsh and Davies, 41.

[150]   O'Brien and Shannon, 41. Also see Dorr, 79; *Quadragesimo Anno*, 88,49-50.

[151]   Henriot et al., 8. Also see Diez-Alegria, 19.

[152]   Diez-Alegria, 20.

[153]   Henriot, 8. Also see Dorr, 94.

to the growth and well-being of the state according to their capacities. Pius XI called for application of the principle of subsidiarity, anticipated the question of option for the poor, and alluded to what was eventually called the common good and affirmative action.[154] Some scholars are of this same view. Oliver F. Williams, for example, affirms that *Quadragesimo Anno* clearly stated that "the role of the state is to be *in the service of* society" and "its role is primarily to facilitate the cooperation and well-being of the "mediating structures."[155] This thought is also in line with the Aristotlean claim, which has an enormous support among scholars, namely, that "the very purpose of the state is the good life or happiness of its citizens."[156] Here the purpose, role, and obligation of the state are clearly stated. The government has the duty to oversee the different activities in the state. In the judgment of Pius XI in specific social contexts, "economic undertakings should be governed by justice and charity as the principal laws of social life."[157] This is a duty the state should accomplish by employing the necessary apparatus.

Pius XI condemned the prevalent unfavorable ideologies of the time. Like Leo XIII, Pius XI decried capitalism and communism. He condemned capitalism because of its "unregulated competition," and he "condemned communism for its promotion of class struggle and the narrow reliance for leadership on the working class."[158] He contended that the evil of capitalism is that it creates a gap between the rich and the poor, and the problem with communism is that it kills initiatives and participation, just as it violates the right to private ownership of property.

A careful reading of Pius XI suggests that justice and charity underlie his condemnation of the two antagonistic ideologies of communism and capitalism. Communism is condemned because it is against justice while capitalism is denounced because it is uncharitable. This makes sense because love and justice are mutually inclusive. Justice without love is inconsiderately harsh, and love breeds justice. The absence of justice breeds strife and hatred.

---

[154] Walsh and Davies, 41. Also see O'Brien and Shannon, 4. According to O'Brien and Shannon, the common good is "a good which included and did not contradict the authentic good of each and every person."

[155] Williams, 14.

[156] Everson, xvii.

[157] Henriot et al, 8.

[158] Ibid., 8. Also see Dorr, 75; Walsh and Davies, 41.

He argued for an alternative that would integrate the positive elements of both communism and capitalism. According to him, the "corporatist principles as an alternative to both capitalism and socialism"[159] is the solution. Here Pius XI reechoed the teaching of Leo XIII, which was directed against the dichotomy between the individual and community, capitalism and socialism. This suggests why he tried to provide an alternative policy that merges the two divergent ideologies.

Quadragessimo Anno of Pius XI furthered the ideas of *Rerum Novarum* by proposing a novel alternative system "based on corporatist principles"[160] as an alternative to capitalism and socialism considered separately. This alternative has been criticized by some scholars. Alegria, for example, argues that creating a corporate order as a solution denies to people "freedom of party and association"[161] and is close to the structure of totalitarian regimes, which practically succumbed to and bent toward capitalist interests. He further contends that this is the reason why the later popes and the Second Vatican Council remained mute about such a suggestion or this portion of *Quadragessimo Anno*. After all, the document had emphasized the right to free and autonomous association. This makes sense because it would be contradictory to suggest corporate order as an alternative solution to both capitalism and socialism as it would mean building one system out of two different and opposed systems. This is impossible and seems a difficult task because as ideologies they are two opposite extremes.

The teaching of *Quadragessimo Anno* resembles that of other Catholic social encyclicals and pastoral doctrines because it addressed questions and advocated development principles present in these other documents. *Quadragessimo Anno*—both implicitly and explicitly—exposed issues, virtues, and principles relevant for human development. These are the principles of human dignity and subsidiarity, human rights, charity, social justice, affirmative action, free association, the common good, and participation. Pius XI also treated the question of ownership of private property and its social orientation and that of the option for the poor.[162] Just as Pius XI demonstrated in his teaching in *Quadragessimo Anno* that the church cares, his successor, John XXIII, did the same in his 1961 encyclical *Mater et Magistra*.

---

[159] Curran, 10.

[160] Dorr, 94. Also see Curran, 10.

[161] Diez-Alegria, 19-20.

[162] O'Brien and Shannon, 41.

C. *Mater et Magistra*: Christianity and Social Progress (1961)— Pope John XXIII

In *Mater et Magistra*, Pope John XXIII continued the encyclical tradition of Leo XIII and Pius XI. His choice of the title of the encyclical, referring to the church as mother and teacher, reechoed the opening paragraphs of *Rerum Novarum* and *Quadragessimo Anno* because it reaffirmed the church's right to teach about the meaning of human life and activities. *Mater et Magistra* affirmed that "the role of the Church is to encourage, stimulate, supplement and complement" the efforts of the people.[163]

Mater et Magistra, however, specifically focused on and emphasized significant developments that occurred after the Second World War. It focused on "aid to underdeveloped nations."[164] John XXIII anticipated the fears in *Populorum Progressio* when Paul VI saw the need to bridge the gap between the poor and the rich and to achieve peace. Consequently, he "set forth a number of principles to guide both Christians and policy makers" to meet this need.[165] John XXIII made a significant contribution to Catholic social thought as previous encyclicals did.

> He called on committed Christians and "all people of good will" to work together to create local, national, and global institutions which would both respect human dignity and promote justice and peace. He emphasized that the growing interdependence among nations in a world community called for an effective world government which would look to the rights of the individual human person and promote the universal common good.[166]

The above reading of the document shows a significant contribution from John XXIII. He articulated crucial principles and conditions necessary for an *integral* human development as Paul VI called it in *Populorum Progressio*. Besides agriculture and the problems related to it such as agricultural technology, health and crop insurance, price management, and just wage for farmers, John XXIII dealt with the traditional issues and conditions—human

---

163 Williams, 15.
164 Walsh and Davies, 81. Also see Curran, 10.
165 Henriot, 8. Also see O'Brien and Shannon, 84.
166 Ibid.

dignity, human rights, justice, peace, solidarity, subsidiarity, active government involvement, and the common good.[167]

Though not explicitly stated, it can be inferred that when the pontiff speaks of "growing interdependence among nations," it is an allusion to the multiplication of social relations and a more effective mutual support among governments and peoples of the various nations, a contention augmented by the fact that John XXIII "argued for state intervention to ensure that property would achieve its social functions," and the underpinning reason for this intervention is that "justice requires that property be used for the common good."[168] This means the state is an apparatus for ensuring that property is used to meet the needs of individuals and the society. John XXIII advocated collaboration at all levels—locally, nationally, and internationally.[169] When he speaks of effective world government, one concludes that the principle of subsidiarity and affirmative action[170] are also implied here because the two are mutually inclusive. This observation is stated in Dorr's reading and interpretation of the document and the text of the document itself.[171] The two principles need to be viewed as mutually inclusive because state action is possible only if an institution such as a government exists, and once such an institution is in place the application of the principle of subsidiarity is essential. In other words, an establishment of a government necessitates the application of the principles of subsidiarity and affirmative action, and an establishment of a government is necessitated by the need to apply the two principles.

In *Mater et Magistra*, "the emphasis on socialization, an increase of network of relations by which individuals are connected to each other"[172] compounds the significance of subsidiarity, association, justice, and solidarity. John XXIII

---

[167] Walsh and Davies, 81. Also see O'Brien and Shannon, 82.

[168] O'Brien and Shanon, 82. Also see Walsh and Davies, 81.

[169] John XXIII, *Mater et Magistra: Christianity and Social Progress* (Washington DC: National Catholic Welfare Conference, 1961), 155-165, 46-49; 169-184, 50-53. Also see Dorr, 116.

[170] Paul VI never used the term affirmative action in *Populorum Progressio,* but the term is used here retrospectively to mean aggressive or positive state action to address situations of injustice.

[171] Dorr, 115. Also see *Mater et Magistra*, 107, 32; 149, 45.

[172] O'Brien and Shannon, 82.

did not overlook this significant factor. Consequently, the document promoted the question of human development through

> its insistence on socialization: the more complex interdependence of citizens that calls for growing state intervention because only the state can deal with such issues.[173]

According to John XXIII, authentic development should emphasize the social dimension of the human person and yet be moderated by the state. This was precisely an advocacy for emphasis on "economic socialism" or socialization, which means "the more complex interdependence of citizens that calls for growing state intervention because only the State can deal with such all embracing issues"; and according to Curran, such emphasis "exists in . . . tension with the older principle of subsidiarity."[174] This means Curran claims that socialization and subsidiarity are mutual extensions of each other. So John XXIII's emphasis continues the previous affirmations of the principle of subsidiarity. This means that economic socialism—collective ownership—and socialization, an initiation of one in such a system, does not hinder the application of the principle of subsidiarity and affirmative action. They are mutually supportive; there is no opposition between subsidiarity and the emphasis on socialization.

The right to private property and a just wage advocated by Leo XIII in *Rerum Novarum* recur in *Mater et Magistra*. John XXIII advocated the right to own private property, but he also insisted on the social dimension of property and condemned the inequality that exists in our world on the basis of ownership.[175] Property can be a possession of an individual, but it is also to be shared with the needy. Natural resources are destined for the good of all. This is one of the reasons for the document's condemnation of inequality in the world. *Mater et Magistra*, therefore, continued the teaching of *Rerum Novarum* by stating that there is a social dimension of property as *Quadragessimo Anno* of Pius XI also advocated.

Like the preceding documents, *Mater et Magistra* grappled with diverse questions and conditions relevant for the integral development of peoples. These included the relational character of the human person, human rights,

---

[173] Curran, 10. Also see Walsh and Davies, 81.
[174] Ibid., 10. Also see Riga, 29.
[175] Ibid., 10.

human dignity, human freedom, peace, justice, subsidiarity, solidarity, participation, the social dimension of property, common good, affirmative action, and option for the poor.[176] Some of these and similar problems were again expounded in John XXIII's following encyclical, *Pacem in Terris: Peace on Earth of 1963.*

D. *Pacem in Terris*: Peace on Earth (1963)—Pope John XXIII

Pacem in Terris is the social encyclical that most broadly advocated and articulated the question of human rights in the context of natural law, at the same time dealing with other questions such as "the relation between authority and conscience, disarmament and development of the common good."[177] Although *Rerum Novarum, Quadragessimo Anno*, and *Mater et Magistra* treated the question of human dignity and human rights, *Pacem in Terris* emphasized human rights and provided other fundamental conditions for integral human development. John XXIII placed Catholic social teaching in an interpersonal context, especially because he clearly emphasized social, economic, legal, and political (civil) rights of the human person.[178] This explains the significance of mutual claims people have upon each other at all levels and in all contexts because they are human but have a divine origin.

Pacem in Terris demonstrated the significance of mutual claims in a social context and actually compounded the importance of solidarity in its definition of human rights. David Hollenbach is of this view. He advocates that solidarity is a precondition for an adequate theory of human rights.[179] The reason for this claim is that a human right is always restricted, especially when it conflicts with the rights of others who are "less able to look after themselves."[180] This means human rights should be defined and exercised in the social context because human beings have a common origin and share human dignity. This is a generally accepted truth and was confirmed especially

---

[176] O'Brien and Shannon, 82.

[177] Ibid., 129. Also see Walsh and Davies, 125.

[178] Henriot, 8.

[179] David Hollenbach, *Claims in Conflict: Retrieving and Renewing the Catholic Human Rights Tradition* (New York: Paulist Press, 1979), 132-133.

[180] Walsh and Davies, 125. Also see John XXIII, *Pacem in Terris: Peace on Earth* (Washington DC: National Catholic Welfare Conference, 1961), 62, 16; 65, 17.

after the "United Nations' Universal Declaration of Human Rights (1948)."[181] The United Nations implied natural law even if it made no explicit reference to it. This is evident in its definition of rights based on the assumption that all people share human dignity.

Similarly, on the foundation of natural law John XXIII developed principles to govern human life. *Pacem in Terris* treated issues of human rights and initiated a dialogue between East and West by articulating different ideologies and movements which deal with socioeconomic issues in the two blocs of the world.[182] *Pacem in Terris* showed that human life has a dual dimension because humans are both individual and social.

Pacem in Terris also dealt with the critical question of war and the arms race, and it underscored the importance of global peace to humankind because the arms race and war retard both individual and national economic progress.[183] Here the question of the importance of peace for human development is introduced as a vital condition. This anticipated one of Paul VI's final appeals in *Populorum Progressio*, calling development "the new name for peace"[184] and underscoring its significance. The development of all demands peace and also means peace for all. This suggests and underscores that the document is concerned about interpersonal relations. It deals not only with individual issues but also with questions that affect all people.

The principle of common good was important to John XXIII especially because of the social character of the issues with which he dealt. Consequently, he considered "the common good as a principle of integration" and advocated that each political community has a common good called "the Universal common good," which transcends the individual good but which cannot be separated from the common good of the entire human family.[185] This notion of common good explains why questions about human rights, peace, participation, ownership, subsidiarity, option for the poor, and affirmative action are closely related. The common good must be promoted by political authority because this is the sole purpose for which political authority is established.[186] Here John XXIII insisted after the example of Leo XIII that

---

[181] Henriot, 8.

[182] Curran, 10.

[183] O'Brien and Shannon, 129. Also see Walsh and Davies, 125; Curran, 10.

[184] *Populorum Progressio*, 76-80, 32-33.

[185] O'Brien and Shannon, 130. Also see Dorr, 116; *Pacem in Terris*, 104, 25.

[186] *Pacem in Terris*, 84, 21. Also see Dorr, 116.

political authority should intervene if the interest of some portion of society should suffer some evil or injustice that it cannot handle. Public authority should intervene to help.[187] Both Leo XIII and John XXIII squarely addressed the question of the role of political authority. If political authority does not serve the common good, it is unjust. This resonates with Aristotle's commonly accepted thought that the purpose of civil authority is to serve the citizens.[188]

In *Pacem in Terris*, John XXIII provided guidelines for ordering relationships between human beings and articulated the ways of handling the relations between individuals and the state. John XXIII did not mention the principles of subsidiarity and affirmative action explicitly in *Pacem in Terris* though he was explicit in *Mater et Magistra* especially regarding subsidiarity. Nonetheless, here, they are implicitly stated as part and parcel of the question of human development. He also treated the ways of ordering international relations by defining human rights in a global context.[189] This is significant because human rights were formally defined in terms of social relations and meant to govern such relations whether between individuals or nations. The definition of human rights provides for smooth and humane social relations. This is probably why John XXIII treated relational issues in the world community.[190] This is a significant contribution because integral human development cannot be achieved without good international and interpersonal relationships.

In *Pacem in Terris*, John XXIII affirmed the following important points for integral human development. First, human persons are social beings. Second, the understanding of human dignity and human rights should apply to all different possible contexts. Third, development is a relational enterprise just as peace is not an individually isolated pursuit. Fourth, the important principles presented by John XXIII in *Pacem in Terris* are the principles of human dignity, human person, and human rights, peace, justice, subsidiarity, participation, common good, affirmative action, and the option for the poor. Finally, all issues of human development need to be coordinated, interrelated, and integrated in order to achieve authentic human development.

---

[187] Curran, 9.

[188] Everson, xvi.

[189] Curran, 10.

[190] Ibid.

E. The Second Vatican Council (1962-1965): Two Significant Documents—GS and DH

To understand the documents of the Second Vatican Council, it is necessary to grasp the situation prior to the council and its consequences because the council was a moment of transition from one era to another. An understanding of this background is also crucial for an understanding of the notion of authentic development, which, to a great extent, was misrepresented in the period preceding the Council. Henriot and others made significant observations to elucidate this point:

> In many respects, Vatican II represented the end of one era and the beginning of a new era. The enthusiasm and energy of the Age of Enlightenment had been spent. This philosophical movement of the eighteenth century, marked by a rejection of traditional social, religious, and political ideas and an emphasis on rationalism, had culminated in the holocaust in Europe and in a world sharply divided. These events had dashed hopes that secular society, based on human reason severed from religious faith, would lead to unending progress. Instead a misguided rationalism had unleashed forces which threatened to destroy the world.
>
> The Church had turned inward in reaction to a rationalistic age which demeaned religious belief. Religion, more and more defined as a "private" affair between the individual and God, was relegated to a marginal role in society. At the same time, the Church channeled its energies outwardly to evangelize the "mission lands" in Africa, Asia, and Latin America.[191]

Despite the very positive and real achievements of the Enlightenment, for instance, its elevation of the importance of reason in facilitating a critical view of life, some people had misgivings about it. As Henriot and others indicate, prior to the Second Vatican Council, there were errors or misconceptions of various kinds and degrees. These mistakes were a consequence of movements claiming to usher in changes for the better. Instead, what happened was indeed the opposite. Second, there was an excessive emphasis on reason as the only and ultimate source of solutions to problems. Third, despite the efforts of

---

[191] Henriot, 9.

the popes to teach people through the various encyclicals, the doctrines of
the encyclicals were not studied or never reached the majority of people. In
other words, the church's efforts to address social issues tended to receive
inadequate results—her influence in the world was diminished. There was
a dichotomy of world view, religion, society and politics, and probably the
human person, especially between one who was a Christian and one who was
not. Consequently, there was some revolution. The holocaust occurred in
Europe and forces that threatened to destroy the church were continuously
making their way into the world.

It was this and like situations to which the Second Vatican Council was
responding through *Gaudium et Spes* and *Dignitatis Humanae*. The conciliar
fathers, particularly in *Gaudium et Spes*, dealt with the social questions, human
dignity, and the role of the church in shaping society.

> They affirmed that the specifically religious mission of the Church
> did give it a function, light, and an energy which can serve to
> structure and consolidate the human community according to
> the divine law.[192]

Such a reaction is tantamount to acknowledging that the role of the church
is crucial in human development and is still more relevant when considered
in terms of integral human development, which this study advocates as the
most authentic notion of development. The rationale for such a claim is that
the church helps contribute to the demands of integral human development
by providing answers, insights, and suggestions for spiritual growth besides
the material growth, which constitutes only a portion of what is true
development.

1. *GAUDIUM ET SPES*: PASTORAL CONSTITUTION ON THE CHURCH IN THE MODERN WORLD (1965)

Gaudium et Spes, one of the sixteen conciliar documents of the Second
Vatican Council, is important reading material for the study of Catholic
social teaching in general and *Populorum Progressio* in particular for three
main reasons. First, the two documents chronologically follow each other; the
latter was promulgated soon after the former. Second, as Krier advances, "in

---

[192] *Gaudium et Spes*, 42, 942-943. Also see Henriot, 9-11.

Populorum Progressio Paul VI was clearly carrying out the vision of Vatican II, which sought to be in dialogue with the world, as church and society addressed current social issues."[193] This view is supported by Richard P. McBrien and Peter Riga, who have acknowledged that "*Progressio . . .* is simply following *The Constitution on the Church in the Modern World* of Vatican II."[194] Finally, *Gaudium et Spes* is a comprehensive, dependable, and authoritative document of Catholic social teaching on which many discourses can be based.

In *Gaudium et Spes*, the conciliar fathers dealt with the Catholic Church's relation to the secular world. The rationale in this approach is that the church, the people of God, is in the world and part of the world affected by different forces of change. Theologically, this is the context in which believers practice their faith, and nonbelievers express their solidarity with the whole of humankind. Consequently, one of the document's main concerns was the paradoxical dichotomy and relationship between faith and practical life.[195]

Gaudium et Spes "presents justice as central both to the issue of poverty and that of peace."[196] This means that peace and people's level of development is determined by how just society is. The creation of peace and people's development call for a critical study of social conditions of the people. The document was fundamentally open to the contemporary situation and even emphasized that "the church can learn from this world" and "must help in the process of evaluating what the world has to offer" whether directly or indirectly.[197] It addressed the question of the role of the church and challenged every church member to look more critically at the church's external activity than at her internal concerns. It challenged people "to read the signs of the times" in the light of the Gospel message and to act accordingly especially because of sociological, technological, and other changes that affect the

---

[193]   Marvin Krier L. Mich, *Catholic Social Teaching and Movements* (Mystic, Connecticut: Twenty-Third Publications, 1998), 155.

[194]   Riga, 13. Also see Richard P. McBrien, "An Ecclesiological Analysis of Catholic Social Teachings" in *Catholic Social Thought and the New World Order: Building on One Hundred Years*, ed. Oliver F. Williams and John W. Houck (Notre Dame: University of Notre Dame Press, 1993), 159.

[195]   McBrien, 156. Also see Curran, 11.

[196]   Dorr, 177.

[197]   O'Brien and Shannon, 164.

world.[198] It advocated that the church has a duty to care for and protect human dignity amidst such changes.

Gaudium et Spes called for respectful dialogue within the Catholic Church and with other churches and nonbelievers. "Respect for others" is crucial because it permits freedom to operate authentically.[199] The council fathers were keen to note that it is necessary for the church to interact with the secular world, but they also observed that church-state relationships should not cause the church to submit to the whims of civil authorities because the church has a prophetic role to defend the poor.[200] The logic of this argument is that if the church identifies only with the state and civil authorities and does not fulfill its prophetic role or forfeits it, there is no defense for the disadvantaged people. This is why the church has always to stand apart and be the conscience of the nation, reminding people when things are going in the wrong direction.

Gaudium et Spes is officially called the Pastoral Constitution on the Church in the Modern World. However, the diverse nature of its contents— "personalism, the social nature of the human person, the relation between the Church and the world, justice, and development"[201]—are relevant issues not just affecting Catholics or Christians or believers but all people. *Gaudium et Spes* treated the fundamental principle for integral human development, namely, human dignity. It placed the human person and human dignity in the context of "human community, human activity in the world and the role of the church in the modern world."[202] It was in this spirit that the council fathers advocated that "social order and development should always work for the benefit of the individual, and they require constant improvement."[203]

The second half of *Gaudium et Spes* addressed intriguing issues such as marriage and family, culture, socioeconomic life, the political community, and the fostering of peace.[204] Further issues addressed by the

---

[198] Ibid. Also see *Gaudium et Spes*, 4-17, 905-917; 21, 920-922; Dorr, 168; Walsh and Davies, 158.

[199] *Gaudium et Spes*, 92, 999-1000. Also see Dorr, 168.

[200] Dorr, 169.

[201] O'Brien and Shannon, 164-165. Also see *Gaudium et Spes*, 1-3, 903-905. For further evidence, see the outline and contents of the text of *Gaudium et Spes*.

[202] *Gaudium et Spes*, 40,933-940. Also see Curran, 11.

[203] Walsh and Davies, 158. Also see *Gaudium et Spes*, 23-32, 924-932.

[204] Curran, 11. Also see Walsh and Davies, 157.

document were proper cultural development and positive intercultural relationships, cultural education, the community of nations, international organizations, and international cooperation.[205] These are vital elements for the integral human development because they either deal with institutions that promote development, or they are components of authentic human development.

Gaudium et Spes provided norms of cooperative and moral life. Its guidelines were for both the developing and developed nations. They are, namely, that developing nations should aim, unequivocally and expressly, at the total development of their citizens; and they should recognize that the foundation of progress is the work, tradition or culture, and talents of their citizens, the tapping of their local resources, and the good example of their most influential personalities, not just foreign aid.[206] Participation and justice are implied here as necessary for integral development.

Second, wealthier nations have a duty to support "less developed nations to achieve their own development."[207] This support should, however, be lent with prudence and mutual consideration of the needs of those to be supported and that of the supporters.

The issue addressed here is that less-developed nations should not expect more support than can be provided and developed nations are not to support to the detriment of their own development. In *Gaudium et Spes*, the conciliar fathers advocated that the most important tasks of the developed nations are "to help the developing nations to fulfill these commitments," undertake within limits what is necessary "for the establishment of world-wide cooperation," and consider "the welfare of the weaker and poorer nations" in their business relations with them because the poorer nations support themselves out of the revenues from such business dealings.[208] Here, the document spells out two requisite conditions for integral human development: solidarity and justice.

Third, to minimize excessive inequalities between the developed and developing nations, the document calls the international community to be the effective coordinator and stimulant of development without injustices or violation of the principle of subsidiarity, thus also calling for organizations that

---

[205] *Gaudium et Spes*, 47-85, 949-995.
[206] Ibid., 86 (a), 995. Also see O'Brien and Shannon, 165.
[207] O'Brien and Shannon, 165.
[208] *Gaudium et Spes,* 86(b), 995; 87,996-997. Also see Dorr, 160.

promote and regulate international commerce.[209] *Gaudium et Spes* addressed the issue of socioeconomic justice. It took a strong stance on the question of international socioeconomic justice and cautioned, as Paul VI did later in *Populorum Progressio,* that if international justice is not pursued the wrath of the less-developed peoples will result in their forceful claims for what they need, which may be a justifiable course of action.[210] The implication of this argument is that there is need for an international institution to regulate the global socioeconomic system, suggesting that the principle of subsidiarity is necessary for the regulation of the economic system. This is what Paul VI later suggested in *Populorum Progressio. Gaudium et Spes,* therefore, identified three vital requisite factors for integral human development—justice, subsidiarity, and solidarity in a spirit of equality.

Fourth, *Gaudium et Spes* advocates a major concern of *Populorum Progressio,* namely, that although it is important to evaluate the economic and social structures, people must guard against whatever offers "material advantage while militating against man's spiritual nature and advancement."[211] *Populorum Progressio* later makes central the issue that development is not only material but also spiritual. *Gaudium et Spes* states that the implementation of such norms is the duty of all and again underscores the importance of participation for human development. It advocates that the role of the church and of every Christian is to support any course of action for international order and efforts to bridge the gap between the poor and the rich—individually, nationally, and internationally—and any action that protects human dignity and promotes human life spiritually and materially.[212] This is the responsibility of the church as an institution and of every individual Christians and all people including nonbelievers. This reinforces the import of the principle of participation, which affirms that authentic integral development involves everybody and benefits all.

Gaudium et Spes manifests an integral character in its treatment of world problems and the Church in the modern world. This view suggests that the document was one of the immediate influences behind Paul VI's thoughts in

---

[209] O'Brien and Shannon, 165. Also see *Gaudium et Spes,* 86 (c), 995; 87, 996-997.

[210] Dorr, 155.

[211] *Gaudium et Spes,* 86 (d), 995-996. Also see *Populorum Progressio,* 14,7.

[212] Williams, 37-38. Also see *Gaudium et Spes,* 88, 997; O'Brien and Shannon, 165.

Populorum Progressio. It outlines the necessary principles and requirements for a good society and for authentic development: the human person, human dignity, human rights, justice, peace, common good, universal solidarity, subsidiarity, affirmative action, option for the poor, and equality.[213] All these elements feature in *Populorum Progressio*. This explains the close relation between *Gaudium et Spes* and *Populorum Progressio* while *Dignitatis Humanae's* teaching is foundational for both *Gaudium et Spes* and *Populorum Progressio*. However, this relation is better seen in the fact that *Gaudium et Spes* initiated the discussion on the theme of development, and their treatises are both critically based on the dignity of the human person.[214]

2. *DIGNITATIS HUMANAE*: DECLARATION ON RELIGIOUS FREEDOM (DECEMBER 7, 1965)

Dignitatis Humanae centered on two crucial issues—human dignity and human freedom. The document was conspicuously an affirmation of conscientious religious freedom, but it actually dealt with "the principle of the dignity of the human person and the freedom of the act of faith."[215] The council fathers had this to say at the introduction of *Dignitatis Humanae*:

> Contemporary man is becoming increasingly conscious of the dignity of the human person; more and more people are demanding that men should exercise fully their own judgment and a responsible freedom in their actions and should not be subject to the pressure of coercion but be inspired by a sense of duty.[216]

While the council fathers recognized that the church has a responsibility toward the wider, secular society, they were also cautious that there should

---

[213] Dorr, 153-154.

[214] O'Brien and Shannon, 165.

[215] McBrien, 158. Also see Williams, 31.

[216] Austin Flannery, "*Dignitatis Humanae*: Declaration on Religious Liberty" in *Vatican Council II: The Conciliar and Post Conciliar Documents* (Leominister, Herefords, England: Costello Publishing Company, 1981), 1,799. Note that here the Council fathers are quoting John XXIII, *Pacem in Terris*, 11 April 1963, AAS 55(1963), 279. Ibid., 265; Pius XII, *Radio Message*, 24 December 1944; AAS 37(1945)14.

be no disrespect for religious views and freedom of religious practice. This position was founded on the fact that all human persons have dignity and rights.[217] This was a reason for their advocacy for religious freedom in *Dignitatis Humanae*. Freedom is an inherent God-given quality and participation in divine qualities. This suggests the gravity of the central character of the human person, human dignity, and human rights in the document. Human dignity is the most imperative principle, a *conditio sine qua non*, for authentic development.[218] The document, therefore, deals with one of the central and crucial elements for integral human development. Human dignity per se is the principle though not emphasized adequately and linked sufficiently to other development factors that guided the authorship of *Populorum Progressio*.

The question of the right to religious freedom was influenced by the experience of the American church and the American bishops who participated in the Second Vatican Council, but the specific advocate and developer of the notion of religious freedom was the American theologian John Courtney Murray.[219] The conciliar fathers adopted the position advocated by Murray though they were initially apprehensive about his views on religious freedom. Although the original intention was to address the question of free practice of religion, there were other implications because attention was drawn not only to the rights for religious practice, but also to the realization that human rights are at the center of the life of a human person and interpersonal relationships, including the process of development. Human rights are founded on human dignity. This is why the foundation of the teaching of *Dignitatis Humanae*, namely, the dignity of the human person, is the most fundamental basis for

---

[217] *Dignitatis Humanae*, 2, 800-801.

[218] Thomas P. Ferguson, *Catholic and American: The Political Theology of John Courtney Murray* (Kansas City, Missouri: Sheed and Ward, 1993), 19 and 81. Human dignity is counted among the first principles of the human person because it is eternal, universal, and immutable. For this reason, it is also considered one of the absolute principles in Christian anthropology.

[219] Paul E. Sigmund, "Catholicism and Liberal Democracy" *in Catholic Social Thought and the New World Order: Building on One Hundred Years*, ed. Oliver F. Williams and John W. Houck (Notre Dame: University of Notre Dame Press, 1993), 59-60. Also see McBrien, 158; Curran, 11. Also see Thomas P. Ferguson, *Catholic and American: The Political Theology of John Courtney Murray* (Kansas City, Missouri: Sheed and Ward,1993), 81.

integral human development. The document addresses the religious-spiritual dimension of the human person by officially acknowledging religious freedom as "based on the very dignity of the human person as known through the revealed word of God and by reason itself," but also "based on the rights of all citizens to be free from external coercion to act against their conscience or preventing them from acting in accord with their conscience in religious matters"[220] both publicly and privately.

Dignitatis Humanae maintains that religious freedom is important for four main reasons.[221] It is a condition to help people achieve "a fuller measure of perfection with greater ease"; it is demanded by the common good of society; it safeguards the rights and duties of the human person in the social context; and finally, the promotion and protection of religious freedom is an all-embracing responsibility of individuals, social groups, civil authorities, the church, and other religious communities.

Development principles presented in *Dignitatis Humanae* revolve around the human person and relationships. Though not all are explicitly spelled out in the document, we can infer that the following issues were addressed by the council fathers: the human person, human dignity, and human rights, participation, common good, and solidarity. One could summarize them as "the principle of the dignity of the human person in the social context."[222] This shows the document's individual and communitarian character and approach to human development and the social question.

IV. THE INFLUENCE OF LOUIS JOSEPH LEBRET IN *POPULORUM PROGRESSIO*

To understand the notion of authentic human development as presented by Paul VI in *Populorum Progressio*, a grasp of Louis Joseph Lebret's life and vision of true development is necessary. This section will treat only the most important aspects of Lebret's life, his influence and contributions to *Populorum Progressio*. A significant foundation for this claim is the comparison of Lebret's definition of development and that of Paul VI in *Populorum Progressio*. Paul VI and Lebret define development in a similar way, and Paul VI quotes Lebret almost verbatim in his definition. Paul VI's views in *Populorum Progressio* many

---

[220] *Dignitatis Humanae*, 2-8, 800-805; 15, 811-812. Also see Curran, 11.

[221] Ibid., 6-8, 803-805.

[222] This is my interpretation.

times replicated the thoughts of Lebret.[223] It is significant to study his life in relation to that of Paul VI because the study facilitates our vision of why they looked at life in a similar way. This claim was supported by Paul VI himself, in *Populorum Progressio*; John Paul II, in *Sollicitudo Rei Socialis*; and Denis Goulet.[224]

A. Louis Joseph Lebret and Paul VI

Lebret was a French planner, priest, and philosopher and a contemporary of Paul VI. He was "born in 1897 to a family of fishermen: his birth place was the hamlet of Minihicsur Rance near Saint-Malo, a major port of Brittany," and at the age of eighteen years, Lebret joined the French naval academy and served his country in that capacity.[225] He served in Belgium, Holland, and in the Middle East during the First World War; and in 1922, he was made an instructor in the naval academy. At the age of twenty-six, he changed his career. He joined the Dominican Order and was later ordained a priest. After ordination, he was appointed a chaplain to a convent in Saint-Malo so that he could recover from his poor health; but he soon abandoned the responsibility, got involved in the social struggles of the fishermen of Britanny, and eventually developed an interest in development and social action because he strongly believed that exploitation and misery at that time were consequences of structural malpractices.[226]

Goulet describes Lebret as a man who respected nature and had immense "curiosity for lands and cultures other than his own, unshakable common sense in the face of life's tragedies, and a person with ever-fresh willingness to take new risks," and one who traveled widely.[227] He observed the circumstances in

---

[223] *Populorum Progressio*, 14, 7.

[224] Denis Goulet, "The Search for Authentic Development" in *The Logic of Solidarity: Commentaries on John Paul II's Encyclical On Social Concerns*, ed. Gregory Baum (Maryknoll, New York: Orbis Books, 1989), 133-134. To understand *Populorum Progressio* and *Sollicitudo Rei Sociallis*, one needs to understand Lebret's notion of development. Also see Denis Goulet, *A New Moral Order: Studies in Development Ethics and Liberation Theology* (Maryknoll, New York: Orbis Books, 1974), 43.

[225] Goulet, "The Search for Authentic Development," 133. Also see Goulet, *A New Moral Order*, 23-24.

[226] Goulet, *A New Moral Order*, 24.

[227] Ibid., 23, 30-31. Lebret traveled to different parts of the world, especially to the Third World Countries including Brazil, Colombia, India, Vietnam, Senegal, the Malagasy Republic, Lebanon, Venezuela, Chile, and Uraguay.

which people lived, their economic activities, and concluded that structural evils could not just be eliminated through individual efforts alone but must be fought by concerted efforts. In the words of Goulet, Lebret believed that:

> chronic structural evils cannot be corrected by subjective goodwill, but only by concerted transformation of structures, a task which presupposes a rigorous and detailed understanding of how structures work. Lebret refused to accept the simplistic choice: *either* efficiency *or* humanization. He understood that efficiency was indispensable; but he also knew that it had to be redefined so as to serve human values.[228]

Lebret advocated a development in solidarity because it takes teamwork to effect development. He contended that planning for development should involve both "decision makers at the summit and communities at the grassroots."[229] Both Lebret and Paul VI strongly invoked participation because the latter concurred with Lebret in *Populorum Progressio* where he advocated that every member of society must contribute to the full development of the society.[230] The principle of participation was strongly invoked here. This involvement, however, demands that the social, economic, political, and cultural circumstances are properly understood. This is why, according to Goulet, Lebret thinks that

> progress or development takes place when freedoms can find their expression in institutions, norms of exchange, patterns of social organizations, educational efforts, relations of production and political choices which enhance the human potential. What is ultimately sought are basic conditions under which all persons may fulfill themselves as individuals and as members of multiple communities.[231]

A careful reading of Goulet suggests the value he attaches to the concern for the common good, freedom, education, social relations, mutual respect,

---

[228] Ibid., 30 and 33.

[229] Ibid., 35.

[230] *Populorum Progressio,*17, 8; 27,12; 65, 27; 70-71, 29; 75, 31. Also see Dorr, "Solidarity and Integral Human Development," 147-148.

[231] Goulet, *A New Moral Order*, 40.

and viable political systems. This calls for an analysis and understanding of how the socioeconomic and political systems operate. He places the human person at the center of the question of development and makes human dignity and human rights important. Efficient work toward development must take this into account and should be judged in terms of how it promotes the dignity and rights of the human person, both individually and communally.

There are similarities in the life and ultimately the experiences and vision of Louis Joseph Lebret and Paul VI. Other than being contemporaries, they were both from families of moderate background though Paul VI was from a richer family background than Lebret; they lived during the First World War and were both interested in defending their countries by fighting during the war though Paul VI was incapacitated by his poor health.[232] Just as Lebret saw the plight of the fishermen and the third world and had poor health at one moment, Paul VI experienced the same. They were interested in cultures other than their own, and they both traveled to many countries in the world, which definitely affected their outlook on life.[233] This explains their interest in the problems affecting the poor and the third world nations. Their common interest in socioeconomic and political issues is probably best explained by these facts too. It was not a surprise that both Paul VI and Lebret would view true development in the same way.

Lebret and Paul VI met during the Second Vatican Council. Paul VI (then Giovanni Battista Montini) was one of the principal figures in the drafting of *Gaudium et Spes*, The Pastoral Constitution on the Church in the Modern World, and Lebret himself was one of those who played an important role in drafting the constitution.[234] This too accounts for how Paul VI and Lebret knew each other and why Paul VI enlisted the help of Lebret in drafting *Populorum Progressio*.[235] Three other reasons possibly account for their relationship. First, both men were writers and interested in the development of poor people. Second, Paul VI lived in France, learned the language and the culture, which he liked. Third, they influenced each other through their

---

[232] Hebbelthwaite, 39.

[233] Hatch, 122-123,195-196, 205-214. Also see Goulet, *A New Moral Order*, 30-31; Barret, 222-225, 262-263; Clancy, 133-137, *Populorum Progressio*, 4, 2-3. Paul VI alludes to his trips to South America in 1960, to Africa in 1962, and his journeys to Palestine and India where he saw abject poverty.

[234] Dorr, 160.

[235] Goulet, "The Search for Authentic Development," 133.

writings; and if Paul VI had to enlist the help of Lebret in drafting *Populorum Progressio*, it was because he already knew Lebret to be an expert in the field of development. These evidences strongly suggest that Lebret exerted influence on Paul VI, especially in his encyclical, *Populorum Progressio*. This view is further supported by Goulet who affirms that

> one explicit and detailed formulation of the requirements of authentic development has been made by the French planner and philosopher, Lebret. Lebret is that rare development expert cited by name in the 1967 encyclical, the text that is commemorated and amplified in the 1987 papal document, *On Social Concern*.[236]

This is an affirmation of the influence of Lebret on the contents of *Populorum Progressio* and Paul VI's trend of thought in the document. Goulet is explicit and confirms that "Lebret served as the major expert advisor to Paul VI in drafting *On the Development of Peoples*."[237]

Lebret used his experiences to meet the development needs of his time and world.

He founded the Institute for Research and Training in Development (IRFED) in 1958 to try to resolve some of the socioeconomic problems of his time. The institute was founded "to prepare future leaders of the Third World for the difficult tasks of development."[238] Lebret died in 1966, just one year before the encyclical *Populorum Progressio,* which he helped to draft, was published.

B. Development and *The Last Revolution*, 1960/ 1965

The Last Revolution, one of Lebret's major, influential, and challenging works was written and first published in 1960 and reprinted in 1965, two years before the promulgation of *Populorum Progressio.* According to George G. Higgins, who wrote the preface of the 1965 edition of *The Last Revolution,* Lebret's main concern was

> the essential causes and remedies for economic, social and cultural misery which plagues the so called underdeveloped countries

---

[236] Ibid.

[237] Ibid.

[238] Goulet, *A New Moral Order,* 31.

and poses such ominous threat to the security and peace of all mankind.[239]

In the work, Lebret impartially critiques what Higgins calls the "established but fallacious values" of the East and the West or, more specifically, of the Soviet Union and the United States.[240] Higgins further affirmed that he was tougher on the United States than on the Soviet Union because he expected a higher standard of performance from a nation which claims to be an example of democracy than from any other nation. According to Lebret, the economic system which the West created made them rich, but it dissociated the West from "the confidence and the friendship of the underdeveloped peoples of the world."[241] Lebret was affirming that the West had created not just a gap but a rift between the rich and the poor together with its own dangers. This vision was eventually made explicit in Paul VI's advocacy for integral human development in *Populorum Progressio*.

Lebret decried the oppressive market system of the West in their dealings with the underdeveloped nations simply because he contended that the West's desire to become even wealthier has blinded them from recognizing, respecting and protecting the rights of other people, especially their rights to the basic essentials of life.[242] He further argued that because there is "greed and immoderate love of possession, there is reluctance of more advanced and consequently richer peoples to take an objective view of the world situation."[243] Here, Lebret raised the question of social and distributive justice. The argument of Lebret was that more advanced and rich nations often make decisions to favor their own interests while the poor continue to suffer and their situation deteriorates. As lack of due good poverty is evil though in itself, it is not immoral, but this kind of injustice is an offense against those who are in dire need. Lebret affirms this by saying that "the greatest evil in the world is not the poverty of those who are deprived but the lack of concern

---

[239]   George G. Higgins, Preface in L. J.Lebret, *The Last Revolution: The Destiny of Over- and Underdeveloped Nations*. Trans. John Horgan (New York: Sheed and Ward, 1965), v.

[240]   Ibid. Also see Goulet, *A New Moral Order*, 36.

[241]   L.J.Lebret, 36.

[242]   Ibid., 137.

[243]   Higgins, vi.

on the part of those who are well off."[244] In other words, the immoral thing is refusing to do something to alleviate poverty.

According to Higgins's reading of Lebret, "money has become a yardstick of everything"; and consequently, education, media, art, and culture are weighed against human persons, especially children, in terms of money, not the value of persons.[245] Higgins's interpretation of Lebret raises a question about the understanding of the dignity and rights of the human person in the Western context. It suggests the conclusion that according to the Western scale of values, human persons other than one's self and one's properties rank last and close to a slave. He aptly demonstrates this contention in his claim that the West's "persistent greed has divorced them from the higher values of human living."[246] In other words, human persons are reduced to "things" and deprived of their dignity and rights when such a yardstick is used. Here, Lebret touches the basic moral or ethical principle for integral human development, namely, the dignity of the human person.

According to Lebret, tampering with such a fundamental principle has a serious negative implication, namely, a revolution, which can erupt spontaneously because of people's constant growth in the awareness of the world situation and their own dignity.[247] This awareness may cause discontent and revolution, but the latter can be avoided by prudent and patient handling of the socioeconomic and political questions. The West or developed nations should, therefore, be cautious to avoid revolution by resolving the problem of the gap between the developed nations and underdeveloped nations or by alleviating the difficulties that confront the poor. He succinctly warned in the following words:

> It is, therefore, clear that if the West resists the change which is being imposed on it, this rejection is suicidal . . . The West can protect itself only by abandoning its introspective attitude.[248]

Lebret was in fact stating that the obliging change, not self-chosen by the West but necessitated by the status quo, is the improvement of the

---

[244] Lebret, 204.
[245] Higgins, vi-vii.
[246] Lebret, 137 and 207.
[247] Ibid., 204-205.
[248] Ibid., 162-163.

condition of the poor, which is a guarantee to avoid their violent reaction. This anticipated what Paul VI later ardently reaffirmed and advanced in strong terms in *Populorum Progressio* to the developed nations in different parts of the document after observing a gap between the developed nations and the underdeveloped nations.[249] Both Lebret and Paul VI were very conscious and cautious about the danger of violent reaction from the less fortunate people.

One of the central and critical views of Lebret, which is also reflected in *Populorum Progressio,* is the measurement and the concept of authentic development. In *The Last Revolution,* he argued that the notion of development can be deceptive. True development, says Lebret, needs to be judged by a comprehensive and careful assessment because something apparent can be claimed to be true development:

> Growth expressed in terms of increased national income per inhabitant can disguise an increase in the incomes of the rich and a corresponding impoverishment and regression in the incomes of the poor. In this case no development has taken place. Genuine development presupposes, in effect, an increase in the standard of living and in human standards which affects the huge, deprived mass of the population. It involves a generalized development of the whole human order, in every man and in all men.[250]

In *Populorum Progressio,* Paul VI articulated the notion of integral human development, which Lebret called genuine development. Both Lebret and Paul VI advocated the development of all people. Lebret advanced one of the significant arguments about authentic development when he observed that the greatest need is the development of the entire world, and what is crucial is the advancement of all people "from a less human form of existence to a more human one" as fast as possible, in solidarity and in the least costly possible way.[251] A careful reading of *Populorum Progressio* shows that this exhortation is present in the document. Dorr even testifies that Paul VI borrowed the concept of development from Lebret, and like Lebret, he emphasized "being more rather than having more."[252] It is evident that the document bears the

---

[249]   *Populorum Progressio,* 9-11, 4-5; 30-32,13-14; 49, 21.

[250]   Lebret, 150-151.

[251]   *Populorum Progressio,* 34, 15; 20,9. Also see Lebret, 209-211.

[252]   Dorr, 182 and 324. Also see Goulet, "The Search for Authentic Development," 134; *Sollicitudo Rei Socialis,* 28, 47-50. Also see *Populorum Progressio,* 20-21, 9.

influence of Lebret because it emphasizes person-centered development and argues for the complete development of all people.

Populorum Progressio and *The Last Revolution* both emphasize the human person, human dignity, human rights, equality, justice, option for the poor, and solidarity as necessary development factors. Lebret advocates a global development in solidarity when he argues that the survival of the West is possible only if it relates liberally without frontiers.[253] The underlying reason here is that the West is not self-sufficient in terms of resources. It depends on the underdeveloped nations for some of the raw materials for its industry. The West also averts the anger of the less developed countries by supporting them. Consequently, the West cannot afford to absolutely discard the less-developed nations in its economic or material endeavors.

One of the components of authentic human development, according to Paul VI, is cultural development.[254] This was not absolutely a novelty in the teaching about human development. Lebret advocated the importance of culture as a component of development. This is evident in his indiscriminate love for cultures:

> Each group has its roots in a certain part of the earth and must find its own formula for collective progress. If it uses Western values as its yardstick, the underdeveloped parts of the world can only lose their zeal for life and lapse into despair.[255]

The term *culture* is implied in the term *values*. Culture is the sum total of a people's way of living, which is in turn determined by their thought patterns and the values they hold. Western cultures are different from the cultures of underdeveloped peoples because they hold different values. Development should occur in the context of a particular culture. It is difficult to attain development out of proper cultural context. Lebret was advocating that people should treasure their own cultures and make them an integral part of the development process and, yet at the same time, respect other people's cultures because they are valuable too.

For Lebret, authentic development involves all people. He advocated participation as a necessary principle for integral development. This is why he contended that integral development is a difficult task even for the wisest

---

[253] Lebret, 207.

[254] *Populorum Progressio*, 40, 17; 72, 29-30.

[255] Lebret, 151.

person because it calls for "a collective will" and understanding.[256] Paul VI expressed this idea in *Populorum Progressio* where he indicated that "every person and all peoples are entitled to be shapers of their own destiny,"[257] everybody is an agent of human development on a personal, local, national, and international level.

Finally, Lebret advocated "a generous welcome to others" and hospitality to emigrant workers.[258] This was a call for openness to foreigners, a call for solidarity and freedom of movement. This call reflects his warning against an introspective attitude if the condition of the underdeveloped people is to be changed, and revolution is to be avoided. This exhortation is also evident in *Populorum Progressio* and expressed in almost the same way *The Last Revolution* presents it.[259]

Lebret's notion of genuine human development, the value of culture in development, and the importance of participation and the requisite conditions for authentic human development are reflected in *Populorum Progressio*. These are some of the significant indicators of the influence of Lebret's thoughts in the document. The significance and influence of Lebret on *Populorum Progressio* is further ascertained by the various evidences in the next section.

C. The Influence of Louis Joseph Lebret on *Populorum Progressio*

Lebret was one of the major influences behind Paul VI's thoughts in *Populorum Progressio*. Lebret contributed a great deal to shape the draft of the document. Paul VI's idea of integral human development is critical like that of Lebret who

> opted for a model of development that promotes community, spiritual fulfillment, and enhancement of creative freedom over mere material abundance, technological prowess, or functionally efficient institutions.[260]

---

[256] Ibid., 211.

[257] *Populorum Progressio*, 17, 8; 15,7-8; 20, 9; 65, 27-28. Also see Dorr, 198-199.

[258] Lebret, 212.

[259] *Populorum Progressio*, 1, 1-2; 17, 8; 67, 28; 69, 28. Also see Dorr, 160, 180-182, 324ff, 389, and 391.

[260] Goulet, "The Search for Authentic Development," 129. Here Goulet is quoting L.J.Lebret, *Montee Humaine* (Paris; Ouvrieres, 1958); Erich Fromm, *To Have or To Be?* (New York: Harper and Row, 1976). Also see Dorr, 160.

Paul VI himself confirms this in *Populorum Progressio,* where he quotes Lebret and speaks of him as being an eminent specialist, thus actually invoking the authority of Lebret's work to support his own arguments and authoritatively confirming that Lebret influenced his notion of authentic development:

> The development of which we are speaking does not extend solely to economic growth. To be genuine, growth must be integral, it must clearly provide for the progress of each individual and of the whole man. In this regard an eminent specialist in the field has rightly and forcefully said: "we do not approve of separating the economic from the human or of considering development apart from the civilization to which it belongs. In our opinion great value is to be placed on man, each man, each group of men and human society as a whole.[261]

Like Lebret, Paul VI "insists that what is in question is the development of each person and of every person"—integral development—which is the theme that runs throughout *Populorum Progressio* and what Paul VI attempts to articulate throughout the document.[262] This explains Dorr's claims that Lebret had great influence on *Populorum Progressio,* and in his treatise on the notion of development, Paul VI quoted from Lebret and followed the approach of Lebret. Dorr contends that "the inspiration of Lebret pervades *Populorum Progressio* and some of the statements in the encyclical are taken almost word for word from Lebret's writings." He clarifies his point:

> At the heart of *Populorum Progressio* lies a notion of integrated development, which Paul VI took from Pere Lebret, the Dominican scholar and activist who died some time before the encyclical appeared.[263]

---

[261] *Populorum Progressio, On the Development of Peoples,* (Washington DC: United States Catholic Conference, 1967), 14, 7. The eminent source and specialist Paul VI is quoting here is L. J. Lebret, O. P, *Dynamique concrete du developpement,* Paris: Economie et Humanisme, Les editions Ouvrieres, 1961, p.28.

[262] Dorr, 181. Also see Goulet, "The Search for Authentic Development," 133; *Populorum Progressio,* 14,7; 17, 8; 18, 9, and 19, 9.

[263] Donal Dorr, "Solidarity and Integral Human Development" in *The Logic of Solidarity: Commentaries on John Paul II's Encyclical on Social Concern,* eds.,Gregory Baum and Robert Ellsberg (Maryknoll, New York: Orbis Books, 1989), 154.

Marvin L. Mich Krier affirms this contention when he explains the competing schools and views of development in the 1960s in relation to Paul VI's view of development in *Populorum Progressio*. According to Krier, one of the schools at that time was the French school that advocated integral development. He refers to the French influence on Paul VI:

> Because he was something of a Francophile already, it wasn't hard for Pope Paul VI to side with the French school. So he asked the French Dominican economist Louis Lebret, O.P., to be the primary editor. Lebret served admirably in that capacity until his untimely death in 1966. Msgr Paul Poupard, another Frenchman picked up the reins and brought the process to its conclusion.[264]

Paul VI was influenced by the French culture, which he experienced and admired, and so it was not a surprise that he would enlist the help of French men like Lebret and Poupard in the writing of *Populorum Progressio*. Lebret's thoughts also affected John Paul II's thoughts in *Sollicitudo Rei Socialis: On the Social Concerns*. Goulet recognizes and acknowledges the influence of Lebret's thoughts in *Sollicitudo Rei Socialis*, which was written to commemorate the twentieth anniversary of *Populorum Progressio*, and he expressly contends that

> Lebret is that rare development expert cited by name in the 1967 encyclical "On the Development of Peoples, the text that is commemorated and amplified in the 1987 papal document "On Social Concern."[265]

Lebret discussed five essential attributes of true development. The first attribute is that development must be finalized, meaning that development "must serve the basic ends—that is, build a human economy and satisfy

---

Here Dorr quotes Francois Malley, *Le Pere Lebret: l'economie au service des homes* (Paris: Cerf, 1968), 99. Also see Dorr, *Option for the Poor*, 391. It is commonly accepted that the text of *Populorum Progressio* was drafted by Monsignor Pavan. But it is clear that "the inspiration of Lebret pervades *Populorum Progressio* and some of the statements in the encyclical are taken almost word for word from Lebret's writings" (Cf. Malley, p.99). Also see Dorr, *Option for the Poor*, 180.

[264] Marvin L. Mich Krier, *Catholic Social Teaching and Movements* (Mystic, Connecticut: Twenty-Third Publications, 1998), 155-156.

[265] Goulet, "*The Search for Authentic Development*," 133.

all human needs in an equitable order of urgency and importance."[266] True development meets human needs according to a properly arranged scale of values. Second, development must be coherent, meaning that it has to address "all problem sectors in a coordinated fashion" without sacrificing one for the sake of another. Authentic development therefore should not be fragmented or segmented. This also features in *Populorum Progressio*.[267] Third, authentic development is homogeneous. Here, Lebret means that development should not be imposed. It should respect and include people's cultural aspirations, their abilities, and their history. *Populorum Progressio* reechoes this view.[268] Fourth, according to Goulet's reading of Lebret, authentic development is self-propelling. This means true development capacitates or empowers people, provides for their autonomy, and minimizes their "dependence, parasitism, passivity and inertia." This recurs in Paul VI's *Populorum Progressio*.[269] Finally, true development is indivisible. This means development should benefit all people, facilitate the attainment of the common good, and bridge gaps between rural and urban populations. Lebret's claim that authentic development is indivisible resonates with Paul VI's core statement in *Populorum Progressio* about authentic human development and other similar statements spread throughout the document.[270]

A careful reading of *Populorum Progressio* reveals a widespread presence of the attributes of authentic human development advocated by Lebret.[271] Chronologically, *Populorum Progressio* was written after Lebret's death. When Paul VI speaks of development for each and all, and as the transition from less human conditions to more human conditions, he does so under the influence of the inspirations of Lebret. This distinction was initially made by Lebret as Goulet states.

> The normative expressions "more human" and "less human" need to be understood in the light of a distinction Lebret considered vital: the difference between *plus avoir* ("to have more") and *plus etre* ("to be more"). A society, Lebret contends, is more human or more

---

[266] Goulet, *A New Moral Order*, 44-45. Also see Goulet, "*The Search for Authentic Development*," 134-135.

[267] *Populorum Progressio*, 14, 7; 23, 10-11.

[268] Ibid., 30, 13; 72, 29-30.

[269] Ibid., 14,7; 23-24,10-11.

[270] Ibid., 14,7.

[271] Ibid.,14,7; 17, 8; 19,9; 23, 10; 30, 13; 47-48, 20-21; 55, 23 and 82, 34.

developed not when men and women "have more," but when all citizens are enabled "to be more." The main criterion of value is not the production or possession of goods, but the totality of qualitative human enrichment. Some material growth and quantitative increases are doubtless needed for genuine development, but not any kind growth or increase at any price.[272]

Authentic development is enhancement of the quality of the life of all people, not necessarily an increase in the quantity of goods. These are interpretations of the thoughts of Lebret, but they typically anticipate Paul VI's thoughts in *Populorum Progressio*. *The Last Revolution* and Goulet's interpretations of the writings and thoughts of Lebret evince the relation and similarity between the thoughts of Lebret and Paul VI about the notion of true human development.

V. Significant Pontifical Documents During Paul VI's Pontificate

A. *Humanae Vitae:* On the Regulation of Birth (1968)

Humanae Vitae, the last and most controversial papal encyclical of Paul VI, was written in 1968. The central issue the document dealt with was the regulation of birth. One reason for reading *Humanae Vitae* in the light of *Populorum Progressio* is to throw some light in understanding the issue of integral human development. *Humanae Vitae* is treated here because it dealt with life, which grounds the fundamental right to life, and human development is all about the necessities for and the quality of human life.

The relationship between *Humanae Vitae* and *Populorum Progressio* is explicit in the question of population and human dignity where Paul VI argues that the problem of rapid demographic growth should be addressed in such a way that human dignity remains unharmed.[273] As part of the

---

[272] Goulet, *A New Moral Order*, 43. Also see Goulet, *"The Search for Authentic Development,"* 134. It is appropriate to mention here that, as manifest in many other parts of *Populorum Progressio*, Lebret's influence is associated with the document, even only on the basis that Paul VI directly quotes him as an eminent expert in development. Also cfr. *Populorum Progressio*, 14, 7.

[273] *Populorum Progressio*, 37, 16.

treatise on integral human development, *Humanae Vitae* is supported by authors like David M. McCarthy who reads the document in the light of *Populorum Progressio* and advocates that it says a lot about authentic human development.

> The framework of *Humane Vitae* is at once social and theological, since it begins with a statement about our cooperation with God and repeatedly turns to concerns about human community.[274]

McCarthy contends that *Humanae Vitae* relates human life to God— the origin and destiny of life—and relates individual human life to other individuals and to the entire human society. In society, lives mutually interact and are affected by God. McCarthy further argues that in *Humanae Vitae*,

> Paul VI proposes that we cannot make the world a better place by denying the procreative character of human sexuality. In HV, he relates the issue of contraception to contemporary social problems, to which contraception is considered by many to be a solution but, in fact, holds out only hollow promises for the goods of life. Contraceptive practices promise relief in a culture where child rearing is an economic liability and a risk to one's personal life style, but Paul VI warns that we will undercut the basic structure of social life if we abdicate our common calling to bear and raise children. Modern development strategies promote advancement by means of eliminating the social and economic drag of having children. Paul VI, in contrast, is convinced that true development necessarily includes the basic human activities of child rearing. HV fits with his wider proposals for authentic human development. True human community cannot be attained at the cost of its own generative character and true development is known through the flourishing of creation of which this generative character is a part.[275]

---

[274] McCarthy, "Procreation, the Development of Peoples, and the Final Destiny of Humanity" in *Communio: International Catholic Review* (Winter 1999), (26), 698. Also see Dorr, "Solidarity and Integral Human Development," 147-148.

[275] McCarthy, 700-701.

The first fundamental issue addressed here is that of the procreative character of the human sexuality and the sexual act itself. On the grounds that the sexual act is procreative in character, the proximate argument is that the procreative element is progressive because it has the potential of generating new life. This is the fundamental element of development within the sexual act. It is from this quality that the unfolding of hidden potentials, properly called development, starts. If this is obstructed, the human species and the divine design are at stake.

Paul VI views procreation and child rearing as constituent elements of true development. According to McCarthy, this shows how *Humane Vitae* is in line with Paul VI's comprehensive proposal for authentic human development. Contraceptive practices militate against integral development because they impede the growth, enhancement, and natural unfolding of life. Paul VI actually made a compelling assertion that procreation is "fundamental to God's design, and as such, the procreative character of sexual acts is not optional."[276] The main problem Paul VI addressed was that of the inherent intended procreative character of sexual acts. Whether sexual acts, initially, have such a character or not is beyond human control. This suggests why Paul VI used strong terms though not without exceptions. The gravity of the problem is confirmed by Hatch, according to whose reading of Paul VI, "the question of birth control represents the most serious present-day confrontation between Science and the Church" because contraceptive practices contradict the original divine plan for human persons.[277] This claim is founded on the divine command to "be fruitful, multiply and conquer the earth."[278] The assertion offers a theological foundation for arguing for human development and raises its social implications for development because of the shared nature and origin of humanity. McCarthy argues that

> questions about our nature are always social because they refer to claims about human solidarity, and these claims are eschatological: true human community is precisely the meaning and mission of the Church . . . . By abiding in continuity with our supernatural end, we will see creation coming to fulfillment which is the very

---

[276] Ibid., 701.

[277] Hatch, 249.

[278] Genesis 1:27-28.

possibility of authentic human community. *Humane Vitae* says nothing less.[279]

McCarthy's argument suggests that the ultimate human community is the eschatological community, the heavenly kingdom of God, and all earthly expressions of solidarity in social life anticipate this ultimate community and solidarity. This is the most authentic and integral human development in the language of *Populorum Progressio*.[280]

McCarthy argues that like *Populorum Progressio*, *Humanae Vitae* features the invitation to participate in the divine activity of creation. For him, *Populorum Progressio*'s call for participation of all in the process of development is reasonable:

> The character of our nature as ordered creation underlies every point and sets the claims of HV within the framework of our participation in God's gracious activity and the fulfillment of our human nature through a supernatural end.[281]

Creation was initially intended to be orderly—a cosmos, not chaos. This order was initiated by divine action, but cooperative human action is to participate in promoting it. This is why all should participate in the maintenance of this order. Participation presented in *Populorum Progressio* is echoed here as necessary for integral human development.[282] If divine intention and human collaboration are separated, the intended end of creation is in jeopardy. It is, therefore, important that the rest of *Humane Vitae* be interpreted with this link between God's activity and human involvement and the supernatural end of humanity in mind. Collaboration and participation in divine activity is one of the theological reasons for integral human development whose climax is union with and participation in the life of God.

Paul VI was concerned about rapid population growth in Southern American and Asian countries as his experiences during international trips

---

[279]   McCarthy, 701-702. Here McCarthy is quoting Henri de Lubac, *Catholicism, Christ and the Common Destiny of Man*, trans. Lancelot C. Sheppard and Sister Elizabeth England, OCD (San Francisco: Ignatius Press, 1988), 48-55.

[280]   *Populorum Progressio*, 16, 8.

[281]   McCarthy, 701.

[282]   *Populorum Progressio*, 27, 12; 65, 27; and 80-85, 33-35.

revealed to him.[283] This concern is relevant because population growth has significant implications for integral human development and procreation. McCarthy acknowledges that "the transmission of human life is a most serious role (*munus*) in which married people collaborate freely and responsibly with the Creator."[284] Procreation is a vital responsibility of married people because through it, they collaborate in integral development intended by God.

Population growth has significant social implications because it is "intimately connected with the life and happiness of human beings."[285] Life has a social dimension because the life of a person affects that of others and vice versa. *Humanae Vitae* advocated that the transmission of life is the most serious duty of married people because human life is always intimately related to other peoples' lives. Whatever undermines human life undermines human society, and vice versa, because of this intimate relationship.

Paul VI observed that population growth raises a number of concerns. The first problem is that the rapid population increase leads to distress in families and developing countries. Consequently, civil authorities could take radical measures to curb population growth that outpaces the requisite resources for decent life, a problem further aggravated by "modern economic conditions, which put an increasing burden on housing and raising large families."[286] Such concerns are real, but they need to be addressed appropriately. Paul VI did not consider state-enforced population control an appropriate solution. An appropriate resolution to the problem of rapid demographic growth is the enforcement of economic justice, resolving problems of urbanization and the first-world consumption, living in human solidarity, and, as John Paul II suggests, taking the question of the inviolability of human life and dignity seriously because "life is always a good."[287] These resolutions help promote human dignity because they provide conducive situations for human life to thrive.

---

283   Hatch, 249.

284   McCarthy, 702. Here McCarthy is quoting *The Papal Encyclicals 1958-1981*, trans. Claudia Carlen, (McGrath Publishing Co., 1981), 223-33. The Latin text is in Peter Harris, et al, *On Human Life: An Examination of Humanae Vitae* (London: Burns and Oates, Ltd, 1968), 107-161. Also see *Humanae Vitae*, 1, 1.

285   *Humanae Vitae*, 1, 1. Also see McCarthy, 702.

286   Ibid., 2, 1. Also see McCarthy, 702-703.

287   John Paul II, *Evangelium Vitae: The Gospel of Life* (On the Value and the Inviolability of Human Life) (Washington DC: United States Catholic Conference, 1995), 34, 60. Also see McCarthy, 703.

Second, population growth results in concern about the person and dignity of women and their place in society. If human progress is to be integral, the concern about women's place is in the context of "conjugal love in marriage" and the "conjugal acts in relation to that love."[288] This is crucial, especially in the context of contemporary views about women's dignity where "reproductive rights (to abortion as well as contraception) have been hailed as grantors of women's equality, autonomy, and bodily integrity."[289] According to Paul VI, contraception is not true progress because its repercussions on the dignity of women are negative. These repercussions include encouragement to disregard the dignity of women, placement of private conjugal life at the mercy of public authority, lowering of morality, loss of respect, disruption of women's psycho-physical equilibrium, and reduction of women to instruments or objects of selfish desires.[290] All these consequences are dehumanizing, not enhancing the life and dignity of women. McCarthy summarizes Paul VI's concern as follows:

> Contraception fosters a lack of reverence for women in so far as it frees up the arbitrary will of men and violates the limits of control set within creation. In *Octogesima Adveniens,* Paul VI rejects "that false equality (for women) which would deny the distinctions laid down by the Creator himself and which would be in contradiction with women's proper role, which is of such capital importance, at the heart of family as well as society. (OA13). Contraceptive practices, Paul, claims, diminish the dignity of women and the integrity of their bodies.[291]

The principal concern here is women's dignity. Contraception dishonors women's dignity and integrity. This vision is relevant because it affirms the respect for the very basic development principle—human dignity.

Aggressive advocacy for liberation of women and promotion of contraception has been partially prompted by the modern economic system, demanding equality of women and men. Liberal advocates call for freedom for women from the burden of child-rearing so that they may also contribute socially and economically to society. The problem with such advocacy is that

---

[288] *Humanae Vitae,* 2, 1.

[289] McCarthy, 706.

[290] *Humanae Vitae,* 17, 11-12. Also see McCarthy, 706.

[291] McCarthy, 706.

children are considered liabilities to economic freedom and growth.[292] The objection is compounded if economic freedom is preferred to child-rearing because human life and dignity are valued less than economic progress. What emerges here is the issue of human dignity in relation to authentic development. However, here the threat is only potential—not real—because the issue here is the attempt to prevent the phenomenon of conception.

Human dignity is the epicenter of true development and defines it. If human dignity is disregarded in the process of economic progress, the result is not integral and authentic development. The strength of *Humane Vitae* precisely lies in its advocacy for respecting human life because life has dignity.

The last area of concern addressed in *Humane Vitae* is the human tendency to claim dominion over self. The issue here is that "humans are attaining control over the body, the mind, social life and even over laws that regulate the transmission of life, a concern also expressed by the Congregation for the Doctrine of Faith nineteen years later."[293] Reproductive and other technologies come with temptations to manipulate human life in the name of progress. Paul VI affirms this position in two of his documents. McCarthy states,

> Paul VI challenges this logic of contraception by objecting to its underlying assumptions about productivity and progress. In *Populorum Progressio* and *Octogesima Adveniens*, he argues that development and progress are false when defined primarily in economic terms. Such progress actually frustrates growth on both personal and social levels.[294]

What Paul advocates here, according to McCarthy, is that contraception excludes the value of life and economic development may not be considered the only development. Second, human life, the human person, and human dignity are the reasons for any kind of development. Finally, exclusive economic growth falls short of Paul VI's understanding of development. The human person is more than material possessions, and what a person owns does not define the person. Persons are defined by the totality of what affects

---

292   McCarthy, 707-708.
293   *Humanae Vitae*, 2, 2. Also see McCarthy, 704; *Instructions on Respect for Human Life in its Origin and on the Dignity of Procreation*, III, 35.
294   McCarthy, 704.

their life and destiny. Consequently, true human development transcends economic progress and embraces all people. This suggests why according to McCarthy, *Populorum Progressio* teaches that "true progress, then, embraces the whole of human community, and it is directed to our eschatological (rather than merely temporal) solidarity."[295] The climax and ultimate realization of integral human development is eternal life salvation of body and spirit. This affirmation resonates with Paul VI's thoughts about holistic salvation, the ultimate integral human development, in *Populorum Progressio*.[296]

Paul VI's consistent argument against contraception is that it does not have a holistic view of the human person as an individual and as a part of the human community. This point of view explains McCarthy's concluding statement about the human tendency to claim dominion over self and develop independently. He says,

> If self-development and the procreative character of human life are disregarded, then progress and human mastery are out of control. The abundance that comes in this reductionist term is inauthentic, self-serving and unjust.[297]

If technology and human culture are defined independently of human persons, problems develop with regard to human life; "technology is inherently disordered, and contraceptive technology is likely to be a symptom of social problems rather than a real solution."[298] The human claims of dominion over self and one's needs ought to take into account the social context of the individual persons as well as the entire community.

Paul VI argued that marital love is not limited to the loving interchange between husband and wife. It must go beyond this to bring new life into being, thus meeting the development of natural potentialities and human social needs.[299] Paul VI is emphasizing that marriage has a social dimension because it is for the promotion of human society. In support of this view, McCarthy contends that

---

[295] Ibid.

[296] *Populorum Progressio*, 16, 8.

[297] McCarthy, 706.

[298] Ibid., 705.

[299] Ibid., 709-712.

> Contraception is certainly a question about the beginning of life, but primarily it is an issue of human solidarity, in accord with the end of creation and our human community with God.[300]

If community is to survive, it is the duty of everybody including married couples. This demands that contraception must be treated in the context and application of the principle of solidarity according to which we need others to be and to become. Without this in view, married couples disregard their relation to the rest of human community and the common good. This argument resonates with James P. Hanigan, who argues that the human person and human actions must be viewed in relation to other people. Explaining the moral agent within community context, he says,

> To recognize the social nature of the human person is to recognize that human beings need one another in order to be what they are-human. Human life is not possible in isolation . . . . Human development cannot take place apart from a human community . . . . To ignore the social dimension of human life, to turn our backs on society, to contemn the social order, is to ignore, turn away from and contemn ourselves.[301]

Hanigan supports the idea of solidarity and its significance in human life. Here, two observations are in order in relation to the notion of integral human development advocated by Paul VI. First, human development that excludes the rest of society falls short of being integral. It is incomplete. Second, excluding society is evil—a lack of due good—because development is not a negation. It is a promotion of potentialities that lie deep within individuals and communities.

It is appropriate to conclude that *Humanae Vitae* reechoes some of the doctrine of *Populorum Progressio*, which advocated that technology, increased productivity, and economic growth by themselves are not the whole of development. They are just a quasi development according to Paul VI. They do not fully make the earth a more suitable living place for human beings.

---

[300]   Ibid., 715.

[301]   James P. Hanigan, *As I Have Loved You: The Challenge of Christian Ethics* (New York and Mahwah: Paulist Press, 1986), 77-78. Also see Dorr, "Solidarity and Integral Human Development," 147.

Human fulfillment must be realized within the context of solidarity with humans and in solidarity with God.[302] In true development, the human person works together with God and other people. This is the authentic progress because it is not opposed to the divine design.

B. *Octogesima Adveniens:* A Call to Action (On the Eightieth Anniversary of *Rerum Novarum*—1971)

Octogesima Adveniens was written in 1971 to commemorate the eightieth anniversary of *Rerum Novarun* and the tenth anniversary of *Mater et Magistra*. It is an apostolic letter written by Paul VI "to Cardinal Maurice Roy, president of the Council of the Laity and of the Pontifical Justice and Peace Commission."[303] The document was written typically in the spirit of *Gaudium et Spes*. It was a response provoked by the Medellin Conference of the Latin American bishops in 1968, which was itself triggered by the Second Vatican Council, especially the discussion of *Gaudium et Spes*.[304]

Gaudium et Spes treated justice in relation to poverty and peace, and Medellin carried forward the same theme by advocating the option for the poor as an act of justice and the need for liberation. The conference made a shift from merely discussing economic issues to making the economic question a part of political discussion. Although the document was directly addressed to Catholics, its impact goes beyond the Catholic community because the community interacts with the world beyond itself. This contention is supported by what O'Brien and Shannon claim.

> *Octogesima Adveniens* emphasized that action for justice was a personal responsibility of every Christian, that this responsibility rested on Christian organizations and institutions, but that it involved both the effort to bear witness to the principles of justice in personal and community life and acting to give those principles life in society.[305]

According to Henriot and others, "Paul VI acknowledged the difficulties inherent in establishing a just social order and pointed to the crucial role of

---

302   *Populorum Progressio*, 34, 15. Also see McCarthy, 721.
303   Curran, 11. Also see O'Brien and Shannon, 263 and 265.
304   Walsh and Davies, 245. Also see Dorr, 206.
305   O'Brien and Shannon, 263.

the local Christian communities in meeting this responsibility."[306] The innate difficulty here is the one of using the same principles, norms, and directives of the Catholic social thought because the circumstances in which people live are not always exactly the same. Involvement of people at the grassroots was considered crucial for building a just society. Similarly, Curran affirms that in this letter Paul VI urged "Christians to participate and contribute to solving the many problems facing individual countries and the world."[307] Participation and cooperation or collaboration are necessary prerequisites to resolve the problem of injustice. Christian communities are, in particular, urged to be involved in critical examination of the contexts in which they live. This is necessary because of the existing variable contexts in the different countries.[308] It was precisely for this reason that Paul VI stated that

> it is up to the Christian communities to analyze with objectivity
> the situation which is proper to their own country, to shed on it
> the light of the Gospel's unalterable words and to draw principles
> for reflection, norms of judgment and directives of action from the
> social teaching of the Church.[309]

The exhortation was written in the spirit of *Populorum Progressio's* teaching about integral human development where Paul VI articulates the issue in terms of the various individual countries and the world community. This reiterates the argument about individual and social dimensions of authentic human development, which is actually a development in solidarity. Paul VI proposes critical analysis of situations in which Christians find themselves as one of the crucial responses to the problem.[310] Here, the emphasis is that people have responsibility to shape their own situations. Like one of its successor documents, *Evangelii Nuntiandi, Octogesima Adveniens* called people to a critical observation, examination, and evaluation of circumstances in which they live to hear the Word of God and to act on it according to the practical situations of their daily life. Precisely, their future is determined by them because it is in their own hands.

---

[306] Henriot et al., 10-11. Also see *Octogesima Adveniens*, paragraph 4.

[307] Curran, 11-12.

[308] O'Brien and Shannon, 263.

[309] Paul VI (Pope), *Octogesima Adveniens: A Call to Action* (Washington DC: United States Catholic Conference, 1971), 4, 2-3. Also see Henriot et al., 11.

[310] Curran, 12.

Paul VI suggests that such a process occurs in three stages or moments: "evaluation and analysis of their contemporary situation," "prayer, discernment, and reflection" on the situation in the light and teachings of the Gospels and the church and "pastoral action which fights injustices"[311] and positively transforms society. This means action should be taken to exercise and defend the course of justice. However, effecting change in the world is the duty of all. This duty ought to be enlightened by and based on the Gospel.

Paul VI made a leap in addressing the social question in *Octogesima Adveniens* because development tended to be limited only to the economic sphere. Paul VI decided to emphasize liberation because the political question is part of the economic agenda, and this suggestion was a shift of emphasis from economics to politics.[312] He made this move because he was convinced that political action should check the power of multinational corporations that create economic difficulties due to their magnitude and power, outpacing small corporations and private enterprises. There was need for a body that moderates socioeconomic relations. Paul VI "acknowledged the significance of the political dimension"[313] but also knew and acknowledged that politics is not an end in itself—it is a means to help achieve human development in different forms.

In *Octogesima Adveniens*, Paul VI also dealt with other issues affecting modern society. These included urbanization and its contingent consequences. For Paul VI, urbanization and industrialization are not necessarily indicators of human development; they are occasions for exploitation and need to be carefully weighed because they sometimes create problems rather than solving them.[314] This viewpoint reechoes Paul VI's notion of authentic development in *Populorum Progressio*.

Octogesima Adveniens also addressed issues of equality and participation, says Curran:

> This document emphasizes the human aspirations to equality and participation; recognizes some legitimate aspects in Marxism, especially as a tool of sociological analysis, condemns liberal ideology, discusses urbanization and mentions environment for the first time.[315]

---

[311] Henriot, et al, 11.
[312] *Octogesima Adveniens*, 20, 11-12 and 44, 24. Also see Dorr, 212-215.
[313] Walsh and Davies, 245.
[314] Ibid.
[315] Curran, 12.

Since these aspirations affect human life, they need to be addressed squarely. Here, Paul VI addressed various issues in the document and did not favor just one political or ideological system. Much as he opposed Marxism, he shows that there is also something good in the Marxist ideology. He also demonstrates that liberal ideology has its own pitfalls. The integral character of his approach is manifested in his ecological concerns and in the diverse nature of themes the document dealt with.

Octogesima Adveniens dealt with various issues. These include justice in personal and community life, participation which expresses personal responsibility in development, solidarity, equality of human persons, common good, charity, global ecology, and the principal ideologies behind many political programs, all of which were treated as significant and necessary for human development.[316] By concentrating on the question of justice, *Octogesima Adveniens* has close ties with *Justitia in Mundo*, which was published the same year.

C. *Justitia in Mundo*: Justice in the World (Synod of Bishops, Rome, 1971)

Justitia in Mundo: Justice in the World is one of the most important documents issued by Rome on the issue of justice in the history of Catholic social thought.[317] It was published in 1971 after the Synod of Bishops convoked by Paul VI as part of the follow-up of the Second Vatican Council and intended to implement the acts of the council, especially to make the church more active and vigilant in pastoral activities and the question of "world justice and peace."[318] *Justitia in Mundo* is like the two documents that preceded it—the Medellin Conference document and *Octogesima Adveniens*—because of its contextual approach to social issues and its theme of social justice.[319] According to the Synod of Bishops, the church has a duty to bring about change in society when that is called for. Consequently, the synod fathers advocated that the transformation of institutions through

---

[316] O'Brien and Shannon, 263.

[317] Dorr, *Option for the Poor*, 228. Here, Dorr states that no Roman document of such gravity and seriousness was ever issued about justice in the history of Catholic social teaching before *Justitia in Mundo*. The document was therefore a landmark in the history of Catholic social thought about justice.

[318] O'Brien and Shannon, 287.

[319] Dorr, *Option for the Poor*, 229.

involvement in social and political issues is a "constitutive dimension of the preaching of the gospel."[320]

Justitia in Mundo centered on the question of justice in the world to be effected through pastoral action. It specifically addressed structural injustice as its core agendum because, according to the bishops, social structures obstruct conversion, structural injustices affect international economic relations, and people need to be liberated from such situations.[321] Development is suggested here as a means to liberation, but it ought to be noted that liberation itself is actually a process of development. Justice is emphasized as a constituent element of evangelization and catechesis. The synod fathers made this clear when they said that:

> action on behalf of justice and participation in the transformation
> of the world fully appear to us as a constitutive dimension of the
> preaching of the Gospel or, in other words, of the Church's mission
> for the redemption of the human race and its liberation from every
> oppressive situation.[322]

Awareness about justice is necessary to help people realize the need to exercise justice in society. They can learn to practice justice if they are taught. Therefore, people need to be reminded of unjust situations where they exist. The synod fathers clearly stated that "the Church must stand with the poor and the oppressed if it is to be faithful to the gospel mandate."[323] Here, *Justitia in Mundo* used the language of the Second Vatican Council, the Medellin Conference, and *Octogesima Adveniens*, which all admitted that differences in local contexts must be taken seriously when addressing social questions.[324]

---

[320] Synod of Bishops, *Justitia in Mundo: Justice in the World* (Washington DC: National Conference of Catholic Bishops, 1971), 6, 34. Note here that the original publication of this document did not have paragraph numbers, but subsequent publications numbered the paragraphs of the document. Also see Williams, 17, and Walsh and Davies, 270.

[321] Dorr, *Option for the Poor*, 229-230. Also see *Justitia in Mundo*, 16, 37 and Walsh and Davies, 272.

[322] *Justitia in Mundo*, 6, 34. Also see Walsh and Davies, 270; Henriot, et al, 11 and 62; Curran, 12, and O'Brien and Shannon, 289.

[323] O'Brien and Shannon, 289.

[324] Walsh and Davies, 268.

Consequently, the synod fathers further advocate that pastoral agents who are in touch with the actual life situations of the people have the duty to discover this and integrate it into their pastoral actions, including evangelization. This suggests that their preaching must be down to earth, and it should touch the real issues affecting the people they minister to. This call also challenges the church as an institution that ministers to society. Walsh and Davies affirm this when they state that "the Bishops admit that the church has itself not always been the very best example of that justice which it now preaches."[325] The church ought to reflect on its functions and relation to the people. It is clear that the document is hinting that the church is also an employer and needs to examine herself about how she treats people she employs. The church should be the protagonist and a living justice as she is also the advocate for justice. Curran's arguments show that this is evident in the bishops' statement in *Justitia in Mundo*.

> The bishops call for significant structural change in our world, based on justice and universal solidarity. The document underscores the need for ecclesial witness to justice in the church's own practical life if the church's teaching is to be credible in the world.[326]

The call for changes in social structures was prompted by the fact that development comes with some negative consequences such as rapid demographic changes or growth, rural stagnation, lack of land reform, massive rural-urban migration and the consequent urbanization, and unemployment caused by technological advancement from all of which people have to be liberated.[327] These are not precisely measures for authentic development because they are not liberating, they are oppressive, dehumanizing, and do not solve problems. The victims of injustice that come out of such situations are migrants, refugees, those persecuted for their faith, those whose rights are restricted, political prisoners, orphans, and nations or regions that are not given opportunities to grow.[328] These are typical indicators of underdevelopment and ought to be overcome.

---

[325] Ibid.

[326] Curran, 12.

[327] Dorr, *Option for the Poor*, 230-231.

[328] *Justitia in Mundo*, 20-26, 38-40. Also see Walsh and Davies, 273-274, and Dorr, *Option for the Poor*, 234.

According to Henriot and others, during the bishops' synod in Rome in 1971, the bishops clearly made their mind known in *Justitia in Mundo*. The document shows that the Bishops linked together the dynamism of the Gospel and the hopes of people for a better world today and in the future.[329] What is implied here is that a dynamic interpretation of the Gospel in accordance with every context is mandatory in the face of people's desperation about what the future holds for them. In other words, people's understanding of justice and their hope to experience it and a good life are determined by the way the Gospel is preached in our contemporary world. What the document advocates is that injustice must be fought by all people in different ways. The document concentrates on and emphasizes the role of the church and calls for the church to actually witness to justice by example.[330] This is evident in its emphasis on integrating justice and evangelization, yet it puts less emphasis on the role of civil institutions and individuals. The document addresses the problem from one side only. Development or eradication of evil in society involves all people. This is true and necessary because the principle of responsible participation is vital for joint development efforts. *Populorum Progressio* is clear about this, but the synod fathers did not emphasize this adequately.

Like other preceding documents, including *Populorum Progressio, Justitia in Mundo* outlined some basic principles and necessary conditions for integral human development. These are justice, participation, solidarity, and, indirectly, human rights. The document also alludes to the option for the poor and the relational or social character of the human person as a necessary consideration.[331]

D. *Evangelii Nuntiandi*: Evangelization in the Modern World (1975—Paul VI)

In 1975, ten years after the Second Vatican Council and eight years after *Populorum Progressio*, Paul VI wrote his apostolic exhortation *Evangelii Nuntiandi: Evangelization in the Modern World*. The document was "not primarily a statement of Catholic social teaching," but is important for the church's involvement in socioeconomic and political issues because it emphasized that

---

[329] Walsh and Davies, 270. Also see Henriot et al., 62, and *Justitia in Mundo*, 5, 33.

[330] Curran, 12.

[331] O'Brien and Shannon, 287.

salvation "is liberation from everything that opposes man"(EN9), thus decisively linking the proclamation of the gospel to the concern about the sort of life people have to live in this world.[332]

Salvation and liberation are used as synonyms here. Paul VI cautioned, however, that evangelization should not be mistaken for human liberation in a political sense, and the church should not be identified with any political system of liberation. The church advocates a holistic liberation, but political liberation falls short of a holistic one. As a mark of the celebration of the tenth anniversary of the closing of the Second Vatican Council, *Evangelii Nuntiandi* "affirms the council's teaching on the active role that the institutional church and individual Christians must play in promoting justice in the world."[333] The specific aspect of liberation addressed in this case is the liberation from situations of injustice. This is to be achieved through preaching and living the Word of God. This lends support to the claim that *Evangelii Nuntiandi* is in continuity with the teaching of the Second Vatican Council, especially *Gaudium et Spes*—which treated justice as one of its central themes—and *Justitia in Mundo*.

Other issues addressed by *Evangelii Nuntiandi* are human rights, solidarity, peace, the human person, development, and liberation in the dual sense— spiritual and material liberation. Henriot and others suggest in *Catholic Social Teaching: Our Best Kept Secret* that in this apostolic exhortation Paul VI was not just advancing Catholic social tradition but was advancing some of the agenda of *Populorum Progressio*, including his idea of integral human development.[334]

Evangelii Nuntiandi emphasized the cultural dimension of liberation.[335] This means besides economic, political, and structural change, it called for change in people's thought patterns and way of life. The theme of liberation and salvation in *Evangelii Nuntiandi* is a resurgence of the same theme of the Medellin Conference and in *Justitia in Mundo*. This shows how *Evangelii Nuntiandi* is in continuity with the issues treated by the two documents which preceded it.

---

[332] Walsh and Davies, 284.

[333] Henriot et al., 66.

[334] Ibid., 67.

[335] Dorr, *Option for the Poor*, 242-247 and 258.

Evangelii Nuntiandi and *Populorum Progressio* are related through *Gaudium et Spes*, which influenced Paul VI's understanding of authentic human development. *Evangelii Nuntiandi* shares with *Gaudium et Spes*, especially where it dealt with issues like family life and life in society besides other issues such as peace, justice, and development. All that *Evangelii Nuntiandi* did was to advocate that the various dimensions of life be changed by the Gospel message. The document has conspicuously manifested notion of integral human development—the growth of the entire person, holistic salvation, and liberation.

In *Evangelii Nuntiandi*, Paul VI confirmed the profound link between "evangelization and human advancement," "development and liberation."[336] Evangelization has an integral character because it is about human liberation and development. It teaches about human rights, duties, family life, peace, justice, development, and liberation and shows that human liberation and solidarity depend on the proclamation of the Gospel message—evangelization—because it creates conversion and collaborative conscience and ultimately transforms people's actual life.[337] On the bases of such interlocking relationships and the authorship of the documents, it is right to suggest that the documents are related in their contents. Henriot and others also affirm this:

> Here he emphasized that preaching the Gospel would be incomplete
> if it did not take into account human rights and the themes of family
> life, life in society, peace, justice and development. Liberation—in
> both its spiritual and its temporal senses—must be proclaimed. The
> plan of the redemption includes combating injustice.[338]

Even if *Evangelii Nuntiandi* does not explicitly deal with integral human development, the tone of the document supports such a conclusion because it is also related to other Catholic social doctrines. For instance, like *Gaudium et Spes*, *Evangelii Nuntiandi* states that the laity have the role and duty to influence the life, thoughts, and actions of people in their work places or environments of life.[339] Similarly, as it explicitly deals with the question of

---

[336] *Evangeli Nuntiandi*, 31, 18. Also see Walsh and Davies, 284.
[337] O'Brien and Shannon, 301.
[338] Henriot et al., 12.
[339] O'Brien and Shannon, 301

evangelization, *Evangelii Nuntiandi* is closely related to *Justitia in Mundo* because of its emphasis that "working for social justice is an essential part of the meaning of the Gospel."[340] This is a significant argument because justice is a virtue upon which the Gospel teachings are centered. However, the Gospel message is more than justice alone.

> Evangelization involves an explicit message, adapted to the different situations constantly being realized, about the rights and duties of every human being, about family life without which personal growth and development is hardly possible, about life in society, about international life, peace, justice and development—a message especially energetic today about liberation.[341]

The issues with which *Evangelii Nuntiandi* dealt show how Paul VI continued to emphasize some of the issues he dealt with earlier in *Populorum Progressio*. These issues are social in nature but directed to liberation of all at all levels, and this coheres with the Christian message of liberation as universal salvation. *Evangelii Nuntiandi* needs to be read in the light of the preceding documents.

The following remarks are in order about *Evangelii Nuntiandi*: First, the document consistently insisted on the social context of people as vital for evangelization. Second, it dealt with questions like justice, human rights, solidarity, peace, the human person, and human dignity. Third, all the questions articulated were centered on the human person and human dignity because this is the object of evangelization, liberation, and total salvation. Fourth, like other documents of Catholic social teaching, *Evangelii Nuntiandi* attempted to address practical life problems. Fifth, the contextual emphasis of the document on issues is significant socially, politically, economically, and spiritually. Sixth, the document and other documents preceding it point to one significant theological fact: namely, that theology, religion, and belief have to be and must be ractical if they are to achieve their real goals. Finally, they can be practical only if they address real issues that lead to true or integral liberation or salvation because theology is an integral enterprise.

---

[340] Curran, 12.

[341] Ibid.

VI. CONCLUSION

This chapter dealt with the biography of Paul VI, forces that influenced his trend of thought, and the development of the Catholic social encyclical and pastoral tradition since Leo XIII's *Rerum Novarum* in 1891. The study suggests that Paul VI was a multifaceted person and a pastor whose life was carefully modeled on the personalities of people he encountered, interacted with from within and without his family. The study suggests why Paul chose to write the encyclical, *Populorum Progressio*: *On the Development of the Peoples,* with an emphasis on the integral character of authentic development.

The treatise of the encyclical and pastoral tradition from *Rerum Novarum* (1891) to *Evangelii Nuntiandi* (1975), apart from *Populorum Progressio,* leads to some significant observations. First, Catholic social teachings before and after *Populorum Progressio* had progressive influences and relationships. The documents prior to *Populorum Progressio* influenced and shaped Paul VI's thoughts in *Populorum Progressio,* and those that succeeded it were in a like manner influenced by it. Second, the arguments that feature in the Catholic social and pastoral tradition gravitate around the *dignity of the human person,* whether they treat human life, human rights, justice and peace, equity, common good, subsidiarity, charity, participation and involvement, option for the poor, affirmative action, solidarity, or ownership of property. This suggests that human dignity is the fundamental principle of Catholic social teaching about development. It is the *imperative moral principle* governing authentic human development. All other conditions for authentic human development gravitate to and circulate around human dignity. Third, the historical development of the teaching of the Catholic social encyclical and pastoral tradition shows that the various questions mentioned above, which are related to the dignity of the human person, are recurrent. Fourth, there have been other social errors in the history of humankind, and they seem to continue to recur. Fifth, the church, the state, and every individual has a responsibility and role to rectify such errors by way of correction or active intervention. Sixth, in order to achieve this, certain principles and guidelines are necessary and should be properly articulated, grasped, and applied. Seventh, considering the historically prevalent circumstances, change or renewal is necessary. This is evident in the study, which shows that Catholic social teaching on human development has been progressive because each document was either innovative or it clarified the doctrine of the preceding documents. Finally, such a vision of the Catholic social tradition suggests that resolutions reached in the past have either been inadequate or inadequately comprehended, applied, and followed. This inevitably suggests that there is some unfinished business, a business that will be treated in the successive chapters of this work. The next chapter, in particular, will present principles, conditions, and guidelines for authentic human development as presented in Paul VI's *Populorum Progressio*. The foundation laid by this chapter is, therefore, necessary for an appropriate understanding of the next chapter.

CHAPTER TWO

The Doctrine of *Populorum Progressio*

I. Introduction

Chapter one was intended to give a background for understanding Paul VI's doctrine in *Populorum Progressio* on the central theme of integral human development. The overarching concern of this chapter is the notion of development and the requisite principles, virtues, and conditions for authentic human development. It will focus on Paul VI's concern in *Populorum Progressio* about four distinct issues: he wanted to articulate the problem of development, outline the significance of a programmatic development for poor countries, denounce injustice, and emphasize the relation between development and peace.[342]

The encyclical has been called the Magna Carta of Catholic teaching on human development.[343] It is the fundamental document of the Catholic Church's teaching about human development because the document "represents a remarkable advance on the previous Church teaching about

---

[342] Marvin L. Mich Krier, *Catholic Social Teaching and Movements* (Mystic, Connecticut: Twenty-Third Publications, 1998), 155.

[343] Mary Synder Hembrow, "Development" in *The New Dictionary of Catholic Social Thought*, ed. Judith A. Dwyer (Collegeville, Minnesota: Liturgical Press, 1994), 280. Also see Peter J. Riga, *The Church of the Poor: A Commentary on Paul VI's Encyclical on the Development of Peoples* (Techny, Illinois: Divine Word Publications, 1968), vii.

human development."[344] It is a foundation for the subsequent teachings on human development. *Rerum Novarum* of Leo XIII (1891), *Quadragessimo Anno* of Pius XI (1931), *Mater et Magistra* of John XXIII (1961), *Pacem in Terris* of John XXIII (1963), and *Gaudium et Spes* of Vatican Council II (1965) had treated some of the issues discussed, but they were treated in less depth than in *Populorum Progressio*. Unlike the previous documents "written from a predominantly European perspective, *Populorum* had international overtones."[345] With the additional influence of *Gaudium et Spes*, it went beyond the influence of the previous documents.

"The understanding of human development worked out by Paul VI in *Populorum Progressio* was a major contribution, relevant" not only for the time he wrote "but also to the world of 1980s"[346] and for our times. This is demonstrated in Paul VI's understanding and definition of human development and social justice and his treatment of diverse issues related to the question of human development. He defined development more deeply and broadly than ever before in any document of Catholic social teaching on development and treated justice from a global, not only national, point of view.[347] This is further evidenced in the statement by the United States Bishops' Conference that *Populorum Progressio* specifically

---

[344] Donal Dorr, "Solidarity and Integral Human Development" in *The Logic of Solidarity: Commentaries on John Paul II's Encyclical on Social Concern*, ed. Gregory Baum and Robert Ellsberg (Maryknoll, New York: Orbis Books, 1989), 144. Also see Peter J. Henriot, "Who Cares about Africa? Development Guidelines from the Church's Social Teaching" in *Catholic Social Thought and the New World Order: Building on One Hundred Years*, ed. Oliver Williams and John H. Houck (Notre Dame: University of Notre Dame Press, 1993), 210.

[345] Julian Filochowski, "Looking Out to the World's Poor: Teachings of Paul VI" in *The New Politics: Catholic Social Teaching for the Twenty-First Century*, eds. Paul Valley (London: SCM Press, 1998), 61. Also see Krier, 155.

[346] Dorr, 143. Also see John Paul II, *Sollicitudo Rei Socialis: On Social Concern* (Boston: Pauline Books and Media, 1987), 41, 77.

[347] Judith A. Merkle, *From the Heart of the Church: The Catholic Social Tradition* (Collegeville, Minnesota: Liturgical Press, 2004), 122. Also see Donal Dorr, *Option for the Poor: A Hundred Years of Catholic Social Teaching* (New York: Orbis Books, 1992), 180.

proposes a Christian vision of the authentic development of people . . . emphasizes the universal destination of created goods and condemns liberal capitalism . . . reinforces the idea of the duty of prosperous nations to help developing nations . . . highlights the widening gap between the rich and poor, and emphasizes that "development" is the new name for "peace."[348]

The problematic issues in development are as old as human history and involve both sad and happy memories—suffering and enjoyment, joy and sadness, sufficiency and insufficiency—involving individuals, nations, and the international community and covering different facets of human life: "political, economic, social, educational, medical, technical and similar fields."[349] Albert T. Dalfovo further asserts that the question of development involves both answers or solutions and questions or problems, and "it is better to reverse the issue and to recognize that development is a question before being an answer, it is a problem before being a solution."[350]

The assertion of Dalfovo is credible because problems precede development. Development simply comes in as solution. Without problems, there would be no need for solutions and development. Development offers solutions but begins with problems, which provoke human thinking and search for solutions to problems. Paul VI's treatise on the question of development gives this picture. His recognition of the prevalent problems provoked him to redefine and articulate the subject of human development more comprehensively than even before Lebret defined it.

This chapter is divided into three main parts. Part one deals with the actual problems Paul VI was addressing. Part two treats Paul VI's general response to the problems and their consequences. Part three deals with ways to attempt to alleviate the situation or resolve the outstanding problems in

---

[348] Robert J. Vitillo and Donna Toliver Grimes, ed., *Principles, Prophecy, and a Pastoral Response: An Overview of Modern Catholic Social Teaching, Catholic Campaign for Human Development*, rev. ed., (Washington DC: United States Conference of Catholic Bishops, 2001), 38.

[349] Albert T. Dalfovo, "The Rise and Fall of Development: A Challenge to Culture" in *African Philosophy*, vol.12, no.1, (Massachussets, Cambridge: SAPINA and ISAP, 1999), 38.

[350] Ibid.

the attainment of integral human development. The requisite principles, virtues, and conditions necessary for integral human development are also discussed in the third part.

II. The Crux of the Problem: The Fundamental Issues

In *Populorum Progressio*, Paul VI addressed a number of urgent problems ranging from "the gap between rich and poor to the differences and tensions between wealthy and impoverished countries."[351] This view suggests that the document treated international development issues. The principal concern of Paul VI was the magnitude of the critical problem of poverty evident in the ever-increasing gap between the rich and the poor and its effects on human dignity. His initial statement succinctly summarizes this fact:

> The development of peoples who are making very great efforts to free themselves from the hardship of hunger, poverty, endemic diseases, and ignorance, who are seeking a more bountiful share in the benefits flowing from civilization demanding that greater value be in fact set upon their qualities as human beings, and who are constantly giving their attention to great growth is gladly and encouragingly viewed by the Catholic Church.[352]

Hunger, poverty, disease, and ignorance directly affected less-developed countries. According to Paul VI, the developed nations had contributed to part of the problems. He listed the core issue regarding integral human development:

> While today we see that men are seeking to find a more secure food supply, cure for diseases, steady employment, increasing personal responsibility with security from oppression and freedom from degradation endangering the dignity of man, better education,

---

[351] Richard P. McBrien et al., eds., *Populorum Progressio"* in *Harper Collins Encyclopedia of Catholicism* (San Francisco: Harper Collins Publishers Inc., 1989), 1033. Also see Riga, 15-16 and 18, and Kevin E. McKenna, *A Concise Guide to Catholic Social Teaching* (Notre Dame: Ave Maria Press, 2002), 65.

[352] Paul VI (Pope), *Populorum Progressio: On the Development of Peoples* (Washington DC: United States Catholic Conference, 1967), 1, 1-2.

in a word while men seek to be more active and consequently to enhance their value, we see at the same time that great numbers are living in conditions which frustrate their just desires.[353]

Paul VI was comprehensive in his attempt to address factors that affect true development. The crucial issues related to authentic development are the questions of meeting the basic needs of life, human dignity, human rights, responsibility and participation, education, and the ultimate satisfaction of the needs of individuals. Peter Riga's observations about the document are helpful for an understanding of the issues raised by Paul VI:

> The social encyclical of Paul VI, *Populorum Progressio*—"On the Development of Peoples"—is the culmination of the voice of the modern popes on the problems and agonies of the men of our day. A note of urgency is one of the letter's outstanding characteristics; Pope Paul obviously considers the problem of poverty and underdevelopment the most pressing and dangerous issue of our day. On the resolution of this issue will hang the balance of peace and, indeed the future of human race.[354]

The crux of the problem raised by Paul VI was that the human dignity was in jeopardy. Paul VI was explicit in pointing this out even if he was not consistent in doing so throughout the document. Human dignity is threatened by the prevalence of misery. This threat may be aggravated by the apparent absence of peace. Paul VI "addressed in *Populorum Progressio* what was clearly the social problem of the age—the division between the rich and the poor nations."[355] It must be added that he did so with foresight and a very close attention to the attendant or related problems. These problems were practical socioeconomic and political issues manifested in the prevalent poverty, ignorance, hunger, and diseases. They were further evident in avarice, inequality, selfishness, cultural degradation, nationalism, racism, and the adversely affected epicenter of human development, namely, human dignity. All of these were indicative of the "growing gap between rich and poor

---

[353] Ibid., 7-8, 10.

[354] Riga, viii.

[355] Filochowski, 61.

nations"[356] and particularly in their understanding of the human person or their failure to take the true notion of the human person seriously.

It should be emphasized that these problems and threats to human dignity were consequences of selfishness, which Paul VI called greed and egoism, besides the problem of a misconstrued notion of human development, which was partially the cause of the other problems mentioned above. It must also be emphasized that all of these issues were related to the human person and particularly human dignity. Riga reminds us that Paul VI's presentation in *Populorum Progressio* shows that "what must remain as the crux of social thought is man—every man and all men."[357] Precisely, human dignity stands at the center of the question and is crucial to development.

Populorum Progressio focused on human community and individuals, their relationships and circumstances in life. The encyclical was concerned with major areas affecting people. These included not only human dignity, but also human aspirations, structural injustice, the role of the church in human development, a new vision of humanism, common good, international socioeconomic and political relations, and peace.[358] Here, it is relevant to suggest that *Populorum Progressio* exhibits the spirit of *Gaudium et Spes,* which intended to offer joy and hope to people in desperate situations as the title of the document states.

A. Socioeconomic and Political Conditions

The socioeconomic and political problems addressed by Paul VI were worldwide. They were rampant that time and being addressed by other religious leaders too. For instance, in many ways, Paul VI grappled with socioeconomic and political situations similar to those confronted by Martin Luther King Jr., although one set of issues was national (that of King) and the other set was international (that of Paul VI). Nonetheless, from a practical perspective, the issues addressed were intimately related, as Hanigan indicates for King.

---

[356] Charles E. Curran, *Catholic Social Teaching, 1891-Present: A Historical, Theological and Ethical Analysis* (Washington DC: Georgetown University Press, 2002), 11.

[357] Riga, 29.

[358] Peter J. Henriot et al., eds., *Catholic Social Teaching: Our Best Kept Secret* (Maryknoll, New York: Orbis Books, 1988), 52.

Concretely for King social evil meant segregation, the second rate status afforded America's black citizens, and economic injustice, the simple disparity between the rich and the poor, the fact that some men had more than enough while others went hungry or homeless. In a formal sense social evil comprehended those institutional elements which put restrictions upon or distorted the development of the human personality.[359]

These are the same evils Paul VI was addressing in *Populorum Progressio*. There is little wonder that there is such a vivid similarity. The two addressed real problems of the world of the 1960s. They both addressed the question of social injustices, the gap between the rich and poor, racism, and the question of human development. King advocated the development of all the citizens of the United States of America in the same manner and in different areas of life. The difference between the two is apparently the level at which they addressed the issues and the methodology they used.

Populorum Progressio opened with a statement on the prevalent phenomenon of inhuman material or economic conditions of people who are attempting to overcome their desperation. Paul VI did not limit this problem to just a national level. Instead, he emphasized the international character of the social question but specifically underscored the development needs of the developing nations.[360] This phenomenon of desperation, according to Paul VI, is evident in the prevalent hardship caused by hunger, poverty, diseases, and ignorance of people who are struggling to liberate themselves from their conditions in order to experience greater human values than what they currently experience.[361] The international problem was, therefore, not only caused by desperation in the underdeveloped countries. It also included the relationship between developed and underdeveloped countries and the dangers of apathy on the side of the rich nations.[362]

---

[359] James P. Hanigan, *Martin Luther King, Jr. and the Foundations of Nonviolence* (Lanham, MD: University Press of America Inc., 1984), 156.

[360] Curran, 11.

[361] *Populorum Progressio*, 1, 1-2. Also see Henriot, 53.

[362] Richard W. Rousseau, *Human Dignity and the Common Good: The Great Papal Social Encyclicals from Leo XIII to John Paul II* (Westport, Connecticut: Greenwood Press, 2002), 263. Also see *Populorum Progressio*, 1-13, 1-7.

1. Poverty and Avarice

Paul VI observed that avarice was one of the causes of the problems. This explains why he addressed the question of ownership of property. However, a caution is necessary according to Paul VI because property is not possessed for the sake of increasing one's power, but for enhancing the dignity of the human person. Avarice must, therefore, be avoided or averted by all. The underlying reason for this global call was that avarice, whether of individuals or families or nations, equally affects both the rich and the poor and "can drive both to *materialism* which stifles their souls."[363] The ultimate end of productive work is not avarice or accumulation of material resources because they are not an end in themselves but are means to an end. Here, Paul VI was addressing an enduring problem. The gravity of the problems caused by avarice or greed was expressed thirty-two years later when the international community was attempting to address and resolve the population and development problem.[364]

Paul VI was prompted to such advocacy because of his personal observations of the ordeal of the poor and the conditions of the rich nations. He alluded to his prepontifical and pontifical trips to various places—South America (1960), Africa (1962), Palestine and India, where he had firsthand observation of the pathetic economic situations there. He stated that such and similar observations were what prompted the Church to request the United Nations to intervene to help the poor.[365] The difficult economic conditions of the less-developed countries were another immediate major cause of concern for Paul VI.

Paul VI's reference and appeal to the UN was an indirect suggestion of the significance of affirmative action, namely, aggressive government intervention on behalf of the desperate poor, on the international or global level, and the significance of the principle of subsidiarity and option for the poor even if not directly stated by Paul VI. He was suggesting that a bigger, more powerful, and capable body that could respectfully but firmly and forcefully intervene on behalf of the poor, especially when they could not handle their own problems, was necessary. Such a body should continue to function and never be obsolete

---

[363] *Populorum Progressio,* 18, 8-9.

[364] *The Rome Statement on the International Conference on Population and Development,* ICPD (Religion Counts, January 1999), 4.

[365] *Populorum Progressio,* 4, 2-3.

at any moment if world affairs are to progress.[366] The significance of such a body would be to regulate the distribution of resources and curb avarice at a global level when necessary.

2. INEQUALITY AND INJUSTICE

According to Paul VI, the inequalities and injustice consequent to technological advancement were problems that needed to be addressed too.[367] Although technology helped to improve the situation of colonial subjects, technological advancements cause rapid inequalities unless their use is well checked to avoid such disparities. However, inequalities are increasing because some nations produce more than they need while others are constantly in need of more or produce less than they need, or they are uncertain of meeting their aspirations of sales of their produce.[368] Paul VI was addressing the problem of what I would call *development fixation* in underdeveloped countries and the opposite in the developed countries. This affirmation confirms the gravity of the growing gap between the rich and the poor. It also confirms the inadequate support for the less-developed nations and their deteriorating situation. There was an imbalance between the steady and rapid growth in developing countries and the stagnation of underdeveloped countries.[369] While underdeveloped nations were not advancing, developed nations continued to advance further and so to increase economic and political differences.

Inequalities were also experiences of regions dependent on agriculture and farmers were aware of their wretched situations in comparison to the industrialists and the prevailing inequalities among them as farmers.[370] These inequalities include possession of goods and the exercise of power. This means that while the minority lived a decent and dignified life, the majority lived in dehumanizing conditions, where freedom is curtailed by those who tended to control most of the resources. Paul VI was addressing the problem of the growing gap between the minority rich and the majority

---

[366] Michael Walsh and Brian Davies, eds., *Proclaiming Justice and Peace: Papal Documents from Rerum Novarum through Centesimus Annus*, rev. and exp. ed. (Mystic Connecticut: Twenty-Third Publications), 223, 241-242.

[367] Ibid., 221. Also see *Populorum Progressio*, 8, 4.

[368] *Populorum Progressio*, 8, 4. Also see Hennelly, 764.

[369] Rousseau, 265. Also see Hennelly, 764.

[370] Rousseau, 265. Also see *Populorum Progressio*, 9, 4-5.

poor, who were totally incapacitated to live humane lives and to work under decent and healthy circumstances. He described the situation as follows:

> For it happens in certain regions that while a small and select number enjoys a most refined culture, the needy meanwhile and the scattered inhabitants, "lack almost every possibility of acting on their own initiative and responsibility, spending their lives in living and working conditions unworthy of human beings."[371]

Paul VI was addressing the theological problem that a growing gap between rich and poor nations inhibits God's intention from being realized.[372] He specifically referred to the universal destiny of natural resources. Here it is noteworthy that the issue of inequality between the rich and the poor is a global reality, even if Paul VI's focus in *Populorum Progressio* was on the problems in the less-developed countries.

3. CULTURE

Conflict of cultural interests or values was another problem Paul VI identified. The encounter between traditional cultures and industrial civilization forges conflicting social structures and creates conflicts between adults and young people because the two categories of people hold divergent cultural values.[373] Paul VI was clear about this problem:

> Then since the traditional civilization is in conflict with recently introduced industrial civilization, it happens without fail that social structures not corresponding to modern needs are almost shattered. Consequently, while adults think that the life either of individuals or families is to be centered as it were in the framework, often times narrow, of this civilization and believe that it is not to be abandoned; the young at the same time consider it a kind of

---

[371] *Populorum Progressio*, 9, 5. Here Paul VI is quoting Vatican Council II *Gaudium et Spes, Pastoral Constitution of the Church in the Modern World*, n. 63, AAS 58(1996), 1085.

[372] McBrien, 1033.

[373] Rousseau, 265. Also see *Populorum Progressio*, 10, 5.

meaningless barrier which keeps them from eagerly advancing to new ways of life in society.[374]

While adults cling to traditional values, youth look at them as obstacles to modern advancement, which they consider as development. According to Paul VI, this tension needs to be eased or eradicated. People constantly deliberate whether to retain traditional cultural institutions and values and forego progress or to discard the culturally rich traditions in favor of modern technology and novel cultural values. Oftentimes, traditional, moral, spiritual, and religious values, convictions, and institutions are discarded and do not have a place in new values and institutions. The principal problem here is the radical break from tradition and the intimate attachment to an inadequately comprehended culture. According to Richard Rousseau, this is a real "breakdown of traditional customs and attitudes."[375] This, according to Paul VI, is where development falls short of its authentic character. This is a plausible assertion because abandoning one culture in favor of another is absorption rather than integrated development, which is open to relevant values. Development is not a matter of discarding old or traditional practices and taking up new ones. Rather, it is an integration of new and old valuable cultural heritage, a continuity of the old in the new. It ought to be noted here that cultural integration is sometimes difficult to achieve but its possibility is what Paul VI's arguments suggest in this case.

The difficulty of uncritical choice of cultural values was the problem that Paul VI thought needed to be addressed. He cautioned developing nations against the attraction to values of wealthy nations whose cultural and technical civilizations and example of hard work and industry, which produced their prosperity to a high degree.[376] Though good in itself, Paul VI contended that temporal prosperity and cultural values of wealthy nations do not meet all human needs, especially spiritual needs. Cultures should be critically examined and only "excellent and useful" values should be sought and developed together with those of the "less wealthy"[377] nations. Paul VI was actually advocating that poor nations should not take up the cultures of the technologically developed and wealthy nations and abandon their own

---

[374] *Populorum Progressio*, 10, 5.

[375] Rousseau, 265.

[376] Ibid., 269.

[377] *Populorum Progressio*, 41, 18.

because of an apparently better and superior nature of the cultural values of the wealthy nations compared to that of the less-developed nations. Here he affirmed that development is not measured in terms of technology and industry alone because they do not define the superiority or inferiority of a particular culture. The significance of a culture is defined by how human it is. As long as cultures of less-developed nations esteem the human person and promote human dignity, they are worthy of retention. This is why, according to Rousseau, Paul VI warned that "developing countries must be careful of simply accepting the values and examples of wealthy nations."[378]

The problem of cultural conflict is sometimes aggravated by those who leave their native countries to study in foreign countries, especially developed or industrialized nations. Paul VI cautioned youth who study in developed countries and eventually lose esteem for their own traditional and cultural values.[379] The problem with such students is that they often attain an excellent education in the developed nations, a knowledge that would be beneficial for their home countries if well integrated with their own culture; but oftentimes, they overlook and disregard the invaluable cultural and spiritual values of their own nations.[380] Besides this, they sometimes abandon their own countries and decide to live in the developed nations. Here, Paul VI addressed the significant issue of loss of skilled labor by less-developed nations to the more-developed ones. When people from the former category of countries refuse to return to their *patria*, they contribute to the slow progress at home but a faster progress in the more-developed nations because instead of being the brains for development and using their skills at their home countries, they add their skills and brains to what the more-developed countries already have. This behavior of expatriate students also partly contributes to the widening gap between the less-developed nations and the developed nations.

4. Population Explosion

Paul VI was concerned about demographic issues in the less-developed countries because of inadequate resources for a decent life. He observed that rapid population growth exceeding "available resources adds its own problems to development."[381] In his judgment, population growth was disproportionate

---

[378] Rousseau, 269.

[379] Ibid., 272.

[380] *Populorum Progressio*, 68, 28.

[381] Rousseau, 268.

to the supportive productivity of developing or less-developed nations. This was threatening decent living conditions. In such cases, resources "badly needed for industrialization and capital investment"[382] are diverted to meet the fundamental or primary needs. According to Paul VI, this does not promote other aspects of development:

> It is not to be denied that accelerated demographic increases too frequently add difficulties to plans for development because the population is increased more rapidly than available resources so that all solutions seem to end in a blind alley.[383]

If population growth outpaces the development or the availability of requisite resources for humane living, it is hard to satisfy the material needs of the people. Alternatively, human needs may not be addressed in morally desirable ways. Paul VI's principal concern was that population explosion was creating difficulties in the development of the third world countries.[384] He feared that the temptation would be the attempt by the legitimate authorities to radically or drastically limit population growth by use of unethical or immoral methods. He wanted demographic problems to be resolved without tampering with human dignity. This is where, according to Paul VI, explosive demographic growth becomes problematic to true human development. This problem was also later recognized and acknowledged by John Paul II in *Sollicitudo Rei Socialis* as an obstacle to development.[385]

5. NATIONALISM AND RACISM

Paul VI observed that nationalism and racism are not supportive of integral human development. According to him, nationalism was often misunderstood and given a negative connotation as expressed in its practice in some countries. It was precisely understood to mean *chauvinism*, which

---

[382] Riga, 50.

[383] *Populorum Progressio*, 37, 16.

[384] Riga, 49.

[385] Peter J. Henriot, "Who Cares About Africa? Development Guidelines from the Church's Social Teaching" in *Catholic Social Thought and the New World Order*, eds., Oliver F. Williams and John W. Houck (Notre Dame: University of Notre Dame Press, 1993), 230. Also see John Paul II, *Sollicitudo Rei Socialis*: On Social Concern (Boston: Pauline Books and Media, 1987), 25, 41-42.

is "blind patriotism."[386] This understanding of nationalism differs from the positive understanding of it as patriotism or love for and defense of one's own country. Paul VI was concerned that nationalism as practiced at that time tended to be a reaction to colonialism and had discriminating overtones, which did not allow for solidarity beyond one's own country. This would not promote integral development. Rousseau's reading of *Populorum Progressio* shows that the primary reason for the inconsonance of nationalism and racism with true development is that they are opposed to the spirit of solidarity and ultimately contrary to the spirit of integral human development.[387] Nationalism and racism—and let it also be affirmed in African and similar contexts that tribalism, caste system, and all sorts of favoritism—are factors that impede integral human development. Initially, nationalism was mainly a problem of newly independent former colonies because these newly independent states wanted to assert themselves as separate entities, but in the course of self-assertion, they were isolating themselves from other nations. According to Paul VI, just as it was before colonial withdrawal, equality based on human dignity and solidarity remains problematic today because of nationalism and racism.[388] Here, Paul VI pointed out that nationalism and racism are enduring problems in the way of development. Nationalism is problematic and an obstacle to integral human development because it

> is divisive and stands in the way of people's genuine advantages, but it causes the most serious harm particularly in those areas where the needs of national economy demand on the contrary the pooling of efforts, or of knowledge, or of financial resources to carry out the plans for economic development and to increase and strengthen commercial and cultural ties.[389]

The problem with nationalism is that it is opposed to the essential conditions or principles necessary for integral human development. These include solidarity, common good, participation, involvement, universal

---

[386] Gove Babcock, *Webster's Third New International Dictionary of English Language*, Unabridged (Springfield, Massachusetts, USA: Meriam Webster Inc. Publishers, 1986), 380.

[387] Rousseau, 272.

[388] *Populorum Progressio*, 62, 26.

[389] Ibid.

charity, peace, and justice. For Paul VI, nationalism and racism were similar. According to him, racism is an international phenomenon. It existed in newly independent states where there was a diversity of people of various backgrounds. The similarity between nationalism and racism, and even tribalism, is that they fragment human community. They are opposed to the spirit of global solidarity, and they promote limits, division, and they are detrimental to national and international community respectively.

Where there is human diversity, tribal wrangles, separatist political affiliations, and factions also develop. Paul VI observed that racism was detrimental to justice, it endangers civil peace and welfare, it obstructs mutual and profitable understanding, and it provokes conflicts based on prevalent injustice. All of these are serious threats to integral human development because they are, by nature, opposed to the spirit of mutual integration and growth. Racism and tribalism have similar effects on human development as nationalism. Paul VI was categorical that racism is

> an obstacle to collaboration among poverty-stricken people and sows the seeds of discord and enmity within countries as often as either individuals or families see themselves deprived of basic rights of the rest of the citizens on account of race or color with contempt for man's inalienable rights.[390]

Paul VI did not explicitly mention tribalism as a problem, but by inference, tribalism rightly falls in the category of problems or obstacles to development because like nationalism and racism, tribalism absolutely does not support solidarity in a wide or universal sense. All three recognize the value of solidarity, common good, participation, involvement, personal responsibility, charity, peace, and justice but to a very limited extent. They do not go beyond the borders of nation, race, and tribe.

B. A Misconstrued Notion of Development

Paul VI decided to redefine human development because he recognized and acknowledged a serious problem with the notion of development. He noted that what many people and governments claimed to be development was in fact a quasi development. The prevalent notion of development at that

---

[390] Ibid, 63, 26-27.

time was exclusively an economic one. This was one of the problems that people needed to confront and find an answer to. Paul VI was of the view hat if authentic development is not properly understood it is still harder to achieve.

Paul VI acknowledged that development is misconstrued if viewed solely from a material point of view, which is devoid of social and spiritual dimensions of a human person. Consequently, he cautioned against two issues regarding development. First, individuals and nations should not consider the growth in supply of possessions their ultimate goal, and neither is it the ultimate goal of true development. Considering the growth in quantity of possessions as development is a mistaken notion of development. The definition of true development is broad.[391] Second, Paul VI acknowledged that development has a twofold effect: positively, it contributes to the progressive growth of the human person; and negatively, development imprisons a person if it is considered "the highest good beyond which one is not to look."[392] The second effect of material growth falls short of integral development because it excludes the ultimate end and meaning of true human development. Material growth is not liberating; authentic development has a liberating dimension.

The problem here is the temptation to think that economic growth alone is complete development and ultimately to make a clear distinction between true development and inauthentic development. Paul VI incessantly and consistently disputed the idea that economic development is the whole of development. According to him, giving priority to material possessions while neglecting real needs of people because of greed or avarice was not true development because it is adversely consequential to the human person. He described the consequence as follows:

> Consequently, the exclusive quest for economic possessions not only impedes man's development as a human being but also opposes his true greatness. For both nations and men who are infested with the vice of avarice give clearest evidence of moral underdevelopment.[393]

Paul VI's emphasis here does not deny the value of material or economic development which constitutes only a fraction of true development. His

---

[391] Riga, 81. This affirmation is well explained in *Populorum Progressio*, 19, 9.

[392] *Populorum Progressio*, 19, 9.

[393] Ibid.

principal concern was human dignity. He contended that as people progress economically or materially, and otherwise, they should also grow morally. Material or economic development should not retard or curtail moral development or overlook human dignity. Though not explicated this way, Paul VI's contention is tantamount to stating that economic development and moral development should have a direct proportionality, not an inverse one. This makes sense especially when conceived in the context of Paul VI's notion of integral human development. Authentic development is all-dimensional and does not retard the growth of people materially and spiritually, economically and morally.

C. Causes of the Problems

Paul VI attributed misconstrued notion of development to three main factors, which he thought played a great role in creating the prevalent situations, which moved him to write *Populorum Progressio*. These were colonialism, neocolonialism with subsequent imbalance of power and wealth, and imbalance in trade relations and economic power in general between the rich and the poor nations.[394]

1. THE EVIL LEGACY OF COLONIALISM

The first cause of poverty, according to Paul VI, is the negative legacy of colonialism.[395] Colonialism left enduring negative effects on the economy of many countries that were left dependent on single export crops subject to sudden and considerable price fluctuations.[396] Although colonizing powers brought to the colonies quality achievements through science and technology and left beneficial results of their presence—diminished ignorance, diminished sickness, benefits of communication, and improved standard of living—in many underprivileged regions, they often perpetuated their own interests, power, domination, and glory, and their departure left precarious economies

---

[394] Filochowski, 61-62. Also see *Populorum Progressio*, 7, 4; 9, 5; 56, 4; 57, 4; 58, 4 and Dorr, *Option for the Poor*, 185.

[395] Merkle, 123.

[396] Rousseau, 271. Also see *Proclaiming Justice and Peace: Papal Documents from Rerum Novarum Through Centesimus Annus*, 221.

in the former colonies.[397] Though Paul VI appreciated the work of the colonialists, he also questioned how disinterested they were in their endeavors and suggested that the lacuna in their endeavors was lack of authentic charity and justice.

The product of colonialism, according to Paul VI, was inadequate to face the hard realities of modern economics. The colonialists widened levels in the world's standard of living, rich people enjoyed rapid growth while the poor developed slowly, and some people produced a surplus while others produced less and were incapable of exporting.[398] Paul VI observed that there was an economic, social, and political power imbalance. There was inequality in the exercise of power, a limited group of people enjoyed refined civilization, and the majority of people were poor, deprived of nearly all possibility of personal initiative and responsibility, and lived under conditions unworthy of human beings.[399]

Paul VI was opposed, though not absolutely, to capitalism or liberal trade. He called into question the fundamental principle of economic liberalism, which was responsible for the socioeconomic and political power imbalance, and requested a moderation in free trade.[400] In the context of the doctrine of the document, it is plausible to affirm here that Paul VI took such a stance because property and subsequently profit are not evil in themselves if they are used to promote human dignity. Promotion and priority of property is bad only when it serves selfish ends, compounds exploitation, and disregards human dignity.

Paul VI contended here that poverty is not merely self-made or caused by natural factors—it is a human creation. Filochowski affirms this assertion. According to him, Paul VI thinks "clearly it is not to be assumed that poverty and underdevelopment result from natural causes or laziness."[401] To affirm that the poor are the cause of their poverty or to blame for their poverty is to presume that poverty cannot be a consequence of other people's attitude or behavior. It is naïve to understand it that way. An integral and critical

---

[397] Dorr, *Option for the Poor*, 186. This view is explicit in *Populorum Progressio*, 57, 24 and Merkle, 123.

[398] Walsh and Davies, 221. Also see Dorr, *Option for the Poor*, 186.

[399] Dorr, *Option for the Poor*, 187.

[400] *Populorum Progressio*, 58, 24; 59, 25; 60,25; 61,25-26. Also cfr., Dorr, *Option for the Poor*, 187.

[401] Filochowski, 63.

consideration of the causes of poverty is called for here. I would suggest that people should see beyond the context of prevalent poverty to its causes and solutions to alleviate it. The concession that laziness is one of the factors that thwarts development is true and ought to be added to any list of obstacles to development. Work enhances human dignity and contributes to material human growth.

2. The Current Neocolonialism

For Paul VI, the prevalent neocolonialism was a significant cause of development problems.[402] The problem with neocolonialism is that it perpetuates political pressure and economic domination aimed at acquiring wealth and maintaining political control by/for a few. It aims at dominance which contradicts the principle of respect for human dignity.[403] According to Paul VI, nationally, neocolonialism promotes economic domination; and internationally, it encourages both economic and political domination of poor countries by rich countries. Here, Paul VI again raised the issue John XXIII had raised in *Pacem in Terris* when he emphasized that "there can no longer exist a world divided into nations that rule and nations that are subject to others."[404] Paul VI was suggesting that colonialism is obsolete. This position was based on the equality of the dignity of people. Although Paul VI apparently thought neocolonialism was a suspicion and a possibility rather than a reality, he never took it for granted, and he addressed problems related to it.[405] It is important to note that neocolonialism was and still exists. Paul VI questioned the motives behind grants and suggested that they should not be given to subdue or curtail the freedom of the recipients; instead, they should promote their dignity.

---

[402] David J.O'Brien and Thomas A. Shannon, eds., *Catholic Social Thought: The Documentary Heritage* (Maryknoll, New York: Orbis Books, 2001), 238. Judith A. Merkle calls Neocolonialism a new colonialism to emphasize that there is not much difference between colonialism and neocolonialism because the subjects are under external domination. Cfr. Merkle, 123.

[403] Dorr, *Option for the Poor*, 186. Also see *Populorum Progressio*, 52, 22.

[404] Riga, 16. Here Peter Riga is quoting John XXIII, *Pacem in Terris: Peace on Earth* (Washington DC: National Catholic Conference, 1963), 42, 11-12.

[405] *Populorum Progressio*, 7, 4; 79, 32-33. Also see Riga, 45.

Paul VI contended that bilateral and multilateral agreements create dependence and bitterness. They should be replaced by systems that substitute dependence and feelings of enhancement, left by colonialism, for systems that build a happier relationship of friendships based on constitutional and political equality.[406] If, under the cover of financial assistance and technical aid, there is political pressure and economic motive aimed at complete domination, then there is something unjust with the arrangement. This frustrates efforts to assist developing nations, financially and technically, and deteriorates to an illusion because benefits accruing from such endeavors would be, at least partially, nullified.[407]

3. Trade and Power Imbalance

Paul VI noted with concern that imbalance in power led to injustice in trade relations and contributed to the poor state of development in the third world nations, which were just beginning to grow or had not yet started growing.[408] He challenged the status quo of international trade relationships and underscored that these relations are arranged to help the rich nations to become richer while poor ones become poorer.[409] Development cannot be integral if trade relationships promote growth in some nations and undermine development in others. This is one of the causes of poverty and underdevelopment in disadvantaged nations. It is also externally determined by the attitude of international trade partners.

Paul VI was concerned about the system of trade between rich and poor nations because it was characterized by an unchanging course to the detriment of poor countries. This was again partly a negative consequence of colonialism. Industrialized nations primarily export manufactured goods, which have constantly increasing prices, while developing countries export raw materials whose prices constantly fluctuated.[410] This is why developing

---

[406]   Rousseau, 270. Also see *Populorum Progressio*, 52, 22.

[407]   *Populorum Progressio*, 56, 24. Also see Rousseau, 271

[408]   Merkle, 123.

[409]   Dorr, *Option for the Poor*, 186. Also see *Populorum Progressio*, 57-60, 24-25. Also see Alfred T. Hennelly, "*Populorum Progressio*" in *The New Dictionary of Catholic Social Thought*, ed. Judith A. Dwyer (Collegeville, Minnesota: Liturgical Press, 1994), 769.

[410]   Dorr, *Option for the Poor*, 186. Also see *Populorum Progressio*, 7, 4; 57, 24.

nations find it difficult to balance their economy or trade. Consequently, they remain poor.

Human persons, human dignity, and human rights are often threatened by malfunctioning socioeconomic, religious, and political systems. An understanding of true development, healthy trade relationships, the exercise of Christian and human virtues, just political arrangements, and just social structures are also significant for the esteem and protection of the human person and the human dignity. From these observations, it is realistic to conclude that—although *Populorum Progressio* dealt with issues such as authentic human development, materialism, a new humanism, technocracy, mutual solidarity, social justice, universal charity, nationalism, racism, and collaboration—the underpinning question it was addressing was that of the defense or protection of human dignity.[411]

In addressing problems prevalent in the global community, Paul VI was making a moral judgment about socioeconomic and political relations between peoples and nations. His ultimate concern was their effect on human dignity—the raison d'etre, the fundamental and ultimate end or reason—of true human development.[412] It would seem right to suggest that every problem he declared immoral was because he judged it to be consequent to an *actus humanus*. That is, he judged each event according to whether it was a human act done freely and after deliberate choice preceded by knowledge. The fundamental cause of the problems is self-concern or self-absorption of individuals and nations. When nations or individuals make choices only in their favor, they deny that other individuals or nations are worthy of the same or similar choices. This idea points to the question of the dignity of other individuals. It prompts the suggestion that structures and systems are necessary for the promotion and protection of the dignity and human rights of individuals and nations regardless of which person or nation. It also suggests that sometimes nations and individuals are responsible to some degree at least according to moral principles, if no impediments such as ignorance, passion, fear, and coercion stand in the way of their decisions and actions.[413]

---

[411] Vitillo and Toliver Grimes, 38.

[412] Riga, 44. Also see *Populorum Progressio,* 21, 9-10; 34, 15.

[413] Timothy E. O'Connell, *Principles for Catholic Morality* (New York: Seabury Press, 1978), 48.

III. PAUL VI'S RESPONSE: GENERAL CONSIDERATIONS

Paul VI's approach to the problem of poverty and underdevelopment was deliberate. He did not approach the problem by beginning with a provision of solutions to the problems at the international or national level without a careful and thorough analysis of the world situation and the causes of poverty and underdevelopment, and neither did he start from the "current conception of economic development."[414] He did just the opposite and started with a statement of the historical concern and involvement of the church, an analysis of the world situation and problems, and later attempted to resolve these problems. Donal Dorr affirms Paul VI's deliberate approach. He thinks that Paul VI did not use the current conception of economic development as a starting point and then modify it. Dorr suggests that this explains why Paul VI's *Populorum Progressio* represents a notable advance on earlier Catholic social documents on the question of human development.[415]

According to Paul VI, "the present situation of the world demands concerted action based on a clear vision of all economic, social, cultural and spiritual aspects" of human life and society.[416] Here, he was hinting at the importance of solidarity, participation or involvement, and respect for socioeconomic and political differences. His ultimate economic response was that rich nations should aid poor nations and international trade should be regulated by social justice.

A. Historical Church Involvement and Contribution

Social justice has always been a concern of the church, and the church has often attempted to resolve some of the social problems including problems of people struggling to come out of situations of hunger, misery, disease, and ignorance.[417] Paul VI affirmed that problems are a fact in human life and the

---

[414]   Filochowski, 62. Also see Donal Dorr, "Solidarity and Integral Development" in *The Logic of Solidarity* : *Commentaries on John Paul II's Encyclical On Social Concern* (Maryknoll, New York: Orbis Books, 1989), 145.

[415]   Dorr, *Option for the Poor*, 181.

[416]   Christine E. Gudorf, *Catholic Social Teaching on Liberation Themes* (Washington DC: University of America, 1981), 21. Here, Gudorf is quoting *Populorum Progressio*, 13, AAS, 59 (1967); 264; translation *Renewing the Earth*, 317.

[417]   Walsh and Davies, 221-222. Also see Rousseau, 264.

church recurrently confronts them. They are true, difficult, and undeniable aspects of the human situation to resolve. Problems defy changes in society. The nature of social problems changes, but as problems per se, they always exist. The church is always aware of this. The Second Vatican Council recommended the importance of the social question in all its ramifications and called for the necessary urgent cooperation of all people.[418] This was an invocation of the principle of participation and the principle of solidarity, both of which are significant for true human development. The historic and future role of the church in promoting integral development cannot and should not be underestimated.[419]

Paul VI stated that historically the church has pursued integral human development and must continue to facilitate it both individually and in solidarity. After the example of her founder, the Catholic Church has never ceased to promote the development of people. For example, missionaries built infirmaries, hospitals, schools, and universities. They taught the natives to tap their resources and to benefit from the resources. They also guarded the natives against the greed of foreigners though at times they acted imperfectly and contrary to Christian doctrine.[420] Paul VI acknowledged that missionaries cherished institutions of the indigenous people and developed them further.

Paul VI insisted that the church must always be attentive to current phenomena, reading and interpreting the signs of the times. His call and advocacy for the church's historical involvement is that it must be alert and critical, especially in situations of maldevelopment. This is a duty the church must continue to cherish within its own ability and jurisdictions so as to establish "on earth the kingdom of heaven"[421] through presenting a view of the human person and human affairs totally.

Currently, this project is undertaken by both groups and individuals, but it demands the concerted effort and action of all who have a clear understanding

---

[418]   *Populorum Progressio*, 1, 2. Also see Merkle,124.

[419]   Merkle, 124. Also see Peter Henriot, "Who Cares about Africa? Development Guidelines for the Church's Social Teaching" in *Catholic Social Thought in the New World Order*, 238.

[420]   *Populorum Progressio*, 12, 6. Also see Hennelly, 764.

[421]   Ibid., 12, 6-7. Also see Henriot, "Who Cares about Africa? Development Guidelines for the Church's Social Teaching" in *Catholic Social Thought in the New World Order*, 239, and also see Rousseau, 265.

of the different facets of political, economic, social, spiritual, and cultural matters. Paul VI mainly focused on and pointed to ecclesiastics and academics or professional people. At this juncture, he introduced the topic of authentic human development by outlining the areas from which efforts need to be pooled together in order to bring about true human progress. He made it clear that the political dimension is an important aspect of human development.

B. Development in Solidarity

Here, Paul VI used the word solidarity to accentuate the idea that people need one another to be and to become, to live and to grow. For development to be true or integral, it must occur in solidarity even if individual members of society are responsible for their own individual development.[422] This means development in solidarity demands individual responsibility. The reason for this call is that everybody is a part of a particular society and the community of the entire human family. Solidarity is an important principle because people need mutual support to grow and to enhance their human dignity, to be what they were originally intended by God. It provides opportunities for mutual exchange of talents and resources necessary for integral development. John S. Mbiti clearly states the expression of solidarity in an African context, which typifies solidarity. He says that the African is convinced of the saying that "I am, because we are; since we are, therefore I am."[423] Among the Lugbara of Uganda, proverbs emphasize the importance of solidarity for development or any achievement. The proverb *"Aluri pa (k)uu ku"*, translated as "the foot of a single person does not sound," means,

> The footsteps of an individual can hardly be heard when walking. There have to be several people walking or dancing for the sound of their feet to be heard clear and far. The inference is that the person who is alone in society or in family cannot accomplish much; his activities have no repercussion. Instead many people together attain far-reaching results."[424]

---

[422] Ibid., 17, 8.

[423] John S. Mbiti, *African Religions and Philosophy* (New York: Frederick A. Praeger Publishers, 1969), 108.

[424] Dalfovo, A.T. Lugbara Proverbs, Rome: Comboni Missionaries, 1990, 57-58 Also see 93 and 225.

According to Dalfovo, the proverb encourages people to cooperate, to work together to be effective in their undertaking. What is precisely encouraged by the proverb is the spirit of solidarity toward meeting individual and community needs. This solidarity extends from the family to people outside the family.[425]

Solidarity is central to integral human development. Paul VI exhorted all people to join together to strive for the complete development of every individual and all people. Paul VI invoked the principles of solidarity, participation, social justice, and global involvement, peace, and common good. These are principles, which the Pontifical Commission for *Justice and Peace*, was established to promote. Paul VI further advocated this view:

> Wherefore, we earnestly exhort all men today to strive by united planning and joint action for the full development of each individual and the common progress of all Mankind.[426]

This view was forcefully reemphasized by John Paul II about twenty years later in *Sollicitudo Rei Socialis*. One of Paul VI's initial responses to the question of human development was that development should necessarily occur in solidarity involving dialogue leading to global plans, if human development is to be integral.[427]

The church's practical action for the cause of human development was the effort to implement the resolution of the Second Vatican Council through the establishment of the Pontifical Commission for Justice and Peace. The purpose of this commission is to conscientize the people of God about the functions entrusted to it in order to promote human development of the poor, to foster international social justice, to aid the less developed countries, and to facilitate their personal and independent development.[428] In 1983, the German

---

[425] John Middleton, *Lugbara Religion: Ritual and Authority among an East African People* (London: Oxford University Press, 1960), 20.

[426] *Populorum Progressio*, 5, 3.

[427] Julian A. Filochowski, "Looking Out to the World's Poor: Teachings of Paul VI," in *The New Politics: Catholic Social Teaching for the Twenty-First Century*, ed. Paul Valley (London: SCM Press, 1998), 63. Also see *Populorum Progressio*, 48-49, 20-21; 50-52, 21-22; 54, 22-23; 60-61, 25; 64, 27; 73, 30; 76-77, 31-32. Also see Henriot, *Catholic Social Teaching: Our Best Kept Secret*, 55, and Walsh and Davies, 223.

[428] *Populorum Progressio*, 5, 3.

bishops emphasized the significance of world peace by advocating both just and sustainable promotion of development in the developing countries in order to create the peace, which Paul VI himself equated to development.[429]

The church's ceaseless call to solidarity, which is a "call to relationship with others reflects the church's awareness of the integral equality of dignity enjoyed by every human being."[430] Paul VI's concern was to foster the dignity of the human person when he advocated development in solidarity. Development in solidarity is vital, according to him, because "there can be no progress toward a complete human development of a person without the simultaneous development of all humanity in the spirit of solidarity."[431] True development is not a solitary process. The development of an individual is related to the development of other individuals and groups. True development involves mutual support among individuals and groups.

Paul VI contended that true development is not just an individual affair and not just the development of an individual. True development is mutual and demands mutual support. According to him, "the complete development of the individual must be joined with that of the human race and must be accomplished by mutual effort."[432] This is why, according to Paul VI, authentic development is both inclusive and exclusive. It is inclusive because no one is outside the claim, and it is exclusive because at the same time it means the whole development of an individual. Whether development is of a whole individual or of the whole of human kind, it calls for mutual support. It is not just a product of an isolated individual effort but of all. This is what explains development in solidarity, collaboration, and unity, which is a development that embraces participation or involvement. Such development, according to Paul VI, is not only relevant nationally but internationally. Authentic human development embraces the whole of humankind, including the past, present, and future generations motivated by the spirit of mutual collaboration, unity, goodwill, harmony of minds, and friendship among individuals and nations.[433]

---

[429] The German Bishops, *Just Peace* (Bonn: Sekretariat der Deutschen Bischofskonferenz, 27 September 2000), 9.

[430] Samuel Gregg, *Economic Thinking for the Theologically Minded* (New York/ Lanham: University Press of America, 2001), 4.

[431] *Populorum Progressio*, 43, 18. Also see Richard W. Rousseau, *Human Dignity and the Common Good: The Great Papal Social Encyclicals from Leo XIII to John Paul II* (Wesport, Connecticut: Greenwood Press, 2002), 269.

[432] *Populorum Progressio*, 43, 18-19.

[433] Ibid., 17,8.

The affirmation here is that in all generations true development is progressive and dynamic, not retrogressive or static.

The realization of integral human development necessitates duties on the part of development agents. Authentic development is possible, according to Paul VI, on the basis of three-faceted natural and supernatural obligations. The first aspect is the "duty of mutual relationship, that is the duty on the part of the rich nations to give assistance to nations still developing."[434] Paul VI was asserting that if rich nations can assist the poor ones, the latter can be helped to move to the development level of the former. Paul VI advocated the importance of solidarity on international level, but the same principle is relevant for social relationships within nations, between individuals and groups or institutions smaller than nations.

Second, there is "the duty of social justice which consists in improving trade relations between the more prosperous and weaker nations."[435] Here, Paul VI explicitly advocated fair conditions for both prosperous and poor countries. He meant that the bargaining powers of developed countries and that of less developed countries must be on par. Both parties should be able to deal with each other without one imposing on the other conditions that do not favor mutual exchange and progress.

Third, according to Paul VI, there is

> finally, the duty of charity to all men by which human relationship for all is promoted in which all must give and receive, in which the progress of some should not impede the development of others.[436]

Paul VI suggested the need to love indiscriminately because it promotes social relationships, and leads to solidarity. Authentic development demands mutual efforts, support, and charity expressed in mutual sharing. Paul VI gave precedence to charity because according to him integral human development depends on charity. He emphasized genuine love, a selfless love. He introduced love as a virtue, not only fundamental to integral human development but the greatest of virtues upon which "the future of civilization depends."[437]

Paul VI's emphasis on solidarity, love, and justice as crucial factors for true development suggests that development is a kind of democracy achieved

---

[434]   Ibid., 44,19.

[435]   Ibid.

[436]   *Populorum Progressio*, 44, 19.

[437]   1 Cor.13: 13. Also see *Populorum Progressio*, 44, 19.

by a democratic process. If it is to be called authentic development, it is *the development of all, by all and for all.* Development of all is integral and a development in solidarity. Development by all is one that involves participation of all in a spirit of solidarity, and hence, democratic. Development for all is one, which takes seriously the spirit of love, solidarity, social justice, and common good and the good of the individual as fundamental elements of development.

Paul VI advocated a selfless human solidarity. He argued that human solidarity is possible only when "mutual suspicions of nations and selfishness" are overcome by "a stronger desire for collaboration and a more profound awareness of human solidarity."[438] Here Paul VI suggested a committed desire for collaboration and deep-seated acknowledgment of the importance of human solidarity and unity in both thought and action.

According to Paul VI, selfless solidarity also demands "common plans of action," coordinated investments, proportionate distribution of "means of production," and organized "sale of products," and assistance to "the more needy nations" to liberate themselves from obstacles to their progress, "and to find, without detriment to their own native character, the means of human and social development."[439] He advocated mutual support on the basis of human solidarity, but he also demanded that this be altruistic. True solidarity is expressed in selfless service; it is essentially for the sake of human dignity.

Development ought to be the special concern of the wealthy nations. This is not just an option for them but an obligation and confers on them a triple duty.[440] First, they have a duty to human solidarity, which calls for aid to the poor nations. Second, they have a duty to observe social justice, which demands equitable trade relationships. Finally, they have a duty to universal charity and collaboration, which demands that the world be made more conducive for living human life, for all peoples. Paul VI's emphasis on this statement suggests how much he thought that the future of the civilization of the whole world depends on the fulfillment of these duties.

1. Aid to the Weak

In addressing the issue of aid to the weak, Paul VI was addressing no problem other than the question of respect for human dignity. According

---

[438] *Populorum Progressio*, 64, 27. Also see Rousseau, 272.

[439] Ibid., 64, 27.

[440] Henriot, *Catholic Social Teaching: Our Best Kept Secret*, 55.

to him, wealth per se is *a divinely ordained good* and a real gift of God to people; but it is, above all, an opportunity for Christians to grow toward their ultimate destiny. Peter J. Riga suggests that, following the Gospel injunction to faithfully serve the cause of the poor, Paul VI devoted the whole of *Populorum Progressio* to "one great appeal for the poor throughout the world."[441] Riga further observes that according to Paul VI,

> a preoccupation with material things has blinded the spirit of many men, particularly in the rich nations. Others must realize that although material goods are absolutely necessary for human dignity, they are not the end of human life but exist only to promote it.[442]

Throughout *Populorum Progressio*, Paul VI addressed the issue of poverty that affected human dignity. He spelled out two distinct categories of people living under different conditions—the weak people who live in less human conditions and the rich who live in more human conditions. According to Paul VI, people who live in less human conditions are those weighed down by material and moral poverty. They include the materially poor and hungry, the less educated, those culturally marginalized, and those oppressed by bad social structures created by abuse of power and wealth, exploitation of workers, and unjust business arrangements and deals.[443] They are destitutes of different sorts who need to be aided. Paul VI consistently and ceaselessly urged that such categories of people and nations should be helped by the rich nations and peoples.[444]

Those who live in more human conditions are people living where there is respect for human dignity, people are oriented to spiritual poverty, there are materially selfless people, and there is cooperation for the common good and a will for peace. According to Paul VI, they are people capable of aiding the disadvantaged people. This is why, in the Gospel spirit, Paul VI made a strong appeal on behalf of the *anawim*—the poor—of the world who were in dire need of the support of the wealthy and referred to their situation as

---

[441] Riga, 18.

[442] Ibid., 114.

[443] *Populorum Progressio*, 21, 9 and 45, 19. Also see Henriot, *Catholic Social Teaching: Our Best Kept Secret*, 55.

[444] Riga, 16. Also see *Populorum Progressio*, 54, 22-23.

being "scandalous and intolerable."[445] Consequently, Paul VI enjoined the world community, especially the communities that are blessed with resources to aid the poor nations. He bluntly suggested that the rich nations should fulfill a threefold duty—"the duty of human solidarity," which suggests mutual consideration and aid, which the rich nations ought to give to the less-developed nations; "the duty of social justice," which calls for the ratification of inequitable trade relations between powerful nations and weak nations; and "the duty of universal charity,"[446] which demands efforts to make a world, which is more human to all people, and all can mutually share their resources without one group progressing at the expense of others. He stated the threefold duty in the document as follows:

> first a duty of mutual relationship, that is a duty on the part of richer nations to give assistance to nations still developing; then the duty of social justice which consists in improving trade relations between the more prosperous and weaker nations; finally the duty of charity to all men by which more human relationship for all is promoted in which all must give and receive, and in which the progress of some should not impede the development of others.[447]

The triple duty Paul VI suggested touches three significant factors for authentic development. According to Peter J. Riga's critical and challenging reading of Paul VI, the latter's theology at this juncture is that if people cannot discover Christ in the numerous suffering people in the world, they cannot find Christ anywhere.[448] People's response to critical situations of need depends on how seriously they take solidarity, justice, and love.

Paul VI commended aid provided by Food and Agricultural Organization, Caritas International, and other groups but stated that elimination of hunger and poverty is not an adequate means to integral development. True development demands "building a world where everybody, regardless of race, religion and nationality, lives a fully human life."[449] This is the integral

---

[445] *Populorum Progressio*, 53, 22. Also see Riga, 22.

[446] Riga, 116. Also see *Populorum Progressio*, 48, 20.

[447] *Populorum Progressio*, 44, 19. Also see the same document 43, 18.

[448] Riga, 117.

[449] Henriot, *Catholic Social Teaching: Our Best Kept Secret*, 52-55. Also see *Populorum Progressio*, 46, 19-20; 47, 20.

development he advocated in *Populorum Progressio*. According to Paul VI, this kind of development calls for generosity, a spirit of sacrifice, readiness to give out of pocket for poor countries and from the fruits of natural resources and the existing technology.

Paul VI further advanced this as a challenge to both individuals and nations, especially the advanced nations who should devote part of their resources for production to meet the needs of the less fortunate. He cautioned against a possible danger of a dual character—spiritual and physical characters—if the poor are neglected. First, spiritually a failure to help the needy will result in divine judgment and punishment; and second, such a failure will arouse the wrath of the weak or poor people against the rich with unpredictable consequences.[450] Succinctly, Paul VI suggested that divine anger and human violence could be consequences of neglect of the needs of the poor. In his judgment, the solution to such eminent dangers is to aid the weak or the poor and to promote the development of all people. The greatest threat to peace, according to Riga's interpretation of Paul VI, is poverty and efforts to address differences between people through development of all people promotes *peace*. This explains why Paul VI eventually considered development as the *new name* for peace.[451]

2. EQUITY IN TRADE RELATIONS

Paul VI was conscious of the need to have a balance of power, economically and politically, nationally and internationally. According to him, imbalance of power was the negative legacy of colonialism and neocolonialism, and he was opposed to the rule of an exaggerated liberal trade system—free trade. In liberal trade arrangements, the ground is not level for all trading partners.[452] Consequently, he called for structural change and an economic and political balance of power. However, Paul VI was not in an absolute opposition to liberal capitalism as Dorr rightly contends. In paragraph 26 of *Populorum Progressio*, Paul VI is clear that he did not suggest a complete elimination of liberal competition or *capitalism*. This is also evident in *Populorum Progressio* where Paul VI only calls for a creation of equal opportunities for trading

---

[450]　*Populorum Progressio*, 49, 21.

[451]　Riga, 15.

[452]　Dorr, *Option for the Poor*, 186-187. Also see *Populorum Progressio*, 59, 25.

partners.[453] In other words, capitalism ought to be modified. The significant and unstated, but underpinning, reason here is the dignity of the human person—labor—and work that deserve recognition but are not as much recognized as profits. Paul VI was aware like other authors that "profit while morally legitimate requires the virtues of generosity and magnanimity."[454] Paul VI was not teaching a new doctrine. The foundation of this teaching goes back to the sacred scriptures and was more vividly explicated by the fathers of the church including Basil the Great (AD 330—379), an "ecclesiastical statesman, reformer of liturgy and social activist."[455] According to Samuel Gregg, he was critical of the rich because of their lack of social consciousness and insists upon sharing as an essential obligation of social justice. His argument was that the resources of nature are meant for all people. Social justice demands that no one be deprived of these resources. Consequently, he advocated equal opportunities, recognition of the dignity of labor, the human person, and the social purpose of natural resources.

The issues Paul VI addressed under this theme were as follows: the North-South economic relationships, long-term progress toward development, and "the international system of trade between the rich and poor" nations characterized by "an unchanging course to the detriment of the poor countries."[456] He also emphasized in light of the foreign aid received by less developed countries that all aid to developing nations is meaningless and ineffective if these nations lose much more than the aid they receive because trade relations and arrangements are unfavorable to them. Free international trade is good and advantageous only when the trading partners are equal.[457] It is unjust if there are disparities between trade partners. If conditions of trade partners are unequal, trade agreements are void. Consequently, Paul VI consistently insisted that free trade between unequal trade partners must be governed by laws of justice.[458] Discussions and negotiations are necessary for equality of opportunity. It must be added that nationalism, racism, and

---

[453] *Populorum Progressio*, 61, 25. Also see Dorr, *Option for the Poor*, 187.

[454] Gregg, 130.

[455] Gen 1:27-29. Also see Gregg, 131.

[456] Alfred T. Hennelly, "*Populorum Progressio*" in *The New Dictionary of Catholic Social Thought*, ed. Judith Dwyer (Collegevile, Minnesota: Liturgical Press, 1994), 769. Also see Walsh and Davies, 221.

[457] Dorr, *Option for the Poor*, 187.

[458] Henriot, *Catholic Social Teaching: Our Best Kept Secret*, 55-56. Also see *Populorum Progressio*, 58, 24; 59, 25.

tribalism—which obstruct justice—have to be eliminated in economic dealings.[459] The rationale here is that norms are essential for establishing more equal and just relations between trading partners. Consequently, Paul VI proposed international agreements with a broad spectrum. According to him, international agreements should establish norms for regulating prices, guaranteeing specified types of production and supporting specific industries. Such regulations promote justice in business relations among peoples and offer positive assistance with immediate and enduring effects.

3. UNIVERSAL CHARITY

Paul VI describes the world as being "sick" because there is lack of concern among people. This world sickness consists less in the unproductive monopolization of resources of nature by a small number of people than in the lack of brotherhood and sisterhood among individual peoples and nations.[460] There are many areas that have not been touched by charity. These areas ought to be reached by true charity, which is indiscriminate, all-embracing, inclusive, and open—even globally. This is the authentic love Paul VI advocated as a crucial virtue for human development. Paul VI understood charity in a broad sense, and Monika K. Hellwig's understanding of charity helps to clarify what Paul VI meant by universal charity because both view charity in a similar way:

> Charity is considered in Christian tradition either as the whole of authentic human communion with God and others, or more narrowly as one of the three theological virtues. In either case it is distinguished from a love of natural attraction, a love of needy desires, a love that simply clings to and aligns itself with the familiar, and from such responses as the instinctive care and protection of offspring. In contrast to all of these, charity is seen as a gift of grace empowering human beings to transcend their nature to share in the creativity and self-gift of God. It is an enhancement of human will to act, as it were, divinely.[461]

---

[459] Dorr, *Option for the Poor*, 187.

[460] *Populorum Progressio*, 66, 28.

[461] Monika K. Hellwig, "Charity" in *The Modern Catholic Encyclopedia*, eds., Michael Glazier and Monika K. Hellwig (Collegeville, Minnesota: The Liturgical Press, 1994), 159-161.

The first sense of charity is in line with Paul VI's understanding of true charity as a virtue necessary for integral development. Authentic charity expresses the relationship between God and the loving agent, and between the latter and fellow human beings who are both objects and subjects of love. This does not exclude the sense of charity presented by Hellwig, namely charity as one of the three theological virtues because theological virtues, which "relate directly to God,"[462] have necessarily to be reflected in a person's relationship with others. This implies that because of the link between charity and the divine will, authentic charity is prompted by an innate sense of human dignity because of the divine origin of human dignity. It affirms that true charity, which is disinterested, is a fundamental virtue for integral human development. This was affirmed by Saint Augustine, according to Hellwig:

> He demonstrates that where each seeks his or her own without regard for others, there will always be conflict, disaster, fear, and suffering. Only when the saving power of divine love transforms human goals and desires, can human society hope for harmony and integration of all its parts.[463]

The above statement suggests how central the virtue of charity is in human life. It is essential for solidarity, participation, association, and common good. Charity is the foundation on which justice and peace are founded, human community is built, and from which protection for human dignity and ultimately respect for human rights comes. It is precisely for this reason that charity is central and has a social dimension, and "it affects all human relationships and all structures of human society from the local to the global."[464] Whether in small or large communities, charity is the propelling force for solidarity, common good, option for the poor, unity among people, and integral growth.

Paul VI specified ways of showing love and made recommendations for a universal charity.[465] First, there is the duty and obligation of hospitality to strangers, an obligation rooted in human solidarity and Christian charity.

---

[462]   Hellwig, 160.

[463]   Ibid. Also see page 153 of the revised and expanded edition of the same work of the year 2004.

[464]   Ibid.

[465]   *Populorum Progressio*, 67, 28; 68, 28; 69, 28; 70, 29.

Second, there should be concern and care for the youth and students, especially those who have left their countries in order to achieve skills that would eventually be helpful for the progress of their own people. Third, people should welcome immigrant workers who want to earn resources for helping and updating the conditions of their families. Finally, financial and educational assistance are crucial, and business people in developing nations should be initiators of social progress and human advancement, helping other people to develop knowledge and skills that would make them responsible and productive. According to Paul VI, all these and similar efforts call for sincere dialogue both internationally and nationally. They also demand that Christians, people of goodwill, government authorities, and educated people commit themselves to this cause.

C. The Invaluable Significance of Culture

Paul VI respected cultures and cultural differences, and he saw in institutions that promoted cultures the solutions to the problem of cultural conflicts. He claimed that besides professional organizations, institutions that promote culture played a significant role in human development. Consequently, he argued that both rich and poor countries have cultures that foster human life and dignity, and these cultures have been handed down from generation to generation through arts, education, and religion. Paul VI asserted that it is a grave mistake to disregard the culture of the poor nations, in favor of that of the rich nations, because the cultures of poor nations also "contain genuine human values."[466] Paul VI was addressing this problem in the following:

> Developing nations, therefore, are to make the correct choice among the things held out to them; let them criticize and reject false values by which the ideal of human life is lowered, but let them accept the excellent and useful and strive to develop them together with their own excellent qualities in accord with their natural abilities.[467]

Paul VI's argument about the value of cultures was deliberate and succinct. If cultures of poor nations are life enhancing, they must be maintained and

---

[466] Ibid., 40, 17.

[467] Ibid., 41, 18.

should not be radically discarded. By affirming the significance of culture, Paul VI recognized the original meaning of the word *culture*, which originated from the "latin *cultura agri* and later *cultura animi*" which referred initially to the improvement and refinement of the person, mainly through education."[468] From the root of the word culture, one realizes the importance and value of each culture in the progress of its people, especially educationally. Dorr similarly supports the idea that culture is important—it must be duly respected—and he argues that the notion of "development proposed in *Populorum Progressio* and understanding of international solidarity"[469] as presented in *Sollicitudo Rei Socialis* offer a strong challenge to any opposition to the culture of one group of people by another.

Paul VI raised a significant issue for the less developed nations, especially where they indiscriminately think that development means discarding one's own culture and taking up a new and different one which seems appealing and progressive and yet does not have regard for the value of the human person, dignity, rights, life, and the human community as such, but instead curtails the enhancement of authentic and genuine human values and needs.[470] Paul VI cautioned developing nations against temptations coming from wealthier nations, lest they lose the best of their patrimony.[471] The significant issue he raised here was that culture and cultural values must be part and parcel of the process of authentic human development. Cultures should be brought to confront one another but be mutually enriching if they are to be part of authentic development. Development outside concrete cultural contexts is utopian because it is out of context of the people being promoted. It remains foreign, and it does not affect the real life of the people and hence is not authentic development.

Cultural imperialism was one of the issues Paul VI addressed in relation to development. He was firm that civilizations, which shaped the life, character, talents, and skills of experts should never "be considered the only one, nor

---

[468] Dalfovo, 42.

[469] Dorr, "Solidarity and Integral Human Development" in *TheLogic of Solidarity: Commentaries on John Paul II's Encyclical on Social Concern,* 150. Also see *Sollicitudo Rei Socialis,* 14, 23-25.

[470] Peter Henriot, "Who Cares about Africa? Development Guidelines from the Church's Social Teaching" in *Catholic Social Thought and the New World Order,* 227. Also see *Populorum Progressio,* 40-41, 17-18.

[471] *Populorum Progressio,* 40-41,17-18.

must it look with disdain on other countries."[472] Paul VI cautioned foreign experts about the danger of cultural imperialism. He called them to a critical study and knowledge of the culture of the people they served so that they would introduce elements of their own culture in foreign countries only when it is appropriate and necessary, but even then ensure that they were properly adapted to the culture of the people they served. This approach to cultural interaction provides for reciprocal or mutual cultural enrichment. The enduring significance of this assertion is evident in emphasis of the *Rome Statement* on the importance of culture during the International Conference for Population and Development (ICDP) as necessary for the harmonious coexistence of people.[473] It was for a similar reason that Paul VI cautioned people adapting to foreign cultures:

> Therefore those who undertake a mission of this kind must see to it that they carefully investigate the history, the special characteristics, the store of knowledge of the country in which they live as guests. From this will follow a contact of one culture with the other by which both will be enriched.[474]

Innovation of development projects must start with a thorough study, understanding, and acceptance of people's culture. Cultural interaction is not only beneficial because of mutual enrichment but because it leads to mutual understanding and knowledge, especially when the interaction involves sincere and genuine dialogue between the principal elements of the interacting cultures. Paul VI made this clear:

> When genuine dialogue between different national cultures is established as in the case between individual men, a fraternal meeting of minds readily has its beginnings. Programs initiated for human development to be implemented by common effort bring nations together if all the chief government officials and the lowest artisan, are enkindled with brotherly love and ardently desire establishment of a civilization of world solidarity. Then a

---

[472] Ibid., 72, 29-30.

[473] *The Rome Statement on the International Conference on Population and Development*, 5.

[474] *Populorum Progressio*, 72, 30.

dialogue will begin based on man but not on the produce of land
or products of technology.[475]

Paul VI suggested that a genuine cultural dialogue is a trust-building
process, which leads to mutual understanding and love. This suggestion is
realistic because without mutual exchange of knowledge and trust, love is
difficult if not impossible. Mutual dialogue and understanding of cultures is
significant not only for human dialogue but also for appropriate action of the
parties involved. Paul VI's argument is logical and simple—mutual cultural
knowledge leads to mutual acceptance and love. However, in real life, mutual
cultural exchange and knowledge does not always necessarily lead to mutual
acceptance and love.

Nonetheless, mutual acceptance and love lead to solidarity. Solidarity
becomes meaningful with dialogue centered on the human person, not on
capital because people realize that the human person is central in the dynamics
of dialogue, relationship, and solidarity. This is possible only if there is a
cultural exchange, which brings to realization the singular but universally equal
human dignity of people. This is again theoretically a plausible assertion, but
practically, there are often difficulties brought forth by individual dispositions
of people to the real vision of the human person and the significance of
mutual cultural exchange.

D. The Primary Significance of Education

The educational background of Paul VI as stated in chapter one and
the educational background of many of his family members and friends
would suggest that Paul VI would attach great importance to education. It
is, therefore, no surprise that he advocated that for development to occur,
education of people is an imperative. Education is a significant factor for
integral human development and constitutes one of the fundamentals for
any attempts to develop human community. For Paul VI, "economic growth"
is founded on "social progress towards which it strives and that primary
education," which introduces literacy is the "prime objective of those planning
development."[476] Education is often insufficiently stressed as a crucial factor
for human development, yet it is actually one of the most basic factors in

---

[475] Ibid.
[476] Ibid., 35, 15.

addition to human dignity and rights, necessary to be grasped, acknowledged, and implemented for authentic human development. Education is important because it creates literacy and knowledge of phenomena and reality. It is a fundamental ingredient for human social knowledge, integration, and consolidation of personal and communal achievements. The ICPD, many years later, underscored the importance of education for human development when it stated that education and good health services are "prerequisites for full participation in human societies," [477] meaning that they facilitate personal involvement and contribution to human development.

Education is a factor for human development because it is a significant social process and a starting point for development. All other human achievements are preceded by education, whatever their form may be. In *Populorum Progressio*, Paul VI suggested that education is "a prime objective of those planning development" besides asserting that "economic growth is above all based on social progress toward which it strives."[478] This assertion is plausible because any social project and progress starts with education about its meaning, prerequisites, value and relevance, the necessities for social growth, what the development process involves, and how it can be achieved. Paul VI demonstrated the importance of education:

> Primary education which teaches the elements of reading and writing is the prime objective of those planning development. The lack of education is no less troublesome than lack of food, for an illiterate is, as it were, a person suffering from starvation of the spirit; but when one knows how to read and write, when he is prepared to perform a task or properly to carry out a function he regains self-confidence and realizes that he can make progress along with others.[479]

Paul VI underscored the significance of education for integral development. However, he emphasized the importance of the formative effect of education rather than literacy because education contributes to development only by transforming human persons and behavior. Paul VI was right to state that the value of education as a stepping-stone for social progress and economic

---

[477] The Rome Statement, 4.

[478] *Populorum Progressio,* 35, 15.

[479] Ibid.

growth is crucial, but his distinction between education and social progress is unnecessary because education is an intimate aspect—constituent facet—of social progress. It is also more plausible to suggest that education is a prime factor in planning and implementation of development rather than the prime objective of planners. The prime objective of planners is development not education.

Education is important because it has a purposeful and liberating effect. It liberates people from ignorance, fear, and incapacity for action and responsibility. Education helps one to get involved and participate in solidarity with others. Paul VI did not directly state the liberating effect of education in *Populorum Progressio*, but this can be deduced from an interpretation of the text. In this case, Paul VI contended that education is a relevant action for development and necessary for the functioning of the principles of solidarity, common good, participation, and freedom as a human right. It makes the dynamics of these principles possible. This also suggests that it facilitates the possibility and functioning of the virtue of charity. Even if Dorr seems to suggest that Paul VI did not emphasize the role of education in making people responsible in society, Paul VI recognized that education helps people to take up tasks along with others.[480] He advocated for both literacy and education for responsibility. This was alluded to when he called for students from the third world to study in the developed nations and return to develop their home countries.

Paul VI affirmed the importance of education in his reference to his message to the members of the UNESCO conference held in Teheran, where the priority he gave to education was clearer than his prior affirmations:

> As we stated . . . "literacy is a basic and primary factor not only for man's social integration but also for his personal enrichment, and for society a most excellent aid to effect growth and development."[481]

Paul VI intimated here that literacy promotes human integrity and individual and societal growth. He praised the initiative of public authorities and international organizations as significant for the promotion of human progress because they equip people to achieve development on their own. This recognition, acknowledgment, and praise suggests that Paul VI

---

480 Dorr, *Option for the Poor*, 200-201.
481 *Populorum Progressio*, 35, 15.

considered education to be the prerogative of all individuals and all national and international institutions, governments, and organizations in pursuit of development.

Paul VI argued that professional educational organizations are important because they facilitate "the principal and primary way of life in the family circle."[482] Here, he conceded that educational institutions are important supplementary organs to the family since development is also founded and dependent on the moral fiber of the family. This shows the significance of participation of all, from individuals to the global community, in the development process. For Paul VI, the role of organizations is crucial to development, but it demands proper planning:

> If these have been established to serve the convenience and interests of their members, their duty is great in regard to their educational function which they can and must carry out. For these organizations, since they instruct and train men, do much to imbue them with an understanding of the common good and obligations which it imposes.[483]

Paul VI suggested here that educational institutions are not established for selfish group or institutional interests but for public interests and must fulfill their duties to that effect. Education is futile and detrimental if it does not meet its goal, namely, the growth of individuals, groups, and society. Education is important, according to Paul VI, because it helps in the instruction, training, and facilitating of people's understanding of the common good and its demands in the development process.

Paul VI was of the view that the value and purpose of education is not limited to just a few people. It is for the good of all people. If education is oriented to personal and selfish goals, it is rendered useless as a starting point for integral human development. In fact, selfish education is one reason for lack of integral human development according to Paul VI. Education should and ought to change people and their lives integrally and be used integrally.

Paul VI's affirmation about the necessity of education in the development process is significant. Education—which many commentators on *Populorum Progressio* and documents of Catholic social teaching have not explicitly stated

---

[482]　Ibid., 37, 17. Also see Hennelly, 770.
[483]　Ibid.

as a crucial practice or, loosely, a principle for human development in the sense that it is a starting point of development—should be emphasized and stated as such. The importance of education lies in the fact that, if properly imparted and used, it is both a curative and preventive action for human development. It enlightens people, makes them aware of the dangers of poverty and its causes, and offers solutions to avoid the tragedy that follows in the wake of poverty.

E. A Credible Notion of Human Development

Etymologically, the word *development* originated from the Latin word *volere*, which means "to roll," and from the root word *veloper*, meaning "wrap," eventually came the old French word *developer* and the later or modern French *developper* or *develop*, which means "unwrap, open out, or to unfold possibilities of something."[484] Most sources agree that the word means "to unfold possibilities of something, to open, to unwrap, and to evolve to a higher stage in function or stature." What is evident here is that to develop or development is not limited to a particular form of growth.

The notion of human development up to 1960s when Paul VI wrote *Populorum Progressio* was predominantly economic. Paul VI believed that the true meaning of *human development* needed to be redeemed. This is evident in his deliberate choice to use the term *development* instead of *economic growth*.[485] Paul VI thought a right notion of development was important, and he attempted to offer in *Populorum Progressio* a novel and credible notion of human development. This fact is attested to by authors like Dorr who says that Paul VI offered a "fresh approach to the understanding of development" in the sense that it was inclusive and avoided violence.[486] Most authors affirm

---

[484] Joseph T. Shipley, *Dictionary of Word Origins* (New York; Dorset Press, 1995), 115. Also see Ernest Klein, *A Comprehensive Etymological Dictionary of the English Language*, Vol. 1 (Amsterdam; Elsevier Publishing Company, 1966), 437.; Walter W. Skeat, *A Concise Etymological Dictionary of English Language* (New York: Capricon Books, 1963), 139; Funk and Wagnalls, *The Readers Digest Great Encyclopedic Dictionary* (Funk and Wagnalls Publishing, 1975), 364; and C.T. Onions et al, *The Oxford Dictionary of English Etymology* (London: Oxford University Press, 1966), 262.

[485] Riga, 29.

[486] Dorr, *Option for the Poor*, 179. Also see Hanigan, 158

the view that the encyclical "maintains that development is the new name for peace and insists on personal and social development in the context of a transcendental humanism."[487] Development is envisioned as not being only economic and of individuals in isolation, but as the growth of every individual who is part of the community. This was the idea Paul VI took from Louis Joseph Lebret's notion of true human development, which Paul VI called integral human development. This is evident in the core statement of *Populorum Progressio*:

> The development of which we are speaking does not extend solely to economic growth. To be genuine, growth must be integral, it must clearly provide for the progress of each individual and of the whole man. In this regard an eminent specialist in the field has rightly and forcefully said: "we do not approve of separating the economic from the human or of considering development apart from the civilization to which it belongs. In our opinion great value is to be placed on man, each man, each group of men and human society as a whole.[488]

This is the central notion of development, which runs through the document and provides the greatest impetus in *Populorum Progressio*.[489] This vision of development, which encompasses all dimensions of the human person and of all people, can transform the thoughts, attitudes, and practical life of individuals, groups, and human society. Paul VI emphasized that this kind of development calls for cooperative promotion of the common good.[490]

Another characteristic of the document was Paul VI's analytical approach in defining human development, says Dorr:

---

[487] Curran, 11.

[488] *Populorum Progressio*,14, 7. The eminent source and specialist Paul VI is quoting here is L. J. Lebret, OP, *Dynamique concrete du developpement* (Paris: Economie et Humanisme, Les editions ouvrieres, 1961), 28. Also see Goulet, Denis, *A New Moral Order: Studies in Development Ethics and Liberation Theology* (Maryknoll, New York: Orbis Books, 1974), 40.

[489] McKenna, 66.

[490] Dorr, 47. Also see *Populorum Progressio*, 14,7; 21, 9-10; 42, 18.

> *Populorum Progressio* represents a remarkable advance on previous
> Church teaching about human development. The advance was
> a conceptual one. By this I mean what is radically new is the
> *framework of understanding* rather than specific details.[491]

Paul VI provided a framework for understanding but not the specifics
for practical implementation or action. This is where his notion of human
development is more theoretical than pragmatic. Paul VI's approach to and
notion of development was also sharply different from that in the previous
Catholic social teaching documents.[492] Reflecting what Lebret had emphasized
in his development ethics, Richard McBrien and others affirm that Paul VI
"is forceful in his insistence that development is spiritual and cultural as
well as economic," and he urges a "complete humanism" that accentuates
"the freely rounded development of the whole and of all men."[493] The
difference was basically in his definition of development because according
to him, authentic development is integral, it is not just economic. Integral
development is a development in solidarity and a development, which
covers all dimensions of human life, social, economic, political, cultural,
psychological, and spiritual.

Paul VI's introduction of the term *integral* in the definition of human
development is what made a radical break from the previous definitions of
development, apart from that of Louis Joseph Lebret on which he heavily
relied. This is what makes the difference between authentic development
and quasi development. Dorr aptly summarizes Paul VI's understanding of
authentic development in *Populorum Progressio*:

> It does not give a privileged place to the economic dimension of
> human development, any more than to cultural, psychological,
> political, ecological, or religious dimension, rather it challenges
> Christians to take full account of the non-economic elements—to
> recognize, for instance, that the protection of the right to free speech

---

[491] Dorr, "Solidarity and Integral Human Development" in *The Logic of Solidarity:
    Commentaries on John Paul II's Encyclical on Social Concern*, 144. Also see Dorr, *Option
    for the Poor*, 180.

[492] Riga, 29. Also cfr. Dorr, *Option for the Poor*, 180.

[493] McBrien, 1033. Also see Goulet, 40, and Walsh and Davies, 221.

may be at least as valuable a part of development as an increase in disposable income.[494]

The document neither gave privilege to economic development nor took the prevalent concept of economic development as its starting point. It outlined basic standards for rendering social changes as authentic human development. It provided a framework and a model of authentic human development. It emphasized the social, political, ethical and cultural character of problems related to development, and the legitimacy and necessity of the church's intervention in this field.[495]

As opposed to what was erroneously claimed to be development up to mid-1960s, Paul VI described what he called integral and sometimes referred to as complete or authentic human development in key paragraphs of *Populorum Progressio*. Many authors, including Peter Henriot, concur that a true definition of human development must be inclusive and centered on the human person, not economics.[496]

Authentic development is integral, meaning it is inclusive of all dimensions of human life. True development provides for the progress of each individual, the whole person, and the whole human family.[497] It is the holistic advancement of individuals and community. Relying on Lebret's work, which was intensely used for drafting *Populorum Progressio*, Riga and others affirm this notion by stating that the human person must develop spiritually, morally, socially, economically, politically and culturally, and it should be added, psychologically and mentally.[498] If some of the above aspects of human life are not developed, authentic development has not occurred.

This notion of authentic development is to some extent idealistic or utopian because there are variable factors that affect development. For

---

[494] Dorr, "Solidarity and Integral Human Development" in *The Logic of Solidarity: Commentaries on John Paul II's Encyclical on Social Concern*, 146. Also see Dorr, *Option for the Poor*, 181-182.

[495] Dorr, *Option for the Poor*, 181.

[496] Henriot, 212-213.

[497] Walsh and Davies, 221. Also see Riga, 29.

[498] Riga, 5. Also see Goulet, 35-37 for further reading and confer O'Brien, David J. and Thomas A. Shannon, eds., *Catholic Social Thought: The Documentary Heritage* (Maryknoll, New York: Orbis Books, 2001), 238.

instance, talents, geographical locations, available basic resources, mental capacities, social possibilities, and physical abilities affect the rate and level of development of individuals and nations. What Paul VI promoted is a notion, which assumes that there are no such variable factors. This is as theoretical as what John Rawls proposes in *A Theory of Justice* and calls the *veil of ignorance* in the original position where all parties are equal in terms of knowledge of relevant requisite principles for justice.[499] This theory presumes that everybody has or lacks the requisite qualities and resources for the exercise of justice, which is a difficult condition to attain in real life.

True and integral human development ought to be advocated for the sake of, among other reasons, human dignity. According to Paul VI, all people have human dignity, and the perfection of "human potentialities is not left to man's good pleasure"[500] because of the origin of the human person, which determines human action. True development is, therefore, the enhancement of human dignity rather than the possession of an abundance of material things.

Efforts and activities toward authentic development are rationally guided. It is not a laissez-faire project—absolutely freely chosen and done—because rational creatures are obliged to direct their lives and their wills to God, who is "the first truth and highest good."[501] Human life is destined for a higher dignity, a life in union with God and a life which transcends human nature. This is the ultimate goal of human life and activity and the aim of true development. Development activity ought to be guided by this fact.

For Paul VI, true and integral human development is a progressive process in which all are involved. Using Lebret's vision of authentic development, Paul VI argued that true development "consists in each and everyone's passing from less human to more human living conditions."[502] He advocated

---

[499]   John Rawls, *A Theory of Justice*, rev. ed. (Cambridge, Massachusetts: The Belknap Press of Harvard University Press, 1999), 11 and 17.

[500]   Denis Goulet, "The Search for Authentic Development" in *The Logic of Solidarity: Commentaries on John Paul II's Encyclical On Social Concern,* eds., Gregory Baum and Robert Ellsberg (Maryknoll, New York: Orbis Books, 1989), 134.

[501]   *Populorum Progressio*, 16, 8.

[502]   Denis Goulet, *A New Moral Order: Studies in Development Ethics and Liberation Theology,* 39 and 43. *Populorum Progressio*, 20, 9. Also see Denis Goulet, "The Search for Authentic Development" in *The Logic of Solidarity: Commentaries on John Paul II's Encyclical on Social Concern*, 134.

the development of the potentialities that are within the individual, but this demands an atmosphere where there is love, friendship, prayer, and contemplation—all of which indicate that the human person is in a progressive process.

There are indicators of *less human* conditions of life and *more human* conditions of life. A less human condition of living is indicated by lack of "the minimum subsistence necessary for life," self-imposed moral deficiencies due to excessive self-love, oppression by social structures with consequent abuse of power or ownership, exploitation of workers, and unjust transactions.[503] Conversely, more human living conditions are characterized by the absence of destitution, possession of basic supplies for life, successful struggle against social ills, broader knowledge, acquisition of culture, increased esteem for human dignity, orientation to the spirit of poverty, cooperation for the common good, the will for peace, and recognition and acknowledgment of God as the highest good, author, and ultimate end of all things. For Paul VI, God's gift of faith and unity in Christian love is also a sign of a more human condition of living.

Development is authentic if all productive activities are directed to the service of the human person, and if they lessen inequalities, remove discrimination, free people from the bonds of servitude and enable them to improve their conditions in the temporal order, achieve moral development, and perfect their spiritual endowments or simply protect the dignity of the human person as consistently taught by the subsequent encyclical and pastoral traditions.[504] These assertions show the gravity of Paul VI's vision of development as "liberation" and his introduction of the term in the question of human development, though he did not use it liberally because it would fall short of integral human development, which looks *"to the absolute God."*[505]

True development is not merely growth in the national domestic product or technological advancement. True development consists in social progress and economic growth, an increase in the capacity of an economy proportionate

---

[503] *Populorum Progressio*, 21, 9.

[504] Ibid., 34,15. Also see National Conference of Catholic Bishops. *Economic Justice for All: Pastoral Letter on Catholoic Social Teaching and the U.S. Economy* (Washington DC: United States Catholic Conference, May 3, 1986), 13, ix.

[505] Julian Filochowski, "Looking Out to the World's Poor: Teachings of Paul VI" in *The New Politics: Catholic Social Teaching for the Twenty- First Century*, ed., Paul Valley (London: SCM Press, 1998), 80-81.

to its people, and equitable distribution of socioeconomic and political wealth. This helps to promote more human social situations of meaningful human life and dignity. This is what Paul VI meant in this passage:

> When we speak of development care must be given both to social progress and economic growth. The increase of national wealth is not sufficient for its equitable distribution; the progress of technology is not enough to make the earth a more suitable place to live in as if it had been made more humane . . . . The predominance of technologists, or *technocracy*, as it is called, if it gains the upper hand in the next generation will be able to bring on evils . . . . Economics and technology lack meaning if they are not turned to the goal of man whom they must serve.[506]

True development goes beyond meeting people's physical or material needs to meeting their spiritual needs. Complete and authentic humanism consists in provision for the development of whole persons without limits to material provisions to the exclusion of God and spiritual values.

> There is no genuine humanism except that which reaches out to God as the absolute, while the duty to which we are called is acknowledged and by which true meaning is given to human life. By no means therefore, is man his own final measure, he only becomes what he must be if he transcends himself.[507]

Full growth is realized in self-transcendence, namely, in being in and with God. True human development is not independent of God. Paul VI introduced the ultimate meaning of human development by giving development a theological meaning besides its material dimension. The true and ultimate realization of the human person is to be found in God, the originator of the human person. This suggests that the climax of the process of the unfolding of human potentialities and self-realization is in the beatific vision and union with God. This is where socioeconomic and political activities and processes should ultimately lead people.

---

[506] *Populorum Progressio*, 34, 15.
[507] Ibid., 42, 18.

Paul VI advocated that development is not merely resolving prevailing problems of people. Consequently, he stated that appeals to aid organizations, groups, and persons for provision of funds—both privately and publicly—and gifts and loans are inadequate for development to be called authentic just as eradication of hunger and poverty and combating destitution are insufficient.[508] He declared that private and communal handouts for eliminating hunger, poverty, and any kind of destitution do not constitute development. This is a sound claim because development is the unfolding of the potential of individuals and groups. Handouts do not promote this unfolding. Instead, they hamper the spontaneous unfolding of potentials or talents. To a great extent, they thwart development because they create reluctance to work, which is a dignified activity. Paul VI was realistic to state that donations and gifts are not development because they do not involve any personal initiatives, involvement, or participation. Important in true development is the

> establishment of a human society in which everyone, regardless of race, religion or nationality, can live a truly human life free from bondage imposed by men and the forces of nature not sufficiently mastered, a society in which freedom is not an empty word and where Lazarus the poor man can sit at the same table as the rich man.[509]

True development is human advancement where discrimination and segregation are absent, there is no injustice, human rights are respected, there is a radical preferential option for the poor, and charity is shown to all people. In quoting Luke16:19-31, Paul VI implied that everyone who can uplift others should do so. The rich man is unnamed and simply refers to anybody capable of elevating the needy from less human to a more human level, even to a level better than one's own. To emphasize the gravity of this issue, Paul VI stated that true development demands generosity, self-sacrifice, and ceaseless efforts on the part of materially blessed people and critical self-examination of all people. Integral development demands that every person capable of support should do something for those who have nothing and are incapable of self-support.

---

[508] Riga, 119. Also see *Populorum Progression*, 47, 20.

[509] *Populorum Progressio*, 47, 20.

Paul VI indefatigably advocated that true development embraces everybody and nation, it is multi-faceted, and depends on various factors. True development consists in socioeconomic, political, spiritual, and moral progress of all people. He argued that

> when we combat misery, and struggle against injustice we are providing not only for man's prosperity but also for his spiritual and moral development and are therefore promoting the welfare of the whole human race.[510]

According to Paul VI, authentic development is not accumulation of wealth for private benefit, neither is it wealth sought for its own sake. Positively, development is economic growth "adjusted to the welfare of the human person and in daily sustenance provided for all the resource as it were, of fraternal charity and clear sign of the help of Divine Providence."[511] True development involves sharing acquired resources with the needy. This sharing of the gifts of God is rooted in love and generosity.

Populorum Progressio suggests the following conclusions regarding Paul VI's notion of development. First, complete development is integral in character. This means development of the whole person because each person has dignity, right, and obligation to attain self-fulfillment. Second, authentic development is not a self-centered or fragmented phenomenon—it has a social dimension. Every individual is part of a community and civilization with its own relational history. All people are bound in solidarity. Each person has to care for the wellbeing of others in human community, including generations yet to come. Third, authentic human development is not only economic; it includes cultural, psychological, ecological, political, and religious or spiritual dimensions of the human person and of all people. Fourth, *Populorum Progressio* offered a novel description of the term *development*. Paul VI linked and equated development to peace. He asserted that "development is the new name for peace."[512] This view suggests that development makes peace, and there is a mutual exchange between development and peace. Development of all people creates a peaceful atmosphere because each member's dignity is respected, protected, and cared for. When an atmosphere of peace prevails, it is conducive for development. The relationship between the two is, therefore,

---

[510] Ibid., 76, 32.

[511] Ibid., 86, 35.

[512] Riga, 143. Also see *Populorum Progressio* 87, 35, 76, 31-32.

an intimate one, and they are mutually indispensable. The document not only linked development to charity and peace but linked peace to justice. Peace is the consequence of charity and justice, just as integral human development is the consequence of charity and justice exercised in solidarity.

Paul VI looked at development in a radically different way from most development experts. The economic, political, psycho-social, and spiritual overtones in the document underscore the fundamentals of Paul VI's notion of integral human development and differentiate his vision of development from others.

F. Means and Models of Change: Violent Revolution or Passive Resistance

Paul VI suggested ways of responding to socially unjust situations. He did not explicitly propose them, but his arguments for a response to evil in society suggest two models of change—confrontational and consensus models of change. Each of these models has both positive and negative consequences.

1. MEANS OF CHANGE: FIVE PRINCIPAL SUGGESTIONS

Paul VI suggested five means of change in *Populorum Progressio*. These are as follows: world relief fund, foreign aid, limited competition, concerted effort, and effective world government.[513] First, Paul VI advocated that there should be a world fund to relieve destitute people. This was a relevant practical expression of love. It suggests the importance of solidarity, charity, justice, option for the poor, the common good, affirmative action, and the principle of subsidiarity. He suggested that nations should work in mutual collaboration to raise such funds. It is from out of the funds that the needs of the poor can be met. The efforts of different people and nations should be well coordinated so that personal interests are checked. Individual nations should also increase their production in order to help their citizens live a dignified life and help improve the conditions of the human race. They are entitled to use the fruits of their labor, but they should not keep their wealth exclusively for their own use.[514]

---

[513] *Populorum Progressio*, 48-51, 20-21, 78, 32. Also see Dorr, *Option for the Poor*, 185-196.

[514] Ibid., 48, 20.

Second, he suggested massive foreign aid in the form of money, goods, skilled labor, especially financial expertise, and agrarian reform.[515] This is a questionable suggestion in the context of the whole document because it encourages dependence and discourages initiative and creativity. It fulfills the demands of solidarity, charity, and common good, but it is against the principle of participation. It is good only at the initiation of the development process. The suggestion supplements the theme of relief to destitute people and concerted effort, but it needs to be implemented cautiously because too much foreign aid also stifles initiatives and creativity. It does not contribute to true development, which demands involvement and participation of all people capable of work. Paul VI himself was aware of this because he warned that development is not just elimination of hunger and poverty or situations of destitution as treated in the preceding section of this chapter.[516] It goes beyond that to a change of attitude toward the material and moral empowerment of people.

Third, he proposed limits of international competitive trading so as to restore equality between the trading partners."[517] Paul VI was never totally opposed to capitalism. He understood that as long as profits accruing from it are used for the enhancement of human life and dignity, they served the right purpose for which resources of nature were made. However, he called for an end to exaggerated liberal capitalism and instead advocated moderation.

Fourth, Paul VI suggested a concerted economic effort for the promotion of development.[518] Nations have to work together in an organized fashion in order to promote the development of peoples. It was for such reason that Paul VI encouraged the nations that are more blessed with resources to help those that are less fortunate. He advocated that this was a way of implementing the doctrine of Second Vatican Council.[519]

Finally, Paul VI thought that a move toward the establishment of an effective world authority would be instrumental for integral development.[520] He encouraged and praised the work of the UN and FAO for this reason. This was a meaningful suggestion for an organ regulating the international

---

[515] Riga, 46.

[516] *Populorum Progressio*, 47, 20.

[517] Dorr, *Option for the Poor*, 196. Also see *Populorum Progressio*, 26, 12.

[518] Ibid., 196. Also see *Populorum Progressio*, 50, 21.

[519] *Populorum Progressio*, 48, 20.

[520] *Populorum Progressio*, 78, 32.

community's socioeconomic and political activities. However, the problem is always management of large organizations or governments, a problem which the UN experiences currently as its efforts and strength are disputable and sometimes defied by individual nations.

2. Models of Change: Consensus and Confrontational Models

Paul VI opposed violence as a way of effecting change. Instead, in his affirmations about response to social evil he implied the possibility of two models of change—the confrontational model and consensus model of which Paul VI preferred the consensus model.[521] His choice was necessitated by the gravity of consequences of the chosen model.

a. The Consensus Model

This is the *top-down model of change* where change is not initiated from the grassroots but from the top. According to Julian Filochowski, the consensus model demands that "changes should be brought about by those at the top—they must agree and then mold others."[522] This approach is questionable because if the bureaucratic structure consists of a corrupt body of people, any change initiated is corrupt, and the possibility of oppression and domination is great. The advantage of this model is that the possibility of violent revolution is minimized.

In the consensus model, change is envisaged as coming from a willing agreement based on reason, emotional appeal, and moral pressure from the various parties involved in the dialogue. This model presupposes that all parties have sufficient goodwill and commitment to justice, which can move them to make concessions. It also presupposes that they are ready to sacrifice self-interest to bring about harmony and promote the welfare of all. These presuppositions do not guarantee that positive change is imminent. Considering the requisite dispositions for initiating a consensus model of change, one is also right to differ from Filochowski's description that it is only a top-down model of change. If all are well disposed it could as well be initiated from the grassroots, hence a top-down model of change.

---

[521] Filochowski, 66.

[522] Ibid. Also see *Option for the Poor*, 203 and 198.

b. The Confrontational Model

Paul VI never intended to recommend the confrontational method, but his vision of the urgency of the need for change suggests this kind of model, which could provide those in dire need of change an alternative model.[523] This contention seems to be a conjecture. The overall tone of *Populorum Progressio* suggests peaceful means of change, not a confrontational approach. The confrontational model suggests that the principal means of change is pressure or threat. It presupposes that those who have power and wealth eventually yield reluctantly, but when there is pressure, they cannot ignore it.[524]

This is a *people-power* model, which demands more "emphasis on the political and critical awareness that could come from education and literacy."[525] For this method to work without serious problems, education is necessary so that people know their role and the consequences of their behavior. This is grassroots-top movement of initiative for change, which implies that power is in the hands of the masses. It suggests a democratic process, which is ideal for true development. This would be the most effective and easiest model of change because more people would be part of the process than if initiated by the bureaucracy.

The problem with this approach is that any socioeconomic and political change is still superficial because it is consequent to coercion and the change may not be genuinely an act of responsibility. The best way to pressurize would be the education of the people, which empowers them to confront the prevalent problem. The eminent danger of the use of this model is violent revolution, which is possible even when the community is educated. The model is contrary to the intention of Paul VI because he warned about the poor venting anger, which would perhaps have undesirable consequences.

This approach supports Martin Luther King Jr.'s advocacy for militant nonviolence, which was intended to appeal to the conscience of the people who perpetuated sinful structures.[526] King opted for a militant nonviolent response for two reasons. First, it was a lesser evil; and second, it was effective. Paul VI was warning the rich about situations and reactions similar to what King was confronting. When poor, deprived, marginalized, and oppressed people cannot tolerate their ordeal anymore, they resort to any way to

---

[523]   Dorr, *Option for the Poor*, 202.

[524]   Filochowski, 66.

[525]   Ibid.

[526]   Hanigan, 150.

achieve results and to save them from their situation with minimum of losses. However, a difference must be acknowledged. While King deliberately chose militant nonviolence as a way of expressing his spirituality, Paul VI was not warning about the danger of the poor expressing a form of spirituality.[527] He was cautioning about the danger of persistent injustice to the poor. Though Paul VI and King affirmed that evil situations should be resolved, their approaches were similar only insofar as they appealed to peoples' consciences and different in that King was actively involved.

There are different views about the value of the confrontational model. Dorr argues that the confrontational model is sometimes necessary and inevitable for social change. Some people think the poor and oppressed should be encouraged "to demand their rights—and organize themselves in such a way that this demand must be heard."[528] These views tend to suggest that Paul VI was leaning toward the idea of organized violence but such a point of view is conspicuously absent in *Populorum Progressio*.

The two models of change are not necessarily beneficial for all parties involved in the development process, and neither are they absolutely incompatible.[529] The problem with both models of change is that disadvantaged people are always at the mercy of the rich and powerful because the development and shaping of each model depends on the determinants of the situation. These include those who have social, economic, and political decision-making powers.

A significant question here is whether Paul VI suggested either of these models in *Populorum Progressio*. The document makes no explicit suggestion of a model. However, Paul VI implied the preferable model to be change through consensus. This conclusion is arrived at only from the indications in the document.[530] The *consensus model* reflects Paul VI's commitment to dialogue, which shows in his conviction that "a more deeply felt need for collaboration and a heightened sense of unity will finally triumph over misunderstandings and selfishness."[531] Though Paul VI warns the rich about the dangers of obstinately remaining complacent, there is no clear indication

---

[527] Ibid., 155.

[528] Dorr, *Option for the Poor*, 197.

[529] Ibid., 200.

[530] *Populorum Progressio* 54, 22-23; 64, 27; 79, 32-33. Also see Dorr, *Option for the Poor*, 196-197.

[531] Dorr, *Option for the Poor*, 196, 200-203. Also see *Populorum Progressio*, 64, 27.

that he favors the confrontational approach in the effort to overcome injustice, oppression. and poverty or underdevelopment in general.[532]

The consensus model appears better than the confrontational model because it is less likely to breed more injustice, but it seems better to suggest that both models need to be integrated or used simultaneously. One without the other may be inadequate or ineffective. Both models can be engaged at the same time. but their application should be intensified according to the nature of the situation being addressed. According to Julian Filochowski, Paul VI suggested in *Populorum Progressio* that education must always precede this integration and application process.[533] A realistic choice of model demands a positive education process, which includes emphasis on the dangers and benefits of each type of model, and any use of a model must be motivated by concern for human dignity.[534]

Paul VI detested the idea of enforcing change or development through violent action. Except when "basic human rights of the human person" and "serious harm to the common good" are at extreme risk, insurrection and rebellion are morally wrong because they "beget new injustices, inflict new inequalities and goad men to new destruction."[535] He objected to resolving injustice and social suffering through active resistance or violence. Paul VI's objection to violence is explained by the fact that violence contradicts development, which he calls the new name for peace. It would be a self-defeating effort to attempt to enforce development by promoting active force or violent resistance. To affirm that Paul VI was justifying revolution of a violent nature as Peter Riga suggests is incorrect and detestable.[536] Violence would defeat Paul VI's statement and suggest that the means justifies the end, which was not his position. He argued for the protection of the human person and dignity; therefore, violence would be contradictory, and his call for universal charity would be contradicted too. Violence is not recommended because it is an emotional, irrational and irresponsible response to problems.

Paul VI was adamant that injustice and suffering ought to be confronted with courage, and not be ignored. Injustices should be analyzed, and people should be taught about confronting injustice with courage and overcome

---

[532]   Ibid., 197.

[533]   Filochowski, 66.

[534]   Dorr, *Option for the Poor*, 200.

[535]   *Populorum Progressio*, 31, 14.

[536]   Riga, 46.

them. He stated that "development demands a bold approach to changes by which things will be thoroughly renovated."[537]

Paul VI's suggestion was relevant because passive observation of social injustices is morally wrong. It is a sin of omission from a Christian perspective. Action ought to be taken to preserve human dignity and to make situations of suffering noble, but only dignified action is morally justifiable. Immediate action is needed, and all people should participate. However, those who hold special responsibility and influence "by reason of their education, position and power" are exhorted to participate extraordinarily.[538] The significance of Paul VI's advocacy for vigorous confrontation of injustice is explained by the rationale that for development to occur, obstacles to it must be removed.

One may conclude that Paul VI, like Martin Luther King Jr., called for active resistance but not a violent one—he called for a *militant nonviolence* as described by Hanigan.[539] King did not advocate physical confrontation but stimulated consciences towards dialogue. This constitutes an active response to unjust situations without violence and is morally justified. Similarly, Paul VI thought participation of all people was important. Though Paul VI was aware that he could not enforce international order, he was also aware that other people could be instrumental in the pursuit of this cause. Statesmen and women, scholars, people of goodwill, especially Catholic Christians and other believers can bring about change in the mentality and structures for change.[540]

For Paul VI, a favorable response to the problem of poverty is beneficial to both the poor and the rich. There is a threefold threat in failure to respond to needs of the poor. Rich people jeopardize "their own highest values by yielding to greed," they invite the "judgment of God" upon themselves, and finally, they call upon themselves the wrath of the poor—"a clear warning to the rich that the oppressed may take into their own hands the challenge to bring about change through a violent action," suggesting that it is "in everybody's interest not to allow such a desperate and risky situation to develop."[541] Paul VI's concern was the risk consequent to the apathy of those who are instrumental in creating the prevalent situation. Julian Filochowski

---

[537] *Populorum Progressio*, 32, 14.

[538] Ibid.

[539] Hanigan, 167.

[540] Filochowski, 64, *Populorum Progressio*, 81-87,

[541] Dorr, *Option for the Poor*, 191. Also cfr, *Populorum Progressio*, 49, 21.

underscores this risk when he explains that Paul VI "offers no further teaching on violent reaction from the oppressed. He simply warns of the risk" and quotes Paul VI himself as saying,

> Lacking the bare necessities of life, whole nations are under the thumb of others: they cannot act on their own initiative; they cannot exercise personal responsibility; they cannot work towards a higher degree of cultural refinement or a greater participation in social and public life. They are sorely tempted to redress these insults to their human nature by violent means.[542]

It is risky to create such a situation because a revolutionary uprising causes new injustices, imbalances and disasters, and produces greater misery. The evil of violent revolution must always be in view. However, this does not mean that evil in society is to be endured passively. What is important is that the situation has to be changed—injustices have to be redressed and overcome. Paul VI is opposed to violent revolution as a way of bringing about radical change because it is ineffective; change introduced in this way is destructive and short lived.[543]

Paul VI was not encouraging revolution though some authors disagree with this assertion. In the context of the whole document and in the context of *Evangelii Nuntiandi*, Paul VI clearly denounced violent revolution:

> We exhort you not to place your trust in violence and revolution: that is contrary to the Christian spirit, and it can also delay instead of advancing that social uplifting to which you lawfully aspire.[544]

Additionally, his advocacy for universal charity as a fundamental virtue for integral human development defies the assertion that he was encouraging violence. Finally, Paul VI would not have called development the new name for peace if he encouraged violence. Paul VI even rejected the use of the term *liberation* as a synonym for *development* for fear it would cause people to rise against unjust regimes.[545] If he considered peace as crucial to development,

---

[542]   Filochowski, 64, *Populorum Progressio*, 30, 13.

[543]   Ibid., 81. Also see Paul VI (Pope), *Evangeli Nuntiandi: On Evangelization in the Modern World* (Boston: Pauline Books and Media, 1975), 37, 21.

[544]   *Evangeli Nuntiandi*, 37, 21. Also see Filochowski, 81.

[545]   Filochowski, 81.

he would not advocate violence as a means or model for change to achieve development.

In *Populorum Progressio*, Paul VI carefully and skillfully advanced three important points about violent reaction to situations of injustice.[546] First, he considered the possibility of a violent revolution, but found it is a futile way of overcoming injustice because it tends to breed the very evils that it wants to overcome. Therefore, it is wrong to argue that Paul VI advocated for a justified revolution. Second, the document specifies the circumstances under which a revolution could occur—flagrant and long-standing violation of human rights and great injury to the common good of the state. It is too exaggerated to read this as Paul VI endorsing the idea of violent revolution. His emphasis on universal love as a fundamental principle of development speaks to this point. Finally, while acknowledging the possibility of a justifiable revolution, the pope very carefully refrained from stating that it would be justifiable or justified under certain conditions. This clarifies the preceding assertions that Paul VI would not advocate violent revolution. Even on the basis of his experience of war and the suffering it causes, as presented in chapter one of this work, he would object to violent revolution. The fact that he notes that there is a possibility of a justifiable revolution does not necessarily mean that he advocated it. He was merely being speculative and foresighted.

This is a view often misrepresented as advocacy for violence. To understand it, one should not lose sight of his statement that development is the new name for peace.[547] What Paul VI suggests is that violent revolution is an inevitable consequence of omission, negligence, and irresponsible behavior—a consequence of lack of development. He argued that "excessive social, economic, and cultural inequalities among nations stir up strife and contention and frequently imperil the peace."[548] Those who respond to such situations with violence are culpable. But due to the negligent people who provoke violence, their degree of culpability is diminished because they are coerced by the prevalent situations and have to fight for their personal dignity. If the bonds of relationship between people are closed, they contribute to peace-making and preservation and promotion of progress.[549]

---

[546] Dorr, *Option for the Poor*, 192-193.

[547] *Populorum Progressio*, 87, 35.

[548] Ibid., 76, 31.

[549] Ibid., 73, 30; 77, 32.

G. Agents of Change

Paul VI appealed to three categories of people—Catholics, Christians, and people of goodwill—but generally, he appealed to all people who value human dignity to effect change.[550] He called for immediate participatory action in solidarity when and where innocent lives are at stake, the burden of poverty amidst inhumane living conditions is great, and world peace and "the very survival of civilization"[551] are at stake. The involvement of all people and nations in these issues is urgent and of grave significance. All people should assume responsibility to make positive change wherever and whenever necessary. Every person and all peoples are to be architects of their own destiny because development is something people do for and by themselves.

Paul VI spelled out some categories of development agents and what is expected of them. These are the Catholic hierarchy—that has the duty of teaching—and the laity, the entire Christian community, and all people of goodwill.[552] Reechoing *Gaudium et Spes* and anticipating *Octogesima Adveniens* and *Evangelii Nuntiandi*, Paul VI advocated that the laity improve the temporal order by free initiative, by planning, and by creativity. As much as possible, they must "permeate not only men's customs and mentality, but also the laws and structures of the civil community with the Christian sense of life."[553] The laity has the responsibility to change things according to Gospel teaching and moral principles. "Without passively waiting for directives, they have the role of infusing"[554] Christian spirit in the mentality, customs, laws, and structures of the communities in which they live, and they also have the duty to bring about basic indispensable requisite reforms. The Catholic laity, especially in developed nations, should offer "their skill and active cooperation to organizations, public or private, civil or religions, which are striving to overcome the difficulties of developing nations," and

---

[550] Filochowski, 64-65. Also see *Populorum Progressio*, 15, 7; 20, 9; 65, 27; 81-87, 33-35. Dorr, *Option for Poor*, 191.

[551] *Populorum Progressio*, 80, 30.

[552] Rousseau, 274-275. Also see *Populorum Progressio*, 81-84, 33-34.

[553] *Populorum Progressio*, 81, 33. Here Paul VI quotes Vatican Council II, *The Decree on the Apostolate of the Laity, Apostolicam actuositatem*, n.7, 13 and 24; AAS 57 (1996), 843, 849, and 856.

[554] Dorr, *Option for the Poor*, 199.

they have the role to disseminate "an international morality based on justice and equity."[555] The laity should be involved in the activities of charitable and humanitarian organizations. Their involvement in development is an application of the principles of participation, solidarity, justice, charity, and common good.

Second, the church has a role in transforming the structures of society that need to be transformed.[556] Paul VI asserted that the church has always been involved in the struggle to transform unjust social structures. In such situations, the role of the church is to offer a global vision of the human person and human relationships as situations require concerted action on a global scale. The entire Christian community is an agent of change. All Christians have the duty to enforce change by helping people to refrain from selfishness and resolve problems such as "egoism and arrogance, disputes and rivalries, and ambitions and injustice" through which, according to Paul VI, the attainment of "a more human life" where everybody is loved and assisted is possible.[557] The challenge Paul VI posits here is a reflection of the teaching of the Second Vatican Council's *Gaudium et Spes, Justitia in Mundo*, and *Evangelii Nuntiandi*, which recommended reading of the signs of the times in addressing issues affecting people.

Paul VI invoked the participation of all people of goodwill to create meaningful and humane living conditions through deep study and love.[558] The difficulty with this injunction is that not everybody may participate or be capable of involvement in a development project. It takes interest, awareness of needs, and commitment to the development process to be involved. This is an obstacle to progress toward what Paul VI calls integral human development. Consequently, the description of true development has to be qualified as integral human development according to possibilities such as natural capacities and resources.

According to Paul VI, people of goodwill may be "delegates to international organizations, government officials, journalists and publishers, educators and teachers."[559] He further contended that in accordance with their capacities

---

[555] *Populorum Progressio,* 81, 33. Also see Dorr, *Option for the Poor,* 199.

[556] Filochowski, 65. Also see Dorr, *Option for the Poor,* 199, and *Populorum Progressio,* 81, 33.

[557] *Populorum Progressio,* 82, 34.

[558] Ibid., 85, 35.

[559] Ibid., 83, 34.

and professions such experts are agents in resolving difficulties in the human situation and in building a new world.

Finally, heads of state and ambassadors are significant agents of change and development. Internationally, the role of "the rich countries and their leaders" and of international agencies such as FAO and the UN is vital.[560] Paul VI emphasized the role of statesmen and women, journalists, and the elite in wealthy states. The role of heads of state is to create unity between their countries and other people, persuasion for contribution toward "the development of peoples and to preserve peace."[561] In poor countries, an important category of agents responsible for change and development are the "experts and development workers, from the rich countries, who work in the poor countries."[562]

Paul VI affirmed that all "people of good will who are aware that peace cannot be attained except through the development of civilization and increased resources" [563] are also agents of human development. Paul VI appealed to the will of individuals to act in the face of injustice and to work for development which brings about peace. For him, ambassadors to international organizations have to work for "a policy of mutual, international cooperation, which is friendly, peace-seeking and interested to replace hostile and senseless confrontations of force and arms" [564] among all people. This means delegates to international organizations or institutions have the duty to make policies that are altruistic and provide for peace and unity rather than unrest. This is how integral and harmonious human development can be promoted. According to Paul VI, the more important agents of change are those who have power, wealth, and influence. The problem with such a suggestion is that such people contribute positively only if they have the right attitude to human needs; otherwise, they can be obstacles to development.

---

[560] Dorr, *Option for the Poor*, 198-199. Also see *Populorum Progressio*, 44, 19; 46, 19; 48, 20; 49, 21; 84, 34; 78, 32 83-85, 34-35; Filochowski, 65.

[561] *Populorum Progressio*, 84, 34

[562] Filochowski, 65. Also see Dorr, *Option for the Poor*, 199, and *Populorum Progressio*, 71-74.

[563] *Populorum Progressio*, 83, 34.

[564] Ibid.

IV. PAUL VI'S RESPONSE TO THE OUTSTANDING PROBLEMS

A. The Right to Private Ownership of Property

Paul VI treated private ownership of property in the light of integral development. According to him, ownership must foster the good of the whole person and of every person.[565] However, Paul VI's understanding of private ownership of property was not novel but related to teachings of the Early Fathers, who had two emphatic doctrines about private ownership of property.

First, the Early Fathers considered property as a means to what they called *autarkeia* or self-sufficiency, which means "property is a means to the relative end of self-sufficiency and self-reliance, which keeps one from being a perpetual burden to others."[566] It is a means to self-determination, self-assurance, moral independence, and freedom to serve others. The fathers advocated that ownership of property must be subordinated to its use. Property is not to be owned for the sake of holding or keeping and showing off. The real value of property is realized only when it is used; otherwise, there is no way of determining its worth. This assertion does not deny that property has potential worth. It only means that it is difficult to determine the value of property apart from its use.

The fathers taught that property's second goal was *koinonia*. Property is to serve in building fellowship between those who have and those who do not have, meaning that it is a means of communion between people, especially the rich and the poor.[567] Property is an instrument for consolidating solidarity. It ought to serve all people in need. The fathers were clear that property is not an end in itself. It is a means to genuine service to human values and needs.[568]

Paul VI did not break radically from Leo XIII or John XXIII regarding private property. All three popes and the Second Vatican Council affirmed the natural right to private property.[569] However, in *Populorum Progressio*, Paul

---

[565] William O'Neill, "Private Property," in *The New Dictionary of Catholic Social Thought*, ed. Judith A. Dwyer (Collegeville, Minnesota: Liturgical Press, 1994), 48-49. Also see *Populorum Progressio*, 14, 7.

[566] Charles Avila, *Ownership: Early Christian Teaching* (Maryknoll, New York: Orbis Books, 1983), 145.

[567] Ibid.

[568] Ibid., 144.

[569] Gregg, 74. Also see *Rerum Novarum*, 15, 9 and Riga, 34-36.

VI treated the right to private property in a social context. Consequently, he called for restraint in the exercise of this right.

Paul VI's claim about private ownership as a principle for integral human development is based on a theology of creation, namely, that "God intends the earth and its goods for use by everyone."[570] Paul VI cited the book of Genesis, "Fill the earth and subdue it"; and using this as a basis, he argued for the right to own property with restraint.[571] He asserted that the text teaches that

> all things of the world have been created for man, and that this task has been entrusted to him to enhance their value by the resources of his intellect and by his toil to complete and perfect them for his own use. Now if the earth has been created for the purpose of furnishing individuals either with the necessities of a livelihood or the means for progress, it follows that each man has the right to get from it what is necessary for him.[572]

Paul VI affirmed the universal destiny of natural resources. Some Ugandan societies acknowledge this contention, namely, that creation is God's gift to all people, not the monopoly of a few people. This is well stated in the Lugbara proverb: "Nyakuni ba piri ma andri ni," literally translated as "the earth is the mother of all" and meaning that the earth can feed everybody by its produce, like a common mother."[573] There is the need to work, which in Catholic social teaching is the means of ownership, to guarantee this motherhood of the earth.

Paul VI acknowledged that people are participants in creation and do so by adding value to the original creation of God. People participate in and continue God's creative activity in the world by working. This makes work blessed, dignified, and noble before God. The dignity of work, individual participation, and use of natural resources are emphasized as crucial for development.

Paul VI affirmed the right to tap resources of the earth through working on the earth. Every person who works can claim the fruits of his/her labor as

---

[570]   McBrien, 1033.

[571]   Genesis1:28. Also see *Populorum Progressio*, 22, 10.

[572]   *Populorum Progressio*, 22, 10.

[573]   Dalfovo, A. T. Lugbara Proverbs (Rome: Comboni Missionaries, 1990), 185

private property, but not absolutely, because of "the destiny of the goods of creation to serve the needs of all."[574] The universal destiny of natural resources is possible if things are ordered according to the principles of justice and charity. Paul VI affirmed that people have the right to what is necessary, not what is unnecessary:

> All other rights, whatever they are, including property rights and the right of free trade must be subordinated to this norm; they must not hinder it, but must rather expedite its application. It must be considered an urgent social obligation to refer these rights to their original purpose.[575]

The right to private ownership ought to remain open to arising needs. The needs of the less fortunate oblige those who are affluent, out of love and justice, to share their resources with the needy. "The rights of all to the goods of the earth supersede not only property rights, but also the right of free commerce."[576] The obligation to leave the claim over property open is based on love; Paul VI also referred to the Early Fathers, particularly St. Ambrose, who argued that the basis for sharing with the poor is the universal destiny of natural resources.[577]

According to Ambrose and Augustine, the affluent do not give from their own resources—they return what belongs to the poor. The universal destiny of resources to meet human needs is the more compelling argument. "No one is allowed to set aside solely for his own advantage possessions which exceed his needs when others lack the necessities of life."[578] This affirmation corroborates the relationships between the right of private ownership, charity, and the common good. It is here that Paul VI "adopts a traditional concept of private property in this encyclical but gives it a different stress," particularly the emphasis on "the social function of private property."[579]

---

[574] Curran, 11. Also David J. O'Brien and Thomas A. Shannon, 238.

[575] *Populorum Progressio*, 22,10.

[576] Gurdorf, 127.

[577] *Populorum Progressio*, 23,10. John 3:17 was Paul VI's theological basis for this assertion.

[578] Ibid., 23, 11.

[579] Riga, 34. Also see *Populorum Progressio*, 22-24, 10-11, 48-49, 20-21.

According to Riga, for Paul VI, "property is always a social responsibility."[580] He agrees with Augustine according to whom "the phenomenon of property must be situated in the context of humanity's solidarity."[581] Paul VI affirmed that sometimes for the sake of the common good, private property can be interfered with, especially when it affects society negatively:

> The common good therefore, at times demands the expropriation of an estate if it happens that some estates impede the common property either on account of their vast size or because of their small or negligible cultivation, or cause extreme poverty to the population or bring serious harm to the country.[582]

In the same spirit as the Second Vatican Council, *Populorum Progressio* was clear that revenues derived from natural resources should not be disposed of at the pleasure of an individual, and excessive profits should not be used for individual benefits. Transfer of excess profits to foreign countries is unjust because the resources of nature are for the benefit of all people.[583] This suggests that human labor is for the good of the human community too. Human labor is good because it is participation in God's creative activity, and so personal industry and creativity are significant contributions to human development.[584]

Paul VI's assertions reflected the thoughts of Thomas Aquinas, who affirmed the right of private ownership but gave ownership a different meaning. According to him, ownership "is merely an extension of the freedom of the person—a necessary extension for successful navigation through life," but essentially, property is for the promotion of the common good.[585] Ownership helps in the cultivation of virtue through the practice of stewardship, generosity and work. Aquinas affirmed the value of work and regarded the benefits accruing from labor as being for the individual as well as others; and labor was, in a way, a custodian of natural resources.

---

[580] Ibid., 35. Also see *Populorum Progressio*, 3, 2.

[581] Avila, 116.

[582] *Populorum Progressio*, 24, 11.

[583] Riga, 35.

[584] *Populorum Progressio*, 25, 11.

[585] Gregg, 71. Also see O'Neill, 789.

This explains why Paul VI was, to a significant degree, opposed to exaggerated free-market capitalism and insisted that the economy must serve the people.[586] He observed that the principal purpose of economic development is not promotion of profits, competition is not "the supreme law of economics," "private ownership of the means of production" is not "an absolute right which recognizes neither limits nor concomitant social duty," and such abusive economic mentalities ought to be rejected because economic progress is for the good of people.[587] Diez-Alegria concedes this claim of Paul VI and succinctly states that what Paul VI "condemns on moral grounds, is private, individualistic profit taken as an absolute itself, to which everything else must be subordinated: the idea that maximizing return on capital is the supreme value."[588] Paul VI rejected the idea of liberal capitalism, though not entirely. He condemned the maximization of profits and their selfish use. When profits are used selflessly to meet needs of people, divine intent is respected. It was for this reason that Paul VI consistently denounced liberal capitalism as the dominant principle for international economic systems.[589]

Paul VI viewed the right to own property in relation to labor and its contribution to development. He argued that "justice demands that we admit that not only the organization of labor but also industrial process made a necessary contribution to promote development."[590] The right to private ownership of property is advocated on the basis of the traditional argument since *Rerum Novarum*—that property is earned through labor. Since work dignifies and it is the causality of production, ownership of what one has worked for is realistic. This is a motivation to work and a positive contribution to development.

Paul VI further argued that what a nation has by virtue of divine providence and its input in the form of labor should first be enjoyed by that nation, but no nation should appropriate natural resources exclusively for its own use.[591] Economic systems and relationships should respect the right to private property. They ought not to turn human beings into objects without

---

[586] Diez-Alegria, 21-22.

[587] *Populorum Progressio*, 26, 12.

[588] Diez-Alegria, 22 and 30. Also see Riga, 38.

[589] Riga, 38, 42. Also see *Populorum Progressio* 7, 4; 26, 12; 34, 15; 52, 22; 54, 22-23; 59, 25; 63, 26; 70, 29.

[590] *Populorum Progressio*, 26, 12.

[591] Ibid., 48, 20; 49, 21.

dignity just for the sake of acquisition of property. Consequently, Paul VI condemned the use of labor as a commodity to be sold for profits, denounced the separation of labor and capital, and considered the exaggerated profit motive of capitalism, which neglects human dignity, as the crux of the problem in current development programs.[592] The problem with the profit motive of capitalism is that it turns values upside down. Profit becomes the end, and human persons become the means. Paul VI denounced private ownership as an absolute right and suggested that the only absolute principle is human dignity.[593]

Samuel Gregg observes that many authors have vehemently defended the right to private property.[594] Some of the reasons for this defense are as follows: private property is a guarantee and security for people who have worked to earn property; private property promotes self-reliance and autonomy—it helps people to actualize virtues such as liberality and magnanimity; and "private ownership is actualized when persons mix their labor with raw materials."[595] Paul VI was aware of these credible reasons, but his concern was that this right was exaggerated and abused. Consequently, he argued for "the common use principle," which advocates that natural resources are destined for common use, not for unrestrained private use.[596] Paul VI acknowledged that

> inequality of wealth is not necessarily unfair. Christianity has always affirmed that many factors must be taken into account when thinking about what constitutes justice in the material realm. These include factors such as need, merit, willingness to take risks and the function performed by a person.[597]

Paul VI's call for the proper exercise of the right to private property was necessitated by the demand of integral human development, the recognition, and acknowledgment that "the goods of the earth are for all people."[598] Paul

---

592   Riga, 40.
593   *Populorum Progressio*, 8, 4; 26, 12; 33, 14. Also see Riga, 43.
594   Gregg, 38.
595   Ibid.
596   Ibid., 38-39.
597   Here Gregg quotes John Finnis, *Natural Law and Natural Rights* (Oxford: Clarendon Press, 1993), 123-77; Also see Gregg, 39. This is not, originally, Gregg's thought.
598   Henriot, "Who Cares about Africa? Development Guidelines from the Church's Social Teaching," in *Catholic Social Thought and the New World Order*, 217.

VI upheld the right to private property but insisted that it is superseded by the right to use the resources of nature.

B. Two Consequential Virtues: Charity and Justice with Peace as Consequence

The relationship between charity, justice, and peace is an intimate one. In Catholic social teaching prior to and after *Populorum Progressio*, the three are consistently linked together. "Justice is an indispensable part of charity," and "justice is a prerequisite for true peace."[599] Charity, justice, and peace are related not only as Christian virtues but also as social virtues. Peace is a consequence of love and justice and comes after the two virtues. Paul VI was not the first person to recognize the value of peace for the human community and its growth. All he taught affirmed Thomas Aquinas who considered peace a significant factor for the well-being of human community.[600]

1. CHARITY

For Paul VI, the social dimension of the human person affects all human relations. The church calls all people motivated by love to heed the call of those who live under evil social, political, cultural and economic conditions.[601] Paul VI invoked the virtues of Christian charity and solidarity as basic principles of liberation and true human development. Charity should be viewed in the context of human solidarity and be given priority in social relationships. Consequently, Paul VI encouraged the practice of fraternity, and charitable organizations such as Food and Agriculture Organization (FAO) and *Caritas Internationalis* that attempt to meet the demands of charity and the material needs of desperate people.[602] According to him, such organizations are necessary and visible expressions of charity because the depraved condition of humanity is caused more by lack of charity than by a monopoly of the resources of nature.

---

[599] Gudorf, 1, and 3 where Gudorf cites various examples of encyclicals to show the relation between charity, justice and peace for either case, but in both cases, *Populorum Progressio* is cited. Also see Gurdorf, 46.

[600] Gregg, 71-72.

[601] *Populorum Progressio*, 3, 2. Also see Riga, 11.

[602] Riga, 116. Also see *Populorum Progressio* 46, 19-20; 66, 28.

Paul VI considered charity a fundamental principle for integral human development. His assertion is justifiable because where there is universal and indiscriminate love among individuals and nations, the possibility of integral development is heightened. It facilitates the process of mutual support among peoples and nations and ultimately integral development. He affirmed extension of "a generous welcome to others" as "a duty of human solidarity and Christian charity" in "households and also cultural institutions of host countries."[603] This suggests that solidarity and charity are foundational for hospitality. By recognizing their mutual bonds, people love each other. Paul VI's concern was young people who tend to be vulnerable to situations, ideologies, and worldviews and need moral and spiritual guidance. In this case, hospitality involves not only love and accommodation, but also moral support and directing the youth.

Paul VI advocated that "emigrant workers too must be welcomed"[604] and be offered decent working conditions as opposed to the fact that they are often left to fate despite their need to support their poverty-stricken family members. The dignity of immigrant workers ought to be respected. Hospitality to aliens was emphasized as an expression of universal charity. It was later reaffirmed as a guiding principle for the international community. *The Rome Statement* of 1999 advised the members of the International Conference on Population and Development (ICPD) to incorporate hospitality to aliens as a vital principle for human development.[605]

Paul VI used the term *charity* as a specific form of Christian love, not a philanthropic act.[606] Charity is not an emotional response to circumstances but a rational, deliberate, and responsible response. He proposed that expatriate experts should be motivated by charity in what they do in foreign countries. Regardless of personal concerns, love must be extended to people in honor of their dignity.

Technical skill should not be valued independently of love. "If then technical skill is necessary the signs and proofs too of genuine love must be joined with it."[607] Paul VI affirmed that technical skill per se is not sufficiently valuable. Its value is determined by how and why it is used to serve others

---

[603]   *Populorum Progressio* 67, 28.

[604]   Ibid., 69, 28.

[605]   *The Rome Statement*, 5.

[606]   Edward Collins Vacek, "Charity," in *The New Dictionary of Catholic Social Thought*, ed. Judith A. Dwyer (Collegeville, Minnesota: Liturgical Press, 1994), 143.

[607]   *Populorum Progressio*, 72, 29.

and expressed in a loving way or not.[608] In emphasizing the significance of universal charity, Paul VI stated that

> programs initiated for human development to be implemented by common effort bring nations together if all, the chief government officials and the lowest artisan, are enkindled with brotherly love and ardently desire the establishment of a civilization of world solidarity. Then a dialogue will begin based on man but not on the produce of the land or products of technology.[609]

For Paul VI, love is the origin of dialogue between nations and collaborative action because it is people-centered. Love breeds solidarity, and solidarity is the beginning of authentic dialogue. According to Paul VI, with true solidarity, dialogue centers on people, not products or technical skills. He made the human person central in the pursuit of development, arguing that education leads to self-betterment and economic and spiritual progress.[610]

Genuine love contributes to integral human development because one "who is animated by genuine love is the one who in particular applies his mental acumen to discourage the cause of misery and find ways to combat them and boldly overcome them."[611] Love is what moves one to devote personal talents, intelligence, wisdom, energy, and abilities to ensure that suffering is abated and development of all is achieved. This suggests, Paul VI says, that authentic development of the human race demands a daring love, a charity that reaches out to others unconditionally:

> Now this striving for a more human way of life does indeed demand effort and entails inconvenience but these very sufferings endured out of love for our brothers and for their benefit can be most conducive to the development of the human race.[612]

Authentic development demands commitment to self-sacrificial charity and a love that is indiscriminate, unconditional, and never hesitates to act. This kind of charity is a biblical demand of discipleship and a social demand

---

[608] Ibid., 72, 29.

[609] Ibid., 73, 30.

[610] Riga, 140. Also see *Populorum Progressio*, 73, 30.

[611] Ibid., 75, 31.

[612] Ibid., 79, 33.

of human community.[613] A loving community can help the disadvantaged to rise to a higher standard, befitting human beings. Though charity is supreme, it must be linked to justice because "it both motivates and completes justice."[614] People are moved to act justly because they love, and love makes justice real and moral.

2. JUSTICE

Paul VI made the notion of justice more expansive than encyclicals before *Populorum Progressio*. He extended the notion of social justice from a national level to an international one and advocated that international social justice is essentially based on human solidarity because human community constitutes a family.[615] Fair treatment among peoples is influenced by their relationships and the inevitable need for each other. Paul VI recognized the significance of the regulation of economic relations between nations so that no party would be exploited. He advocated commutative justice. He dealt with a situation of exchange involving legal contracts, which stipulate—directly or indirectly—the requisite conditions of the agreements or contracts entered into. This is typical of commutative justice, a justice exercised in exchange of commodities or services.[616]

Paul VI envisioned that protective agreements were necessary. Consequently, he suggested that bilateral and multilateral agreements must be honored because of the social relations they create on the basis of political and juridical equalities. He further thought that these agreements need to be governed by justice, which is a fruit of sincere collaboration and respect for human rights and dignity.[617] The implication of this view is that justice must protect the human person, rights, and dignity. The view is credible because all principles for integral human development are founded on the most fundamental principle of the human dignity. If human dignity is understood, recognized, and acknowledged, respect for human rights and the human person, solidarity, and ultimately the exercise of justice is more easily achievable.

---

[613] Cfr. Mt. 5:38-48.

[614] Gudorf, 3. Gurdorf quoting *Evangelii Praecones*, June 1951, AAS 43 (1951): 518, para.71; *Quadragesimo Anno,* May 15, 1931, AAS 23 (1931): 223-224, para.137; *Pacem in Terris*, April, 11, 1963, AAS 55 (1963): 302-303, para.167.

[615] *Populorum Progressio* 5, 3; 44, 19; 48,20. Also see Riga, 11.

[616] Gudorf, 2 and 30. Also see *Populorum Progressio*, 61, 25-26.

[617] *Populorum Progressio,* 52, 22; 54, 23.

From Paul VI on, the requirement of justice for human development has been consistently emphasized and supported. For example, justice was one of the principal developmental elements underscored during the ICPD. The Rome Statement affirmed that justice is an important and protective component against poverty and disparities of wealth and societal unity.[618] Similarly, Paul VI had earlier argued that solidarity is easily undermined by injustice. When nations attempt to work in collaboration and mutual agreement, they should ensure that there are no variable trade relations, which exist between richer and poorer countries because steady relationships provide hope and confidence for poor nations. [619] Otherwise, their fears that aiding nations can take back their aid any time may be aggravated.

Paul VI affirmed "the need for social justice to govern world trade."[620] Less-developed countries depend on exportation of raw materials, which are less valuable than the products of developed nations and "subject to very great and sudden price changes and are consequently far outclassed by the increasing value of industrial products."[621] This variation contributes to the gap between developed and underdeveloped nations. The phenomenon incapacitates less-developed countries, competing with industrialized countries. Costs of goods from industrialized countries claim more money from the unindustrialized countries than their income. Paul VI concluded rightly that "for this reason nations struggling against poverty become still poorer, but those endowed with all resources are enriched with even greater wealth."[622] Injustice in international trade relations persists in relationships of unequal bargaining powers, capacities, and possibilities.

According to Paul VI, international trade relations are good and just only if "the parties involved do not differ too much in resources," and it is unjust if "very unequal situations obtain between countries"; and it was for the same reason, according to Paul VI, that "the fundamental principle of liberalism as the norm of commercial transaction is called into question."[623] Paul VI did not condemn economic liberalism or capitalism—absolutely. He simply called for moderation in the system. As long as the profits of a capitalist serve the needs of human dignity and are not used for needless selfish interests, he

---

618   The Rome Statement, 5.
619   *Populorum Progressio*, 44, 19.
620   Curran, 11.
621   *Populorum Progressio*, 57, 24.
622   Ibid., 58, 24.
623   Ibid.

had no problem. The aspect essentially questioned is that capitalism gives rise to economic inequalities. Inequalities at the same time provide opportunities for free trade because the poor cannot favorably compete with the rich. To allow people to make economic transactions without agreements that favor both trading partners is unjust and faulty because the more powerful can manipulate situations for selfish ends, thus disregarding the common good.

Paul VI raised many challenging issues. First, he questioned the sense of a claimed or supposed solidarity. When nations or individuals get into trade relationships, they express their need for each other, but true solidarity is not selfish or exploitative. True solidarity benefits all parties involved. Where there is authentic solidarity, there is justice. Second, there is no justice in relationships when one party suffers or is exploited. Third, though it could happen in any economic system, liberalism is inconsonant with justice and solidarity or at least makes them difficult to achieve. The terms of a just agreement may not be honored, or mutual needs are disregarded or become selfish. Partners fail to see their need for one another, and this makes the principle of economic liberalism questionable. Finally, Paul VI suggested the principle of subsidiarity and an option for the poor to regulate economic justice. According to him, regulation of trade relations demands an authority that intervenes when smaller groups are unable to resolve their problems.

Paul VI argued for the exercise of justice, freedom, and equity. He observed that free competition is beneficial only to those who have stronger bargaining power. It is unjust that the weaker or poorer parties are compelled to succumb to stronger ones because they have no alternative. This would be an act of commutative injustice, a violation of human freedom, and immoral because it is coercion. Paul VI suggested that there should be objective rationality in economic relations. Human reason endowed with divine assistance should discern what needs to be done. Economic relations should be governed by ethical principles. If not, the so-called collaborative relation or solidarity is not authentic or relevant and integral human development is impossible.

Paul VI advocated justice on the basis of Christian understanding of the social character of people. He asserted that justice must be based on "responsibility to others," restrained inviolability of private property, and "the universal destination of material goods" or "the common use principle," and that "completely equal standards are necessary" [624] for just economic competition or trade. Paul VI outlined conditions necessary for justice to

---

[624] Gregg, 6. Also see *Populorum Progressio*, 61, 25.

flourish: people need to be responsible for each other, take the common good seriously, be selfless in the use of property, and deal on even economic grounds.

Paul VI praised the work of large industrial groups operating in foreign countries. He advocated and urged "industrialists, merchants, the leaders and representatives of these large organizations" to deal with the less-developed countries disinterestedly; their principal motive should be "social development and human progress."[625] Justice should govern employer-employee relations. "No one should unjustly be subjected to the arbitrariness of others."[626] They should help nationals to participate in shaping development in their countries and do this by training and involving them in the leadership and general business of their organizations. Paul VI suggested that joint participation of specialists and nationals of countries they serve is necessary because different skills supplement each other and meet the needs of integral development. This means solidarity is a necessary partner of justice because it expresses how much people need each other and treat each other according to their genuine needs.

For Paul VI, justice makes two important demands.[627] First, it demands that experts who work in nations other than their own do not dominate but serve. Paul VI advocated just action on the part of those whose skills benefit those who lack requisite skills for development. Second, justice demands that experts are free from exaggerated patriotism—an inordinate love of their country—and unjust discrimination. Their patriotism should not jeopardize the life, dignity, and culture of the people in the nations they serve. They should refrain from giving preeminence to their own culture, knowledge and experience, and their countries of origin.

Several authors agree that in his treatise of social justice in *Populorum Progressio*, Paul VI moved the focus from a national to an international level.[628] Prior to the document, "justice was primarily a matter of ensuring the proper distribution of *existing* wealth and resources"; the novelty of the document is that "it could be seen in terms of the production of increased resources which would be used to overcome poverty and to ensure that those who have little

---

[625] *Populorum Progressio*, 70, 29.

[626] Ibid.

[627] Ibid., 72, 29-30.

[628] David J. O'Brien and Thomas A. Shannon, 238. Also cfr. Dorr, *Option for Poor*, 184.

could catch up with those who have more."[629] This means justice—like option for the poor, affirmative action, and subsidiarity—consists in improving the conditions of those who are poor and incapable. The document affirmed the worldwide dimension of justice in human development and the role of solidarity between the rich and the poor.

In *Populorum Progressio*, Paul treated the three types of justice—social justice, commutative justice, and distributive justice. Social justice is more explicit in his vision of human solidarity and mutual relationship. The commutative dimension is clear in his treatise on the balance in trade relations. The distributive dimension is treated in his attempt to address the plight of nations marred with poverty, ignorance, disease, and other maladies. However, his advocacy for distributive justice should be read in light of the right to private ownership of property and the promotion of the dignity of the human person because the use of property also reflects justice. This suggests that general justice as understood by Thomas Aquinas, namely, as justice whose direct object is "the welfare of entire community—the common good," [630] and what Christine E. Gudorf calls social justice as justice of the status quo or the social order is present in Paul VI's vision of justice.

3. PEACE

At the end of *Populorum Progressio*, Paul VI equated his overarching theme of human development to peace. This shows how significant a condition peace is for development. Both the church and state should always pursue peace. Its pursuit should be directed to the defense of human dignity—the principal focus in the struggle for peace as Paul VI had stated in 1965 in his address to the United Nations assembly.[631] Peace is also a product of the practice of justice, and since love and justice are necessarily linked, then peace is also a product of love. It can rightly be called the fruit or consequence of charity and justice.

Paul VI's doctrine of peace promoted the teaching of his predecessors. For example, Pius XI, in *Quadragesimo Anno*, and John XXIII, in *Pacem in Terris*, had clearly affirmed that peace is an important and a unique

---

[629] Dorr, *Option for Poor*, 179.

[630] Gudorf, 2.

[631] The German Bishops, *A Just Peace* (Bonn: *Sekretariat der Deutschen Bischofskonferenz*, 27 September 2000), 57-58.

condition to be established. It is crucial to integral development of peoples but delicate because it can be disrupted easily by "excessive social, economic, and cultural inequalities among nations."[632] For Paul VI, the consequence of inequalities among nations and even individuals is often controversy and fighting, but "peace is not simply to be reduced to the elimination of all war, as if it consisted in a precarious balance of power."[633] True peace is not just the absence of war.

Peace is an earned harmonious life, tranquility in relationship, consequent to unity of mind, and a deeply heart-rooted reconciliation. Justice and charity are crucial for authentic human development, but "a more perfect form of justice" [634] is a prerequisite for peace. True peace is tranquility of heart and mind, a real transformation, and an absence of fears and concerns. A balance of socioeconomic and political power is not a guarantee for enduring peace. True peace is a consequence of satisfactory living circumstances for all.

The French bishops argued that true peace is created by a rational influence on people's political wills and intentions. Peace is not forced through threats or intimidation. Consequently, they preferred the French word *dissuasion* for *deterrence*, which has the English equivalence of dissuasion and the German word *abschreckung*, which is derived from the German verb *abschreken*, meaning to deter, put off, plunge in cold water—all of which give a sense of force or conditioning.[635] This German term does not exactly depict the sense of the English word *dissuasion*. Instead, it conveys the sense of deterrence just as the United States Bishops' English equivalent of deterrence, which gives the sense of intimidation and fear even though the latter can influence people's wills.[636] The French rendering of deterrence is preferred because it does not convey the sense of intimidation, and it is "the deterrence of the strong by

---

632 *Populorum Progressio*, 76, 31.

633 *Populorum Progressio*, 76, 32. Also see Rousseau, 273; *Gaudium et spes*, 78; and National Conference of Catholic Bishops, *The Challenge of Peace: God's Promise and Our Response* (Washington DC: United States Catholic Conference, May 3, 1983) 68, 21.

634 Ibid., 76, 32. Here Paul VI is quoting John XXIII, *Pacem in Terris*, AAS 55 (1963), 301.

635 Harper Collins, *German-English Dictionary* (New York: Harper Collins Publishing Company, 1989), 5.

636 James V. Schall, ed., *Out of Justice, Peace: Joint Letter of the West Germany Bishops* (April 18, 1983) and *Winning the Peace: Joint Pastoral Letter of the French Bishops* (November 8, 1983) (San Francisco: Ignatius Press, 1984), 19. Also cfr. *Winning the Peace*, 28,110;

the weak."[637] This notion of deterrence is plausible because it resonates with the original sense of peace as derived from the Hebrew word *shalom*. Both OT and NT, *shalom* had an integral meaning of general welfare. The word meant health or peace and a comprehensive welfare, which Saint Augustine referred to as the tranquility of order, meaning a true harmony with self and environment.[638]

For Paul VI, authentic peace is not given and taken without labor, it is earned. Peace is something to work for ceaselessly and progressively in accordance with the original harmony divinely instituted. Paul VI's vision of true peace is a product of the harmony of mind and heart within oneself and with people in a communal environment. For this reason, peace is rightly called "a quality of relationship between persons and nations."[639] It is a fruit of authentic love and justice. Consequently, Paul VI "argued for economic justice as the surest way to peace."[640]

This is a credible argument because people disagree and fight on the basis of whether they are justly treated or not. Social, economic, political, religious, cultural, and educational injustices are fundamental causes of disharmony. They directly affect human rights and human dignity, which is the overriding principle for the integral development of the human person and communities.

If true development is the new name for peace as Paul VI claimed, then peace is the work not only of an individual person or a single nation, but of all.[641] It involves action in solidarity. Contributions of nations and people toward peace are significant, but they needed to be corroborated and coordinated. This is what Paul VI meant when he said,

> Since nations are each the architects of their own development they assume a task and responsibility of such magnitude that they will never be able to accomplish it if they live in isolation.[642]

Out of Justice, Peace, (4.3.2), 136-151,78-82; *Just Peace*, 2, and *The Challenge of Peace: God's Promise and Our Response*, 162-177, 51-56.

[637] *Winning the Peace*, 28, 110.

[638] Gerald O'Collins and Edward F. Farrugia, 195.

[639] McBrien, 1033.

[640] David J. O'Brien and Thomas A. Shannon, 238. Also cfr. Dorr, *Option for Poor*, 184, and Henriot, *Catholic Social Teaching: Our Best Kept Secret*, 53.

[641] Gudorf, 37. Henriot, *Catholic Social Teaching: Our Best Kept Secret*, 53.

[642] *Populorum Progressio*, 77, 32.

True development is not the achievement of one nation, and it is the achievement of peace, which Paul VI equated to development. The achievements of peace and development are hard tasks in isolation. Peace and solidarity are necessarily related. For this reason, Paul VI stated that

> agreements between poorer nations of the same region on mutual assistance, common programs of broader scope to help them, likewise other agreements of greater importance made to coordinate plans of action with other nations are, so to speak, so many milestones of this road which leads to peace while it promote progress.[643]

Paul VI asserted that personal or individual efforts need to be supplemented with coordinated external efforts and support to attain true peace and true human development. The road to true peace and development is hard, involving, and demanding individuals and nations to pool their efforts, talents, and resources. Similarly, the French bishops later affirmed in 1983 that to build peace requires courage, effort, and willingness on the part of all parties involved in the peace building process, and what needs to be understood and attended to are the ideologies and intentions of people in conflict.[644] This is a credible affirmation because true peace can only be built when worldviews and the intentions of conflicting parties are reconciled. Above all, the peace-building process involves critical analysis of situations, mutual understanding, and sincere dialogue.

For Paul VI, there is no distinction between the fruit of peace and the event of human development because "development is synonymous with peace," a view commonly affirmed by many interpreters of *Populorum Progressio*.[645] The credibility of this assertion is based on the vision that when and where there is development, there is peace and when there is peace the possibility of development is eminent. This was why Paul VI called development the new name for peace.

Henriot supplements Paul VI's assertion by stating that there is a twofold connection between development and peace, which flows from the text of the document. First, "a world filled with poor and oppressed people will not be

---

[643] Ibid.

[644] *Winning the Peace*, 17, 109.

[645] *Populorum Progressio*, 87, 35; 76-77, 31-32; 83, 32. Also see Filochowski, 64 and Henriot, *Catholic Social Teaching: Our Best Kept Secret*, 56.

a peaceful world"; and second, "a world preparing for war or actually waging war will not be a world where people move from less human to more human conditions."[646] This statement realistically explains the equation of peace to development. Henriot suggests here that development is the cause of true peace. If development is not authentic, peace is a dream or falsely claimed. Second, war contributes nothing to the development of people.

Development and peace are necessarily mutually supportive. Peace-loving peoples, regions, and nations develop. Truly developed peoples, regions, and nations are peaceful, not only because they are developed, but also because they understand that the disruption of peace retards human progress, diminishes human dignity, and creates more problems for society and individuals.

Paul VI's introduction of development as a synonym for peace shows a break from previous papal teachings regarding the relationship between social justice and the status quo and consequently called for a careful understanding of justice.[647] Paul VI stated that civilization is partially manifested in charity and justice, which are antecedents to peace. The inseparable relation between love and peace confirms the relation between peace and solidarity. John Paul II later succinctly stated that the achievement of peace requires "the practice of the virtues that favor togetherness and which teach us to live in unity, so as to build unity by giving and receiving a new society and better world."[648] This summarizes the requirements of true peace and some of the requirements of true development.

C. Three Contextual Principles: Subsidiarity, Option for the Poor, and Affirmative Action

1. SUBSIDIARITY

The principle of subsidiarity was introduced into Catholic social teaching by Pius XI in his encyclical *Quadragessimo Anno*, where he stated that the principle is the important guiding norm for the restoration of social order.[649]

---

[646] Henriot, "Who Cares about Africa? Development Guidelines from the Church's Social Teaching," in *Catholic Social Thought and the New World Order*, 222.

[647] Gudorf, 37.

[648] Ibid., 150.

[649] Michael Allsop, "Subsidiarity, Principle of," in *The New Dictionary of Catholic Social Thought*, ed. Judith A. Dwyer (Collegeville, Minnesota: Liturgical Press, 1994), 928.

According to Pius XI, subsidiarity is "that most weighty principle which cannot be set aside or changed, it remains fixed and unshaken in social philosophy.":

> Just as it is gravely wrong to take from individuals what they can accomplish by their own initiative and industry and give it to the community, so also it is an injustice and at the same time a grave evil and disturbance of right order to assign to a greater and higher association what lesser and subordinate organizations can do. For every social activity ought of its very nature to furnish help to the members of the body social, and never destroy and absorb them.[650]

Pius XI suggested that if smaller bodies or groups or individuals can meet their needs, larger bodies like the state should not interfere. Conversely, smaller bodies should not transfer to the larger bodies like the state what they are able to do for themselves. It would constitute mutual injustice if smaller bodies shunned their responsibilities and bigger bodies usurped responsibilities of smaller bodies and vice versa. The explanation is that the principle of participation demands that all people contribute to the common good according to their abilities. The teaching about subsidiarity was continued by John XXIII in *Mater et Magistra* and *Pacem in Terris*.[651]

Paul VI advocated for a mediating body to resolve conflicts when individuals or groups are incapable of supporting themselves. In case of

> conflict between acquired private rights and the primary needs of the community it pertains to the public authorities to seek a solution to these functions with the active participation of individuals and social groups.[652]

Paul VI suggested that the common good, affirmative action, participation, and an option for the poor are related to the principle of subsidiary.

---

[650] Pius XI, *Quadragesimo Anno: On Reconstructing the Social Order* (Chicago, Illinois: Outline Press, 1931), 79, 46.

[651] Allsop, 929.

[652] Here, Paul VI is quoting the letter of cardinal secretary of state to Catholic men attending social life studies at Brest published in *L'homme et la revolution urbaine* (Lyons, Chronique Sociale, 1965). Also see *Populorum Progressio*, 23, 11.

When small or weak communities make efforts but cannot handle conflicts or support themselves, then stronger or larger bodies such as public authorities should intervene. Affirmative action is implied here because subsidiarity advocates necessary intervention of stronger or larger bodies on behalf of the poor or the weak. It boosts the participation or involvement of all people. Paul VI emphasized the significance of the principle of subsidiarity:

> It is the function of public authorities to establish and enjoin the objectives to be attained, the plans to be followed and the means to achieve them; also to stimulate the energies of all involved in this common activity. But they must be careful to associate the projects of individuals and intermediary agencies with this kind of work.[653]

According to Paul VI, intervention by superior bodies must be limited— they should not take away what individuals and smaller groups are capable of doing. To do so would usurp rights of these bodies to function freely and to attain self-fulfillment. Respect between the smaller bodies and the superior ones is an imperative. The limits of each are defined by what the small bodies are capable of doing. Encroaching on the freedom or rights of individuals or smaller groups kills initiative and participation, ultimately encouraging dependence. It also denies the dignity of an individual's work and personal dignity. However, the principle is fraught with, at least a flaw, because it is not easy to determine what smaller bodies can or cannot do for themselves.

Paul VI thought that projects of "individuals and intermediary agencies" should not be associated with public authorities because this leads to collectivization and arbitrary economic management, which deprives individuals and groups of people of their freedom and exercise of basic human rights.[654] The second part of the principle of subsidiarity is that when individuals and intermediary groups are capable, the intervention of public authority is unnecessary. This part of the principle protects capable individuals or intermediary bodies and limits the intervention of public authorities to necessary moments only.

Paul VI did not explicitly use the term *subsidiarity*, but it is apparent in his assertion in *Populorum Progressio* that

---

[653] *Populorum Progressio*, 33, 14.

[654] Ibid.

this international cooperation which embraces the whole world demands institutions which prepare the way for it, coordinate, and direct it until a new judicial order is established which all recognize as fixed and firm.[655]

Paul VI was suggesting that it is necessary to have an international structure or authority to govern activities within the international community and organizations with international orientations and overtones. He reiterated "the need of international authority to coordinate the establishment of just political and economic spheres."[656] Such a body is necessary when nations need support though they should act on their own. Institutions act as mediators or coordinators for different groups, but they should unite people and nations, and create effective international judicial and political systems.[657] In other words, an international government or body should have effective guidelines for directing and developing the world community.

Paul VI emphasized the importance of the United Nations Organization, which was already established. The principle of subsidiarity was intended to restore social order in relations between smaller groups and larger ones, to restore autonomy of groups, and to state the right relations between associations and and the larger society.[658] This was important because integral human development depends on mutual relations and dealings among individuals, groups, communities, and nations.

2. PREFERENTIAL OPTION FOR THE POOR

As alluded to in chapter one, Paul VI's trips to different continents influenced his vision of the world and shaped his writing of *Populorum Progressio*. Riga says that "it is evident that the Pope's travels put him into direct contact with the poor and that he was shocked to see the extent of human degradation throughout the globe."[659] It is no surprise that Paul VI's concern for the poor was emphatic and empathetic.

---

[655] Ibid., 78, 32.

[656] Allsop, 729.

[657] *Populorum Progressio*, 78, 32.

[658] *Quadragesimo Anno*, 49, 34-35. Also see Allsop, 928.

[659] Riga, 24. Here Riga refers to *Populorum Progressio*, 4, 2-3.

The condition and dignity of the poor was the crux of the problem Paul VI addressed in *Populorum Progressio*; it was inevitable that he should suggest a principle directly related to the problem. Consequently, he proposed the principle of an option for the poor as a way of resolving these problems. The principle invokes the spirit of sacrifice directed toward resolving the problem of poverty in society. This is a dominant demand of *Populorum Progressio*.[660] Option for the poor is an invitation to give priority to care for and to protect the human dignity of disadvantaged people. This is a call to all to act in solidarity for the empowerment of the weak in society.

Paul VI declared that "the more needy nations" should be helped to liberate themselves from what retards their progress "and to find, without detriment to their own native character, the means of human and social development."[661] Here, he advocated a preferential but not exclusive action which favors the disadvantaged people. Their needs are not specified in the document, but it can be inferred from previous doctrine that they are socioeconomic, political, and spiritual because he emphasized integral human development. For Paul VI, opting for the poor demands their liberation from obstacles to progress—namely, poverty, disease, ignorance, and injustice. He cautioned that this should not be done at the expense of their cultural values.

Paul VI urged nations to emulate the examples of nations that have replaced military service with social service directed to the poor and needy after the example of Christ's preaching.[662] He suggested that money allocated for destructive military equipment should be constructively used for promoting the dignity and meeting the needs of people. People who are stricken by poverty and ignorance should not be ignored; those who possess resources have responsibility to show compassion to them.[663] Prompt action is imperative where suffering is evident.

According to Paul VI, opting for the poor is not optional for the rich. Riga suggests that, according to Paul VI this means that for the rich it constitutes a duty, "not an 'act of charity' out of their superfluity [par.44]."[664] To say

---

[660] Ibid. Also see *Populorum Progressio*, 4, 2-3; 9, 4-5; 12, 6; 18-19, 8-9; 21, 9; 45, 19.

[661] *Populorum Progressio*, 64, 27.

[662] Paul VI was making reference to Christ's teaching in Matthew 25; 35:36.

[663] *Populorum Progressio*, 74, 31. Here Paul VI referred to Mk 8: 2.

[664] Riga, 25. Riga quotes *Gaudium et Spes*, art.69 which also reechoes here the teachings of the Fathers and Doctors of the Church who taught that people are obliged to aid the poor and to do so not only out of their superfluous goods.

that it is a duty for the rich to give to the poor needs to be well defined. If they have not met all their basic needs, they are not bound by the obligation to help the poor. This is the advocacy Paul VI made. Those who have are obliged to give to the poor when they (the poor) are unable to procure resources by their own strength. If they are capable but simply lazy, their lack of resources does not constitute an obligation on the side of the rich. There is an optional dimension of gift to the poor if circumstances surrounding the gift are critically scrutinized. Justice would at least speak to this effect. To say that opting for the poor is not an act of charity is contestable. It would suggest that Paul VI used the term charity liberally while he actually used it in the strict sense of Christian charity or gift motivated by true or selfless love, which demands sacrifice. When one person gives to another, that person does so out of love.

Paul VI advocated that the church as an institution should defend the poor. She has the responsibility to teach and to remind the rich of their obligation to support the weak.[665] This too is not an optional responsibility for the church and must necessarily constitute part of her responsibilities as later advocated by *Evangelii Nuntiandi* and *Justitia in Mundo*. A further implication of this call is that, as a protagonist of the principle of option for the poor, the church must also physically do something to alleviate the condition of the weak in society. Paul VI never overlooked the church's historical involvement in the struggle for the improvement of human conditions. He encouraged the church's continued involvement to support the weak in society.

3. AFFIRMATIVE ACTION

The term *affirmative action* was not part of the vocabulary of Paul VI's teaching, neither was it explicitly coined and used that time or earlier, but his teaching in *Populorum Progressio* speaks to that effect because it addressed the need for deliberate action to address the helpless condition of the disadvantaged people of society. The term is used here to mean assertive government intervention on behalf of the weak and disadvantaged people. This is not different from affirmative action, which is a "legislated, judicial and administrative mechanism" used for addressing problems caused by social structures so as to offer hope for minorities to participate, contribute, and

---

[665] Ibid., 27.

improve their conditions.[666] Affirmative action captures the thought of Paul VI about integral human development because it is "a program to diminish the present effects of past discrimination and to prevent its future occurrence."[667] Similarly, Paul VI was addressing the problem and the causes of differences in socioeconomic and political status of people.

Paul VI contended that individual initiatives and competitions are not a guarantee for successful development because they can exacerbate the problem of the widening gap between the rich and the poor. Instead of improving living situations, "the resources and power of the rich become even greater and the distress of the needy increased and the enslavement of the oppressed aggravated."[668] In case of two conflicting parties, a third party is inevitably necessary to resolve the conflicts. Here, government intervention becomes necessary.

Paul VI addressed questions of social justice, common good, option for the poor, and human dignity. These are problems that individuals may not be able to handle on their own. It was for this reason that he advocated some sort of world authority and approved the organization of the United Nations, as a force to help when smaller communities are incapable of handling their development needs. This is why he stated that "programs therefore are necessary to encourage, stimulate, coordinate, supplement and supply the deficiencies of the activity of individuals and intermediary agencies."[669] The affirmation here is that a government should rectify situations of disadvantaged people.

An unjustifiable discrimination or arbitrary differentiation on the basis of race, sex, tribe, or age contradicts integral human development just as it is counter to affirmative action because it renders its victims alien, forgotten, dispensable, and insignificant objects in decision-making as well as the allocation of resources.[670] This is a problem Paul VI addressed in *Populorum Progressio*, and why he emphasized the importance of related principles such as solidarity, common good, option for the poor and subsidiarity, and affirmative

---

[666] Philip J. Chmielewski, "Affirmative Action," in *The New Dictionary of Catholic Social Thought*, ed. Judith A. Dwyer (Collegeville, Minnesota: Liturgical Press, 1994), 12.

[667] Ibid.

[668] *Populorum Progressio*, 33, 14

[669] *Populorum Progressio*, 33, 14. Paul VI is quoting *Mater et Magistra* AAS 53 (1961), 414.

[670] Chmieleski, 12.

action. Although Paul VI never used the term *affirmative action*, he applied it in his teaching in *Populorum Progressio*.

D. Two Significant Social Principles: Common Good and Solidarity

1. COMMON GOOD

Paul VI advocated that the common good is crucial to human development, and it imposes obligation on all people.[671] The common good is a reflection of the social character of human persons. The notion of the common good is closely related to Aristotelian anthropology and the Thomistic vision of the goal of law. Thomas Massaro spells out this assertion:

> Aristotle's anthropology begins with the claim that the human person is by nature a social animal, a being of the polis. Every person is a part of the polis and the end of the polis is the common good. The purpose of law, therefore, is to govern the relation of a person to his or her true good, or genuine happiness. Aquinas borrows this notion when in his "*Treatise on Law*" he asserts that "everyone is ordained to the common good."[672]

The idea of common good is at once relational, moral, and legal. It is relational because human persons are naturally social beings, and they have the affinity to relate with one another and must be protected by the political community. It is also relational because the common good is "the end of the social whole."[673] It is moral because it provides some norm for ordering people's life; "it implies and requires recognition of the fundamental rights of persons."[674] It is legal because the common good is sometimes promoted

---

[671] *Populorum Progressio*, 38, 17.

[672] Massaro, 10. Thomas Massaro is quoting Aristotle. *Politics*, 1. 2, and St. Thomas Aquinas, *Summa Theologica*, I-II, q.90, a.2. Translation from the English Blackfriars edition, 60 vols. (New York: McGraw-Hill Book Co. 1966).

[673] Jacques Maritain, *The Person and the Common Good*, trans., John J. Fitzgerald (Notre Dame, Indiana: University of Notre Dame Press, 2002), 49.

[674] Ibid., 51.

through enforcement of laws or norms directed to create conditions for people to live gratifying or self-fulfilling lives.

It is because of its social nature that the common good is related to social justice, solidarity, human rights such as the right to private ownership of property, option for the poor, affirmative action, peace, participation, and other virtues, conditions, and principles for integral development. In this regard, other than human dignity, the common good is the most inclusive of the principles for integral human development. This is suggested by Jacque Maritain's observation, which aptly describes it:

> Thus, that which constitutes the common good of the political society is not only: the collection of public commodities and services—roads, ports, schools, etc, which the organization of common life presupposes; a sound fiscal condition of the state and its military power; the body of just laws, good customs and wise institutions, which provide the nation with its structure; the heritage of its great historical remembrances, its symbols and its glories, its living traditions and cultural treasures. The common good includes all of these and something much more besides—something more profound, more concrete and more human. For it includes also, above all, the whole sum itself of these; a sum which is quite different from a simple collection of juxtaposed units . . . . It includes the sum of sociological integration of all civic conscience, political virtues and sense of right and liberty, of all the activity, material prosperity and spiritual riches, of unconsciously operative hereditary wisdom, of moral rectitude, justice, friendship, happiness, virtue and heroism in the individual lives of its members. For these things all are, in a certain measure, *communicable* and so revert to each member, helping him to perfect his life and liberty of person. They all constitute the good human life of the multitude.[675]

Maritain advocates a consolidation and integration of conditions that contribute to human growth and perfection. All of these are some of the "values which combine overlapping and sometimes competing concerns for both individuals and communities" and make the common good "an umbrella term for describing patterns of human agency which allow for the protection

---

[675] Maritain, 52-53.

of such values."[676] As a condition for integral growth, the common good is defined as "the sum total of conditions of social living, whereby persons are enabled more fully and readily to achieve their own perfection."[677] The common good is not just the sum total of individual interests or goods. It is a condition or circumstance that allows total growth of people of the community in question. Jacques Maritain succinctly states this:

> The common good of the city is neither the mere collection of private goods, nor the proper good of a whole which, . . . relates the parts to itself alone and sacrifices them to itself. It is the good *human* life of the multitude, of a multitude of persons; it is their communion in good living. It is therefore common to both *the whole and the parts* into which it flows back and which, in turn, must benefit from it.[678]

According to Paul VI, at times for the sake of the common good, ownership of property can be interfered with especially when it affects the wider human society negatively. He encouraged people's cooperation for the common good because it facilitates people's lives.[679] Paul VI linked private ownership of property to the common good and the original divine intention about natural resources. Revenues derived from natural resources should not be disposed of at the pleasure of an individual, nor should excessive profits be used for one's benefit only. The resources of nature are for the benefit of all people. Through such assertions, Paul VI implied that resources of nature must be used for creating possibilities for people to realize their self-perfection. They are good only for human participation in God's creative activity through personal industry and creativity, which are significant contributions to human development.

Paul VI stated that the common good is related to the right of ownership. The explanation for this assertion is that the life and dignity of people and

---

[676] Massaro, 11.

[677] David Hollenbach, "Common Good," in *The New Dictionary of Catholic Social Thought*, ed., Judith A. Dwyer (Collegeville, Minnesota: Liturgical Press, 1994), 193. Also see John XXIII, *Mater et Magistra: Christianity and Social Progress* (Washington DC: National Catholic Welfare Conference, 1961), 65, 21, and *Gaudium et Spes*, 26, 927.

[678] Maritain, 50-51.

[679] *Populorum Progressio*, 21, 9-10; 23, 10-11.

the common good itself are jeopardized if the wealthy and powerful withhold resources meant for the good of all.[680] This explains why, according to Paul VI, the common good is the public good and a necessity for a decent life. His notion of the common good was close to that of John XXIII in *Mater et Magistra* where he says of the common good: "This embraces the sum total of those conditions of living, whereby men are enabled more fully and more readily to achieve their own perfection."[681] This means the common good is an aggregate of requisite conditions for individuals to realize their self-fulfillment to the most perfect possible degree. Natural resources constitute part of the conditions necessary for a decent human life. According to Paul VI, natural resources must be used for the promotion of human community; and if they are not, the community can claim them.[682] For this reason, Paul VI argued that

> the common good, therefore, at times demands the expropriation of an estate if it happens that some estates impede the common prosperity either on account of their vast size, or because their small or negligible cultivation, or cause extreme poverty to the population or bring serious harm to the country.[683]

The common good compels an individual to abdicate personal rights of ownership for the sake of community. This is especially necessary if what an individual owns obstructs development of community or does not contribute to the growth of society. The attainment of the common good involves dynamic exchange between an individual and community or among members of the community.

From the foregoing arguments, it is right to concur with Jacques Maritain that the common good goes beyond the individual and beyond community. He says that "the common good of the city implies an intrinsic ordination to something which transcends it."[684] The common good is a condition that is not a monopoly of an individual, neither is it a monopoly of community; but it is promoted by both, and it promotes both. The common good goes beyond individuals constituting community, yet it is achieved in and by the individuals constituting community.

---

[680] Krier, 73.

[681] *Mater et Magistra*, 65, 21. Also see Massaro, 11.

[682] Krier, 159. Also see *Populorum Progressio*, 24, 11.

[683] *Populorum Progressio*, 24, 11. Also see Michael Walsh and Brian Davies, 222.

[684] Maritain, 51.

2. SOLIDARITY

Paul VI emphasized universal human solidarity for integral human development as he stressed the necessity of universal charity. It was because of the significance of solidarity that his emphasis on "universal human solidarity and fraternity" [685] dominated *Populorum Progressio* more than any of the previous encyclicals. However, Paul VI was not the first person to raise the significance of solidarity in human life. His advocacy for solidarity in *Populorum Progressio* is in line with Thomas Aquinas, John Chrysostom, Pius XI, John XXIII, and the Second Vatican Council fathers, especially in *Gaudium et Spes,* that emphasized the necessity of solidarity for human life.[686] Paul VI advanced the teaching on solidarity by emphasizing its importance for true human development.

Solidarity is the guiding principle for integral human development according to Paul VI.[687] Paul VI also thought that one must first understand the human person to understand human solidarity. The human person, according to him, must be defined in relation to other humans because the person is a social being and belongs to society and to the family in particular, which defines a person initially. Paul VI was of the view that people should also define themselves independently. Citing the social structure in the developing nations, he advocated that "ancient social institutions, however characteristic of developing regions are still necessary for a time, but their excessive force must gradually be diminished."[688] However, he never disregarded the family ties that define initial human identity. Families forge unity and mutual assistance, leading to acquisition of wisdom and harmony in personal rights, which "with other social requirements constitutes the foundation of society."[689]

The origin of solidarity is in the family because solidarity within the family is what is extended beyond it. Solidarity leads to harmony and a better understanding of the human person, rights, and relationships both within and outside the family. This affirmation facilitates the understanding

---

[685] Riga, 30. Here Riga cites the outstanding paragraphs in *Populorum Progressio*, which treat the subject of solidarity, Cfr. *Populorum Progressio* 1, 1-2; 6, 3-4; 15, 7-8; 17, 8; 20, 9; 22, 10; 27-28, 12-13; 34, 15; 39, 17; 42, 18; 47, 20; 65, 27-28; 79, 32-33; 86, 35. Also see Matthew L. Lamb, "Solidarity," in *The New Dictionary of Catholic Social Thought*, ed., Judith A. Dwyer (Collegeville, Minnesota: Liturgical Press, 1994), 909.

[686] Gregg, 77. Also see Avila, 103 and Lamb, 909.

[687] Filochowski, 63. Also see *Populorum Progressio*, 48-49, 20-21; 76-77, 31-32.

[688] *Populorum Progressio*, 36, 16.

[689] Ibid. Here Paul VI is quoting *Gaudium et Spes*, 52, 956.

and appreciation of the equality of human dignity. Consequently, the universal value of the human person and human rights can be recognized. This recognition promotes mutual acceptance, respect, unity, and enhanced solidarity. Equality of human dignity is the basis for the claim that solidarity should be infinite both temporally and spatially.[690]

Solidarity is fundamental for Paul VI because without solidarity progress toward development is deceptive. There must be a "simultaneous development of all humanity in the spirit of solidarity."[691] Solidarity is not only to be exercised among individuals. It should also be expressed locally, nationally, and internationally. For this reason, developed nations and peoples have a duty to help less fortunate nations.[692] The principle of solidarity is a compelling reason for rich countries to help the poor ones. People need one another to be and to become better. Consequently, developed nations have the obligation to support the less-developed nations.

More-developed and less-developed nations need to live in solidarity, but this demands a spirit of dialogue. For Paul VI, dialogue creates understanding and a smooth working relationship among nations. It is a burning necessity because it provides well-articulated conditions for functioning, and it encourages and facilitates mutual support. Loans can be more properly used, their repayment is less problematic, capital is loaned without ulterior motives, and poor nations receiving loans can maintain their independence and integrity and avoid interference from the aiding and developed nations. This ensures that there is no mutual violation socially, economically, or politically. Paul VI advocated solidarity with freedom:

> Since sovereign states are involved, it is their exclusive right to conduct their own affairs, to determine their policy, and to choose the form of government they prefer. This, then, is indispensable that nations collaborate with each other without constraint and with equal dignity, that they at the same time work at creating a civil society truly worthy of man.[693]

---

690   Lamb, 909.

691   Henriot, "Who Cares about Africa? Development Guidelines from the Church's Social Teaching," in *Catholic Social Thought and the New World Order*, 220. Also see *Populorum Progressio*, 43, 18-19.

692   *Populorum Progressio*, 48, 20. Here, Paul VI Quotes *Gaudium et Spes*, 86, 995.

693   Ibid., 54, 23.

For Paul VI, collaborative action is important and should be performed ceaselessly. He stated that "this common task without doubt demands constant, prompt, concerted action."[694] Action in solidarity ought to keep pace with needs, and all efforts to meet needs should be pooled together. It is ceaseless in the sense that even when external assistance has long stopped, solidarity between the collaborating nations should continue.[695]

Paul VI thought that solidarity is the fruit of joint national and international efforts of government officials and the grassroots individuals. This demands participation, a spirit of understanding, collaboration, love for the common good, and an attitude of selflessness, which are crucial for integral human development.[696] Consequently, he advocated that "individuals, social groups, and whole nations" should devote all their "wisdom enthusiasm and charity" to help the disadvantaged to progress.[697] This suggests that the fruit of solidarity animated by charity is the preferential option for the poor, care for the common good, and affirmative action. It indicates the significance of solidarity for integral human development and evinces that it is related to option for the poor, the common good, and affirmative action.

According to Paul VI, human solidarity is possible only when "mutual suspicions of nations and selfishness" are overcome by "a stronger desire for collaboration and a more profound awareness of human solidarity."[698] This demands "common plans of action," coordinated investments, proportionate distribution of means of production, and organized sale of products, and it requires that "the more needy nations" should be helped to liberate themselves from what retards their progress and "find without detriment to their own native character, the means of human and social development."[699]

The vision of solidarity presented by Paul VI in *Populorum Progressio* was expanded and reemphasized by John Paul II in *Sollicitudo Rei Socialis*. The latter called solidarity a virtue with eight requisite conditions. Solidarity demands interdependence, trust, collaboration, an enduring commitment to serve common good, a spirit of self-sacrifice, transformation of interpersonal relationships to a point where the wealthy take responsibility for the weak,

---

694 Ibid., 55, 23.
695 Michael Walsh and Brian Davies, 223.
696 McKenna, 67.
697 *Populorum Progressio*, 75, 31.
698 Ibid., 64, 27.
699 Ibid.

participation by the weak, and mutual respect of interests.[700] According to him, solidarity demands that there be no domination, oppression, or exploitation of one nation by another; and nations must resist hegemony and imperialism.[701]

John Paul II asserted that solidarity demands and leads to radical change in society because it empowers people "to oppose diametrically the desire for profit and the thirst for power, and the sinful structures arising out of choice of profit and power"[702] at any cost. It calls people to live responsibly in harmony with their environment. He cautioned about ignoring solidarity. Individuals and nations that exploit others instead of respecting them may grow rich, but they are not truly developed because they ignore the crucial moral dimension of human development in solidarity with others.[703]

The principle of solidarity demands collaboration, participation, and responsibility for others. It fits well in the treatise of integral human development. Paul VI thought that solidarity should yield efficacious results as later reemphasized by John Paul II. Consequently, solidarity dominated the teaching of *Populorum Progressio*.[704] The importance of solidarity for integral human development lies in the fact that it facilitates selfless joint movement toward growth.

E. Necessary Conditions: Association and Participation

Association and participation are akin to the principle of solidarity, according to Paul VI, although documents issued after *Populorum Progressio* are more emphatic about their positions as prerequisites for integral human development than he suggested in the encyclical. Nonetheless, *Populorum Progressio* never neglected the significance of association and participation in integral human development.

---

[700] Lamb, 909.

[701] Dorr, "Solidarity and Integral Human Development," in *The Logic of Solidarity: Commentaries on John Paul II's Encyclical On Social Concern*, 148-149.

[702] Ibid., 150. Also see John Paul II, *Sollicitudo Rei Socialis: On the Social Concerns* (Boston: Pauline Books and Media, 1987), 26, 42-45; 34, 61-63; 38, 69-72.

[703] Ibid., 151. Also see *Sollicitudo Rei Socialis*, 9.9.

[704] Riga, 29. Also see *Populorum Progressio*, 1, 1-2; 6,3-4; 15,7-8; 17, 8; 20, 9; 22, 10; 27-28, 12-13; 34, 15; 39, 17; 42, 18; 47, 20; 65, 27-28; 79, 32-33; 86, 35.

1. Association

Solidarity is the reason for association, and it embraces participation, which promotes it. People associate to build organizations because they need to uphold, preserve, protect, and promote each others' dignity. Paul VI was clear about this in his encouragement of organizations such as the UN and FAO. However, he was discriminate in his choice and suggestion of associations. Social actions that rest on the philosophy of materialism and atheism are detestable from a Christian point of view, especially if they have "no regard either for the religious outlook directing life to its eternal and final goal, or for freedom, or for human dignity"[705] because social organizations are established to serve people and to liberate them from desperate circumstances of life. Any association that falls short of this goal does not contribute to true human development. Social organizations and associations have as their objective the promotion of the human person and human dignity. Integral human development is possible "through dialogue and cooperation with others."[706]

Paul VI reiterated his support of associations by recognizing and acknowledging charitable organizations such as FAO, *Caritas Internationalis*, and other groups operating everywhere to help meet the needs of desperate people.[707] These and similar organizations are to be emulated because they promote people.

2. Participation/Involvement

The emphasis on participation as a principle for integral development was not Paul VI's own idea. He was promoting the doctrine of *Quadragesimo Anno* of Pius XI who advocated that "humanization of production demands the participation of all involved."[708] Paul VI encouraged participation by advocating that every person and all peoples are entitled to be shapers of their own destiny.[709] He made this appeal in many parts of *Populorum Progressio*. According to a significant number of authors including Dorr, participation is

---

[705] *Populorum Progressio*, 39, 17.

[706] Riga, 108.

[707] *Populorum Progressio*, 46, 19-20.

[708] *Quadragesimo Anno*, 53-54, 36-37.

[709] *Populorum Progressio*, 15, 20; 65, 27-28. Also see Dorr, *Option for the Poor*, 198.

one of the document's most important contributions because "development is something people have to do for themselves."[710]

Circumstances demand that individuals change their lives and the society in which they live. The significance of participation is in promotion of authentic development is evidenced in self-fulfillment people experience when they do things for themselves and their community. They realize their worth, the significance of their initiative, and creativity. What people realize is an unfolding of their talents, which is development.

For Paul VI, human persons created *imago Dei* are called to cooperate with God in creation and to perpetuate the creative activity to perfection. This is possible because of the intellectual power and sensitivity with which God has endowed people. Anyone who engages in work cooperates with God and participates in God's work of creation and "leaves imprint of himself upon them while at the same time refining his persistency, skill and power to think."[711] This suggests that work is also a means to participate and to be united.

Participation in solidarity or unity demands mutual respect for human rights and collaboration. In other words, where there is true solidarity and unity, there is freedom too. According to Paul VI, world unity "must allow all peoples . . . to be the architects of their own fortune."[712] Unity and solidarity are significant for complete development, but they should not diminish personal involvement. Instead, they ought to promote participation. People need not entrust their future entirely in the hands of other people. Paul VI urged that international relations, interpreted broadly, should consider seriously that regard and friendship; they should "be expressed in assistance with mutual respect and collaboration" with "individual nations accepting with full conviction their obligation and duty to promote the improvement of all."[713] This assertion is significant because it points out that participation is not only a duty, it is also a right.[714]

Participation is also seen in the work of expatriate experts involved in developing countries. Their presence in these nations should be one of helping and collaborating with the people to bring about development.[715] Paul VI

---

[710] Dorr, *Option for the Poor*, 198.

[711] *Populorum Progressio*, 27, 12.

[712] Ibid., 65, 27.

[713] Ibid.

[714] Robert J. Vitillo and Donna Toliver Grimes, 9.

[715] *Populorum Progressio*, 71, 29.

advocated the value of participation of the people who need to develop. He also suggested that a facilitating leadership is necessary for the involvement of the people. This means participation demands, which stimulates people's thoughts and activity.

Participation is important for authentic development because it is the responsibility of the entire human race to heal and prevent miseries due to disease, poverty, ignorance, and other social moral evils. Everyone must be devoted with "firm determination to combat underdevelopment to the extent of his strength and resources."[716] Such a demand to participate wholeheartedly calls for a selfless attitude that goes beyond an individual and extends to the needy. It also demands maximum participation according to one's capacity.

Participation is demonstrated in joint action to enforce change. According to Paul VI, immediate participatory action of all people capable of contributing in solidarity is called for in situations and moments where innocent lives are at stake, the burden of poverty amidst inhumane living conditions is great, and world peace and "the very survival of civilization"[717] are all at stake. In other words, the involvement of all people and nations in such moments is an urgent need and of grave significance. All people should assume the responsibility to make positive change. Paul VI was also attentive and focused on the importance of the value and role of the lowest artisan. True development calls for recognition, acknowledgment, and involvement of—even—the least as long as they have the abilities to perform and are capable of contributing to the enhancement of human life, person, rights, and dignity.

V. CONCLUSION

The treatise in this chapter leads to the following conclusions: First, Paul VI's vision of development in *Populorum Progressio* is paradigmatic in the sense that he provides an archetype notion of development, which reduces other notions of development to just a portion of what he called integral human development. Though Paul VI's conception of development appears paradoxical because it seems challenging and practical and at the same time idealistic or practically difficult, meaningless, contradictory, and sometimes utopian, it has truth and presents an enduring challenge of Catholic doctrine on human development. This is evinced in the fact that all Catholic social

---

[716] Ibid., 75, 31.

[717] Ibid., 80, 30; 81, 33-34.

doctrine before *Populorum Progressio* gravitated toward the document and those after it emanated from the document or reechoed it. The theme running through all of them is concern for the human person, which constitutes the center of all development and development problems.

Second, *Populorum Progressio* is pragmatic because it treated issues that still affect people. Paul VI placed the social issue, particularly, that of human development in a global context offered an interpretation of the causes of unrest and presented charity and justice as the sources of true peace and development. Paul VI rejected the basic laws of capitalism, especially its laissez-faire principles for liberal pursuit of ownership of property, its profit-oriented tendency, its inclination to absolute reliance on free trade in the world economy. However, he was not opposed to the entire practice of capitalism. According to him, if profit promotes human dignity, it is in accordance with divine design.

Third, Paul VI emphasized justice—the right of the poor nations to aid from the wealthier nations—and argued that in situations of extreme need the poor have the right to claim the property of the rich. They may also be justified to use nonviolent pressure or force to seek solutions to their problems. Precisely, it emphasized social justice and the social dimension of property.

Fourth, in *Populorum Progressio*, Paul VI offered a vision of development, which takes place on an individual level as well as communal level—an integral human development. This notion of development includes all dimensions of human life—namely, the economic, cultural, political, social, psychological, educational, and spiritual aspects of life. It is based on the recognition of supreme values of human dignity and the destiny of the person and the acceptance of faith, which opens individuals to union with God.

Fifth, *Populorum Progressio* underscored the importance of development, which Paul VI equated to and called the new name for peace, one of the principal prerequisites for development. The document suggests that requisite principles for integral human development are of diverse nature but all of them are interrelated. None of them is dispensable for authentic human development because each plays a unique role and contributes to the support of other principles and ultimately integral human development. Their basic relationship is founded on the principle of human dignity. All the principles, virtues, and requisite conditions govern and direct human activity to the protection and care for the dignity of the human person.

Finally, human dignity per se is the indisputably contending principle and reason for the existence of other principles, conditions, and virtues.

This point will be emphasized in the next chapter which will explain the centrality of the human person, human dignity and human rights. The chapter will advocate the significance of a relevant anthropology and explore the relationship between different development principles, virtues, and requisite conditions

CHAPTER THREE

Populorum Progressio and an Anthropology for Integral Human Development

I. INTRODUCTION

The principal concern of this chapter is to show that a relevant anthropology is necessary for integral human development, which Paul VI suggested in *Populorum Progressio,* because true development is the enhancement of all people through respect for the human person, human dignity, and human rights. Chapter two treated Paul VI's doctrine in *Populorum Progressio,* the meaning of integral human development and the problems and causes of lack of integral human development. It revealed Paul VI's concern for both the *individual* and *community,* which are significant terms in both chapter two and this chapter. They are the reasons for Paul VI's introduction of the term integral human development in redefining development. The chapter also outlined Paul VI's suggestions for attaining integral development. He attempted to resolve people-related or people-centered problems. The problems not only affected people, they were also caused by people; and the suggestions to resolve them were virtues, conditions, and principles related to people. This suggests that the problems originated from conflicting anthropologies.

Paul VI's major concern was the human person, but his goal was not a treatise of theological, philosophical and social anthropology. This chapter focuses on the notion of the human person, human rights, and human dignity—all of which are necessary for authentic human development. It treats an anthropology for *Populorum Progressio.* Critical readers of Paul VI question the adequacy of the application of Christian or theological anthropology in *Populorum Progressio.* Robert Royal, for example, notes that if there was a step backward, it was not his adherence to Catholic principles, but his failure to bring the church's views of the human person fully to bear on the current developmentalist orthodoxies. This failure resulted in contradictory messages in his text.[718]

Royal suggests that Paul VI needed to critically apply Catholic or Christian anthropology to facilitate the question of integral human development and the application of principles, virtues, and conditions necessary for it in the current contexts. It was not Paul VI's intention to do an anthropological treatise as such. However, Royal's observation shows a failure in the application of Christian anthropology in *Populorum Progressio*. This chapter attempts to construct an anthropology relevant for integral human development, but Paul VI should be credited for his vision of the human person in terms of development because throughout *Populorum Progressio* he made references to anthropological notions such as person, dignity, and rights. This chapter will attempt to emphasize these anthropological elements and show their significance in the application of the doctrine of *Populorum Progressio*.

It is necessary to treat and understand the human person, dignity, and rights because of the pluralistic nature of human community, both locally and globally. Above all, it is an imperative to construct a relevant anthropology because "the ultimate determining factor" and litmus test or measure of true development "is the human person."[719] An anthropology is necessary in the study of *Populorum Progressio* because the document addressed problems affecting human dignity and involved people of diverse sociocultural, economic, and political backgrounds. There are racial, tribal, ethnic, and class differences, yet all people have equal dignity. This is the central critique Paul VI suggested in *Populorum Progressio*. In light of this statement, it is realistic to concur with John Mary K. Kabyanga that

---

[718] Robert Royal, "*Populorum Progressio* (1967)" *A Century of Catholic Social Thought: Essays on Rerum Novarum and Nine Other Key Documents*, eds., George Wiegel and Robert Royal (Washington DC: Ethics and Public Policy Center, 1991), 117.

[719] Matthew Habiger, "Papal Tradition on the Distribution of Ownership," in *Curing World Poverty: The New Role of Property*, ed., John H. Miller (Social Justice Review: Saint Louis, Missouri, 1994), 3. Here, Matthew Habinger, verbatim, quotes the statement of Archbishop Renato R. Martino, Apostolic Nuncio, head of the Holy See delagation to the United Nation Conference on Enviroment and Development, Rio de Janeiro, June 4, 1992.

the problem of the theology of development as a starting point is no
longer merely that of the split between the body versus the soul, the
temporal versus the spiritual and the kingdom versus eschatology.
The problem is man himself.[720]

The problem here is anthropological. Kabyanga argues that true
development starts with a right understanding of the human person. It is from
the understanding of the human person that the temporal and spiritual, the
kingdom and eschatology can be integrated well. This is a credible vision because,
theologically, ultimate integral human development is realized at the end times
when all people are united with God and with each other. This assertion
suggests why Kabyanga advocates people's individual and collective striving.
Chapter three is significant because it attempts to explain the human person; it
shows whether the concept of the human person is the same for all people, and
how different visions of the human person can be explained and reconciled.

The chapter is divided into six main parts. The first part deals with
contending notions of the human person. It treats the development of
the African communitarian notion and the Euro-American notion of the
human person. The second part deals with the notion of human dignity,
its meaning and origin, the universality and equality of human dignity, and
the significance of the universality and equality of human dignity. The third
section treats human rights from the liberal and communitarian points of view
and attempts to establish the universality of human rights. The fourth part
is an anthropology for *Populorum Progressio*. It attempts to demonstrate how
Paul VI viewed the human person, human dignity, and human rights. The
fifth section is an attempt to reconcile liberal and communitarian notions. It
shows difficulties in reconciliation of these notions and how the difficulties
can be overcome. The last part attempts to establish an ultimate principle for
integral human development and how it is a link between other principles
for integral human development.

II. CONTENDING NOTIONS OF THE HUMAN PERSON

The two contending notions of the human person are the individualist or
liberal notion and the communitarian notion. David Bohr states that people's

---

[720] John Mary K. Kabyanga, *Towards Integral Human Development: To Be More Rather Than
to Have More, The Contributions of Fr. Louis Joseph Lebret, O.P.* (Wisconsin, Sparata:
Prell Books, 2004), 30.

search for self-understanding is "the basic quest for life, and the question Who am I? has been intensified due to "cultural pluralism."[721] This question suggests why it is necessary to understand the human person from different perspectives and to attempt to judge whether it is right to prefer only one vision of the human person.

Cultures affect people's thought patterns and their vision of reality. Consequently, cultural differences explain differences in the vision of the human person. From a Catholic, and generally a Christian believers' point of view, "the human person is central, the clearest reflection of God among us."[722] The scriptures ground an understanding of the human person. Catholic social doctrine suggests that "the book of Genesis provides us with certain foundations for Christian anthropology" such as the "inalienable dignity of the human person,"[723] the principle of *imago Dei*, human freedom and the social nature of human person, and the meaning of human activity in the world.

A. Development of the Notion of the Human Person

The notion of the human person developed over time. Classically, Boethius (ca 480—ca 524) defined the human person as *rationalis naturae individua substantia*, meaning that the human person is "an individual substance of rational nature."[724] The principal elements of this definition of the human person are rationality and individuality. The human person is an individual with the ability to think or reason. This defines the human person inadequately because the human person is defined independently of other people and the prevalent environment. It denies the notion that the human person is a social being. However, rationality distinguishes the human person

---

[721] David Bohr, *A Catholic Moral Tradition: In Christ, A New Creation* (Huntington, Indiana: Our Sunday Visitor Publishing Division, 1990), 66.

[722] Robert J. Vitillo and Donna Toliver Grimes, eds. *Principles, Prophecy, and a Pastoral Response: An Overview of Modern Catholic Social Teaching, Catholic Campaign for Human Development*, rev. ed. (Washington DC: United States Conference of Catholic Bishops, 2001), 5.

[723] Pontifical Council for Justice and Peace, Libreria Editrice Vaticana, *Compendium of the Social Doctrine of the Church* (Washington DC: United States Conference of Catholic Bishops, 2005), 17.

[724] Gerald O'Collins and Edward G. Farugia, *A Concise Dictionary of Theology*, rev. and exp. ed. (New York: Paulist Press, 2000), 199.

from other creatures but identifies one person with other people and "only humans are honored with the term *person*."[725] No other individual being is called person, except what has naturally been endowed with rationality.

Later, the human person was defined on the basis of "relationship, incommunicability, self-consciousness, freedom, duties, inalienable rights, and dignity."[726] The notion of human person is so lofty that it cannot be easily captured, but there are certain traits specific to a human being. The human person is an individual but also a social being, aware of his/her existence and activities as an individual. A human person is endowed with the ability to choose, to make inevitably obliging claims on other human persons, to act responsibly, and to be accountable for his/her actions. The human person has worth, which other human individuals have, but which other creatures do not have. This notion of the human person is more balanced than the preceding one because it includes individuality and communality.

Like Thomas Aquinas, Bonaventure considered a person as "a distinct substance possessing dignity."[727] This notion of person emphasizes individuality and dignity. This dignity of a person provides gravity for the claim that the human person, human dignity, and human rights are at the center of integral human development. Later, Immanuel Kant (1724-1804) viewed the human person as "an absolute that may never be used as a means but must always be respected as a moral end-in-itself."[728] The Kantian vision of the human person, like the biblical notion, places the human person at the peak of creation. It reflects the singular identity of the human person. The human person is never a thing. After God, in rank, the human person is the master of creatures other than human beings, can make responsible use of them for his/her own good, but cannot be equated to the things (s)he uses to meet his/her needs. The rest of creation is a means to help the human person realize fulfillment. The Kantian notion of the human person suggests a vision of the human person who is more an absolute individual than a social being. Jacques Maritain developed Kant's vision of the human person in relation

---

[725] James B. Reichmann, *Philosophy of the Human Person* (Chicago: Loyola University Press, 1985), 208.

[726] O'Collins and Farugia, 199.

[727] Thomas D. Williams, *Who is My Neighbor?: Personalism and the Foundations of Human Rights* (Washington DC: The Catholic University of America Press, 2005), 155. Williams is quoting St. Bonaventure in *I sent*, dist.23, art.I. q. I, Resp.

[728] O'Collins and Farugia, 199.

to or based on the Aristotelian and Thomistic visions. Maritain stressed the idea of the individuality of human person in relation to personality but distinguished the two:

> Outside of the mind, only individual realities exist. Only they are capable of exercising the act of existing. Individuality is opposed to the state of universality which things have in mind. It designates the concrete state of unity and indivision, required by existence, in virtue of which every actually existing or possibly existing nature can posit itself in existence as distinct from other beings.[729]

Maritain emphasizes that the human person is a distinct individual. Individuality is the principle which explains the identity or distinction of a person from the rest of the community. However, this is not a sufficient definition of the human person according to Maritain. He thinks that "personality is the subsistence of the spiritual soul communicated to the human composite," and it "signifies interiority to self" and yet "of its essence requires a dialogue in which souls really communicate, especially to God, "the absolute source of sufficiency."[730] In defining individuality and personality, Maritain asserts that individuality is a reality of the human person to be asserted and respected as such, but human affinity to relate or communicate, especially as an expression of his/her spiritual and personal nature may not be ignored without denying the human person a truly human characteristic of being communal or social. He affirms that individuality and personality are distinct from each other but inseparable when predicated of the human person: "our whole being is an individual by reason of what is in us which derives from matter, and a person by reason of that in us which derives from Spirit."[731] Personality pertains to the spiritual reality, and the concrete individual pertains to material reality.

The contemporary definition of the human person has relational overtones, even if it takes the individuality of a person seriously. This is probably because at one moment, there was an overemphasis on the individuality of persons and liberal expression of freedom and claims for personal rights. The contemporary

---

[729] Jacques Maritain, *The Person and the Common Good*, trans., John J. Fitzgerald (Notre Dame, Indiana: University of Notre Dame Press, 2002), 34.

[730] Ibid., 41-42.

[731] Ibid., 43.

theological notion of the human person resonates with the philosophical assertion that "every human person is distinct from every other, yet at the same time all are truly human."[732] In both theology and philosophy, the individual and social dimensions of the person are significant for understanding the human person. They provide an integrated and balanced vision of the human person. Gerald O'Collins and Edward G. Farrugia note that

> today, to overcome the notion of persons as autonomous selves, some stress the way persons are always persons-in-relationship, constituted through relations with other persons and the environment.[733]

The contemporary notion of the human person is a summation of notions of the human person developed over time. It is relational not only to fellow human beings but also to the rest of creation. It tends to combine the individualist or liberal and the social or communitarian visions of the human person in order to give a better notion of the human person. Paul VI's vision of the human person in *Populorum Progressio* is suggestively in the category of the contemporary notion. This is, at least, implicit in his advocacy for integral human development. The contemporary notion of the human person is preferable because it takes seriously the individuality and the social nature of the human person.

The human person may be defined from different points of view by different people depending on what emphasis they prefer or think is fundamental for the definition of the human person. Louise Marcil-Lacoste is aware of this and observes five perspectives from which a person could be defined. First, *logically*, "a person is an entity distinct from a mere thing."[734] The dignity of a person is what makes distinction between a person and other creatures. Theologically, this claim is explained in terms of the principle of *imago Dei*. The dignity of the human person is directly endowed by God in whose image and likeness the human person is created. Since the human

---

[732] Reichmann, 252. Also cfr. Karol Wojtyla, Cardinal (John Paul II). *The Acting Person*, trans., Andrzej Potocki (Dordrecht: D.Reidel Publishing Company, 1979), 293.

[733] O'Collins and Farugia, 199.

[734] Louise Marcil-Lacoste, "Women as Persons," in *The Human Person*, vol. LIII, ed. George F. McLean (Washington DC: The American Catholic Philosophical Association, 1979), 78.

person is created in the image and likeness of God the human person has an "inherent dignity that must not be violated."[735]

Second, from a *moral* point of view people are entitled to special treatment on account of their inherent and inviolable dignity as beings created in the image of God. This means, in Kant's famous phrase, that persons are "ends-in-themselves and sources of value in their own right."[736] The dignity of the human person is again the ground for such claims. The unique treatment of a person differentiates the *person* from *things* and limits the relationship between the person and God who is an end—the absolute being. The relationship of the human person to God is one of creature to creator.

> As God's image the human person lives constitutively *in relation*
> to God. This means every dimension of his existence and finitude,
> his creaturely needs and his mortality.[737]

The relationship between the human person and God is one of dependence where the human person owes existence and functionality to God. Human activity is due to God, the ultimate principle of activity.

Third, from a *legal* point of view, "a person is a being who has legal rights and duties. In this context, one would insist that persons alone are responsible and that rationality is a precondition for responsible action."[738] Here, the qualifications of a person are stated. A person is one who can make claims on other people and is at the same time responsible in relating to others because of the endowment with reason. A person has duties or obligations toward other people because of this endowment with reason.

Fourth, from a *metaphysical* point of view "persons ought to be defined primarily by reference to self-consciousness."[739] Persons are aware of themselves as existing individual entities. This does not suffice to define a person because

---

[735] Russel W. Davenport, *The Dignity of Man* (New York: Harper and Brothers, 1955), 231.

[736] Marcil-Lacoste, 78.

[737] Eberhard Schockenhoff, *Natural Law and Human Dignity: Universal Ethics in an Historical World*, trans., Brian McNeil (Washington DC: The Catholic University of America Press, 2003), 229.

[738] Marcil-Lacoste, 78.

[739] Ibid.

relationship with others and environment is also crucial. Metaphysically, there is relationship to oneself, and this constitutes the individuality and the totality of the human individual in a social relationship. The individuality of a person is a significant element of the definition of a human person. It is also important to note that "the relationship of a human person *to his own self*" is not "a conscious relationship of the intellect to itself, but is a total unity of human life embracing body and soul."[740] This means the human person exists as an individual entity, a totality, distinct from other things, but there is a relational dimension of the individual because of the spiritual dimension of the human person. The identity and distinction of an individual from others involves the totality of a person as a conscious individual agent who is aware of this consciousness. Here, there is also an emphasis on the rational aspect of the human person.

Finally, since the human person has a unique *role* in relation to the rest of creation, the "definition of the concept of person is based on the concept of role."[741] The human person has "a God-given mission to preside (Gen. 1:26) over all created things."[742] The human person is also related to these creatures in terms of responsibility. The human person is the crown of God's creation, commissioned and entrusted with a task "to serve his Creator in the representative function of establishing God's peaceful sovereignty over Creation."[743] This alone does not suffice to define the human person adequately. The dominion of the human person over creation must be a responsible one. This means the human person is a steward and a *co-operator*[744] with God in the enhancement of creation.

Since a human person is viewed differently, depending on the point of view from which the human person is defined, the claim that "such variations

---

[740] Schockenhoff, 232-233.

[741] Marcil-Lacoste, 78.

[742] International Theological Commission, *Proposition on the Dignity and Rights of the Human Person* (Washington DC: United States Catholic Conference, 1986), 6. Also see Pontifical Council for Justice and Peace, *Compendium of the Social Doctrine of the Church*, 52.

[743] Schockenhoff, 234.

[744] I prefer the term *co-operator* with God in creation to the term *co-creator*, which John Paul II has often used. It is a term many secular sciences would prefer to use today. I am of the opinion that creation is *ex-nihilo*, it is from nothing, except for the creative power of word which is God's prerogative.

in meaning are important sources of ambiguities when talking of persons"[745] is compelling and intriguing. Therefore, if the concept of the human person varies, integral human development is problematic because human dignity and human rights are not conceived in a uniform way.

Attributes often associated with the human person are spirit, soul, image of God, human dignity, body, intelligence, ability to love, and moral responsibility.[746] Here, it is significant to note that human dignity is founded on these attributes of the human person; and for the same reason, the human person has inherent and inviolable dignity. Paul VI's *Populorum Progressio* advocates that a totality of these attributes should be protected and enhanced. Consequently, a right vision of these attributes is necessary for integral human development.

The human person, as the image of God, is a relational being in four ways: human relation to God, other human beings, self, and creation. As Thomas D. Williams suggests, according to his reading of Augustine, "the human person is, therefore, an intermediate end in himself and also a being for God, his ultimate end," meaning that the human person is

> a true and inviolable end in himself and must be treated as an end; on the other hand; one person cannot constitute the final end for another, or for himself, since man is made to find his total fulfillment in union with God.[747]

This assertion suggests that the human person is ultimately subject only to God. Other human beings may not, therefore, do as they please with fellow human beings because they are all (intermediate, not ultimate) ends in themselves. God is the ultimate reference for defining the human person even when the human person is defined in relation to other human beings. Consequently, the Catholic Church has consistently and emphatically stated that

> the human person may never be thought of only as an absolute individual being built up by himself, as if his characteristic traits

---

[745] Marcil-Lacoste, 78.

[746] Timothy E. O'Connell, *Principles for Catholic Morality* (New York: The Seabury Press, 1978), 58-59. Also see Michael Novak, "Human Dignity, Human Rights," in *First Things*, no.97 (New York: Institute on Religion and Public Life, November 1999), 41.

[747] Williams, 163.

depended on no one else but himself. Nor can the person be thought of as a mere cell of an organism that is inclined at most to grant it recognition in its functional role within the overall system. Reductionist conceptions of the full truth of men and women have already been the object of the Church's social concern many times.[748]

The unity and totality of the individual person are significant. That "man was created by God in unity of body and soul"[749] is the consistent teaching in the Catholic Church. The notion of the unity of the human person is significant for Paul VI's advocacy for integral human development, which is not only the development of all people but also the development of the whole individual. Here, the anthropology implicit in Paul VI's teaching in *Populorum Progressio* is affirmed to be relevant for integral human development. According to "Aristotelian-Thomistic ontology, the human person, unlike non-personal existents, is a totality in which the fullness of creaturely reality is present in a unique manner."[750] The human person is a climax and summary of divine creation. In a way, the contention is that creation subsists in the human person. However, the superiority and distinctiveness of the human person over the rest of creatures is what is stated in this claim. It is also important to note that while the human person is not like other creatures—not a thing—persons are still both objects and subjects because they can initiate action directed to other beings and actions can also be directed to them. Thomas D. Williams has clarified this by asserting that persons are "rational subjects of action" but also "rational objects of action."[751] The assertion is plausible because human beings can rationally initiate activity and also rationally direct activity toward other human persons or receive rationally initiated activity from other human beings. I think this is partially why human persons are responsible for what they do and how moral culpability may be judged.

---

[748] Pontifical Council for Justice and Peace, *Compendium of the Social Doctrine of the Church*, 56.

[749] Ibid. The consistent series of quotations the Pontifical Council for Justice and Peace made in this regard suggests emphasis on integral character of a human person, expressed in the unity of the physical and spiritual dimensions of the human person.

[750] Schockenhoff, 230.

[751] Williams, 125. Also see O'Connell, 60.

The human person is social and this fulfills God's plan of love, which is theologically based on "the mystery of God as a Trinitarian love."[752] The relationship between the three persons—a relation of love—is the ultimate fulfillment and reflection of the social nature of the human person. No relationship goes beyond this in perfection. Every loving human relation is a reflection of the Trinitarian love to some degree. This element of interpersonal relationship is a significant aspect of the definition of human person because it grounds human rights, which are mutual claims.

Relationship to other human beings—namely, shared humanity and the fact of two genders—suggests the universality of human personhood, human dignity, and human rights. The vertical relationality of human existence with God is extended in the horizontal relation with other human beings. Here, there is a relationship of "the dependence of the human person on *a human 'thou.'*"[753] According to Eberhard Schockenhoff, this horizontal relationship of dependence is captured by Genesis 1:27 where both male and female are created in God's image. This is where the equality of personhood must be sought. This is further affirmed in Genesis 2:8-14, which shows only humans are equal and other animals do not meet the standard of personhood and both genders are complimentary though different. That "they complement each other's shared humanity in a comprehensive manner which includes mutual understanding and dialogue"[754] is, according to Eberhard, a significant and realistic statement. It spells out that man and woman are distinct only in gender but not in human personhood. This distinction or differentiation of gender does not affect equality of human personhood. This assertion facilitates the understanding of the equality of the dignity of the human person.

The vision of the human person has varied over time and from one person to another. Noticeable in historical development of the notion of the human person are two outstanding positions. First, the human person is defined as an individual entity distinct from and independent of other human persons or an individual in relation to other people. The definitions emphasized the individual dimension of the human person or the social dimension of the human person. Second, the human person is defined in terms of rationality as opposed to the rest of creation. It is in the light of such visions that the

---

[752] Pontifical Council for Justice and Peace, *Compendium of the Social Doctrine of the Church,* 16.

[753] Schockenhoff, 230.

[754] Ibid., 231.

distinction between the communitarian notion of the human person and the individualist notion should be viewed.

B. The Communitarian View of Person

The communitarian defines a human person in a social context, not in isolation from other persons and the rest of creation. A typical communitarian vision of the human person is what Placide Tempels offers in his study of the Bantu of the present Democratic Republic of Congo, which Bujo correctly suggests is applicable even to "modern Black Africa."[755] Tempels describes the human person as a personal living force who participates in the force and being of God, the supreme, complete, and perfect force; and the human person is "the dominant force among all created visible forces."[756] However, the emphasis in the communitarian vision of the human person is on community rather than the individual although this does not mean that the individual is negligible. The individual has a personal conscience and is responsible or accountable for his/her actions which is primarily based in the heart according to most African societies and ethical thought.[757] Much of the communitarian vision of the human person is summarized by David Fergusson:

> The communitarian . . . is more impressed by the essentially social nature of the human being. Then self is formed by its roles, attachments, and relationships with other people, institutions, communities, and traditions. Concepts of what is right and how society should be organized always presuppose some vision of the common good.[758]

The human person is an individual affected by the actual context of life. The individual lives in and interacts with the environment. The individual is

---

[755]   Benezet Bujo, *Foundations of an African Ethic: Beyond the Universal Claims of Western Morality*, trans. Brian McNiel (New York: Crossroad Publishing Company, 2001), 113.

[756]   Placide Tempels, *Bantu Philosophy*, trans. Rubbens A (*Paris: Presence Africaine*, 1959), 64-65.

[757]   Benezet Bujo, *Foundations of an African Ethic: Beyond the Universal Claims of Western Morality*, 151.

[758]   David Fergusson, *Community, Liberalism and Christian Ethics* (Cambridge: Cambridge University Press, 1998), 139.

partly externally determined, not absolutely self-determined. As Stanley M. Harrison states, "persons are irreducibly social beings, where this is taken to mean that *being-with* others is necessary in order to be a person."[759] Harrison's assertion is correct because people's personalities or characters are molded by and in the community in which they live and with which they interact. This explains why a right vision of the human person is that the human person is social, has an individual identity, and yet is in a growth process which is a consequence of interaction with other people and the environment in which the person lives. This idea is also expressed by the African scholar, John S. Mbiti, whose view is consonant with that of Harrison. He states that according to an African, "the individual can only say: 'I am, because we are; and since we are, therefore I am.'"[760] The significance of the community for an individual and the individual for the community is also underscored in this statement. This is appropriately equated by Uzukwu to Martin Luther King Jr.'s statement in one of his speeches for advocacy for equality of people and human rights. According to Uzukwu, the idea of relatedness underlies or is consonant with with Martin Luther King Jr.'s *dream* speech for a free nonracial America in 1961 when the latter stated, "Strangely, enough, I can never be what I ought to be until you are what you ought to be. You can never be what you ought to be until I am what I ought to be."[761]

---

[759] Stanley M. Harrison, "Charles S. Peirce: Reflections on Being a Man-Sign," in *The Human Person*, vol. LIII, ed. George F. McLean (Washington DC: The American Catholic Philosophical Association, 1979), 98.

[760] John S. Mbiti, *African Religions and Philosophy* (New York: Frederick A. Praeger Publishers, 1969), 108. Also see Uzukwu E. Elochukwu, *A Listening Church: Autonomy and Communion in African Churches,* 37. According to Uzukwu, the emphasis of the statement is that one is human because of others, with others, and for others. Here, Mbiti and Uzukwu are quoting a Sotho, South African, proverb—"Motho ke motho ka batho ka bang," which means "I am because we are, and since we are, therefore I am" and altenatively meaning, according to Uzukwu, "I belong, therefore I am." Here, Uzukwu is quoting A. Boesak, "Le Courage et la fierte d'etre noire," in A. M. Goguel and P. Buis, eds. *Chretiens d'Afrique du sud face a l'apartheid* (Paris: L'Harmattan, 1978), 262.

[761] Uzukwu E. Elochukwu, *A Listening Church: Autonomy and Communion in African Churches,* 37. Here, Uzukwu is quoting J. H. Cone, *Martin & Malcom & America* (Maryknoll, New York: Orbis Books, London: Fount, 1993), 80.

A person is a creature made in the image and likeness of God and endowed with freedom of thought and action, responsibility to respond, and enter into dialogic relationship with God—the absolute "I."[762] The human person has the ability to think freely and responsibly, take initiative to communicate and relate with others. The climax of this communication and relationship is the one with God. This thrusts into the communitarian vision of the human person that the human person, whether extravert or introvert, is actually relational. Joseph Fichtner agrees with this vision. According to him, it is only when a person transcends whatever is selfish and enters into fellowship with God that the person is complete and fulfilled. The climax of the communitarian element of the human person is expressed in the communion with the divine community. In fact, the human person is considered the image of God because (s)he becomes person through

> relationship to the whole of the world, through openness and accountability to the world, to its end, and to the Thou in community. This is in fact a relationship with God and this proposal stands in contrast to definitions of person that focus primarily on conscious spiritual individuality.[763]

The emphasis in the quotation again is on the social nature of the human person. Human personality develops and is shaped by the environment through the interaction of the person with others or the environment and the interaction with the Creator. This vision of the human person is opposed to the individualist vision, which emphasizes the individuality, freedom, and autonomy of the human person. The communitarian theology of the human person, therefore, consistently views a person as

> a being in solidarity with the cosmos and with God. Corporeally he gathers up the world within himself but spiritually he transcends

---

[762] Joseph Fichtner, *Theological Anthropology: The Science of Man in his Relation to God* (Notre Dame: University of Notre Dame Press, 1963), 38.

[763] Philip Hefner, "*Imago Dei*: The Possibility and Necessity of the Human Person," in *The Human Person in Science and Theology*, ed. Niels Henrik Gregersen et al. (Grand Rapids, Michigan: William B. Eerdmans Publishing Company, 2000), 74.

it, raises it to the level of his own existence, and in turn is open and accessible to his creator.[764]

The human person is viewed here as a being shaped in and by society, but (s)he is an individual who exists as a distinct entity and even transcends society in as far as (s)he relates to God. Therefore, the human person is not only social by nature, but also a sacred being because of the relationship with God. This communitarian view of the human person is reaffirmed by Philip Hefner whose understanding of Tillich suggests that

> being a person is constituted both by a cognitive process of perceiving and understanding oneself in one's world, and also by a moral process of responding in relationship to the world. Formally, then, the person is defined in relationship.[765]

Communitarians define the human person relationally, not independently or as an isolated individual. Even in the contemporary African context, a person is defined in terms of clan or blood relationship as well as relationship beyond blood or clan because, as Alexis Kagame suggests, according to Bujo, "fellowship based on blood extends to include non-blood relationship."[766] This means relationship is also just based on the fact of being human. The life of an individual is affected by others, and (s)he affects the lives of others, too. This assertion supports the commonly accepted Aristotelian view that the human person is a political animal and social being. It suggests why communitarians think that "we realize our dignity and rights in relations with others in community."[767] The human person ought always to be defined relationally. This is a valid foundation for mutual respect for human rights and human dignity. The communitarian vision of the human person is fundamentally based on the idea that "individuals actualize their full potential through the virtually unlimited enhancements that community life offers . . . persons can

---

[764] Fichtner, 34.

[765] Hefner, 84.

[766] Benezet Bujo, *Foundations of an African Ethic: Beyond the Universal Claims of Western Morality*, 113. Also see Uzukwu E. Elochukwu, 36.

[767] Vitillo J. and Toliver Grimes, 9. Also see Benezet Bujo, *Foundations of an African Ethic: Beyond the Universal Claims of Western Morality*, 157.

develop most successfully by drawing on the talents and accomplishments of others."[768] According to Andrew N. Woznicki,

> [the] feeling of deep esteem for each and every human person is the corner stone of building any community life of all men, which Cardinal Wojtyla described as participation in terms of a relation of man to man.[769]

Human community is founded on every human being. The respect for the dignity of every person is the foundation for a social or community life and acknowledgment of a participatory or shared dignity. Unless universality of human dignity is acknowledged, community life is not possible or authentic.

C. The Individualist/Liberal View of the Human Person

The liberal notion of the human person seems diametrically opposed to the communitarian notion. It begins with the idea of self-consciousness or subjectivity as a fundamental basis of humanity. The human person is depicted as being aware of his/her existence as a person. Ray S. Anderson expresses the foundation of the liberal notion of the human person in the following words:

> I experience my own humanity as a subjective reality. I am a center of feelings, reactions, hopes, fears, opinions, motivations, and

---

[768] Machan Tibor, *Private Rights and Public Illusions* (New Brunswick/London: Transaction Publishers, 1995), 65-66. Machan also partly quotes his own work, *Human Rights and Human Liberties* (Chicago: Nelson-Hall, 1975), 74-77. Jacques Maritain emphasized this idea in his book, *The Person and the Common Good*, 61, 73-74.

[769] Andrew, N. Woznicki, "The Christian Humanism of Cardinal Karol Wojtyla," in *The Human Person*, vol. LIII, ed. George F. McLean (Washington DC: The American Catholic Philosophical Association, 1979), 32. Woznicki is quoting "Osoba; podmiot I wspolnota Rozniki Filozoticzne," 2 (1976), 5-39. The social nature of the human person is also strongly emphasized by the International Theological Commission, which affirmed that "human beings are created as social beings." Cfr., *International Theological Commission*, 6.

desires. Other persons exist for me. That is, they are within range of my own perception of reality, either as other subjects whose feelings, motivations and desires interest or threaten me, or as objects along with other phenomena in the objective world.[770]

This vision of the human person is centered on the individual and defies relationship with other individuals. At its social best, other human persons affect one's life positively to a minimum possible degree. Otherwise, they affect the individual negatively. This, however, still suggests that other people are not absolutely excluded from an individual's life although the vision does not seem to acknowledge the basic relationship between persons. It shows an individual as an absolutely independent and distinct entity from other people. The underlying principle emphasized in this notion of the human person is the principle of individuation and unrestrained freedom and use of reason.

However, some scholars think that the liberal notion of the human person does not necessarily neglect the communal elements in the human person though its emphasis is on the individual. This raises the question whether it is necessary to categorize the vision of the human person into the communitarian vision and the individualist vision. Woznicki responds to such a question:

> In view of the mutual relation between men, participation in humanity is based on mutual primacy of "I" in regard to each other, as being regarded as person, constituting ties which are always secondary to the personal one. In other words, the mutual participation of "I" in the other person is by the same token indicative of the primacy of personal subjects over the community.[771]

While it is right to acknowledge that the difference in the understanding of the human person by both communitarians and individualists is a question of the emphasis on one dimension of human person to the neglect of the other, it should also be acknowledged that the individual always comes before community. This is the argument Woznicki attempts to raise when he refers

---

[770] Ray S. Anderson, *On Being Human: Essays in Theological Anthropology* (Grand Rapids: William B. Eerdmans Publishing Company, 1982), 55.

[771] Woznicki, 32.

to the *I* as the primary element of relationship between people. The mutual relation of people is the interaction of the various *I*'s, and these various *I*'s are constituents of the community. The individual should not get lost in the community; instead, the individual should be emphasized so that a community makes sense and the human person can be called a social being.

In terms of human rights, the inevitable tendency is to view the human person as a liberal bearer of rights. As Fergusson states, "liberalism asserts the right of each person to free and equal treatment" [772] and views human rights as entitlements of individuals. This is a Kantian vision of the human person supported by scholars like Karol Wojtyla (John Paul II), who was strongly of the view that the human person is a being endowed with dignity, which is "an excellence that calls for special regard"; a person is "a thinking and willing subject, capable of making decisions," a subject not to be subordinated by other subjects, "never to be used *merely* as a means to an end for another person," and by natural right, a person "deserves to be treated as an end-in-himself" [773] According to Thomas D. Williams, Wojtyla thinks that the person must remain inviolate by fellow human beings and even God the Creator. [774]

Though credible from a practical point of view, this idea is subject to challenge because of the social nature of the human person and the significance of interdependence in human life. Even from the very fact of differences in people's talents and abilities, such an argument falls short of practical needs. The principles of participation, solidarity, association, or involvement, common good and subsidiarity would be rendered useless if the social aspect of the human person was ignored because these principles recognize and affirm the significance of using one's talents for the good of others. From this point of view, the human person can still be considered also a means for other people to thrive. However, what is clarified and ought to be noted here is that human dignity may not be tampered with in such a process, an assertion Kant affirmed by stating that "we should not only ever use each other partially as means." [775] Human dignity is an end in itself, and so the human person may not be treated merely and only as a means. This is the categorical imperative of Kant's *Metaphysics of Morals* that suggestively

---

[772] Fergusson, 139.

[773] Williams, 159.

[774] Ibid., 160.

[775] Ibid., 161.

offers a significant argument for the respect of the individual, human rights, and human dignity.

The foregoing study shows two contending notions of the human person and two extreme emphases in the notion of the human person. The first emphasis is on the social dimension of the human person, which represents the communitarian vision of person. The second emphasis is on the individual dimension of the human person, which depicts the vision of the liberals or individualists. In both cases, the opposite dimension is not excluded absolutely. Consequently, the following conclusions are in order: First, the social and individual dimensions of the human person are both significant in a total definition of a human person. Second, each of the notions of the human person suggests the possibility or potential for reconciling the communitarian and liberal visions of the human person and human rights. Third, there is also a paradoxical dimension of the definition of the human person, says Thomas Massaro:

> Maritain holds out a paradox for investigation: humans are beings of inestimable and inviolable value, transcending any temporal or political order, yet they find themselves and realize their dignity only by participating in (and in so doing, subordinating themselves to) the community. The human person simultaneously transcends and is subordinate to the common good.[776]

Here, the paradox is that the human person is both a social being and an autonomous individual who acts freely—a person is communal and individual. One is an individual by reserving sovereignty to self, and social because the human person remains open to other people and open to God, interacts with God, and "reserves ultimate sovereignty to God alone."[777] Maritain views the human person as having both immanent and transcendent dimensions but the aspirations for transcendence are immanent. These two opposite traits inhere in the same person. This suggests some uniting element in the human person in the vision of the communitarian and the liberal. This connecting element also explains why some liberals have rightly conceded that "the self cannot be understood apart from the social roles and attachments. Any fulfilled life is one in which the self is committed to

---

[776] Thomas J. Massaro, *Catholic Social Teaching and the United States Welfare Reform* (Collegeville, Minnesota: The Liturgical Press, 1998), 15.

[777] Ibid.

goods that are essentially social."[778] The ultimate suggestion of the preceding arguments is that radical separation of the communitarian and individualist notions of the human person is unnecessary. As Linda Zagrzebski suggests, it suffices to view a person as a rational individual substance, self-conscious or aware of his/her existence as an entity with a capacity to act deliberately and responsibly to attain an end, and may do so not only for his/her own sake but also for the sake of others.[779]

III. Human Dignity

A. Meaning and Origin

The meaning and origin of human dignity can be viewed both philosophically and theologically. The operative notion of human dignity depends on who defines it. The notion of human dignity articulated here rejects an understanding of dignity that disregards the qualities of universality, durability, and invariability. This means human dignity is lasting and does not change according to circumstances. A notion of human dignity which excludes the idea of associating human dignity with only certain capacities and conditions of life is more preferable than its opposite because human dignity never depends on the individual person's characteristics and circumstances of living. Patrick Verspieren observes that a concept of dignity defined in terms of capacities and conditions of life denotes that human dignity is "the capacity to decide and act for oneself, what may be called autonomy and independence, and the quality of the image of oneself that one offers to others."[780] A definition of human dignity that considers dignity as autonomy and a liberal expression of personal freedom as opposed to the classical vision of freedom as "the inalienable value of the person" [781] demanding respect because of the enduring character of human dignity regardless of prevailing temporal or social circumstances is out of question.

---

[778] Ferguson, 147.

[779] Linda Zagrzebski, "The Uniqueness of Persons," in *Journal of Religious Ethics*, vol. 29. no.3 (Washington DC, 2001), 405-410.

[780] Patrick Verspieren, "Dignity in Political and Bioethical Debates," trans. John Bowden, in *The Discourse of Human Dignity, Concilium*, ed. Regina Ammicht-Quinn et al. (London: SCM Press, 2003/2), 18.

[781] Ibid., 18-19.

According to Williams, Aquinas considered the origin of human dignity to be "personhood" defined in terms of the rational character of the human person, and he defined human dignity as "the distinguishing characteristic of personhood."[782] Bonaventure concurred with Aquinas in his definition of human dignity. In the definition of both Aquinas and Bonaventure, human dignity marks the difference between a human person and other creatures. This definition of human dignity also establishes the intimate link between human personhood, human dignity, and human rights. The trio are inseparable and necessary for defining each other. The human person comes first, but there is concurrence or simultaneity in their occurrence.

"One classic definition of the enlightenment philosophy is that dignity is that which has no price, which cannot be bought or sold," a definition derived from Kant's vision of "the human being as an end in itself and a prohibition against total instrumentalization which follows from that."[783] Kant clarified the definition of dignity by distinguishing between price and dignity which he called "*innern werth*, an intrinsic value."[784] Kant affirmed that dignity was different from price because price measures the value of a thing and equates it to another thing of the same value, but human dignity cannot be equated to the value of any other thing. This invaluable worth inheres in all people. The notion suggests the singular and invaluable character of human dignity as a necessary principle for real development because it does not exclude anybody from possession of dignity. Human dignity is a transcendental human quality. Kant attributed the foundation of the dignity of human nature to autonomy, a view which is disputed because autonomy, value, and moral norms are founded in God, not just human nature, even if it participates in divine nature.[785] It seems right to concur with those who dispute Kant's view that the origin of the dignity of the human person is merely autonomy because freedom or autonomy does not ultimately originate from an individual. Individual

---

[782]   Williams, 155.

[783]   Ammicht-Quinn is quoting Immanuel Kant, *Grunndelegung zur Metaphysiik der Sitten*, in Werke, ed. W. Weishchedel, Frankfurt am Main, 1968, VIII, 68. Also see Ammicht-Quinn, "Whose Dignity is Inviolable? Human Being, Machines and the Discourse of Dignity," trans. John Bowden in *The Discourse of Human Dignity, Concilium*, ed. Regina Ammicht-Quinn et al. (London: SCM Press, 2003/2), 40. Also Cfr. Williams, 155.

[784]   Williams, 155. Also see Linda Zagrzebski, "The Uniqueness of Person," in *Journal of Religious Ethics*, vol.29, no.3 (Washington DC, 2001), 402.

[785]   Ibid., 155.

freedom or autonomy is a participation in divine nature and confined within divine freedom which is ultimate.

While philosophy does not state that human dignity originates from a definite being other than human person and nature, theology explicitly affirms that human dignity has its foundation in God. Human dignity originates from without the human person. It is a gift and a participation in the nature of a greater being than the human person.

> Theological foundations of human dignity and rights include creation
> in the image of God (Gen.1:26-27), the Trinitarian concept of God,
> redemption by Jesus Christ, and the call to a transcendent destiny.[786]

This idea is succinctly stated by *Gaudium et Spes*, which affirms that "an outstanding cause of human dignity lies in man's call to communion with God. From the very circumstance of his origin, man is already invited to converse with God."[787] This conversation leads a person into a communion with God. This is an essential statement about human dignity and human rights. All other explanations of human dignity and human rights revolve around this idea. The grounding of the notion of human dignity on the idea of creation in the image of God is, however, often questioned from a secular point of view. It is considered a religious view of human dignity in the same way human rights are some times branded. According to Michael J. Perry, people argue that the notion of human dignity and human rights are religious because "there is . . . no intelligible . . . secular version of the conviction that every human being is sacred. The only intelligible versions are religious."[788] Such objections are refutable, according to Regina Ammicht-Quinn, on the basis of the assertion that

---

[786] Milburn, J. Thompson, *Justice and Peace: A Christian Primer* (Maryknoll, New York: Orbis Books, 1997), 94. Also see O'Collins and Faruggia, 114. Also cfr. Ammichdt-Quin, 40-41. This is the most commonly advocated and accepted theological foundation for the definition and arguments for both human dignity and human rights.

[787] Massaro, 7. Also see Austin Flannery, ed. "*Gaudium et Spes*: Pastoral Constitution on the Church in the Modern World," in *Vatican Council II: The Conciliar and Postconciliar Documents* (Leominister, Herefords, England: Costello Publishing Company, 1981), 19, 918.

[788] Michael J. Perry, *The Idea of Human Rights: Four Inquiries* (Oxford: Oxford University Press, 1998), 5 and 11.

> On the human level the dictum about human beings as the image of
> God has two shades: representation and affinity . . . representation
> means that human beings are not alone. They are wholly themselves,
> but not just themselves. If one looks at them they are transparent
> to another reality. Affinity means that human beings are not alone.
> They are wholly themselves, but not just themselves. If they look
> at themselves, at the same time they see the other.[789]

As individual entities, human beings are representations of God. As complete individuals, they tend toward union with God and reflect God and fellow human beings. This observation seems to concur with Perry's view that the concept of human rights, based on human dignity which is an attribute of human personality or human beings, is "inescapably religious"[790] because it is an idea that reconciles beliefs about interpersonal relationships and how people are bound to each other and to the Ultimate Reality or God. This is theologically correct. The question here is, who defines or interprets human rights and human dignity and from what perspective the person is doing this—a believer or a nonbeliever? There is, therefore, a religious notion of human dignity, and there is also a secular notion. The notion is not necessarily religious, but the notion is just better articulated in religious or theological terms. Nonetheless, this does not make a difference in human dignity as such because it does not depend on religion or any other circumstances and status. To claim it makes a difference in itself is to deny the universality of human dignity. It would seem that Perry has stated that the notion is inescapably religious because any notion of human dignity other than the religious notion is already contained in the religious notion.

Human dignity is worthiness, not value, but it is the basis of value and what makes human beings different from things and animals, although *human dignity* and *human worth* are rather recent, twentieth-century terms.[791] Human persons have something that resembles God. It is for this reason that the idea that "God created us in His image . . . is the basis of human dignity."[792]

---

[789] Ammicht-Quinn, 42.

[790] Perry, 12. Also see pages 14-15 of the same work.

[791] Enrique Dussel, "Dignity: Its Denial and Recognition in a Specific Context of Liberation," trans. Paul Burns, in *The Discourse of Human Dignity, Concilium.* ed. Ammichht-Quinn Regina et al. (London: SCM Press, 2003/2), 95-97.

[792] Bohr, 74.

Theological anthropology often advances three basic reasons for the claim that human persons are created in God's image. First, they are rational. Second, they are created free and have ability to make choices. Third, they are capable of interpersonal relationships. This last characteristic captures the idea of human persons created in the image of God because God is a community of relationships between Father, Son, and the Holy Spirit, which David Bohr calls "a Trinity of personal relationships or Tri-Unity."[793] This Trinitarian element of the definition and origin of human dignity is also significant for understanding the human person and human rights as being relational too. It ought to be reflected in the treatise of the human person, human dignity and human rights.

Machan Tibor defines human dignity in terms of the capacity for moral responsibility for actions rationally evaluated and consciously and freely chosen.

> Human dignity is the capacity of individuals to be morally responsible. Moral responsibility, in turn arises because human beings are capable of free choice and rational thought, rational consciousness and the ability to make choices make an individual a moral agent since his decisions can be made in accordance with a rational standard in which some actions are right while others are wrong.[794]

Freedom and the ability to choose constitute significant defining elements of human dignity. Since rationality and freedom are traits of the human person, it is reasonable to say that human dignity is an individual's moral capacity to act responsibly. It is also the ability to make choices, which accounts for human responsibility for deliberate behavior. Consequently, it is right to say that when people's ability to choose is impeded, their human dignity is denied because human dignity is a moral capacity for responsible action.

From a social point of view, human dignity is also based on self-respect and the respect for others. This idea is well expressed in the traditional religion of the Lugbara. The word *ru* or *ruta*, which means respect or honor or fear, explains some unique quality in every human person, and it is the reason for

---

[793] Ibid., 75.

[794] Machan, 62.

respecting or honoring every person.[795] This means there is something shared or mutual about human dignity and human persons. A further reason for such a respect consists in what John Paul II often referred to as a sincere feeling and great esteem for the human person, as described by Macan Tibor:

> The most vital social condition for any person is the honoring of his or her dignity. If someone's dignity is destroyed, all other benefits that person reaps from others amount to very little and certainly serve as no compensation. Trading one's dignity is akin to selling one's soul; it takes away one's essential identity as the human being one is.[796]

The honor and respect for human dignity is a foundation for understanding human rights. Its significance is in the idea that human dignity is the core of the being of the human person and accounts for becoming the human person. The human person is defined by human dignity on which human rights are based. The very attributes, which define human dignity—namely, intellect or rationality, freedom, and the capacity for responsible action or choice, and the capacity for interpersonal relationship—are the reasons for people to claim certain rights.

In human dignity, there is singularity and universality. The feeling of the presence of human dignity in other people is something unique in the human person and in all people. Ammchidt-Quinn, citing John Baptist Metz, suggests that "radical vulnerability is a negative formulation of dignity" necessary for understanding human dignity, meaning that the "human dignity is unassailable."[797] Human dignity cannot be tampered with without an opposing reaction in response. This claim is credible because human dignity is the most sensitive element of the human person in the sense that it is easily tampered with by others, and yet nobody wants it to be tampered with. This is probably an argument that defies the claim that the notion of human dignity is essentially or "inescapably religious" because every human being is sacred as Michael Perry suggests.[798] Human dignity is the reason for

---

[795] John Middleton, *Lugbara Religion: Ritual and Authority among an East African People* (London: Oxford University Press, 1960), 21.

[796] Machan, 65.

[797] Ammicht-Quinn, 44.

[798] Perry, 5.

the claim of the inviolability of human integrity. It is the worth that every person has and that demands

> that the human being must not be treated as a mere means to some other end (such as, for example, the state), but must be regarded as an end in himself. His self-fulfillment is an indispensable goal of human life, and the society is backward, unjust, even evil, that does not promote it.[799]

This vision of the importance of human dignity clearly shows that an institution, religious or civic, that does not respect and promote human dignity ought not to claim to be developed. The view also affirms the recognition of the universality of human dignity, which will be treated in depth in the next section. The same view was, at least indirectly, expressed in the Universal Declaration of Human Rights where the drafters of the document never linked human rights to religion and never thought that one had to adhere to a particular religion in order to accept the existence of human rights.[800] The International Theological Commission, using Kantian categories of thought, emphasized the gravity of the recognition and respect for human dignity in the following words:

> Man appears not as an object and instrument to be used but as an intermediate end in himself, whose welfare both personal and ultimately as a being for God must be our aim. Man enjoys a spiritual, soul, reason, freedom, conscience, responsibility, an active role in society.[801]

The constitutive elements of human dignity were stated by the commission as important. These elements make the human person valuable and different from other beings. It was for this reason that the commission advocated that "all personal relationships between people must be conducted in such a way that this fundamental human dignity be given full honor, and the needs of self

---

[799] Davenport, 230.

[800] Johannes Morsink, *The Universal Declaration of Human Rights: Origins, Drafting, and Intent* (Philadelphia: University of Pennsylvania Press, 1999), 125.

[801] International Theological Commission, 5.

be fulfilled to the best of our ability."[802] The commission suggested that the virtues of justice and love are crucial for the enhancement of human dignity. Likewise, Paul VI advocated in his theory of integral human development that this dignity should be enhanced in all people. The basic reason in both cases is that human dignity is equal in all because all are created in the divine image and likeness. The equality and common origin of human dignity from God also explains why the dignity of each person is realized in community, should be recognized by the community or other individuals, and is protected by the community or other individual persons. This shows the social and the universal dimensions of human dignity. It is for this reason that Catholic social doctrine emphasizes "community as a necessary locus"[803] for the awareness and promotion of human dignity.

Three concluding statements prompted by the above treatise are as follows: First, the origin of the idea of human dignity is the idea that all people are created in the image and likeness of God or at least a being that human persons recognize and acknowledge to be greater than every human person. Second, because of their common origin, all people share in divine qualities such as rational faculty and the ability to make free decisions or choices though to a limited extent as compared to their creator. Third, secularists consider these assertions to be religious. Consequently, human dignity is variously defined, but the ideas principally expressed are tantamount to calling human dignity a connatural value, inherent value, inborn worth, or "an innate worth."[804] It is an immeasurable value, an invaluable worth, in monetary or equivalent terms. It is also an invariable worth under every circumstance of time and place. It is an ontological value. The idea is not necessarily religious because even those who are not religious recognize human dignity.

B. Universality and Equality of Human Dignity

The main issue treated here is whether human dignity is spatially and temporally universal and equal in all people of all. The focus of the arguments will be the assertion that everybody has human dignity regardless

---

[802]   Ibid.

[803]   Massaro, 9.

[804]   Ibid., 7.

of disabilities.[805] The explanation of the universality and equality of human dignity is traced to the origin of human dignity.

> Each person is created as an *imago Dei*; collectively we are deemed by our Creator to be good. Even the power of sin, original or actual, in no way cancels this bestowal of dignity. Our status as children of God sets humans apart from the rest of the created order. [806]

Human dignity is the participation of all rational beings endowed with the ability for free choice in the intelligence of God or divine qualities. The arguments advanced by Thomas D. Williams about the universality and equality of human dignity are compelling. He argues from the very nature of the human person, which according to him, is the same in all people. It is in this nature that human dignity should be located. Consequently, he states that

> If this dignity inheres in man's nature as a free and intelligent being, it can be predicated equally of all members of the human race. In order to be universal, personal dignity could not be a function of intelligence, abilities, accomplishments, moral worth, or baptism, for these factors vary from person to person. It must rather be a function of the human being simply by virtue of his humanity, of his personhood, a natural quality that cannot be acquired or lost. The very expression "human dignity" implies that dignity resides in human nature itself and thus ensures a fundamental ontological equality among all people.[807]

The universality and equality of human dignity, according to Williams, is its inherence in human nature. Human dignity is beyond human ability or creativity. It defeats conditions created by individual human persons

---

[805] Pontifical Council for Justice and Peace, *Compendium of the Social Doctrine of the Church*, 64.

[806] Massaro, 6.

[807] Williams, 153. Also see Vitillo and Toliver Grimes, 5. Here, the same affirmation is made. Namely, that each person possesses a basic dignity that comes from God, not from any human quality or accomplishment, not from race or gender or economic status.

and communities. The vision of the universality and equality of dignity of all people has not only been the idea of the Catholic Church or any other religious group. The inherence, inviolability, universality, and equality of dignity and rights "of all members of the human family" were affirmed by "the Universal Declaration of Human Rights proclaimed by the United Nations on 10 December 1948."[808] The assertion is also reechoed in the assertion of John Paul II who contended that "the dignity of the human person is a transcendent value, always recognized as such by those who sincerely search for the truth."[809] The general consensus is that all human beings have dignity. Human dignity is beyond any human conditions or making because it does not derive from the will of the human person. The preceding arguments support the assertion that the universality and equality of human dignity is explained by the idea that

> every person is created by God, loved and saved in Jesus Christ and fulfills himself by creating a network of multiple relationships of love, justice and solidarity with other persons while he goes about his various activities in the world.[810]

That all people were created by God and in the image and likeness of God explains why human dignity is universal and equal. However, this claim can be contested on the basis that it is only a religious claim and may not be held as such by nonbelievers. Nonetheless, the problem is whether nonbelievers can adequately account for the origin of human dignity, which transcends individual persons and embraces all people. If the common origin of dignity is denied, then universality may have to be denied, and the very idea of human dignity or humanity makes no sense at all. Hence, human dignity and its universality should be affirmed.

---

[808] Paul Valadier, "The Person who Lacks Dignity," trans. John Bowden in *The Discourse of Human Dignity, Concilium*, ed. Regina Ammicht-Quinn et al. (London: SCM Press, 2003/2), 49. Also see Morsink, 329. Also cfr. H. Weston Burns, "Human Rights," in *Human Rights in the World Community: Issues and Action*, eds. Pierre Richard Claude and Burns H. Weston, 2nd ed. (Philadelphia: University of Pennsylvania Press, 1992), 419.

[809] J. Vitillo and Toliver Grimes, 6. These authors are quoting John Paul II's message on the World Day of Peace, 1999, Message No.2.

[810] Pontifical Council for Justice and Peace, *Compendium of the Social Doctrine of the Church*, 17.

That the dignity of the human person is inviolable and "the whole of the Church's social doctrine"[811] develops from this assertion or principle is generally an accepted assertion because the social doctrine is all about the promotion of the human person. The idea of the universality and equality of dignity applies to all human sexes or genders:

> "Male" and "Female" differentiate two individuals of equal dignity, which does not however reflect a static equality, because the specificity of the female is different from the specificity of the male, and this difference in equality is enriching and indispensable for the harmony of life in society.[812]

The firm assertion of the Catholic social doctrine is that man and woman are complementary physically, sociologically, and ontologically. This complementarity does not, however, mean that either of the two has greater dignity. The meaning of human dignity and human person would change if there was any differentiation in the dignity of men and women.

> Man and woman have the same dignity and are of equal value, not only because they are both, in their differences, created in the image of God, but even more profoundly because the dynamic of reciprocity that gives life to the "we" in the human couple, is an image of God.[813]

Significant to note is that equality of dignity is not affected by differentiation in sex or gender, stature, socioeconomic standing, or political standing. What is stated here is that human beings complement each other in many different ways because they are social. The idea that both men and

---

[811]   Ibid., 50.

[812]   Pontifical Council for Justice and Peace, *Compendium of the Social Doctrine of the Church*, 64.

[813]   *Catechism of the Catholic Church*, 2nd ed., trans. United States Catholic Conference (Citta del Vaticana: Libreria Editrice Vaticana), 2000, 2334, 561. Also see the same document, 371, 94. Also cfr. Pontifical Council for Justice and Peace, *Compendium of the Social Doctrine of the Church*, 51. The statement was not original from the council because it quotes the Catechism of Catholic Church.

women are social also demonstrates individual inadequacy and the need for others on account of their talents and abilities or capacities. This affirmation does not disqualify the assertion that all people are created in the image and likeness of God. Difference in dignity is only in what Williams calls *moral* dignity but not what he calls *ontological* dignity. This means the root of the offence against the equality of human dignity is sin in both its "personal and social"[814] dimensions because division, which also explains claimed differences in human dignity, has both personal and social aspects. Any sin is an abuse of freedom with the consequences of alienation from God, alienation from others, and alienation from self as the Pontifical Commission for Justice and Peace advocates. According to the Pontifical Council for Justice and Peace, the affirmation of the equality of the dignity of human persons is also theologically founded on the idea that God loves and cares for everybody and "shows no partiality."[815]

According to Thomas D. Williams, scholars like Fortin disapprove of the idea of the universality of human dignity on the grounds that it is approved only in a limited way by Christian anthropology.[816] Williams argues that Fortin can be refuted on the basis of the distinction between "*ontological* dignity, common to all human beings by reason of their nature, and a *moral* dignity, which reflects the consistency with which a person lives according to moral truth," meaning that while "moral dignity can be acquired and also forfeited, ontological dignity remains constant, since the rational nature on which it rests endures independent of moral choices."[817] Williams's argument is based on the nature of the human person, which is a quality shared by all human beings. On this basis, the universality of human dignity can be affirmed, whether by Christian anthropology or any category of people who take human nature seriously. According to the argument of Williams, the actual universality of human dignity is explained in the ontological dimension of dignity, not the moral dimension. The argument of Williams is more credible than that of Fortin. To argue that the universality of human dignity is approved only in a limited way by Christian anthropology is to deny the very idea of the

---

[814] Pontifical Council for Justice and Peace, *Compendium of the Social Doctrine of the Church*, 53.

[815] Ibid., 63. Also cfr. Acts 10:34, Rom. 2:11, Gal. 2:6, Eph. 6:9, Gal. 3:28, Rom.10: 12, 1 Cor 12:13, Col. 3:11.

[816] Williams, 154.

[817] Ibid., 156.

universality of human dignity. Second, it would suggest that the idea of human dignity is necessarily religious or Christian, which is not true. The fact that human dignity is not necessarily a religious notion suggests the affirmation of the universality of human dignity.

Williams plausibly argues that ontological dignity is a quality per se while moral dignity is a quality attached to an action, not independent of any action. In other words, human dignity is not contingent or dependent on any factor.[818] The credibility of this argument is affirmed by the idea that if human dignity were contingent on prevalent circumstances, one would only sensibly talk of degrees of human dignity or human dignity varying from person to person. It would make less sense to talk of human dignity generally. Instead, it would even be better to talk of human dignities. Consequently, it is plausible to state that since *moral* dignity is just a quality attached to an action, it defies the idea of universality. Universality of human dignity can only be predicated of the *ontological* dignity.

Since human dignity is inherent in the human nature, the affirmation of the universality of human dignity is credible. Hence, Williams's distinction between ontological dignity and moral dignity is intelligible and plausible. It facilitates the distinction of a contingent dignity and a universal, invaluable, inviolable, and durable or enduring dignity, which is typically a human dignity. Further reflection on the source of morality, Williams suggests points to a transcendent and universal source, which is an ontological source. Consequently, one can conceive an ontological dignity, which is universal. The universality of human dignity ultimately implies an ontological human dignity of which what Williams calls *moral* dignity is part because the ultimate source of morality is God who is the *Ultimate Being* and also the source of human dignity.

C. Importance of the Vision of Universality and Equality of Human Dignity

Paul VI's principal concern in *Populorum Progressio* was the integral development of peoples. The vision of universality and equality of human dignity is important for Paul VI's vision of integral human development for a number of reasons. First, the "conditions of equality and parity are

---

[818]   Ibid., 154.

prerequisites for the authentic progress of the international community."[819] If all are to develop or be helped to develop, they must be seen as having equal worth because they are creatures of God and in the likeness of God. This way, they can be treated in the same way or at least with the same consideration. The recognition of human dignity and human rights, which are based on human dignity, is necessary for the integral promotion of the progress of peoples.[820] Recognition of the dignity of all people is an impetus for a struggle for the promotion of all peoples. The gravity of this assertion can be seen in light of Karol Wojtyla's statement that *humanness* is "concretized in every man just as much as it is in myself" and this humanness "unites human beings."[821] When people recognize in others what they know, they have and treasure they can be moved to act selflessly. This offers possibilities for integral human development.

Second, the awareness and recognition of the universality and equality of the dignity of every person helps "safeguard and promote human dignity only if it is done as a community, by the whole community."[822] This suggests that the awareness and recognition of human dignity is everybody's responsibility if integral human development is to be achieved. This recognition can be promoted through the applications of Paul VI's integral human development principles of solidarity, association, common good, and participation. Since all people are created in the image and likeness of God and participate in some way in divine dignity, human dignity can be affirmed as equal in every person. Promotion of freedom, justice, and peace in the world and in any

---

[819]   Pontifical Council for Justice and Peace, *Compendium of the Social Doctrine of the Church*, 63. This quotation is based on references to John XXIII, Encyclical Letter *Pacem in Terris*, 47-48: AAS55 (1963) 279-281; Paul VI Address to the General Assembly of the United Nation (5 October 1965), 5: AAS 57 (1965), 881; John Paul II, Address to the Fifth General Assembly of United Nations (5 October 1995), 13: *L'Osservatore Romano*, English edition, 11 October 1995, 9-10.

[820]   Morsink, 315.

[821]   Karol Wojtyla, Cardinal (John Paul II), *The Acting Person*, trans. Andrezej Potocki (Dordrecht: D. Reidel Publishing Company, 1979), 293. Humanity and community should be "based on the mutual primacy of each other," meaning that there should be a mutual recognition of human dignity, human rights, and human persons. Cfr. Woznicki, 32.

[822]   Pontifical Council for Justice and Peace, *Compendium of the Social Doctrine of the Catholic Church*, 63.

society demands the recognition of the inherent worth, also expressed in human rights, of every human being.[823]

Third, the human person is defined by attributes such as body, soul, spirit, intelligence, conscience, freedom, and sense of responsibility. All these attributes contribute to the foundation of human dignity. Since these attributes are under normal circumstances shared by all people, "all human beings, since they are God's creation and endowed with the same fundamental characteristics deserve the highest consideration."[824] It should also be added that the universality of human dignity demands that all people be responsible. That all human beings have dignity is the principal thesis in human dignity talk. The emphasis of the International Theological Commission is that there is no exception in treating people respectfully because all share the same attributes originating from the same source. This assertion reaffirms that human dignity is an objective reality. For these reasons, it seems right to concur with Williams:

> To say that persons are to be treated in a certain way, then, is not an expression of a philanthropic sentiment to which others may or may not subscribe, it is a statement about the true nature of things. Human dignity is a quality which demands a certain response from us.[825]

Fourth, the respect for human dignity, which facilitates the development of all, demands an application of "the principle of reciprocity" or Jesus's golden rule "Do to others what you would like done to you . . . be merciful as your heavenly father is merciful."[826] This principle of reciprocity is founded on the notion that the human dignity is a shared quality or value and should always be recognized as such. As Michael Perry suggests, the 1948 Universal Declaration of Human Rights, which was proclaimed by the United Nations suggests this universality in its recognition, in the preamble of the document, of "'the inherent dignity . . . of all members of the human family and of the dignity and worth of the human person,'"[827] thus recognizing and acknowledging the

---

[823] Morsink, 313.

[824] International Theological Commission, 6.

[825] Williams, 153.

[826] International Theological Commission, 5.

[827] Perry, 12.

universality of human dignity. The affirmation suggests that human beings should treat each other in a dignified manner.

Finally, the universality of human dignity brings to our awareness that human dignity is an ontological reality inherent in human nature. As an ontological reality, it is not contingent on any person or factor. Nobody can give another person human dignity. Human dignity *is* (it exists) in human beings. Although it can be abused, violated, and denied, it cannot be taken away. It ought to be protected, defended, and promoted or enhanced.

IV. HUMAN RIGHTS: THE INDIVIDUALIST AND COMMUNITARIAN NOTIONS

A number of observations are necessary before delving into the question of human rights. First, the concept of human rights is polyvalent, and it developed over time. Most human rights studies trace the origin of human rights to the ancient Greek foundation of stoicism at the time of Zeno who initially suggested the universality of rights on the basis of the universal law of nature.[828] Second, this section is a treatise of two supposedly different and hardly reconcilable concepts of human rights—the Euro-American individualist and the African communitarian concepts of rights. The goal of this section is to examine the two concepts of human rights and to attempt to establish the universality of human rights. Some definitions of human rights will be interjected to help support the positions of the two philosophies of human rights. Here is one viewpoint:

> Human rights address situations where power is being exercised in such a manner as to control human beings by manipulation or coercion so that they are unable to affirm their dignity and humanity fully.[829]

This means human rights are immunities or protections against forces that interfere with the exercise of human freedom and consequently abuse of human dignity. It suggests that the claims of one person are limited by claims of other people.

---

[828] Burns, 14.

[829] Alan D. Falconer, "Right, Human," in *The New Dictionary of Theology*, eds. Joseph A. Komonchak et al. (Wilmington, Delaware: Michael Glazier, 1987), 899.

Third, it is significant to note, as the magisterial teaching presents, that human "dignity forms the basis of rights."[830] Hence, a correct notion of human rights depends on the right understanding of human dignity. The preceding section is therefore crucial to this section. Finally, I will attempt a synthesized definition of human rights using ideas of other authors, which I consider to be inclusive of both Euro-American individualist and African communitarian notions of human rights, especially with consideration of the reconciling Roman Catholic notion of rights.

Michael Perry's vision of human rights points to two major perspectives on human rights—the individualist and communitarian notions. He states that the idea of human rights suggests that "each and every person is sacred—each and every human being is inviolable; has an inherent dignity and worth; is an end in himself; or the like."[831] This aspect of the idea of human rights emphasizes the individuality of a person as a distinct entity. The vision gravitates to the liberal notion of the human person and human rights. The second part of the idea of human rights is that

> because every human being has inherent dignity, certain choices should be made and other choices should be rejected; in particular certain things ought not to be done to any human being and certain other things ought to be done for every human being.[832]

This dimension of the idea of human rights points directly to the relational character of rights, and so it has communitarian overtones because claims one makes on other people are reciprocally applicable. There is mutual obligation in claiming and exercising rights. Rights are related to individuals as well as community.

A. Individualist Notion of Rights: The Euro-American Model

The Western liberal concept of human rights, like any other vision of rights, is a consequence of political, social, and economic power or authority. Contextually, Donnelly thinks that the Western concept of human rights

---

[830] Williams, 148.

[831] Perry, 5-6.

[832] Ibid., 6. This same view is also advocated by Williams, 148.

is characterized by "a perpetual and . . . obsessive concern with individual dignity, personal autonomy and property."[833] Human rights are viewed as protections or immunities from external aggressions against individual freedom. This contention suggests that

> the liberal tradition interprets a right as an immunity from coercion; a right in this sense is understood as a circle of protection within which the person is guaranteed a sphere of freedom from intervention by the state or other organized forces in the society.[834]

This seems to be the reason why Western philosophical anthropology views individuals or persons as dominantly motivated by self-interest when making claims upon others or for themselves.[835] However, it would seem that, according to Donnelley, the individual character of human rights is reasonable in the absence of alternative protection of the dignity of the individual person. If an individual's dignity, which defines or determines freedom, is to be protected and the individual is incapable of doing this, some other external and capable force has to protect it. This very concern gravitates toward the possibility of thinking that the dichotomy between an individualist and a communitarian view of the human person is unnecessary in the human rights dialogue because their mutual complementarity is suggested here. An individual's claim to be protected as a being that has dignity is inevitably valid and necessary because human dignity is the basic human principle. Society has a duty to support and protect the individual. This means the individual also needs society. To be society, individuals should also exist because society is constituted by individuals.

---

[833] Jack Donnelly, *The Concept of Human Rights* (New York: St. Martin Press, 1985), 80. Also see Asmarom Legesse, "Human Rights in African Political Culture," in *The Moral Imperatives of Human Rights: A World Survey*, ed. Kenneth W. Thompson (Washington DC: University Press of America, 1980), 124.

[834] Bryan J. Hehir, "Human Rights and U.S. Foreign Policy," in *The Moral Imperatives of Human Rights: A World Survey*, ed. Kenneth W. Thompson (Washington DC: University Press of America, 1980), 10.

[835] Donal Dorr, "Solidarity and Integral Development," in *The Logic of Solidarity: Commentaries on John Paul II's Encyclical on Social Concern*, eds. Gregory Baum and Robert Ellsberg (Maryknoll, New York: Orbis Books, 1989), 147.

The Western concept of human rights was much impacted by Lockean thought.[836] Bryan J. Hehir states that according to John Locke, the concept of human rights has nothing to do with the notion of shared responsibilities; "the person enters civil society with rights but not bound by social responsibilities," and the individual is presented as being a "self-sufficient" entity in need of society because "protection of life, liberty and property is too arduous outside some kind of social setting," meaning that "a person is social by necessity."[837] This suggests that according to Locke people are merely conditioned to be social because they, individually, are incapacitated to meet some of their needs. Even here, one can still notice that the individual cannot absolutely stand independently of society. Whether it is out of necessity or not, individuals need society or community because society is built on the basis of values commonly shared by its members. Two of the commonly shared qualities are natural equality of dignity and freedom. These are the foundations or reasons for the unity of all people; they are not qualities of differentiation.

The USA Virginia Bill of Rights had Lockean tones in some aspects. The June 1776 document had the following to say in its first clause:

> All men are by nature equally free and independent, and have certain inherent rights, of which, when they enter into a state of society, they cannot, by any compact, deprive or divest their posterity: namely, the enjoyment of life and liberty, with the means of acquiring and possessing property and pursuing and obtaining happiness.[838]

Four important observations are significant at this point. First, the main emphasis of the above statement is that individuals precede society and determine it. This is an area of fundamental difference between Western individualist and African communitarian concepts of a human person in relation to society because the notion of human rights is comprehended in terms of the individual in the Western context while it is centered on community in the African communitarian view. Generally, it is observed that

---

[836]   Maurice Cranston, *What Are Human Rights?* (New York: Basic Books Inc. Publishers, 1962), 2.

[837]   Hehir, 8.

[838]   Cranston, 2.

"liberalism asserts the right of each person to free and equal treatment."[839] For the African communitarian, the individual and the community are inseparable. It is true that the individual and community are in mutual need, but in the order of phenomenon, there is a flaw because the individual is not given precedence over community. However, this does not mean that African communitarianism entertains unequal treatment. Consequently, like the individualist vision, the freedom or individuality of a person is still significant. Second, the foundation of natural equality is not specified in the document. Rights are only said to be inherent. The source of inherence is unstated in the clause. If it is on the ground that human nature is the same, the sameness of this nature has yet to be accounted for. However, in the mind of the founding fathers expressed in various ways—the American motto In God We Trust, the Pledge of Allegiance, and the national anthem—this clause does not exclude the idea that the equality of nature is grounded in God. This fact is also evident in the July 1776 Declaration of American Independence. Third, although the clause is refined in the Declaration of American Independence of July 1776, which states that "all are created equal and endowed by their Creator with certain inalienable rights . . . ,"[840] both statements still manifest the individual and liberal character of human rights in the Euro-American concept. Finally, such a view of rights tends to create a dichotomy between the individual and the society or community—the Western view and the African one.

According to David Hollenbach,

> In the neo-scholastic documents it is "reason" which gives persons the power to make history, to understand their social relationnships, to be self-determining and to be obedient to God's law without loss of personhood and freedom.[841]

Reason commands human action and life. It explains the demand for responsibility for one's actions. This is why it defines the human person and, specifically, human dignity. Reason impacted the Western concept of human rights in the sense that it helped define rights as responsible freedom. If freedom is a natural quality of all people, then rights may not be considered

---

[839] Fergusson David, 139.

[840] Ibid.

[841] David Hollenbach, *Claims in Conflict: Retrieving and Renewing the Catholic Human Rights Tradition* (New York: Paulist Press, 1979), 124.

absolute prerogatives of an individual or few individuals. In the Western context, because every person is by nature free, everybody has rights. The corollary implication is that it suggests that one person's rights are restrained by another person's rights. This is why in every context, rights have always to be interpreted as mutual claims. In this sense, there are never absolute rights in any context. According to Bujo, this idea is similarly deepened by Kant's emphasis on the *autonomy* of a person on the basis of the faculty of rationality or the general law (the categorical imperative), making autonomy the chief characteristic of the Western concept of human rights.[842] Bujo suggested that this autonomy was not just a laissez-faire freedom but autonomy for self-realization. This autonomy again belongs to everybody, but in relation to the autonomy of other people.

The preceding contentions suggest that the emphasis on the autonomy of the individual or personal freedom is, historically, a constant contention in the Western tradition of human rights. Hollenbach's claim that the Western concept of human rights emphasizes the right of the individual, and consequently, his assertion that all rights are commonly founded on "the freedom of the individual person"[843] is a testimony to this contention. The emphasis of freedom as foundation for rights supports individual liberty but in relation to the liberty of other individuals or groups because all people are naturally endowed with freedom. On account of this fact, the social dimension of the individual's life is not secondary as it seems in practical life. Benezet Bujo's view is not different either. Quoting Kant, he suggests that in the Western school of thought based on Kant's *Metaphysics of Morals*, there is one original right:

> Freedom (independence of another person's constraining arbitrariness) is the sole, original right, to which every human being is entitled on the basis of humanity itself, as long as this freedom can exist together with every other freedom in accordance with a general law.[844]

---

[842] Benezet Bujo, *The Ethical Dimension of Community: The African Model and the Dialogue Between North and South* (Nairobi: Pauline Publications Africa, 1998), 144.

[843] Hollenbach, 13.

[844] Bujo, 144-145. Bujo makes reference to I. Kant, *Die Metaphysik der Sitten*. Rechtslehre AB 45, in ders. Werke in Sechs Banden, hrsg. V.W. Weischhedel, Bd. IV. 345 (Publisher's translation).

Even if freedom is the sole original right, it seems right to infer from this quotation that freedom and, consequently, human rights are not absolute. Rights call for duties or obligations—rights and duties or obligations are correlative. One person's freedom is limited by other people's freedom, implied in the general law or the categorical imperative, which proposes that other people have similar freedoms or rights. A laissez-faire interpretation of freedom, hence, is irrelevant. This suggests that, just like human dignity, an adequate concept of human rights gravitates around a commonly shared element in human persons.

Bujo contends that according to the Euro-American vision of rights

> at the core is the concept of the the dignity of the individual: being human justifies the claim to certain rights. The emphasis falls upon the individual, not upon society; the single person should be respected as such and not on account of 'the relationship to others.'[845]

The autonomous respect of an individual is based on the dignity of the individual, which is universal at the same time. Human dignity and human rights are, in turn, based on and defined in terms of natural freedom. This view promotes Hollenbach's assertion that human rights are "ramifications and extrapolations of individual freedom," human rights are consequences and expressions, projections and expansions of human freedom, hence rooted in the fundamental rights to liberty as H. L. A. Harts affirms.[846] He further advances that people capable of choice have the right of liberty or freedom from coercion or restraint, and they have the liberty to do any action that is never coercing or restraining or injurious to any other person.[847]

Harts's vision of rights, according to Hollenbach, is that rights are negative in the sense that they are defenses of liberty. This seems an extremely liberal notion of rights. However, the second part of Harts's definition points to an element of rationality and responsibility, implied in the ability to choose. A right is freedom to do what is morally right and necessary, but it should not obligate others nor may it thwart the liberty of others by restraining them. Its expression should not hurt any other human person. This Western vision

---

[845] Ibid, 144. Bujo quotes L. Swidler, *Die Menschenrechte*, 98.

[846] Hollenbach, 14.

[847] Ibid. Hollenbach is quoting H. L. A. Harts, "Are There Any Natural Rights," in Olafson, *Society, Law and Morality*, 173.

suggests why Robert Audi and Nicholas Wolterstorff think that many people have rightly argued that "the very concept of liberal democracy implies restraint"; in other words, "the ethic of the citizen in a liberal democracy incorporates its restriction because the concept of liberal democracy implies this restriction."[848] Such an understanding of human rights does not seem to give an absolute character to human rights. It is within limits of charity, justice, peace, common good, subsidiarity, solidarity, option for the poor, and respect for human dignity. If rights are absolute, for example, the right to private ownership of property, then we must also deny the social nature of human person because it would mean the human person is independent or does not need other persons for whatsoever reason. As long as there is no absolute freedom, there are no absolute rights for one's rights are restricted by another person's rights.

The emphasis on the individual is valid, but it ought to be affirmed with emphasis on community. If *humanness* and *human dignity* are shared by all, a conscious individual always fights to promote and protect the duo. This protection, however, is the responsibility of the individual and community or society. It is the duty of both the individual and society because society facilitates individual efforts and the individual contributes to the efforts of the community. Consequently, society or community and the individual cannot determine or facilitate human rights independently of each other.

Although Bujo does not deny that there are communitarian elements in the Euro-American liberal notion of human rights, he says, "They are always concerned with the individual's self-realization."[849] This may not be read negatively only. It positively affirms individual freedom. However, to some degree, this is where the Western individualist concept of rights and the African communitarian concept conflict with each other. The problem here is that of mutual exaggeration of individuality or communality at the expense of the other and of an individual's relation to community or vice versa. The conflict of rights remains unresolved if such emphasis is not moderated.

Western philosophy of human rights manifests that rights emanate from the needs and the good of the individual. They are based on the command

---

848   Robert Audi and Nicholas Wolterstorff, *Religion in the Public Square: The Role of Religious Convictions in Political Debate* (Lanham: Rowman and Littlefield Publishers Inc., 1997), 151.

849   Ibid.

of reason and human freedom, and they are legally determined through mutual agreements. Rights are liberal exercises of freedom. They are freedom from external "interference of the exercise of one's rights."[850] In this sense, rights are negative, or "they are immunities from interference by others."[851] This suggests that rights always have communal orientation. This is evident, especially where an individual's claims conflict with or obstruct the rights of another individual.[852] Since one person's rights are limited by the rights of another person or other people, rights are not absolute at all. This notion of rights does not deviate from the Roman Catholic vision:

> In the nineteenth century, the Roman Catholic Church clearly rejected the liberal concept of human rights on the grounds that the individual was being elevated to such a position that social cohesion and the common good were being undermined.[853]

A liberal notion of rights would be characterized by absoluteness, but the idea of absolute rights has been refuted in the Western world too. The basic reason for this refutation is the mutual relationship between people. Mary Ann Glendon affirms that an absolute human right is an illusion and a harmful vision of rights. When one claims an absolute or mandatory right, one hurts other people too. Such claims are irrational and do not deserve the name human rights, says Glendon:

> When we assert our rights to life, liberty, and property, we are expressing the reasonable hope that such things can be made more secure by law and politics. When we assert the rights in an absolute form however we are expressing infinite and impossible desires—to be completely free, to possess things totally, to be masters of our fate and captain of our souls.[854]

---

850   Hehir, 8.
851   Hollenbach, 14.
852   Bujo, 149.
853   Falconer, 903.
854   Mary Ann Glendon, "'Absolute' Rights: Property and Privacy," in *The Essential Communitarian Reader*, ed. Amitai Etzioni (Lanham: Rowman and Littlefield Publishers, 1998), 113.

The argument of Glendon has gravity and serious implications. It draws attention to the idea that we are limited and our rights are limited. It suggests that to claim absolute rights is to initiate a conflict of rights. The exercise of rights demands mutual respect and some compromise. The significance of the argument lies in the thought that rights are protections or immunities, and claims demanding responsible action from the side of both the right bearer and those upon whom claims are laid or from whom the respect of rights is demanded. To deny this, according to Glendon, is to shun one's responsibilities, and "the implication is that no one else is affected by the exercise of the individual right in question."[855] This is not possible because rights are exercised in social contexts and have social implications too. It is important to note, as Hollenbach suggests in relation to social justice, that in the Western context, "human rights have a social as well as individual foundation."[856] People make individual claims and do so with the awareness that there are other individuals who constitute society and make similar claims.

B. Communitarian Notion of Rights: The African and the Third World Model

The foundation of the African concept of human rights is the African understanding of the human individual. As stated earlier, according to John S. Mbiti, an African thinks that "the individual can only say: 'I am, because we are; and since we are, therefore I am.'"[857] This African saying emphasizes the value of the individual within the community, not an individual dissociated from community. The importance of community is emphasized not only in a secondary sense but also in a primary sense without disregarding the individual. Both community and the individual are placed on par. This idea is suggested by Mbiti's affirmation that "the individual does not and cannot exist alone except corporately."[858] For Mbiti, and many who interpret him, the individual constitutes just a portion of the entire community because "only in terms of other people does the individual become conscious of his own being, his duties, his privileges and responsibilities toward himself and towards

---

855   Ibid.

856   Hollenbach, 55.

857   John S. Mbiti, *African Religions and Philosophy* (New York: Frederick A. Praeger Publishers, 1969), 108.

858   Ibid.

other people."[859] The African individual and community are complementary and actually mutually inclusive.

However, this notion of the individual does not exclude individual identity. This means individual identity is not lost in the community. While the individual is identified with community, he/she is at the same time distinct from it, asserts Placide Tempels:

> The Bantu cannot be a lone being. It is not a good enough synonym for that to say that he is a social being. No; he feels and knows himself to be a vital force, at this very time to be in intimate and personal relationship with other forces acting above him and below him in the hierarchy of forces. He knows himself to be a vital force, even now influencing some forces and being influenced by others.[860]

The individuality and independence or freedom of a person is evident, according to Tempels, but the conscious individual person is also aware of the influence, on him or her, of other people and the environment in which one lives. Some African authors support this contention. For example, Deusdedit R. K. Nkurunziza is in line with Tempels and thinks that man is an active constituent part of society involved in the promotion of the well-being of other members of society.[861] The individual is not lost in society. In a response to the question, "Does individuality get lost in the African communitarian view of a person?" Bujo explicitly says that "the statement that in Africa the community alone matters and not the individual is hardly right."[862] He argues that the individual is singular, inexchangeable, and responsibly related to the community by solidarity while at the same time retaining his/her identity. The argument that the individual does not get lost in the community in the African communitarian view of person is consistent. It is also supported by the fact that in the African context each person is responsible for his/her actions and punishments are administered according to responsibility for actions.

---

[859] Ibid.

[860] Placide Tempels, *Bantu Philosophy* (Paris: Presence Africaine, 1959), 68-69.

[861] Deusdedit R. K. Nkrunziza, *Bantu Philosophy of Life in the Light of the Christian Message: A Basis for an African Vitalistic Theology* (Frankfurt am Main: Peter Lang, 1989), 183-184.

[862] Bujo, 147.

The second factor that individuates the African person is name. Authors like Tempels and Bujo argue to this effect. Temples argues that besides the physical appearance of an individual, the name is an outstanding factor of individuation, "the name is not just a simple external courtesy, it is the very reality of the individual" because "the name expresses the individual character of the being."[863] According to Bujo, the concept of names is what typically points toward the difference between the Western and African notions of an individual. He argues that in African context

> There are no family names, in the Western sense, which are transmitted from father to son. Every child has its own name, depending on the circumstances of birth. The name of the individual characterizes him/her as a historical being, in its uniqueness.[864]

Bujo's contention suggests that there is an individuation of the human person in African society. A person is different from the community. Bujo's contention also amounts to the idea that there is something communitarian in the Western world, expressed here in terms of names because if one name is passed from parents to children, there must be something that binds their lineage too. The issue at stake is that the communitarian element in the Western world is emphasized in the concept of names but not as much in their concept of rights of the individual in relation to society. This is the paradox of theory and practice, which is outside the scope of this work but requires further investigation.

The foregoing paragraphs suggest the following conclusions as affirmed by Uzukwu and Bujo: First, in African social and theological anthropology, individual freedom is recognized as such; an individual remains free within society. According to Uzukwu E. Elochukwu,

> The autonomy and right of the individual subject are enjoyed in relationship in communion. Indeed the "freedom" of the individual is "for" the construction of a better community . . . . It is not principally understood in terms of "freedom from" an oppressive society.[865]

---

863 Tempels, 70 and 74.
864 Bujo, 147.
865 Uzukwu E. Elochukwu, *A Listening Church: Autonomy and Communion in African Churches* (Maryknoll, New York: Orbis Books, 1996), 44.

The positive element in Uzukwu's assertion is that freedom is considered as a virtue in the sense that it is a disposition of the human person to do good for herself/himself and for others. The *common good* is in view in the exercise of freedom. This suggests that African societies advocate responsible freedom.

Second, the African concept of human rights is based on the African understanding of the individual in the context of society. This is because relationship is "not simply a way of living in which the subject must realize itself," but "it is the essential element of personhood. One is human because of others, with others, and for others."[866] This is what earns the African notion of human rights the description communitarian concept of rights. The African sees individuals' rights in a relation of mutual interaction. They can at most be mandated or confirmed in a community context. Therefore, it is appropriate to describe the African notion of human rights as the *African social concept of human rights*. This assertion is explained by the authentic communitarian vision that rights are never absolute individual claims. This vision supports the assertion that in a communitarian vision of the human person "the conception of what is right and how society should be organized always presuppose some vision of the common good. In this respect, the good presupposes the right."[867] This suggests that the common good makes the individual impose claims on others, but it also obliges the person claiming rights to accept similar or the same claims from others for their own good.

Third, human rights are founded in the community without disregarding the individual although the emphasis seems to be more on community than the individual interests or claims. Bujo affirms this view by claiming that "human rights here do not emanate from the individual but are extended from community to the individual."[868] Bujo's argument is grounded on the idea that in the African context, "only within the lineage, that is the kinship, can one be a human being," without forgetting human dignity and right because "to be human is something that has to be learned right from childhood together with others."[869] This assertion suggests why the African notion of human rights seems not to allow deviation, heroism, and the individual's overwhelming influence on society.[870] The problem with such a vision of

---

[866]   Ibid., 37.

[867]   Fergusson, 139.

[868]   Bujo, 151.

[869]   Ibid.

[870]   Legesse, 125.

rights is the limitation of individual freedom. It is the crux of the African understanding of human rights and a point where it seems to deviate radically from the Western notion of human rights.

C. The Universality and Equality of Rights

The primary concern of this section is to attempt to show that human rights are universal and relative. It is generally acknowledged that human rights are claims persons have on other people on account of being human. This acknowledgment shows the mutual character of rights and points to the idea of the universality of human rights, and it suggests that human rights are not absolute.

The universality of human rights is affirmed on the basis of the common origin, nature, and dignity of people. The affirmation of the universality of human dignity also suggests the universality of human rights. The basic argument for the universality of human rights is that God created people in his image and likeness as is explicit in Genesis 1:27-28. Many scholars hold this position. Joseph Massaro expresses the idea as follows:

> Every human being is a person; that is, his nature is endowed with intelligence and free will. Indeed, precisely because he is a person he has rights and obligations flowing directly and simultaneously from his very nature. And as these rights and obligations are universal and inviolable, so they cannot in any way be surrendered.[871]

On the basis that people have the same nature originating from the same source, every human being has rights prompted by this universal nature, and these rights are the same everywhere. This argument does not, however, suggest that people have the same rights everywhere, but it suggests that certain rights (human rights) are commonly shared and so are universal. The assertion also suggests that rights are sometimes *relatively absolute* as long as they are founded on human nature. For instance, the right to life of an innocent person is always to be respected everywhere and by all people. I would like to suggest here that the right to life is a *relative, absolute* right. As long as one maintains innocence, the right to life is absolute; but in the event that innocence ceases, the right to life ceases to be absolute—it becomes a

---

[871] Massaro, 14. Massaro is quoting John XXII, *Pacem in Terris*, paragraph 9.

relative right. The quality of inviolability or inalienability of human dignity makes the right to life relatively absolute. Thompson speaks to this point by affirming that human rights are claims made on the basis of human nature and so are equal, universal, and cannot be taken away from people or be surrendered by people:

> Human rights are rights that one has simply because one is human. Such rights are held equally by all humans, and they are inalienable. Human rights are rooted, then, in a theory of human nature.[872]

The idea of the equality and universality of human rights is, however, controversial. People like McIntyre reject the idea of the universality of human rights and even the idea of human rights per se. Such contention or denial suggests a vision of rights as a laissez-faire exercise of human freedom. Williams states that according to McIntyre,

> to speak of "rights of man" is to speak of a presumably universal phenomenon. Yet whereas needs and wants are universally experienced and thus universally intelligible, rights claims presuppose social and ethical structures that are not universal.[873]

The principal claim of McIntyre seems to be that human rights depend on local social structures and institutions. It is true that some rights depend on established local social institutions and structures. Some civil rights, for instance, fall into this category. A distinction ought to be made between human rights and civil rights. Civil rights are entitlements of a person by virtue of being a citizen. These would vary because of differences in institutional and legal structures, and not necessarily be universal. Human rights are claims people have on other people by virtue of being human. These are rooted in human nature and so are universal. The denial of universality of human rights is a denial of the universality of human nature. This does not, however, exclude the existence of universal human rights, for example, the innocent person's right to life. Whether by religious people or unbelievers, civilized or uncivilized people, the right to life and other related rights such as the right to food and decent living are often treasured.

---

[872] Milburn, 4. Also see Burns, 17.

[873] Williams, 55.

The universality of human rights was affirmed by John XXIII because human dignity is universal, and all people are created by God in the divine image, and they deserve the reverence that is due to God because "human nature" is a partial reflection of "divine nature."[874] This assertion grounds the universality of rights because human rights are based on human dignity, which originates from God. If human dignity and human nature and their universality are affirmed, the same affirmation should be granted to the possibility of the affirmation of at least some human rights. Conversely, the denial of the reality and universality of human nature, dignity, and rights should be predicated of human nature, human dignity, and human rights.

The study of human rights in this section is typified by Williams's vision of rights. Williams outlines characteristics of human rights as follows: First, "a right is something one has" in the sense that it is the power to make claims on others, meaning that it is distinct from its bearer but "within his ownership or jurisdiction."[875] Second, a right is "a transitive term: always a right to something."[876] This means a right is a claim to do or to have something or a demand for protection against something or action. Third, a right is not a tangible thing; it is "a moral power or capacity or in more classical language, a *faculty.*"[877] And as such, it is a stable quality to do or to claim or to have something. Fourth, Williams suggests that as a moral quality, a right is important because it determines the quality or type of claims one lays upon others. In other words, rights are not needless burdens laid upon other people or unrealistic demands from others. The importance of this understanding of rights is evident in the pragmatic characteristics of human rights. Finally, human rights "describe a reciprocal relationship," meaning that "an assertion of right is other-directed and therefore passes from the sphere of personal morality to the juridical sphere."[878] Any claim on others invokes the reciprocal acceptance of the same claim from others. It invokes corresponding duties, obligations, and responsibilities on the part of the rights' claimant. This shows how rights are necessary for ordering people's relationships in society.

---

[874] Milburn, 88. Also see Massaro, 147. Also cfr. Massaro, 7.

[875] Williams, 4-5.

[876] Ibid., 5.

[877] Ibid., 5-6.

[878] Ibid., 7.

V. The Anthropology of *Populorum Progressio*

The principal concern of Paul VI in *Populorum Progressio* was the human person, particularly the development of the human person. This too is the central concern of the Catholic social doctrines. Since the promotion and the good of the human person is the center of attention in both cases, it is relevant to suggest that a Christian anthropology is necessary for the promotion of the human person and, in particular, for Paul VI's advocacy for integral human development. Paul VI never explicitly defined the human person or undertook a categorical anthropological study for this purpose. However, in many ways, he mentioned, implied, and dealt with traits that define the human person. The intention of this section is to explicate areas of the anthropology of *Populorum Progressio* necessary for integral human development.

A. The Human Person

Paul VI touched upon issues like human freedom and the creation of the human person in the divine image. The freedom of a human person, which can also be properly called a right, is what partly determines a person as an individual. It also constitutes a defining element of the dignity of a person in terms of valuing the nature of the human individual as free and divinely endowed. Paul VI made the important assertion that

> man is a man only in so far as being the master of his own actions and the judge of their importance, he himself is the architect of his progress and this must be in keeping with his nature which the Creator gave him and the possibilities and demands of which he freely assumes.[879]

Autonomy or freedom—the ability to judge and to act responsibly—defines the human person. Paul VI did not veer from the views of other theological anthropologists who define the human person in terms of intellect and responsibility. A responsible action is first an intellectual activity because it involves judgment. Neither was Paul VI different from Kant who emphasized autonomy as a defining characteristic of a human being. He was in line with

---

[879] *Populorum Progressio*, 34, 15.

traditional Catholic creation theology founded on Genesis 1:26-28, which grants the human person dominion over the rest of creation.

The free nature of the human person facilitates people's ability to interact with their environment, particularly, fellow human beings. Consequently, the human person is, in part, defined in terms of other humans because the person is a social being and belongs to society and family, which defines an individual. Paul VI advocated that persons should be defined and define themselves individually because an exclusively social definition of the human person, typical of "ancient social institutions" of the "developing regions,"[880] impairs the basic human rights. He mentioned the individual's right to marry and to procreate. Paul VI suggested that the individual person should be recognized as a distinct entity and always as such even if he/she lives in and is a part of society. He cited social structures such as the institution of the family in the developing nations as an example.[881] Such rights as to form family should be protected. Paul VI advocated that old social and institutional definitions and arrangements are necessary only temporarily.

According to Paul VI, "excessive force" from ancient social institutions in developing regions "must gradually be diminished."[882] Though Paul VI was not explicit, his contention suggests that he was opposed to an exaggerated community ethos, which would cause the individual to disappear or be a negligible component of human society. He advocated that the exercise of individual freedom must be permitted. This means that the identity of the individual must be intact, yet the individual should be seen as part of the human family, dependent on it for personal fulfillment. He advocated for family ties that define initial human identity and forge unity, mutual assistance leading to acquisition of wisdom, and harmony in personal rights. However, he further argued that social family values are instrumental for humane living. Family is fundamental and the first enriching school, and together "with other social requirements constitutes the foundation of society."[883] True solidarity starts in the family. This implies that solidarity based on family relations has positive effects. It leads to harmony and a better understanding of the human person, rights, and relationships and builds a solid community. This assertion is realistic for four reasons. First, it suggests that human dignity is

---

[880] Ibid., 36,16.

[881] Ibid., 37,16.

[882] Ibid., 36,16.

[883] *Gaudium et Spes*, 52, 956. Also see *Populorum Progressio*, 36, 16.

universal and equal in all people. Second, as a consequence of the assertion, the human person and human rights can be recognized as having universal value. Third, it facilitates unity and mutual respect for human dignity and human rights. Finally, it suggests a typically communitarian element of the notion of the human person, dignity, and rights.

The above discussions also suggest the following conclusions: First, Paul VI's vision of the human person incorporates both the communitarian and liberal notions of the human person. This assertion is confirmed by his vision of human rights, especially the right to private ownership of property. He affirmed that the individual has the right to own private property, but this is not an absolute right in the face of ardent need. When there are people or individuals in dire need, one should relinquish the right to private ownership in order to save or promote the right to life. The individual's right to private ownership of property is subordinate to the demands of the common good or the needs of the community or its members, especially in moments of ardent need. Second, Paul VI defined the human person as an individual endowed with qualities such as intellect and freedom or autonomy, which are exercised within the context of fellow humans and the rest of creation. Finally, like other philosophical and theological anthropologists, he asserted that a human person is not a thing and is different from the rest of creation, which is meant to serve human needs.

B. Human Dignity in *Populorum Progressio*

The persisting principal concern of Catholic social teaching is the human person and the promotion of the dignity of the person.[884] Similarly, the epicenter of the teaching of *Populorum Progressio* is the *dignity of the human person* based on the fundamental principle of *imago Dei*, meaning that all people are created in the image of God. *Imago Dei* is the principle on which human dignity and human rights and all other principles of humane living and relationship are grounded. It is also the principle of universality and equality. All human beings are made in God's image. They have a value different from that of other creatures by virtue of their unique relationship

---

[884] Peter J. Riga, *The Church of the Poor: A Commentary on Paul VI's Encyclical on the Development of Peoples* (Techny, Illinois: Divine Word Publications, 1968), 29. This view is accepted the by a majority of scholars of Catholic social doctrine.

with God, and they cooperate with God and participate in God's governing and creative activity in the world.[885]

Paul VI did not categorically state that human dignity is the foundational principle for authentic development, but it was the reason for his advocacy for integral human development. He was motivated to take a stance for integral human development because there is "an integral equality of dignity enjoyed by every human being."[886] However, Paul VI presumed that the centrality of human dignity and human rights were already acknowledged as such and emphasized enough. His approach to the issue of integral human development suggests that the dignity and rights of the human person were already understood by all as basic for human development. Consequently, he tended to weaken the stance that human dignity is fundamental because all human beings are created in the image of God and participate in divine qualities and dignity. This principle runs throughout the entire Catholic social teaching because it is the reason for the institution of the church.[887]

The church has a duty to defend and protect this dignity and is always concerned about the dignity of all people who constitute society. The evidence of the centrality of human dignity in modern Catholic social teaching is *Gaudium et Spes*, which provides the core of the thesis that human dignity is the foundational principle for true development. According to Peter Henriot, the document confirms this in its statement that "the human person is the source, the center and the purpose of all socioeconomic life."[888] All development efforts are motivated by this fact, and they are directed to the human person. When they fall short, they are not efforts toward authentic development.

---

[885] Karl Rahner and Hebert Vorgrimler, *Theological Dictionary*, ed.Cornelius Ernst, trans. Richard Strachan (New York: Herder and Herder, 1968), 222. Also see Gen.1: 26ff, James T. Bretzke, *Consecrated Phrases: A Latin Theological Dictionary*, 2nd ed. (Collegeville, Minnesota: The Liturgical Press, 2003), 61. Also see O'Collins and Farrugia, 114. Also see Riga, 31.

[886] Samuel Gregg, *Economic Thinking for the Theologically Minded* (New York: Lanham, 2001), 4.

[887] Peter J. Henriot, "Who Cares about Africa? Development Guidelines from the Church's Social Teaching," in *Catholic Social Thought and the New World Order*, eds. Oliver F. Williams and John W. Houck (Notre Dame: Notre Dame University Press, 1993), 216.

[888] Ibid., 211. Also see *Gaudium et Spes*, 63, 968-969.

Human dignity and human rights are at the center of the human person, and this is why human dignity is the overriding principle for integral human development.[889] All development initiatives should attempt to address the problem of degradation and abuse of the human person, human dignity, and human rights. It should be stated here that human dignity is also central to the question of integral human development because it is an *invariable principle*. It is immutable not just because it is equal in all people by virtue of being *imago Dei*, but also because it does not depend on any variable factors such as economic status, political status, social status, religion, or age.[890] Human dignity is not determined or defined by any of these variable factors. The whole of paragraph six of *Populorum Progressio* is devoted to the question of the dignity of the human person, which should be recognized in endeavors towards development.[891]

Like many other proponents of the central position of the human person and dignity in development issues, for Paul VI, human aspiration must first try to protect human dignity.[892] This is why people seek and do what they advocate. The quest for food, cure for diseases, the search for employment, personal responsibility, security and protection from oppression, desire for education, private ownership, socioeconomic progress worthy of humans and enhancement of human values, and freedom from any threat to human dignity; all of these contribute to protection or defense or enhancement of human dignity. They are genuine human aspirations, which people desire to achieve by their own power through the available resources. The problem is that many people live in conditions that frustrate these natural, human, and genuine desires.[893] In *Populorum Progressio*, Paul VI expressed his deepest concerns for human dignity and demonstrated the invaluable character of human dignity.

When newly independent or less-developed nations overcome frustrating conditions and gain their legitimate human enhancement, they can become part of the international struggle for true human development. Here, Paul VI emphasized human dignity, the human person, and human rights. They

---

[889] Filochowski, 63.

[890] Gregg, 4.

[891] David J. O'Brien and Thomas A. Shannon, eds., *Catholic Social Thought: The Documentary Heritage* (Maryknoll, New York: Orbis Books, 2001), 238.

[892] Henriot, 216.

[893] *Populorum Progressio*, 6, 3-4.

are strongly invoked and advocated as reasons for every effort favorable to development.

Since human dignity is at the center of the human person, it is unjust to deprive a person of any opportunities that enhance human dignity. Human dignity is enhanced by work because work is dignified. Work has dignity because it is a divine design, mandated by God's command to our first parents to fill the earth and subdue it. The Pontifical Commission for Justice and Peace affirms that "even though these words do not refer directly and explicitly to work, beyond doubt they indicate it as activity for man to carry out in the world."[894] Work is a duty of all who are capable of work. When people capable of work are deprived of this duty or shun this duty, their dignity is depraved/corrupted, and this is an injustice. Oftentimes, this injustice is detestable because it affects the very being of people.

Paul VI was aware of the invaluable significance of human dignity:

> For when entire populations, deprived of necessities of life, are so subjected to the domination of others that they are denied any self initiated activity, responsibility, attainment of higher culture, and participation in social and public life, men are easily tempted to remove by force the injustice done to human dignity.[895]

When the core dimension of a person is attacked, there is the inevitable reaction in self-assertion by fighting back in self-defense. Here, Paul VI addressed the question of the significance of people's self-determination expressed in self-fulfillment. Individual and social self-determination and assertion or private and public self-determination and assertion of a person is an indication of the need to protect and enhance human dignity. One way of asserting oneself is work. Paul VI meant that human dignity is enhanced by human involvement and participation in work. He was also suggesting, like other theological anthropologists, that the human person should also be defined in terms of responsibility expressed through dominion over the rest of creation other than human persons and God. Denying a person such

---

[894]   Robert Sirico, A and Zieba Maciej, *The Social Agenda: A Collection of Magisterial Texts* (Citta del Vaticano: Pontifical Council for Justice and Peace, 2000), 133. Also see John Paul II, *Laborem Exercens: On Human Work* (Washington DC: United States Catholic Conference, 1981) 4, 11-13.

[895]   *Populorum Progressio*, 30, 13.

an opportunity means tampering with a very basic principle and reason for efforts toward human development. Human dignity, which *is* (exists) because the human person, is created *imago Dei* is attacked. This assertion is credible because if the human person is created in God's image and does not contribute to and participate in work (s)he does not cooperate with God in God's creative activities. This deprivation is an injustice because the human person is emptied of the core of human existence, and human dignity is devoid of its meaning and credibility. It is because of such offenses against human dignity that forceful uprisings are often inevitable.

Paul VI was concerned that the population explosion could adversely affect human dignity because

> accelerated demographic increases too frequently add difficulties to plan for development because population is increased more rapidly than available resources so that all solutions seem to end in a blind alley.[896]

If population growth outpaces the development of available resources, it is either too hard to meet the material needs of people or their needs may be addressed inadequately. This militates against human dignity, and its consequence is the temptation to attempt to address the shortage of material supply by drastically limiting population growth using methods that disregard human dignity and the value of the human person. This would mean the possibility of violation of human dignity and human rights. It explains why, according to Paul VI, wild demographic growth is problematic to authentic development.

Social actions that rest on the philosophy of materialism and atheism are detestable from a Christian point of view especially if they have "no regard either for the religious outlook directing life to its eternal and final goal, or for freedom, or for human dignity."[897] The sole reason behind Paul VI's assertion is that social organizations are established to serve people and to liberate them from desperate circumstances of life. Social organizations should work for the enhancement of the human person and dignity.

The purpose of natural resources is also the enhancement of the human person and human dignity. Individually, nations must work to improve their

---

[896]   Ibid., 37,16.
[897]   Ibid., 39,17.

production both quantitatively and qualitatively "to give the life of all their citizens truly human dignity and give assistance to the common development of the human race."[898] Paul VI advocated that national products must meet the needs of both the nationals and nonnationals whose life and dignity need to be promoted. Private ownership must give way and be rendered powerless when there is excess after meeting the needs of the nationals. National private ownership of property including technology and expertise is not an absolute right according to Paul VI. Consequently, he suggested that affluent countries should train teachers, engineers, technicians, and scholars to serve the less-developed people with their knowledge and skill.[899] Paul VI linked ownership of private property, including professional skills and talents, to human dignity. The right to private ownership of property is forfeited in the face of need, precisely, for the sake of promoting or protecting human dignity.

According to Paul VI, the work of experts who move to countries other than their own should enhance human dignity. This suggests that the work of both expatriate and domestic experts should help change human conditions and improve the quality of life of people. Their work should preserve, promote, and protect human dignity. This too is the reason for the practice of charity and hospitality. It seems right to accept Henriot's thesis that "integral human development requires respect for all human rights and is itself a human right"[900] because development is a natural aspiration of all, and so it constitutes a right. The logic of this assertion is that human rights are based on the dignity of the human person, and this aspiration is directed toward the promotion of human dignity.

Human person, human dignity, and human rights are the enduring principles for authentic human development. These are the consistent and recurrent principles of Catholic social teaching. Human dignity in particular is central to any teaching related to authentic human development. International conferences including the International Conference on Population and Development (ICPD) of 1994 have given priority to people over markets and emphasized equality of people's rights.[901]

---

[898]   Ibid., 48, 20.

[899]   Riga, 121. Also see *Populorum Progressio*, 48, 21.

[900]   Henriot, 216.

[901]   *The Rome Statement on the International Conference on Population and Development (ICPD)* (Religion Counts, January 1999), 4.

C. Human Rights in *Populorum Progressio*

Human dignity and human rights are intimately related because human rights are based on human dignity; they are affirmations of the existence and recognition of human dignity. It must be added that human rights are also protections for human dignity.[902] The assertion here is that there is a mutual exchange between human rights and human dignity. Human dignity is recognized and respected if human freedom and self-determination are inviolate.

Populorum Progressio did not treat human rights in depth the way its predecessor document *Pacem in Terris* did, but Paul VI did not overlook human rights. In fact, his treatise on human dignity, the common good, subsidiarity, participation, association, and justice are a treatise of human rights. However, his treatise on human rights was more focused and emphatic on the right to ownership of property. In treating this right, there are actually two contending rights—the right to free access to use resources of nature and the individual's right to own property.

According to Peter Riga, in the thought of Paul VI, the right to ownership of property is subordinated to the right of the usage of the fruits of one's talents and the protection of health, suggesting that conservation of life comes before the right of property.[903] Paul VI does not object to the right to own property. He objected to the absolute claim for the right and emphasized the limited nature of the right to use property; and the obligation to share with those who lack the means of livelihood because the resources of nature are destined for the good of all people. Paul VI's affirmation of the universal destiny of natural resources, with his predecessors, sets limits to the right of private ownership of property and the exclusive use of property.[904] He consistently emphasized that the right of ownership of property was limited by other virtues, conditions, and principles necessary for human growth, including the principle of the common good.[905]

Apart from property rights, Paul VI affirmed other rights such as the right to free trade, the right to life, and the right to have a family, but he subordinated

---

[902] Gregg, 4.

[903] Riga, 91.

[904] *Populorum Progressio*, 22, 10.

[905] Ibid., 23,11.

all to the universal destiny of goods of nature. Consequently, with regard to ownership of property, he insisted that "the absolute right of private property is a grave aberration."[906] Absolute ownership violates the real meaning of the the right to private ownership of private property. Paul VI treated the right to life, the right of families, "the rightful freedom of married people," and "the most inalienable rights of matrimony and procreation," which Paul VI thought if taken away means the destruction of human dignity.[907] Paul VI did not elaborate these affirmations enough, but his reference to procreation draws attention to the divine plan and the means through which human persons manifest the image of God and also promote human life and society. In stating that parents have the right to determine the number of children they wish to have, he advocated that parents' human rights go with responsibility to the community and their children. Therefore, exercise of rights should be in a responsible fashion because they have corresponding duties, and they should promote human dignity and the human person.[908]

Paul VI advocated the right to development of the less-developed peoples and the right to development of all peoples as the theme of the encyclical suggests.[909] This view reflects not only Paul VI's mind. It was also what the drafters of the Universal Declaration of Human Rights stated and referred to as "full development on the part of individual."[910] The evidence that this was what he advocated is to be understood in the light of the entirety of *Populorum Progressio*. The whole document focused on the issue of true or complete human development. In terms of rights, its gravity is on the question of the right of everybody and all people to develop.

Riga's reading of Paul VI, which I think is correct, suggests that the right to development is globally to be promoted through international relationships.[911] The explanation for this affirmation is the social nature of the human person and practical life which demands interaction with others. This affirmation calls for international collaboration, associations, and participation in human development. It also demands world unity and government which promotes

---

[906] Riga, 91.

[907] *Populorum Progressio*, 37, 16.

[908] Riga, 109.

[909] *Populorum Progressio*, 64, 27.

[910] Johannes Morsink, 210.

[911] Riga, 133.

"the rights and dignity of the human person,"[912] a body Paul VI strongly suggests and evinces in his support for the United Nations.

Paul VI's advocacy for development of the peoples sums up his treatise on human rights. The right to property is the most extensively treated individual human right in *Populorum Progressio*. However, the issues he addressed in the whole document are rights-related because he addressed threats to human dignity, which is the foundation for human rights. For instance, there is no doubt that when he addressed the injustices of the time, he was at the same time suggesting that those who were being treated unjustly had a right to fair treatment.

At the beginning of this chapter, I made an allusion to Robert Royal's claim that Paul VI failed to articulate true development in light of the church's views of the human person.[913] In fairness to *Populorum Progressio*, it is questionable whether a critique of failure of application of Christian anthropology is well grounded because *Populorum Progressio* dealt with concerns about people. Paul VI never devoted a section of the encyclical to anthropology necessary for understanding integral human development. He was not making an anthropological treatise per se. However, his treatise of development was in light of the Christian understanding of the human person. His principal concern was the development of peoples and the reasons for lack of integral development of peoples and the requisite principles, virtues, and conditions for integral human development, although an explicit anthropology would have facilitated his articulation of the question of development. However, anthropology features in his espousing of the requisite principles, virtues, and conditions for integral human development as outlined in the document.

VI. Reconciliation of Notions: The Need for an Inclusive Vision

A. Impediments to Reconciliation of the Concepts

A number of factors stand in the way of reconciliation between Western individualist concepts of the human person, human dignity, and human rights, and African communitarian notions. This section outlines some conspicuous

---

[912] Ibid., 135.

[913] See footnote number 1 of this chapter.

obstacles to the process of dialogue between liberal and communitarian anthropologies.

In the first place, dialogue is facilitated by language because it is a real communication medium and exercise. One of the difficulties in the dialogue between liberal Western anthropology and communitarian third-world anthropology, particularly regarding the notion of human rights, is the language for communication. According to Asmarom Legesse, the main problem is that "different societies formulate their conception of human rights in diverse cultural idioms."[914] Practically, this makes the articulation of the concept of rights problematic. The need to develop a better and inclusive language is real. This need is suggested by the shared human nature. Human beings are "by nature dialogical creatures."[915] Persons have the ability for mutual exchange of views, and because of this ability, they can arrive at a consensus. The medium of this mutual exchange is speech. Speech itself is "essentially other oriented."[916] It facilitates this mutual exchange of views through language. A mutually intelligible language for articulating the notion of human rights is necessary.

Second, there is the problem of a distinct individual as opposed to other individuals or society/community. In this line communitarian, critics of liberalism think that the latter needs community only for self-security.[917] Uzukwu succinctly states this idea:

> While the African social definition of a person displays the human person as subsistent relationship—in other words, the person as fundamentally "being with" and "belonging to"—Western philosophy lays emphasis on the absolute originality and concreteness of the human person, a "being-for-itself" . . . . However, Western

---

[914] Legesse Asmarom, "Human Rights in African Political Culture," in *The Moral Imperatives of Human Rights: A World Survey,* ed. Kenneth W. Thompson (Washington DC: University Press of America, 1980), 124.

[915] Gregory Baum, *Essays in Critical Theology* (Missouri, Kansas City: Sheed and Ward, 1994), 19.

[916] Ibid.

[917] Michael Walzer, "The Communitarian Critique of Liberalism," in *Political Theory: An International Journal of Political Philosophy,* vol.18, no.1, eds. Tracy B. Strong et al. (Newbury Park, California: Sage Publications, Inc., February 1990), 8.

systems wish to guard against the dissolution of the person in relationship. The "I" is already constituted before it ever chooses to be related. The autonomy and the incommunicability of the "I" are fundamental.[918]

Uzukwu is addressing the question of a radical separation between the individual and community. The problem here is the one of the notion of the human person. He suggests that it is the problem of resolving the "I-you," "I-they," and "we-they" relationships and differences. If this is true, it is a real problem in the attempt to reconcile the individualist West and the communitarian African visions of rights, person, and human dignity. It is also a problem manifested in cooperative action, especially in pluralistic contexts. In light of Uzukwu's assertion about the Western vision of a person as not emphatically related to others, it would be questionable how rights could exist in the West if rights are claims persons have on other people. This in itself is enough to suggest that the individual is not really exclusively autonomous. One would even wonder how organizations or associations that are characteristic of the west as opposed to the communitarian Africa could exist without people relating to and defining themselves in relation to other people. However, Uzukwu recognizes the interaction between the individual and community in the Western context. This idea is suggested by his assertion that right from medieval times, Western philosophy—phenomenology and existentialism—recognized the importance of relationship for self-realization of the individual.[919] The issue raised by Uzukwu is only the issue of emphasis on community and the individual independently of each other.

Josef Fuchs acknowledges this difficulty:

> The "I" and the Others are personal individuals and not simply identical, with the exception of personal dignity in which we are all equal. But the human concreteness in which personal dignity is incarnate is not the same in different human beings, even if the dignity itself is the same for all: this concrete difference is the source of difficulty.[920]

---

[918] Uzukwu, 42-43.

[919] Ibid., 43.

[920] Brien McNeil, *Moral Demands and Personal Obligations*, Josef Fuchs, trans. (Washington DC: Georgetown University Press, 1993), 2-3.

The assertion that individuals are different should be acknowledged. It impacts their existential relations and claims on one another. Similarly, Mark G. Kuzewski is of the idea that "the main problem is liberalism's voluntaristic notion of a person."[921] Such a notion of person creates a plurality of nationalities, personalities, and interests with a consequent rift between one individual and another or other groups of individuals. To argue for a commonly shared concept of human dignity and human rights on such basis is problematic. Consequently, a common denominator for understanding rights and human person is called for here. A foundation that unites, modifies, and facilitates relations between individuals is needed.

The third problem, closely related to the second, is the one of the concept of *the self*. Liberal individualism and communitarianism look at the self differently. Walzer's contention suggests this. According to him, communitarian critics of liberalism think that

> Liberalism . . . is founded on the idea of a presocial self, a solitary and sometimes heroic individual confronting society, who is fully formed before the confrontation begins . . . . The critics are commonly said to believe in a radically socialized self that can never 'confront' society because it is from the beginning, entangled in society, itself the embodiment of social values.[922]

The assertion here is that for liberals the individual comes before society or community because society is constituted by individuals while communitarians contest such assertion. The issue here is whether the self is predetermined or at least shaped by society or developed in community. The appropriate response is an affirmation of the latter—the individual is shaped or influenced by the community although the community is affected by the life of the individual. The liberal tradition of the human person and rights recognizes this but emphasizes that the individual comes before society, which is right, while the communitarian vision tends to emphasize community more than the individual. This suggests why Western individualist notions of human person and human rights and African communitarian concepts are contending notions though not mutually exclusive.

---

[921] Mark G. Kuzewski, *Fragmentation and Consensus* (Washington DC: Georgetown University Press, 1997), 51ff.

[922] Walzer, 20-21.

The fourth impediment to reconciliation of Western and African concepts of human rights is the difference in the conception of the notion of human freedom. Bujo claims that according to Kant,

> freedom is the sole, original right, to which every human being is entitled on the basis of humanity itself, as long as freedom can exist together with every other freedom in accordance with a general law.[923]

Freedom is part of Kant's categorical imperative that ought to be respected. This seems to be why in the Western context freedom is often conceived as "freedom from interference of the exercise of one's rights"[924] or freedom from oppressive systems. It is freedom as liberation. On the other hand, in the African conception, freedom is viewed as freedom for promoting community. The major difference and problem is the West's laissez-faire notion of freedom as opposed to the conservative African notion of freedom which is limited by society.

The last significant problem in the dialogue between notions of person and rights is that of degrees of values so that "when forced to choose between basic values, societies rank them differently."[925] This problem is present in the ways the Western world and Africans or the third world in general look at the individual and community, value them, and outline the nature of the human person and human rights. The difference in visions is also manifest in what the two traditions want to protect, what their needs are, and the circumstances in which individuals and communities find themselves, economically, socially, and politically. A few problematic enduring questions are inevitable here: Is there any culture that can claim superiority for its values? On what grounds can such claims be made? Finally, are hierarchies of values important in the dialogue about human person, human dignity, and human rights?[926] These questions invoke further elucidation about the place and significance of hierarchy of values in anthropology. They will not be investigated here, but they stimulate further reflections on the issue of human person, human dignity, and human rights.

---

[923] Bujo, 144-145.

[924] Hehir, 8. Also see Uzukwu, 41.

[925] Asmarom, 124.

[926] The provisional answer to these questions is no. To give a definitive answer, a thorough investigation is necessary.

From the foregoing discussion, there are three areas of differences between the Euro-American vision and the African communitarian visions of person and rights. First, there is difference in the *starting point* of the notion of rights or the human person. While the Western notion starts with individual freedom, the African communitarian notion starts with the community. Second, there is difference in *emphasis* on the individual and community. While the Western liberal vision emphasizes the individual more than the community, the African communitarian notion emphasizes the community more than the individual. Third, there is difference in *limitation* of the individual or community. While in the Western context the individual tends to limit community, in the African communitarian view, the community tends to limit the individual. These issues and similar problems further raise the question as to whether the notions of the human person, human dignity, and human rights from the Euro-American and African communitarian points of view can be reconciled. The next section of this work tries to show how and how far some of these difficulties can be resolved. It attempts to show the mutually inclusive aspects of Western-liberal and African-communitarian concepts. The mediating factor is the Roman Catholic understanding of the human person and human rights.

B. Reconciling Notions: The Roman Catholic Tradition

Even if there are some differences between the liberal and communitarian anthropologies, they can be reconciled. Their reconciliation is a necessary factor for the attainment of integral human development. In the attempt to resolve the conflicts between the Euro-American liberal notion and the African communitarian anthropological concepts, Roman Catholic tradition is necessary for mediation. A number of observations are, however, necessary at the outset.

First, the Roman Catholic Church acknowledges that human dignity and human rights exist, and they initially originate from God. Second, the church looks at herself as a community of the people of God consisting of individual persons. These two statements suggest the conviction in the Roman Catholic tradition about the import of both the individual and community. From the Roman Catholic point of view, the possibility of the reconciliation of the Western individualist and the African communitarian concepts of rights lies in the proper understanding of the individual, the community, their origins, and mutual interaction. Other arguments revolve around this conviction. Third, the attempt to reconcile the two notions of rights is based on the consistent modern Roman Catholic tradition often "dominated by one basic theme—an unshakeable affirmation and vigorous defense of the dignity and rights of the human person."[927] David Hollenbach's remarks about the Catholic tradition are significant for acknowledging its mediating role, especially in Catholic human rights tradition:

> Catholic rights theory is far removed from individualist or libertarian social philosophy. The theory presented in the encyclicals is "personalist", not individualist, and it recognizes that persons are essentially social and institution building beings.[928]

This statement supports the social and political thoughts of Aristotle, later developed by Aquinas, one of the principal architects of Catholic theology based on philosophical principles or categories. According to Aquinas, the sociopolitical orientation of a person is natural, but it does not exclude the individuality of a person. The Roman Catholic tradition precisely emphasizes both the individual and society. The moral injunction provided by the personalist vision of the human person is close to, if not like, the Kantian categorical imperative forbidding the use of the human person as a means to an end, but it has also the "positive content (Thou shalt love!)," not only the "negative content (Thou shalt not use)."[929] It differs from other theories of human rights by its balanced emphasis on both the individual and the social dimension of the human person and its introduction of human dignity, originating from God, into the human rights arguments.

The two visions of human rights can be reconciled. The attempt to reconcile the liberal and communitarian concepts of rights is treated under five subthemes: human dignity based on the principle of *imago Dei*, which is the greatest concern of the Catholic documents, the question of the individual versus community, the concept of freedom, the problem of language, and the diversity of values.

1. Human Dignity: The Fundamental Solution

Human dignity is the most important principle in the Roman Catholic human rights arguments. Its importance lies in the assertion that

---

[927] Hollenbach, 42.

[928] Ibid, 97.

[929] Williams, 164.

human dignity is not a concept which derives its meaning from a particular class or genus of human action. It has a reality in all situations, independent of the kinds of actions and relations which give them structures.[930]

The dignity of the human person has a transcendent origin—it is an ontological reality. This assertion has been the consistent emphasis of the Roman Catholic magisterial doctrine since Leo XIII's encyclical, *Rerum Novarum (1891)*. Besides affirming the equality of human dignity in all people, the basic and enduring statement of Leo XIII is that "man precedes the State," suggesting that "the worth of human beings . . . is the standard by which political and legal institutions are to be evaluated."[931] The priority of the individual and human dignity is stated here. This is not, however, an absolute contention that emphasizes only the individual. Leo XIII also invaluably united the two crucial dimensions of the human person—the individual and social dimensions—in his formulation of rights and duties. According to Williams, three elements of the document account for this fact: human dignity, social interaction, and social institutions which Leo XIII proposed. This suggests that any claim and exercise of rights is not detached from concrete situations and other individuals or groups. Catholic social thought preceding *Populorum Progressio* was based on the affirmation of human dignity and the social nature of the human person. Paul VI was aware of this and suggested this affirmation in his treatise of the right to private ownership of property.

In his encyclical *Quadragesimo Anno*, Pius XI also emphasized the dignity of the human person as the foundation of human rights. Hollenbach says that

> all of Pius XI's claims about respect for persons' claims to material, bodily, and even psychological necessities are ultimately founded on a characteristic of the person which transcends any and all of these needs.[932]

Rights are *claims* dependent on and defined in terms of human dignity. They are not arbitrary claims. They are claims commonly shared by all on the

---

[930] Hollenbach, 90.

[931] Ibid., 43 and 45.

[932] Ibid., 51.

basis of a human characteristic that transcends needs, interests, and desires. The assertion suggests that human dignity—the transcendent characteristic of persons—comes even before claims (rights), needs, desires, and interests. There is no authentic human right without human dignity. Human dignity necessarily precedes human rights and the demand for satisfaction of human needs, interests, claims, and desires. This affirmation explains the call for respect for human rights, human dignity, and the human person. Robert Audi and Nicholas Wolterstorff concur with the affirmation and state the *respect* for persons is a central notion in ethics and also for citizenship.[933] This suggests that according to the duo, liberal democracy emphasizes the importance of mutual respect in ethics and human relations.

To acknowledge that human dignity deserves respect demands that it should not be arbitrarily abused for selfish interests because it is an honorable quality shared by all. Both Western individualist and African communitarian rights advocates need to incorporate this idea in order to reach a consensus about the notion of human rights because it creates a possibility of uniting the individual and community. Human dignity is an *absolutum* and a *conditio sine qua non* for determining human rights. Without human dignity, there are no human rights even if human rights in turn protect human dignity. To reconcile the Western and the African notions of human rights, a common denominator—which at the same time is the ultimate foundation for articulating the concept—is necessary. Without such a foundation, any human rights concept is arbitrary, and the two trends of thought cannot be united because they each argue from different foundational determinants of human rights. For individualism and communitarianism to be reconciled, the notion of human dignity should be accurately articulated and grasped.

Robert A. Evan's contention that human dignity needs to be seen as a quality bestowed on all by God—"something that people have, rather than something they earn or are granted by family, society or government"[934] is crucial for reconciliation between the individualist vision of rights and the communitarian vision. Human rights are not determined by individuals, community, social structures, or institutions. They are determined by God through human dignity, which is an ontological reality. It is only when any

---

[933]　Audi and Wolterstorff, 172.

[934]　Robert A. Evans, "From Reflection to Action," in *Human Rights: A Dialogue between the First and Third Worlds*, eds. Robert A. Evans and Alice Frazer Evans (New York: Lutherworth Press, 1983), 247.

concept of human rights takes seriously the transcendent dimension and origin of the human person that a common notion of human rights is possible. This is what the Western individualist and the African communitarian concepts need to incorporate as the basis of their explication of the notion of the human person, human dignity, and human rights in order to arrive at a consensus view of human rights.

2. PRUDENCE IN THE PRIORITY OF INDIVIDUAL OR COMMUNITY

The main issue addressed in this section is the relation of the individual to community. It is partly the problem of the *Sitz-im leben* of the development of the human person or personhood. Although human dignity is, at least in Roman Catholic tradition, the ultimate foundation of rights—the understanding of the individual in relation to community—is crucial for the right understanding of human rights. Therefore, the issues are particularity and universality, unity, and plurality.

Pius XI's encyclical, *Quadragesimo Anno*, emphasized the transcendental origin of the dignity of the human person in relation to community.[935] Although the document is more concerned with issues of social justice, it touches the question of human rights. This is evident in its basic contention that "liberalistic individualism which subordinates society to the selfish use of the individual" should be avoided because the individual is in "organic union with society," and by mutual collaboration, "the attainment of earthly happiness is placed within the reach of all."[936] The individual is recognized but not independently of community because the two are tied together by a mutual relationship. Leo XIII's emphasis on the primacy of human dignity is reaffirmed and the role of institutions in mediating and shaping human rights is stated by Pius XI, too.[937] Similarly, Bujo describes a communitarian point of view in the African context:

> Although the individual is embedded in the community, he or she is a unique and inexchangeable being, who has irreplaceable tasks within a community. The individual has to act in solidarity with

---

[935]　Hollenbach, 51-53.

[936]　Ibid.

[937]　Ibid., 55.

the lineage, while retaining his/her identity as well as showing the responsibility entrusted to him or her.[938]

According to Bujo, individuality does not get lost—it is not subordinated to community. This is a point emphasized by John Paul II in the entirety of *Sollicitudo Rei Socialis,* where the individual and community are on par and viewed as necessarily related. Prior to this, John Paul II, then Karol Wojtyla, emphasized that when a person is viewed in the context of community, humanness should be seriously considered because it unites people, it is shared by all people, and "it puts into the forefront man's relation and subordination to a given community."[939] The individual is a distinct portion of community.

In his attempt to resolve the issue of the relation of the individual to society, Pius XII emphasized social morality using the notion of "responsible citizenship."[940] The term *responsible citizenship* is significant in the reconciliation of the Western individualist and African communitarian concepts of human rights because it suggests a notion of rights which combines both notions. It shows mutual concern of individuals as well as that of an individual and community. A responsible citizen is not eccentric. In other words, a responsible citizen does not deviate from community but is an individual conscious about duty toward self and toward others.[941]

John XXIII's emphasis, in Mater et Magistra, on the dual context of human dignity and rights is important. In the document, he stresses that interdependence is vital because "human dignity can only exist within a consciously developed context of human interdependence."[942] This means persons need to understand that they are dependent on each other and there is something worthy in other people. Unless this conception exists, it is difficult to recognize the dignity of other people. This is a reality present in the African notion of the human person, but not much deepened by the Western notion of the human person. Western anthropology of rights, therefore,

---

[938] Bujo, 148.

[939] Wojtyla, 293.

[940] Hollenbach, 56-59.

[941] Ibid., 63. Pius XII emphasized the reciprocal relation between rights and duties, namely, that to every right corresponds the duty that this right be protected by both the subject of the right and others or society.

[942] Ibid.

needs to seriously consider that "it is in the belief in human interrelatedness, human reciprocity, that the key for solving the problem of human rights is to be found."[943] It is when people recognize equality of dignity and mutual responsibility that the possibility of global human rights becomes real. This assertion calls for a mutual relationship in which there is not an overemphasis of distinctions. Instead, the distinctions of I and You or They, and the We and They melt into a We relationship and human identity. This suggests that people need to understand that they are dependent on each other, and there is no need for tribalism or parochialism. This manifests a recognition of the universality of human dignity and equality of rights of all without losing sight of the distinct individual.

The notion of interdependence reflects the biblical teaching on the equality of persons, which is vital in the conception of equality of human dignity. This equality of dignity is based on the fact that all are created in the image of God. This is a fact extant in the sacred scriptures (Cfr. Genesis 1:26-27). Both the Old Testament and the New Testament emphasize the equality of the dignity of the human person. This biblical view of human dignity is distinct from Western and African communitarian concepts of rights, which can be inferred from the contention of Montgomery, who asserts that the

> biblical approach to human dignity cannot he identified with the barren extremes either of eighteenth century western liberal philosophy or Marxist-Socialist collectivisms.[944]

The biblical vision of human dignity can be utilized for reconciling the liberal and communitarian visions of human rights because it stands in between the two. What the liberal notion and the communitarian notion of rights need is emphasis on human dignity as the foundation of human rights. Once this foundation is incorporated into both, their reconciliation is less problematic because at this point, they have a common and transcendent ground for articulating the notion of human rights and the human person.

The Roman Catholic principle of the common good can also contribute to the dialogue between the liberal and communitarian human rights concepts because it places rights in both a social and an individual context. As

---

[943] Evans, 248.

[944] John Warwick Montgomery, *Human Rights and Human Dignity* (Grand Rapids, Michigan: Zondervan Publishing House, 1986), 209.

Hollenbach states, *Mater et Magistra* defines the common good as "the sum total of those conditions of social living, whereby men are enabled more fully and more readily to achieve their own perfection."[945] This principle is vital for resolving the conflict between the individualist and communitarian notions of human rights because it joins the good of each person to the good of all, the good of community. It shows that Catholic tradition rejects extremes of individualism and communitarianism but incorporates elements of both to build a tradition of its own. The principle combines both elements because the promotion of the common good calls for the promotion of the rights and the good of every individual member of the community. It considers both the individual and community important. The Western individualist who emphasizes freedom, concreteness and autonomy of the individual, and the African communitarian, who stresses the communal character of persons, can feel comfortable with the principle of common good, even if not absolutely, because the elements of the two notions are included in this principle. The principle is, therefore, necessary in the attempt to resolve the conflicts between the individualist and communitarian notions because it provides checks and balances in the course of articulating the notion of human rights. As Hollenbach suggests, society is necessary for founding, supporting, conditioning, and limiting human rights.[946] Society checks extremes of individualism and at the same time protects its individual members. Both the society and the individual need one another for a balanced self-conception.

The dual emphasis of the value of community and the individual is further noticed in two other Roman Catholic documents—*Pacem in Terris* and *Gaudium et Spes*. First, according to Hollenbach, *Pacem in Terris* underscores the importance of both social and communal rights and acknowledges rights stressed by both the liberal democratic tradition and socialism as crucial in the human rights talk. The principal norm for acknowledgment of rights emphasized in both traditions is *human dignity*. Such rights, as listed by Hollenbach, include: *life-related rights,* rights concerning adequate *standard of living,* moral and cultural values, religious activity, family life, economic life, assembly and association, freedom of movement, and political rights.[947] These rights are all claims relevant in both liberal democratic and socialist settings on the basis of the universality of human dignity. The two concepts of

---

[945]   Hollenbach, 64.

[946]   Ibid.

[947]   Ibid., 66-67.

rights—the individualist concept and the communitarian concept—fall under either of these trends or ideologies. They can be reconciled by applying John XXIII's vision of human rights strongly established on human dignity.

Second, the Vatican Council II's *Gaudium et Spes*, advocates that "if persons in society possess a transcendental worth, then the structures of social organization are confronted with claims to serve and protect personal dignity."[948] That the dignity of every human individual is important is stated here. Community ought to protect the individual dignity and rights. This is an idea that features in both the Western and African contexts of human rights though with a difference in degree of emphasis. In the Western context, unlike in the African context, "relationship is not constitutive of the being of humans . . . it is fundamental to human existence."[949] This is where one of the fundamental differences between the Western individualist and the African communitarian notions of person and rights lies. However, similarity is evident because social relationship is still fundamental for human existence.[950] Here, one notices that the difference between the Western and the African notion of the human person—the self and human rights—gets more blurred, a signal for the possibility of reconciliation of the two, though the notion of the human person as a social entity seems to be more conspicuous in the African concept of person than in the Western vision. The document unites the Western and the African notions of person by its recognition of the value of "social interdependence and the essential social nature of the human person."[951] The communal dimension of persons, which also features in both Western and African contexts, is affirmed though the African communitarian vision tends to emphasize the communal dimension more than the Western individualist vision, which is more concerned about individual rights than about society. This conciliar view of the human person points to the possibility of reconciling the two trends of human rights arguments because the document presents human persons as being in a dialogical relationship. The notion of rights derived from both individual and social understandings of the human person projects human rights as being in constant conversation.

---

[948] Ibid, 70

[949] Uzukwu, 43.

[950] Bujo, 144, 148. Also see Uzukwu, 43.

[951] Hollenbach, 73.

One of the fundamental and reconciling concepts in the Roman Catholic human rights tradition is the one of *solidarity* introduced into the rights talk by John Paul II in his encyclical *Sollicitudo Rei Socialis*. The document affirms the value of solidarity in the following terms:

> Solidarity helps us to see the "other"—whether a person, people or nation—not just as some kind of instrument with a work capacity and physical strength to be exploited at low cost and then to be discarded when no longer useful, but as our "neighbor", a "helper" (Cfr. Gen.2: 8-20), to be a sharer, on a par with ourselves, in the banquet of life to which all are invited by God.[952]

Solidarity is closely related to the principle of common good. Its import in the human rights dialogue is its emphasis on the individual's commitment to community. Like the notion of interdependence, it stresses the fact that people need each other to be and to become better. This point is well taken by the African notion of the human person because "the value of life consists in solidarity and participation of the individual entities in the totality of the whole reality."[953] The main issue is that solidarity constitutes the essential trait of Africans. The *Sitz-im Leben* of a fully developed person is community and communal relations because community is for meeting the needs of the individual as well as the entire society. This is why human need and—it should be added—human dignity or right is "the basic criterion of behavior."[954] Solidarity, hence, defines the self in terms of society or other selves and vice versa. If this definition of the self and community is acknowledged, reconciliation of the individualist and the communitarian notions of rights can be visualized because there is no more clear distinction between the individual person and the community since they define, or are defined, in terms of each other.

---

[952] John Paul II, "*Sollicitudo Rei Socialis*: On Social Concerns," in *The Logic of Solidarity: Commentaries on John Paul II's Encyclical on Social Concern*, eds. Gregory Baum and Robert Ellsberg (New York: Orbis Books, Maryknoll, 1989), 42. Also cfr. *Sollicitudo Rei Socialis*, paragraph 39.

[953] Nkrunziza, 150.

[954] Ibid. Also see page 151.

Finally, the Roman Catholic principle of *subsidiarity* is vital for the reconciliation of Western and the African concepts of human rights because it facilitates the dialogue in human rights. Verbatim, the principle is stated as:

> Subsidiarity is a fundamental principle of social philosophy, fixed and unchangeable, that one should not withdraw from individuals what they can accomplish by their own enterprise and industry. So, too, it is an injustice and at the same time a grave evil and a disturbance of right order to transfer from the larger and higher collectivity functions which can be found and provided by the lesser and subordinate bodies. In as much as every social activity should, by its very nature, prove a help to the members of the body social, it should never destroy or absorb them.[955]

The principle of subsidiarity advocates that the independent decisions and actions of the individual and the intervention of community are legitimate when it is reasonable and necessary for both the individual and society. The individual is recognized as much as the community on account of natural competence to decide and to act. In other words, society's interference with the individual's right to decide or act for the good or promotion of his/her dignity is a violation of rights. And the society's refusal to intervene to save an *individual* from a violence against his/her rights, when the individual is incompetent, is itself a violence against the dignity of the individual. Conversely, the individual's refusal to act for the protection or promotion of his/her rights or dignity, when capable, is a self-inflicted violation of dignity and rights, contrary to the spirit of solidarity and common good. The individual's refusal of community intervention, when he/she is incapable, is another self-inflicted violation of rights and dignity.

From the foregoing analysis, the principle of subsidiarity seems to suggest an incorporation of both individual and communal exercise of rights. But it does so within limits of reason, necessity, and competence. It permits both individual and communal exercise of rights provided that the consequences do not violate the individual's rights and duties and the rights and duties of others in community. This is where the liberal human rights advocate recognizes that rights are not absolute claims, and the communitarian rights

---

[955] John XXIII, *Mater et Magistra: Christianity and Social Progress* (Washington DC: National Catholic Welfare Conference, 1961), 63, 17.

advocate should not suppress the individual's exercise of rights unnecessarily. The solution to the problem of limits of the exercise of rights seems to be extant in the Roman Catholic principle of subsidiarity.

With regard to the individual's relationship with society, in the context of human rights, the following points are crucial: An appropriate understanding of the human person is necessary to resolve the conflict between the two human rights concepts. The human person needs to be understood as "an individual with intellect and will: the capacities of insight and judgment, choice and decision, an individual able to inquire and to choose."[956] Persons should be conceived both as subjects and objects of experience and "the moral subject can be, in a way, a plurality of persons or selves within a single individual human being."[957]

Considering the two conceptions of the human person jointly, it is noticeable that both subjective and objective dimensions of a human person are stated. This is what explains the interior tensions in an individual in a process of deliberation, choice, and self-affirmation or determination. It suggests that one person coexists with many persons within him/herself; there is in each person a community, if not of persons, of views or opinions. If this can happen within an individual, there is also a possibility for it to happen with an individual in relation to an outside community, even if the opposite is also true. This shows that the individual and the community are inseparable at least at certain moments, and so the individualist notion of rights and the communitarian notion can be reconciled.

In an attempt to bring consensus between the individual and the community with regard to rights, Kuczewski aptly suggests that "the self regains contents via knowledge and participation in the community of which he/she is a member."[958] There is a mutual exchange between the individual and the community. As far as there is such exchange, the individualist concept of rights and the communitarian notion of rights are not radically separated. There is a possibility of the reconciliation of the two on the basis of this mutual exchange. Proposing a radical interdependence between the individual and society, Kuczewski reaffirms this in the following words:

---

[956] Michael Novak, *Free Persons and the Common Good* (New York: Madison Books, 1989), 134.

[957] Michael J. Sandel, *Liberalism and the Limits of Justice* (Cambridge: Cambridge University Press, 1982), 8 and 63.

[958] Kuczewski, 45.

> We need to define the self as essentially related to community. The
> community must be a constitutive of the individual's identity . . . .
> This makes possible, a positive notion of rights. The communitarian
> is able to embrace a value of rights as basic guarantees that enable the
> individual to discover his or her values and higher preferences.[959]

The social element of the human person is again stated here. From this assertion, it is right to agree with Walzer that "the liberal ideology of separatism cannot take personhood and bondedness away from us. What it does take away is the sense of personhood and bondedness."[960] This means that personhood is not exclusively an individual reality because it is developed and achieved in community. It is personhood that unites individuals. The individual and community are inseparable. What separates the individual and community is the loss of sight of this fact. In relation to rights, the contention is that rights cannot be absolutely individual claims regardless of community. This assertion is augmented by the contemporary Roman Catholic notion of the common good, which includes both the individual and the community. The individual and the community have a mutual obligation of promoting the good and rights of one another because an "individual stands in an ultimate relation to the community and vice versa."[961] In other words, there is a moment of coincidence of both the individual and the community or their interests. This is why, in rights claims, both individual or personal good and the common good have to be valued equally. This way neither individual rights nor the claims of community are given priority. Instead, both are placed at the same level. Consequently, the problems of individual or communal absolutism and the one of overemphasis of only one dimension of the human person and rights disappear.

It seems plausible to conclude, as Uzukwu advocates, that an unbalanced view of the human person is problematic only when priority is given either to the individual or the community alone because overemphasis on either of them makes the survival of the other problematic.[962] The point here is that overemphasis of one means the death of the other. There is, hence, a need for balanced emphasis on both the individual and the community. The solution

---

[959]   Ibid., 51.

[960]   Walzer, 10.

[961]   Kuczewski, 45.

[962]   Uzukwu, 44.

to reconcile the Western and the African notions of the human person and human rights is to strike a balance of emphasis. Jacques Maritain suggests a solution, but it is plausible to concur with Thomas D. Williams, who says,

> Maritain holds out a paradox for investigation: humans are beings of inestimable and inviolable value, transcending any temporal or political order, yet they find themselves and realize their dignity only by participating in (and, in so doing, subordinating themselves to) community. The human person simultaneously transcends and is subordinate to the common good.[963]

This affirmation stands out as paradox because of the mutual dependence of both the individual and the community while at the same time subordinating the former to the latter. Indeed, such a solution is a paradox because it suggests the importance of both the individual and the community. As a solution to the problem, it shows how important both the individual and community are in suggesting a notion for the human person, human dignity, and human rights. This could be considered one of the core arguments for the universality of human rights and dignity. Massaro argues and suggests that Maritain's solution to the conflicting vision of human person and human rights is the human person's "immanent aspiration for transcendence," and subsequently

> Maritain insists on the ultimate inadequacy of any social, political or economic system which fails to acknowledge the spiritual nature of persons, possessing as they do aspirations which surpass their temporal needs.[964]

The insistence of Maritain is credible because of the dual dimension of the human person—the material and the spiritual dimensions. The spiritual tends to the communal while the material tends to individuation. The two dimensions, therefore, do not need to be radically separated as if they are absolutely independent of one another and do not exist in the same person.

---

[963] Massaro, 15.

[964] Ibid. Massaro is quoting Maritain Jacques, *The Person and the Common Good*, 1-4. This quotation is from the original source, not the English translation by Fitzgerald J. John.

3. A RIGHT CONCEPT OF HUMAN FREEDOM

A proper notion of human freedom is necessary for a credible understanding of human rights. At least from a Christian perspective, rights and duties are correlative notions rooted in the social nature of persons. This implies that freedom as a right is exercised in the context of society and should be defined in a social context. Rights cannot be liberally exercised, because "the deepest meaning of freedom is 'freedom for' engagement with others in society."[965] This is a point also stated by John XXIII, who, according to Hollenbach, contends that rights are not "a jumble of *ad hoc* claims."[966] They are mutual claims. This affirmation is plausible because if human rights are not defined in terms of mutual human relationships, there would be an endless list of rights.

Hollenbach advocates that *Dignitatis Humanae* provides a solution for the problem of the foundation of rights, their mutual relationship, and institutionalization. It is concerned with interaction and relationship of persons. The assertion is realistic on the basis of his affirmation that the concern of the arguments in the document is

> for the person and his or her freedom to act in society. The state may not substitute itself for the responsible citizen. It may regulate, which is to say it may order, human interaction. For *Dignitatis Humanae*, as for Pius XII, order is an ordering of freedom. Only thus is it possible to understand the common root of both personal and social rights and to see their essential interrelationship with each other.[967]

This document offers advocacy for freedom in social context. Its assertion is not an advocacy for liberal freedom because the exercise of freedom is limited by society. The document suggests a responsible exercise of freedom. The exercise of freedom, and ultimately all rights, should be within the limits of social good and demands. John Paul II combines both views by affirming, in *Sollicitudo Rei Socialis*, that human freedom and respect are related to

---

[965] Hehir, 9.
[966] Hollenbach, 68.
[967] Ibid., 77.

solidarity on both individual and communal levels.[968] Freedom with mutual respect is, in other words, important for solidarity.

A reconciliation of the African communitarian notion of freedom with the Roman Catholic understanding is not a problem because the African notion is not libertarian—it emphasizes freedom as "freedom for construction of a better community."[969] Bujo affirms this view, in the African context, by stating a view consistently emphasized by the Roman Catholic social doctrine as necessary for understanding human dignity and rights:

> Freedom has always to keep in mind the communitarian dimension and can only be developed within the community. Without communitarian relationship there is no identity for the African person. Only together with others can one become a human person and achieve individual freedom, which again should be exercised in a communitarian manner.[970]

A careful reading of this statement suggests that it is rather hard for the individualist rights notion to be reconciled with the communitarian notion and the Roman Catholic vision. However, the problem could be resolved because both notions express that there is individual human freedom. The main problem is how freedom is exercised and the context of its exercise. The possibility of reconciliation of the two views of freedom lies in the acceptance of the view that no absolute rights exist—a point noted in the African communitarian context and less emphasized in the Western vision of freedom. I think this is the aspect of freedom most difficult to reconcile in the two visions of freedom and human rights.

According to Robert Evans, "human dignity"—and I suggest not human freedom—"is the Foundation for nurturing and protecting human rights"[971] because human freedom is just an expression, or an outgrowth, of human dignity. The self-determination of an individual can only be authentic and dignified if it does not neglect the dignity of other persons. Any claim for absolute self-determination is excessive. It oversteps the limits of freedom and

---

968 Ibid., 146.

969 Uzukwu, 44.

970 Bujo, 148.

971 Evans, 247.

denies that there are actually and often conflicts of rights. Freedom needs to be conceived as a relational reality because it is limited by the freedoms of other individuals or community. In other words, as a right, freedom is a *prima facie* right. To reconcile the liberal and the communitarian concepts of rights, a balance of emphasis of individual freedom and the freedom of others ought to be maintained. These observations make credible Bujo's assertion:

> Because of one's humanity and independently of "personal conditions, political constellations and historical circumstances," everyone shall claim human rights, whereby one's self-determination, that is freedom, should be "compatible" with that of all others. Freedom which is understood in this way could be called the only yardstick of human rights. At the same time, it is apparent that freedom, which is shown in autonomy, does not support arbitrariness, but stresses to the highest degree reasonable and responsible self-determination. This confirms human dignity which belongs to each and everyone in an equal manner.[972]

The importance of this statement lies in one issue Bujo raises. He raises the issue of lack of responsible individual claims in the liberal Euro-American concept of human rights. His contention is that any claim by an individual without regard for others contradicts the authentic meaning and demands of human rights. Rights are exercised with the consciousness that other people also have rights, and rights' claimants have obligations to fulfill toward others and themselves.

4. COMMON LANGUAGE AS A SOLUTION

The Western individualist and the African communitarian notions of rights need an inclusive language to articulate the notion of rights and, consequently, to eliminate some of the prevalent conflicts between them. The two trends of human rights advocacy have been influenced by the cultural contexts of the people. This in turn has affected their way of thinking. The basic reason for the need for an inclusive language is that the two trends of thought use different types of language to describe human rights. Michael Novak observes that

---

[972] Bujo, 145.

two types of languages are associated with liberal individualism and communitarianism. Liberalism's language is the one of rights and freedom while that of communitarianism is of learnt virtues and common good.[973]

These two distinct types of language create a dichotomy of vision between liberal individualism and communitarianism. An inclusive language is needed in the formulation of a *concensus concept* of human rights. This means the languages of individualism and communalism should be modified rather than claim precedence. They should both constitute elements of the notion of human rights.

It seems inevitable to conclude from the above arguments that the problem of rights language can ultimately be resolved by the use of the Roman Catholic traditional language of human dignity—transcendent worth shared by all—solidarity, common good, subsidiarity, interdependence, transcendent and equally shared values, dual dimension of the human person, individual and social constitution and determination of the self, and mutual responsibility. The language of I-you, I-they, or we-they ought to be replaced by we. This last terminology is crucial because it neither excludes the individual as opposed to other individuals nor community or society as opposed to the individual.

5. A SYNTHESIS AND CONCLUSION

An uncritical study of the Western individualist and the African communitarian concepts of human rights would suggest that the two visions cannot be reconciled. A critical analysis suggests that reconciliation of the two notions is possible. The difficulty in reconciling them lies, first, in the absence of emphasis on a common foundation—the dignity or the inherent worth of the human person. Second, besides the problems of language, understanding the constitution and determination of the self, the concept of human freedom, and the diversity of values, the problem lies in overemphasis on only one aspect of the human person, discrepant language, and vision of the foundation of human rights. The two concepts of human rights, independently considered, emphasize different but vital domains of the human person and, ultimately, human rights. These emphases seem a dichotomy in such philosophies of human rights. Such a dichotomy impairs the right vision of human rights.

---

[973] Novak, 159.

The solution for reconciling the two visions lies in placing the Western individualist and the African communitarian concepts of human rights on par. An analysis of the two philosophies of human rights and their constituent elements suggests a possibility for reconciliation of the two.

The Western individualist and the African communitarian concepts of human rights are distinct but not absolutely contradictory because community is not totally independent of the individual and vice versa. This possibility is suggested by the Roman Catholic human rights tradition, especially as expressed in the doctrines of human dignity or the human person as an *imago Dei*, the common good, responsible freedom, subsidiarity, solidarity, and interdependence. The Roman Catholic tradition of human rights has consistently avoided extremes of the individualist and the communitarian understanding of rights by introducing the notion of human dignity derived from a common transcendent source—God—as the foundation of its arguments about human rights. By steadily maintaining that the dignity of an individual is not detached from occasions of encounter with other individuals in society or community, Roman Catholic tradition suggests a unitary nature of human rights and the possibility of reconciliation of the two concepts. The inclusive element of the two dimensions of the human person seems to be more manifest in the African concept of human rights than in the Western notion. Consequently, it seems easier for the African concept of human rights to fit the Roman Catholic tradition than the Western concept. However, traces of the communal aspect of the human person are present in the liberal concept of rights. The difference is the degree of emphasis.

A sound concept of human rights integrates crucial concepts such as human dignity, individual, community, liberty, and equality. This assertion suggests that the individual and the community should not be mutually exclusive. It is plausible to conclude a treatise on the theme of reconciliation of Western and African concepts of human rights with an inclusive definition of human rights. Relying on various definitions of the human person, human dignity, and human rights, the following definition seems reconciliatory:

> Human rights are mutually responsible, moral and just political, civil, economic, social and cultural claims or entitlements, immunities or protections and powers of either an individual or other individuals who constitute society, exercised for the sake of the individual and society on the basis of their equal transcendent

worth which may not be violated by any other individual or group of individuals.[974]

From this definition and the preceding discussion, the following observations are noteworthy for the reconciliation of the Western and the African concepts of human rights. First, the individualist view of human rights fits well in categories of rights such as legal or civil and contractual rights. Second, rights are neither egoistic nor suppressive, neither considering the individual's selfish interest only nor the community's conditioning and suppressing of individual identity only. Rather, they are just claims of individuals or the community that do not harm any individual or the community. Finally, in terms of entitlement, rights are not a guarantee of authority for individual claims regardless of community and vice versa. Instead, they are claims or immunities of an individual and community in dialogue. This dialogue is founded on the transcendental worth, the dignity of the human person, which is the common characteristic of all people. Therefore, human dignity and the mutual relationship between the individual and the society are vital for reconciling Western and African concepts of human rights. Although possibilities of reconciliation are apparent, an absolute reconciliation is utopian. It is not a guarantee because of differences in the foundations of arguments, dispositions to reconciliation, thought patterns and contextual experiences. An inclusive vision of the human person and human rights is grounded on the assertion that all people have equal dignity. The assertion is founded on the idea that all people have the same origin, and they are *imago Dei*. The principle of *imago Dei*, from which the social dimension of a person is derived, forms the basis for the reconciliation of the notions of human person and human rights because

Personality, that spiritual side of man tends by nature to communion, in virtue of its value and dignity and of its needs. The

---

[974] This is my suggested definition of human rights arrived at on the basis of my readings about the human person, human dignity, and human rights. The definition shows that human rights are not absolute. In other words, human rights are *prima facie* because they may be overridden at certain times and under certain circumstances. However, they may not and should not be selfish claims. They should protect and provide for the good of people.

knowledge and love, the freedom and responsibility, that enrich
and enable the personality require relationship with other persons
because personality is identical with a creative spirit that wants to
communicate whatever treasures it has. Likewise personality stands
in need of dialogue with others because of its deficiencies derived
not so much from itself as of its material individuality.[975]

An individual should be recognized as such, but because the individual
person shares something with other persons, one remains open to incorporate
others in one's life. Human dignity is not an absolute personal claim; it is
universal. Human rights cannot and may never be absolute personal claims
because they require similar responses or obligations. There is something
mutual and obligatory because human dignity prevails in each case, which
calls for respect because of human dignity. Anderson's view of the individual
and community is significant for understanding this assertion:

> The determination of humanity in general as being with others does
> not dissolve individual beings into corporate being, but results in a
> determination of humanity in its singularity as well as its plurality.
> This singularity, however, is expressed as reciprocity of being of one
> with the other and also, to an extent for the other.[976]

The individual should be recognized as a unique being but is part
of a community and exists in community. This contention calls for
acknowledgment of uniqueness in plurality without destroying the social
element or dimension of the human person. Human person, human dignity,
and human rights should be viewed in the contexts of both the individual
and the community. No context should be given precedence or be more
emphasized than the other. This claim is supported by Mary Ann Glendon's
vision and argument about rights:

> The exaggerated absoluteness of our American rights dialect is all
> the more remarkable when we consider how little relation it bears
> to reality. There is a striking discrepancy . . . between our tendency
> to state rights in a stark unlimited fashion and the common sense

---

[975] Fichtner, 35.
[976] Anderson, 45.

restrictions that have to be placed on one person's rights when they collide with those of another person.[977]

The argument is that it is unrealistic to claim absolute individual rights. This is a strong argument because rights are relational, and as such they have both individual and communal dimensions, none of which is to be neglected in the exercise or recognition of rights—claims, duties, and responsibilities.

There is, however, some paradox in understanding the human person and rights in both Western-individualist and the African-communitarian contexts in relation to the question of integral human development. Sometimes in the so-called individualistic societies, such as in the Western world, a better degree of integral development is attained while societies that are acknowledged as communitarian, for example, African societies tend not to flourish integrally or cooperatively. This paradox may be resolved through acknowledgment and esteem for the human person and the universality of human dignity and human rights.

C. The Importance of Reconciliation of Notions

An understanding of the human person, human dignity, and human rights is vital because it is related to all people. Consequently, the principal focus of this section is the human person, human dignity and human rights that tend to be variously conceived. An understanding of the human person and human dignity are crucial because it is through this understanding that human dignity can be viewed as an inalienable (God-given) element, which forms the foundation of human rights.[978] This also helps people to rethink their vision of persons, their dignity and rights, and eventually try to work for authentic human development. They would, for example, rethink their conception of human development and their action plans for human development. The issue of human development would not be just a matter of semantic activity, but a process of transforming people's thinking and practical life.

Divergent views of the human person make application of principles for integral human development difficult because principles may be applied in a relative manner depending on which vision of human person, human dignity, and human rights is emphasized. For instance, a principle like that of common

---

[977] Glendon, 108.

[978] Reichmann, 213.

good may be considered of less gravity if human person, human dignity, and human rights are individualistically viewed. Just as various principles are insufficient, independent of each other, there is a need to reconcile the notions of human person, human dignity, and human rights because they are also defined by each other. Such reconciliation is necessary for integral human development since it provides for integration of visions.

The communitarian views a person to be social, human dignity as shared because of its common origin and human rights as mutual claims and entitlements. Human rights necessitate fulfillment of obligations and responsibilities or duties, and freedom is a "freedom from" leading to a "freedom for" responsible behavior or action. The individualist views a person as an independent or distinct entity, human dignity is not necessarily shared, but individuals have their dignity, and human rights are claims to protect the individual. Rights are more commonly considered as "freedom from" binding conditions leading to "personal or individual gratification" without "freedom for" obligation toward others. If there are such divergent visions of human rights integral human development is difficult to achieve.

There is need to balance the vision of human persons, human dignity, and human rights. Any claim of "absolute rights" has the negative consequences of "tending to down-grade rights into mere expressions of unbounded desires and wants."[979] Such claims arise if there is exaggerated emphasis on the individual dimension of the human person and freedom. The consequence is the tendency to make rights absolute as if the person claiming rights does not affect or relate with other individuals. If both individuals and community are seriously considered in the question of rights, there is mutual responsibility or duty. It is here that the elements of care for others and mutual respect are expressed. Consequently, love, justice, peace, care for the common good, application of the principles of subsidiarity, solidarity, participation, and association are possible. These principles, virtues, and conditions provide fertile ground for integral development to flourish. For instance, local, national, and global integral development can be achieved. Exaggerated political tensions, economic differences, nationalism—which breeds hatred for nonnationals—tribalism, racism, or ethnicity can be tempered. It is possible to achieve these for at least two reasons. First, a single vision of the human person facilitates a uniform vision of human dignity, human rights, and people-related problems. Second, it facilitates the vision of human rights

---

[979] Glendon, 113.

and duties or responsibilities. It makes easy the application of the golden rule or mutual relation and action—do unto others what you want done to you—in terms of human rights.

VII. THE ULTIMATE PRINCIPLE: ITS RELATION TO OTHER DEVELOPMENT FACTORS

A. Human Dignity: The Ultimate Principle for Integral Human Development

The ultimate principle for integral human development is human dignity. Any social teaching starting with any of the principles as most fundamental—for instance, the common good as Todd David Whitmore advocates—is questionable because it falls short of the assertion that human dignity is the ultimate principle.[980] Human dignity is the ultimate principle because it defines the human person and it is the foundation for human rights. Since Catholic social doctrine has the human person as its ultimate goal, principles related to the human person are foundational. All other virtues, principles, and conditions required by integral human development and emphasized in Catholic social teaching are related to each other through human dignity.

In order to be fair to Whitmore, there is no doubt that the common good is a necessary condition for the human person, human dignity, and human rights to thrive, but it is not what is pursued as an end. The common good is a means or stepping-stone to protect or promote human dignity. The right and ultimate starting point of any morally sound social reflection and teaching and integral promotion of people is human dignity. Any Catholic social doctrine is ultimately addressing human issues and specifically issues that affect the dignity of the human person. This is the indispensable principle, contrary to Whitmore's suggestion of the common good. Any talk about the common good is ultimately directed to the dignity of the human person.

It is true that both common good and human dignity are transcendent principles in the sense that they are not exclusive qualities of an individual. However, only human dignity is the most basic or fundamental principle. This argument is better understood from the idea that any attempt to develop or

---

[980] David Todd Whitmore, "Catholic Social Teaching: Starting with the Common Good," in *Living the Catholic Social Teaching: Cases and Commentary*, eds. Kathleen Maas Weigert and Alexia K. Kelly (Lanham: Row and Littlefield Publishers Inc., 2005), 59.

to address a social issue is an attempt to solve problems, which affect human dignity. The principle of common good creates conditions for the success of the attempts to resolve the problems.

Whitmore's order of priority calls for a rearrangement, which first takes human dignity more seriously and provides the common good for the enhancement of a dignity which already exists. If Whitmore's argument for starting with the common good is "the empirical observation that all persons are social,"[981] which is affirmed by many authors, he also should note that social nature of people is partly explained by what they fundamentally share. The fundamental trait, which human persons share, is human dignity. There is, at least, no ground to affirm that the common good is a quality or an experience of every person. Human dignity remains the basic principle around, which other principles are built either to protect it or to enhance it. It is for this reason that Milburn Thompson argues that the dignity of the human person, realized in community, is the foundation of Catholic social teaching and its theory of human rights.[982]

The common good is a significant principle for integral human development because it is profound in depth and breadth. It includes many other virtues, principles, and conditions, which Maritain emphasizes as necessary for human thriving.[983] The common good is a comprehensive notion, which appears to subordinate human dignity. It is a necessary condition for the human person, human dignity, and human rights to thrive, but it *is not* what is pursued in social contexts as *an end*. Instead, it constitutes a means, a stepping-stone to an end, which is the promotion or enhancement of the human person, human rights, and human dignity. It is called for because human dignity demands it. This does not contradict the assertion that common good is a relevant starting point to reflect on human dignity. In fact, the latter affirms the importance of the universality of human dignity. To affirm the common good is to affirm the universality of human dignity.

Two visions of human dignity suggest themselves as interesting here and probably account for differences in the vision of the human person. But one vision is critical for acknowledging the universality of human dignity. These are the vision of human dignity as *ontological* dignity, which is the dignity common to all human beings by reason of their nature, and human dignity as

---

[981] Whitmore, 65.

[982] Thompson, 94.

[983] Maritain, 52.

moral dignity, which is the reflection of the "consistency with which a person lives according to moral truth."[984] The ontological dignity is a requirement for moral dignity because the origin of morality is God—the ontological and the *absolute being* or being itself. The ontological dignity is the ground for the intelligibility of moral dignity. From the perspective of believers, the ultimate principle is called *imago Dei* principle—namely, the human person created in the image and likeness of God, the absolute being from whom human dignity or inherent worth emanates. This idea is emphatic in the thoughts of Maritain:

> The deepest layer of the human person's dignity consists in its property of resembling God—not in a general way after the manner of all creatures, but in a *proper* way. It is the image of God.[985]

The affirmation of the principle of *imago Dei* consistently points to the idea of the universality of human dignity and its ultimate and ontological character. The principle, therefore, weakens the moral dignity theory because moral dignity suggests a difference between the dignity of one person and another. It denies the universality of human dignity and suggests that human dignity is variable or dependent on variable factors. Consequently, it defies the idea of the ultimate character of human dignity as the ultimate principle for integral human development. It is for this reason that ontological dignity, which expresses the ultimate nature of human dignity, is preferable to moral dignity as it constitutes what may hesitantly be called human dignity.

B. The Relationship between Human Dignity and Other Development Factors

The ultimate and uniting principle of integral human development is human dignity because all other principles of Catholic social teaching protect or promote human dignity and are based on human dignity. Theological anthropology suggests that human dignity is the ultimate expression of the divine quality, which is the ultimate principle in the human person. Consequently, the interrelationship among the principles for integral human development is also based on human dignity.

---

[984] Williams, 156.

[985] Maritain, 42.

Succinctly, the relationship between the principles of human development may be stated as follows: All the virtues, principles, and conditions for integral human development—namely, charity, human person, and human rights, participation, subsidiarity, common good, justice, peace, preferential option for the poor, affirmative action, solidarity, and association—are related to each other through human dignity. However, charity or love also plays a vital role in the establishment of this relationship because it "constitutes the fundamental content of what is 'due' to human dignity," and "it also mediates between dignity and particular human rights."[986] Human dignity calls for love or charity. Love or charity is expressed in the different facets of the principles for integral development of peoples as proposed by Paul VI in *Populorum Progressio*.

Love, peace, and justice are virtues necessary for integral human development. One significant observation about their relationship to the common good is that they manifest the moral dimension of what is properly called the common good. The significance of their relation is that the common good is based on "justice and moral goodness."[987]

Human rights are based on human dignity and they promote or protect human dignity. The recognition of human rights is indicative of the recognition of human dignity. Charity is a manifestation of the recognition of human dignity. The purpose of justice is respect and promotion of human dignity and human rights. Justice is a sign of respect and recognition of human dignity. It is at the same time founded on human dignity, and it also protects and promotes human rights.

Peace is pursued for the sake of human dignity. It is related to justice because justice provides the foundation for peace. Peace is also related to love because it is the fruit of true love or charity. It is related to solidarity, common good, and participation because its attainment demands joint action of people.

The principle of subsidiarity, which advocates that bigger bodies should allow smaller bodies or individuals to do for themselves what they are capable of, is a recognition and promotion of the self-worth of individuals and smaller collectivities because it allows them to work according to their abilities. Human person, human dignity, and human rights are also related to the principle of subsidiarity through the exercise of human rights. Rights first

---

[986]   Williams, 164.

[987]   Maritain, 53.

suggest the existence of an individual even though rights are relational. This also suggests that the individual always comes prior to the family or society, and so the individual should be given precedence over any kind of collectivity. Human constitution in the divine image and their destiny to eternal life "is the origin of those primordial rights which political society must respect, and which it may not injure when it requires the service of its members."[988] Respect for the human person, human dignity, and human rights is suggested in the principle of subsidiarity, but the individual who is given precedence over a collectivity is also defined against the backdrop of community or collectivity. This links the human person, human rights, and human dignity to solidarity and common good and ultimately to subsidiarity.

Preferential option for the poor is emphasized or called for in order to protect or promote the dignity of the poor. It is, therefore, recognition of the dignity of the disadvantaged. Similarly, affirmative action or aggressive government intervention on behalf of those discriminated against or disadvantaged falls into this category. Any such intervention is for the protection or promotion of the dignity of such vulnerable people.

The principle of the common good is related to the human person, human dignity, and human rights. Common good implies that there is some shared quality among people, and a person is a reflection of the entire community. Such a reflection or mirroring depends on the exercise of respect for human persons, human dignity, and human rights. The common good partially consists in respect for and the promotion of human rights and human dignity. Human dignity and human rights contribute to the common good because human rights protect human dignity, and they are founded on human dignity. They mutually help each other and create part of the conditions demanded by common good as necessary for human flourishing.

The principle of common good is also related to solidarity, association, and participation because all of these suggest that human dignity is recognized. Solidarity suggests that there is inner worth in every person, and this is why people need one another to be and to become. Common good is demanded for the promotion and protection of human dignity. Association is possible on the basis of recognition of the value or worth of the other. Participation by all is also based on the understanding that other people have something to offer. They should be given a chance to contribute because they have inherent worth.

---

[988] Ibid., 75.

From the above observations, it is proper to make the following assertions: First, it is important to emphasize the relationship among the different virtues, principles, and conditions for integral human development because they are dependent on each other directly or indirectly, and thus complementary. To consider the significance of the principles absolutely individually is to deny what Paul VI advocated and called integral human development. Second, the application and functioning of each principle is facilitated by and directed to the same purpose or goal—the protection and enhancement of human dignity. This constitutes a reason for the assertion that human dignity is the ultimate principle and link between all the principles. Each of the principles is based on and directed to human dignity. All other principles, conditions, and virtues necessary for integral human development are related to each other and should be treated as part and parcel of one another. Third, to argue that the various principles for integral human development are independent of one another is to fragment and destroy the integrity of the human person, human dignity, human rights, and integral human development. Since all the principles, virtues, and conditions are based on and directed to human dignity, they are related to each other through human dignity. Therefore, it is realistic to affirm that none of the principles, virtues, and conditions for integral human development is dispensable.

VIII. Conclusion

The "litmus test" for authentic human development is how much the life, the dignity, and rights of the human person are esteemed, cared for, and protected—both individually and collectively. This test depends on a proper understanding of the human person, human dignity, human rights, and true human development. From the investigations in this chapter, a number of conclusions can be drawn. First, there are diverse *anthropologies* both secular and religious. Consequently, though difficult, there is need for an anthropological consensus if the integral human development advocated by Paul VI and the subsequent Catholic social doctrine is to be achieved. If there is no unitary vision of the human person, integral human development remains *utopian*. Paul VI did not provide this vision explicitly. He presumed it was already in place, but his advocacy in *Populorum Progressio* suggests that there is one true way of conceiving the human person.

Second, the *human person* is often viewed from both the liberal Euro-American point of view and the conservative or traditional African communitarian point of view—a representative of the vision of the less-developed nations. These visions affect not only the vision of human rights and human dignity, but also the vision of human development. There is, therefore, a need to seek a reconciliatory vision of the human person—a universal notion based on the origin and nature of the human person—in order to guarantee a possibility for integral development of people and individuals. Such a vision should embrace the private, individual, and the social or public dimension of the human person and the material and spiritual dimensions. The human person should be viewed as a two-dimensional reality—as an individual entity and as a social entity. This requires acknowledgment of the mutual subordination of the individual and society, which Jaques Maritain refers to as "reciprocal subordination and mutual implication."[989]

Third, acknowledgment of the universality of *human dignity* is crucial to the possibility of integral human development. This acknowledgment calls for a reconciliatory notion of human dignity, which may best be described as an ontological dignity because this description is inclusive and captures the transcendent aspect of human worth. On the basis of the ontological character and the universality of human dignity, integral human development may alternatively be defined as the promotion of the human dignity of all people or the universal promotion of human dignity.

Fourth, just as it is the case with human dignity, *human rights* should be acknowledged as reciprocal claims and entitlements with reciprocal or mutual obligations. A reconciliatory notion of human rights is also necessary for integral human development. If such an understanding or notion of rights is lacking, the consequences are conflicts of rights and the practical impossibility of integral human development. Human rights have universal dimensions, but not all human rights are absolute.[990] If rights are viewed as being absolute they remain subjective claims lacking a binding or compelling force.

Fifth, in the context of general Christian anthropology and the anthropology in the Catholic doctrine, *Populorum Progressio* is less explicit in its *anthropology*; but its teaching suggests an anthropology, which is consonant with the rest of Christian anthropology, especially the Roman Catholic anthropology. Paul VI's anthropology could not be more explicit than what

---

[989] Maritain, 65. Also see pages 61, 73, and 75 of the same work.

[990] Michel Perry is of this view too, but suggests that some human rights as moral and legal international rights should be absolute. Cfr. Perry, 7, 88, and 105.

Populorum Progressio suggests because his treatise was not fundamentally anthropological. However, his concern was anthropological because he treated the development of the human person.

Sixth, there are *obstacles* in reconciling the different visions of the human person, human dignity, and human rights. These difficulties can be overcome and need to be overcome, if integral human development is to be attained. The human person, human dignity, and human rights should be defined in terms of their origin, freedom, and intellect. Human persons are ends in themselves, not just means to an end. However, it is necessary to observe that people are intermediate ends in relation to God because God is the only absolute end and only God can make absolute claims.

Seventh, the question of the *universality* of the notion of the human person, human dignity, and some human rights is significant for integral human development because such a vision offers the possibility for the recognition of every person. Paul VI never got directly into the question of the universality of the notion of the human person in *Populorum Progressio*. However, his advocacy for integral human development suggests that he understood the universal nature and dignity of the human person. Human dignity is precisely why he advocated integral development. There should, therefore, be universal validity to the notion of the human person, human dignity, and basic human rights. Human dignity, without exception, should be conceived universally as a valid claim. The distinction between ontological dignity and moral dignity facilitates the understanding of the universality of human dignity fully expressed in the ontological dignity.

Eighth, it is necessary to acknowledge that there is a *relationship between the different principles* for integral human development. No principle for integral human development is independent. This relationship needs to be established, stated, and explained so that the application of one principle of integral human development is done according to how it is related to other development principles.

Finally, it seems appropriate to suggest that the *solution for reconciling* the different notions of the human person, human dignity, and human rights is a *holistic anthropology*. This conclusion suggests an anthropology, which establishes both the individual and social dimensions of the human person and how they relate and operate within the same person. It is on account of a holistic vision of the human person that there is a possibility of integral human development. This is what Paul VI suggested as fundamental for integral human development.

CHAPTER FOUR

Integral Human Development in *Populorum Progressio*: Challenging Uganda's Development Claims

I. INTRODUCTION

This chapter investigates the extent of the challenges of the doctrine of Pope Paul VI's encyclical *Populorum Progressio* to Uganda's development claims, especially since its independence from British colonial rule on October 9, 1962. Until very recently, the World Bank and other Western organizations—the protagonists in the attempts to help African and other less developed countries to develop—often include Uganda among their development promotion success stories, especially since 1986.[991] Whether the claims originate from Uganda or from outside Uganda, they stand to be challenged by the doctrine of *Populorum Progressio* and some current observations about Uganda. A recent African survey of Uganda's development claims contradicts and questions such claims. Economically, Uganda is currently "classified as one of the 26 poorest countries in the world where more than half of the households live below the poverty line."[992] According to "the African Development Report 2005, compiled by the African Development

---

[991] George B. N. Ayittey, *Africa in Chaos* (New York: St. Martin Griffin, 1999), 11-12.

[992] Arthur Bainomugisha, "The Empowerment of Women," in *Uganda's Age of Reforms: A Critical Overview*, ed. Justus Mugaju (Kampala: Fountain Publishers, 1999), 95.

Bank," Uganda is rated as "eleventh from the bottom among African countries with less than $300 per capita."[993]

The chapter attempts to establish how much the development principles, virtues, and conditions stated in *Populorum Progressio* have been integrated into Uganda's development endeavors. It attempts to demonstrate successes and failures of development in Uganda. In line with some of Paul VI's contentions in *Populorum Progressio*, Josephine Bweyale strongly suggests that development in Uganda

> has been deterred in all dimensions of life. Even morals have degenerated drastically, cherished cultural values have been suppressed under the guise of modernity. One wonders whether development means immorality and loss of one's identity.[994]

The above statement of Bweyale, the preceding claims, and the subsequent statements about development help one to make a provisional claim about Uganda at the beginning of this chapter. Uganda's development claims, since its independence in 1962, are in many ways below the standards set by *Populorum Progressio*, which advocates integral human development.

The loci of the arguments and contentions in this chapter are human life, the human person, human dignity, and human rights as consistently implied or explicitly stated and emphasized in the three preceding chapters. These are the critical principles around, which human development revolves. All other principles of integral human development Paul VI advocated in *Populorum Progressio* are grounded in and linked to these fundamental principles.[995] They shall be and should always be emphasized and acknowledged.

---

993   Martin Luther Oketch, "Uganda Is Not a Medium Income Country," in *Daily Monitor* (Kampala, Uganda, February 2, 2006), 22aa. This statement suggests that Uganda is the eleventh last country among countries with a per capita of less than $300. In other words, Uganda's per capita is better than of only ten African countries that have a per capita of less than US $300.

994   Bweyale Josephine, "The Christian Churches and the Peace Building Process," in *Developing a Culture of Peace and Human Rights in Africa: African Peace Series*, vol. 1, eds. Nkrunziza, R.K Deusdedit and Mugumya Levis (Kampala, Uganda: Konrad Adeenauer Stiftung (KAS), 2003), 57-58.

995   A number of paragraphs in *Populorum Progressio* allude to these basic principles for integral human development. Cf. *Populorum Progressio*, 1, 1-2; 5-6,3; 14-17,

Denis Goulet, a development ethicist, contends that "development is an ambiguous term used both *descriptively* and *normatively* to depict a present condition or to project a desired alternative."[996] When the term *development* is applied to Uganda and yields magnanimous conclusions about the development level in the country, those who draw such conclusions have not cared about the idea that there is ambiguity in the notion of development. This is why it is realistic to acknowledge what Goulet states as an often mistaken notion of development:

> Development is equated to aggregate economic growth, the creativity of modern institutions and the spread of consumer aspirations and professional ambitions. In the most fundamental sense, however, none of these is development; at best they may be social changes capable of facilitating genuine development.[997]

Authentic development is not just a socioeconomic and political change. Diverse notions of true human development and the human person were advocated in history because of uncritical considerations. It seems right to construe that "most economic or political paradigms of development define it as a process of structural change in which external forces shape and transform people's lives."[998] This claim about development is supported by the assertion that "during the early 1960s there were competing notions of development."[999] However, the question to be investigated in this chapter is partly whether development is from without or from within a person, community (society), or a nation.

7-9; 20-23, 9-11; 28,13; 30,13; 32, 14; 36-37,16; 39,17; 42,18; 48, 20-21; 50, 21; 64-65, 27 and 71, 29.

[996] Dennis Goulet, *Development Ethics: A Guide to Theory and Practice* (New York: The Apex Press, 1995), 1.

[997] Ibid., 141.

[998] Susan Reynolds Whyte and Michael A. Whyte, "The Values of Development: Conceiving Growth and Progress in Bunyole," in *Developing Uganda,* eds. Bernt Holger Hansen and Michael Twaddle (Kampala: Fountain Publishers, 1998), 227. Also see Marvin Krier L. Mich, *Catholic Social Teaching and Movements* (Mystic, Connecticut: Twenty Third Publications, 1998), 155.

[999] Marvin Krier L. Mich, *Catholic Social Teaching and Movements* (Mystic, Connecticut: Twenty-Third Publications, 1998), 155.

Several authors, institutions, and governments have differences of opinion regarding the notion of human development, the requisite principles and their challenges to, and practicability in the diverse human situations. A majority of these claims are based on limited reflections, examination, and interpretations of the notion of development and the human person. They have not adequately expressed and emphasized the most fundamental elements for authentic human development—the human person, human dignity, and human rights. This factor ultimately makes the achievement of true human development difficult. These assertions also suggest why integral human development is not readily possible and cannot be practically achieved in most, if not all, countries including Uganda.

The meaning of development has been misconstrued by many people in Uganda, in the same way Paul VI suggested in *Populorum Progressio* as presented in chapter three. Mahmood Mamdani suggests that there is misunderstanding of human development in Uganda:

> It used to be that the analysis of a politics of underdeveloped countries was informed solely by the dualism of the traditional and the modern . . . . The traditional was retrogressive, the modern was progressive.[1000]

Mamdani's statement reflects the way development is conceived by the majority of Ugandans. In contemporary Uganda, development is also conceived differently among the various ethnic groups as Twaddle and Hansen suggest by acknowledging that there are "conflicting models of development which continue to influence Museveni's Uganda."[1001]

It is critical to note that the "starting point and term of reference" of the Fathers of the Second Vatican Council "was the kind of economic development to which governments all over the world were committed," and because they were discontented with the notion of development at that time, they "set out to correct and expand this conception, to produce a more integral

---

[1000] Mahmood Mamdani, *Politics and Class Formation in Uganda* (New York and London: Monthly Review Press, 1976), 1.

[1001] Michael Twaddle and Hansen Holger Brent, "The Changing State of Uganda," in *Developing Uganda*, eds. Holger Bernt Hansen and Michael Twaddle (Kampala: Fountain Publishers, 1998), 10 and 12.

and balanced conception of human development."[1002] Paul VI's doctrine of integral human development in *Populorum Progressio* continued the spirit of the Second Vatican Council and suggests a persistent challenge to a failure of authentic development in Uganda and other countries.

Therefore, the fundamental thesis in this chapter is that the development claims in Uganda, though not excluding other nations, fall short of authentic human development because the notion of integral human development advocated by Paul VI in *Populorum Progressio* presents pertinent challenges to the status quo in contemporary Uganda. Paul VI's vision of human development includes all dimensions of a person and all people. This is evident in his core statement and challenge in *Populorum Progressio*:

> The development of which we are speaking does not extend solely to economic growth. To be genuine, growth must be integral, it must clearly provide for the progress of each individual and of the whole man. In this regard an eminent specialist in the field has rightly and forcefully said: "we do not approve of separating the economic from the human or of considering development apart from the civilization to which it belongs. In our opinion great value is to be placed on man, each man, each group of men and human society as a whole.[1003]

Paul VI was convinced that, if this vision of development is seriously taken and applied, it could transform people's thoughts and attitudes and, eventually, their practical life situations. The transformation advocated by Paul VI is holistic. Such a vision and transformation is particularly necessary in the Ugandan context.

The chapter is divided into three main parts. Part one treats the statement of the problem in a general way, and in fact, it is a precis of the Ugandan situation. Part two is a study of the situation of Uganda in the light of the development principles, virtues, and factors or conditions in Populorum

---

[1002] Donal Dorr, *Option for the Poor: A Hundred Years of Catholic Social Teaching* (New York: Orbis Books, 1992), 180.

[1003] Paul VI (Pope), *Populorum Progressio, On the Development of Peoples* (Washington DC: United States Catholic Conference, 1967), 14, 7. The eminent source and specialist Paul VI is quoting here is L. J. Lebret, OP, *Dynamique concrete du developpement* (Paris: Economie et Humanisme, Les editions ouvrieres, 1961), 28.

Progressio as treated in chapter two and chapter three. Part three offers some recommendations for Uganda's development.

II. PROBLEM STATEMENT: A *PRECIS* OF THE UGANDA CONTEXT

The problematic situation in Uganda is at once realized when one traces the origin of the name of the country. "The name of Uganda was derived from the ancient kingdom of Buganda."[1004] When the British wanted to name their protectorate, which included Buganda and other ethnic or tribal groups, the Baganda wanted the country to be called Buganda. The British refused because the dominance of Buganda was already causing tension. Moreover, Buganda was Britain's favored ethnic group of what would later be called Uganda. To make it a neutral name and avoid further tension, the letter *B* was simply omitted; hence, the name Uganda emerged as the name of the British protectorate and has remained the name of the nation to date.

Uganda became independent on October 9, 1962. Justus Mugaju suggests that at that time it was relatively developed compared to other third world countries in the world, but "shortly after independence, the country degenerated into tyranny, chaos, violence, war, economic collapse and moral degeneration."[1005] He states that in most of the period from 1971-1986, there was widespread lawlessness although lawlessness predates 1971. About a million people lost their lives, many were imprisoned, and some others went into exile. This was hardly a period of human development in Uganda. It is necessary to note that the development referred to here is integral or authentic development, which Alice Tuyizere, like Paul VI, has suggested "is people centred and guided by values of peace, justice, equality and genuine participation in a democratic way."[1006] It is correct, however, to say that the critical statement regarding the situation in Uganda is that—to a significant

---

[1004] Richard Nzita and Mbaga-Niwampa, *Peoples and Cultures of Uganda* (Kampala: Fountain Publishers, 1997), 1.

[1005] Justus Mugaju, "The Historical Context," in *Uganda's Age of Reforms: A Critical Overview*, ed. Justus Mugaju (Kampala: Fountain Publishers, 1999), 10. Also see George B. N. Ayittey, *Africa Unchained: The Blue Prin6t for Africa's Future* (New York: Palgrave Macmillan, 2005), 204-206.

[1006] Tuyizere Alice, "Introduction of Peace Education in Secondary Schools: A Strategy for Promotion of Peace in Uganda," in *Developing a Culture of Peace and Human Rights in Africa: African Peace Series*, volume 1, eds. Nkrunziza,

extent—true, or integral human development has not been evident in Uganda since its independence. This claim is supported by the following observation by Adrian K. Ddungu, which shows the recurrent situation in Uganda since independence:

> The endemic obstacles to integral development in Uganda are very well known, namely: ignorance, disease, poverty, exploitation, instability, political manipulation, greed, selfishness among those who control power and money, gross injustices and corruption in most sectors of society, and the absence of a clear and correct people and life-centred vision of development.[1007]

The national disparity of development in Uganda may also be explained by the people's division along "religious, regional and ethnic lines, and the colonialists' politico-administrative way of doing things,"[1008] which emphasized these divisions and made them the basis of their administration. Hence, there is need for unity in the country and care for the common good of the people of Uganda. The dual principal elements of Uganda's national motto and national anthem, respectively—For God and My Country and "United free for liberty / Together we will always stand"—are constant reminders to the people about the need of their efforts toward this unity and common good.[1009] Integral human development is possible in a country if there is national unity. Unfortunately, disunity is one of the issues Ugandans have to wrestle with in order to advance together as citizens of a nation.

R. K. Deusdedit and Mugumya Levis (Kampala, Uganda: Konrad Adeenauer Stiftung (KAS, 2003), 74.

[1007] Adrian K. Ddungu, "Church-State Cooperation in Promoting Integral Development—A Supplement," in *Church Contribution to Integral Development*, eds. Joseph Therese Agbasiere and Boniface K. Zabajungu (Eldoret, Kenya: AMECEA Gaba Publications, 1989), 24. This element has continued to date when, unfortunately, many unsuspecting Ugandans believe that the country has advanced so far. Also see Paul Gifford, *African Christianity: Its Public Role* (Bloomington, Indiana: Indiana University Press, 1998), 116.

[1008] Ondoga Amaza Ori, *Museveni's Long March: From Guerrilla to Statesman* (Kampala: Fountain Publishers, 1998), 223.

[1009] George W. Kakoma and Peter Tynard, "Uganda," in *National Anthems of the World*, eds. T. M. Cartledge, W. L. Reed, Martin Shaw, and Henry Coleman (New York: Arco Publishing Company Inc., 1978), 456.

Since its independence, and even prior to that, tribal or regional allegiances militated against any nationwide nationalist movement in Uganda. The people could not come together as a consolidated or united front. There is no doubt that "deep north-south divisions"[1010] have characterized the history of postindependence Uganda. This is reminiscent in the persistent disunity in the country today. This element of disunity, which recurs in the relationships among Ugandans to date, predates Uganda's independence. Paul Gifford says this of preindependence Uganda:

> In the run up to independence, the rise of any properly nationalist movement was hindered because the Baganda, seeking a separate state, refused to countenance any proposal which treated Buganda as an integral part of greater Uganda.[1011]

There is a tribalism or there are tribalisms, as some would suggest, which tend to impede national unity and, consequently, integral human development.[1012] The tribal constitution of the country compounds the difficulties in applying the principles Paul VI offered in *Populorum Progressio*. In treating the question of integral human development in Uganda, one deals with a heterogeneous context—"the three main groups of Eastern Africa— Bantu, Nilotic and Nilo-Hamitic—all meet in Uganda."[1013] Other than this, "political parties tend to divide the people along ethnic, religious and such other non-political lines resulting in unnecessary conflict,"[1014] a reason for which the NRM government denied multiparty politics for Ugandans for twenty years. Such a denial could be considered a genuine political reason because it helped to temper the political situation in Uganda, but it is opposed

---

[1010] USAID, Democracy and Governance Assessment: Republic of Uganda, 2005 (Burlington, Vermont, USA: ARD Inc., November 2005), vii.

[1011] Paul Gifford, *African Christianity: Its Public Role* (Bloomington, Indiana: Indiana University Press, 1998), 114.

[1012] Vincent, Okot Oburu, "The Church's Role in Promoting National Unity," in *Church Contribution to Integral Development*, eds. Joseph Therese Agbasiere and Boniface K. Kabajungu (Eldoret, Kenya: AMECEA Gaba Publications, 1989), 101.

[1013] International Bank for Reconstruction and Development, *The Economic Development of Uganda* (Baltimore: John Hopkins Press, 1962), 6.

[1014] Ondoga, 201.

to democracy and freedom of association and infringes on the human, civil, social, and political rights of Ugandans.

The commission from the International Bank for Reconstruction and Development, on the request of the Uganda government, emphasized the gravity of the ethnic division in the country by asserting that there is still evident division that runs across Uganda between the Bantu-speaking people, who are mostly in the south and central lake region of the country, the Nilo-Hamitic-speaking people to the northeast of the country, and the Nilotic-speaking people of the north, and the Sudanic-speaking people west of the river Nile in the north of the country besides the Hamitic-related pastoral class, the Bahima, in the western part of the country. Uganda consists of twenty-four to thirty-four or more ethnic groups within these major divisions.[1015] It seems correct to suggest that religion or Christianity in particular and the claims of Uganda's so-called *broad-based government* have not overcome this effect of ethnic diversity.

The pluralistic context of Uganda is suggested by the diversity of cultures exemplified in the different languages spoken all over the country and the diverse vision of human, social, political, and economic relations and trends of thought. "There are diverse cultural groups speaking more than thirty-three languages,"[1016] although other authors give lower figures. The issue of language is outstanding and needs a careful and critical consideration.[1017] A real mutual understanding is necessary because of the ethnic diversity in the country. Besides the people of African descent, there are people of Indian and European descent. Although the latter two groups constitute a small percentage of the population, they are economically and politically more

---

[1015] Tarsis B. Kabwegyere, *Politics of State Formation and Destruction in Uganda* (Kampala: Fountain Publishers, 1995), 19. Also see Paul Gifford, *African Christianity: Its Public Role* (Bloomington, Indiana: Indiana University Press, 1998), 133. The 1995 Constitution of the Republic of Uganda indicates that Uganda's indigenous communities as on 1 February 1926, numbered about 56. Cfr. Government of Uganda, *Constitution of the Republic of Uganda* (Entebbe: Uganda printing and Publishing Corporation, 22 September, 1995), 189-191.

[1016] Nzita and Mbaga-Niwampa, ii.

[1017] Franz, Pfaff, "People's Participation in Development," in *Church Contribution to Integral Development*, eds. Joseph Therese Agbasiere and Boniface K. Kabajungu (Eldoret, Kenya: AMECEA Gaba Publications, 1989), 155.

influential and powerful than the indigenous people and a significant force to reckon with.[1018]

Kabwegyere suggests such a pluralistic social constitution by acknowledging that there is "diversity in terms of social scale and social organization."[1019] At the advent of colonialism, some of the groups were socially, economically, and politically powerful while others were not, and the social organizational structures varied in magnitude—some were organized on a small scale while others were organized on a large scale. The advantaged positions were further strengthened by the colonial administration and continued to the postindependence period. They are partly responsible for the conflicts that started soon after independence.[1020] They were, principally, tensions between superiority and inferiority. These tensions and other diversities suggest difficulties of achievement of integral human development—a real challenge to Uganda today.

Another problem is uneven development in and among individuals, contrary to the consistent teaching of *Populorum Progressio* in the global context.[1021] This disparity in Uganda's development is the effect of overemphasis on the diversity in the country. Consequent to the political, ethnic, religious, and language diversity, there is conspicuous tribalism, ethnic animosities, persistent political division, segregation, discrimination, and factionalism.[1022] There have been and there are, for instance, still "post-independence and political factions" like "pro-Baganda" and "anti-Baganda"[1023] factions. At this

---

[1018] International Bank for Reconstruction and Development, 6.

[1019] Kabwegyere, 19.

[1020] Ali A. Mazrui, *Violence and Thought: Essays on Social Tensions in Africa* (New York: Humanities Press, 1969), 148-149. Also see Paul Gifford, *African Christianity: Its Public Role* (Bloomington, Indiana: Indiana University Press, 1998), 114.

[1021] *Populorum Progressio*, 8, 4; 29, 13; 34, 15 and 76, 31-32. Also cfr. Peter Riga, *The Church of the Poor: A Commentary on Paul VI's Encyclical on the Development of Peoples* (Illinois: Divine Word Publications, 1968), 67.

[1022] The discrimination talked of here is not only on ethnic or tribal basis but also gender oriented. See Aili Mari Tripp, "Local Women's Association and Politics in Contemporary Uganda," in *Developing Uganda*, eds. Bernt Holger Hansen and Michael Twaddle (Kampala: Fountain Publishers, 1998), 120. Also see Vincent, Okot Oburu, 102.

[1023] Twaddle and Hansen, 12.

point, it is important to reflect on the observation of Ali Mazrui, a renowned East African scholar:

> Ethnic pluralism, in much of Africa, tends to be among the most politically sensitive of all the social issues. The risk of violence between tribes is at the centre of Africa's twin-crises of identity and integration.[1024]

Mazrui is contending that division is imminent and unity is hard to achieve because of ethnic differences and tensions. This is a problem to be addressed if African nations, including Uganda, which have such characteristic tribal or ethnic diversity, are to achieve integral development. The cattle-rustling by the Karamojong and the frequent conflict between them and their neighbors, a problem that demands some solution, is a testimony to this fact.[1025] The problem here is one of cultural differences, which require mutual education, understanding and acceptance of cultures, especially those aspects of culture, which are enhancing to the human person and human dignity and promote human development.

Considering the fact that even neighboring ethnic groups are in frequent disagreement and tension, the issue remains serious for both the church and state to resolve. Caution is needed here because the Karamojong, for example, may have to be approached and treated according to their background without imposing certain values on them. For instance, a political system which centralizes activities is contrary to their sociopolitical setup, which is *acephalous* and even "the very word chief does not exist: because among them nobody can impose on others his or her will."[1026] Other than corruption, injustice, ignorance, and illiteracy, exploitation of the poor and the weak is another problem, which compounds the social distinction of the elite.[1027] Also

---

[1024] Mazrui, 155. Also see Okot, 98.

[1025] Bruno Novelli, "Church and Development for Nomads," in *Church Contribution to Integral Development*, eds. Joseph Therese Agbasiere and Boniface K. Zabajungu (Eldoret, Kenya: AMECEA Gaba Publications, 1989), 144.

[1026] Ibid., 144.

[1027] Paul Gifford, *African Christianity: Its Public Role* (Bloomington, Indiana: Indiana University Press, 1998), 115-116. Also see Twadle and Hansen, 2 and 5. Also see Mahmood Mamdani, *Politics and Class Formation in Uganda* (Kampala: Fountain Publishers, 1999), 233-235.

featuring clearly in Uganda are problems such as: poverty, unemployment, prejudice and social stratification, dependence syndrome, an ever-widening gap between the rich and the poor, recurrent wars, and political instability.[1028] In 1994, Uganda was unable to meet 50 percent of its debt service obligations because of its inadequate foreign currency earnings.[1029] It was "among the world's five poorest countries" in 1991 and in "1998 when Uganda sent troops into DRC"[1030] (Democratic Republic of Congo), the economy was much affected.

There has also been a considerable violation of human dignity and rights, which are central to Paul VI's thoughts on human development. Uganda's additional crucial historical problems are as follows: a bad education system, cultural superiority and inferiority, and socioeconomic and political confrontations, and "mutual suspicions."[1031] Corruption, which is one of the aspects of NRM's target in the ten-point program, which aimed at elimination of corruption is also a great force to reckon with and major factor yet to be overcome in Uganda today.[1032] Contrary to NRM government's initial plans to overcome corruption, George B. N. Ayittey offers evidences of Uganda's escalating corruption. Acording to him, the corruption in Uganda permeates all levels of Ugandan society, and the Uganda Debt Network (UDN) recently reported that

> Uganda has been ranked among the most corrupt countries of the world . . . 80 percent of business in Uganda pays a bribe before accessing a service . . . . In the year 2000, transparency

---

[1028] Susan Dicklich, "Indigenous NGOs and Political Participation," in *Developing Uganda*, eds. Michael Twaddle and Bernt Holger Hansen (Kampala: Fountain Publishers, 1998), 149. Also see Twadle and Hansen, 1-2 and 10.

[1029] Nalugala, Reginald, and Richard Mutua, "A Practical Approach to Empowerment of the Poor in Kenya," in *The Poor Discover Their Own Resources: A Practical Approach to Poverty Reduction in Urban and Rural Areas in Africa* (Nairobi: Pauline Publications Africa, 2002), 17.

[1030] Legget, 12. Also see "Uganda," in *Oxford Encyclopedic World Atlas*, 6th ed. (New York: Oxford University Press Inc., 2002), 222.

[1031] Ondoga, 183.

[1032] Phares Mutibwa, *Uganda since Independence: A Story of Unfulfilled Hopes* (Kampala, Uganda: Fountain Publishers, 1992), 180.

International ranked Uganda as the third most corrupt country in the world . . . .[1033]

While the police, judiciary, and the health department are rated **the** most corrupt institutions in the country, the World Bank Mission sent to investigate Uganda in 1998 pointed accusing fingers to President Museveni's brother, Salim Saleh; the then Vice President Specioza Wandira Kazibwe; and even President Museveni himself, collaborating with the presidents of Rwanda and Burundi to plunder the resources of the DRC.[1034] The simplest conclusion here is that it is not a development to move from the goal of fighting corruption to being part of the efforts for the promotion of corruption—an evident self-defeating (contradictory) development plan or prophecy.

Anthony J. Regan, like many authors, states that "Uganda is divided along overlapping complex religious, ethnic, regional and economic lines."[1035] Divisions and conflicts are sometimes consequences of multiculturalism or ethnic diversity. In themselves, multiculturalism and ethnicity are not bad, as Gregory Baum contends as he addresses a similar problem in a Canadian context.[1036] Neither does Paul VI condemn cultural diversity in *Populorum Progressio*. He actually encouraged the promotion of culture and respect for other cultures. However, the contentions of Paul VI and Baum also call for a critical reflection about the problematic aspects of multiculturalism or ethnicity, at least from a Christian perspective. Dominant groups in a diverse community may not overlook people of the same community with different cultural, racial, and ethnic backgrounds because they all have dignity before God who created all of them. Baum suggests this point in his critical and crucial statement, a statement still more crucial for Uganda, a nation characterized by "religious, ethnic, regional and economic"[1037] diversity:

[1033] George B. N. Ayittey, *Africa Unchained: The Blue Print for Africa's Future* (New York: Palgrave Macmillan, 2005), 208.

[1034] Ibid., 208-209.

[1035] Anthony J. Regan, "Decentralization Policy: Reshaping State and Society," in *Developing Uganda*, eds. Michael Twaddle and Bernt Holger Hansen (Kampala: Fountain Publishers, 1998), 161.

[1036] Gregory Baum, *The Social Imperative: Essays on Critical Issues that Confront Christian Churches* (New York: Paulist Press, 1979), 203.

[1037] Regan, 161.

Since God has created humanity made up of different peoples and
different traditions, it is intolerable that the dominant group in a
country should despise the less successful groups and make some
people feel badly about their ethnic or racial background. To expose
children to a climate in which they are made ashamed of their own
heritage is a grave social sin.[1038]

Baum's vision is socioculturally and psychologically important for
authentic integral human development. Families, institutions, and ethnic
groups contribute socially, culturally, and psychologically toward integral
human development. It is the responsibility of all these social groups to impart
to their members that "every human person is distinct from every other, yet
at the same time all are truly human."[1039] This responsibility depends on good
and proper personality development, which is the duty of the government,
the religious institutions, families, ethnic communities, and educators. The
individual human person is ultimately decisive, but this is impacted by the
primary educators and formators. Reichmann confirms this view:

One's racial, cultural and educational backgrounds function as
a significant influence on the kinds of decisions one will make,
but they do not determine these decisions, nor is their influence
ultimately decisive.[1040]

One of the greatest challenges to Uganda's development claims, Peter
Henriot asserts, is that "integral human development anywhere requires
integral development everywhere."[1041] This contention suggests that
what Paul VI affirms in *Populorum Progressio* is that a true development
is not fragmented. Dorr's reading of *Populorum Progressio* rightly shows
that "Paul VI provides a basis for integrating personal development with

---

[1038] Baum, 203.

[1039] James B. Reichmann, *Philosophy of the Human Person* (Chicago: Loyola University
Press, 1985), 252.

[1040] Ibid., 212.

[1041] Peter J. Henriot, "Who Cares about Africa? Development Guidelines from the
Church's Social Teaching," in *Catholic Social Thought and the New World Order:
Building on One Hundred Years,* eds. Oliver Williams and John H. Houck (Notre
Dame: University of Notre Dame Press, 1993), 219.

community development and reconciling national development with global development."[1042] According to Paul VI, integral human development is both individual and communal.

Nationally, integral development calls for national participation besides other requisite factors. Such participation is possible when there is a common medium of communication. Unfortunately in Uganda, there is the problem of language differences because at least thirty-three languages are spoken. On March 31, 1967, because of cultural and language diversity, Apollo Milton Obote—the then President of Uganda—adopted the position of the British and reiterated that English shall be the national or official language used for education, politics, and economics.[1043] This was an attempt to solve the problem of language, but another problem has been created, namely, the problem of a majority not knowing the national and official language of the country. This means participation of the majority is curtailed because the official language favors the minority. Political participation since Uganda's independence has always been the privilege of powerful minorities.[1044] This is explained by the fact that change of government has always come through coups. A slight change developed in the 1990s when people started electing representatives to parliament and government offices. However, whether everybody who participated in these elections understood what it is all about is still questionable.

Uganda's political history shows that the country never had a smooth transition of governments. From the time of Benedict Kiwanuka to the time of Pres. Yoweri Kaguta Museveni in 1986, there were successive coups.[1045] Each time, change of government occurred by force of arms. It has mostly been a *traumatic* history as some people describe it.[1046] When Prime Minister Milton Obote took over power from Kabaka Edward Mutesa—the king and president or head of state at independence—by force of arms in 1966, he abolished the four kingdoms: Bunyoro, Toro, Ankole and Buganda, forcing Buganda

---

[1042] Dorr, 182.

[1043] Pfaff, 155.

[1044] Ibid., 156.

[1045] Bweyale, 58.

[1046] Ronald Kassimir, "Uganda: The Catholic Church and State Reconstruction," in *The African State at A Critical Juncture: Between Disintegration and Reconfiguration*, eds. Leonardo A. Villalon and Philip A. Huxtable (London: Lynne Rienner Publishers, 1998), 235.

which had an apparent federal status to come directly under the control of the central government of Uganda. He abrogated the 1962 constitution and introduced a new constitution in 1967, and in 1969, he banned "all opposition parties."[1047] Obote's popularity continued to sink among the different institutions and categories of people in Uganda.[1048] One coup after another continued to occur in Uganda from then on.[1049]

In 1971, Milton Obote was overthrown by Idi Amin Dada who expelled all Asians from Uganda in 1972.[1050] He attempted to invade Tanzania and annex part of its territory in and around Kagera to Uganda, and he was in turn overthrown by a coalition of Tanzanian forces and Ugandan exiles who formed themselves into the Uganda National Liberation Army in 1979.[1051] A provisional government was established under the military commission headed by Paul Mwanga who was assisted by Yoweri Museveni. Yusufu Lule and Godfrey Binaisa were leaders shortly: each one was overthrown, eventually, to pave way for Milton Obote to return to power when rigged elections were held in 1980 and Uganda People's Congress (UPC) party under the presidency of Milton Obote was declared the winner. He soon was overthrown by the army under the leadership of Tito Okello-Lutwa in 1985.[1052]

While Tito Okello-Lutwa attempted negotiation with the opposition forces, the most significant of which was National Resistance Army/National Resistance Movement (NRA/NRM), the latter refused but pretended to be in favor of the negotiations then taking place in Nairobi, Kenya.[1053] As talks continued the NRA was making its way to Kampala—the capital city—to capture power, and they did so under Yoweri Kaguta Museveni in 1986 when they captured Kampala and dissolved the Military Council.[1054]

The NRM established what it called a *broad-based government* with representatives of all groups; elections were held in 1989 to the Constituent Assembly dominated by Museveni's supporters, to write a constitution, which was published in 1993 and promulgated in 1995, and the constitution

---

1047 Gifford, 114. Also see USAID, 4.

1048 Mugaju, 24.

1049 Kassimir, 235. Also see USAID, 4.

1050 Mutibwa, 91-92.

1051 Ibid., 125.

1052 Ibid. Also see pages 138-147 and 163-169 of the same source.

1053 Mutibwa, 169.

1054 Gifford, 114.

allowed only no-party democracy.[1055] This was actually a one-party system of government, and that one party was NRM. Technically, all other parties were banned, and there was no multiparty democracy for at least twenty years. There has been political unrest and instability, with its brutality, in the north and northeastern part of Uganda during these twenty years, and it is likely to persist.[1056]

The political system used in Uganda since independence shows similar patterns with just slightly modified differences. There has been consistent failure of democratic governance, a dictatorship of one kind or another, and expression of self-interest. This claim can be substantiated by the ardent request and plea of the Catholic Bishops of Uganda in their appeal to the members of parliament when they say: "the 'self-seeking politics' that has characterized Uganda's politics for several years since independence should be shunned."[1057] This is not just a statement defying the past. It is also addressing the currently prevailing situation in the politics of Uganda.

Prior to independence, the economy of Uganda was flourishing but not controlled by the natives in much the same way the political system was not in their control. It was a situation where much of the economic destiny of Ugandan nationals was not in their own hands. There was simply no economic and political participation of the indigenous people, or it was minimal. Paul Gifford has properly stated this case:

> Within the Protectorate, Indians—normally called "Asians" and originally brought in to build the East African railway—were encouraged and assisted to engage in business and trade; Africans received no such assistance. Asians were given a place on the Legislative Council, something denied to Africans until after the Second World War when Britain had accepted that decolonization was inevitable.[1058]

From the point of view of education in Uganda, for a long time, too much emphasis has been laid on academic education instead of practical training.

[1055] Ibid., 115.

[1056] Ibid., 116.

[1057] Catholic Bishops of Uganda, *Towards A Democratic and Peaceful Uganda Based on the Common Good* (Kisubi, Uganda: Marianum Press, November 2005), 14.

[1058] Gifford, 113-114.

Much of the education people have received is not related to practical or actual daily life situations and needs, although recently emphasis is being made on the significance of vocational institutions and the study of practical Sciences.[1059] This more theoretical and less practical system of education has been a persisting pattern since colonial times.

In conclusion, the principal factors impeding or causing development difficulties in Uganda are as follows: cultural diversity, socioeconomic and political variations, religious views, and general disunity. All of these may be explained in terms of limited anthropology. These factors have often made it difficult to implement or apply the necessary virtues, conditions, and principles for integral human development. The lack of application of these virtues, conditions, and principles primarily presents pertinent challenges to the church, the state, and individual citizens and groups of people living in Uganda although the challenges go beyond this limit.

III. CHALLENGING UGANDA'S DEVELOPMENT CLAIMS: THE CHOICE BETWEEN CONFRONTATION AND MUTUAL RESPECT

The overarching challenge of Paul VI's teaching in *Populorum Progressio* to the socioeconomic, religious, and political context of Uganda, according to Benedict XVI, was "the scandal of underdevelopment as an outrage against humanity,"[1060] and the very concept of authentic development, which he articulated in the document. The principal and durable challenge is the respect for human dignity. True development is the moral growth of the human person and all possible dimensions of growth for each and everybody—a concept whose practical manifestations are lacking in Uganda, even spiritually, but also socially, politically, economically, and culturally due to marginalization of some sectors of the population.[1061] The fundamental

---

[1059] J. C. B. Bigala, "The Church's Contribution to Education," in *Church Contribution to Integral Development*, eds. Joseph Therese Agbasiere and Boniface K. Zabajungu (Eldoret, Kenya: AMECEA Gaba Publications, 1989), 168-170. Also see pages 176-177 of this work.

[1060] Benedictus PP. XVI, "Jesus at the sight of the crowds was moved with pity" (Mt. 9: 36), message of Pope Benedict XVI for Lent 2006 in *Arua Diocese Bulletin*, no.69 (Arua: Arua Diocese Communication Department, March 2006) 1. Benedict XVI backed his assertion by quoting *Populorum Progressio*, 21, 9.

[1061] USAID, 57.

challenge is, therefore, the respect for the human person, human dignity, and human rights expressed in the complete growth of an individual and all people. This challenge is manifest in the different facets of human life. Addressing Uganda's development problems, Adrian K. Ddungu reaffirms Paul VI's idea of development:

> Integral development is opposed to *dichotomized* development. The former aims at enabling all men and women to be inspired, directed and assisted in developing, as fully as possible, in various dimensions of life: educational-physical, socio-personal, moral-cultural, economic-political, spiritual-religious. Integral development should appropriately take into account the fact that a human being is made up of body, soul and mind. To develop integrally, people need to plan for all their material and spiritual needs in an holistic manner, without undue imbalances.[1062]

Ddungu's contention is clearly the reiteration of the doctrine, especially the definition of true development in *Populorum Progressio*. He suggests that both church and state leaders should serve people without dichotomizing their lives, without separating the spiritual and the material dimensions of the human person. This is one of the general challenges of the document. However, the document challenges the Ugandan context in the various facets of the life of the nation as explained below.

A. The Anthropological Challenge: The Challenge of Mutual Respect

The main challenge here is to respect and protect people's dignity. In dealing with the anthropological challenges, we deal with the most crucial elements of the question of human development. Human development is directly related to the human person who has dignity, free will, rationality, rights, and eternal destiny.[1063] The gravity of the anthropological challenge ought to be seen in the light of peace; the fact that the anthropological

---

[1062] Ddungu, 21.

[1063] Lorenzo Servitje Sendra "Reevaluating Private Enterprise," in *Curing World Poverty: The New Role of Property*, ed. John H. Miller (Saint Louis, Missouri: Social Justice Review, 1994), 83.

challenge underlies all other development principles, virtues, and conditions suggested by Paul VI; and finally, the situation in which people of Uganda as citizens of the secular society and members of the church live. In relation to issues affecting the people of Uganda, the Executive of the Association of Major Superiors of Religious Institutes in Uganda (AMSRIU) made the following challenging statement about the situation of the Internally Displaced People (IDP) in the war-torn northern Uganda and northeastern Uganda:

> This appalling situation in the camps is a crime against humanity! It is a big challenge to each and all of us. We have to do all that is possible to bring it to an end.[1064]

The challenge in this case is not only the need to recognize the human person, human dignity, and human rights but also to respect them. The human person, the respect for human rights, and ultimately, human dignity with which every person is gifted by God, whatever background the person comes from, should be acknowledged and respected. These areas constitute the challenge of mutual respect, which *Populorum Progressio* consistently suggests and which was emphasized in chapter three of this work. Similarly, in a global context, Bernard Haring and Valentino Salvoldi suggest that it is significant to have an appropriate anthropology in order to have the possibility of an integral human development:

> One hopes for the advent of an era in which an authentic world community can be created in which the dignity of each one and the fundamental rights of all are recognized and in which every nation understands that it cannot think of its own welfare without interesting itself in the welfare of all nations.[1065]

Human dignity and human rights are the consistently challenging anthropological principles for integral human development. Mutual respect

---

[1064] The Executive Association of the Major Superiors of Religious Institutes in Uganda, "Live by the Truth and the Truth Will Set You Free," in *Arua Diocese Bulletin*, no. 68 (Arua, Uganda, February 2006), 7.

[1065] Bernard Haring and Valentino Salvoldi, *Tolerance: Towards an Ethic of Solidarity and Peace*, trans. Edmund C. Lane (New York: Alba House, 1995), 60. This is a reference to *Pacem in Terris*, paragraph 68.

for them is tantamount to mutual human development. In the Uganda context, we are dealing with what the 1995 Constitution of the Republic of Uganda also clearly acknowledges as being beyond the control of any person when it affirmed that "fundamental rights and freedoms of the individual are inherent and not granted by the state."[1066] While the constitution aptly affirms the fundamental character of the human person, rights, and dignity, the challenge to the government is to help people to protect and enhance these elements.

One specific challenge, among others, to the Uganda government and to the church is the 2000 Kanungu tragedy,[1067] where people of a religious sect—the Movement for the Restoration of the Ten Commandments of God (MRTCG)—were burnt to death. Although the government issued arrest warrants for the culprits, after more than four years, or more now, no arrest has been made.[1068] The local governments in the areas where the movement had establishments were not negligent or careless about the people, their rights, and dignity. Indeed, they attempted to make arrests of the propagators of this religion on discovering that they were promoting dangerous ideas, but the arrests were condemned by higher government officials.[1069] This is one of the significant anthropological challenges to the

---

[1066] Government of Uganda, *The Constitution of the Republic of Uganda* (Entebbe: Uganda Printing and Publishing Corporation, 22 September 1995), 20.

[1067] Kanungu is a place in Western Uganda in the Archdiocese of Mbarara. The Kanungu tragedy is an incident that happened on March 17, 2000, when many people belonging to an apocalyptic religious group called the Movement for the Restoration of the Ten Commandments of God, founded in Mbarara Archdiocese in Western Uganda, were killed by a fire deliberately ignited by the leadership of the group, who were breakaway Catholics including two excommunicated Catholic priests—Dominic Kataribabo, a former junior seminary rector, and Joseph Kasapurari, known to and a former classmate (in the Major Seminary at Ggaba) of the author of this work after purportedly having received a vision about the end of the world with the new millenium. Also see Narcisio Bagumisiriza, *The Kanungu Tragedy 17th March 2000 and Details of Related Discoveries: The Movement for the Restoration of the Ten Commandments of God* (Kisubi: Marianum Press, 2005), 4-7.

[1068] Narcisio Bagumisiriza, *The Kanungu Tragedy 17th March 2000 and Details of Related Discoveries: The Movement for the Restoration of the Ten Commandments of God* (Kisubi: Marianum Press, 2005), 73.

[1069] Ibid.

citizens and, above all, the government of Uganda, which has the duty to protect the citizens from being harmed. A government that cares about its citizens should have prevented such a tragedy by enforcing laws through national security agents. It should have pursued this case and informed citizens of the findings. Both the Catholic Church and the Protestant Church made vain attempts to thwart the growth of the religious movement.[1070] Their efforts needed to be supplemented by the government. This is where a healthy church-state relationship is invaluable to resolve issues affecting people's dignity and rights.

The constitution of Uganda suggests that the Ugandans are equal in some regard and should recognize each other as such. Vincent Okot Oburu also speaks to this effect in an attempt to explain the role of the church in promoting national unity in Uganda. Unity can only be attained if there is mutual recognition among the citizens of Uganda:

> Many Ugandans have not fully recognized people from other tribal or ethnic groups, as being fellow citizens, with equal rights and duties: in the social, political and economic life of the country.[1071]

The above statement is consonant with what Ali A. Mazrui construes as a crucial challenge to Africans and others, including African intellectuals. It is what he calls self-contempt, which must be conquered prior to recognition of this invaluable human dignity. The African can begin to recognize human dignity in a fellow African if (s)he can recognize and appreciate her/his own dignity and culture with the values that it contains and reach out for a self-accepting attitude. Mazrui emphasizes this issue of mutual respect for human dignity and culture:

> This in turn requires the growing toleration of some of the least respected, in western terms, of those aspects of indigenous culture. If an African intellectual can begin to concede dignity to the physical nakedness of the Karimojong men, or to the use of red ochre on the skin of the Masai, or invocation of supernatural forces

---

[1070] Ibid.

[1071] Okot, 97.

to help determine election, the African intellectual is on his way to transcending his own cultural self-contempt.[1072]

The ordinary African and African intellectuals ought to acknowledge that all people have dignity and overcome degradation of their own cultures. Respect for human dignity and culture are at the center of Mazrui's advocacy. The *Karamojong,*[1073] who are pastoralists, are some of the sectors of Ugandan population that have not developed much. They are very much like their Kenyan and Tanzanian counterparts—the *Masai,* who are also pastoralists—and some of the least developed groups in Kenya and Tanzania. Mazrui actually construes that this fact about these people and their culture does not constitute them into people with less dignity than the so-called developed ethnic groups. The greatest challenge here is to respect culture and recognize human dignity, human rights, and the person of every Ugandan and of people beyond Uganda.

Another principal anthropological challenge is to recognize a "common understanding of man and woman, and of their dignity, human rights and needs, and their final destiny."[1074] The anthropological dimension of the human problem, therefore, concerns the way human persons view a human being. This is the central challenge in every human relationship. When the human person is misunderstood and there is no consensus in the definition of the human person, conflicts are inevitable, and integral human development is at stake. It was essentially the question of slavery, which violates the essential aspects of the human person, which caused the troublesome split and civil war

---

[1072] Ali A. Mazrui, *Political Values and the Educated Class in Africa* (Berkeley and Los Angeles: University of California Press, 1978), 18.

[1073] There is variation in the way this word is used and written. In some sources, it is written Karimojong and in others it is written Karamojong. In both cases, it refers to the people. The region or place/area is called Karamoja. In reality, the region is called *Karamoja,* not *Karimoja,* and the people are called the *Karamojong,* not *Karimojong.* This is a region in northeasten Uganda. It is bordered by Kenya in the east and in the north by the Sudan. The people are pastoralists although they do some little cultivation. It is one of the least developed parts of Uganda. The difference in writing the word(s) is explained by the different backgrounds of the authors of books.

[1074] Ddungu, 21.

in one of the world's greatest nations—USA—for about a decade beginning in 1860.[1075] This further shows the gravity of the anthropological challenge.

The violation of human dignity is a universal problem, and Uganda is not an exception. In the Uganda context, this problem is aggravated by the diversity of ethnicity in the country. The different ethnic groups have their own philosophies and world vision and, in particular, unique visions of the human person. This accounts for the variation of social and political relations among the ethnic groups in Uganda.

The most dominant ethnic group in Uganda is the Bantu group who constitute over 50 percent of Uganda's population.[1076] Although there are different names of Bantu tribes, this ethnic group covers the area in the whole of southern Uganda, parts of eastern Uganda, and western Uganda. They constitute a group that has a distinct cosmological and anthropological vision though similar in many ways to the ethnic communities that occupy the northwestern, northern, northeastern, and some eastern parts of Uganda because there is some shared vision of the human person.[1077] However, there are variations in the vision of the human person in the context of the entire human family. In light of this fact, one of the challenges of *Populorum Progressio* to the Uganda context is the vision of the human person. To illustrate this point in the context of Uganda, it is relevant to consider two examples, the Bantu vision of the human person, and that of the Lugbara of West Nile, which are not extremely different from the vision of other ethnic groups in Uganda and African ethnic communities.

Placide Tempels studied the Bantu, not those in Uganda, but the Baluba of the Belgian Congo (current Democratic Republic of Congo, or DRC) in Central Africa, who are akin to the Bantu of Uganda. According to him, the study was exclusively from the Bantu philosophy of life, not from a Western point of view. He asserts that among the Bantu a person—*muntu*—is a full, lofty, and vital force or personal force, part of creation, in relation with family, clan brethren, descendants, patrimony of his/her land, creation and God but above-created material or visible beings, and a causative agent that exercises

---

[1075] James W. Garvey, *St. Paul Cathedral Parish: The Early Years, 1834-1903* (Houston, Pennsylvania: J.Pohl Associates, 2005), 27.

[1076] Nzita and Mbaga-Niwampa, 2.

[1077] Tempels, 61.

vital influence.[1078] This description of the human person shows the relational and social character of the human person. According to Tempels, the Bantu think that this personhood grows or increases with acquisition of material goods and diminishes with loss of possessions.[1079] The reason is that the person is a vital force, and this force depends on what the person owns, contrary to the strong notion that human dignity is invariable under all circumstances. This notion of the human person is, therefore, questionable; it contradicts Christian anthropology, which upholds the view that human dignity is not contingent upon any temporal circumstances or factors.

The *muntu* is an individual being distinct from other people. The marks of distinction are the native name of the person which expresses the "very reality of the individual" and the "visible appearance"[1080] of the person. These traits of a person are shared by other ethnic groups. However, these definitions of the human person were, initially, limited to each ethnic group as Benezet Bujo suggests, and I would like to agree with Bujo that there has been a development in the vision of the human person in most African contexts.[1081] This suggests that the extension of the term *person* beyond blood or tribal relationship with the same connotation was a later vision of the human person which was probably influenced by Christianity and Western philosophy.

Often those who belong to ethnic communities other than one's own are considered foreigners and at most not considered as human as those in one's ethnic circle. Consequently, they may be treated differently from those who belong to one's ethnicity. This is the probable explanation for strife, discrimination, or segregation in African communities including that of Uganda. For example, the traditional Lugbara of northwestern Uganda categorized some people as *juru or anyi'ba*—foreigners—which means one who does not fit exactly in the immediate definition of people related to oneself by blood, though considered *ba* or person worthy of respect but not

---

[1078] Placide Tempels, *Bantu Philosophy*, trans. Rubbens A. (Paris: Presence Africaine, 1959), 64-68.

[1079] Ibid., 67.

[1080] Ibid., 7074.

[1081] Benezet Bujo, *Foundations of an African Ethic: Beyond the Universal Claims of Western Morality*, trans. Brian McNeil (Crossroad Publishing Company: New York), 24.

exactly the same as the immediate people.[1082] This suggests that the human person is defined according to the degree of the relationship of the person being defined and according to the one defining the human person.

Many ethnic groups in Uganda, and elsewhere, view the human person in a similar way, meaning that they view the human person in limited contexts. These ways of conceiving the human person contribute to the preferential treatment of people and constitute problems in understanding and achieving integral human development. The definition of the human person according to ethnicity or relationship contributes to a fragmented vision of the human person. The various visions are limited to the ethnic groups. Historically, this can be explained by limited worldviews that people had because the world basically consisted of their immediate environment. Their worldviews never went far beyond their ethnic groups. This is why *persons* tend to be those belonging to one's ethnic community.[1083] Consequently, all others are either less persons or nonpersons. They may be treated fully humanely or less humanely. This is a problem and challenge to national solidarity, the common good, unity, and integral development. It is an aspect of the human problem to be addressed, especially by government, religious leaders, and educational institutions in the country.

One of the principal concerns of colonial states, including Uganda, emerging from the colonial era was "nation building" and "national integration"; but once this was achieved, the problem after independence was "the elite/mass gap."[1084] Kabwegyere rightly affirms Binder's contention that the key issue for national integration in developing nations is "the relationship between a modernizing elite and a traditional mass—the point being that there exists a gap, which must be bridged if countries are to be integrated. To him, national integration requires that the gap be closed."[1085]

Uganda has been a victim of this kind of elite-traditional mass gap since independence and continues to be subject to such a situation. There is a gap between the elite who constitute the minority and the majority of the

---

[1082] John Middleton, *Lugbara Religion: Ritual and Authority among an East African People* (London: Oxford University Press, 1960), 9. Also see John Middleton, *The Lugbara of Uganda* (New York: Holt, Rinehart and Winston, 1964), 49.

[1083] Ibid.

[1084] Kabwegyere, 4

[1085] Ibid. Here Kabwegyere quotes L. Binder, "National Integration and Political Development," *American Political Science Review*, September 1964, 624 and 627.

population that is not formally educated or not educated at all. This gap has continued to create tension between the traditional vision of life and the modern vision, which is often considered a foreign vision or lifestyle. Consequently, the notion of human development is affected too. It is also here that there is a failure, in the Ugandan context, of the right notion of human development in the light of *Populorum Progressio*, which advocates the promotion of cultures and different cultural values emphasized in chapter two of this work. The principal argument for this assertion is that every culture has some value, and no culture may claim total superiority over other cultures. Each ethnic group and culture should be considered in its own context and right.

The cultural issue calls for discretion. Some aspects of two cultures may not be able to blend well while other aspects may be able to blend well, but no culture should be branded and dismissed as absolutely irrelevant as advocated by Paul VI.[1086] The crucial social challenge here is the possibility of integration of different cultures, which demands a critical study.[1087] This is a process that facilitates the growth of solidarity in the country and, ultimately, solidarity with cultures outside the country. An adaptation of cultures is insufficient to build social bonds between people because it may not facilitate a unitary vision of the human person, human dignity, and human rights. In light of the teaching of *Populorum Progressio* Uganda's plural cultures, tribal or ethnic diversity are real challenges to integral growth.[1088] The document never mentioned tribalism as a bad practice, but in the global context, it considered racism and exaggerated nationalism as opposed to integral development. However, by interpretation and inference, tribalism which displays the negative elements of exclusivity and discrimination—characteristic of racism and nationalism—belongs to the latter categories. As Kabwegyere rightly suggests, it is an "enemy to national

---

[1086] *Populorum Progressio*, 41, 18.

[1087] The critical study I suggest here means or involves examination of cultural elements that are similar and those that are different. In other words, a critical study ought to bring different cultures to mutual confrontation and reconciliation.

[1088] Examples to illustrate this fact are as follows: the tensions between the Baganda and other Bantu groups, the tension between the Bantu tribes in general and the Nilotic tribes, the Nilo-Hamitic and the Sudanic tribes. This has actually split Uganda into two major social, political, and economic blocs—north, northwest, and northeast *versus* the southern and western Uganda.

integration."[1089] In Uganda, it is perhaps this fact which accounts for the extant difficulties in social interaction, inappropriate mutual ethnic visions, and discrimination in economic and political activities, except where there are personally vested interests.

One of the major challenges in the political field is the role of government to protect the citizens, to promote all the people of the nation, and to protect or promote their rights and dignity. Promotion of justice and peace and the implementation of affirmative action and preferential option for the poor all contribute positively to human development. They are significant indicators that the anthropological challenges to human development are being addressed. A political system that does not provide for such possibilities and the care of people is called into question because it neglects human needs and thwarts development. This has been and still is a challenge to all governments of Uganda since its independence in 1962.[1090] There is discrimination on the basis of tribes or ethnic communities whenever a new government takes over, of course, often by force of arms, meaning that there were/are often regional, economic, religious and political marginalization or discrimination, and human rights abuses.[1091]

Currently, in the northern part of Uganda, the socioeconomic and political atmosphere is not supportive to the respect for human persons. This is evident not only in the twenty-year-old ongoing war in the region, but also in the fact that many people are living in dehumanizing conditions created by the dual fighting factions.[1092] The challenges to be addressed here are to help both sides to understand and accept the values and dignity of human life and the consequential significance of peace. The process calls for cooperation from both the indigenous people and those supporting the course of peace. If no change is made, it is either because the indigenous people are not developed enough to understand the value of their dignity as persons, or they are

---

[1089] Kabwegyere, 5.

[1090] Mugaju, 28-39. From the time of Uganda's independence up to this moment (2006), there are portions of the population of Uganda whose human development needs are either not being met at all or are utterly neglected. A typical example here are the people who are in war-torn regions of Uganda and those who are internally displaced—actually refugees in their own country.

[1091] Justus Magaju, 22-27.

[1092] Catholic Bishops of Gulu Archdiocese, Nebbi, Arua, and Lira, *Peace is Love* (Kisubi: Marianum Press, 2000), 23 and 32.

intentionally suppressed. In either case, it is also the duty of the state and the church to perform, though the church is doing the best according to her capacity. The two institutions need to ceaselessly address issues like arbitrary arrests, detentions without court trials, and obstruction of justice.

Another critical anthropological challenge to religious institutions, the government, and cultural and social sectors such as education is to explain and help people understand the human person, human dignity, and human rights. It is the challenge to educate people about these basic values or principles. The mutual relationships between people regardless of religion, ethnic or racial origin, and political affiliations need to be understood if people are to respect one another. Education about the human person and human dignity ought to be *a continuous pastoral imperative* for religious institutions as much as it should be a priority in sociocultural, educational, and political institutions.

In the field of religion, a number of issues also require attention. Religion or the church has a duty, like the state, to protect and promote the human person, human rights, and human dignity. There is no doubt that the church in Uganda has consistently and frequently taken this responsibility very seriously. This is evident, especially in the case of the Catholic Church, in the eighteen pastoral letters that the Catholic bishops of Uganda have written since independence, beginning with *Shaping Our National Destiny*, which was issued on the occasion of Ugandan independence from the British, October 9, 1962, to *Towards a Democratic and Peaceful Uganda Based on the Common Good* published in November 2005.[1093] For example, one of their most extensive pastoral letters, namely, *With a New Heart and a New Spirit*, which was issued in 1986 at a very critical time in the history of Uganda, devoted "nearly a whole chapter on the need for respecting human rights"[1094] and on the whole covers many human issues, which are critical even to Uganda of today. They present enduring challenges to the political system in Uganda and

---

[1093] See the page (not numbered) preceding page 1 of Catholic Bishops of Uganda, *Towards a Democratic Uganda Based on the Common Good* (Kisubi: Marianum Press, November 2005).

[1094] Abraham Kiapi, "Church Defence of Rule of Law and Human Rights," in *Church Contribution to Integral Development*, eds. Joseph Therese Agbasiere and Boniface K. Zabajungu (Eldoret, Kenya: AMECEA Gaba Publications, 1989), 87. The document and the chapter referred to here is Catholic Bishops of Uganda, *With a New Heart and a New Spirit* (St. Paul's Publications, Africa, 1986), chapter 2.

have been the reason for some of the improvements in Uganda's economic and political systems in the past few years. However, one serious question to ask—and a retrospective challenge to the Uganda Catholic hierarchy—is why there was a lapse in their address of *national social issues* from the time of the pastoral letter *Shaping Our National Destiny* published in 1962, to 1979 when *Reshaping Our Nation* was written.[1095] This was a lapse of seventeen years of not addressing Uganda's intense socioeconomic and political problems during very stormy years in the history of Uganda.

Religious institutions also stand to be challenged where there is no respect for human life. Killing or fighting is sometimes encouraged by some religious leaders. Outstanding examples are the Movement for the Restoration of the Ten Commandments of God (MRTCG), a breakaway religious sect, which on March 17, 2000, and earlier, killed at least 893 people in the name of an apocalyptic vision that was to be realized imminently.[1096] This and armies like Holy Spirit Mobile Forces (HSMF) of Alice Lakwena and the Lord's Resistance Army (LRA) of Joseph Kony that claim to fight for the moral, political, and economic rehabilitation of the people in the name of the Lord are serious challenges to religious institutions.[1097] They show that to some extent religion is a failure. They question how effective religion is in the life of our people.

There are different religious denominations, and it is not infrequent to notice religious discrimination. In fact, just before independence Ugandans were already divided along religious lines because the main political parties were formed along the lines of religious denominations.[1098] The questions to grapple with are two. Either the teaching of the church or different religious denominations has bounced against people who call themselves believers or Christians—but actually they are not—or the teaching has been inadequate, especially about human dignity, its universality and equality. This failure

---

[1095] See Catholic Bishops of Uganda, *Towards a Democratic Uganda Based on the Common Good* (Kisubi: Marianum Press, November 2005), especially the page after the cover page where there is the list of the pastoral letters of Catholic Bishops of Uganda.

[1096] Bagumisiriza, 90.

[1097] Heike Behrend, "The Holy Spirit Movement's New World: Discourse and Developments in the North of Uganda," in *Developing Uganda,* eds. Holger Bernt Hansen and Michael Twaddle (Kampala: Fountain Publishers, 1998), 246-247. Also see Bweyale, 62.

[1098] Bweyale, 59.

is seen not only when different religious denominations encounter each other. It is also evident in politics and general social interaction involving the same people who are believers. The anthropological challenge is tied to the challenges of solidarity, justice and the common good, and to all other development principles, virtues, and conditions or factors. In a context like Uganda, they should always be addressed simultaneously.

One of the greatest challenges to the church in Uganda is to help people express God's love for all people. This love for people is partly expressed through the church's active participation in fighting unjust social structures, economic organizations, and political systems that humiliate people and subject them to misery. This is a constituent dimension of the church's true mission and what makes the church relevant to humankind.[1099] This perspective suggests that one of the significant challenges to religious institutions, the government, and individuals, especially Christians, is to remain relevant to people by protecting their fundamental rights and helping them to meet their needs.

B. Universal and National Charity: The Challenge of Authentic Love

At the outset, it is important to note that similar to human dignity, the issue of charity or love is a crucial one and ties together all other development principles Paul VI advocated in *Populorum Progressio*. What ties charity and human dignity together is the fact that they are directly related to the human person. Although both justice and charity are compelling virtues, charity must always come first because every person is "the object of charity."[1100] Benedict XVI reemphasized the centrality of love, asserting that in a global context and interdependent world, economic, social, or political projects cannot substitute "that gift of self to another through which charity is expressed."[1101]

[1099] Frederick Drandua, *Let Me Live: A Cry of All Those Killed by a Neighbour under Whatsoever Circumstances* (Arua, Uganda, November 1994), 15.

[1100] Michael D. Greancy, "Charity or Justice: Where Is the Hope of the Poor ?" in *Curing World Poverty: The New Role of Property*, ed. John H. Miller (Social Justice Review: Saint Louis, Missouri, 1994), 55

[1101] Benedictus PP. XVI, Benedictus PP. XVI, "Jesus at the sight of the crowds was moved with pity" (Mt. 9:36), message of Pope Benedict XVI for Lent 2006 in *Arua Diocese Bulletin*, no. 69 (Arua: Arua Diocese Communication Department, March 2006), 2.

In other words, the sincere gift of oneself and one's talents is the climax of the expression of love. The testimony to this is God's *sacrificial self-gift* in the person of Jesus Christ. A brief treatise of the theme of charity anticipates the fact that the treatise on virtues, conditions, and other principles for integral development touches the question of charity.

Universal charity is a love "without discrimination of tribe, religion and nation."[1102] This claim is consonant with the theological summary of Paul VI's advocacy for integral human development. Integral human development should be manifested in physical and public love. This is possible if individuals are receptive to all people of different backgrounds regardless of mutual or personal knowledge and evenness of development in the country. The challenge to Uganda is the observable continued segregation and discrimination, initiated by its successive leaders, with consequent irregularity in development and social interaction.[1103] In a context such as Uganda, the challenge of love is compounded by what David M. McCarthy suggests as true love. According to him, "love requires that we will what is good."[1104] Love is not only an emotional feeling, it is a duty and expressed in a rational or deliberate good action. In the context of Uganda, its principal challenge is that people deliberately act to stop segeragation and discrimination. This, in other words, should be the good they will—love should have what McCarthy calls the "critical elements of willing and the good."[1105]

McCarthy suggests that it is the rational and deliberate character, which makes love an authentic human act and thus gives it its moral dimension. True love ought to be viewed against the backdrop of "both doing good and having good reason for what we should do."[1106] This contention suggests that much as it is difficult to define love, true love can be seen expressed in genuine action that is gratifying to both the agent of love and the object of love. The challenge for Ugandans is to grasp this fact and appreciate it in order to show national and universal charity.

[1102] Catholic Bishops of Gulu Archdiocese, Nebbi, Arua, and Lira, 11.

[1103] Bweyale, 59.

[1104] David M. McCarthy, "Love in Fundamental Moral Theology," in *Moral Theology: New Directions and Fundamental Issues, Festschrift for James P. Hanigan*, ed. James Keating (New York/Mahwah, NJ: Paulist Press, 2004), 184-185.

[1105] Ibid., 186.

[1106] Ibid.

One of the greatest challenges of the call to universal charity is the questioning of people's apathy. This challenge is directed in a special way to Catholics, and other Christians, because they constitute the majority of Uganda's population and contributed much to the formulation of the motto of the country—For God and My Country.[1107] Showing love in the most critical or difficult moments is indicative of the authenticity of love. Patriotic citizens stand by their agonizing fellow citizens in times of trouble. The political situation in northern and northeastern Uganda reveals the contrary. Parts of the country have quietly watched these affected regions suffer for many years. In a bid to break this silence, John Baptist Odama had this to say:

> I want to remind the indifferent world that the people of Northern and North-Eastern Uganda, Acholi, Langi, Teso, Karamojong, Lugbara, Madi, Alur, and many others subjected to such atrocities are part of Uganda and the whole humanity who should enjoy equal rights, responsibility and dignity.[1108]

The named peoples constitute a segment of the country whose people are of Nilotic and Nilo-Hamitic origin, distinct from the rest of the Ugandans, most of whom are Bantu-speaking people. Even if the statement of Odama were not broadly interpreted, it is still tantamount to the assertion that there is lack of national charity. This challenge is still more compelling to Catholics who, denominationally, constitute the majority of the population of Uganda—40 to 50 percent of the population.[1109] The challenge is prompted by the apathy manifest in the silent observation of many who do not care about what some parts of the country are suffering. This claim is supported by the observation of Ian Legget:

> There is remarkably little national concern about the atrocities that are being perpetrated against the people of the north, and an apparent lack of understanding among southern Ugandans about

---

[1107] Ronald Kassimir, 233.

[1108] John Baptist Odama, *I Have Seen the Humiliation of My People and Heard Their Cry (Ex.3: 7)* (Gulu, Uganda, 29 June 2003), 2-3.

[1109] Kassimir, 233.

the sheer scale of the humanitarian and economic crisis that has evolved.[1110]

This statement shows the gravity of the situation in northern Uganda, a portion of one nation. The challenge of the statement is again compounded by the reality of the "predominantly Christian character or constitution of Uganda's population."[1111] Uganda is a nation that boasts of being at least 86 percent Christian (48 percent Catholic and 38 percent Protestant) and a religious or a God-loving nation expressed in Uganda's motto: For God and My Country.[1112] Where is the love of God and concern and care for fellow children of God in this case? Uganda is a nation that proclaims, partly, in its national anthem:

> United free for liberty, together we'll always stand. Oh Uganda the land of freedom, our love and labour we give, and with neighbours all, at our country's call, in peace and friendship we'll live.[1113]

The national anthem rightly expresses, in resonance with Christian anthropology, de facto the end of true love as "sharing our lives" with others and our "fulfillment in the love of God."[1114] Just considering the fact that citizens of Uganda are spread from north to south and from east to west of the country, an attitude of indifference as stated (above) by Legget is one of the greatest challenges to the government and the religious leaders of Uganda, and to every Ugandan, in the context of the true end of love. It ought to be overcome. In light of the stated end of love, the motto and the national anthem have no meaning, or they are just decorations and words to be proud of but not lived in real life.

The Catholic Church in particular has tried to be an instrument of love in many different ways though it needs to do more. For instance, the efforts of

---

[1110] Ian Leggett, *Uganda, the Background, the People, the Issues: An Oxfam Country Profile* (Kampala: Fountain Publishers, 2001), 27.

[1111] Michael Twadler and Holger Bernt Hansen, "The Changing State of Uganda," in *Developing Uganda*, 6.

[1112] Catholic Bishops of Uganda, *With a New Heart and a New Spirit* (Kisubi: Marianum Press, 1986), 70.

[1113] Kakoma and Wyngard, 456.

[1114] McCarthy, "Love in Fundamental Moral Theology," 188.

the Uganda Catholic bishops to establish the Centenary Rural Development Bank (CERUDEB). This is one of the best serving, if not actually the best serving local bank in the country. It serves people without discrimination in terms of employment and economic sevices, expressed in its motto: "Unite, Love and Serve."[1115] This is a symbolic and traditional Catholic expression of universal love besides what the Catholic Church practices in other services such as schools, orphanages, hospitals or health care services, and other areas.

Political representation should be a testimony of true and national or universal love in the country, but this again is a failure. True love shows itself in many ways, but the challenges of true or universal love are seen in the results when there is universal love:

> Social life will be peaceful, mutual help will be given more freely, dialogue and consequent mutual understanding will pave way to friendship, to a real culture of heart and *civilization of love*. Such love, it is abundantly clear, cannot be confined to attraction towards others, nor simply to good feeling. These may be only the beginning of the process towards real love. Real love is above all a decision of the will controlled by reason.[1116]

The real challenge of love to anyone is to build a civilization or a culture of love. This is something not forced upon a person or groups of people. It is a deliberate action consequent to a reflection and a realization of the value of people and the obligation to love them. Such a love is indiscriminate, goes beyond any borders, shows in mutual recognition and peace.

The challenge of charity or love is the invitation to love indiscriminately, meaning that love be extended even to one's enemies as Jesus Christ taught.[1117] In addressing the problem of socioeconomic and political instability in northern Uganda, John Baptist Odama had this to say to the people of the region about the mission of the church:

> Every Christian faithful and every God-fearing person knows that our faith is a mission we are to accomplish. This mission for us

---

[1115] Mark Leopold, *Inside West Nile: Violence, History and Representation on an African Frontier*, (Oxford: James Currey, 2005),22.

[1116] Catholic Bishops of Gulu Archdiocese, Nebbi, Arua and Lira, 13.

[1117] Mt.5:38-48.

is strictly peaceful, loving and respectful of the dignity in human persons of all walks of life.[1118]

The reason for this advocacy is simply the imperative nature of the Christian mission because of the centrality and universality of human dignity. Universal love is, therefore, called for because of universality and equality of human dignity. Besides, this "love is the badge for all Christians," and its "social expression"[1119] is solidarity. Teaching or preaching and practicing charity is one of the principal functions of religion. There is no doubt that church or religious leaders often like to do acts of charity.[1120] In fact, the practical expression of charity in the church is evident in the social services that the church renders through education, hospitals, orphanages, baby care homes, and homes for the elderly and the blind. However, one other challenge to the church in preaching and living charity is that it should always take into account the socioeconomic and political situations in which people live. It is good to preach universal love, but it is also significant to let the masses know their rights and the injustices that are perpetrated by other people against them; if the church preaches love without considering different circumstances, she can also prepare ground for injustice and abuse of human rights and human dignity.[1121] The attempts the Uganda Catholic Bishops Conference made to resolve the crisis in Kabale Diocese of Catholic symbolized their collegial spirit and love for each other and the church in Uganda.[1122] The efforts of the bishops toward resolving the problem also shows that they were determined to thwart the cause of injustice resulting from abuse of human rights and human dignity. They would not have acted immediately to resolve the issues if this were not the case.

C. Universal Destiny of Natural Resources: The Challenge of Private Ownership

The study in chapter two treated the basis on which Paul VI argued about ownership of property. It spelled out that his teaching was founded on the

---

[1118] Odama, 1.

[1119] Catholic Bishops of Gulu Archdiocese, Nebbi, Arua and Lira, 14-15.

[1120] Pfaff, 160.

[1121] Ibid.

[1122] Gifford, 123-124.

creation theology. God created the earth and its resources for the good of all people, and this mandate was given to the first people when God told them to "be fruitful, multiply, fill the earth and subdue it."[1123] The articulation of the principle of ownership of property as indicated in the chapter suggested that ownership takes into consideration the work of the property owner and the needs of those who gravely lack the basic resources for their livelihood. This understanding of ownership is based on the interpretation and meaning of the quotation from the book of Genesis. Concisely, the text suggests that the mandate or command to conquer the earth through work is a fulfillment of a divine precept; and even though people earn property by their labor, they should not forget that they are only God's ambassadors and custodians—they are stewards of divine property originally intended for the benefit of all.[1124]

When property owners have met their basic needs and have extra resources, the universal destiny of the resources of nature demands that they help those who do not have resources to meet their basic needs out of the surplus. Much as the owner of the goods or natural resources has the right to own these goods by virtue of having worked for them, (s)he has at the same time a duty to meet other people's needs after meeting her/his own because these resources are meant for the good of all people according to divine design. However, if the person lacking the basic goods necessary for living is capable and has possibilities for acquiring them, but is negligent or simply lazy, the application of the principle should be made with care and caution. Such persons could be denied such support except when in danger or under threat to their life. Merely supporting the needy without critical consideration of their abilities and possibilities available to them would also contradict participation, solidarity, and the common good to which everybody should contribute.

The principle of ownership of property challenges every citizen to live in a spirit of universal charity, solidarity, and preferential option for the poor. One of the issues raised by this principle is how socioeconomic and material resources of a nation are used or shared among the citizens. Some critical observers have suggested that

> if the religious, political, and ethnic divisions which have proved
> to be so destructive in Uganda are to be reduced and replaced

---

[1123] Genesis, 1: 28. See *The New Jerusalem Bible* (New York: Doubleday, 1985), 18.

[1124] Eugene H. Maly, "Genesis," in *The Jerome Biblical Commentary*, vol. 1, eds. Raymond E. Brown et al. (Englewood Cliffs, New Jersey: Prentice-Hall Inc.), 11.

with a stronger sense of nationhood and national identity, the role of economic and social developments as a means of minimizing differences rather than accentuating them will be critical.[1125]

The principle touches the issue of human equality and socioeconomic justice. It challenges the church, government, and the people of Uganda about the poverty of certain people and parts of the country and the widely growing gap between the rich and the poor. The claimed economic growth of Uganda does not mean that all Ugandans are beneficiaries of the currently prevailing policies and resources. It is noticeable that "there has been growth in inequality, and an increasingly common feeling that some people and some parts are doing very nicely, while others are being left behind."[1126] An example for citation is the comparison between Karamoja or any other place in the north and northeast and Kampala in the south or any other lake region area such as Mbarara in the west of the country.[1127]

> Any visitor to Uganda who has the opportunity to go to the north, as well as to spend time in Kampala and the fertile crescent around Lake Victoria, would be struck by the remarkable contrast between the two. Kampala and the towns of the south and west are thriving. Business is good, and the signs of growth and wealth are evident all around: in the houses being built, the goods available in the shops and markets, and the number of vehicles on the roads. Kampala is one of the safest and most pleasant cities in Africa. Travel north for four to five hours to the town of Gulu, however, and the landscape changes completely. Gulu has experienced growth in the last ten years, but it is an expansion of cheap investments and hurried construction, signs of flight from an unsafe and increasingly abandoned countryside.[1128]

[1125] Leggett, 10.

[1126] Ibid., 3.

[1127] Ibid., 27.

[1128] Ibid. Gulu is an undisputable reference point in terms of violence or absence of true peace, but northern Uganda includes and ought to include northwestern Uganda and northeastern Uganda, if one speaks of less developed or neglected areas of northern Uganda.

The quotation above evinces the disparity of socioeconomic and political development in Uganda. Gulu is referred to here because it is one of the outstanding areas affected, similar situations prevail elsewhere in the country. All of these support the claim that there is no integral development in Uganda.

The problem of private ownership of property in Uganda dates back to the early 1950s when cooperative unions and other business organizations were established, but they were dominated by the rich farmers "who controlled the committees and thus the use of surplus funds"[1129] and grossly mismanaged corporate resources. They denied poor people the right to use resources of nature. This behavior contradicts the limited nature of the right to own private property as espoused in chapter two.

One of the principal challenges of the right to ownership of property is to ignore the fact that ownership of land is an ownership of the source of human livelihood. The problem of ownership of land was aggravated by the 1975 Land Reform Decree, which created opportunities that undermined customary ownership of land, especially in northern and northeastern Uganda, which was formerly considered Crown Land in the colonial times and later called Public Land after independence.[1130] The consequences of this decree were undesirable and resented by those who are educated about the value of land because the "customary land tenure system has been seriously eroded by the middle class gaining advantage over the 'ordinary people.'"[1131] The system opened the way for the rich who can afford to buy land from the poor and to do so at will. Such a system not only disfavors the poor and illiterate populace, it is unjust or immoral because it deprives them of their source of living.

The land decree is disadvantageous because it opened way for the use of the land "in northern and northeastern Uganda to capitalist relations of production"[1132] as suggested by Amaza Ori Ondoga. Ondoga suggests that people in these regions, and other regions of Uganda confronted with similar situations, were denied the right to own land; they were unjustly treated and discriminated against by the prevailing laws. Similar discrimination is also observable in the unjust traditional system of land ownership where women who are "childless, widowed, disabled, separated/divorced, or with only girl

---

[1129] Mamdani, 233-234.

[1130] Ondoga, 196.

[1131] Ibid.

[1132] Ondoga, 196.

children often have little or no recourse to land since they cannot even rely on men for access to land."[1133] The fact that there is no preference for them as poor people in need of the support of government and because they are human beings means a denial of their dignity and rights. This deprivation and injustice to women is also expressed in the practice that even if a woman and the husband jointly acquired land, the woman cannot claim ownership because the land titles are registered in the name of the husband.[1134]

The above system of the ownership of land recurs to date. It has compounded the problems of poor people when the rich continue to purchase the land of the poor, depriving them of ownership of their livelihood. As Aili Mari Tripp states, "Land is the most important resource in Uganda because much of the population depends on it for their livelihood."[1135] Moreover, many of those who sell their land are not aware that they are depriving themselves and their future generation of a precious ownership and life, or they are unable to anticipate the grave and eminent danger into which they are heading. Such "commodification of land"[1136] poses a grave threat to the poor people who own nothing but their plots of land. People, therefore, need to be educated about the value of land, and this is a challenge to be confronted by the government, religious institutions, and the educational institutions in the country.

The economic system was unjust because economic activities were controlled by Asians until 1972 when Idi Amin expelled them from Uganda, and some of them were unjustly deprived of their citizenship and their property.[1137] The Asians had earned what they were deprived of through their own hard work. The indigenous people had the right and duty to meet their economic needs. The Asians were deprived of resources they had earned by

---

[1133] Aili Mari Tripp, "The Politics of Women's Rights and Cultural Diversity in Uganda," in *Gender Justice, Development, and Rights*, eds. Maxine Molyneux and Shahra Razavi (Oxford: Oxford University Press, 2002), 421.

[1134] Ibid.

[1135] Ibid. The gravity of this statement is compounded by the fact that 86 percent of Uganda's population is rural, and majority of these people live in abject poverty

[1136] Commodification of land is used here, negatively, because customary ownership of land gives people freedom to own land, but it also allows people to sell it to anyone willing to purchase it. This is unfortunate for the poor who easily lose land, their major source of survival. Also see Ondoga, 198.

[1137] Mamdani, 236.

working for them. It was a vicious circle of injustice—a deprivation of either party of the right to own property. The Asians should not have been forcefully deprived of their property, but they also needed to realize and acknowledge that the indigenous people required necessities for survival and had the right to participate in their own development.

One test for true development of a nation is the number of beggars in the nation and their distribution according to regions or the number of poor people and their distribution according to the regions of the country. The 86 percent of the population of Uganda, which live in the countryside, constitute the majority of the population, and they are actually the poor of the nation.[1138] Those who own businesses, especially in the urban areas, are called to question whether their businesses are exclusively for themselves or also for the benefit of their needy neighbors, who might be haunting the rich deeply in their consciences. Kampala has more beggars today than ever before, yet Uganda is said to be developing faster than ever before. Such claims are not tenable because one of the litmus tests for the development of a nation is the number and care for the poor people in that nation.

The challenge of ownership in a political context is how government uses the resources of the country. It can also be seen in how widely spread economic development is in the country. Though partly the legacy of precolonial economic differences and the colonial reinforcement, while the southern, southeastern, and western parts of Uganda are developed and have good socioeconomic infrastructure, the north, northwestern, and the northeast are not.[1139] This disparity makes the use of government grants or foreign aid to Uganda questionable in terms of its distribution for developing the country. The proper use of resources is demanded by just social and economic order, and it is required by the sense of responsibility expected of anybody in public service because (s)he is "accountable not only to the nation but also to God, and God will be the final judge."[1140] The challenge of integral development to the government of Uganda and the nation's economic planners is that the ownership of the wealth of the nation means

---

[1138] Edward K. Kirumira, "Developing a Population Policy for Uganda," in *Developing Uganda,* eds. Holger Bernt Hansen, and Michael Twaddle (Kampala: Fountain Publishers, 1998), 185.

[1139] Legget, 55-56.

[1140] Catholic Bishops of Uganda, *With a New Heart and a New Spirit,* 28. Here, the bishops are quoting G. S., 75.

provision of better opportunities and solutions to problems confronting the poorest regions of Uganda.

Matthew Habiger has rightly pointed out that ownership is important for the stability and confidence or security of society: "it is inherent in the nature of men and women that they have some claim to material goods for a sense of security for themselves and for all their dependents."[1141] The principle of ownership of private property also calls to question the ownership of property in both Christian institutions and other religious institutions. Many times conflicts between religious leaders and members of the groups arise over resources and their distribution. The challenge to religious institutions in this regard is about sharing or use of personal property and donations given to members, community leaders, priests, religious, bishops and pastoral agents, or whoever is entrusted with such responsibility. Such a state of affairs further challenges one to reflect on why churches split and why there are many independent churches, radical or fundamentalist religious sects even within Christian institutions. The problems are sometimes doctrinal or ideological, but they are also related to ownership of property.[1142] There are sometimes squabbles about the wealth or property of religious institutions. The examples Gifford gives of the crises in the churches in Uganda suffice as adequate testimonies to this assertion though there are other examples besides these.[1143] It is the problem of ownership or access to property, and the question goes beyond this to the self-concern of individuals. The temptation to high standards of living is one of the factors that forces religious people to "live above their means."[1144] It contributes or leads to dishonesty and corruption, not only in religious institutions but above all in civil or political institutions. One of the challenges of the right to own property is, therefore, the challenge to shun undue self-concern, and hence a challenge to think of the common good. This is a great challenge because people always want a mutual determination of allocation of resources. At the same time, each person aspires to receive a share and members of the institutions also question whether government is the owner and the one in charge or the people, whether

---

[1141] Matthew Habiger, 1.

[1142] Gifford, 152.

[1143] Ibid., 123 and 125.

[1144] Luke Mbefo Nnamdi, *The True African: Impulses for Self-Affirmation* (Onitsa, Nigeria: Spiritan Publication, 2001), 138.

the superior of the religious community or his/her delegate or members of the religious institution are the owners and custodians.

D. Subsidiarity: The Challenge to Promote Initiatives

As stated in chapter two, the principle of subsidiarity is crucial for social order. It is a principle Paul VI considered necessary for resolving conflicts of rights between individuals and communities.[1145] It is necessary in both secular and religious institutions. The challenge of the principle of subsidiarity is threefold: the issue of the priority of government versus the priority of intermediate groups or institutions, the priority of intermediate groups or institutions versus that of families, and the priority of families versus individual family members. The main issue in each case is who does what and when. The principle of subsidiarity demands that smaller groups or individuals should do for themselves what they are capable of without the interference of the bigger bodies; and when they are not capable, the bigger bodies should intervene, which means smaller groups or individuals should not expect larger bodies to do for them what they are capable of doing for themselves.[1146] Families and small groups are challenged that they can only be helped when they are incapable of fruitfully helping themselves in carrying out their missions. "Even the United Nations" and other aiding organizations should be helpful and function according to the principle of subsidiarity and promote "the autonomy of single states,"[1147] and the states respect the principle of solidarity and subsidiarity.

The main problems here are government or state control of development projects and services, which people could otherwise manage on their own. For instance, if people or regions are able to provide or raise funds for building power stations, they should be allowed to do so. Second, there are certain things toward, which people could contribute, but some people simply do not cooperate. Such attitudes also exist where people expect to be given things or expect that things should be done for them. To give is often the expectation of people from the state or government, nongovernmental

---

[1145] *Populorum Progressio*, 33, 14.

[1146] Pius XI, *Quadragesimo Anno: On Reconstructing the Social Order* (Chicago, Illinois: Outline Press, 1931), 79, 46.

[1147] Haring and Salvoldi, 59.

organizations (NGOs), the church or religious institutions or individuals people imagine are rich, while they would be able to do some of the things themselves using personal or local resources. Pres. Yoweri Kaguta Museveni's call for participation in poverty eradication is crucial to any development endeavors: "But Government does not work alone. Poverty-eradication is the business of all the citizens of Uganda. We all contribute."[1148]

The political development of the different regions of a country depends on the ability of the local regions or government intervention when the regions are incapacitated. This means that a proper application of the principle of subsidiarity is crucial. In the political arena, a similar attitude as in the socioeconomic fields is one of the main problems affecting other aspects of development in some parts of Uganda. For instance, the promotion of political efficiency depends on creation of a conducive situation in the country or the particular region. Peace is one of the relevant factors, and a typical example of a factor whose promotion demands coopertion. Its promotion depends on all people besides the government.[1149] Government may contribute, but the support of the indigenous people who know the mentality and the culture of the region is equally necessary. In addressing such a situation in northern Uganda, the bishops of the affected areas had this to say:

> Above all the Acholi themselves, each and every one of them, must help and join the efforts for a peaceful solution of all the violence and insurgency. We ask all citizens of Uganda to share our difficulties and understand us.[1150]

The bishops suggest that there is sometimes some regional and individual indolence where many people are expected to contribute toward a given course such as peace making. The main challenge is that sometimes people expect government to make peace. At other times, government expects the local people to provide conditions necessary for peace. The problem is that both the local people and government are equally in dilemma. There is a fine

---

[1148] Yoweri Kaguta Museveni, "Forward," in *Poverty Eradication Action Plan (2001-2003)*, vol. 1 (Kampala: Ministry of Finance, Planning and Economic Development, February 2001), ii.

[1149] Catholic Bishops of Gulu Archdiocese, Nebbi, Arua, and Lira, 38-48. Read paragraphs 60-60.

[1150] Ibid., 55.

line between the role of government and that of the local people or agents of peace. Consequently, the expectation of peace is uncertain because there is no clear definition of who does what.[1151] The local people look toward the state or government to solve all the local political problems and vice versa. This is a difficulty in the application of the principle. It is one aspect of the challenge of subsidiarity in the political context, and it needs to be clarified.

Another political challenge in the application of the principle of subsidiarity is the situation where there is a possibility of conflict between church and state regarding development projects. While history has shown that the church and state have cooperated in helping to meet the needs of the citizens who are also members of the religious institutions as Pres. Yoweri K. Museveni stated, "We in government commend serious development efforts, and we will do all that is possible to assist the church in such endeavours,"[1152] the possibilities of conflicts of interest cannot be ruled out completely because there is no fine definition of limits of responsibility. Second, such conflicts often arise when there are personal interests or ulterior motives involving particular projects. However, the principle is favorable for advancement because it clearly stipulates that what smaller groups can do for themselves should not be taken over by larger bodies.[1153] For instance, if a religious institution is able to manage a particular project for its people, who constitute part of the nation, the state or government should not thwart its efforts. It is helping the state and relieving it of some of its responsibilities to care for the people though this is also a responsibility of the church. The church cares for both the spiritual and material needs of the people, and it has done this consistently in the past and even to date.[1154] It is for this and similar reasons that Museveni's contention is significant and should be taken seriously by

---

[1151] The principle of subsidiarity provides directives for action, but the definition of limits of action are not provided, and they indeed are hard to provide because the principle is circumstanctial. This is the greatest problem in the application of the principle of subsidiarity in every situation—religious, political, economic, and social.

[1152] Yoweri K. Museveni, "The Relationship Between Church and State," in *Church Contribution to Integral Development*, eds. Joseph Therese Agbasiere and Boniface K. Kabajungu (Eldoret, Kenya: AMECEA Gaba Publications, 1989), 20.

[1153] The principle of subsidiarity has already been explained. For a deeper comprehension of the principle, see chapter two and chapter three of this work.

[1154] *Populorum Progressio*, 1, 1-2.

any political leader. Moreover, such efforts contribute to solidarity and the common good of the nation.

In the religious field, people have sometimes failed to handle local religious problems effectively. The principal reason is also the difficulty in drawing the line between the roles of individuals, local religious institutions, and national or regional authorities. The second difficulty is autonomy, which is often given to the individual local religious authorities. The limit of their authority is not clear, and it is difficult to explicitly know whose responsibility begins where. Two examples of this challenge can be cited here.

The first example of the difficulty or challenge in the application of the principle of subsidiarity was apparent in the crisis in the Catholic Diocese of Kabale in western Uganda in the 1990s when the diocese was split into two major factions—those who were probishop Barnabas Halem'Imana, the then ordinary of the diocese, and those who were opposed to him.[1155] The dispute in Catholic Diocese of Kabale was about the management of the resources of the diocese and the relationship of the bishop to priests of the diocese and of some of the priests (Rwandese Tusi and Hutu) to the Rwandese Patriotic Front (RPF). Apparently, it was an ethnic dispute and the bishop's relation to the security forces of Uganda.[1156] The application of the principle of subsidiarity was an apparent failure. The bishop of the diocese, the priests, and religious and pastoral agents could not resolve the division and strife among themselves and the people in the diocese. Neither could other people in the diocese resolve the problem. The alternative option was the Uganda Catholic Bishops Conference, but they could not resolve the problem immediately; and radically because, according to Catholic Church law (canon law), though the ordinary of a diocese is in collegiality with other bishops,[1157] he is still autonomous

---

[1155] Gifford, 123.

[1156] Ibid., 123-124. In these pages, Gifford suggests that the causes of the dispute were as follows: economic, social, and political—namely, tribal differences, inefficiency in the administration of the diocese, failure to implement the acts of the 1985 synod of the diocese, allegations of political ties between the bishop, some of the Rwandese priests and their counterparts, the Rwandese rebel fighters who infiltrated Rwanda from Uganda, and the bishop's relationship with Uganda security forces.

[1157] The Canon Law Society of Britain and Ireland, *The Code of Canon Law in English Translation* (London: Collins Liturgical Publications, 1983), 336-341, 58-59.

as the ordinary of that diocese.[1158] Consequently, the crisis dragged on for a substantial period.

Rome did not intervene to handle the crisis directly or personally. It expected the people of the diocese together with the ordinary or the Catholic Episcopal Conference of Uganda to resolve the crisis. It was not until a commission of inquiry consisting of canonists from among the Uganda bishops and one priest-canonist was sent to look into the issue, make a report to the bishops' conference; and "in mid 1994 the report was completed and outlined four options. It was considered at a plenary meeting of the Catholic bishops, and Halem'Imana himself chose the option that he resign."[1159] This technically shows that he was not dismissed by the episcopal conference or his opponents or the bishops' conference.

One thing again to be observed here is the difficulty or challenge of drawing a clear line between the intervention of the superior body and the freedom of the smaller body. The lines remain fine and unclear. This is often the difficulty in applying the principle of subsidiarity. Bernard Haring and Valentino Salvoldi suggest that the church's central administrative authority

> should avoid presenting itself as a suffocating central organization which takes everything on itself, controls everything and gives directives to every part of the world, to the detriment of what the local and synodal authorities can decide for themselves.[1160]

Since there is a fine line between authorities in as far as the application of the principle of subsidiarity is concerned, the contention of the duo should be taken with a lot of caution too. While people should or can be left to do for themselves what they are capable of, it is sometimes not easy to know who is capable of doing what. Conversely, it is not always easy to determine when a superior body should intervene to help a smaller group or if it should not. The greatest challenge of the principle of subsidiarity is the difficulty of its application because of the fine lines between the ability of smaller bodies and that of larger bodies.

The second example is the Church of Uganda (COU) crisis, which happened in the Diocese of Busoga, beginning on August 20, 1992, when the

---

[1158] Ibid., Canon 381, 67-68.
[1159] Gifford, 124. Details of the report of the commission are not contained in this source.
[1160] Haring and Salvoldi, 59.

dean of the cathedral resigned on several grounds including corruption and irresponsible leadership.[1161] The community was also split into two—those who supported bishop Bamwoze—the then bishop—and those who wanted him out of office. Just as in the case of the Catholic Diocese of Kabale, Bishop Bamwoze could not resolve the crisis, and neither could the Church of Uganda community in the diocese do it. They appealed to the archbishop, Yonah Okoth, who found it hard to resolve the issue because he was himself subjected to violence in the same way Bishop Bamwoze was.[1162] There was no way of resolving the conflict except to try to employ some extraecclesial organs or agents. Consequently, government or state organs and agents were involved to curb the problem.[1163] In the context of the nation, the principle worked but not within the limited context of the administrative structure of the Church of Uganda. The bid to involve state organs or agents was indicative of the difficulty of the application of the principle of subsidiarity within COU as an institution.

Another challenge of this principle in the religious field is economic. There is often, as Yoweri K. Museveni remarked in 1989, three years after coming to presidency, the tendency of expectation of help from elsewhere as if Uganda does not have resources that could be tapped for its development.[1164] This is a real problem with religious institutions. This problem is also real with the government of Uganda, which depends on "the international community for 55 percent of its budget."[1165] Many national, regional, and local seminaries and individual dioceses have for years expected to be helped by the churches or religious institutions in the developed world. This is the seemingly enduring dependence syndrome. It considerably challenges the plans, initiatives, and efforts of the churches or religious institutions in Uganda in over 120 years of Christianity in Uganda. The Catholic Church's expectation of funds from Propaganda Fide[1166] and other organizations or associations for several decades

---

[1161] Gifford, 124-125.

[1162] Ibid., 127.

[1163] Gifford, 125-130.

[1164] Yoweri K. Museveni, "The Relationship between Church and State," in *Church Contribution to Integral Development*, 20.

[1165] Ayittey, *Africa Unchained: The Blue Print for Africa's Future*, 207.

[1166] This is the Roman Catholic congregation that takes care of the Catholic Church teaching. It is mostly referred to as the Congregation for the Propagation of the Faith.

suggests needs that are more than just the support for crucial things. The need is apparently for daily and annual financial support. Such needs suggest rather an extremely loose interpretation of subsidiarity, universal charity and the right of ownership of property, which leads to a sit-down-and-wait attitude. It also undermines the principle of participation or involvement. This challenge is critical because it invites all to further reflect about living within one's own means. It is sometimes the wish to live beyond one's personal means that makes people behave unethically in order to achieve what they want. This is the case, especially when the expected aid is not forthcoming as it initially was.

E. Common Good: The Challenge of the Requisite Conditions for Development

The principle of common good challenges us to acknowledge the social character of human beings. It is closely related to social justice, solidarity, option for the poor, and affirmative action, notwithstanding the fact that it is also intimately connected to universal love and human dignity. As the sum total of conditions necessary for fostering the well-being of every member of community, it challenges every person to contribute in various ways to creating this situation.[1167] Common good challenges everybody that development is not possible without other principles, virtues, and conditions required by integral human development. In every context, including that of Uganda, it challenges all to embrace universal love, social justice, peace, subsidiarity, preferential option for the poor, association, participation, and education.

The challenge of the common good in the social and economic context is well expressed in the 1995 Constitution of the Republic of Uganda, but it needs to be actualized in the socioeconomic life of the people. The constitution aptly suggests that the citizens of Uganda should be patriotic and loyal, "engage in gainful work for the family and the common good, contribute to the national development and the well-being of the community."[1168] As the supreme law of a country, it is fitting that the constitution incorporates the idea of the common good because as law the constitution is meant to foster the good of the people. It creates an orderly situation and gives people a sense

---

[1167] John XXII, *Mater et Magistra: Christianity and Social Progress* (Washington DC: National Catholic Welfare Conference, 1961), 65, 21. Also see *Gaudium et Spes*, 26, 927.

[1168] Government of Uganda, 10.

of direction. That law is for the good of people is an idea consistently asserted by outstanding legal students including Thomas Aquinas.[1169] The stipulation of the 1995 constitution is, therefore, a positive theoretical contribution that needs to be actualized. The actual positive contribution is real if corruption, discrimination, and marginalization of some people or regions of Uganda are eradicated. Although these are serious challenges, as Lisa Cahill Sowle suggests, despite human weaknesses, one can entertain hopes that "the common good can become a reality and not merely a utopian illusion because humans have an innate capacity to build a just society"[1170] although not without commitment and serious efforts. Second, people are rational and have the ability to know the requirements of common good or social life, and to establish "certain important values from their moral and social experience."[1171] However, the challenge here is the one of the proper use of intellectual capacities. The intellectual capacity has sometimes been deliberately and wrongly used. This misuse is the problem to guard against.

Another challenge of the principle of the common good is that "in a society of persons, the common good is for each individual an end which (s)he must serve and to which one must subordinate one's particular life or interest."[1172] Any service for the cause of the common good demands that people of the community are considerate or less self-concerned. It means each person renders service for other people. This is a great challenge because the human tendency is often first to try to satisfy the ego. On the basis of such demands of the common good, one of the challenges of the common good presented by the Catholic bishops of Uganda is that "politicians and political parties should desist from sacrificing the common good for selfish ends."[1173] This is a critical challenge because it touches the idea that if Ugandans are only self-concerned, they cannot attain the common good. Common good is achieved when people know that they need each other to survive, grow,

---

[1169] Thomas Aquinas, *Summa Theologiae: A Concise Translation*, ed. Timothy McDermott (Allen, Texas: Christian Classics, 1991), 280.

[1170] Lisa Sowle Cahill, "The Global Common Good in the Twenty-First Century," in *Moral Theology: New Directions and Fundamental Issues, Festschrift for James P. Hanigan*, ed. James Keating (New York/Mahwah, NJ: Paulist Press, 2004), 236.

[1171] Ibid., 237.

[1172] Frederick Drandua, 11.

[1173] Catholic Bishops of Uganda, *Towards a Democratic and Peaceful Uganda on the Bases of the Common Good*, 9.

and develop. The Uganda bishops aptly emphasized this need of unity and solidarity in the following words:

> Unity in diversity should be among important ingredients of pluralistic political dispensation that Uganda has embraced. With unity as a starting point and the pursuit of the common good for all citizens of Uganda as a fundamental political principle, we can be assured of a peaceful political transition and greater future prosperity as a country.[1174]

The principle of the common good presents a special challenge to the government, which has a unique role. According to Ddungu, "the state exists for promoting the common good of its citizens and other residents."[1175] This means the role of the state is to create conditions that help all people and groups to fully develop themselves. Such conditions include all kinds of justice—commutative, social, distributive, and legal—peace, efficient public service, goodwill, education, unity, truth, responsibility, the spirit of sharing, and love.[1176]

The principle of the common good is, therefore, a common challenge to all people of Uganda. Politically, the challenge of the principle of common good to Ugandans may be viewed in the light of what the bishops' conference stated recently:

> All of us should unite in solidarity adhering to the values and principles of the common good. Political diversity should be rooted in this common good around which all party programmes should revolve.[1177]

Common good demands solidarity of the people or their unity in action despite the ethnic differences in Uganda. The statement of Uganda Catholic bishops is significant when interpreted in relation to the significance of the colors of the Uganda flag. The Uganda flag has three colors—black, yellow,

---

[1174] Ibid., 10.

[1175] Ddungu, 22. Also see GS, no.74, which Ddungu quotes.

[1176] Ibid. Ddungu is quoting GS, no.76.

[1177] Catholic Bishops of Uganda, *Towards a Democratic and Peaceful Uganda Based on the Common Good*, 4.

and red, in this order. Black is the color of the skin of the people and shows that Uganda is a black African nation; yellow stands for the abundance of sunshine, which Uganda enjoys as an equatorial country because of its location—4 degrees north and 2 degrees south of the equator; and red stands for oneness or brotherhood/sisterhood in blood.[1178] All three colors symbolize what the people of Uganda commonly share. Besides the colors of the Uganda flag, there is one similar symbol of unity—the motto of Uganda: For God and My Country.[1179] The motto suggests a selfless commitment to the cause of Uganda. All these symbols strongly suggest and point to the common good of the nation.

The challenge of the principle of the common good is that it imposes on people—believers and citizens alike—the responsibility to care for others. The principle imposes on people an ethical or moral responsibility they must fulfill as their conscience directs them. Bernard Haring and Valentino Salvoldi suggest to this effect that "the ethical category of responsibility obliges me not to bury talents I have received but to multiply them for the advantage of all."[1180] The challenging obligation is to use one's talents for the benefit or good of the community. In this spirit, the church has made great contributions to the common good of Uganda through its spiritual and social services to the people of the nation. Ddungu has carefully observed and affirmed this in the following words:

> In fulfilling its mission, the church here in Uganda, as elsewhere, has from the very beginning been laying emphasis upon assisting in providing the following services: education and health care, assistance to the needy and the disadvantaged, integral evangelization, which makes people holistic in their thinking and acting; promotion of the means of social communication for educating people's consciences and attitudes; and improvement of food production, water, shelter, environment, family and community life for all. The church has provided personnel and structures for the realization of most of the above services.[1181]

[1178] "Uganda" in *Oxford Encyclopedic World Atlas*, 222. Also see McKnight, 366.
[1179] Catholic Bishops of Uganda, *With a New Heart and a New Spirit*, 70.
[1180] Haring and Salvoldi, 63.
[1181] Ddungu, 23.

If there are any institutions in Uganda that give priority to the common good, it is the religious institutions that are ranked among the first, especially the Christian churches. The Catholic Church and the Protestant churches have consistently shown concern for the common good and done what it requires from the time of the first Christian missionaries up until today. If they are to be commended for their work this is one of the areas where they should be complemented. If the churches have done so much to contribute to the common good, others are also capable of doing the same. However, the final challenge I would like to adopt from Cahill is what she describes as "James Hanigan's diagnosis of 'the human problem', namely as 'not that we do not know what we should do, but that we do not want to know and do not want to do it'."[1182] It is not that nobody knows the right things to do and how to do them. The problem and challenge is simply human obstinacy or negligence—people deliberately refuse to know and do the right things. This is the reality of the immoral or sinful dimension of human character.

F. Justice and Equality: The Challenge of Equality and Fairness in Social Diversity

Justice is one of the most challenging principles for integral human development. It is called for by the human need to coexist, it requires and at the same time leads to human coexistence, which is often complicated by individual interests. As Reinhold Niebuhr suggests, the difficulty of human coexistence is a perennial one, and human society will always have to deal with the question of justice necessary for "the preservation and fulfillment of human love."[1183] In treating the question of justice in this section, our concern is about people who suffer injustice, but it should be noted that in reality the main concern is about the attitude of those who do injustice. The best explanation or supportive assertion in this case is what the Nichomachean ethics, which resonates with the Christian view suggests. Namely, it is worse to do injustice than to suffer injustice because the latter does not involve vice,

---

[1182] Cahill, 242.

[1183] Reinhold Niebuhr, *Moral Man and Immoral Society: A Study in Ethics and Politics*, indroduced by Langdon B. Gilkey (Louisville Kentucky: Westminister John Knox Press, 2001), 1.

and so it is not blameworthy while the former involves some form or degree of vice and is blameworthy.[1184]

Paul VI was clear in his expansion of the notion of justice, from being a national social justice to international social justice, that the virtue is based on the principle of human solidarity.[1185] As some of the preceding sections of this work espoused, Uganda is a nation that has a pluralistic ethnic constitution. The virtue of justice is both a significant value and a challenge in such a context, at least on the basis of understanding justice as fairness or giving each person his or her due, though what is due to each person is often difficult to determine. Justice and its pursuit is, nonetheless, a moral imperative to both religious institutions and the civil society.[1186] The moral obligation that at once confronts the church leadership, the Christian community, the Uganda government, the citizens, believers, and leaders, in relation to justice, is the recognition of and respect for the equal dignity and freedom of all people. This idea is also clearly stipulated in the Ugandan constitution and stands as a serious challenge to all. The constitution states that "all persons are equal before and under the law in all spheres of political, economic, social and cultural life and in every other respect."[1187] The real challenge is that it is not enough to verbalize the equality of people while in real life there are critical differences in treatment of peoples or regions as has been the case in the history of Uganda and still persists. A typical example here is that since the establishment of British protectorate West Nile

> was used as a labour reserve, gazetted as a "closed area" from which outsiders were excluded and systematically underdeveloped in favour of the cash-crop agriculture of southern Uganda.[1188]

This is a problem that also affected some parts of Uganda as indicated in some of the subsequent paragraphs of this subsection. This differential

---

[1184] Aristotle, *Nicomachean Ethics*, trans.Terence Irwin (Indianapolis/Cambridge: Hackett Publishing Company, 1985), 147.

[1185] *Populorum Progressio*, 2, 5; 44, 48.

[1186] Norman G. Kurland, "Economic Justice in the Age of Robot," in *Curing World Poverty: The New Role of Property*, ed. John H. Miller (Social Justice Review: Saint Louis, Missouri, 1994), 62.

[1187] Government of Uganda, 20.

[1188] Mark Leopold, 12.

treatment recurs in West Nile to date, and the evidence is what Mark Leopold has stated. Namely, that "the economic, social and political marginality of Arua has persisted."[1189]

From socioeconomic and political points of view the issue articulated here is, therefore, that of the recognition of the rights of people, the equality of their dignity, and treating them according to these rights and needs in a fair manner. Justice can only be achieved if people understand and accept that they have mutual rights and obligations. The demands of justice may be imposed by religious or civil law. This means that justice sometimes demands some form of coercion, as Reinhold Niebuhr also suggests.[1190] This view was also upheld by Martin Luther King Jr., says Deotis J. Roberts:

> King believed in a strong and aggressive leadership by government authorities to sponsor civil rights and social justice. However when government is on the side of injustice, King believed Christians had the responsibility to apply moral pressure to compel unwilling authorities to yield to the mandates of justice. Government has a responsibility to help control antisocial and immoral behavior through the process of law . . . . For King the state is fulfilling the divine purpose for its existence when it reflects love and justice, when it creates and preserves the well-being of humans intended by God in Christ. This, in King's judgement, would be a community where integration has replaced segregation where economic justice has eliminated poverty, where a just order has supplanted violence and chaos. On the other hand, a state is evil and sinful when it formulates and sponsors policies that are divisive, unjust and violent.[1191]

Here, the state is portrayed to be potentially both good and evil, which is right especially from a Christian perspective in light of the history of secular states. Religion should be its corrective counterpart. However, King suggests

---

[1189] Ibid. Also see page 147 of the same source.

[1190] Niebuhr, 3.

[1191] Deotis J. Roberts, *Bonhoeffer and King: Speaking Truth to Power* (Louisville, Kentucky: Westminister John Knox Press, 2005), 80. Here, Roberts is partly quoting Baldwin, "On the Relation of the Christian to the State," 99. Here, a reference has also been made to Michall G. Long, *Against Us but for Us: Martin Luther King Jr. and the State* (Macon, GA: University Press, 2002), xv.

a nonviolent pressure. According to me, it seems good to argue that King also advocates that from a Christian point of view a true act of justice does not demand physical coercion because it is motivated by love. Justice demands that mutual responsibility and obligation are recognized and accepted as such by all.

Viewing justice in reference to the salaries of the public or civil servants, justice remains a significant challenge to Uganda. The challenge is compounded by the legal or constitutional claim that

> under "the rule of law," every citizen has the right to receive a just return for his labour: whether manual or mental. In conducting economic, and cultural affairs of the state, every government must realize that the rights of the individual, include provision for just and favorable conditions of work, fair and adequate renumeration [sic] which can ensure the worker and his family a standard of living worthy of human dignity. It is the duty of the government to take all possible action to promote the economic and social welfare of the people and of the nation as a whole.[1192]

Such issues have not been raised for nothing. Neither are they new, even in modern Uganda. Although Levis Mugumya claims that teachers' salaries are in accordance to the service they render, there is a poor salary scale for teachers in particular.[1193] For example, primary school teachers are currently paid, monthly, UShs 150,000 (an equivalent of US $82), and secondary (high) school teachers receive, monthly, UShs 200,000 (an equivalent of US $110).[1194] This salary scale suggests that the average annual income of a secondary

---

[1192] Kiapi, 81-82.

[1193] Mugumya Levis, "Human Rights: An Insight into Uganda's Education Sector," in *Developing a Culture of Peace and Human Rights in Africa: African Peace Series*, volume 1, eds. Nkrunziza, R.K Deusdedit and Mugumya Levis (Kampala, Uganda: Konrad Adeenauer Stiftung [KAS], 2003), 117.

[1194] Recently, the government of Uganda increased the salary of primary school teachers to the level of the Secondary school teachers' salary effective from July 2006. Instead of UShs 150,000, they receive UShs 200,000. This increase is still inadequate considering the needs of the teachers and their families or dependents. Cfr. Gerald Walulya, "Government to Raise Teachers' Pay to Shs 200,000," in *Daily Monitor* (Kampala, Uganda, April 19, 2006). Currency exchange rates

school teacher is about UShs 2,400,000 (US $1,320). On average, excluding children in the primary schools, a family takes care of the education of three children in secondary schools with an *estimated* term average expenditure of UShs 120,000 for tuition, UShs 25,000 for stationery, and UShs 30,000 for pocket money and transportation in a rural area. This means a year's expenses on the three secondary school students amounts to a total of UShs 1,575,000 (US $875), leaving a balance of UShs 825,000 (US $ 458) for the rest of the family needs, viz., feeding, health care, school supplies of children in primary schools, clothing, etc., for a whole year.

The annual estimates suggest that these salaries cannot sustain the teachers and their families for a month. Though government has attempted to raise the salary of teachers by UShs 20,000 (an equivalent of US $11) after their peaceful demonstration in 2005, the teachers still clamor that the salary increase is "still below the average cost of living."[1195] The challenge to the government is to ensure that these teachers, and all employees, are paid a living wage—not "a killing wage as it is often called in Uganda"[1196] because the meager salaries are incapable of sustaining employees and their families or dependents. The Uganda National Teachers Union (UNATU) study in April 2005 made some interesting revelations:

> 71% of teachers spend their very meager salaries on feeding and educating their children; . . . 69% of Uganda's teachers do not do any other job to supplement their abysmal incomes. The teachers "survive on debts and handouts. They live as beggars."[1197]

It is unjust to treat civil servants the way these teachers are treated just because they have no alternative opportunities for their livelihood and that of their families. The gravity of the injustice to the teachers is aggravated by

---

indicated are of the date just indicated. The currency exchange rates are often in flux within a short time. Cfr. www.monitor.co.ug/news.

[1195] Gerald Walulya, "Government to Raise Teachers' Pay to Shs 200,000," in *Daily Monitor* (Kampala, Uganda, April 19, 2006). Also cfr. www.monitor.co.ug/news.

[1196] Vali Jamal, "Changes in Poverty Patterns in Uganda," in *Developing Uganda*, eds. Holger Bernt Hansen and Michael Twaddle (Kampala: Fountain Publishers, 1998), 83.

[1197] K. Mulera Muniini, "Raise Teachers' Salaries," in *Daily Monitor* (Kampala, Uganda, April 30, 2006). Also cfr. www.monitor.co.ug/news.

the fact that money is drained by the defense ministry, sometimes encouraged from without, there are ghost soldiers and ghost teachers, or people are paid when actually not teaching or even out of the country.[1198] The real challenge is to pay workers a just wage. Here, a just wage is understood to be

> the way of responding to the economic rights of every person which lay claim to adequate food, clothing, shelter, education, working conditions, health care, retirement protection—all that is needed for the full and integral development of the human person.[1199]

The just wage is what provides for the barely comfortable life of the workers, their families, and dependents. In other words, as Frank D. Almade suggests, it helps the employee to meet just the basic necessities of life. It is the minimum pay and "equal pay for equal work done."[1200]

While the evil of injustice is perpetrated against Uganda's civil servants, the level of corruption is also growing. The statement of AMSRIU is a testimony here: "Corruption continues to be rampant and it is ineffectively challenged."[1201] Economic and social justice demands that the resources of a nation are used for the benefit of all and especially the needy or less fortunate citizens. Unfortunately, as Ronald Kassimir states, Ugandans have transformed "in popular parlance their national motto from 'For God and My Country' to 'For God and My Stomach.'"[1202] The expression typically depicts the politics and mentality of corruption and self-concern. In light of this assertion, the inevitable challenge for the Uganda government, the citizens, rich regions, and civil or public servants is to undo the colonial legacy of the uneven distribution of the country's resources.[1203] While the central region, especially around the capital of Kampala, and the lake region have

---

[1198] Twaddle and Holger Bernt, 6. Also see Legget, 12. Also see Ayittey, *Africa Unchained: The Blue Print for Africa's Future*, 207.

[1199] Frank D. Almade, *Just Wages for Church Employees* (New York: Peter Lang, 1993), 117.

[1200] Ibid., 123.

[1201] The Executive Association of the Major Superiors of Religious Institutes in Uganda, 7. Also see Ayittey, *Africa Unchained: The Blue Print for Africa's Future*, 208-209.

[1202] Kassimir, 233.

[1203] Mugaju, 14.

reasonable infrastructure and economic standing, and a few other parts are wealthy, other areas are not.[1204] Even the so-called wealthy regions have beggars, and the majority of the country lives in dire poverty. The challenge here is that many of the poor are unaware and not concerned about the differences between their conditions and that of the well-to-do. They need more and real education, a further challenge to a sincere government and civil or public servants, and religious institutions.

Labor for large estates or plantations of tea, coffee, and sugar are obtained from the poor regions of the nation, a routine which was arranged during the colonial times. For instance, those from Kigezi and Ankole, in western Uganda, and West Nile, Acholi, Teso, and other northerners were considered strong and courageous, hence good fighters and thus good candidates for the military and any hard labor.[1205] These regions have been and are some of the poorest regions of Uganda. Consequently, in the subsequent years the recruitment, and employment at Kakira and Lugazi sugar estates was provided by the western, northern, and northeastern regions of Uganda. Such were, and are still, some of the factors that contribute to "ethnic animosities and prejudices, which eventually became stereotypes of the 'developed' south and the 'backward' north,"[1206] which suggest or are a testimony to the regional imbalances in the country. Vali Jamal is of the same view when he affirms that there is "the North-South divide"[1207] in terms of income distribution or economic differences.

The unaware and unsuspecting people thought, and some still think that going down country Uganda is getting to heaven. To date, some of the civil servants or government agents, who should be at least slightly enlightened, in some of these regions encourage the youth to get recruited for these kinds of work, either out of ignorance or because the agents and the youth are bribed. Uganda is historically known for government intimidation of and bribes to politicians to silence them and any religious leaders who raise sensitive political issues.[1208] It is not a surprise that the responsible people are bribed to contribute to such unfair treatments of certain sectors of the country. This constitutes an actual injustice.

[1204] Legget, 27.

[1205] Mugaju, 14-15. Also see Mark Leopold, 12.

[1206] Ibid.

[1207] Jamal, 75.

[1208] Bweyale, 71.

This practice of labor recruitment occurs mainly in specific political regions of Uganda while there are capable people in the regions where the estates are located and they need money too, as the general poverty situation in Uganda suggests, and they too could work in these estates.[1209] Two conclusions are inevitable. First, the poor regions are discriminated against and targeted for use as instruments of development in some regions of the nation without being remunerated adequately. This is social and economic injustice. Second, every able citizen is expected to contribute to the progress of the nation as demanded by solidarity, justice, common good, and participation but surely not at the expense of the respect for human dignity. No citizen ought to be subjected to such unfair treatment.

In any unjust political and economic system or process, people are often disgruntled and sometimes fight each other. Injustice has caused the decline of many nations and regimes or governments. Justice is, hence, a crucial virtue for government, public servants, and every citizen. Where it is lacking, there is no peace. Reinhold Neibuhr speaks to this point in his assertion that in addressing injustices in society, "violence can therefore not be ruled out on *a priori* grounds."[1210] He suggests, as Paul VI did in *Populorum Progressio*, that violence is not desirable, but it is an inevitable consequence regardless of the rightness or the morality of the purpose to be achieved. Otherwise, where there is justice, there is peace and stability.

In the context of Uganda, Okot observes that "instability, insecurity, war and various other forms of violence that have been suffered in this country have largely been consequences of economic imbalances."[1211] The imbalances reflect the degree of injustice in Uganda. These imbalances suggest that governments in the past did not create conditions to promote development of the nation. While it is necessary to acknowledge that there are differences in circumstances and abilities of the people, it is also good to accept that certain conditions can be corrected, and they should be corrected or improved for the sake of the growth of the people. This is a challenge to both the former and the current government of Uganda.

Three types of justice that challenge the Ugandan context must be delineated because all of them are part and parcel of the question of justice as a virtue necessary for human growth. First is *commutative justice*, which

---

[1209] Mugaju, 14-15.
[1210] Niebuhr, 172.
[1211] Okot, 105.

requires that when people make private contracts or agreements, they should keep the contracts and there must be equality between the goods and the services or work offered and the reward given for them.[1212] This type of justice presents a challenge to business people, who cheat with weighing scales and the quantity of work done by employees and the remuneration paid to them for the work done. It puts into question the deceptive advertisements through any communication medium.

The second type of justice is *distributive justice*, which demands that public goods of a country "such as its natural resources, be used to satisfy the basic needs of all the people, especially the under-privileged[sic], the poor and the powerless."[1213] Distributive justice is a challenge to the government of Uganda in relation to lack of hydroelectricity in the West Nile region, Karamoja, and any region in that country that is not supplied with hydroelectricity despite exporting electricity to Rwanda or other neighboring nations.

Finally, there is *legal justice*, which "demands that all citizens contribute according to their ability to the promotion of the welfare of society: by supporting public institutions, which serve the common good of all the citizens."[1214] This aspect of justice again challenges the rich regions of Uganda such as Kampala or the central region, and the lake region in general, to respond to the needs of the poor regions which receive less of the resources of Uganda, including electricity already referred to above.

Heroism is one of the challenges of the virtue of justice to the religious institutions and leaders in addressing the issue of injustice in both civil and religious communities. The challenge for anyone addressing questions of injustice is to accept to be heroic and exercise the virtue of courage, even when the cause being pursued is unpopular to the government or civil society and their sympathizers. A challenging example suggested here is the difficult time during the reign of Idi Amin as president of Uganda. While his reign was marked by lots of injustices, persecutions, and confiscation of the property of Asians and their expulsion, including those who were Ugandan citizens, no church authority dared to confront him or government organs to demand justice.[1215] One of the main challenges of that time, and during

---

[1212] Kiapi, 82.
[1213] Ibid.
[1214] Ibid.
[1215] Gifford, 118.

similar moments in our time, is that of accepting the consequence of the fulfillment of one's prophetic mission or to be a *Christian hero*.

According to Gifford, only the Makerere University students of that time dared to protest the expulsion of the Asian-Ugandan citizens and the confiscation of their property when they marched into the city.[1216] They proved to be more prophetic and heroic than the religious leadership in the country at that time—a country dominantly Christian. This was a real challenge and a failure of the religious leadership or the Christian churches' prophetic leadership and mission at a time when it was most needed. They constitute the majority of the population and needed to pool their efforts together early enough to address issues.[1217] Whether it was fear or prudence, the challenge was the one of the choice between love and hatred, justice and injustice, between mutual respect and confrontation. This, unfortunately, is a frequently neglected responsibility, says Peter Kanyandago:

> We have to acknowledge, especially, we the church leaders, that in the past, sometimes, we have feared to expose and endanger ourselves individually, or as an ecclesial community and institution, that we have been too prudent.[1218]

However, one has to acknowledge that it was the church, especially the Christian churches, which remained the only formidable and unbroken institution providing support and strength and the best place of refuge for the populace at the difficult times during the reign of Idi Amin and later, even to date.[1219]

The problem of the need to address the issue of injustice affects not only the civil society, but also religious institutions. This assertion is suggested by the fact that the church is not only a divine institution, it is

---

[1216] Ibid.

[1217] Ibid., 119.

[1218] Peter Kanyandago, "A Biblical Theology of the Rule of Law, and Due Respect for Basic Human Rights," in *Church Contribution to Integral Development*, edS. Joseph Therese Agbasiere and Boniface K. Zabajungu (Eldoret, Kenya: AMECEA Gaba Publications, 1989), 71. Here Kanyandago quotes C. Stuhlmueller, "What Price Prophecy," in *The Way* (September 1980),167-175, where the author develops the idea that there is a price upon being a prophet.

[1219] Gifford, 119-120.

also a human institution—it is both holy and sinful. However, this is not a justification to excuse or exempt the church from being affected by the problem of injustice. The church has also treated this issue of just pay in parts of several of her social teachings and documents.[1220] On account of this assertion, the question that the church needs to address is also whether in practice she offers just or living wage for her employees or not. Peter Kanyandago suggests that to this question, in the context of Uganda, the dominant answer is *no* because the majority of church employees are paid meager salaries.[1221] They are often expected to render service as their *Christian contribution*. The fact is, however, that they and their families or communities need material resources to live. This fact is often minimized or neglected. The greatest challenge in this regard is that if the church or religious institutions are not just, "our action and call" to people "for a more just world"—our function as religious leaders and institutions—"will not be credible."[1222] In other words, the mission and ministry of the church or religious institutions become obsolete.

Another challenge of the virtue of justice to religious institutions in relation to the commitment to be examples of justice for the civil society or other people and institutions is that of reexamining our lifestyle. Above all, it important to note that "every just social order can be judged according to the service it provides for the people who live under it."[1223] This challenge confronts the civil society as well as religious institutions. In relation to such a situation, Peter Kanyandago strongly charges,

> if we are honest with ourselves, we will recognize: that there is concentration of wealth to particular areas of the church, mainly in clerical circles. Justice calls for an equitable sharing of the goods of the world. Failure to share and distribute the wealth of the world is to disregard the will of the Creator. It is also an offence to the poor, which can provoke reactions of frustration and violence, which can hamper the church's mission, as happened during the French revolution.[1224]

[1220] Almade, 79ff.

[1221] Kanyandago, 72.

[1222] Ibid.

[1223] Habiger, 9.

[1224] Kanyandago, 72-73.

Religious leaders and institutions are challenged here to reflect on their attitude toward possession of natural resources, their attachment to these goods, and their application of the principle of ownership of natural resources. This is a critical challenge because the religious—not just religious by profession of the vow of poverty, but all members and leaders of religious groups or institutions—are the very teachers or advocates of these principles. This challenge also invokes the application of the principles of preferential option for the poor, affirmative action, common good, and solidarity.

The challenge of justice or its opposite—injustice—is equally critical to religious institutions, governments, various groups, and individuals because the question of justice or injustice involves lawlessness, greed, and unfairness or their opposites. The Nicomachean ethics, which, in my judgment, is in line with Christian ethics, says it all about justice in relation to law and fairness: "What is just will be both what is lawful and what is fair, and what is unjust will be both what is lawless and what is unfair."[1225] The real challenge here is to be just and to act lawfully.

G. Preferential Option for the Poor: The Choice between Priority and Self-Interest

The question of the preferential option for the poor is and has always been one of the principal concerns of the church. The church in Uganda has also been the champion and protagonist of the teaching and application of the principle.[1226] The 2006 Lenten message showed the gravity of the option for the poor. After frequent references to *Populorum Progressio* in his 2006 Lenten message, Benedict XVI alluded to the statement of Blessed Teresa of Calcutta that "the worst poverty is not to know Christ."[1227] His message shows the

---

[1225] Aristotle, *Nicomachean Ethics*, 117.

[1226] Anna Mary Kayonga, "The Church's Role in the Care of Orphans and Destitutes," in *Church Contribution to Integral Development*, eds. Joseph Therese Agbasiere and Boniface K. Kabajungu (Eldoret, Kenya: AMECEA Gaba Publications, 1989), 217.

[1227] Benedictus PP. XVI, "Jesus at the sight of the crowds was moved with pity" (Mt. 9:36), message of Pope Benedict XVI for Lent 2006 in *Arua Diocese Bulletin*, no.69 (Arua: Arua Diocese Communication Department, March 2006), 2. This is a teaching, though not stated, based on Mt. 25:31-36 because true knowledge of Christ means practically identifying with him and doing what he wants

significance of the option for the poor especially when he states that to care for the poor is to live the Christian message because Christ identified himself with the poor; liberating the poor means Christ is recognized in them.

As treated in chapter two, option for the poor is a principle that Paul VI would not have overlooked because, in *Populorum Progressio*, he was addressing the problem of the poor peoples of the world. It was the issue of the degradation of human life and dignity.[1228] The principle is necessary for a poor country, purportedly said to be developing, like Uganda. In Uganda, there are economic disparities.[1229] These disparities demand or call for the Uganda government, the church, and organizations capable of providing assistance to apply this principle of positive discrimination in favor of the most disadvantaged people of Uganda.

Yoweri K. Museveni acknowledges this fact and states that "the poorest part of the country, the North, has made much slower progress than other areas, mainly because of insecurity."[1230] The poverty due to insecurity in northern Uganda is a challenge to stop fighting, but it is also a challenge to ceaselessly help war-ravaged and consequently poor regions in parts of northern and western Uganda that have been affected by "chronic insecurity, resulting in social dislocation and economic underdevelopment."[1231]

Despite their critical financial situation, the economically poor often shoulder more financial burdens than affluent people. They pay for the basic needs of life more expensively than the rich. The majority of the rich live in urban areas, and the poor live in the rural areas or in the countryside. Over 66 percent of Ugandans live below the poverty line, "on less than US $ 15.00 per month."[1232] While cultural practices and individuals contribute to such a pathetic situation, the situation demands that government allocate more development funds to help the poor address their needs. It calls for the government and the church to educate people and to create enduring systems

---

done for him and for others. In this text, it is clear that Christ and the poor are identified together—they are not differentiated.

[1228] Peter Riga, *The Church of the Poor: A Commentary on Paul VI's Encyclical on the Development of Peoples* (Techny, Illinois: Divine Word Publications, 1968), 24.

[1229] Leggett, 56.

[1230] Yoweri Kaguta Museveni, "Forward," in *Poverty Eradication Action Plan (2001-2003)*, vol. 1, ii.

[1231] Leggett, 3.

[1232] Ibid., 64.

that can create conditions for the poor to improve their lives. The government attempted to address the problem through its Poverty Eradication Plan, introduced in mid-1990s after an agreement with the International Monetary Fund (IMF), which was "designed to wipe out poverty within 20 years;"[1233] but the conditions of the majority of the people remain poor.

The results of the Poverty Eradication Plan are hardly noticeable on a general observation of the situation in Uganda. In the urban areas, where there is more money in circulation and there are more possibilities for employment, basic needs are less expensive than in the rural areas where there is less money; and there are no lucrative businesses and employment opportunities. Vali Jamal's testimony about the situation, at least up to 1998, supports this contention. He states that "around 35 per cent of the rural population and 16 percent of the urban population are now shown to be in poverty," but because "the rural areas comprise over 88 percent of the total population, poverty is very much a rural phenomenon in Uganda, with over 90 percent of the total poverty."[1234]

The rich are often in serious pursuit to purchase the land of the poor, which is their livelihood. They try to do so at giveaway prices. There is a challenge here because rich people, who could improve the situation of the poor, neglect the poor, forfeit their responsibility to help the poor, contrary to Paul VI's exhortation in Populorum Progressio.[1235] The neglect of the poor is not only an injustice. It also shows that the rich are motivated by self-interest and do not recognize the dignity of the poor.

Politically, governments have not come up with feasible projects to help promote poor citizens. Even if Uganda's poverty reduction strategy has well-outlined plans for the reduction of poverty in the country as indicated by the 2000/2001 development report, the results are far from reaching the desired goal.[1236] The weak and the poor are consistently neglected or marginalized. They are not listened to politically. Yet they are the people whose votes are often sought by politicians. They seem to exist as citizens only when elections are close and during elections. They are often promised

---

[1233] Ibid.

[1234] Jamal, 80-81. Some authors suggest that the rural population comprises 86 percent of Uganda's total population. The same percentage of Ugandans are poor.

[1235] Populorum Progressio, 74, 31. The biblical foundation Paul VI used here is Mk. 8:2.

[1236] World Bank, World Development Report, 2000/2001: Attacking Poverty (Oxford: Oxford University Press, 2001), 22.

heaven on earth before and at the time of elections. Once elections are over, politicians do not deliver on their promises. Their votes are solicited with money, which is not even sufficient for a decent meal. This is not what the poor would opt for if they had bargaining powers. Neither is it an option that promotes their life, dignity, and rights. Instead of giving precedence to the needs of the poor over the rich, the rich give precedence to themselves over the poor.[1237] The problem here is that of distortion of the order of priority of values. Even if "poverty eradication is the central objective of the Government of Uganda"[1238] and it were achieved, Uganda would still be far from being called truly developed if the poor are not part of human development. I would like to appropriate the suggestion of Anna Mary Kayonga to help us understand and improve the condition of the poor. She suggests that to help the poor, we need to

> enter into solidarity with the poor in concrete ways: by sharing their lives, sorrows, joys, hopes, and fears . . . . Solidarity with the poor also means that we must break complicity with those who oppress the poor, and that we must oppose the causes of evil. This calls for the transformation of the unjust structures, which institutionalize destitution.[1239]

The poor are often the victims of corruption by government and civil leaders and individuals who are self-concerned. While external aid and loans are solicited for them and in their name, they almost never benefit from the foreign aid. All they receive depends on the political giants. This is precisely why the forgiveness of debts of Uganda, which was forgiven 67 percent of its debts in 1995, makes no sense for a country where there is rampant discrimination, injustice, and corruption.[1240] Uganda claims that corruption

---

[1237] The Bishops of Africa, "Forgive Us Our Debts: Open Letter to Our Brother Bishops in Europe and America," in *The African Synod: Documents, Reflections, Perspectives*, ed. Maura Browne (Maryknoll, New York: Orbis Books, 1996), 115. The African bishops are quoting the Pontifical Commission for Justice and Peace, *An Ethical Approach to the International Debt Question*, 1986.

[1238] Yoweri Kaguta Museveni, "Forward," in *Poverty Eradication Action Plan (2001-2003)*, Vol. 1, ii.

[1239] Kayonga, 218.

[1240] Gifford, 116.

is now minimized, but actually, proportionately it has been aggravated. The 2003 World Development Report shows that 39 percent of the total number of the known and reported bribes were paid.[1241] Since the corruption is prevalent in Uganda, forgiving its debts aggravates corruption. It encourages more corruption on the part of those who administer the funds and adds to the marginalization, exclusion, and misery of the poor. It promotes an option for the rich, not an option for the poor. This is where the request of African bishops during the African synod, and the later advocacy of John Paul II in preparation for the jubilee year, that debts of poor countries should be forgiven seems rather ridiculous and may be accepted reservedly.[1242] As pastors, their request makes sense because it shows their concern for the needy and poor. The forgiven debts are intended to relieve governments so that they may help unfortunate citizens. The concern of the bishops and the pontiff is the dignity of the human person. It was this kind of concern that attracted the African bishops to propagate the idea of an "uncompromising solidarity with the poor and to make their cry known."[1243] However, in reality, those who are forgiven are the corrupt officials who are beneficiaries of loans and grants that the government receives. They make forgiveness of debts problematic and perhaps even immoral, especially if those who forgive the debts are aware of the prevalence of corruption.

Uganda is a religious country and dominantly a Christian one—48 percent Catholic and 38 percent Protestant, though some authors suggest that Catholics constitute 49.6 percent and Protestants are 26.2 percent of the population of Uganda.[1244] Religious institutions have been the chief protagonists of the principle of the preferential option for the poor. The poor have often been a priority of religious institutions because they understand that they are one of the reasons the church was instituted. The Christian churches are perhaps the more leading religious institutions in this regard since the colonial times. They built and continue to build schools, colleges, formation houses, hospitals, orphanages, and other development institutions that meet

---

[1241] World Bank, *World Development Report, 2005: A Better Investment Climate for Everyone* (Oxford: Oxford University Press, 2005), 246.

[1242] The Bishops of Africa, 114.

[1243] Ibid.

[1244] Gifford, 119. Gifford cites David Barrett, ed., *Encyclopedia of Christianity* (Nairobi: OUP, 1984), 686.

the needs of the poor.[1245] They are the ones that speak more strongly on behalf of the poor and try to educate the poor to come out of their situations. Adrian K. Ddungu affirms this assertion:

> The church in this country is committed to community development, with special emphasis upon women, youth, and rural people's development; and upon uplifting of the condition of the poor and the oppressed.[1246]

The initiatives of the church in making a preferential option for the poor are definitely a noble cause. Ddungu's statement is true, but it is also questionable whether all churches or religious institutions, used here as a generic term for believers, are committed to this cause. Second, option for the poor may also have negative consequences and present extra challenges. This suggests why, recognizing and citing Laurenti C. Magesa's very significant view, Kanyandago alludes to the possible danger of helping the poor as "aggravating their dependence."[1247] He specifically states that according to Magesa "true generosity liberates unto freedom, enabling individuals and peoples to take charge of their own life."[1248] In other words, any help rendered to the poor should improve their condition but at the same time help them to be self-reliant. The danger of perpetual donation or assistance is that it can lead to perpetual dependence. This is counterproductive to authentic development.

After independence in 1963, the state took over the management and the policies of schools and a majority of schools became public or government-aided schools.[1249] It was too expensive for poor people to educate their children because they could not afford the costs of education previously much

---

[1245] Okot, 106. Also see Ddungu, 23. Here also cfr. page 24, footnote number 5, which is an emphasis on the church's preferential option for the poor in Uganda.

[1246] Ddungu, 23.

[1247] Kanyandago, 74.

[1248] Ibid. Here, Kanyandago quotes L.C. Magesa, "The Priority of Justice Over Charity," in *AFER* 29, no.6, December (1987), 353; see also Rupper's reaction to this article in "Platform," in *AFER* 30, no.2, April (1988), 113-114.

[1249] J. C. Ssekamwa and S. M. E. Lugumba, *A History of Education in East Africa* (Kampala: Fountain Publishers, 2001), 150.

subsidized by the church. The quality of formation also declined and continues to decline. In 1997, Universal Primary Education (UPE) was introduced in Uganda to help the poor attain at least a primary education, but this meant "only four children per household benefit"[1250] would be given free education though in practice UPE remained open. This was a positive implementation of prior plans for the future development of Uganda, but its implementation was not ready for 1997 or the implementation was either poorly planned or unplanned. Consequently, the standard of education has worsened and UPE cannot be considered a favorable option for the poor. Education is a crucial factor in development. It is for this reason that some people send their children to schools where they can receive relevant, well-founded, and profitable education even if that means paying very expensively for it.

The study in this section shows that the "poverty in Uganda is a development problem," and it calls for a "development strategy involving all sections of the population."[1251] This is a critical challenge to the government of Uganda, religious institutions, and especially the planners of development strategies in the country.

H. Affirmative Action: The Challenge of Genuine Government Intervention

One of the priorities for any good government is to address the past injustices of discrimination and marginalization. This priority is significant because if not addressed violence or disharmony may creep into society. In Uganda, different categories of people—women, disabled people, and minorities for instance—have suffered and many of them still suffer injustices. The government of Uganda (NRM government, in particular) has tried to address some of these issues.[1252] The challenge which confronts the nation

---

[1250] Mugumya, 115.

[1251] Jamal, 85.

[1252] Mary R. Mugyenyi, "Towards the Empowerment of Women: A Critique of NRM Policies and Programmes," in *Developing Uganda*, eds. Holger Bernt Hansen and Michael Twaddle (Kampala: Fountain Publishers, 1998), 133. Here, Mugyenyi makes reference to Yoweri Kaguta Museveni, "Speech by the President of the Republic of Uganda on the occasion of the Closing of the 1st Conference on Women and Health," in 1989, reproduced in *Agenda: A Journal about Women and Gender*, no. 6:10.

and the church or religious institutions persistently is that women need to be included and promoted more than ever before. Mary Mugenyi underscores this point:

> Developing Uganda takes men and women. Gender should therefore be on the agenda of development dialogue more so in Uganda where women constitute a 53 percent majority of the population; they contribute 80 percent of agricultural labour and 90 percent of domestic labour and are almost exclusively responsible for the health and nutrition of their families and communities.[1253]

There is no doubt that in the field of education there has been promotion of women. Government has done so by providing opportunity for female students to go on to higher institutions of learning with poorer academic grades than male students. The problem with this effort in the positive discrimination or affirmative action is that "if access is not open to all at the lower levels, then affirmative action of affording females to enter higher institutions of learning" will not achieve its goal of "eliminating equality and injustice."[1254] The academic requirement for admission to higher institutions of learning is less for female students than for the male students in terms of their academic performances. This arrangement merely perpetuates the vicious circle of discrimination and injustice. It has helped promote female students who often perform poorly in subjects like mathematics and the physical sciences. The number of women admitted to higher institutions has grown since the inception of this program. However, the problem the program could create is that of encouraging female students to be lazy. They may become reluctant to fully apply themselves in studies. Positively, the plan helps male students to work hard in order to perform extremely well so as to be admitted to the higher institutions of learning. The arrangement still contributes to a difference between female students and the competing male students in terms of how much they learn or accomplish in their education.

[1253] Ibid.

[1254] Deusdedit R.K. Nkrunziza, "The Role of Civil Society in Peace Building: The Case of Uganda," in *Developing a Culture of Peace and Human Rights in Africa: African Peace Series*, vol. 1, eds. Nkrunziza R. K. Deusdedit and Mugumya Levis (Kampala, Uganda: Konrad Adeenauer Stiftung [KAS], 2003), 116.

Uganda's education system has also been discriminating on the basis of subjects taught in schools. Some subjects are traditionally considered too hard for female students and so become mainly the prerogative of male students, and other subjects are considered fitting for female students only. For instance, mathematics, carpentry, construction, and experimental sciences in general are still considered male subjects while home economics, needle work, and tailoring are considered women subjects.[1255] This discrimination has not been adequately addressed. In addition to this difficulty, certain cultural values and practices need to be examined, evaluated, and remodeled or abandoned altogether to help improve women's situation in relation to men. This suggests that there are still many obstacles to be overcome if women's level of development is to match that of men.[1256]

Paul VI's proposal of the significance of the principle of affirmative action emphasized the importance of bodies or organizations like the United Nations (UN) as presented in chapter two. However, the implementation of the principle is not without challenges as Bernard Haring and Valentino Salvoldi suggest.

> The United nations still does not have the power to impose its will, nor does it have a legally authorized and authoritative representative. The time has not yet arrived to courageously propose such a world authority because up till now the narrow concept of the sovereignty of the Nation State still holds.[1257]

This state of affairs does not help a nation like Uganda, which has problems it is unable to resolve by itself. A typical example of this is the twenty-year-old war, which has ceaselessly continued in northern and northeastern Uganda. Another challenge besides the apparent weakness of the UN currently is that should it happen that the organization becomes legally authorized and has an authoritative representation, there would be an absolute power or body that would impose its ideologies on people regardless of cultural differences in the world. The UN decisions in this case would override the positive elements of cultures which—*Populorum Progressio* suggests as indicated in chapter two—are necessary values and constituent elements for human development.

[1255] Ibid., 120.
[1256] Mugyeni, 135ff.
[1257] Haring and Salvoldi, 61-62

If a feasible world-body or authority that moderates global life and activity is to be established, it must be by "virtue of free consent" and promote the "spirit of liberty and of co-responsibility."[1258] This consensus is not easy to achieve, whether globally or nationally, because of differences of tribe, race, ethnicity, and ideologies.

Politically, in the history of Uganda from independence up to 1980s, women, disabled people, and youth less actively participated in Uganda's politics. However, since the NRM government took over the administration of Uganda, women, the disabled people, and youth have been given opportunities for political participation. They are all represented in the parliament. The integration of women into political positions with men is one of the greatest positive achievements of the NRM government in the field of affirmative action.[1259] In Uganda's political history, the first woman vice president, Wandira Kazibwe, was appointed in the period of NRM, and the number of women ministers and members of parliament and, in general, women's involvement in political affairs increased during this time.[1260] This is a positive innovation by the NRM government—it was not just an affirmative action, it was also an option for the poor.

The innovation is a positive attempt at the promotion of women and enforcement of affirmative action. However, in the context of true development based on the dignity of the human person, at least a problem remains unresolved. While women are definitely recognized to have the same dignity as men, there is a social discrimination, which penalizes men or places some artificial barrier in the way of men who qualify for certain jobs or educational levels but are left out because of such affirmative action policy.

Although the implementation of the principle of affirmative action is the responsibility of the government, religious institutions can contribute to the implimentation of the principle by way of suggestions to the government to formulate and affect practicable affirmative action policies. The rationale here is that the Christian churches have often strongly spoken and acted on behalf of women and marginalized people based on the equality of human dignity. This is, however, questionable regarding Islam, which differs in its tradition

---

[1258] Ibid., 61.

[1259] Mutibwa Phares, 189.

[1260] Aili Mari Tripp, "The Politics of Women's Rights and Cultural Diversity in Uganda," in *Gender Justice, Development, and Rights*, eds. Maxine Molyneux and Shahra Razavi (Oxford: Oxford University Press, 2002), 425.

about women from the Christian denominations. Religious institutions need to contribute toward implementation of affirmative action because it is the responsibility of religious institutions to act as a conscience to the nation by reminding government of the existence of situations that need to be aggressively addressed by the state, and in particular, "religious leaders should be concerned about the overall needs of the people they lead."[1261] If the church, its members, and organizations do not fight to change the evil conditions under which humankind lives, "it will become identified with injustice and persecution."[1262] When the church or religious institutions and communities identify with injustice and persecution, they are obsolete and questionable.

I. Solidarity: The Challenge of Nonfragmented or Segmented Solidarity

Solidarity is a necessary and "an urgent moral imperative"[1263] and a challenge to humanity created by God out of God's love for all people. One of the critical challenges of the principle of solidarity is the challenge to transcend self, family, tribe or ethnicity, race, and nationality. In view of this perennial problem, the idea that human beings are social, they have an affinity to unity, and they are coresponsible for one another has been persistently emphasized.[1264] The gravity of the challenge of the principle of solidarity is founded on love and the universality of the principle of human dignity much emphasized in chapter three, which is shared by all people, and human affinity to unity and coresponsibility. To many people, this is an unquestionable assertion. Human dignity is the concern of the Association of the Major Superiors of Religious Institutes in Uganda (AMSRIU) when reflecting on the situation in Uganda. They allude to people being wounded because their dignity has been affected, and they affirm that these wounds

---

[1261] Kakooza Teresa, "Promotion of Adult Education for Women," in *Church Contribution to Integral Development*, eds. Joseph Therese Agbasiere and Boniface K. Zabajungu (Eldoret, Kenya: AMECEA Gaba Publications, 1989), 190. Kakooza is quoting Drandua F., Bishop of Arua, "Message on Radio Uganda," 26 December 1988.

[1262] Ibid. Here, Kakooza is quoting J. Nyerere, "Rebelling against Slums," in *Freedom and Development*, 214 and 220.

[1263] Habiger, 6.

[1264] Haring and Salvoldi, 55-57

"presently hinder us from forming a family where, each in spite of our tribal, religious and political differences recognizes the other as a brother and a sister to love and respect."[1265] Similarly, Denis Goulet also contends that

> all agree that beyond differences of race, nationality, culture, or social organization a common "human-ness" is present. This factual unity of a shared humanity is the first ontological basis for solidarity among humans.[1266]

Solidarity is an outstanding challenge to Uganda. One of the programs intended for Uganda's development since 1986 or earlier is the consolidation of national unity and elimination of all forms of sectarianism as advocated in one of NRM's ten-point programs for Uganda.[1267] The program suggests the significance of the principle of solidarity. However, the practical application of the principle remains questionable in Uganda. In spite of the historical fact that one of the significant paragraphs in the national anthem of Uganda is "United free for Liberty together we will always stand,"[1268] a critical observation reveals flaws in how Ugandans actually live this significant verse of their national anthem. This verse of the anthem initially suggests unity, thus solidarity among the people of the nation as expressed in the phrase "together we'll always stand." A further challenge of the principle of solidarity in light of this verse is that every Ugandan needs not only be tolerant to others but needs a true spirit of unity. Every Ugandan who seriously craves solidarity should adopt and apply the suggestion of Bernard Haring and Valentino Salvoldi that "every search for unity between human beings implies first of all that this unity be accomplished within self."[1269] Unity with others or love for others is a consequence of integrity within oneself and love for oneself and subsequently within a small group or community. This is an interior challenge to love all and to be in solidarity people. It is not an advocacy for selfishness or self-concern. The contention suggests that self-acceptance and self-love are positive steps toward acceptance of others.

[1265] The Executive, Association of the Major Superiors of Religious Institutes in Uganda, 7.

[1266] Goulet, 63.

[1267] Mutibwa, 180.

[1268] Kakoma and Wynard, 456.

[1269] Haring and Salvoldi, 17.

In the Ugandan social and economic context, there is some kind of solidarity, but it is a fragmented or segmented solidarity. Solidarity in Uganda, like in African and other contexts beyond Uganda and Africa, is in most cases fragmented because it is often based on ethnic or similar backgrounds.[1270] Even within people of the same ethnic groups, there are often microgroups based on classes or social, economic, and political status. An example to illustrate this fact is the statement of the Catholic bishops of Gulu Archdiocese—Nebbi, Arua, and Lira—as they addressed the problem of the war in northern Uganda:

> The Acholi are divided among themselves: there are the fighters, their supporters, their sympathizers, the profiteers of this situation and the peace loving people (90%). Moreover there are the Acholi soldiers in the UPDF who fight Acholi fighters (LRA) and they themselves join other societies who in different ways oppress civilians in Acholi territory.[1271]

This disunity within the same ethnic community could be predicated of other ethnic groups in Uganda and beyond. In such cases, the kind of solidarity expressed may be called segmented or stratified solidarity, which is unchristian and opposed to what Paul VI advocated in *Populorum Progressio* and which was reemphasized by John Paul II in *Solicitudo Rei Socialis*. In Uganda, fragmented solidarity has been exacerbated by a lack of a common or mutually intelligible language. This is an added challenge to Uganda.

Solidarity has also been negatively impacted by differences in economic development. Long before the current situation, various problems related to the lack of solidarity were discussed by the commission from the International Bank for Reconstruction and Development in 1960:

> In order to cement unity of the country and to maintain stability, the Government cannot afford to neglect the economic and social developments of certain areas where the yields to investment in purely economic terms, may not be the highest available. The Government has also to avoid neglect of certain fields of investment such as the law and order services, where economic

---

[1270] Ayittey, *Africa in Chaos*, 60.
[1271] Catholic Bishops of Gulu Archdiocese, Nebbi, Arua, and Lira, 39.

returns tend to be unduly discounted merely because they cannot be measured.[1272]

Questions about enforcement of justice and absence of discrimination, tribalism, or regionalism are directly cited here by the commission set by the International Bank for Reconstruction and Development. If some regions or people of the country are not discriminated against and justice is allowed to take its course, the possibility of peace and unity is high; but if justice is at stake, peace, unity, and, consequently, solidarity are also at stake. This is in the spirit of *Populorum Progressio* that affirms these principles, conditions, and virtues as being crucial for integral development. What the commission advocated was integral development in the regional dimension of Uganda. Consequently, the commission further suggested that

> a balance must be struck between positive measures to develop the economy as rapidly as possible and measures to conserve the conditions essential to such development, the chief of which are the unity of the country and the maintenance of law and order and good relations with neighbouring countries.[1273]

Rapid economic development ought to go with the possibility and development of the means to sustain it. The principle of the common good is also partially invoked here as necessary for economic and social growth. Second, solidarity which is necessary for economic growth goes beyond the solidarity of the nation. Uganda's challenge is to show this solidarity with its neighbors instead of fighting with them as has been the case with Tanzania and Kenya at Idi Amin's time and Rwanda, Sudan, and the Democratic Republic of Congo (DRC) during the reign of Museveni's NRM government.[1274]

The notion of solidarity is neither necessarily Christian nor exclusively sociopolitical. Solidarity is also an expression of responsible attitude and action extended toward others, but it has a more theological or Christian overtones than sociopolitical one because God is the Christian ethical foundation of

---

[1272] International Bank for Reconstruction and Development, *The First Five Year-Development Plan, 1961/62-1965/66,* (Entebbe, Uganda: Uganda Government, 1961), 8.

[1273] Ibid.

[1274] Legget, 12.

the principle of solidarity.[1275] God is the creator of all people, and all people are created *imago Dei*. Consequently, because God is also a family or a solidarity of three persons, the ultimate source of solidarity is God. This ought to be recognized. However, in a pluralistic sociopolitical context like the one of Uganda the real challenge of the principle of solidarity is what the 1995 constitution of the Republic of Uganda expressly states, "Every effort shall be made to integrate all the peoples of Uganda while at the same time recognizing the existence of their ethnic, religious, ideological, political and cultural diversity."[1276] The constitution rightly advocates that there should be unity in diversity. The constitution's teaching in this regard is in line with the Catholic social tradition and Paul VI's teaching on the respect for culture, and the dignity of all. The critical national challenge is the one to implement what *Populorum Progressio* and the constitution of Uganda stipulate.

In Uganda, the political arena is one of the areas where the principle of solidarity is much violated. National political solidarity is, at its best, an apparent failure in Uganda. This is manifest in the political history of the country. For example, the West Nile region has been in a marginal position—at the periphery—since the inception of colonial administration in the region and continues to be so.[1277] The different ethnic groups have struggled and fought for political power, and one political party has often stood in strong opposition to the others. The existence of political factions since independence are not unfamiliar to the majority of Ugandans.

One of solidarity's greatest challenges to religious institutions is that "religion has frequently contributed to making . . . conflicts 'holy,'"[1278] thus justifying divisions, as Bernard Haring and Valentino Salvoldi contend. Uganda is a religious and especially a "Christian Country"[1279]—about 48 percent Catholic and 38 percent Protestant. The Muslims constitute about 8-10 percent of the population. The contention of Haring and Salvoldi has proved to be true in the religious history of Uganda. At the initiation of Christianity in Uganda, there were conflicts between these religious

---

[1275] Haring and Salvoldi, 63.

[1276] Government of Uganda, 3.

[1277] Mark Leopold, *Inside West Nile: Violence, History and Representation on an African Frontier* (Oxford: James Currey, 2005), 80.

[1278] Haring and Salvoldi, 1.

[1279] Catholic Bishops of Uganda, *Be Converted and Live: Pastoral Letter of the Uganda Catholic Hierachy* (Kampala: Marianum Press, Kisubi, 1981), 6.

denominations.[1280] Even if open religious wars occurred between Christians and Muslims and even between Catholics and Protestants in the nineteenth century (1880s), there has been a fairly good balance and harmonious coexistence and relations between the different religious denominations. However, this has not been without flaws in the subsequent years. Around the year 1976, there was "Muslim-Christian violence in Ankole,"[1281] the home place of Pres. Yoweri Kaguta Museveni, in western Uganda.

There is often stronger solidarity according to religious affiliations than interdenominational solidarity. This is an issue president Yoweri K. Museveni has often cited and emphasized as negative since 1986 when he came to power, probably because of his 1976 personal experience of the Muslim-Christian conflicts in Ankole. He sees religious differentiations as one of the divisive factors in the country, an idea that challenges all Ugandan believers about the true meaning of religion. Museveni's view is not different from the above concession of Bernard Haring and Valentio Salvoldi. Religion needs to be conceived, principally, as a reunion with God and fellow human beings. The word *religion* is derived from the Latin word *religare*—to reunite what was once united with God but has since been disunited.[1282] Religion should and must be an instrument of justice, unity, reconciliation and, consequently, solidarity. The critical challenge at this juncture is for Ugandans, especially Catholics and Protestants, to reconsider the Christian and moral character of solidarity and desist from using the historical idea that colonialists sowed seeds for Catholic and Protestant conflicts and disunity as scapegoat.[1283] Ugandans now have a moral responsibility and obligation to correct the mistakes of the past of which they are aware.

However, ecumenical efforts have made possible the establishment of joint Christian activities. One clear example of positive interdenominational solidarity is Uganda Joint Christian Council (UJCC).[1284] The UJCC which was founded in 1964 consists mainly of Catholic, COU, and Orthodox

---

[1280] Museveni, 18

[1281] Gifford, 119.

[1282] Michael J. Perry, *The Idea of Human Rights: Four Inquiries* (Oxford: Oxford University Press, 1998), 14.

[1283] Bweyale, 66.

[1284] Catholic Bishops of Uganda, *Towards A Democratic and Peaceful Uganda Based on the Common Good*, 6. UJCC is the visible sign of some working relationship between different Christian denominations in Uganda.

representatives.[1285] It needs to be expanded to include other Christian religious groups, which are not part of the council. This kind of association and solidarity has not been readily possible with the Muslims because of some significant differences in religious doctrine and practice and structural organization. These phenomena show yet another aspect of the failure of solidarity among the religious denominations in Uganda.

There were, however, times in Uganda's religious and political history when all the three major religious denominations—Catholics, Protestants and Muslims—have worked together. A typical example, according to Paul Gifford, was when, during Idi Amin's presidency, the situation in the country was at its worst and the leaders of the three religious denominations, especially the COU Archbishop Luwum and Emmanuel Cardinal Nsubuga convened a meeting and invited all the bishops and senior Muslim leaders to meet and share their concerns with Idi Amin.[1286] This is an evidence of a joint heroic and prophetic action of leaders of different denominations in a spirit of mutual support and solidarity, although according to Paul Gifford, the death of the Protestant archbishop, Luwum, as a consequence of a joint prophetic and heroic action of the religious leaders dulled the Catholic-Anglican relation because the latter thought the former were not sincerely ready to confront the government squarely.

Mazrui observes that in most African countries including Uganda, which he cites as an example, Muslims have been ready to accept Christians democratically elected to be heads of states, but Christian countries have been less ready to accept a Muslim who is democratically elected to head Christian countries.[1287] Perhaps this is an area that needs a critical study. Gen. Idi Amin Dada, a Muslim, though not democratically elected served for eight years as the head of state of Uganda that is predominantly—about 86 percent—Christian. However, here there is need to consider the fact that he came to power through a military coup and ruled with brutality and an iron hand.[1288] This was the reason he was able to hold power for so many years.

The issue raised by Mazrui should be critically studied, weighed, and considered. Though it is not the intention of this study to go deep into that,

---

[1285] Bweyale, 67.

[1286] Gifford, 119.

[1287] Mazrui, *Political Values and the Educated Class in Africa*, 145.

[1288] Bweyale, 60.

the issue is intriguing to Ugandan Christians. Are they being discriminatory against the Muslims, or is it because the Muslims have not provided capable leadership for Uganda or the Muslims themselves are discriminatory? The precise answer is the Christian constitution of the population of Uganda and the, historically, different religious ideologies reflected in the political leadership of Uganda. There is certainly a significant difference in the vision of Christians and Muslims. Consequently, there is not much religious and political solidarity between Christians and Muslims.

Ugandan Catholics seem to have a greater sense and degree of unity and national solidarity than the Anglicans and the Muslims. However, this sense of solidarity has not always been consistent in the Catholic Church as pointed out by Paul Gifford.[1289] Gifford correctly states that when Martin Luluga was appointed an auxiliary bishop of the Diocese of Gulu, he was welcome. Later, as the ordinary of the diocese, he was held in suscipicion and resented; Bishop Emmanuel Wamala received a cool reception from the Baganda of Kampala Archdiocese in 1988 when he was appointed the archbishop of Kampala because he was a Muganda from the diocese of Masaka. However, despite such phenomena, there is Catholic solidarity. There are four Catholic national major seminaries in different regions of Uganda, and Namugongo, the Uganda martyrs basilica and national shrine, is a national centre for pilgrimage for all Catholics in Uganda and beyond.[1290]

Within the internal ordering of the mainstream churches or religions in Uganda—Catholics, Protestants, and Muslims—there have been, to this day, elements of tension and division too. These show a failure of solidarity in the different religious denominations. Muslims, including those in Uganda, are often characterized by fighting and divisive behavior even among themselves.[1291] In the 1990s, Catholics and Anglicans were no exceptions to similar conflicts and divisions. A Catholic example is the diocese of Kabale in western Uganda, where the community was divided into two factions—those who were probishop Barnabas Halem'Imana and those who did not support him.[1292] The episode was based on ethnic and political differences and allegations of some corruption. The consequence was that "the entire diocese became polarized and, when all Church groups

---

[1289] Gifford, 137-138.

[1290] Ibid., 139.

[1291] Here Gifford is quoting *The New Vision*, 3 November 1986, 1.

[1292] Gifford, 122-123.

ceased to exist, effectively collapsed."[1293] In 1992, a similar event occurred in the COU (Church of Uganda) in the Diocese of Busoga. The Christian community was also split into those who were pro-Bishop Bamwoze—the then bishop of the diocese—and the anti-Bamwoze because it was alleged that he was dysfunctional or irrelevant and had practically forfeited his role and position as bishop and pastor by not fulfilling his duties, and so another bishop should be elected.[1294]

Despite these episodes, there are elements of solidarity among the religious institutions in Uganda, especially in the Catholic and the Anglican churches. A clear example of the expression of solidarity is the fact that there are a good number of bishops in Uganda, both Catholic and Anglican, who serve among people who are of ethnic backgrounds other than their own. In the Catholic Church, the following dioceses have bishops from outside their ethnic backgrounds: Nebbi, Gulu, Lira, Kotido, Moroto, Kasese, and Jinja. This is nearly half of the number of Catholic dioceses in Uganda. In the Anglican Church, the outstanding example is the archbishop of Kampala, Joseph Orombi, who is an Alur from Nebbi in northwestern Uganda but is serving among the Baganda in the south of the country although also in a national capacity as an archbishop.

From the foregoing treatise on solidarity, the following conclusions can be made: First, true solidarity is all-embracing, and it demands mutual openness. This can be a spontaneous process based on the virtue of universal charity and recognition of the universality of human dignity. Second, where spontaneous and inclusive solidarity is not forthcoming, especially in the political context, some form of coercion may be necessary as the situation in Kabale Diocese and Busoga diocese.[1295] Niebuhr suggests,

> All social co-operation on larger scale than the most intimate social group requires a measure of coercion. Where the factor of mutual consent is strongly developed, and where standardized and approximately fair methods of adjudicating and resolving conflicting interests within an organized group have been

---

[1293] Ibid.

[1294] Ibid., 124-129.

[1295] The problems or situations in the two dioceses, one Roman Catholic Diocese of Kabale and the other COU Diocese of Busoga were partially resolved because there was some form of pressure, either externally or internally as explained above.

established, the coercive factor in social life is frequently covert, and becomes apparent only in moments of crisis and in the group's policy toward recalcitrant individuals.[1296]

The normal way of building unity and solidarity is the spontaneous one, but there are certain moments when force is necessary to complete the process of solidarity, especially in the case of those who are simply stubborn. Such measure of force is inevitable to hold a state or an institution together. In such a case, it is a matter of choosing between two evils—use of force to bring people together or escalating disunity among people. In a situation where people are informed and cooperative force is not necessary. Therefore, people need to comprehend and accept their own situation as well as that of other people in order to build solidarity. Therefore, education for peace, unity, and solidarity is a crucial endeavor. This suggests that force is sometimes an inevitable part of the building of social cohesion because of

> the limitation of the human mind and imagination, the inability of human beings to transcend their own interests sufficiently to envisage the interests of their fellowmen as clearly as they do their own.[1297]

J. Peace: The Most Delicate Challenge to Uganda

The term *peace* is used here in the Jewish and Christian sense of *shalom* or general well-being and harmonious life in human community as explained in chapter two. In this sense, peace also implies security. It is in this context that the condition or factor of peace remains an impending and delicate challenge in Uganda and shows the failure of yet another claim of Ugandan government to provide security to all people in Uganda and to their property as stipulated in the ten-point program of the NRM.[1298]

While peace is the desirable thing and what human persons often seek, human history has consistently shown violent moments. Bernard Haring and Valentino Salvoldi have rightly argued that human history has been continuously filled with conflicts, even if people have loved to live peacefully:

[1296] Niebuhr, 3-4.

[1297] Ibid., 6.

[1298] Mutibwa, 180.

From ancient times human beings have struggled to live peacefully
side by side, having recourse for the most part to the exclusion
or marginalization to keep under control whole social groups or
"castes" defined on the basis of their economic activity, their wealth,
their ancestry or their race.[1299]

This is true to a great extent in various societies. One evidence in Uganda
is what Mark Leopold suggests of the West Nile people. He contends that the
real expectation of the people is that government has to deliver or be relevant
to them by meeting their needs or expectations.[1300] This is a demand not only
relevant for the people of West Nile or marginalized regions of Uganda, but
for any person who cares about human life and human dignity. Paradoxically,
despite the fact than human beings are social and have the affinity to unity,
they also have the tendency to strive to dominate and to resist domination.
Consequently, there are conflicts and a noticeable absence of peace among
people.

Considering seriously what Bernard Haring and Valentino Salvoldi
suggest, peace is the most delicate challenge to efforts toward integral human
development because "it represents *per se* the moral progress of humanity
decisively oriented towards unity. Unity and peace, when liberty unites them,
are sisters."[1301] If there is unity amidst expression of human freedom, there
is real peace. Peace is crucial and demands factors such as concern for the
common good, justice, and love, and it is a consequence of these significant
factors. The challenge of peace is compounded, in the Ugandan context, by
the prevailing ethnic, political, economic, and religious diversity. Peace is the
brainchild of justice and love because justice and love lead to peace. However,
charity ranks higher than justice and true Christian justice is a consequence
of charity.[1302] Any violation of justice is a violation of charity.

Peace is a result of just and charitable mutual action. While justice precedes
peace, some integral education is necessary for attainment of peace. It is not
until all people understand, accept, and live the true meaning and value of

---

[1299] Haring and Salvoldi, 1.
[1300] Mark Leopold, *Inside West Nile: Violence, History and Representation on an African Frontier* (Oxford: James Currey, 2005), 46.
[1301] Haring and Salvoldi, 67. The duo are quoting Paul VI, *Messagio per la giornata del pace,* January 1971 in *Acta Apostolicae Sedis* 6 (1971), 8.
[1302] Greancy, 54-55.

peace that it can actually prevail. This is why peace is a delicate principle or condition for integral human development in Uganda.

If asked whether people are economically and socially peaceful in Uganda, the fair answer to the question is both yes and no. The rich have economic peace of mind and heart but not social peace because they always live under the fear of the attack from the poor. Consequently, all they tend to do is build physical and social walls instead. On the other hand, the poor are economically, and even socially, not peaceful because they lack the necessities for a comfortable life. Besides that, if they are poor because of the injustices in society or because of the rich people, deep in their hearts, the poor cannot be comfortable at all. The evidence is to be seen in what has been happening in the north and northeastern part of Uganda, where, according to AMSRIU,

> After twenty years the government has failed to resolve this scandalous conflict! Meanwhile, nearly two million of IDP (Internally Displaced People) are obliged to live in desperately inhuman conditions. About 1000 IDP people die every week to the shame of the Government and all of us. In their desperation, some commit suicide! Concerning the IDP, we find the letter of Mahmood Mamdani (Daily Monitor of 4-12-05) quite appropriate.[1303]

One of the principal challenges of peace as a necessary condition for true or integral development is human confrontation with the dignity of other people. We ought always to keep in mind that every person is important, everybody matters, because of their human dignity.[1304] The question of justice and equality are also significant because true peace is founded not only on the respect for human dignity, but it is also founded on the respect for human rights and on justice and equality.[1305] All principles, virtues, and conditions necessary for human development are related to human dignity. Violation of any one of them is an automatic violation of human dignity.

Since its independence from the British in 1962, the transition of government in Uganda has consistently been through armed force or wars.

[1303] The Executive Association of the Major Superiors of Religious Institutes in Uganda, 7.

[1304] Oskar Wermter, *Politics for Everyone and by Everyone: A Christian Approach* (Nairobi: Pauline Publications Africa, 2003), 129.

[1305] Haring and Salvoldi, 67.

There is yet no hope that it will ever happen peacefully. After each new government comes to power, it claims to be working for peace, but time has proven them to be public liars because authentic national peace has never been achieved at any time in Uganda's history since independence. One part or some parts of the country may have just relative or apparent peace, but other parts of the country are at war either physically with neighbors or the wrong ethnic groups or interiorly in their minds and hearts of people because they are not in harmony. They are disgruntled because of what is actually happening in the country.

The years 1966-1967 were characterized by the strife between Milton Obote and the Kabaka of Buganda and led to the eventual invasion of Kabaka's palace at Mengo and ultimately to his flight into exile in England.[1306] Soon thereafter was the strife between Obote and Idi Amin who eventually took over power from Obote by force in 1971.[1307] From 1971-1985 when Amin, Obote II, the Military Commision, Yusufu Lule, Godfrey Binaisa, and Tito Okello Lutwa were in power and Museveni launched a guerrilla war (1980-1985) in the Luwero triangle, there were untold sufferings and killings in Uganda. In these years, the affected people were in Lango, Acholi, West Nile, and Luwero. During this period, Archbishop Luwum—an Anglican—was killed (by Amin's men), the home district of the Anglican archbishop Silvanus Wani was vandalized (by Obote's men),[1308] and from 1980-1985 (during the reign of Obote, Tito Okello Lutwa, and Museveni), there were untold massacres in the Luwero triangle. From 1987-1995, as George Ayittey records, there were also many killings and assassination attempts of both Ugandan nationals and expatriates. For example, Hussein Musa Njuki, a newspaper editor, was killed in 1995; Andrew Lutakome Kayira, a political activist, was killed in 1987; Charles Owor, district administrator of Nebbi, was ambushed and killed in 1993; and "Peter Forbes, a Canadian Reseacher and his colleague John Ongom were murdered by government security men, and Monsignor Fredrik[sic] Drandua, a Catholic bishop of Arua,"[1309] providentially escaped an assassination attempt in 1994. These are just some of the known indicators of violence in postindependence Uganda.

[1306] Mutibwa, 37-39.

[1307] Ibid., 78ff.

[1308] Gifford, 120-121.

[1309] Ayittey, *Africa in Chaos*, vi-vii.

Paul VI's message of peace from *Populorum Progressio* persistently challenges Ugandans. According to Vincent Okot Oburu, Paul VI in one of his messages on the World Day of Peace, insisted that peace depends on everybody and is, therefore, a challenge to everybody.[1310] In this context, the struggle for peace is a challenge to all Ugandans. People should not be apathetic because a region where one comes from or lives is not affected by any fighting or anything that affects the peace of the residents of that place, region, or nation. In fact, any knowledge or news of fighting, hunger, epidemics, or any form of discrimination and injustice in any part of the country should be enough to disrupt the relative peace within every Ugandan citizen and beyond. It is on the bases of such assertions that the words of Paul VI, as stated by Vincent Okot Oburu, become more forceful:

> Peace will never be without a hunger and thirst for justice; it will never forget the effort that has to be made in order to defend the weak, to help the poor, to promote the cause of the lowly. Peace will never betray the higher values of life, in order to survive.[1311]

Currently, there is the dilemma and uncertainty among the people of Gulu, Kitgum, Lira, parts of Soroti and Karamoja, and sometimes people of West Nile region about their security. Who provides security for them and who is their enemy—the Lord's Resistance Army (LRA) or National Resistance Army (NRA) or Uganda People's Defense Forces (UPDF). These people question themselves about who commits atrocities in their region. The challenge to the current government is whether they are human beings deserving peace, at least, if not citizens or part of Uganda. Lack of peace has affected their political, social, and economic output or contribution to the country. Since 1986, they have been—and perhaps they will continue to be—dependent. A government that claims to be the protector of people ought to do something for the peace of all its citizens. This is also the real demand of common good as Jacques Maritain affirms.[1312]

[1310] Okot, 63. Also see Catholic Bishops of Uganda, *Towards a Democratic and Peaceful Uganda Based on the Common Good*, 12.

[1311] Ibid. Okot is quoting Paul VI, "Peace Too Depends on You," World Day of Peace, in *Ways of Peace*, 1986, 63.

[1312] Jacques Maritain, 52-53.

There are "more than 300,000 Acholi who are displaced in Acholi land itself and living in protected camps and in other parts of Uganda."[1313] They are refugees on their own land and in their own country. To claim there is peace in Uganda is false. With regard to peace, what is true about Uganda is to affirm that there is only relative or fragmented peace.

There is no doubt that the government has tried to fight for peace and tried to protect some of the people in the named regions. The so-called *protected camps* have been created to keep people safe and provide some measures of peace. However, it is questionable whether these camps are actually protected because sometimes people have been attacked and abducted from them or they are subjected to untold sufferings.[1314] In other words, the camps are unprotected and unsafe to a very considerable extent. Besides these factors, the camps are undignified habitations because people are not able to work for themselves. They cannot fully exercise their human rights. While to some extent a relative peace has prevailed, critical caring and loving people who have witnessed the actual conditions of the people living in the affected parts of the country are still apprehensive about the possibility of continuous disharmony and the reversal of the peace process.[1315] This is not a far-fetched apprehension because peace processes have failed many times in the history of Uganda.

Religious institutions in Uganda are often confronted by—and they have also frequently confronted—the challenge of peace. The Catholic bishops of Uganda have consistently done this. In two consecutive years, 2004 and 2005, they have reiterated the importance of peace for Uganda's development, not only now but also in the future.[1316] While the bishops acknowledge positive developments in Uganda since they issued their pastoral letter, A Concern for Peace, Unity and Harmony in Uganda, they repeated their appeal for peace in the 2005 pastoral letter, Towards a Democratic and Peaceful Uganda Based on the Common Good:

> We must all build peace in our hearts as individuals; we must build peace in our families and communities and then we shall

---

[1313] Catholic Bishops of Archdiocese of Gulu, Nebbi, Arua, and Lira, 39.

[1314] Odama, 4.

[1315] Catholic Bishops of Uganda, *Towards a Democratic and Peaceful Uganda Based on the Common Good*, 3-4.

[1316] Ibid., 4.

be able to build peace in our nation. This is a big call we want to make to our pastoral agents, all leaders in the country to build a culture of peace, security and tolerance among all individuals and communities in Uganda.[1317]

The real challenge of peace is the challenge of united efforts to create peace as was discussed in chapter two. It is also a challenge to love, to foster solidarity, and to work for the common good. The challenge of peace is a call to all people to contribute toward the tranquility and harmony of the country, socially, politically, and economically. Deusdedit R. K. Nkurunziza has rightly observed that the NRM government has not "given the civil society and NGOs their full participation as key stakeholders of peace keeping, peace-making and peace building"[1318]; yet in the past twenty years, the government has provided no feasible solution to the problem of insurgency in northern and northeastern Uganda. This challenge also confronts these groups to which government has consistently denied participation and the entire nation. The involvement of the civil society in the peace-building process and good governance in any part of Uganda is fundamental for far reaching results and ought not to be neglected.[1319]

One of the considerable challenges the question of peace poses for religious institutions is their failure to achieve the goal of effective preaching of the gospel of love and peace. While most of the churches have often intervened to negotiate for peace between warring factions, they have often not been successful because the powers that be or the warring parties have not cooperated adequately. Instead, they have often fought for their own, and often selfish, interests. To date, the seeming failure of the efforts of the religious leaders in Uganda can be seen in the last twenty years of war in northern and northeastern Uganda, particularly in Gulu, Kitgum, Lira, Apach, Soroti, and Karamoja in the northeast of the country. There is only a minimum success. The real failure is suggested by the frustration of the Catholic bishops of Uganda about the failure of government to resolve the situation in these regions. This is evident in their plea:

[1317] Ibid., 2. Here, the bishops of Uganda made reference to their 2004 pastoral letter *A Concern For Peace, Unity and Harmony in Uganda*, paragraph 9 page 2.

[1318] Nkurunziza, 23.

[1319] Ibid., 25.

> We once again reiterate our call to Government to do all it can
> to end the war in the North without any further delays. We do
> understand that significant achievements have been recorded in
> terms of security of people and property—reduction in abductions,
> security on roads and the surrender of many Lords resistance army
> (LRA) fighters—thanks to the government and to the Amnesty Act
> and the efforts of Ms. Betty Bigombe and the different religious
> and political groups in northern Uganda.[1320]

While the bishops acknowledge the successes so far recorded, they are still emphatic that more needs to be done to improve the situation in the region. There is still a significant degree of desperation, insecurity, and suffering among the people of Northern and Eastern Uganda.[1321] This again consistently demands a concerted effort of all parties.

In relation to the situation in northern Uganda, another challenge to religious institutions is to embody what true religion teaches. The LRA who have fought since the NRM government came to power in 1986 claim to be a religious faction that wants to run Uganda according to the Ten Commandments of God—thus claiming the fight to be a religious war.[1322] They have killed many, abducted and raped women, and subjected many people to torture. By so doing, they denied that the commandments advocate love of all and care for all and harmonious coexistence. One would question this type of religion and its authenticity. This is a challenge to religious institutions because they are to unite people to God and to one another. Here is again a failure in understanding what religion is. In this case, religion is also practically an utter failure because it has not united people but divided them instead. This same failure can be ascribed to the killers at Kanugu, who are believed to be the religious leaders,[1323] a story which the government

---

[1320] Catholic Bishops of Uganda, *Towards A Democratic and Peaceful Uganda Based on the Common Good*, 5.

[1321] Ibid.

[1322] Odama, 3.

[1323] I explained the Kanungu tragedy earlier on in this chapter under the subtheme of *Anthropological Challenges*. Here, I am making reference to the same incident, especially regarding the unapprehended culprits of the incident. They are believed to be not only members of the religion but the leaders, who instead of offering peace destroyed lives of many people.

ceased to follow and which makes one question whether the government is there to protect the people of Uganda and whether it cares about the life and dignity of its citizens.[1324] The challenges of peace in Uganda are as follows: development of a real culture of universal love, justice, mutual understanding, and consideration for the common good of the country. However, the critical challenge in the actual pursuit of peace is that true peace is durable, not restricted to a few people and not a temporary cessation of violence, and "peace must be pursued and rights defended within moral restraints and in the context of defining other basic human values."[1325] The methodology for pursuing peace should always take into account the dignity of the human person and the desire to care for everybody.

The attainment of peace requires some specific strategies. One strategy is peace education, which promotes tolerance and mutual trust among people of different backgrounds.[1326] The principles of this education are the following: respect for and defense of human dignity and rights; that the individual is not subordinate to the state; stewardship of natural resources and their destiny; defiance of discrimination; participation in social, religious, cultural, and political life of people; and the understanding of solidarity, charity, sense of dialogue and negotiation, common good, and justice.[1327] This education ought to be carried out nationally and to the different categories or classes of people. It should constitute part of the education curriculum of Uganda from the lowest level to the highest. It should, as in the real sense of religion, be part and parcel of the obligation of all religious institutions.

K. Association: The Challenge of Laissez-Faire or Restricted Association

The principal problems related to freedom of association among the people of Uganda—both nationally and locally at the level of ethnic groupings and similar smaller groupings—is the inability to transcend culture, religion,

---

[1324] Bagumisiriza, 73.

[1325] United States National Conference of Catholic Bishops, *The Challenge of Peace: God's Promise and Our Response* (Washington DC: United States Catholic Conference, 1983), 33.

[1326] Tuyizere, 76.

[1327] Ibid., 77.

ethnicity, and political differences.[1328] These had partial roots in the colonial administration that favored some sectors of the population and disfavored others. There are a few associations such as the Farmers Associations and Cooperative Societies, but they are neither widespread nor viable institutions. On the whole, there are few credible economic associations or organizations.

When Uganda got independence from the British, it immediately imprisoned itself consistently in a system of one-party politics though nominally there were political parties in the early postindependence years. The first Ugandan leaders after independence seemed never to believe in democracy and its attendant values such as justice and the respect for human rights and the common good.[1329] One of the greatest political challenges and difficulties regarding association in the history of Uganda since independence has recurrently been that of not giving opportunity for a multiparty political system. One regime after another resented multiparty politics for extensive periods of time. This was most observable in the eight years of Idi Amin's military rule[1330] and twenty years of Yoweri K. Museveni's partly military rule and the later years of a seeming civilian administration.[1331] Freedom of political association in the form of political parties was banned. The second regime of Milton Obote and recently that of Yoweri Kaguta Museveni (February 2006) were perhaps the only ones that allowed different political parties to function. Nonetheless, all the presidents of Uganda since independence have used the army as personal machinery for limiting the activities of other political parties.

On a positive note from 1986 or in the last twenty years, the government of Uganda has been careful in following any attempts by groups of people to form new parties. Radical groups that have tendencies to disrupt the smooth functioning of the government and the nation have been restricted, especially

---

[1328] Mugaju, 12-16.

[1329] Mugaju, 17.

[1330] Idi Amin ruled Uganda from January 25, 1971-April 11, 1979 when he was overthrown by force. In all these years, he suppressed political parties.

[1331] Yoweri Kaguta Museveni came to power by force of arms in January 1986 and established what he called the movement system of government, which was apparently one-party system, which continued until February 23, 2006, when there were elections on party basis. It was a return to multiparty politics after a lot of pressure from the Ugandan populace and some international governments.

radical political groups with evil ideologies. President Museveni has particularly feared the formation of new political associations or parties formed along lines of religion. Muslim parties are among some of the dreaded ones probably because of their character and the experiences during Idi Amin's regime. Mazrui's explanation is perhaps one of the best to understand apprehensions about some Muslim groups. He suggests that radicalism in Islamic politics is because Islam "has not only a tradition of submissive following but also, paradoxically, a tradition of rebellious leadership."[1332]

Since the role of government and religion is to help people to meet their needs and to protect or care for them, any political party that does not meet such standards or goals is, prudently speaking, not permissible because it defeats the purpose of these institutions. This has basically been the fear of the NRM government. However, the banning of political parties by the NRM government in the last twenty years is not democratically positive.[1333] The preceding argument is a support only for the prevention of the development of radical political groups that would create unrest, not for the banning of political parties per se. The legislative branch of the government (the parliament) and the constitution of the country, which is the supreme law of the country, should be invoked, though not manipulated to satisfy individual interests.

The challenge of the principle of association is that of the choice between liberal freedom for association and conservative limitation of freedom for association. If people are allowed too much freedom to form associations, the consequence could be anarchy or lawlessness. If they are too much restricted from associations, the consequence could also be a violent explosion of anger and revolution. The historical reaction of the "anti-Buganda sentiments"[1334] of non-Baganda, created by the colonial administration, better illustrates the possibility of such reactions. In either case, the consequences are negative and undesirable. This is the dilemma and challenge to the political situation in Uganda. There should, therefore, be a balance or moderation.

There is freedom of religion and freedom of associations. Religious institutions are themselves associations. An authentic religious association

---

[1332] Mazrui, *Political Values and the Educated Class in Africa*, 149.

[1333] NRM government prohibited multiparty politics from 1986 upto 2006 when there was the first multiparty presidential and general elction in Uganda after twenty years.

[1334] Mugaju, 13.

ought to promote the human person, dignity and rights, and universal charity. The principal challenge to religious groups is that they should establish microassociations within the same larger group. In Uganda, the Catholic Church has perhaps performed better than other religious institutions in this regard.[1335] Its structural organization provides for different associations and movements for people of various categories or different age groups in order to meet different needs of people. The structural organizations of the associations run from the lowest level of the church through the diocesan level to the national level. Other Christian denominations have made attempts to do the same, but they have not matched the level of the structural organization in the Catholic Church. Muslims have associations of their own but they are more fragmented because of the various sects extant within the religion.

L. Participation or Involvement: The Challenge of Ethnic and Cultural Diversity

Participation suggested in this section means involvement of all people in the development project. It means that every person including people who are not experts in decisions and actions related to issues affecting them is part and parcel of every decision related to their life, as Goulet suggests.[1336] If people, including nonexperts, do not participate in deciding what affects them, they may even have no enthusiasm for practical action necessary for their development. Depriving them of participation in determining their own fate constitutes an injustice—namely, social, economic, and political injustice. Participation is important because not only one person or a group of few individuals or a party has all the right answers and solutions to problems.[1337] The more people are involved, the more easily solutions can be sought to problems and the more ideas can be enriched.

[1335] The Catholic Church's excellence in religious associations is in terms of both structural organization and the number of Catholic associations in the country and how the associations cater for the different age groups from five years to the aging people.

[1336] Denis Goulet, *Incentives for Development: The Key to Equity* (New York: New Horizon Press, 1989), 159.

[1337] Wermter, 19.

Paul VI underscored the significance of the principle of participation. He emphasized that "every person and all people are entitled to be shapers of their own destiny."[1338] As treated in chapter two, he advocated that all people need to be involved in the development process. Museveni similarly states that "government does not work alone. Poverty-eradication is the business of all citizens of Uganda."[1339] Though Museveni does not state it clearly or explicitly, in a way, he suggests that participation is a right.

The exercise of this principle or right is problematic in pluralistic contexts not only because people have no opportunity, but also because people are sometimes passive. Mark Leopold has remarked this of the Lugbara and the Alur in their historical past where he suggests that they have been "passive victims,"[1340] meaning that for a long time they have faced problems without getting involved in confronting them. They observed situations without doing anything about the prevalent problems while they should have been part of the problem-solving process. This kind of attitude is a challenge to people who do not care to participate in confronting issues affecting them or society in general.

While every time one thinks of a nation one, at least theoretically, thinks that it is an independent entity with united citizens. Most countries either think this is what they are or this is what they want to be or they are working to build. However, the actual situation is often different on close observation. This is true even of the most homogeneous community. Uganda is no exception to such a phenomenon, especially considering its ethnic and racial diversity. It is for this reason that one of the greatest challenges to the people of Uganda, the church or religious institutions, and the state is that "development should involve the participation of the broad mass of the people and not only of a few. People have to be involved in the work of their development . . . man can only develop himself. He cannot be developed by another."[1341]

For a long time, in the economic history of Uganda, economic activities were dominated by expatriates or naturalized citizens. Trading merchandise

---

[1338] *Populorum Progressio*, 15, 20; 65, 70. Also see Dorr, 198.

[1339] Yoweri Kaguta Museveni, "Forward," in *Poverty Eradication Action Plan (2001-2003)*, vol. 1, ii.

[1340] Mark Leopold, *Inside West Nile: Violence, History and Representation on an African Frontier* (Oxford: James Currey, 2005), 80.

[1341] Pfaff, 27.

and industrial activities were, for instance, dominated by the Asians while the indigenous people were economically and even socially marginalized.[1342] When Idi Amin became Uganda's president in 1971, he expelled all the Asians in 1972 regardless of whether they were Ugandan citizens or not, confiscated their property and entrusted it to the custodian board. Idi Amin declared what he called *economic war* and decided to Africanize economic activities.[1343] This in itself was cruel and unjust. However, Amin's intention was to entrust the economy of the country to the indigenous Ugandans. It was an effort to give indigenous Ugandans the opportunity for economic participation. It was at this time that Ugandans started to, more closely and critically, learn to do business and manage their economy.

This was an effort toward economic participation although often uncritically and negatively viewed by many outsiders and some Ugandans. It was a clear message to the indigenous Ugandans that they could and ought to do business or take care of their economy just like the expatriates. This action is, however, opposed to James P. Bailey's contention that "economic activity is one way people participate in, and benefit from, the community; barriers to participation in the economy are to be challenged."[1344] In this context, a careful observation suggests that Idi Amin is not exclusively to blame for the expulsion of Asians from Uganda and economic businesses. Those who established an economic system that excluded the indigenous people of Uganda—precisely the British colonial masters[1345]—are also to blame. However, the injustice of Idi Amin was that of confiscating the property of the Asians and expelling even those who were Ugandan citizens. Amin's Africanization of the economy was also a failure because it led to what came to be known as the *Magendo economy*, which "was characterized by speculation, hoarding, smuggling and black marketeering."[1346] This means customers paid high prices for commodities not because the commodities were worth the prices charged, but because business people created shortage of supply in order to raise prices and reap high profits. This was also injustice

---

[1342] Leggett, 22

[1343] Mugaju, 28. Also see Leggett, 22-23.

[1344] James P. Bailey, "Asset Development for the Poor," in *Journal of the Society of Christian Ethics*, 24, 1 (2004): 52.

[1345] Leggett, 22.

[1346] Mugaju, 29.

to the citizens who offered the market for the business people involved in the promotion of such economy.

Another notable challenge with regard to the application of the principle of participation is that participation is determined by the type of development required or in question. Certain areas of development require specific skills or technical know-how while others do not. As Goulet suggests,

> different kinds of development require different forms of participation. A "people-centered" development requires participation which assigns priority to satisfaction of basic needs among the poor, to job creation, self-reliance, and the active preservation of cultural diversity obviously requires a form of participation in which non-elites play an active role in the diagnosis of their own problems. If on the other hand, a top-down, growth oriented approach to development is adopted by a particular country, it is most likely that whatever participation does occur will not be generated by the people themselves from below. Rather, participation will be imposed by the government for the purpose of rallying the populace to implement activities planned for it. In this case bottom-up participation will generally be confined to resistance against imposed plans and projects, or to micro "do-it-yourself" activities.[1347]

The critical challenge is to determine what kind of participation is needed in different development projects. The frequently made mistake is to impose on people that they should be involved or for the people to think that they do not have to be involved in a particular development project. This squares with the difficulty of applying the principle of subsidiarity. The solution to this problem ought to be sought in appropriate education that provides for the requisite expertise.

From a political point of view, at the outset, it is necessary to note that one of the main challenges of the principle of participation is that no person, no government, or political system should ever be considered irreplaceable or indispensable.[1348] Each person or system contributes in its own way. Each one has advantages and disadvantages, weaknesses and strengths.

[1347] Goulet, *Development Ethics: A Guide to Theory and Practice*, 95-96.

[1348] Gardner Thompson, *Governing Uganda: British Colonial Rule and its Legacy* (Kampala: Fountain Publishers, 2003), 352.

The question of political participation in Uganda is of profound importance because the political history of the country shows how much, to date, true political participation was lacking in one regime after another. It has consistently been a questionable issue from the time of independence to the present time.[1349] The colonial masters designed the political administration in such a way that the Baganda—the most dominant ethnic group in Uganda and the first to encounter and interact with the international world—would be more involved in and take charge of political administration. From then, and especially from the time of independence from the British in 1962, this trend of limited political participation has persisted. What Thompson Gardener affirms is perhaps one of the strongest assertions that testify to this claim:

> Participatory democracy based on political parties has been no more welcome in the latter period than in the former. At both times political parties have been seen as the tool of individual opportunists, and of interest groups based on ethnicity and/or religion, if not class. First Cohen and colonialism, then Museveni and the Movement: each has sought to manage political aspiration and pressure, while inhibiting the growth, exercise and significance of parties.[1350]

When Milton Obote forcefully grabbed power from Kabaka Edward Mutesa with the help of Idi Amin, the then military commander, it was a reaction to the lack of involvement or the limited involvement of the people who were marginalized, especially people of northern Uganda. The consequence was that when Obote himself took over power, he allied more with the northerners, particularly people of his tribe: the Langi, the Acholi, and the Luo in general.[1351] This was one of the reasons for Idi Amin's overthrow of Obote and his promise to unite all Ugandans. It was welcome news to most Ugandans but soon frustrated when Idi Amin decided to ally with and mostly involved the Kakwa, Nubians, and Sudanese and alienated the rest of the people of Uganda.[1352]

[1349] Pfaff, 156.

[1350] Thompson Gardner, 350-351.

[1351] Mugaju, 26.

[1352] Ibid., 26 and 30.

Disgruntled by this state of affairs Ugandans in exile reorganized themselves to expel Idi Amin with the help of Tanzanian troops. No sooner was this successfully achieved than one overthrow after another occurred between 1979 and 1980, from Yusufu Lule through Godfrey Binaisa to Obote II.[1353] When Obote returned to the presidency for a second time in 1980, a clique of Luo and a few *extra-luo supporters* took control of Uganda. However, they were soon divided among themselves—a division of the Acholi against the Langi, leading to the overthrow of Obote, a Langi, by Tito Okello Lutwa, an Acholi.[1354] The latter was overthrown by Yoweri Kaguta Museveni, a Munyakole from Western Uganda, in January 1986. He promised to make a *fundamental change*, establish what he called *a broad-based government*, which would provide for the participation of different categories and ethnic groups of people.[1355] He did this, and it seemed to work satisfactorily in the first five years of his regime; but as he clung to power the spirit of participation continued to wane, especially from the point of view of ethnic representation, religious representation and participation of political parties.

One of the positive contributions of the NRM government that captured the idea of participation was the constitutional review and writing process. This involved the election of representatives from different areas or regions of the country and different walks of life to the constituent assembly.[1356] The result was the review of the 1967 constitution and the writing and promulgation of the 1995 Constitution of the Republic of Uganda. This was a positive achievement. However, this constitution has posed a challenge of its own. The implementation of the constitution has already been questioned. Thompson Gardener has doubts of its actual use. According to him, many written constitutions, including the current one of Uganda, have not been lived and only "few if any written constitutions achieve the iconic status of the American."[1357]

What one observes in Uganda is political association or participation based on ethnicity, religion or political convenience and political parties. One of the challenges *Populorum Progressio* presents here is that ethnic or

---

[1353] Leggett, 23-24. Also see Mugaju, 33-34.

[1354] Mugaju, 38.

[1355] Tarsis Kabwegyere, "Politics of Democratisation," in *Uganda's Age of Reforms: A Critical Overview*, ed. Justus Mugaju (Kampala: Fountain Publishers, 1999), 43. Also see Leggett, 25 and cfr. Mugaju, 39.

[1356] Ibid., 49.

[1357] Thompson Gardner, 249.

any other type of discrimination is opposed to the spirit of integral human development, universality of human dignity, solidarity, the common good, justice, and universal charity. A similar trace of discrimination is also reflected in the number of politicians according to religious denominations. From the time Muslims lost in the religious wars in 1889, long before Uganda's independence and even before a proper establishment and consolidation of colonialism, they have at best remained at the periphery of Uganda's political, economic, and social life.[1358]

Compared to Catholics and Protestants, Muslim politicians are very few; but according to Gifford, "there are far fewer Catholics in top political positions"[1359] than Protestants. This is perhaps one of the reasons why the Catholic leadership has been asking pastoral agents such as priests, religious, catechists, and justice and peace commissions in the country to educate people and be prudently and impartially involved in political affairs and to help people to adopt just ways of being part of the political process.[1360] The Protestant practice of discrimination is believed to have originated in the preindependence days, when Catholics thought that Anglican politicians, the Church of England, and the Archbishop of Canterbury cheated the Catholics, and the Church of Uganda (COU) are intimately tied to the state—a feeling of discrimination, which lasts up to the present day.[1361]

Participation in the political process is important because each citizen has civil or political rights to exercise. When political participation is lacking, something has not been done by those responsible for the public good. Precisely, people have either not been adequately educated or their participation has been deliberately curtailed or prevented by state/government agents. It is for similar reasons that the Catholic bishops of Uganda and other people have insisted that the government should create a level ground for all to participate and compete favorably, political activities should be fully demilitarized, and people should be provided full civic education so that they can freely and fully participate in the political process in Uganda.[1362] In other

---

[1358] Gifford, 122.

[1359] Ibid., 117.

[1360] Catholic Bishops of Uganda, *Towards a Democratic and Peaceful Uganda Based on the Common Good*, 15.

[1361] Gifford, 117.

[1362] Catholic Bishops of Uganda, *Towards a Democratic and Peaceful Uganda Based on the Common Good*, 8.

words, human freedom for political participation should not be limited by any external coercion. These requests have been emphasized because the vital principle of participation has been gravely neglected or abused by the political systems in Uganda. They are a call to radical change in the systems. It is also for the same reasons that citizens are urged to "avoid passivity or 'I do not care' attitude."[1363] They are being reminded of what many have neglected in the past even up to recently—namely, their rights, their civic or political duties or responsibilities to their country and particularly the need to work for the common good of the nation.

The reminder of the Catholic bishops of Uganda is significant, especially to the Catholic community, because for long in its history, Catholic involvement in politics has been minimal. The observation of Gifford is a testimony to the significance of the encouragement of the Catholic bishops of Uganda to the Catholic population to participate in politics. He says, "The Anglican church is smaller, but is much more powerful politically. All Uganda's heads of government (except Amin) have come from Anglican background."[1364] It is possible that Catholic political passivity in the course of Uganda's political history is responsible for their lagging behind the Anglicans or Protestants politically. It is now time for the Uganda Catholic population to realize the importance of political involvement, as Sean P. Kealy says:

> It seems clearer than ever, that there is no real choice between political involvement and non-involvement for the church. All questions are ultimately religious and in need of theological reflection in a never-ending circle.[1365]

This challenging issue raised by Kealy is real. The issue or suggestion has been exemplified in the ceaseless teaching of the Uganda Catholic bishops from the time of Uganda's independence until today. The Uganda Catholic population faces this challenge in a real and special way because of the fact that it is behind the Protestant population in participation in politics. The previous and recent advocacy of the Uganda Catholic bishops also amounts to some very crucial issues in the church-state relationship. They are suggesting,

---

[1363] Ibid., 114.

[1364] Gifford, 139.

[1365] Sean P. Kealy, *Jesus and Politics* (Minnesota, Collegeville: The Liturgical Press, 1990), 22.

as Robert Audi and Nicholas Wolterstorff contend, that "concentration of power in a religious group as such easily impairs democracy, in which citizens should have equal opportunities to exercise political power on a fair basis."[1366] Beyond this fact, Christian mission and duty call all Christians to the fulfillment of this mission. They should learn from the example of Jesus Christ's mission in the world of his time with its attendant problems. Jesus himself was "far more politically minded and far more concerned with the political life of his nation in relation to God's all-embracing purposes than many pious Christians have often supposed."[1367]

Within the individual religious institutions, the question of participation needs to be addressed. The challenge here is people's participation in the religious life or activities in the country. We mentioned earlier that Uganda is dominantly a Christian country with Catholics leading numerically. There are also other religious denominations. The question at this juncture is the one of the representation of the religious denominations and their involvement or participation in Uganda's political and religious sectors. The Catholic bishops of Uganda have raised in their pastoral letter *With a New Heart and a New Spirit* that some Christians think that the call to holiness is for priests and religious.[1368] This issue should also be extended to people's general participation in the country. The civil population ought to be encouraged to participate and should participate in the life of the nation. Unfortunately, the civil population in Uganda often looks to the government or head of state for solutions to their problems, thinking that "power belongs to the head of state" and forgetting that the power of the head of state "is delivered by the people" because in a truly democratic system "real political power rests with the people, the governed and not with the governor."[1369]

The populace of Uganda should be educated to know that participation in the affairs of the country affecting them is their right. For any Christian and person who values morals, participation as Goulet suggests, should be seen

---

[1366] Audi, Robert, and Nicholas Wolterstorff, *Religion in the Public Square: The Place of Religious Convictions in Political Debate* (Lanham: Rowman and Littlefield Publishers Inc., 1997), 6.

[1367] Kealy, 22.

[1368] Catholic Bishops of Uganda, *With a New Heart and a New Spirit*, 49.

[1369] Mugumya, 26.

as "a *moral incentive* that empowers hitherto excluded non-elites to negotiate new material incentives for themselves."[1370] The suggestion of Goulet is not merely a motivation or an encouragement of people's involvement but also a statement of fact about the significance of participation in personal and communal development. The ultimate participation is one where people whose life is affected by decisions related to their life are part of the decision-making process.

M. Education: The Challenge of Universal, Integral, and Relevant Education

The significance of education was much emphasized during the Second Vatican Council on the basis of human dignity. The council members were clear that "all men of whatever race, condition or age, in virtue of their dignity as human persons have, an inalienable right to education."[1371] A correct understanding of education is crucial to the understanding of its significance and application. While education may be equated to instruction, teaching, guidance, inculcation, indoctrination, initiation, and similar terms, the definition, and significance of education suggested by the Catholic bishops of Uganda suffices for our purpose here: education is "a means to develop the character, intellectual abilities and moral stature of individuals" and "the civilization of a society is a product of education."[1372] There is no development without education whether formal or informal education.

At the outset, it should be observed that the formal educational system in Uganda was initiated by the Catholic and Protestant missionaries and

---

[1370] Denis Goulet, *Incentives for Development: The Key to Equity*, 160.

[1371] Austin Flannery, "*Gravissimum Educationis*: Declaration on Christian Education," in *Vatican Council II: The Conciliar and Postconciliar Documents* (Leominister, Herefords, England: Costello Publishing Company, 1981), 1,726. The council members quote Pius XII, Radio Message 24 December 1924: AAS 35 (1943), 12; 19; John XXIII. Encycl. *Pacem in Terris* 11 April 1963: AAS 55 (1963), 259ff; Also cf. United Nations Universal Profession of the Rights of Man, December 1948.

[1372] The Uganda Episcopal Conference, *Education Policy 1997* (Kampala: Kisubi, 1997),1.

also Muslims.[1373] They are the true protagonists of formal education in the history of education in the country. They continued administering schools until 1960s when the school system was taken over by the government of Uganda, and "since the mid-1960s, church influence in education has been significantly reduced through the nationalization of the school system."[1374] This government initiative was not without some negative consequences in the educational system and management in the country, yet education is one of the crucial factors for human development. Postindependence Uganda witnessed a significant change in the education system and administration when government assumed direct responsibility for financial administration of schools because financial initiatives of the churches declined.[1375] This was not, however, only a miscalculation on the part of the government; it was also negligence on the part of the churches that were aware of the importance of education.

The purpose of education as a strategy or factor for integral human development is that it makes the public aware of their conditions and alternative possibilities. Education promotes this awareness "in order to win their intellectual and political support for a normatively better future."[1376] Education helps people to improve their lifestyle because to change a people's way and standard of living, one needs to influence their thoughts, understanding, and convictions or vision of life. Effective education can do this.

Since 1970, higher education has rapidly grown in Uganda, but the growth has only been in terms of the number of people enrolled, not the nature and the structure of the education system adapted to the needs of the country.[1377] A significant indicator of postindependence decline in Uganda's educational growth or development and standards is what George B. N. Ayittey has stated, "In the 1950s Makerere University in Kampala, Uganda, used to be proudly called 'the Harvard of Africa.' Today it is in a state of dilapidation."[1378] Although ranked as one of the eleven to fifteen top African universities today, Ayittey's observation does relate the inside

---

[1373] Ibid., 2.

[1374] Kassimir, 243.

[1375] The Uganda Episcopal Conference, *Education Policy 1997* (Kampala: Kisubi, 1997), 3.

[1376] Goulet, 193.

[1377] A. B. K, Kasozi, *University Education in Uganda: Challenges and Opportunities for Reform* (Kampala: Fountain Publishers, 2003), 1.

[1378] Ayittey, *Africa in Chaos*, 42.

story of Makerere University, which is the first and actually the biggest of the four state universities where the leadership of the nation is educated. The dilapidation he has mentioned should be further read beyond physical dilapidation of the structures to the moral or ethical decay of the university as told by numerous students and many administrative staff members including some of the former academic staff like Mamood Mamdani. If the future leadership of a nation is educated in and by such an institution, the future of development in the nation is also at stake, and the nation's claims for development are questionable, to a great degree. As the conciliar fathers suggested, education should help people "to develop harmoniously their physical, moral and intellectual qualities."[1379] This is the kind of education integral human development calls for.

From 1970 to 1995, "government commitment to funding education was fairly consistent."[1380] However, the educational system and curriculum in Uganda since independence has remained traditional in the sense that it has not been oriented to the formation for integral human life. Education is dominantly helping people to be literate and informed socially, scientifically, religiously, historically, and politically. Even this is not adequately done. The suggestion of the International Bank Committee that more work needs to be done to "widen the range of human knowledge about Uganda's physical and human resources and how they can best be developed"[1381] is a recommendation to be noted. Oftentimes, even today, the country relies on the expertise of expatriates to try to understand itself and its needs better. This is a significant sign that there is still much work to be done. However, some of the new universities are attempting to address the needs of the country. For instance, "Nkumba University offers a variety of programmes that are linked and related to the job market."[1382]

For the first time in Uganda's education history, the Catholic Bishops Conference of Uganda was able to think more aggressively of integral education for living a good life in accordance with their stipulations in the 1997 education policy.[1383] The Uganda Catholic bishops decided to open

---

[1379] Austin Flannery, "*Gravissimum Educationis*: Declaration on Christian Education," in *Vatican Council II: The Conciliar and Postconciliar Documents*, 1,727.

[1380] Kasozi, 13.

[1381] International Bank for Reconstruction and Development, 10.

[1382] Kasozi, 145.

[1383] The Uganda Episcopal Conference, *Education Policy 1997* (Kampala: Kisubi, 1997), 9.

Uganda Martyrs University. The relevance of the university is based on its philosophy, asserts A. B. K. Kasozi:

> The philosophy of the Uganda Martyrs' University is derived from Catholic Christian philosophy of the human person. Accordingly, its aim is to develop individuals who combine career competence with a sense of moral responsibility both at the individual and social level.[1384]

The Catholic bishops of Uganda decided to establish Uganda Martyrs University (UMU) to counteract the immoral atmosphere in the country—an atmosphere that militates against crucial virtues and principles such as love, justice, peace, participation the common good, the human person, human rights, and human dignity. It seems to be a success story of education in Uganda's history because the graduates of the university are doing well in real work situations. They constitute some of the best and relevant personnel in institutions where they work. They provide some of the labor force the moral situation in Uganda calls for. The Institute of Ethics and Development Studies is particularly oriented to help students live a decent life. The relevance of UMU is also seen in the fact that it has designed a curriculum that attempts "to address social concerns," and it delivers "quality higher education with a moral emphasis"[1385] to pursue the goal of relevance and moral as well as academic excellence. Its emphasis on moral development is evident in what Kasozi states:

> The teaching of moral values is integrated in and is part of the curriculum of all other disciplines. It is core to UMU teaching. Acceptable moral values and their seeping into the general society, particularly the educated elite, is a legacy that UMU strives to contribute to the Ugandan society through higher education.[1386]

This is the kind of education system Uganda needs today if it is to develop integrally. Hence, UMU offers for the education system in Uganda a model of education to emulate even at the level of primary and secondary school

---

[1384] Kasozi, 146.

[1385] Ibid.

[1386] Ibid., 147.

education. From a social point of view, a challenge that confronts Uganda's education system is the unequal access to higher education. This is a problem that can be traced to the early times in the history of Uganda. It should be considered a critical challenge because

> it was the means by which southerners, particularly Baganda, came to dominate the affairs of the country. The education system had been started by the missionaries and the first schools were located in Buganda.[1387]

Traditional attitudes toward education have also often favored men more than women, who are often considered more resourceful in making wealth, good for marriage, and domestic work.[1388] In such cases from a Christian anthropological point of view, the female gender is discriminated against, and the understanding of human dignity and human right is flawed. This is gender inequality or discrimination in education in terms of gender. To achieve integral development is difficult because of the traditional or cultural attitude about the education of women. It is this attitude which creates this gender inequality, a fundamental social injustice that must be eliminated before a positive step can be made toward increased education of women. This cultural factor also militates against the promotion of the common good and the operation of the principle of participation or involvement, which were much encouraged by Paul VI as crucial for integral development and especially recommended by the Second Vatican Council.[1389]

The education system in Uganda provides for little socioeconomic and political education. It is only in the higher institutions of learning that political science is taught. At lower levels, civics is taught but does not address real or serious political issues and problems. For instance, serious questions like those of human rights, human dignity, and peace, which are important for political stability, are not part of the education curricula.[1390] Even in the higher

---

[1387] Mutibwa, 9.

[1388] Kasozi, 131ff

[1389] Cfr. Austin Flannery, "*Gravissimum Educationis*: Declaration on Christian Education," in *Vatican Council II: The Conciliar and Postconciliar Documents*, 1, 727.

[1390] Tuyizere, 77. Alice Tuyizere aptly suggests here some of the very fundamental, virtues, conditions, and principles Paul VI suggested for integral development as relevant for peace education in secondary schools.

institutions of learning, these issues are taught to people who have specialized in political sciences. This means that a large sector of the population grows up to be politically ignorant. If politicians triumph over the populace during elections, it is because they prey on the ignorance of the masses.

There is no question that "education is primordial in the development of a country; it is a prerequisite for civilization and a progressing society can be judged by the quality of its education."[1391] Consequently, one principal challenge to the Uganda government is to ensure that the whole population is educated. Education would help the nation to achieve its enduring goals since independence—namely, the fight against disease, poverty, and ignorance as advocated first by Milton Obote and continued by the majority of the successive leaders. Without good, relevant, and integral education it is difficult to achieve these goals.

In 1997, Uganda government introduced Universal Primary Education (UPE).[1392] This innovation was partly a solution to the problem of ignorance, sickness, and poverty and partly to promote the political or personal agenda of the NRM government. Nonetheless, the attempt seems to be an utter failure because the products, in the form of quality education, are extremely poor. This is basically because there are no adequate rooms, school supplies, and other necessary facilities for the students. Pedagogically, this is not right because in such circumstances students do not receive the badly needed integral education or formation. When there are too few teachers, the students cannot be assisted adequately. For example, in the year 2000, there were fifty-nine students for every primary school teacher.[1393] In such a case, there is no adequate follow-up of students. Consequently, they cannot be adequately and effectively helped. Compared to the 1970 ratio of teacher to students, which was thirty-four students for every primary school teacher, there is a much better opportunity to help students than in times UPE came into effect about thirty years later.[1394] The UPE program is relevant and necessary, but its implementation started without sufficient planning and resources. At most, it only contributed to some political successes for certain individuals, not the nation, because it was used for political propaganda.

[1391] Mugumya, 114.

[1392] Ibid., 115.

[1393] World Bank, World Development Report, 2004: *Making Services Work for the Poor* (Washington DC: World Bank and Oxford University Press, 2003), 259.

[1394] World Bank, World Development Report, 1994: *Infrastructure for Development* (Oxford: Oxford University Press, 1994), 216.

Equal participation in provision of education according to different religious denominations is significant. Uganda's history has revealed that some religious denominations have been deliberately discriminated against for religious and political reasons. Justus Mugaju observes that "the Anglicans became the de facto established church in Uganda," and Catholics have often felt "outsiders in the politics of their own country."[1395] The attempt to close some Catholic Teachers Training Colleges—especially Lodonga Teachers Training College, on March 31, 1999, even if equal opportunity for all districts was one of the explanations for the closure of some teachers' training colleges—is a sign of the failure of implementation of the principle of equal participation or opportunity.[1396] Yet the same year, the best performing teachers training college was the Catholic-founded Lodonga Primary Teachers College (PTC), one of the teachers' training colleges slated for closure together with Mbarara, while Kalangala and Ajumani that were not viable were favored by the policy of closure.[1397] In the year 2006, the same college has been the best performing teachers' college in the whole of Uganda with 79.9 percent of the students passing their final national examinations and the best student of the nation's PTCs emerging from the same Lodonga PTC out of the forty-seven PTCs nationwide.[1398] This is a challenge the ministry of education never adequately addressed until the Catholic bishops questioned the prevailing events.

Church contributions to education in Uganda have been invaluable. Ddungu notes that "since Vatican Council II (1965), the church in Uganda has made significant efforts to promote 'development education' in order to conscientize people to social and economic development."[1399] This contribution has been through formal and informal education which the church worked hard to promote wherever it was possible.

One of the principal educational challenges to Christian religious institutions in Uganda is the teaching of Christian Religious Education (CRE). This has declined since the government took over the administration

---

[1395] Mugaju, 15.

[1396] Odubuker Picho Epiphany, an oral informant, principal of Lodonga Teachers Training College, interviewed on May 11, 2006. The informant is a Catholic priest and director or principal of the college who personally fought hard to successfully block the closure of the college.

[1397] Ibid.

[1398] Ibid. Interviewed on September 19, 2006.

[1399] Ddungu, 23.

of most schools, and a joint syllabus was established. Religious institutions need to ensure that the standard of religious education taught in schools improves to that of 1963 when government took over the management of schools from church institutions.[1400] This has meant that some aspects of the Christian faith where there are differences, especially between the Catholics and Protestants or other Christian denominations, are either not taught or not adequately emphasized because the syllabi are ecumenical although this in itself is positive in the sense that it shows some element of solidarity among religious groups.

Another critical challenge in the field of education, especially to Catholics, is the problem of educational monopoly. The Protestants should be commended for their ecumenically forthcoming attitude and shrewdness, founded in the colonial period because the colonial masters of Uganda were dominantly of Protestant background.[1401] As referred to earlier in this chapter, one issue remains challenging to religious institutions and political leaders of Uganda. It is the Protestant attitude of insistently and consistently trying to dominate both the political and the educational sector in the country. A typical example is already cited above, the attempt by the government ministry of education or parliament, coincidentally or otherwise dominated by Protestants, to close some targeted teachers' training colleges in the country. An analysis of the event showed that most, if not almost all colleges slated to be closed, were Catholic-founded. The challenge to Catholics in such a case is to question how genuine ecumenical endeavors have been in the past and whether government is not violating the equalitarian principle according to which "the state may not give preference to one religion over another" and also to some extent the neutrality principle, which states that "the state should neither favor nor disfavor a religion as such or give positive or negative preference to institutions or persons simply because they are religious."[1402] In either case, the Catholic Church is a victim. If a parliament or a government ministry discriminates against certain sectors of the nation's population, its sense of justice and respect for this principle is questionable.

The Catholic Church and other Christian churches emphasize that religious or moral education should be compulsory in Catholic schools,

---

[1400] J.C. Ssekamwa, and S.M.E. Lugumba, *A History of Education in East Africa* (Kampala: Fountain Publishers, 2001), 150.

[1401] Gifford, 117.

[1402] Audi and Wolterstorf, 4.

especially on the secondary school level.[1403] However, Christian churches in general face the challenge that in many schools CRE is neglected or not emphasized enough. Even if churches can have their programs for catechesis, one thing to be remembered is the constant or ongoing need for practical catechesis. The continuity of such a progressive process of religious education is interfered with in schools if their directors do not consider the question of religious education seriously, whether they are primary schools or institutions of higher learning.

As a conclusion of the various critical challenges of Paul VI's vision of integral human development to Uganda, I would like to adopt what Luke Mbefo Nnamdi states about Ghandi's vision of some of the great challenges or evils that confront humanity and actually obstruct true human development:

> To Ghandi has been ascribed the seven-fold catalogue of deadly sins, namely: wealth without labour, religion without sacrifice, politics without principles, commerce without morality, pleasure without conscience, education without character and finally science without humanity.[1404]

The reason for the appropriation of Ghandi's vision as stated by Mbefo is that the statement captures the challenges I have outlined in light of *Populorum Progressio*. It also captures some of the recommendations that feature in the subsequent section. Finally, the vision of Ghandi as stated by Mbefo points to the real sources of dishonesty, corruption and lack of true human development.

IV. SOME RECOMMENDATIONS

A. Integral Education

Education is perhaps the most crucial social factor of human development. The significance of education is seen in the fruits of human activity and in the quality of life of people. The critical statement made by Adam Smith, as

---

[1403] The Uganda Episcopal Conference, *Education Policy 1997* (Kampala: Marianum Press, Kisubi, 1997), 10.

[1404] Mbefo Nnamdi, 144-145.

quoted by Reinhold Niebuhr, is significant reminder and summary of the
contributions of education toward human development.

> An instructed and intelligent people are always more decent and
> orderly than a stupid one. They feel themselves each individually
> more respectable and more likely to gain the respect of their
> lawful superiors . . . . They are disposed to examine and are more
> capable of seeing through the interested complaints of faction
> and sedition, and they are upon that account less apt to be misled
> into any wanton or unnecessary opposition to the measures of
> government."[1405]

The principal concern of this section is to make some suggestions for
Uganda. One of the greatest challenges for educational development is whether
education is relevant to people's development needs.[1406] A relevant formal and
informal education helps people to critically see other people's conditions and
their own situation, their needs and their roles, and to compare their own
situation with that of other people and to realize that they have a dignity that
deserves respect and a certain standard of living. It helps people to reflect and
strive to find alternative ways of living. The knowledge of good and evil or
right and wrong is at the foundation of any moral or ethical behavior and
reflection.[1407] Uganda's educational institutions, whether public or private,
religious or secular, should emphasize education about moral or ethical values
and help students to differentiate what is evil and detrimental to society from
values that promote society. Any suggestions for education should attempt
to meet these and similar standards.

Integral education suggested here means the complete education of
the student. The education recommended here is what Levis Mugumya
describes, after the example of Paul VI, as an appropriate education to which
all people have rights, the type of education which aims at "developing an
individual's personality, talents, mental and physical abilities to their fullest
potential."[1408] It facilitates attainment of the goals of the type of education

---

[1405] Niebuhr, 121. Niebhur is quoting Adam Smith, *Wealth of the Nations*, Bk. V, ci.

[1406] Kasozi, 125.

[1407] Deotis J. Roberts, 58.

[1408] Mugumya, 119. This is a reference to articles 28 and 29 of the Convention on
the Rights of the Child.

(integral) suggested. Integral education is a comprehensive education for human enhancement and promotion of society, an education that helps people feel comfortable almost everywhere. Such education incorporates or integrates the history, geography, cultures, politics, economy, and religions of peoples and should help students "to develop a sense of civic responsibility"[1409] as is the goal in most North American countries. J. C. B. Bigala affirms this as the goal of education:

> Integral education should promote the welfare of individuals and of society through providing intellectual, occupational and professional skills, social, moral and spiritual development.[1410]

The significance of education for national integration and development is invaluable. As Matthew Habiger states, "Education to solidarity is an urgent necessity of our day."[1411] It is one of the first factors necessary to achieve peace and national unity or integration. It helps develop "in the heart of every individual and in the activities of every society a true sense of *stewardship* and *solidarity*."[1412] Besides being a necessary factor to achieve peace and national unity, education is a "driver of development."[1413] Consequently, the leadership of the churches should help the government to ensure that from the lowest level to the highest level, education continues to provide for the possibility of peace, unity, and development.

While universal primary education is a positive or relevant innovation because it benefits not only individuals but all categories of people, the ministry of education ought to improve the UPE program in Uganda. The ministry should improve and expand plans for primary education by providing the requisite conditions for effective universal education, viz., adequate housing, adequate and regular payment of teachers' salaries, and any necessary pedagogical resources or requirements.

Uganda's Poverty Eradication Report suggests that "the introduction of UPE with free education for four children in every family has transformed the

---

[1409] Kasozi, 60.

[1410] Bigala, 167. Bigala is quoting J. C. Ssekamwa and T. F. Kasibante, eds., *Education Today: A Guide for Parents and Teachers in Uganda* (Kisubi, Marianum Press), 2.

[1411] Habiger, 6.

[1412] Ibid., 5.

[1413] Kasozi, 13.

situation of enrollment"[1414] in primary schools since 1997. Universal primary education is a positive proposal of the education system for Uganda because for a long time over 50 percent of Uganda's population was illiterate. The theoretical and practical significance of the system is compounded by the necessity of education as a basic factor for authentic human development. It would meet the need of education for all or the development of all. However, the eminent question is whether UPE meets such needs and the requisite standards.

Even if UPE is at the lowest level of education, it needs to be planned well for a solid educational foundation. To date, UPE seems a failure because of the poor products in terms of students as stated earlier, even if some 60 percent of parents are said to be "satisfied with the quality of their children's education" while "40% are not."[1415] The intriguing question this survey prompts is: Who were the respondents in the survey—the rich or the poor, politicians or ordinary citizens, the educated or the uneducated? Where and with whom the survey was conducted determines the validity of the above results. It is not the purpose of this work to investigate this, but it provokes further thinking, especially in light of the real observable fruits of UPE.

UPE has pushed many people to school because tuition is not required. Those who had no hope to reach a primary seven standard are now attempting to do so and attempting to assert their right to education.[1416] This seems to many people to be a success. Unfortunately, the success is only in the quantity of students not the quality of their education. UPE's failure is real because education does not meet its real ends stated above—peace, national unity, and development in general. The input in terms of teaching and formation is poor, and consequently, the output in terms of the quality of students or their performance is also poor. For instance, it is incredible and shameful that some students complete seven years of primary education, and they are not capable of fluent reading in their local languages, let alone in English, which is their second language. In other words, the transformative consequence of UPE is minimal. While government advocates improvement in "both quality

---

[1414] Ministry of Finance, Planning and Economic Development, *Poverty Eradication Action Plan (2000-2003)*, vol. 1 (Kampala, February 2001), 136.

[1415] Ibid.

[1416] Mugumya, 115.

and quantity of primary education,"[1417] in reality, it is a failure. Some of the propagators of UPE are reluctant to send their children to public/government schools. They prefer to send them to private or well-managed schools, sometimes not just within Uganda but outside Uganda.[1418] This says volumes about whether UPE is really helpful to the people of Uganda though it is a relevant innovation.

Teachers have not been well paid and are not promptly paid. Where does motivation come from? It is not only the question of motivation. Justice demands that they ought to be given what they and their families need to survive. The challenge for the government is to recognize and enforce education, without prejudice, as the propelling force behind people's development.[1419] The challenge to teachers is to contribute to the development of Uganda through the education they provide. Teachers ought to teach students what can transform their life and the condition of the nation. Uganda's development depends on the kind of education they provide, the process it involves, and what the education contributes and does not contribute to the nation and its citizens.

The idea that the first goal of education is to "prepare people for life"[1420] is very significant; and it should direct the process of education. Education needs to be oriented toward development because it is one of the crucial factors for the development of people. It is for such a reason that Kasozi thinks that university education and universities in Uganda "must direct curriculum changes that address national needs"[1421] of Uganda. Their curriculum should include development ethics and any development-related themes as core subjects of study. The need for education that helps enhance and integrate human development challenges the human mind that

> there is also the urgent need to generate on a greatly expanded scale those human skills and knowledge that are essential to increase productivity and hence to accelerate economic growth. This is a problem for education and training. Increased productivity is

---

[1417] Ssekamwa and Lugumba, 149.

[1418] K. Mulera Muniini, "Raise Teachers' Salaries," in *Daily Monitor*, April 30, 2006.

[1419] Kasozi, 13.

[1420] Ssekamwa and Lugumba, 149.

[1421] Kasozi, 15.

not of course the only goal of education. Another essential goal
is equipping people with knowledge to advance a country's entire
cultural, economic, and political level.[1422]

A critical study of the context intended for development is crucial for
development planning. Education should, therefore, help people to accomplish
knowledge needed for development. This need calls for "co-operative
education"[1423] and adaptation. Education should be adapted to the real needs
of people. Adaptation of education is necessary for the progress of people and
a nation, but it demands a critical study of contexts to be developed. There
are other crucial requisites for development, which education for development
should incorporate. Lawrence Harrison has aptly stated this:

> What makes development happen is our ability to imagine,
> theorize, conceptualize, experiment, invent, articulate, organize,
> manage, solve problems, and do a hundred other things with our
> minds and hands to contribute to the progress of the individual
> and humankind. Natural resources, climate, geography, history,
> market size, government policies and many other factors influence
> the direction and pace of progress. But the engine is human
> creativity.[1424]

Education for development should first help people to develop their
potential and be creative. It should help people think in a practical fashion and
be able to construct practical solutions from the pieces of information they
have been able to lay their hands on. This is very crucial to integral human
development and should be promoted by all educational systems. Creativity
is at the root of every development, and "the society that is most successful at
helping its people—all its people—realize their creative potential is the society
that will progress the fastest."[1425] A cooperative education system is one where

---

[1422] Committee for Economic Development, *How Low Income People Can Advance
their Growth: The Lessons of Experience* (New York: The Research and Policy
Committee for Economic Development, 1966), 32.

[1423] Kasozi, 61.

[1424] Lawrence E. Harrison, *Underdevelopment Is a State of Mind: The Latin American Case*
(Lanham: The International Affairs, Harvard University and Madison Books, 1988), 2.

[1425] Ibid.

industries and educational institutions work together in training students. It is both theory and practice—a type of internship or apprenticeship. Human creativity for development should also be expressed in the different sciences and arts as Rose-Marie Rychner suggests,

> Art needs to be more than aesthetics; it focuses on its potential to shape people's characters both as individuals and as social beings. Artists in Uganda see their role primarily in the promotion of peaceful development of political order and stability.[1426]

Fine art is not just something to be enjoyed or a beauty to be beheld. Much as it has the capacity or power to affect or shape people's vision of reality, it should be used to influence people's developmental process by providing powerful teaching aids. The Ugandan pedagogy should make a maximum use of the gifts of fine art by involving its talented fine artists. Education in fine arts should continue to be vigorously rejuvenated and used to fight ignorance, poverty, and diseases such as HIV/AIDS that has tarnished the image of the health of Uganda since the 1980s.[1427] Media and all literature should not be colored by or used for the realization of some personally profiteering objectives. It should be at the true and disinterestsd service of the nation. Media ought not to be used merely for propaganda or promotion of individual or personal interests.

Positive objectives can be achieved through an education system that drills people in upholding and living according to moral values such as already stated of and propagated by UMU.[1428] This means that part of what education should do is to teach people to be honest and sincere in and with the media. Those who communicate should be sincere and recipients of media information should be critical, not naïve as to take what they read and hear for gospel truth. The integrity of media should be manifested in what they communicate to the public. Ugandan media should be used for true, responsible moral, political, and socioeconomic formation of the citizens. It should be at the true and disinterested service of the nation.

[1426] Rose-Marie Rychner, "The Context and Background of Ugandan Art," in *Uganda: The Cultural Landscape,* ed. Richard Breitinger (Kampala: Fountain Publishers, 2000), 263.

[1427] Ibid.

[1428] A. B. K. Kasozi, 146-147.

Education should help people to grasp the true meaning of development. The actual purpose of education is the development of peoples. It aims at helping people to aim at "struggle against illiteracy, support of political, social and moral development process, improving the general state of health, stimulation of economic development and improve the material living conditions of the individual."[1429] Human enhancement demands a critical vision of development and development theories, even questioning the understanding of development as promoted by the developed nations because often times they do not have a full view of development. Denis Goulet makes a critical and important observation to this effect:

> It is not a case of sound development being exported to sites unsuited to receive it, but rather that the very conception of development transferred is itself distorted at its point of origin.[1430]

Education systems should adopt methodologies that foster participation of the people that are practically relevant depending on the contexts in which a particular category of people find themselves. In other words, "participatory pedagogy, including techniques that encourage more initiative and cooperation at lower levels" of the system and emphasize seminars and case-method at upper levels"[1431] of education and society should be encouraged in the school systems. This helps people adapt their approaches according to the type of community they deal with.

Continued church involvement in education and educational institutions is necessary for an integral education. Religious institutions have a long tradition of providing education in Uganda and other countries, and they should continue this spirit or mission of providing education. The church should, therefore, continue to be present in educational institutions on all levels—universities, higher institutions of learning, secondary schools, and primary schools.[1432] Parish priests should also be personally involved in teaching

---

[1429] Kakooza, 185-188. Here, Kakoza quotes Lowbler H., *Mass Education*, eds. Lars Olof Edstrom, Renee Erdos, and Roy Prosser (the Dag Hammarskold Foundation, 1970).

[1430] Goulet, 184.

[1431] Bigala, 177.

[1432] Kasozi, 8.

Christian religious education even in primary schools. This is even more significant than elevating the educational standards or knowledge of those who have already received substantial or adequate religious education—those in higher institutions and universities, especially if their religious education has already been well catered for. Training in character, morality, or ethics should help reinforce "practical life skills."[1433]

The education needed for integral human development is one that helps people to live decent, moral, or responsible practical life, which shows true faith and civility. Education detached from God breeds broken relationship with God, other people, and self, and ultimately, as Deotis J. Roberts asserts, it is the "foundation for sinful, evil-ridden community."[1434] In the context of Uganda, this demands that the education curriculum should be revised; both quality and quantity of education should be critically considered so as to produce people who are well prepared for life.[1435] It ought to be noted that education can become a menace if not well directed. Much as it can be a powerful instrument for creating peace, for example, it can also be used as an instrument for creating disharmony. As Niebuhr contends, "When the educational process is accompanied by a dishonest suppression of facts and truths, it becomes pure propaganda."[1436] Education can be used to meet the needs or achieve the goals of educators. This indicates that education can be used as an instrument for conflict making and conflict resolution. Consequently, Niebuhr suggests that educational process alone is inadequate to resolve conflicts, its established goals ought to be moral or ethical and adhered to. Therefore, the value of education and its moral dimension ought always to be judged according to the purpose it serves, especially the enhancement of human dignity.

B. Practical Political Democracy

Democracy is new to Uganda and perhaps does not really exist in its true sense. From the time of Uganda's independence up to today, democracy has been ignored by one leader after another. After Museveni's address to

---

[1433] Ibid.

[1434] Roberts, 59.

[1435] Ssekamwa, 149.

[1436] Niebhur, 245.

the Catholic bishops of Uganda in 1986, just five months after he came to power, the bishops responded after three weeks by writing the pastoral letter *With a New Heart and a New Spirit*, suggesting among other statements of support to cooperate in the development of Uganda with clear guidelines that even if they would not identify with any particular political grouping Uganda should return to parliamentary democracy, universal suffrage, general elections, and multiparty politics, which guarantees "freedom of assembly and association."[1437]

However, there were moments when Ugandans had a glimpse of democracy. For instance, the process of the review and rewriting of the 1967 Uganda constitution is generally acknowledged to have been democratic in terms of presentation and the process of electing representatives.[1438] However, there is much to be desired from Uganda's democratic processes. The principal reason for apprehension about practical political democracy is well stated by George B. N. Ayittey, twenty-one years after NRM came to power: "Uganda is a defacto 'one-party state' with the political arena dominated by Presudent Museveni's National resistance Movement."[1439] Uganda needs the following things for true democracy:

1. Tolerance

In a practical political democracy, tolerance should be understood as unconditional mutual acceptance despite differences and undesirable factors. The basis of tolerance has been articulated by Bernard Haring and Valentino Salvoldi as being the recognition and respect for the equality of people, but they add to this description:

> The concept of tolerance to which we are referring is based on that positive attitude as opposed to others which draw from nonviolence the strength to endure evil rather than to inflict it on others.[1440]

[1437] Kassimir, 240-241.

[1438] Tarsis Bazana Kabwegyere, *People's Choice, People's Power: Challenges and Prospects of Democracy in Uganda* (Kampala: Fountain Publishers, 2000), 119.

[1439] Ayittey, *Africa Unchained: The Blue Print for Africa's Future*, 208.

[1440] Haring and Salvoldi, 4.

Tolerance demands nonviolence among people. To have democracy, tolerance is necessary. In a pluralistic context like Uganda, tolerance leads to peace, but peace is also a necessary condition for tolerance to flourish. This suggests that peace education should also be given to the citizens. Peace education "is an indispensable strategy" not only for promoting tolerance but also "mutual trust of people belonging to different backgrounds."[1441] There should be mutual political acceptance, an acceptance embraced for more than the sake of avoiding conflicts and hostile exchanges. The notion of tolerance suggested here is tantamount to Paul VI's advocacy for peace where he rejected violent reactions to situations of injustice as explained in chapter two. There should be ungrudging and sincere mutual political acceptance and exchange of views or ideologies.

Tolerance is a relevant and necessary suggestion for a country like Uganda that has been war-torn for years—a country struggling to attain some solidarity, which has been hard to achieve because of its ethnic, religious, social, economic, and political diversity. All these diversities demand some tolerance. Political tolerance, in particular, demands an end to Uganda's many years of apparently one-party system, rule of military juntas, and so-called "no party democracy."[1442]

The tolerance suggested here should be based on the most fundamental principle for integral human development much emphasized in this study and especially in chapter three, namely, the human person and human dignity. That is, "the basis for tolerance is the equality of all people by nature and their aspiration to the same destiny, 'happiness.'"[1443] There should be a mutual understanding, and nobody's rights should be trampled upon by anybody.

2. Impartial Democracy

A well-defined, understood, and applied democracy is necessary. However, I would not suggest a new definition. The word *democracy* comes from the Greek word *demos,* which means "people," and *kratos,* "strength" or "power"—people power or government by the people.[1444] The traditional

---

[1441] Tuyizere, 76.

[1442] Ondoga, 202.

[1443] Haring and Salvoldi, 4.

[1444] *The New International Webster's Quick Reference Our Nation Notebook,* 1.

definition of democracy as "government of the people, by the people, and for the people," serves the purpose of achieving integral human development, which has been stated in chapter two as a democratic process itself. It should be a democracy that provides for a less self-seeking service and a more selfless attitude of the political and civil leadership. This notion of democracy is also preferable because it fits well in the federal system of government I suggest for Uganda in this chapter. As Oskar Wermter suggests, true democracy is and should always be "based on deeply-held convictions of the fundamental equality of all human beings, the unity of the human race and the value and dignity of the human person."[1445]

Democracy demands service in accordance with the stipulations of the national constitution, which is the supreme law of a nation, without changing the constitution for personal convenience or interests. The Catholic bishops of Uganda have hinted at such whimsical changes of the constitution as a possible enduring contentious issue in the history and future of Uganda.[1446] They need to be avoided by all means because a constitution, as the supreme law of the country, should be a lasting ordinance. Moreover, by its very definition, a law is not for personal convenience—it is "an ordinance of reason, for the general good, made by whoever has the care of the community, and promulgated."[1447] What people ought to guard against is that all these conditions may be fulfilled in a law-making process, but they may also be initiated and imposed by a few powerful people for their personal good, not the good of the entire community for whom the law is intended. Other than this issue, another challenge is that laws may be made and promulgated by the responsible people, but their correct application may be inhibited by just a few others or an individual.

Impartial democracy demands that government function according to constitutionally just laws.[1448] It should always be kept in mind that while the government is established to take care of the people—the citizens—and to promote their good and protect them from any external aggressions, the

---

[1445] Wermter, 18.

[1446] Catholic Bishops of Uganda, *Towards a Democratic and Peaceful Uganda Based on the Common Good*, 3.

[1447] Thomas Aquinas, *Summa Theologiae: A Concise Translation*, ed. Timothy McDermott (Allen Texas: Christian Classics, 1989), II. 9. 90, 4.

[1448] Kiapi, 79.

authority of government is derived from the people through the constitutional law of the country, which determines "what a government can or cannot do."[1449] Therefore, the constitution should always be acknowledged and respected as the supreme law of the country. It should not be manipulated at the whim of a president or anybody else who assumes authority or may be entrusted with the responsibility of the care for the nation. The laws of the nation, including those which govern the behavior of public authorities or servants, should be fair, not oppressive and arbitrary, because the government is an instrument of service to people, it is "the trustee of the public interest of its people,"[1450] not an institution and instrument for the oppression of its citizens.

Another characteristic of an impartial democracy is expressed in the role of the army in the life of the nation. Amaza Ori Ondoga claimed that the National Resistance Army (NRA), now called Uganda People's Democratic Forces (UPDF), is "a peoples' army."[1451] This claim is questionable because honest Ugandans would agree that Ugandan leaders have been notorious, since independence, for using the military for personal political interests. The evidence is the series of coup d'état that have occurred in Ugandan history and have been effected by the army. While the current constitution of Uganda is clear that the army should be and is a neutral body, not owned by the head of state, any political party or the president, even if he is the commander in chief of the armed forces, Uganda's leaders have consistently and in a very protracted way used the army to achieve their personal ends.[1452] This is contrary not only to Christian-ethical norms but also to the 1995 Constitution of Uganda, which includes the following statement:

> The Uganda Peoples' Defence Forces shall be non-partisan, national in character, patriotic, professional, disciplined, productive and subordinate to the civilian authority as established under this constitution.[1453]

[1449] Ibid.

[1450] Ibid.

[1451] Ondoga, 225.

[1452] USAID, Democracy and Governance Assessment, 59.

[1453] Government of Uganda, 134.

Election contestants are aware that if they contest the results of any election, they and their supporters could be in trouble. This is so, especially if the incumbent president is proclaimed winner and they and the populace are dissatisfied about the atmosphere of fear and force created by the army at the time of elections. This has been the consistent reason for those who lose elections to run to exile or to seek refuge in the bush. They have no defense because the commander in chief owns the army. This constitutes injustice, lack of participation, violation of freedom of speech or human rights, and an absence of a minimal democracy. The 2005 USAID assessment of democracy and governance in Uganda provides a clear evidence about the "ownership or personalization" of the army:

> Despite the constitutional provisions that require the UPDF to answer to Parliament and the people of Uganda, in practice the separation of military and Movemnet as political organization is ambiguous, and the top military command is drawn predominantly from the southwest. The role of the army is inextricably linked to the president who is the chairman of the Movement and the commander-in-chief of the armed forces. The army has become an integral part of politics, evidenced in the manner in which the Movement leadership has used it for different political interventions beyond Uganda's borders without Parliament's approval, such as the case in the Democratic Republic of Congo (DRC).[1454]

It is probably for the gravity of the need to nationalize the army that the November 2005 pastoral letter of the Catholic bishops of Uganda expressed the bishops' gratitude about parliamentary resolutions to limit the role of the army though USAID assessment is suggesting that it does not happen in practice. The November 2005 report of the Uganda bishops states in part:

> With Uganda's nasty past the destructive role of the army in politics cannot be taken lightly. We are happy that the army will no longer be represented in the Parliament. This is a positive development especially in the era of multiparty political dispensation.[1455]

[1454] USAID, Democracy and Governance Assessment, 7.

[1455] Catholic Bishops of Uganda, *Towards a Democratic and Peaceful Uganda Based on the Common Good*, 13.

The religious leaders should help the populace to understand such critical issues. They should also help people and the government to understand and ensure that there is equality before the law, the legislative and the executive wings of government support the judiciary system and functions, the judiciary is independent in executing its functions, rights of individuals should be respected, and "government must be the representative of the majority of the citizens."[1456] The question of equality before the law is closely related to the anthropological principle treated in depth in chapter three of this work. The legal equality is and should always be based on the principle of *imago Dei*. All people are created with equal dignity. It is precisely for this reason that the rights of individuals—civil, political and human rights—should be respected. Similarly, Abraham Kiapi contends that justice and true democracy have certain requirements:

> The just laws . . . must be impartially administered. All people are, and must always remain, equal before the law. The law must be consistently and equally applied to all citizens. The status: whether by birth, marriage, social standing, political importance or economic opulence, must not be allowed to interfere with the administration of the law.[1457]

The independence of the judiciary is crucial because it is the overall controlling force in the country. It is not above the law. It is and should always be the custodian and the authoritative interpreter of the law and its application. Second, justice condemns bribery as unfair and a discriminatory practice. This in turn suggests that

> the legislative and executive arms of the state must not interfere with the decisions of the judiciary in the courts of law, over particular cases. The administration of justice must be the sole prerogative of the courts of law . . . . Judges and magistrates must not be influenced by extraneous matters, foreign to the facts established from the submitted evidence and in accordance with the applicable law.[1458]

[1456] Kiapi, 80.

[1457] Ibid.

[1458] Ibid.

The question of political participation is also suggested by the people's choice of whom to entrust with the authority to care for the needs of the nation. Governments should not be chosen by only a handful of people. There should be a general consensus of the citizens about the government of the state. The issue confronting Uganda, as Nkrunziza suggests, is "to create a self-sustaining and empowered civil society that does not depend on handouts from the state."[1459] The challenge is to create a civil society that detests bribes from government and a state which is founded on truth, universal charity, justice, option for the poor, affirmative action, subsidiarity, and common good.

3. A Federal Political System for Uganda

A federal system of government would be helpful to the integral human development in Uganda. Ugandan political discussion introduced the notion of federalism, but the type of federalism under debate was the type of government, which the Buganda government of Mengo wanted and actually referred to as federo[1460]—not in the ordinary sense of federalism. It is the type federalism to which Milton Obote was opposed and which led him to abrogate the 1966 constitution and introduce his 1967 constitution.

According to the 1966 Constitution of Uganda,

> only one region-Buganda-was given separate and substantial powers independent of the center. The Buganda Lukiko controlled public services, local government, its public debt, and had separate powers of taxation; furthermore, its revenue was supplemented by grants from the state, as specified in the constitution. It had its own court system, and subject to the control of the Uganda inspector-general, its own police force. It selected its assembly indirectly, through the Lukiko rather than by popular vote. None of these powers could be altered by the Uganda parliament without the two-thirds concurring vote of the Lukiko.[1461]

[1459] Nkurunziza, 27.

[1460] Ondoga, 188.

[1461] Mamdani, 242-243. He is quoting Emory Bundy, "Uganda's New Constitution," in *East African Journal* (July 1966): 25.

This is the type of federalism Buganda demanded in 1993 from the NRM government. The Buganda region was denied this privilege precisely because such demands do not provide enough executive powers for the central government over Buganda. Neither is the federal system advocated here one which provides for too much power to the central government at the expense of the lower structures.[1462] It would also be an injustice to grant this only to Buganda while other regions never enjoy similar privileges and power. The term federo as understood by the Baganda—and officially introduced, probably to distinguish it from federalism generally understood—is disputed and the meaning untenable in the pluralistic context of Uganda.

The federal system of government suggested here is one which provides for all regions of the country equally. This should be debated and agreed upon in the parliament after intense consultation with the masses. It should be a system accepted by consensus because it does not discriminate against any region or ethnic group. The federalism suggested here is one that is unitary. It should provide for true unity in diversity. It is the United States and Canadian systems that I suggest.[1463] The framers of the American federal system aimed at strengthening the national government, but they also aimed at "the division of power between the national government and the states."[1464] The type of federalism understood by the majority of the Baganda—which is evidently different, undesirable, and not accepted by majority of the people of other regions of Uganda—is not feasible in Uganda because the latter is a pluralistic society. The model of American or Canadian or German and other federal systems, independent of ethnic understanding of federalism is much more suitable for Uganda. The American federal system was intended to ensure that "government would not be dominated by any one group and that there were adequate safeguards to protect individuals and states."[1465] This is a democracy relevant for a nation with people of diverse ethnic groups and divided along ethnic lines.

This is one of the critical and unresolved problems in Uganda's political system and structures. However, it should be addressed. In their November 2005 pastoral letter, the Catholic bishops of Uganda are very clear about

---

[1462] E. L. Henry, "Government," in *New Catholic Encyclopedia*, 2nd ed., vol. 6 (New York: Gale, 2003), 377.

[1463] Ibid.

[1464] Paul Soifer et al, *American Government* (Cleveland, Ohio: Hungry Minds, 2001), 8.

[1465] Ibid., 10.

the contentious nature of this issue and speculate that the controversy over federalism is "likely to remain so for an unforeseeable future."[1466] The federalism suggested here is not only for the Baganda or certain sections of the country. It should be one uniformly designed for the whole of Uganda and work according to the same general or national stipulations. In other words, the federalism suggested here is that which is amiable to people of the different parts of the country and helps to promote national unity.

This kind of federalism helps the promotion of even development in a country. Decentralization that has been introduced by the NRM government cannot be equated to federalism, and it does not adequately meet the needs of the different regions.[1467] Federalism suggested here should not be according to the traditional claims of the kingdom or monarch beneficiaries. It should not be equated to an instrument or a way to return to the so-called traditionally owned things—ebyafe or "our things"—which contradicts the very principle of ownership of property because nobody has absolute ownership of resources of nature. The notion of federalism presented by the Mengo government also contradicts the principles of universal charity, option for the poor, common good, justice and equity, and the principle of solidarity advocated in Populorum Progressio. To suit our purpose, federalism should be defined anew. It ought not to be seen as exclusivity as the Mengo government suggests because Uganda is one country. In any case, unity would foster participation or involvement, regional responsibility built on personal responsibility.

Federalism should not be equated to monarchies. For example, federalism understood as "the act of unity in a league by agreement of each member to subordinate its power to that of the central authority in common affairs"[1468] suffices to be a starting point from which we can build our own federal system although not without invoking the insights, support, and understanding of other nations, especially those who have already established the system and it has so far worked well. Here, we maintain our own autonomy as an independent nation to choose what suits us best as a nation. We should also not just duplicate the Western federal system but use it to help us develop our own.

[1466] Catholic Bishops of Uganda, *Towards a Democratic and Peaceful Uganda Based on the Common Good*, 3.

[1467] Anthony J. Reagan, 164ff.

[1468] *Webster's New Universal Unabridged Dictionary*, 2nd ed. (New York: Simon and Schuster, 1979), 671.

4. Affirmative Action Policies

In the context of the discussion here, what is suggested as affirmative action is an aggressive government intervention and action on behalf of those historically marginalized or discriminated against. This is a notion akin to the American vision that initiated the notion of affirmative action in the question of political democracy and social justice.[1469] The government and the religious institutions should together develop policies that help people who have been gravely marginalized or discriminated against in the past.

The care for groups that have been marginalized or oppressed in the past has to be effected, for instance, for the benefit of women, some parts of western Uganda, and northern and northeastern regions of Uganda that have experienced discrimination since the colonial times and especially in at least the last twenty years. Specific minority communities such as the Lugbara, Alur, Kakwa, Madi, Karamojong, Banyarwanda, Pokot, Basamia, the Bakonjo, and the Muslim community in Uganda should be given some preferential treatment owing to their past history of being marginalized or overlooked.[1470] They should be more adequately supported, especially economically.

The first four tribes named here are often not counted or immediately thought of when talking about northern Uganda. To many people, northern Uganda consists only of Gulu and Lira or the Acholi and the Langi. West Nile region is often excluded and only considered labor reserve as from the colonial times although it is not the only region marginalized this way.[1471] The Baganda have been, politically, viewed with great suspicion because of their privileged position and being instruments of the expansion of colonial administration in Uganda before and after independence.[1472] Politically and socially, they should also be integrated and treated without further suspicions. The affirmative action in progress, especially in relation to women and their education and involvement, should be continued with more emphasis. It should more powerfully and ceaselessly address the bad influence or effect of cultures that perpetuate discrimination against women and any disadvantaged groups.[1473]

[1469] Philip J. Chemielewski, "Affirmative Action," in *The New Dictionary of Catholic Social Thought,* ed. Judith A. Dwyer (Collegeville, Minnesota: Liturgical Press, 1994), 12.

[1470] Mugaju, 1. Also see page 15 of this work.

[1471] Leopold, 80.

[1472] Ibid., 13-14.

[1473] Bainomugisha, 89ff.

Affirmative action policies and application of the principle of the preferential option for the poor should be applied in such a way that there is room for those who are helped to exercise their abilities and not be recipients only. Government and the church have the responsibility or duty to help the poor and marginalized and to create possibilities for them to function for their well being, but the former have no obligation or duty to do everything for the latter. The citizens should also be helped to understand and acknowledge this and the fact that they have also responsibility to meet their own needs instead of waiting for handouts.

5. HEALTHY CHURCH-STATE RELATIONSHIP

This subtheme provokes the question whether the church is a political institution or trying to be one. The answer to such a question is what Sean P. Kealy suggests, "No church can completely escape a political dimension to its activities and its influence"[1474] though this is not its primary role, even if other churches have made politics their primary concern. For true development, which is integral to occur, the cooperation between the church and the state is crucial. Consequently, it demands that the relationship between the two institutions is healthy and good to promote human persons both as citizens and as people who belong to religious communities or institutions. They should have a close working relationship because they are for the promotion of the same people. This contention suggests that though distinct from one another, church and state are necessarily related and should not be radically separated. They can be separated as institutions, but not when it comes to dealing with certain individual issues affecting people. Robert Audi and Nicholas Wolterstorff suggest that the two are necessarily related because "there is no sharp distinction between moral and political issues."[1475] The suggestion is relevant because the duty of both the state and the church is to help people to live upright lives, be responsible citizens and believers. I think it is right to suggest that while the church promotes *Christian or religious morality* the state promotes *political or civil morality*. The equivalent word, which captures the notion of morality in both religious institutions and civil society, is *responsibility*. The church and state try to make and expect people to be responsible.

[1474] Sean P. Kealy, *Jesus and Politics* (Collegeville, Minnesota: The Liturgical Press, 1990), 17.

[1475] Audi and Wolterstorff, 43.

Paul Gifford states that "since Museveni's accession to power church-state relations have been of less importance."[1476] Gifford suggests that the church-state relationship has not been emphasized since 1986. While this is not a positive observation, the assertion is only theoretically correct. Practically, it is not correct because the two institutions have often, whether expressly indicated or not, demonstrated their need for each other in certain critical moments. Gifford himself noted that Museveni and some government agents were involved in resolving the crisis in the COU Diocese of Busoga and in other issues.[1477] According to Ronald Kassimir in his address to the Catholic bishops of Uganda in 1986, five months after his ascendance to power, Museveni made explicit that

> the National Resistance Movement is not opposed to the role of the churches and religion, if they can be used positively. The Movement expects the Churches to assume their rightful place in the development of nations and is indeed committed to the support and encouragement of the spiritual and moral rehabilitation of our society. This direction is exactly in consonance with the programmes of the National Resistance Movement which is concerned, among other things, with the restoration of morality and human dignity.[1478]

The initial statement Museveni made about church-state relations is a crucial one. If church-state relationship continues to evolve in this line, there are good future prospects for the joint efforts toward the development of the people of Uganda. To ignore this relationship is to divide the nation because both institutions work for the good of the same people. That the church and state are each autonomous should always be in sight of the leadership of either institution, thus maintaining the autonomy of the sphere or power of each. However, the spirit of dialogue and conversation between the two institutions is always crucial. They also need to be mutually supportive. The cooperation between church and state helps to effectively promote and achieve the common good in the different contexts of time and place.[1479] There are

---

[1476] Gifford, 122.
[1477] Ibid., 129 and 140
[1478] Kassimir, 238-239.
[1479] Ddungu, 23. Here, Ddungu refers to GS, No.76.

times the church needs the support of the state and vice versa. There are also times when the two institutions correct each other or assist one another with suggestions. If there was a reasonable relationship between the government and the MRTCG (Movement for the Restoration of the Ten Commandments of God), the March 2000 tragedy might have been avoided.[1480] Here, the proper application of the principle of subsidiarity is also vital.

It is important to note that working at odds with each other or independently, neither the church nor the state can achieve much in liberating the people of Uganda from their problems and lead them into true development. Consequently, the struggle to help develop Uganda should be done in unity and solidarity between the church and state. Ddungu has emphasized this point of view:

> The state and the church in Uganda have a *joint responsibility*, based on *common interest* and *mutual obligation* for reshaping the present and the future of this nation. The shared responsibility should promote harmonious coexistence, effective dialogue and cooperation.[1481]

Church-state relationship should be characterized by mutual understanding of the goals of both institutions and the needs of the people they serve. There should be no deliberate antagonism. Instead, there should be dialogic relationship evidenced in harmony between church and state. Ugandan heads of state should learn from the nasty experiences of church-state relationship in the history of the country; for instance, the one that led to the murder of the Anglican archbishop Luwum by Amin and the invasion of the Anglican archbishop Silvanus Wani in October 1981 by Obote's Uganda National Liberation Army (UNLA) and created tensions and animosities.[1482] There are other similar incidences of strife between civil leaders and religious leaders, but they have not been documented or may not be known. All such cases

---

[1480] Bagumisiriza, 90. Details of the tragedy that could possibly be avoided if there was close communication between government and religious leaders has already been explained earlier in this chapter. See and read under the subsection entitled *Anthropological Challenges.*

[1481] Ddungu, 24.

[1482] Gifford, 120-121

do not give a picture of love, solidarity, concern for the common good, and development of the state and religious institutions.

This issue remains crucial in the history of the relationship between the two institutions because of the radical attempt to separate church and state. The significant separation emphasized here is often the separation of powers or domains of action/function. However, one should also carefully consider the issues Mazrui raised, namely, that "it is too often taken for granted that to separate Church and State is also to separate religion and politics. In practice this conclusion is seldom sustained."[1483]

Mazrui's contention that although church and state may be separated, religion and politics have refused to be separated up to today is sound.[1484] Two questions need to be answered in order to understand Mazrui. Who constitutes the church and who constitutes the state? In many instances, those who constitute the state also constitute the church or religious institutions. If the same people constitute both institutions, though functioning in different capacities, and at the same time they have to be faithful to their commitments, how is it possible to separate religion and politics? This actually forces one to ask whether the two institutions are not for the good of those who constitute them, which indeed is why they exist.[1485] If they are for the good of people, then they are meant to procure a due good—the good they owe to people—for people who should be viewed as spiritual and material in constitution. This affirmation is not a denial that there are certain things that differ in the two institutions. It is an affirmation against a radical separation of religion and politics, church and state, which is often advocated by political leaders to secure their position when they feel threatened.

C. Balanced Socioeconomic and Political Policies

1. SELFLESS INTERESTS AND RELEVANT DEVELOPMENT INNOVATIONS

First, Uganda needs promotion of disinterested development innovations. This means development projects should be well directed according to

---

[1483] Mazrui, *Political Values and the Educated Class in Africa*, 143.
[1484] Ibid., 144.
[1485] Gerald O'Collins and Edward G. Farugia, *A Concise Dictionary of Theology*, rev. and exp. ed. (Paulist Press: New York/Mahwah, 2000) 43.

government policies that help people to understand that whatever they want to do privately or publicly is not entirely for their personal interests. The intentions of development projects should not be self-concern. Self-concern was one of the reasons for economic and political disaster in Uganda's efforts in the DRC.[1486] The reason for the failure of most projects is that as soon as they are started, everybody wants personal benefits immediately. This attitude should be discouraged through moral education. People who undermine development projects should be prosecuted for the sake of the common good even if the projects are private establishments. Government should ensure that development enterprises undertaken by foreign organizations or countries are not established for ulterior motives. The responsible people and the entire nation should also be educated about such policies. According to Denis Goulet, there is a high possibility for vested interests to dominate socioeconomic and political development because the investing nations or organizations

> correctly perceive that alternative development strategies are a threat
> to their own power, wealth, social status, and global mobility, all of
> which depend on their partnership with foreigners.[1487]

This suggests that government agents or the state should be disinterested in the way they look at private development initiatives or innovations. Government should not consider private individuals and private institutions as threats to its general control or grip of the country as long as these innovations or initiatives are not merely for personal interests; and these individuals or groups can make development innovations for themselves and the people. This question is tied to the one of the principle of subsidiarity, which permits smaller bodies to do for themselves what they are able to and prohibits larger bodies from interfering with such initiatives.

Relevant innovations must be the priority in domestic development strategies, not just idealistic innovations. Laurenti C. Magesa suggests "a distinctive African vision of development."[1488] He proposes here a vision of

---

[1486] Legget, 12.

[1487] Goulet, *Development Ethics: A Guide to Theory and Practice*, 188.

[1488] Laurenti C. Magesa, "Theology for Integral Human Development in Africa," in *Church Contribution to Integral Development,* eds. Joseph Therese Agbasiere and Boniface K. Zabajungu (Eldoret, Kenya: AMECEA Gaba Publications, 1989), 120.

development as liberation, not just some model adopted from outside. This should, according to him, be based on the understanding and cherishing of the human person, human rights, and human dignity. It is precisely in these areas that Ugandans need some form of liberation. Denis Goulet cautions about wholesale importation of development ideals or models:

> Strategies were exported from industrially advanced countries to societies where cultural, psychological, social, and political soil was uncongenial to them. Most Western agents of change were insensitive to these differences. Introducing the wage system and the commercial mentality, for example, to people who for centuries have lived on the edge of subsistence, shatters their fragile social cohesion.[1489]

Goulet rightly cautions nations as they make development strategies. It is good to make innovations or strategies according to models of foreign nations. However, what is adopted by the countries struggling to develop should be feasible. This of course demands that there should always be a team that is able to make critical feasibility studies before strategies are made, confirmed, and implemented.

2. ACTIVE PARTICIPATION OR INVOLVEMENT OF THE EXPLOITED AND OPPRESSED

Hard work is one of the significant recommendations for human development. This is well summarized in the Lugbara proverb: "Alio oraa okpo ni" or "Alio ma aroo okpo ni," translated as "The medicine of poverty is strength," which is explained as follows:

> The remedy for a state of poverty is strength, namely, strenuous work; this is the antidote that will cure poverty. The proverb suggests that hard work is also preventive medicine to avoid falling into the painful condition of poverty. By envisaging work as the genuine cure for poverty, the proverb implicitly condemns other deceptive surrogates like begging or relying on the property of others, which do not really relieve one's poverty.[1490]

[1489] Goulet, *Development Ethics: A Guide to Theory and Practice*, 184.

[1490] A. T. Dalfovo, *Lugbara Proverbs* (Rome: Comboni Missionaries, 1990), 56.

Poverty is a serious challenge to the apathy of those who think they may or should not contribute to development by every means. It is still a more serious challenge if there are people who think that they have nothing to offer. This indeed is a negative attitude, which unfortunately, many ordained ministers, religious leaders, and lay people have cultivated and maintained in both political and socioeconomic fields.[1491] Enlightened religious and civil leaders should help such people and all oppressed people to appreciate self-involvement in their developments as individuals and as groups and to discover the value of self-reliance and especially to do away with the "survival mentality."[1492]

In Uganda, lack of development is sometimes blamed on or "traced to overt colonialism, economic exploitation, racial discrimination, or less overt forms of social control."[1493] To a great extent, such blame merely serves polemical purposes. Development is possible when people are aware of their own current conditions and convince themselves that they can actually come out of such conditions using their own efforts and available resources. Therefore, all people including the disadvantaged and the poor should be educated that the evils that confront them are no longer tolerable, there is a better alternative for them, and "large numbers of oppressed people must become convinced that changes proposed to them can succeed."[1494] Such a conviction cannot be achieved from the blue. People must be taught or educated, whether formally or informally, depending on the learning and understanding capacity of the people in question. Second, as Goulet contends, "great leaders must appear at the horizon to help the weak to overcome their passivity and accept risk"[1495] although such leaders are rare.

Participation or involvement of the poor and oppressed also demands education about the value of hard work. The Lugbara proverb—"Nga bori nya bori, which means "Already done, already eaten"[1496]—says much about the value of work and should be invoked for a further understanding. It

---

[1491] Pfaff, 161.

[1492] Patrick Kutu, "The Rural Poor: Protagonists of Their Empowerment," in *The Poor Discover Their Own Resources: A Practical Approach to Poverty Reduction in Urban and Rural Areas in Africa* (Nairobi: Pauline Publications Africa, 2002), 36.

[1493] Goulet, *Development Ethics: A Guide to Theory and Practice*, 189.

[1494] Ibid., 189-190.

[1495] Ibid., 190

[1496] Dalfovo, 183.

means when a person has worked hard that person has also assured himself or herself of food and sustenance. The poor and weak should be helped to realize the importance of hard work, especially if they are capable of being productive. Therefore, it is important that the poor, weak, or handicapped people are helped to develop "positive-thinking about life and self."[1497] They ought not to develop a crippling attitude, surrender to fate, and think that they are useless and incapable of anything.

The oppressed or exploited people are those who suffer because of injustice or they are mentally or physically or materially incapacitated. Their incapacity may be no fault of theirs but due to unjust structures or sicknesses. When they have the ability to be productive it is necessary to involve them and strengthen their participation.[1498] Such involvement and participation could be through establishment of institutions. Such institutions could be organizations or associations of such people, especially when they are mentally capable or institutions established and managed with the assistance of capable people who help involve them in decision-making so that they have a say in improving their life and they can protect themselves against those who are intent on exploiting them.[1499]

3. STRONG AND HEROIC LEADERSHIP

Achieving development demands formidable leadership. Without people prepared intentionally for supervision of national, regional, local, and private development projects, the attainment of development remains a mere dream. This requirement is necessary especially at the grassroots. Goulet suggests relevant and significant qualities, which I think serve the need for Uganda to promote effective development leaders. First, development leaders should have "an intuitive grasp of the larger historical dimensions latent in local struggles."[1500] This means the leader must be aware of the explanation behind the persistent struggles of the people in the past and the present. This is a significant quality because a leader should be informed since (s)he sometimes acts as the conscience of the people. A leader determines the will of the people

---

[1497] Kutu, 34.

[1498] Nalugula and Mutua, 19.

[1499] Ibid.

[1500] Goulet, *Development Ethics: A Guide to Theory and Practice*, 190.

toward the achievement of the general good of the people.[1501] Second, a leader has "the ability to reconcile multiple class alliance."[1502] This means that a good leader has the ability to influence people across ethnic, regional, and professional categories and bring them together for positive purposes which are for the good of these different categories. This means a good leader is one who has the ability to foster universal love and solidarity. Third, a trait of a good development leader is moral and physical courage.

> Courage enables them to run risks, to persevere in the face of defeat, to reject temptations to compromise along the way, and to face death unflinchingly. At the very least, symbolic death must be faced in the form of politically suicidal decisions necessary to preserve integrity.[1503]

A true leader should be ready to make serious sacrifices so that good may be achieved not just for oneself, but for all. Frederick Drandua notes that if good is to come out of an evil situation there is need for heroic leadership.[1504] Drandua has argued that in order to change a bad status quo one should also be guided by one's conscience and remain faithful to the demands of divine law. This is one of the greatest challenges imposed upon Christians if not all believers. It is a real challenge in the sense that "heroism is sometimes called for in order to remain faithful to the requirements of the divine Law."[1505] A Nigerian proverb supports the significance of the suggestions and arguments of Goulet and Drandua. Luke Mbefo Nnamdi quotes the proverb as stating that "the possibility of losing one's life is not a sufficient reason for refusing to fight for a just cause."[1506] The trio emphasize that the virtue of courage is necessary in the efforts toward true development. They also suggest as Mbefo explicitly states that the ultimate human concern must be the care for the human person who has a God-given dignity.

[1501] Aquinas, *Summa Theologiae,* I. 6. 105, 3.

[1502] Goulet, *Development Ethics: A Guide to Theory and Practice,* 190.

[1503] Ibid.

[1504] Drandua, 14. This idea was emphasized by John Paul II in his address and message for the World Day of Peace in 1990. Also see Habiger, 8 and 13.

[1505] Ibid.

[1506] Mbefo Nnamdi, 138.

An observation is necessary here in the light of the doctrine of *Populorum Progressio*. This advocacy is not encouraging violence. It is in line with Paul VI's teaching because of its emphasis of moral courage. Just as Paul VI and Martin Luther King Jr.—the 1960s protagonists of development, love, justice, and peace were opposed to violence as a solution to face injustice—Drandua, Mbefo, and Goulet call for a pressure that is governed by Christian values or moral principles and common sense. A critical reading of their texts implies that they do not think or suggest that a good leader is violent, and violence is a moral means to achieve any objective.

The fourth quality of good development leaders is the ability to effectively and tacitly "communicate their own vision of possible success to less imaginative or less experienced masses," and the final quality of a good leader "is the ability to learn quickly from their mistakes."[1507] A good leader for development should be capable of articulating his/her ideas and plans in an intelligible fashion and should be quick to realize or discover why mistakes happened in the past and what should be done to rectify or avoid them.

4. Innovations that Aim Higher

Uganda has had some poverty reduction goals, especially from around the year 2000 or a little earlier. For instance, reduction of the under-five mortality rate, universal primary education, reduction of the rate of infection in human immunodeficiency virus /acquired immunodeficiency syndrome (HIV/AIDS), and the reduction of fertility or births, but so far the results are not conspicuous.[1508] In Uganda, asset development policies for the nationals, with greater emphasis upon the poor, is necessary for any development. In particular, it is more important for integral development in a context such as that of Uganda where development is absolutely fragmented; there are critical economic differences between people. As James P. Bailey infers from the teaching of Leo XIII, this is the way for closing the gap between the rich and the poor.[1509] The poor should be helped to save money and to build assets. The significance of this suggestion is compounded by Bailey's assertion that

---

[1507] Goulet, *Development Ethics: A Guide to Theory and Practice*, 190-191.

[1508] World Bank, *World Development Report, 1994: Attacking Poverty*, 22.

[1509] Bailey, 67.

> income-based approaches to poverty reduction help address
> the injustice of economic arrangements, but they need to be
> complemented by asset-development policies that help give the
> poor greater access to the economy and greater control over
> their lives.[1510]

Development demands that capital is derived from income, but it also demands that part of the income is saved for future development or any eventualities. It is for this reason that Bailey's suggestion that a combination of both asset-based and an income-based approaches to the problem of poverty are more preferable and in line with Christian ethics than the exclusive use or application of an income-based approach to the problem. Any strategies or policies that the government or any development institution attempts to make for uplifting the condition of the poor should consider this suggestion seriously. The suggestion provides two alternative options to be applied jointly although the asset-based approach is more reliable because of enduring results and advantages and the possibilities it offers, especially in moments of economic upheaval.[1511]

The government should, therefore, employ and engage experts to develop and articulate policies that facilitate the savings and asset development of the poor people. Assets are valuable things owned by a person or group of people or business, namely, the resources such as cash, machinery, equipment, and estate as opposed to one's income that is used for the daily running of affairs.[1512] The policies would particularly help people who live on resources from hand to mouth and perpetually lack the basic necessities of making livelihood. This is the main problem confronting the majority of Ugandans. For instance, in 1993, 55 percent of the Ugandan population lived below the poverty line; and in 1992, about 36.7 percent of them had lived on an income below US $1 a day, and 77.2 percent were below an income of US $2 a day.[1513] It is difficult to envision how people in a situation of poverty would save money or purchase and develop assets on their own, especially in a situation as in Uganda, where the majority of people are not well educated. However, some authors suggest that with support and incentives from institutions, such as the state and other organizations, there is a possibility for the poor people

---

[1510] Ibid., 52.

[1511] Ibid., 57-58.

[1512] *Webster's New Universal Unabridged Dictionary*, 112.

[1513] World Bank, *World Development Report, 199: Attacking Poverty*, 281.

to "substantially increase their savings."[1514] While it is true that the state is instrumental for people's development, the development of people should be based on individuals and smaller groups. This is also in line with the development principle of subsidiarity. The grassroots growth, however, ought to move toward including a larger number of people.

Denis Goulet's suggestion that there should be transition from micro to macro arenas of action strongly supports the idea that development is a progressive process:

> Grassroots movements must not become mere havens for disenchanted anti-modernists, a kind of parallel counter-culture, and no matter how self-sufficient or viable. On the contrary their goal is to serve as an alternative development paradigm for the entire nation, to lead it into a new way of being modern, one which safeguards national culture and traditional values.[1515]

5. POPULATION POLICIES

The rate of development of a country partly depends on the number of people who constitute it. The governments of Uganda have not been consistent in following demographic changes even from the time of colonial administration.[1516] Negligence about population growth is sometimes counterproductive to any socioeconomic and political planning and development because development processes or people's needs cannot be monitored well.

From the moral standpoint, the church has the duty to address the population and family issues, at least in a pastoral letter and articulate clearly the stance of the church as she has done on several other social issues. The Uganda Catholic bishops should, therefore, emulate examples offered in history regarding population and family issues. Historically, from Pius XII to John Paul II, popes have "stepped into the picture of family planning and population control."[1517] The religious leadership in Uganda should help

---

[1514] Bailey, 52.

[1515] Goulet, *Development Ethics: A Guide to Theory and Practice*, 192.

[1516] Kirumira, 185

[1517] Herbert F. Smith, "The Proliferation of Population Problems," in *Why Humanae Vitae Was Right: A Reader*, ed. Janet E. Smith (San Francisco: Ignatius press, 1993), 399.

the government, in conjunction or consultation with religious leaders and educational institutions, not to attempt to stipulate radical demographic policies. As Herbert F. Smith proposes, the recommendation offered by John Paul II urging the "the development and the teaching of NFP" (Natural Family Planning) in his apostolic exortation on the family, and inviting "married couples, doctors and experts"[1518] to help in instructing all married people and young adults, before marriage, should be seriously considered. A frequent or constant oversight in demographic changes, the reasons for the variation and facilitating the knowledge of the government, the church, and people and assessment of their condition and planning for the promotion of a dignified life for the people of Uganda are necessary priorities in demographic matters.

One of the challenges for the government and the church or religious institutions in Uganda, and the citizens, is the question of opposing views about population as suggested by Edward K. Kirumira:

> It is worth noting that the population debate in Uganda is also peculiar in that, much as the emphasis may be placed on the stand of the churches, for example, it is virtually impossible to characterize opposing views. The churches, government and public opinion are equally likely to adopt pro-natalist as anti-natalist positions.[1519]

This is a pertinent problem that needs to be resolved because of the differences in the stance about population growth—the prolife group and the antilife group. The former is the position the churches ought to maintain. The Catholic Church is clear on this and stands for life, and this position endures until today. The validity of the position is in the fact and value of human life and human dignity. Life is the greatest gift of God to be protected and nourished. It would also be logically correct to recommend that the Catholic Church, in particular, should help the government to understand and adopt the same position because every government has the duty to create conditions that favor the flourishing of its citizens. Creating conditions that protect life should be the priority of Ugandan government. This is what the churches or religious institutions should foster in their various communities. Like the government, they are to safeguard people—created in the image of God with

---

[1518] Ibid., 399-400. Here Smith makes reference to John Paul II, *On the Family* (Washington DC, United States Catholic Conference, 1981), 30-31.

[1519] Kirumira, 188.

both biological and spiritual values—and help create conditions that promote the God-given dignity of people in their care.[1520]

Population explosion is one of the main problems hindering human development. It was also one of the concerns of Paul VI in *Populorum Progressio*. His concern, as presented in chapter one, was the rapid demographic growth; but principally, it was human dignity.[1521] This concern developed out of Paul VI's historical experiences in the less developed countries or world—namely, Asia, Africa and Latin America. These parts of the world had similar concerns. The experiences and concerns testify that rapid population growth in low income countries is a serious issue in human development. This experience is more evident in the majority of large-sized families in the rural areas.[1522] It does not only hinder human development, it also causes human suffering. Overpopulation is a serious problem that affects the well-being of the human person.

> The experience of the past decade offers convincing evidence that if low income countries are to develop rapidly they must avoid or extricate themselves from the "population trap," by which we mean rates of increase in population growth so large that they approach the feasible rates of increase in economic output, thus preventing significant growth in per capita output.[1523]

The rate of population increase should not out-pace the ability to comfortably maintain the population. The Committee for Economic Development was definitely not making suggestions for population control from a religious perspective. The concern of committee about population growth is growth in the per capita output of the nation, "yet human resources are the key to unlocking all resources,"[1524] as Smith suggests. In other words, production is not possible without human labor. Our concern here is the maintenance and enhancement of human dignity and the human person.

[1520] Dietrich von Hilderbrand, *The Encyclical Humanae Vitae: A Sign of Contradiction, an Essay on Birth Control and Catholic Conscience* (Chicago: Franciscan Press, 1969), 45.

[1521] *Populorum Progressio*, 37, 16.

[1522] Kutu, 31.

[1523] Committee for Economic Development, 30.

[1524] Smith, 397.

However, the committee's contention should not be considered just from a secularist point of view. The suggestion has in view the dignity of the human person and the value of human life. This assertion is better explained by the contention of Dietrich von Hilderbrand, which suggests the divine intention with regard to procreation and demographic growth. He believes that, when necessary or if there is a compelling reason to avoid conception, it can only be by means of natural birth control:

> It is clear, therefore, that in the intention itself of avoiding another child for serious reasons there is not a trace of irreverence toward the mysterious fact that God has entrusted the birth of a person to the spousal love. We see that only during relatively brief intervals has God himself linked the conjugal act to the creation of a man . . . . The fact that conception is restricted to a short time implies a word of God. It not only confirms that the bodily union of the spouses has a meaning and value in itself, apart from procreation, but it also leaves open the possibility of avoiding conception if this is desirable for serious reasons.[1525]

Hilderbrand is apparently suggesting that life may not be brought into the world to experience or cause needless suffering. His suggestion, however, has to be taken with caution. There is possibility of making every reason to control birth a serious one. This is where the church or religious leadership of Uganda ought to intervene as a conscience of the nation to define or outline the serious reasons in a pastoral letter, as suggested earlier in this section. They should make it abundantly clear that the aim of family planning is to help parents to "rear their families in dignity and happiness,"[1526] as suggested by Mother Teresa.

Most of Uganda may not yet be overpopulated in the real sense, but some parts are experiencing demographic explosion. Kigezi is one of the regions consistently affected by population growth since the colonial times. This was a consequence of the over-propagation of children, the immigration of people from Rwanda due to famine, and the encouragement from the chiefs, whose

---

[1525] Hildebrand, 47.

[1526] Mother Teresa, "Planning Something Beautiful for God," in *Natural Family Planning: Nature's Way-God's Way,* eds. Anthony Zimmerman et al. (St. Cloud, Minnesota: De Rance Inc., 1980), 2.

salaries depended on the number of people under their jurisdiction at that time.[1527] This has resulted in land shortage in Kigezi or the Kabale region in southwestern Uganda, where some people are migrating to neighboring areas, which are less densely populated. As early as 1946, some of the people from the Kigezi region settled in Ankole after negotiations and agreements with the chiefs in the latter region.[1528] As the population continued to grow in Kigezi, further negotiations were made with the leadership in Toro; and some of the people of Kigezi moved to Toro, and even until recently, they have been migrating to Toro.[1529] It is good to take precautions before the situation worsens, but the measures taken should conform to moral values, not just economic values, as suggested by the Committee for Economic Development in the following passage:

> So long as unrestricted population growth continues, resources that might otherwise be available for investment will have to be used for current consumption. The expanded outlays for food and for basic health services will limit the resources available for education and for improving skills . . . . Clearly, the fundamental purpose of economic development—to raise living standards and broaden man's opportunities for a more enriched life—is being put in jeopardy.[1530]

The concerns of the committee are real, but they lack balance of emphasis. The critical issue addressed by the committee is that unrestricted population growth does not allow investment because the immediate daily needs of people ought to be satisfied. This concern is related to the question of asset development treated earlier in this chapter. When material resources are limited, provision for education and eventually improvement of skills are also affected. Consequently, development is also affected because improved skills, which are actually acquired through education, are lacking, and there are no savings or assets for further development. The validity of this assertion is founded on the fact that family expenditure is always proportionate to

---

[1527] Paul Ngologoza, *Kigezi and Its People* (Kampala: Fountain Publishers, 1998), 76-77.

[1528] Ibid., 96.

[1529] Ibid., 97.

[1530] Committee for Economic Development, 30-31.

the size of the family. The more people there are in a family, the higher the expenses and vice versa. It is right to conclude from this assertion that "large family size tends to increase poverty over the generations."[1531] This is one fundamental fact about which population-study and religious institutions should inform the government and educate the masses. It is encouraging to know that government has taken keen interest in issues of population increase and quality.[1532] However, in a context like that of Uganda, which is affected by the AIDS pandemic, restricted population—just from a secular, not moral point of view—affects labor force negatively. AIDS needs to be checked because the "size and quality of labour force"[1533] are particularly affected by it. The government concern and interest in population issues should yield a dignified life of the population of Uganda. It ought to be in a manner that promotes both moral and material development of individuals and of the nation.

The question of population has often been controversial in Uganda because of ethnicity and religion.[1534] The church leaders in Uganda should through the populace, ensure that the government does not exploit the controversy for political purposes. It should explain the real significance of censuses, namely, for integral development planning and human promotion. It is significant to emphasize here that church institutions, especially the Catholic Church, should ensure that addressing the question of population does not undermine the fundamental principle of human dignity. Human dignity and innocent human life should always be protected by any laws of Uganda. Uganda should not be developed materially at the expense of human life, human dignity, and morality.

The church or religious institutions ought to be and have the challenge to be informed of the demographic issues of Uganda. They also have the duty to disseminate such information and their judgement and recommendations about such knowledge to the masses. They should regularly and squarely confront national population problems. This is necessary because radical

---

[1531] Ministry of Finance and Economic Development, 132.

[1532] Ibid.

[1533] Maryinez Lyons, "Aids and Development in Uganda," in *Developing Uganda*, eds. Holger Bernt Hansen and Michael Twaddle (Kampala: Fountain Publishers, 1998), 199.

[1534] Kirumira, 187.

secular solutions may be suggested in the name of human development. The Committee for Economic Development, for instance, suggested that

> to meet the population problem effectively, programs of family planning must play a part. Parents should have access to family planning information services. Such access is not merely indispensable to producing desired results with respect to economic development but is consistent with human dignity and the right of men and women everywhere to be aware of the problem and contribute to its solution.[1535]

Though seemingly relevant, the type of family planning advocated by the committee is not specific, while from a Catholic perspective, the recommended method is Natural Family Planning (NFP). The main concern in family planning should be about the rural population which constitutes the majority of Uganda's population. About 86 to 89 percent of Uganda's population lives in the countryside.[1536] Of this percentage, the majority are young people, less educated, and who marry when they are not prepared for marriage and the implications of family life. The countryside is where the church or religious institutions should intervene aggressively to stipulate and explain relevant population and family planning procedures. The guidelines should, however, be morally justifiable or desirable. It is for this reason that the church in Uganda, especially the Catholic Church, should spearhead this endeavor of addressing demographic issues and articulate its position regarding family planning clearly in the course of this endeavor. The following reminders are of grave importance:

First, Uganda's Poverty Eradication policy states that "family size is an individual choice,"[1537] but people need to be helped to make choices responsibly and morally, and they should be assured of a minimized infant mortality rate. Second, as Anthony Zimmerman states, while we may not and "we do not sit in judgement on which family is better or more heroic," it ought to be made abundantly clear that "in regard to family size couples are

---

[1535] Committee for Economic Development, 31.
[1536] Kirumira, 185.
[1537] Ministry of Finance, Planning, and Economic Development, 132.

not subject to arbitrary government interference."[1538] Parents should propagate children according to the possibilities of caring for them. As Zimmerman further suggests, "When parents omit family planning and accept children as they come, they act laudably so long as this is within the bounds of prudent human foresight."[1539] This assertion is reasonable and does not contradict the position of the Holy See.

Third, the *responsible parenthood* recommended by Paul VI in *Humanae Vitae*—which, among other elements of responsible parenthood, suggests that parents should propagate children knowing that they will be taken care of—should be seriously considered.[1540] It is immoral and against human dignity to propagate life that is subjected to suffering or dehumanizing living conditions.

Finally, Uganda has so far been blessed to a great extent with regard to population issues. Michael Twaddle and Holger Bernt Hansen correctly state that "successive governments have been keen not to antagonize religious groups, especially the Catholic Church with regard to methods of population control and prevention of AIDS.[1541] Catholics, as well as Protestants, should maintain their stance on population policies and keep developing deeper and convincing explanations and the underpinning reasons for their explanations and stance. Consequently, it is important that Catholics and Catholic leadership and institutions, in particular, maintain and articulate the Catholic position, which Matthew Habiger quotes from Archbishop Renato R. Martino:

> The position of the Holy See regarding procreation is frequently misinterpreted. The Catholic Church does not propose procreation at any cost. It keeps on insisting that the transmission of, and the caring for human life must be exercised with an utmost sense of responsibility. It restates its constant position that human life is sacred; that the aim of public policy is to enhance the welfare of families; that it is the right of the spouses to decide on the size of the

---

[1538] Anthony, Zimmerman, (The Coodinator), "Large families, Child-Spacing, and When to Start NFP," in *Natural Family Planning: Nature's Way-God's Way*, eds. Anthony Zimmerman et al. (St. Cloud, Minnesota: De Rance, Inc. 1980), 77.

[1539] Ibid.

[1540] Paul VI, *Humanae Vitae: On the Regulation of Birth* (Rome, 1968), 10, 6-7.

[1541] Holger Bernt Hansen and Michael Twaddle, 13.

family and spacing of births, without pressures from governments or organizations. This decision must fully respect the moral order established by God, taking into account the couples responsibilities toward each other, the children they already have and society to which they belong. What the Church opposes is the imposition of demographic policies and the promotion of limiting births which are contrary to the objective moral order and to the liberty, dignity and conscience of the human being.[1542]

6. UGANDA'S INTERNATIONAL REPUTATION

The United Nations Universal Declaration of Human Rights as a charter to be followed by all nations, including Uganda, which is a member of the United Nations, is one thing that comes to mind when thinking of international laws. What the UN advocates in its charter is conspicuously present in the 1995 Constitution of the Republic of Uganda.[1543] What Uganda has incorporated from the UN should not just remain theoretical. It needs to be studied again and again by the citizens through both formal and informal education. By virtue of being a member of the international family, it is suggested that Uganda needs to ensure that its citizens are duly educated about their rights, and this is an essential aspect of the education of the citizens in and out of schools. They should have a distinctive vision of human dignity and know and understand human rights and civil rights and any other freedoms.[1544] These should always be explained and understood in a social context as well as the context of an individual based on human dignity as the principal and commonly shared foundation.

The government should always ensure that there is "respect for international law."[1545] This contention is significant in the context of integral human development. Development cannot be achieved in isolation. No person or nation is self-sufficient as Lebret observed, according to George Higgins's reading of the former, as stated in chapter one of this work. The respect for

---

[1542] Habiger, 7. Matthew Habiger, verbatim, quotes Archbishop Renato R. Martino, Apostolic Nuncio, Head of the Holy See Delegation to the United Nations Conference on Enviroment and Development, Rio de Janeiro, 1992.

[1543] Government of Uganda, 20-39.

[1544] Magesa, 120.

[1545] Kiapi, 81

international law is a mutual demand on nations. Uganda is not an exception if it is to develop with the help or support and cooperation of other countries. This call is particularly important with regard to Uganda's relationship with her immediate neighbors. While the government of Uganda has the duty to protect the citizens of the country from external aggression, it should not invade neighbors or other nations for selfish economic and political interests under the guise of protecting the people of Uganda. This is clearly stipulated in the 1995 constitution, and it should be respected.[1546] It ought always to be kept in mind that both domestic stability and the stability of the global community depend on the spirit of universal charity, mutual respect, and a serious consideration for international law because "events in one country can affect other nations or even the whole world."[1547]

One factor that guarantees national dignity and good reputation in the global context is peaceful or amicable coexistence of a nation with its neighbors and other nations. Amaza Ori Ondoga, a deceased staunch NRM propagandist, contends that Uganda's relationship with the neighboring countries was stormy before 1986.[1548] He did not categorically state the fact that thereafter its relationship with the neighboring countries continued to be sour until today. For instance, Uganda is the context in which the RPF invasion of Rwanda in 1990 can be better understood.[1549]

Uganda has had a series of wars that have drained its meager resources and cost her lots of lives. This is a trait of the nation since independence with just a few interludes of quiet periods in its history. Another evidence that remains a challenge and contradicts or refutes Amaza Ori Ondoga's implication that after 1986 Uganda had good relations with other countries or its neighbors is what has recently been cited by AMSRIU in their strong statement:

> According to the verdict of the International Court of Justice (ICJ), the UPDF committed in the Democratic Republic of Congo (DRC) horrendous inhuman acts of torture and killings, incited ethnic conflict, trained child soldiers and looted the Congo to the

---

[1546] Government of Uganda, xxiii(i)b-c

[1547] Kiapi, 81.

[1548] Ondoga, 169.

[1549] Mahmood Mamdani, *When Victims Become Killers: Colonialism, Nativism, and the Genocide in Rwanda* (Princeton, New Jersey: Princeton University Press, 2001), 159.

tune of 10 billion dollars. This debacle has ruined the reputation of our country and has brought enormous shame to the whole nation! The government is answerable to all this.[1550]

Uganda should work hard and maintain a status that befits a nation that claims to be developed or developing. Uganda ought to become conscientious about the human person, human life, human rights, and human dignity regardless of sex, age, state of health, ethnicity, nationality and social, religious and political affiliation, and status. For instance, the provision of material support to the RPF to return to Rwanda without coming back to Uganda was near to, if not an active participation in, the invasion of Rwanda.[1551] Above all, it never took into consideration the dignity and the value of the lives of those who would eventually suffer. It was an undignified support. Peaceful coexistence with neighbors ought to be taken seriously. This issue has been repeatedly emphasized by the Catholic bishops of Uganda in many of their pastoral letters but especially in the 1986 letter, *With a New Heart and a New Spirit.*[1552]

The tendency to be at war with neighboring countries has colored especially the reign of Idi Amin and the NRM government.[1553] This tendency should stop, and Uganda should radically change its foreign policy of fighting in order to secure resources for the country or certain individuals and provide peace for the neighbors and its citizens instead of fear and unrest. Peace would also provide both the opportunity to get to work and to develop. The sum total of our being created in the divine image and not to be used as objects should be maintained in our international relationship. Neither should we use other nations and peoples and their resources for our selfish interests as it; unfortunately, it happened in the DRC where, according to George B. N. Ayittey,

> President Museveni himself, together with the presidents of Rwanda and Burundi, were directly accused by a United Nations panel of

---

[1550] The Executive, Association of the Major Superiors of Religious Institutes in Uganda, 7.

[1551] Mahmood Mamdani, *When Victims Become Killers: Colonialism, Nativism, and the Genocide in Rwanda,* 183-184.

[1552] Catholic Bishops of Uganda, *With A New Heart and A New Spirit,* 21-25.

[1553] Ayittey, *Africa Unchained: The Blue Print for Africa's Future,* 205, 207.

taking advantage of the civil war in the Democratic Republic of Congo and engaging in systematic plunder of the country's mineral resources. The United Nations Panel of Experts on the Illegal Exploitation of Natural Resources and Other Forms of Wealth of Congo . . . found "mass scale looting" of stockpiled minerals, coffee, timber, livestock, and money by the armies of Rwanda, Uganda and Burundi. Military and government officials then exported the diamonds, gold, and a composite mineral called coltan to line their own pockets and enrich a network of shell companies owned by well-connected associates.[1554]

The same report continued to show how these countries had increased exports in minerals, which they had in little deposits or they were not known to be producers of prior to the civil war. For instance coltan, niobium, and diamond, which Uganda does not have, were being exported by Uganda. Policies for international relations should be clearly articulated and provide for a sincere and uncompromised autonomy of the nation and its neighbors. Any foreign policies that are costly to domestic policies in terms of affecting the development of the people of Uganda should not be encouraged or executed.

The 1995 Constitution of the Republic of Uganda suggested that in terms of international relationships, Uganda would promote "the national interests of Uganda."[1555] I would like to strongly suggest here that the national interest should not be liberally interpreted to mean the invasion of other nations and designed to ransack or deplete their economic resources to enrich Uganda or a few individual Ugandans.[1556] This is a violation of the right to own private property, it is injustice and uncharitable. The national interest proposed here should be understood to be selfless national interest.

A dignified nation respects, promotes, and protects the rights of its citizens and resident aliens, not just the personal interest of a few individuals. This picture is partly reflected through the political processes at home. A country where there is coup d'etat occurring with alarming frequency, where leaders cannot relinquish power without physical or armed force, where foreign nationals rush out of the country before or during elections, and elections

---

[1554] Ayittey, *Africa Unchained: The Blue Print for Africa's Future*, 209-210.

[1555] Government of Uganda, 9.

[1556] Leggett, 12. Also see The Executive AMSRIU in *Arua Diocese Bulletin*, 7.

are rigged, where the legal system is broken and losers cannot concede their defeat with dignity and must escape to the bush to begin again the vicious circle, is not dignified at all. This is one area where concerned Ugandans are always apprehensive before, during, and after elections.[1557] This is not the type of nation anyone would like to be part of. Neither can it be respected internationally nor represent the dignity of a true nation.

D. Relevant and Sound Religious Policies

Religion is perhaps the most fundamental element or aspect of education contributing toward integral human development because the climax or fulfillment of integral development is realized in the religious dimension and life of the human person. Religion contributes greatly to the moral fibre of society.[1558] Its contributions need to be positively effective to achieve complete human progress. For this reason, I concur with Bujo who points out what he thinks John S. Mbiti rightly observes, namely that

> religious beliefs, values, rituals and practices are directed towards strengthening the moral life of each society. Morals are the food and drink which keep society alive, healthy and happy. Once there is a moral breakdown, the whole integrity of society also breaks down and the end is tragic. (The last point does not apply to Africa alone) This is why communities in Africa are very much interested in the individual ethical conduct. And the individual's growth in wisdom depends on the ethical health of the community as a whole.[1559]

1. INTERDENOMINATIONAL COOPERATIVE ACTION

Uganda's religious institutions need a more genuine faith, love, and cooperation. They also need sincerity, honesty, transparency, and less time-wasting in the name of diplomacy, which easily ends in lies and flattery. The good

---

[1557] Catholic Bishops of Uganda, *Towards a Democratic and Peaceful Uganda Based on the Common Good*, 11.

[1558] Catholic Bishops of Uganda, *With a New Heart and a New Spirit*, 41.

[1559] Benezet Bujo, *Foundations of an African Ethic: Beyond the Universal Claims of Western Morality*, 156. Bujo is quoting John S. Mbiti, *Introduction to African Religion*, 2nd ed. (Nairobi/Kampala, 1996), 70-71.

example, which religious leaders set is crucial for the different denominations and the rest of the nation. Such cooperative actions are already in progress in the Uganda Joint Christian Council (UJCC), which is important in the follow-up of political processes in Uganda and should be encouraged to continue its work.[1560] However, such cooperation needs to be extended to other spheres of human life and activity and should include more people than so far accommodated. In other words, a more broad-based cooperation is suggested here.

Any cooperative action demands some tolerance between the different denominations too. I would like to adopt the three levels of tolerance suggested by Bernard Haring and Valentino Salvoldi. These are "the personal sphere, the micro-social sphere and the macro-social sphere"[1561] of tolerance. By the personal sphere, they affirm that one should first be able to forgive oneself before pardoning other people. Second, one should be able to tolerate those with whom one relates closely or intimately on the level of the smallest groups such as family. It is precisely this ability one translates into larger social relations. Finally, by macrosocial sphere, they suggest that one should be able to tolerate or forgive people who are furthest in terms of social and blood relation and interaction—those in the larger social setting or sphere such as people of other tribes, races, sociopolitical and religious ideologies, and nationalities.

2. LEADERSHIP FORMATION AND PROMOTION

Leadership formation referred to here is both religious leadership and civil leadership. The Catholic Church can be commended for the formation of her religious leadership in the country—no church in Uganda matches her efforts in this regard. The Anglican Church or, in general, Protestant churches in Uganda are to be praised for being aggressive in the preparation of civil leaders—a real challenge to the Catholic Church.[1562] The Catholic Church needs to do much more in this regard and learn more from the Protestant counterparts. While the Catholic Church has the means and ability to educate people—and actually excels in this regard, de facto numerically and otherwise—inferior Protestants unquestionably tower over Catholics in the political arena of Uganda. The Catholics and Muslims ought to question their own planning for preparing leaders in the future.

[1560] Catholic Bishops of Uganda, *Towards a Democratic and Peaceful Uganda Based on the Common Good*, 6.

[1561] Haring and Salvoldi, 6-7.

[1562] Gifford, 117.

There is no doubt the Catholic Church has done a lot in the field of education, but we need to ask if this has been done with very specific intentions and orientations, especially in preparing people for the crucial areas of economics, civil service, and politics. The religious preparation of leadership has, no doubt, been well done though not without flaws. For instance, good planning for the aggiornamento, especially of priests as recommended by the Catholic Church law and of religious and other crucial pastoral agents and church employees has often not been well implemented.[1563]

The Second Vatican Council suggests differences in the formation in the Catholic seminaries—both minor and major—religious institutions, and universities according to the levels or ages and circumstances. However, formation should help students to be more aggressive in combating the harsh situations of poverty, injustice, and any situations of immorality. The conciliar fathers were explicit concerning seminary formation that it ought to be a pastoral oriented formation but also a comprehensive training where all elements of seminary formation—spiritual, intellectual, and disciplinary— "should be coordinated with this pastoral aim in view."[1564] The Uganda Martyrs University was established for such a purpose and should be commended for what it is doing, but other institutions should emulate this example as well.

The curriculum designed and followed in religious institutions should help them prepare to face difficulties and to live decently and help them to understand that this is demanding in terms of preparation and their personal input. The *imperative value* to be strongly inculcated in all participants in educational or formation programs should be the *value and dignity of work* and of the *value of the human person*. This contention points to the suggestion that there is an inevitable need for an integral education of the candidates to priesthood and religious life because their impending future ministry is the service of people, and this demands a spirit of hard work and an appreciation of the human persons they encounter is various sorts of problems.

In this vein, the Second Vatican Council fathers were explicit that students preparing for priesthood should be helped to cultivate openness of "their

---

[1563] The Canon Law Society of Britain and Ireland, *The Code of Canon Law in English Translation* (London: Collins Liturgical Publications, 1983), Canon 384, 68-69.

[1564] Austin Flannery, ed., "*Optatan Totius*: Decree on the Training of Priests," in *Vatican Council II: The Conciliar and Postconciliar Documents* (Leominister, Herefords, England: Costello Publishing Company, 1981), 4,711.

hearts in a spirit of charity to various needs of fellow men."[1565] The ability to freely accept to do humanly undesirable physical work should, therefore, be one of the main conditions for promoting a student intending to be a priest or religious, not just excellent theoretical academic performance. The fundamental reason for the emphasis on the value of work is that the majority of people are apparently addicted to free handouts. Ronald Kassimir has rightly observed this of the Catholic Church:

> The relative wealth of the Church, enhanced greatly by its access to international Catholic donor community, has led to dependence on transnational Catholic networks, and to patronage relations with the laity that are not conducive to mobilization.[1566]

Formation programs ought to help candidates to be self-reliant and to prepare a leadership that is not patronizing to the people it serves. This is the grave mistake of the past still being perpetuated. Many also think that education is only for those doing white—collar jobs. This indeed is one of the critical challenges to white-collar-job seekers, perpetual dependents, bishops or religious leaders and superiors of dioceses, and congregations in terms of attitude and the requisite formation for pastoral agents.[1567]

Continued teaching of practical subjects or sciences should be encouraged as part of leadership preparation, even in seminaries and formation houses of religious and other pastoral agents, not just studies in humanities. A more all-round formation than what we have today is necessary for the formation

---

[1565] Ibid., 19, 722. The fathers are quoting Paul VI, encycal letter *Ecclesiam suam*: AAS 56 (1964), *passim*, especially pages 635f and 640ff.

[1566] Kassimir, 237.

[1567] The real problem here is that pastoral agents—catechists as well as priests—and members of religious communities or institutes of consecrated life come out of formation house expecting that everything they need will automatically be provided by whoever their superiors are. In a situation like in Uganda, at least in the majority of the dioceses, entertaining such thoughts is a dream and really utopian because of the financial conditions. The question to which every person should find an answer and work to realize the answer is, what can I do to help myself and the religious institution or others?—not, what can others or the religious institution do to help me? Or not, who can do something to help me? This last question is of a desperate person and at the same time undignified in relation to a normal human person.

of future leadership in the church and the civil society. Good leadership needed by the church and society today does not just consist in humility and charity. Charity should help people to relentlessly pursue the cause of justice, respect for the dignity and rights of people, peace, reconciliation, option for the poor, and affirmative action. Many examples from the scriptures suggest how Christ either changed values or invigorated them and overturned the undesirable situations of his time aggressively.[1568] The leadership of people today should do likewise.

Catholics and Muslims in Uganda have lagged behind for a long time. This is not necessarily because they—especially Catholics—are incapable, but because there was not critical planning on their part. It is appropriate and right to suggest that Catholics and Muslims and other religions that are in this category in Uganda have to try to live up to this challenge while their Protestant counterparts who have done much better in this regard should continue with the same spirit. However, all groups other than Catholics need to do much more to improve their formation of religious leadership because they are far-behind Catholics.

3. Effective Basic Religious Communities: Relevant Ongoing Catechesis

Small Christian or religious communities provide an ideal opportunity for easy interaction, for practical living of faith and for sharing experiences— joys and sorrows—and for mutual encouragement. Historically, they have played a significant role in the life of the church, especially in proclaiming and developing love of God and mutual love of people.[1569] Therefore, they can provide an avenue for the promotion of integral development of people. Consequently, I suggest here basic religious communities, not only basic Christian communities, because it would be good if all religious institutions organize themselves in small groups too. It is African and easier for people to interact freely and act more responsibly in their small groups. This kind of organization leads to an easy possibility for practical action. Small Christian communities have been and are fundamental pillars of the church.[1570] The idea of small/basic Christian communities was first initiated in the early church

---

[1568] See Mt. 5:17-20; 38-48 and Lk 6:27-36; 10:34-36; 12:49-53.

[1569] Thomas A. Kleissler et al., *Small Christian Communities: A Vision of Hope for the 21st Century* (New York: Paulist Press, 1997), 7.

[1570] Catholic Bishops of Uganda, *With a New Heart and a New Spirit*, 51.

in the Acts of the Apostles, but it was activated in East Africa in 1976 by the AMECEA bishops, and it was to be considered a priority.[1571] However, it needs to be more emphasized in the current situation of the Catholic Church in Uganda because not every diocese and religious institution in Uganda has effectively established such communities as required. Neither has it remained a priority in every diocese. If it does, its effectiveness needs to be emphasized in every local situation.

A strong community and development foundation depends on strong basic communities or individuals.[1572] As part of their ongoing formation program, church leaders or religious institutions should incorporate the social teachings of religious institutions, emphasize the notion of authentic human development, and encourage people to study the social teachings of the church. The social teachings of the of Catholic Church treat a diversity of themes critical to social, economic, political, and cultural matters—all of which affect people directly. The people should be informed of these issues. These should no longer be down played as Peter Henriot and others suggest.[1573] They should be part and parcel of evangelization and ongoing catechesis.

Small Christian communities are ideal places for educating people and for helping them to implement their education. Churches or religious institutions should use these small communities to inculcate religious values and the requisite ideas for true human development. Significant themes already treated, e.g., population policies, democracy, tolerance, the value of the human person, human dignity, human rights, and all necessary principles for human development should be taught to members of the SCCs/ BCCs. This is the way to empower them and to make them to realize that they are spiritually, economically, socially, culturally and politically effective instruments, and above all, invaluable for the promotion of general human society.

4. Family and Parental Involvement and Participation

The family is a significant basic institution; good parents and good family provide good foundation for the education of children and their eventual

---

[1571] Ibid., 50.

[1572] Kleissler, 8.

[1573] Peter J. Henriot et al., eds., *Catholic Social Teaching: Our Best Kept Secret* (Maryknoll, New York: Orbis Books, 1988), 3.

personality development.[1574] Family is where love and peace begin and are nourished. Developed people and families contribute to personal and general human development. The family, also a foundation for small Christian or religious communities, is "an intimate communion of life and love"[1575] and hence fundamental for human development. This is an issue parents ought to consider carefully. However, education is not one moment of achievement, nor is it a responsibility of one person or a few groups of people. As a point of reflection for all, not only West Nile, it is worth pondering on Mark Leopold's suggestion that "Amin was at least as much a creation of West Nile's past as he was a shaper of its future."[1576] His past upbringing affected his life and the future of West Nile. Precisely, the life of one person affects others and their future too. Hence, education of one person affects other people too and is the responsibility of all in the society to ensure that people are offered moral education.

Education involves as many people as can provide for a needed education. A comprehensive education involves parents, teachers, and religious agents. Precisely, it involves parents, the church, government, and society.[1577] Such education should above all emphasize moral values and the significance of hard work in human life as a dignified activity or an activity that promotes the dignity of the human person. This means any institution or nation needs a coordinated education system. It demands cooperation from leaders at different settings, spheres, and levels.

Parents, teachers, and the church's pastoral agents and community need to cooperate in the education of young people as suggested by the conciliar fathers.[1578] They should do so through collaboration in various ways, not independently. They should promote mutual exchange of information about the children's behavior. They should sincerely share their personal experiences and knowledge of the children so that at every moment and stage of their life the children are assisted where there is need. This is

---

[1574] Catholic Bishops of Gulu Archdiocese, Nebbi, Arua, and Lira, 61

[1575] Catholic Bishops of Uganda, *With a New Heart and a New Spirit*, 56.

[1576] Leopold, 6.

[1577] The Uganda Episcopal Conference, *Education Policy 1997* (Kampala; Marianum Press, Kisubi, 1997), 4-5 and 19.

[1578] Austin Flannery, ed., "Gravissimum Educationis: Declaration on Christian Education," in *Vatican Council II: The Conciliar and Postconciliar Documents* (Leominister, Herefords, England: Costello Publishing Company, 1981), 3-5, 728-731.

necessary because discontinuity in the formation process causes flaws in the education process and frustrates the efforts and enthusiasm of interested education agents.

Parents, teachers, and religious agents need to follow or apply such significant development principles as solidarity, participation, and more especially subsidiarity. They should recognize their need for one another. They each should do their part in formation. Where their counterparts are responsible and capable, they should avoid unnecessary interferences or transfer of responsibilities to other people. This means parents should not leave the burden of bringing up children entirely upon teachers or religious leaders and vice versa. Neither should the latter two think that their colleagues in formation should do it by themselves. The trio—teachers, parents, and religious agents—should not take over the burdens or responsibilities of the children when the latter are capable. As Bernard Haring and Valentino Salvoldi suggest, "In the family parents must educate their children not to have recourse to them when they can obtain by their own efforts a determined result."[1579] Parents should intervene to help their children only when it is absolutely necessary. Children should be given education for independent living rather than for dependence.

V. CONCLUSION

A number of conclusions may be drawn from the study in this chapter. First, one of the principal challenges to Uganda is that its successive leaders since independence have neglected—to a great degree—human dignity, human rights and human person, universal love, and justice as basic principles and virtues. These principles and virtues would supplement feasible strategies for developing the country as a unit. The leaders assended to power with divisive mentalities and prejudices. The people need to be helped to be sincerely, mutually intelligible and united in their view of life, and especially the crucial principles for true human development. These are as follows: the human person, human dignity, human rights, democracy, justice, participation, affirmative action, option for the poor, subsidiarity, common good, and ownership of property, charity, peace, and association.

Uganda needs a theology, sociology, economics, education, and politics of human development, which makes the dignity and the rights of the human

---

[1579] Haring and Salvoldi, 59.

person central and recognizes and acknowledges human dignity as *the most fundamental principle* for true human development.

The question addressed in this chapter was whether Uganda's development claims face the challenges of Paul VI's vision of human development. *Populorum Progressio's* challenges to Uganda are suggested by the claim that

> *Populorum Progressio* does not give a privileged position to the economic dimension of human development any more than to the cultural, psychological, political, ecological or religious dimensions. Rather it challenges Christians to take full account of the non-economic elements—for instance to recognize the value of different cultures and of basic human rights.[1580]

Paul VI was cautious about limiting the number of criteria for true human development. He advanced the thoughts of Lebret to clarify his point of view. They are thoughts that question development claims, including that of Uganda.

> Growth expressed in terms of increased national income per inhabitant can disguise an increase in the incomes of the rich and a corresponding impoverishment and regression in the incomes of the poor.[1581]

The challenge and concern of Lebret and Paul VI is that development should be judged from different perspectives. Imbalances in the distribution of resources and the growing gap between the rich and the poor are indicators of lack of true development. He suggested that "the greatest evil in the world is not the poverty of those who are deprived, but the lack of concern on the part of those who are well off."[1582] Balanced distribution of resources is consequent to love, care, or concern for the needs of all regardless of tribe, socioeconomic and political status, cultural background, and political or religious affiliation. From the study in this chapter, this is the very opposite of the status quo in

---

[1580] Dorr, 182.

[1581] Louis Joseph Lebret, *The Last Revolution: The Destiny of Over- and Underdeveloped Nations*, trans. John Horgan (New York: Sheed and Ward, 1965), 150. Also see *Populorum Progressio,* 8, 4.

[1582] Ibid, 204. Also cfr. *Populorum Progressio,* 66, 28 and 9, 4-5.

Uganda where there is inadequate psychological, social, cultural, political, economic, and spiritual human development, properly called integral human development.[1583] A further challenge to Uganda is that

> progress or development takes place when freedoms can find their expression in institutions, norms of exchange, patterns of social organizations, educational efforts, relations of productions and political choices which enhance the human potential. What is ultimately sought are basic conditions under which all persons may fulfill themselves as individuals and as members of multiple communities.[1584]

Common good, freedom, education, harmonious social relations, mutual respect, and relevant or democratic political systems are indicators of real development. The Ugandan context does not adequately provide for the requisite conditions that facilitate the enhancement of the lives of individuals as well as communities. It is such a state of affairs that the central aspects of *Populorum Progressio* challenge.

Paul VI was concerned about the development of the entire person— spiritually, economically, culturally, politically, psychologically, and socially— and of all people in a similar fashion. The development of all is also the responsibility of all. According to him, true development is realized in a spirit of solidarity and participation, which are not so much the Ugandan spirit as the study in this chapter shows. This assertion was emphasized in Paul VI's claim:

> But each man is a member of society and therefore belongs to the entire community of men. Consequently not merely this or that man, but all without exception are called to promote the full development of the whole human society.[1585]

[1583] Aidan Southall, "Isolation and Underdevelopment: Periphery and Centre," in *Developing Uganda*, eds. Holger Bernt Hansen and Michael Twaddle (Kampala: Fountain Publishers, 1998), 254.

[1584] Denis Goulet, *A New Moral Order: Studies in Development Ethics and Liberation Theology* (Maryknoll, New York: Orbis Books, 1974), 40.

[1585] *Populorum Progressio*, 17, 8. Paul VI made this point clear right from the opening section of the document, stating, "We earnestly exhort all men today to strive

The statement evinces that the human person is a social being. It is also an evidence of the crucial need for a right understanding of the human person and human responsibility. The fact that there is always an intimate relation between persons remains challenging to Ugandans.

In the context of integral human development, such a claim challenges the practice of dependence, segregation, discrimination, tribalism, regionalism, and division, which are some of the characteristic problems of Uganda.[1586] These practices suggest a misguided understanding of the human person, an understanding which radically differentiates one person from another and, consequently, leads to a misconception of human dignity and human rights. They also explain why one of the core problems of Uganda, a challenge of *Populorum Progressio,* is insufficient respect for the human person, dignity and rights. At the heart of the document is "the concern for the human person and all people."[1587] All the arguments and principles of the document suggest this assertion or gravitate toward it.

The study in this chapter attempted to demonstrate that the practical application of the doctrine of *Populorum Progressio,* to a great extent, is questionable in the case of Uganda. The document calls for an acknowledgement and respect for the value of human life—the dignity and the rights of the human person. The principles, virtues, and conditions that enhance the human person and dignity are necessary for the promotion of the human person as Paul VI advocated in the document. The major concern of this chapter was to establish that he status quo in Uganda does not, to a great extent, reflect the doctrine of Paul VI in *Populorum Progressio* because Uganda condones attitudes, practices, and behaviors inconsonant with the teaching of the document and many of the prevailing attitudes, practices, and conduct in Uganda are counterproductive to complete human development.

---

by united planning and joint action for the full development of each individual and the common progress of all mankind," 5, 3.

[1586] Whyte and Whyte, 12. Also see Regan, 161, and Mari Aili Tripp, "Local Women's Association and Politics in Contemporary Uganda," in *Developing Uganda*, eds. Holger Bernt Hansen and Michael Twaddle (Kampala: Fountain Publishers, 1998), 120.

[1587] *Populorum Progressio,* 1, 1-2; 5-6, 3; 14-17,7-9; 20-23,9-11; 28,13; 30,13; 32,14; 36-37,16; 39,17; 42,18; 48,20-21; 50,21; 64-65,27, and 71,29. Also see Henriot, 219. Henriot argues that integral human development is anywhere and everywhere. This suggests that uneven development as in Uganda is not any close to being called integral human development.

GENERAL CONCLUSION

In this study, the forces that influenced Pope Paul VI's vision of true human development, which he called integral human development, the development principles in *Populorum Progressio* were outlined, interpreted, and applied to the context of development in Uganda. The overarching conclusion from the study and application of the principles is that the development claims of Uganda do not meet the standard of development advocated by Paul VI in *Populorum Progressio*. This conclusion is based on an anthropology relevant for integral human development—precisely, a critical notion of the human person and human rights, and an understanding of and respect for human dignity. Such an anthropological vision implies what Denis Goulet calls ethical rationality which, he suggests,

> takes as its goal the creation, nurture, or defense of certain values considered worthy for their own sake—freedom, justice, the inviolability of persons, the "right" of each to a livelihood, dignity, truth, peace, community, friendship, or love.[1588]

I suggested in the study that, in the context of Uganda, education for development is imperative for attaining integral or authentic human development. The scope and challenge of education about human dignity and moral principles is that it must respect and promote human dignity. This

---

[1588] Denis Goulet, *Incentives for Development: The Key to Equity* (New York: New Horizon Press, 1989), 150-151. Values are considered more important than practical results because what matters is whether actions are right or wrong or if they are just or unjust.

ought to be emphasized and accepted as one of the most crucial challenges of *Populorum Proressio* to Uganda. The doctrine of human development in the document is a perennial challenge to all individuals, groups or institutions, tribes, races, and nations.

The study grappled with a number of questions in the context of Uganda and Paul VI's vision of integral human development in *Populorum Progressio*. The principal question addressed in chapter one of the study was as follows: Why and how Paul VI conceived of development the way he did? The answer to this question is, his childhood experieces, encounters with people of different life experiences, and his international trips and professional experiences all shaped his understanding of human development as presented in *Populorum Progressio*.

In chapter two, I grappled with the problems Paul VI was addressing and attempting to resolve and what he suggested about true human development in *Populorum Progressio*. Precisely, I outlined such problems as poverty, avarice, inequality and injustice, cultural development, population explosion, nationalism, and racism or tribalism—all of which affect humankind. There was also a misconstrued notion of human development, which had gained ascendancy, and Paul VI thought should be reconstructed or corrected and replaced. Consequently, he suggested a notion of human development that considers everyone as the subject and object of development. He called this integral human development. It was this very notion, which I applied to Uganda's development claims to ascertain whether Uganda's development claims match the standards set by *Populorum Progressio*. To attain this kind of development, Paul VI suggested principles such as solidarity, the common good, right to private ownership of goods, universal charity, aid to the weak, and equity in trade relations. He proposed other development principles and conditions such as: peace, option for the poor, subsidiarity, affirmative action, association, and participation. He identified education as a necessary means for development. I used the principles to interpret the situation in Uganda and discovered that some attempts were made to apply them, but few attempts were successful and many principles for authentic human development have been violated.

In chapter three, I dealt with the core principle for integral human development, namely, human dignity as related to human person and human rights. Paul VI's teaching about integral human development and the principles for integral human development are relevant, but he presumed that the understanding of the human person, the value of human life, human dignity, and human rights did not need to be emphasized and related to other development principles. This argument was necessary and inevitable as suggested by Peter Henriot's reading of *Gaudium et Spes.*[1589] Paul VI mentioned and many times referred to human dignity, human rights, and the human person in *Populorum Progressio* but loosely or implicitly related them to other principles for integral human development in the said document.[1590]

The principles need to be explained, related, and emphasized because they are fundamental starting points for arguing for and developing an authentic understanding of integral human development.[1591] They are a means to a focused view and comprehension of integral human development and efforts toward its achievement. The importance of underscoring the understanding of the human person, rights, and dignity can never be emphasized too much because a relevant political, social, economic, and religious system is the one that provides "goods and services essential to a life of human dignity."[1592] Consequently, I contended that human dignity and a proper understanding of the human person and human rights is the foundation from which integral human development can be explained, understood, and achieved. However, human person, human dignity, and human rights need to be understood both individually and collectively. This is significant because

> To recognize the social nature of the human person is to recognize
> that human beings need one another in order to be what they

---

[1589] Peter J. Henriot, "Who Cares about Africa? Development Guidelines from the Church's Social Teaching," in *Catholic Social Thought and the New World Order: Building on One Hundred Years*, eds. Oliver Williams and John H. Houck (Notre Dame: University of Notre Dame Press, 1993), 211.

Also see Austin Flannery, ed., *"Gaudium et Spes,"* in *Vatican II Council: The Conciliar and Post-conciliar Documents* (London: Costello Publishing Company, 1981), 63, 968-970.

[1590] *Populorum Progressio,* 1,1-2; 5-6,3; 14-17,7-9; 20-23,9-11; 28,13; 30,13; 32,14; 36-37,16; 39,17; 42,18; 48, 20-21; 50, 21; 64-65, 27; and 71, 29.

[1591] Henriot, 211.

[1592] Charles Avila, *Ownership: Early Christian Teaching* (London: Sheed and Ward, 1983), 154.

are—human. Human life is not possible in isolation . . . . Human
development cannot take place apart from a human community.[1593]

This vision and similar notions situated the understanding of the human
person and integral development in the context of both the individual
and community. Development is, exclusive and inclusive, individual and
communal. In the study, I reiterated that the principles for integral human
development such as charity, justice and equity, participation or involvement,
common good, subsidiarity, solidarity, preferential option for the poor, and
peace as presented by Paul VI in *Populorum Progressio* should be explained
in relation to an appropriate understanding of the fundamental principles—
human person, human dignity, and human rights—without which they are
superficial and do not make much sense. This is a call where the real need for
an understanding of the human person or a relevant anthropology is necessary
for integral human development.

Since Paul VI's basic intention in *Populorum Progressio* was not,
fundamentally, to suggest an anthropology for development, a relevant
anthropology needed to be constructed from his frequent references to the
human person, human rights, and human dignity in *Populorum Progressio*.
The anthropology facilitates a practical application of his advocacy for integral
human development. The human person, human dignity, and human rights
were the center of my arguments against Uganda's development claims. All
other principles stated or implied in *Populorum Progressio* are necessary for
human development but human dignity is the de facto basic principle to
be recognized, underscored, understood, and acknowledged as *the genesis* of
integral human development. This is the monumental task and challenge of
Paul VI's teaching on integral human development in *Populorum Progressio*.

That the basis and focal point of all arguments in the work is human
dignity is evident and consistent from the first chapter to the last chapter. In
the study, I postulated that all arguments about integral human development
should protect or promote the human dignity of all people. Consequently,
on the basis of human dignity integral human development is consistently
and emphatically presented as the development of the entire individual and
of all individuals regardless of age, sex, socioeconomic and political status,
tribe, race, and color.

[1593] James P. Hanigan, *As I Have Loved You: The Challenge of Christian Ethics* (New
York and Mahwah: Paulist Press, 1986), 77.

In chapter four, the fundamental and recurrent issue I addressed was whether or not the development initiatives and efforts undertaken in Uganda respect, protect and enhance human life, the human person, and human dignity and rights. To some extent, certain government and church initiatives promote the human person and human dignity, but they do not reach the extent suggested by the notion of integral human development according to Paul VI's doctrine in *Populorum Progressio*. I showed in chapter four that the teaching of *Populorum Progressio* regarding integral human development is relevant and offers enduring pertinent challenges in the Ugandan context. I applied the principles in the document to the context of Uganda. A conclusion from the application of the principles yielded the suggestion that the development claims of Uganda do not meet the standards of development advocated by Paul VI in *Populorum Progressio*. This conclusion is based on the understanding and respect for human dignity—the overriding human development principle in *Populorum Progressio* and any Catholic social doctrine. The most fundamental principle for integral human development is human dignity, but the most fundamental factor is the practical education about human dignity and all other development principles.

In the study, I made suggestions for the context of Uganda. Education about human dignity and moral principles that respect and promote human dignity is, among other suggestions, to be emphasized and accepted as the most crucial challenge if Uganda is to measure up to the doctrine of human development in *Populorum Proressio*. The challenge of the document is, however, a perennial challenge to all individuals, groups or institutions, tribes, races, and nations.

The document is current, relevant, and challenging to the *status quo* in Uganda. The notion of integral human development presented in *Populorum Progressio* and its application to Uganda showed the challenges of the document to the context of Uganda. The prevailing situation in Uganda guarantees the need for implementation of the teaching of the document to interpret and confront the social, political, economic, and religious structures or systems in the country.

Paul VI provided excellent principles for integral human development and appealed to the altruism of the agents of development. The wealthy nations have the liberty to support the poor nations. I have argued in the study that in the Ugandan context, the most crucial and effective action is relevant and effective education and empowerment of smaller groups and individuals in addition to the responsible actions of top administrators and managers of institutions and structures. As Louis Joseph Lebret argued, development is a simultaneous responsibility and action of individuals, those at the grassroots, and those in the topmost administration and management of institutions and structures.[1594]

Institutions and structures that can counteract or combat prevalent evils need to be created, well established, and supported. The operation of existing structures should be improved. This demands that both individuals and groups are conscientized about their mutual rights and responsibilities. Conscientization contributes to creativity and enables people to raise appropriate questions in the proper context—those in charge of institutions and structures. Educational programs and systems are crucial in this effort. All of these need careful research and planning, which is possible only with relevant education. As Denis Goulet contends, development process demands a clearly articulated plan in terms of goals, analysis of development process, comprehensive guidelines for the various sciences, and a coherent theoretical framework.[1595] This is a process that demands more than a fickle, shallow, and irrelevant education. The needed education ought to be centered on the human person—a challenge to individuals, the church, and the state. The church, the state, and individuals are a failure if they cannot defend and protect the human person, human dignity, and human rights. Both institutions and individual members belonging to them are for the good of the human person.

Finally, it is important to note that the notion of integral human development presented in *Populorum Progressio* sets extremely high standards of the notion of human development. It is the litmus test for authentic human development. Any claims of development, even by the most developed countries, fail to measure up in terms of reaching the standards set in *Populorum Progressio* because each society has elements of the abuse of the human person, human rights, and the human dignity. However, this does not mean that the document is *utopian*, nor does it excuse continued efforts to work for the integral development of all people. The standard is an enduring challenge to individuals, peoples, groups and nations to, ever faithfully, try to strive to do better in developing themselves and others. The standard of development advocated in *Populorum Progressio* will always stand in strong

---

[1594] Louis Joseph Lebret, *The Last Revolution: The Destiny of Over- and Underdeveloped Nations*, trans. John Horgan (New York: Sheed and Ward, 1965), 211.

[1595] Denis Goulet, *A New Moral Order: Studies in Development Ethics and Liberation Theology* (Maryknoll, New York: Orbis Books, 1974), 18-19.

opposition to development claims, and it will be judged and challenged, only by whether people have become *more human beings* and *less nonhuman beings* than ever before—whether there is a "qualitative human enrichment"[1596] or not. This is a challenge to governments, religious institutions, any human society or grouping, and to both those who have adequate material possessions and those who do not.

[1596] Denis Goulet, *Development Ethics: A Guide to Theory and Practice*, 6-7.

BIBLIOGRAPHY

Allsop, Michael. "Principle of Subsidiarity." In *The New Dictionary of Catholic Social Thought*. Ed. Judith A. Dwyer. Collegeville, Minnesota: Liturgical Press, 1994 (927-929).

Almade, D. Frank. *Just Wages for Church Employees*. New York: Peter Lang, 1993.

Amaza, Ori Ondoga. *Museveni's Long March: From Guerrilla to Statesman*. Kampala: Fountain Publishers, 1998.

Ammicht-Quinn, Regina. "Whose Dignity is Inviolable? Human Beings, Machines and the Discourse of Dignity." In *The Discourse of Human Dignity, Concilium*. Trans. John Bowden. London: SCM Press, 2003/2 (35-45).

Anderson, Ray S. *On Being Human: Essays in Theological Anthropology*. Grand Rapids: William B. Eerdmans Publishing Company, 1982.

Aristotle. *Nicomachean Ethics*. Trans. Terence Irwin. Indianapolis/Cambridge: Hackett Publishing Company, 1985.

Aquinas, Thomas. *Summa Theologiae: A Concise Translation*. Ed. Timothy McDermott. Allen, Texas: Christian Classics, 1991.

Audi, Robert and Nicholas Wolterstorff. *Religion in the Public Square: The Place of Religious Convictions in Political Debate*. Lanham: Rowman and Littlefield Publishers, Inc., 1997.

Avila, Charles. *Ownership: Early Christian Teaching*. Maryknoll, New York: Orbis Books, 1983.

Ayittey, B. N. George. *Africa in Chaos*, New York: St. Martin's Griffin, 1999.

___. *Africa Unchained: The Blue Print for Africa's Future*. New York: Palgrave Macmillan, 2005.

Babcock Gove. *Webster's Third New International Dictionary of English Language*. Unabridged, Springfield, Massachusetts: Meriam Webster Inc. Publishers, 1986.

Bagumisiriza, Narcisio. *The Kanungu Tragedy 17th March 2000 and Details of Related Discoveries: The Movement for the Restoration of the Ten Commandments of God*. Kisubi: Marianum Press, 2005.

Bailey, P. James. "Asset Development for the Poor." In *Journal of the Society of Christian Ethics*. 24, 1 (2004); 51-72.

Bainomugisha, Arthur. "The Empowerment of Women." In *Uganda's Age of Reforms: A Critical Overview*. Ed. Justus Mugaju. Kampala: Fountain Publishers, 1999 (89-102).

Barrett, William E. *Shepherd of Mankind: A Biography of Pope Paul VI*. Garden City, New York: Doubleday and Company, 1964.

Baum, Gregory. *The Social Imperative: Essays on Critical Issues that Confront Christian Churches*. New York: Paulist Press, 1979.

___. *Essays in Critical Theology*. Kansas City: Missouri: Sheed and Ward, 1994.

Behrend, Heike. "The Holy Spirit Movement's New World: Discourse and Developments in the North of Uganda." In *Developing Uganda*. Ed. Holger Hansen Bernt and Michael Twaddle. Kampala: Fountain Publishers, 1998 (245-253).

Benedictus PP. XVI. "Jesus at the Sight of the Crowds, was Moved with Pity (Mt.9: 36)": Message of Pope Benedict XVI for Lent 2006. In *Arua Diocese Bulletin*. No.69, Arua: Arua Diocese Communication Department, March 2006 (1-2).

Bigala, J.C.B. "The Church's Contribution to Education." In *Church Contribution to Integral Development*. Ed. Joseph Therese Agbasiere and Boniface K. Zabajungu. Eldoret, Kenya: AMECEA Gaba Publications, 1989 (167-178).

The Bishops of Africa. "Forgive Us Our Debts: Open Letter to Our Brother Bishops in Europe and America." In *The African Synod: Documents, Reflections, Perspectives*. Ed. Maura Browne. Maryknoll, New York: Orbis Books, 1996 (114-116).

Bohr, David. *A Catholic Moral Tradition: In Christ, A New Creation*. Huntington, Indiana: Our Sunday Visitor Publishing Division, 1990.

Bretzke, James T. *Consecrated Phrases: A Latin Theological Dictionary*. Second Edition. Collegeville, Minnesota: The Liturgical Press, 2003.

Bujo, Benezet. *The Ethical Dimension of Community: The African Model and the Dialogue between North and South*. Nairobi: Pauline Publications Africa, 1998.

____. *Foundations of an African Ethic: Beyond the Universal Claims of Western Morality*. Trans. Brian McNiel. New York: Crossroad Publishing Company, 2001.

Burns, H. Weston. "Human Rights." In *Human Rights in the World Community: Issues and Action*. Ed. Richard Pierre Claude and Burns H. Weston. Second Edition. Philadelphia: University of Pennsylvania Press, 1992 (14-18).

Bweyale Josephine. "The Christian Churches and the peace Building Process." In *Developing a Culture of Peace and Human Rights in Africa: African Peace Series*. Vol. One. Ed. R. K. Deusdedit Nkrunziza and Mugumya Levis. Kampala, Uganda: Konrad Adeenauer Stiftung (KAS), 2003 (57-72).

Cahill, Sowle Lisa. "The Global Common Good in the Twenty-First Century." In *Moral Theology: New Directions and Fundamental Issues, Festschrift for James P. Hanigan*. Ed. James Keating. New York/Mahwah, N.J.: Paulist Press, 2004 (233-251).

The Canon Law Society of Britain and Ireland. *The Code of Canon Law in English Translation*. London: Collins Liturgical Publications, 1983.

Catechism of the Catholic Church. Second Edition, Trans. United States Catholic Conference, Citta del Vaticana: Libreria Editrice Vaticana, 2000.

Catholic Bishops of Gulu Archdiocese, Nebbi, Arua and Lira. *Peace is Love: Pastoral Letter On the Occasion of the Great Jubilee*. Kisubi: Marianum Press, 2000.

Catholic Bishops of Uganda. *With A New Heart and A New Spirit*. Kisubi, Uganda: Marianum Press, 1986.

____. *Be Converted and Live: Pastoral Letter of the Uganda Catholic Hierachy*. Kisubi, Uganda: Marianum Press, 1981.

____. *Towards A Democratic and Peaceful Uganda Based on the Common Good*. Kisubi, Uganda: Marianum Press, November 2005.

Chemielewski, Philip J. "Affirmative Action." In *The New Dictionary of Catholic Social Thought*. Ed. Judith A. Dwyer. Collegeville, Minnesota: Liturgical Press, 1994 (12-16).

Clancy, John G. *Apostle for Our Time: Pope Paul VI*. New York: P. J. Kennedy and Sons, 1963.

Clifford, M. Anne. *Introducing Feminist Theology*. Maryknoll, New York: Orbis Books, 2001.

Committee for Economic Development, *How Low Income People can Advance their Own Growth: The Lessons of Experience*. New York: The Research and Policy Committee for Economic Development, 1966.

Congregation for the Doctrine of the Faith. *Instruction on Respect for Human Life in its Origin and on the Dignity of Procreation: Replies to certain Questions of the Day*. Rome, 1987.

Coombs, H. Philip and Manzoor Ahmed. *Attacking Poverty: How Non-formal Education can Help*. Ed. Barbara Baird Israel. Baltimore and London: John Hopkins University Press, 1974.

Cranston, Maurice. *What are Human Rights?*. New York: Basic Book, Inc, Publishers, 1962.

Cronin, Kieran. "Defining 'Group Rights'." In *Irish Theological Quarterly*. Co. Kildare, Ireland: Pontifical University, Maynooth, 2004, Vol. 69. No.2. (99-115).

Curran, Charles E. *Catholic Social Teaching, 1891—Present: A Historical, Theological and Ethical Analysis*. Washington, D.C.: Georgetown University Press, 2002.

Dalfavo, Albert T. "The Rise and Fall of Development: A Challenge to Culture." In *African Philosophy*. Vol.12, No.1, SAPINA, 1999 (37-49).

____. *Lugbara Proverbs*. Second Edition, Rome: Comboni Missionaries, 1990.

Davenport, W. Russel. *The Dignity of Man*. New York: Harper and Brothers, 1955.

Ddungu, K. Adrian, "Church State Cooperation in promoting integral Development—a Supplement." In *Church Contribution to Integral Development*. Ed. Joseph Therese Agbasiere and Boniface K. Zabajungu. Eldoret, Kenya: AMECEA Gaba Publications, 1989, 21-26.

Dicklich, Susan. "Indigenous NGOs and Political Participation. In *Developing Uganda*. Ed. Holger Bernt Hansen and Michael Twaddle. Kampala: Fountain Publishers, 1998 (145-158).

Diez-Alegria, Jose Maria. "Ownership and Labour: The Development of Papal Teaching." In *Concilium, Rerum Novarum: A Hundred Years of Catholic Social Teaching*. Ed. John Coleman and Gregory Baum. London: SCM Press, 1991(18-23).

Donnelly, Jack. *The Concept of Human Rights.* New York: St. Martin Press, 1985.

Dorr, Donal. "Solidarity and Integral Human Development." In *The Logic of Solidarity: Commentaries on John Paul II's Encyclical On Social Concern.* Ed. Gregory Baum and Robert Ellsberg. Maryknoll, New York: Orbis Books, 1989 (143-154).

____. *Option for the Poor: A Hundred Years of Catholic Social Teaching.* New York: Orbis Books, 1992.

Drandua, Frederick. *Let Me Live: A Cry of All Those Killed by a Neighbour, Under Whatever Circumstances.* Arua, Uganda, 25 November 1994.

Dussel, Enrique. "Dignity: Its Denial and Recognition in a Specific Context of Liberation. Trans. Paul Burns. In *The Discourse of Human Dignity, Concilium.* Ed. Regina Ammichht-Quinn et al. London: SCM Press, 2003/2 (93-104).

E.L., Henry. "Government." In *New Catholic Encyclopedia*, Second Edition, Vol.6, New York: Gale, 2003, (375-377).

Evans, Robert A. *Human Rights: A Dialogue Between the First and Third Worlds.* Ed. Robert A. Evans and Alice Frazer Evans. New York: Lutherworth Press, 1983.

Everson, Stephen. Ed. *Cambridge Texts in the History of Political Thought, Aristotle, The Politics.* Cambridge: Cambridge University Press, 1988.

The Executive, Association of the Major Superiors of Religious Institutes in Uganda. "Live by the Truth and the Truth will set You Free." In *Arua Diocese Bulletin.* No. 68, Arua: Arua Diocese Communication Department, February 2006, (7).

Falconer, D. Alan. "Right, Human." In *The New Dictionary of Theology.* Ed. Joseph A. Komonchak, et al. Wilmington, Delaware: Michael Glazier, 1987 (899-904).

Ferguson, David. *Community, Liberalism and Christian Ethics.* Cambridge: Cambridge University Press, 1998.

Ferguson P. Thomas. *Catholic and American: The Political Theology of John Courtney Murray.* Kansas City, Missouri: Sheed and Ward,1993.

Fichtner, Joseph. *Theological Anthropology: The Science of Man in his Relation to God.* Notre Dame: University of Notre Dame Press, 1963.

Filochowski Julian. "Looking Out to the World's Poor: Teachings of Paul VI." In *The New Politics: Catholic Social Teaching for the Twenty-First Century.* Ed. Paul Valley. London: SCM Press, 1998.

Flannery, Austin, Ed. "*Gaudium et Spes*: Pastoral Constitution on the Church in the Modern World." In *Vatican Council II: The Conciliar and Postconciliar Documents.* Leominister, Herefords, England: Costello Publishing Company, 1981 (903-1014).

____. "*Dignitatis Humanae*: Declaration on Religious Liberty." In *Vatican Council II: The Conciliar and Postconciliar Documents.* Leominister, Herefords, England: Costello Publishing Company, 1981 (799-812).

____. "*Gravissimum Educationis*: Declaration on Christian Education." In *Vatican Council II: The Conciliar and Postconciliar Documents.* Leominister, Herefords, England: Costello Publishing Company, 1981 (725-737).

____. "*Opotatam Totius*: Decree on the Training of Priests." In *Vatican Council II: The Conciliar and Postconciliar Documents.* Leominister, Herefords, England: Costello Publishing Company, 1981 (707-724).

Fuchs, Josef. Trans. Brien McNeil. *Moral Demands and Personal Obligations.* Washington, D C: Georgetown University Press, 1993.

Funk and Wagnalls. *The Readers Digest Great Encyclopedic Dictionary.* Funk and Wagnalls Publishing, 1975.

Garvey W. James. *St. Paul Cathedral Parish: The Early Years, 1834-1903.* Houston, Pennsylvania: J. Pohl Associates, 2005.

The German Bishops. *A Just Peace.* Bonn: Sekretariat der Deutschen Bischofskonferenz, 27 September 2000.

Gifford, Paul. *African Christianity: Its Public Role*. Bloomington, Indiana: Indiana University Press, 1998.

Glendon, Mary Ann. "'Absolute' Rights: Property and Privacy." In *The Essential Communitarian Reader*. Ed. Amitai Etzioni. Lanham: Rowman and Littlefield Publishers, 1998 (107-114).

Goulet, Denis. *A New Moral Order: Studies in Development Ethics and Liberation Theology*. Maryknoll, New York: Orbis Books, 1974.

____. "The Search for Authentic Development." *In The Logic of Solidarity: Commentaries on John Paul II's Encyclical On Social Concern*. Ed. Gregory Baum and Robert Ellsberg. Maryknoll, New York: Orbis Books, 1989 (127-142).

____. *Incentives for Development: The Key to Equity*. New York: New Horizon Press, 1989.

____. *Development Ethics: A Guide to Theory and Practice*. New York: The Apex Press, 1995.

Government of Uganda. *The Constitution of the Republic of Uganda*, Entebbe: Uganda Printing and Publishing Corporation, 22nd September 1995.

Granfield, P. "Paul VI, Pope." In *New Catholic Encyclopedia*. Second Edition. Volume 11. Washington, D C: The Catholic University of America, 2003 (26-33).

Greancy, D. Michael. "Charity or Justice: Where is the Hope of the Poor?." In *Curing World Poverty: The New Role of Property*. Ed. John H. Miller. Saint Louis, Missouri: Social Justice Institute Review, 1994 (51-60).

Gregg, Samuel. *Economic Thinking for the Theologically Minded*. University Press of America. Oxford/ New York; Lanham, 2001.

Gudorf, Christine E. *Catholic Social Teaching on Liberation Themes*. Washington, D C: University of America, 1981.

Guitton, Jean. *The Pope Speaks: Dialogues of Paul VI with Jean Guitton*. Trans. Anne and Christopher Fremantle. New York: Meredith Press, 1968.

Habiger, Matthew. "Papal tradition on Distribution of Ownership." In *Curing World Poverty: The New Role of Property*. Ed. John H. Miller, Social Justice Review: Saint Louis, Missouri, 1994 (1-13).

Hanigan, James P. *As I Have Loved You: The Challenge of Christian Ethics*. New York and Mahwah: Paulist Press, 1986.

_____. *Martin Luther King, Jr. and the Foundations of Nonviolence*. Lanham, MD/London, England: University Press of America, Inc. 1984.

Haring, Bernard and Valentino Salvoldi. *Tolerance: Towards an Ethic of Solidarity and Peace*. Trans. Edmund C. Lane, New York: Alba House, 1995.

Harrison, E. Lawrence. *Underdevelopment is a State of Mind: The Latin American Case*. Lanham: The International Affairs, Harvard University and Madison Books, 1988.

Harrison, M. Stanley. "Charles S. Peirce: Reflections on Being a Man-Sign." In *The Human Person*. Vol. LIII. Ed. George F. McLean. Washington, DC: The American Catholic Philosophical Association, 1979 (98-106).

Harper Collins *German-English Dictionary*. New York: Harper Collins Publishing Company, 1989.

Hatch, Alden. *Pope Paul VI*. New York: Random House, 1966.

Hebblethwaite, Peter. *Paul VI: The First Modern Pope*. New York: Paulist Press, 1993.

Hefner, Philip. "*Imago Dei*: The Possibility and Necessity of the Human Person." In *The Human Person in Science and Theology*. Ed. Niels Henrik Gregersen, et al. William B. Eerdmans Publishing Company, Grand Rapids, Michigan, 20009 (73-94).

Hehir, Bryan J. "Human Rights and U.S. Foreign Policy: A Perspective from Theological Ethics." In *The Moral Imperatives of Human Rights: A World Survey*. Ed. Kenneth W. Thompson. Washington, D C: University Press of America, 1980 (1-23).

Heike, Behrend. "The Holy Spirit Movement's New World: Discourse and Developments in the North of Uganda." In *Developing Uganda*. Ed. Bernt, Holger Hansen and Michael Twaddle, Kampala: Fountain Publishers, 1998 (245-253).

Hellwig, K. Monika. "Charity." In the *Modern Catholic Encyclopedia*. Ed. Michael Glazier and Hellwig K. Monika. Collegeville, Minnesota: The Liturgical Press, 1994 (159-161).

Hembrow, Mary Snyder. "Development." In *The New Dictionary of Catholic Social Thought*. Ed. Judith A. Dwyer. Collegeville, Minnesota: Liturgical Press, 1994 (278-282).

Hennelly, T. Alfred. "*Populorum Progressio*." In *The New Dictionary of Catholic Social Thought*. Ed. Judith A. Dwyer. Collegeville, Minnesota: Liturgical Press, 1994 (762-770).

Henriot, Peter J. "Who Cares About Africa? Development Guidelines from the Church's Social Teaching." In *Catholic Social Thought and the New World Order*. Ed. Oliver F. Williams and John W. Houck. Notre Dame. University of Notre Dame Press, 1993 (201-243).

Henriot, Peter J, et al., *Catholic Social Teaching: Our Best Kept Secret*. Maryknoll, New York: Orbis Books, 1988.

Higgins, George G. "Preface." In Lebret, L. J. (Louis Joseph). *The Last Revolution: The Destiny of Over-and Underdeveloped Nations*. Trans. John Horgan. New York: Sheed and Ward, 1965 (v-viii).

von Hilderbrand, Dietrich. *The Encyclical Humanae Vitae: A Sign of Contradiction, An Essay on Birth Control and Catholic Conscience*. Chicago: Franciscan Press, 1969.

Hollenbach, David. *Claims in Conflict: Retrieving and Renewing the Catholic Human Rights Tradition*. New York: Paulist Press, 1979.

____. "Common Good." In *The New Dictionary of Catholic Social Thought*. Ed. Judith A. Dwyer. Collegeville, Minnesota: Liturgical Press, 1994 (192-197).

International Bank for Development, *The First Five Year Development Plan, 1961/62-1965/66*. Entebbe, Uganda: Uganda Government, 1961.

International Bank for Reconstruction and Development, *The Economic Development of Uganda*. Baltimore: John Hopkins Press, 1962.

International Theological Commission. *Proposition on the Dignity and Rights of Human Person*. Washington, D C: United States Catholic Conference, 1986.

Jamal, Vali. "Changes in Poverty Patterns in Uganda." In *Developing Uganda*. Ed. Holger Hansen Bernt and Michael Twaddle. Kampala: Fountain Publishers, 1998 (73-97).

John XXII. *Mater et Magistra: Christianity and Social Progress*. Washington, D C: National Catholic Welfare Conference, 1961.

____. *Pacem in Terris: Peace on Earth*. Washington, D C: National Catholic Welfare Conference, 1963.

John Paul II. *Sollicitudo Rei Sociallis: On the Social Concerns*. Boston: Pauline Books and Media, 1987.

____. *"Solicitudo Rei Socialis*: On Social Concern" in *The Logic of Solidarity: Commentaries on John Paul II's Encyclical On Social Concern*. New York: Orbis Books, Maryknoll, 1989 (1-62).

____. *Laborem Exercens: On Human Work*. Washington, D C: United States Catholic Conference, 1981.

____. *Evangelium Vitae: The Gospel of Life* (On the Value and the Inviolability of Human Life). Washington, D C: United States Catholic Conference, 1995.

Kabwegere, Tarsis Bazana. *People's Choice People's Planner: Challenges and Prospects of Democracy in Uganda*. Kampala: Fountain Publishers, 2000.

_____. *The Politics of State Formation and Destruction in Uganda*. Kampala: Fountain Publishers, 1995.

_____. "Politics of Democratisation." In *Uganda's Age of Reforms: A Critical Overview*. Ed. Justus Mugaju, Kampala: Fountain Publishers, 1999, (40-50).

Kabyanga, John Mary K. *Towards Integral Human development: To Be More rather than to Have More, The Contributions of Fr. Louis Joseph Lebret, O.P.* Wisconsin, Sparata: Prell Books, 2004.

Kakaire A. Kirunda, "Population growth may fail Development Goals" in *Daily Monitor*. Kampala, Uganda, September 21, 2006.

Kakoma, W. George and Peter Wyngard. "Uganda" in *National Anthems of the World*. Ed. T.M. Cartledge, et al. New York: Arco Publishing Company, Inc., 1978 (456).

Kakooza, Teresa. "Promotion of Adult Education for Women." In *Church Contribution to Integral Development*. Ed. Joseph Therese Agbasiere and Boniface K. Zabajungu. Eldoret, Kenya: AMECEA Gaba Publications, 1989 (183-191).

Kanyandago, Peter. "A Biblical Theology of the Rule of Law, and Due respect for Basic Human Rights." In *Church Contribution to Integral Development*. Ed. Joseph Therese Agbasiere and Boniface K. Zabajungu. Eldoret, Kenya: AMECEA Gaba Publications, 1989 (63-76).

Kassimir, Ronald. "Uganda: The Catholic church and State reconstruction." In *The African State at A Critical Juncture: Between Disintegration and Reconfiguration*. Ed. Leonardo A. Villalon and Philip A. Huxtable. London: Lynne Rienner Publishers, 1998 (233-253).

Kasozi, A.B.K. *University Education in Uganda: Challenges and Opportunities for Reform*. Kampala: Fountain Publishers, 2003.

Kayonga, Anna Mary, "The Church's role in the Care of Orphans and Destitutes." In *Church Contribution to Integral Development*. Ed. Joseph Therese Agbasiere and Boniface K. Zabajungu (Eldoret, Kenya: AMECEA Gaba Publications, 1989, (213-223).

Kealy, P. Sean. *Jesus and Politics*. Minnesota, Collegeville: The Liturgical Press, 1990.

Kiapi, Abraham. "Church Defence of Rule of Law and Human Rights." In *Church Contribution to Integral Development*. Ed. Joseph Therese Agbasiere and Boniface K. Zabajungu. Eldoret, Kenya: AMECEA Gaba Publications, 1989 (77-96).

Kirumira, K. Edward. "Developing a Population Policy for Uganda." In *Developing Uganda*. Ed. Holger Hansen Bernt and Michael Twaddle. Kampala: Fountain Publishers, 1998 (185-193).

Kirunda, Kakaire A. "Population growth may fail Development Goals" in *Daily Monitor* Kampala, Uganda, September 21, 2006. Cfr. www.monitor.co.ug/news.

Klein, Ernest. *A Comprehensive Etymological Dictionary of the English Language*. Vol. 1, Amsterdam; Elsevier Publishing Company, 1966.

Kleissler, A. Thomas, et al. *Small Christian Communities: A Vision of Hope for the 21st Century*. New York: Paulist Press, 1997.

Krieg, Robert Anthony. *Karl Adam: Catholicism in German Culture*. Notre Dame: University of Notre Dame Press, 1992.

Krier, Marvin L. Mich. *Catholic Social Teaching and Movements*. Mystic, Connecticut: Twenty-Third Publications, 1998.

Kuczewski, Mark G. *Fragmentation and Consensus: Communitarian and Casuist Bioethics*. Washington, D C: Georgetown University Press, 1997.

Kurland, Norman G. "Economic Justice in the Age of Robot." In *Curing World Poverty: The New Role of Property*. Ed. John H. Miller, Social Justice Review: Saint Louis, Missouri, 1994 (61-74).

Kutu, Patrick. "The Rural Poor: Protagonists of Their Empowerment." In *The Poor Discover Their Own Resources: A Practical Approach to Poverty Reduction in Urban and Rural Areas in Africa*. Nairobi: Pauline Publications Africa, 2002, (27-37).

Lamb, L. Matthew. "Solidarity." In *The New Dictionary of Catholic Social Thought*. Ed. Judith A. Dwyer. Collegeville, Minnesota: Liturgical Press, 1994 (908-912).

Lebret, L. J. (Louis Joseph). *The Last Revolution: The Destiny of Over—and Underdeveloped Nations*. Trans. John Horgan. New York: Sheed and Ward, 1965.

Legesse, Asmarom. "Human Rights in African Political Culture." In *The Moral Imperatives of Human Rights: A World Survey*. Ed. Kenneth W. Thompson. Washington, D C: University Press of America, 1980 (123-138).

Leggett, Ian. *Uganda, the Background, the People, the Issues: An Oxfam Country Profile*. Kampala: Fountain Publishers, 2001.

Leo XIII. *Rerum Novarum: On the Condition of Labor* (Of the New Things). Washington, D C: National Catholic Welfare Conference, 1891.

Leopold, Mark. *Inside West Nile : Violence, History and Representation on an African Frontier*. Oxford: James Currey, 2005.

Lorentzen, Lois Ann. "*Gaudium et Spes*." In *The New Dictionary of Catholic Social Thought*. Ed. Judith A. Dwyer. Collegeville, Minnesota: Liturgical Press, 1994 (406-416).

Lyons, Maryinez. "Aids and Development in Uganda." In *Developing Uganda*. Ed. Holger Hansen Bernt and Michael Twaddle. Kampala: Fountain Publishers, 1998 (194-206).

Magesa, C. Laurenti. "Theology for Integral Human Development in Africa." In *Church Contribution to Integral Development*. Ed. Joseph Therese Agbasiere and Boniface K. Zabajungu. Eldoret, Kenya: AMECEA Gaba Publications, 1989 (113-123).

Maly H. Eugene. "Genesis" in *The Jerome Biblical Commentary*. Vol.1, Ed. Raymond E. Brown, et al. Englewood Cliffs, New Jersey: Prentice-Hall, Inc., 1968 (7-46).

Mamdani, Mahmood. *Politics and Class Formation in Uganda*. New York and London: Monthly Review Press, 1976.

_____. *When Victims Become Killers: Colonialism, Nativism, and the Genocide in Rwanda*. Princeton, New Jersey: Princeton University Press, 2001.

Maritain, Jacques. *The Person and the Common Good*. Trans. John J. Fitzgerald. Notre Dame, Indiana: University of Notre Dame Press, 2002.

Marcil-Lacoste, Louise. "Women as Persons." In *The Human Person*. Vol. LIII., Ed. George F. McLean. Washington, DC: The American Catholic Philosophical Association, 1979 (78-87).

Massaro, Thomas. *Catholic Social Teaching and the United States Welfare Reform*. Collegeville, Minnesota: The Liturgical Press, 1998.

Mazrui, A. Ali. *Violence and Thought: Essays on Social Tensions in Africa*. New York: Humanities Press, 1969.

_____. *Political Values and the Educated Class in Africa*. Berkeley and Los Angeles: University of California Press, 1978.

Mbefo, Luke Nnamdi. *The True African: Impulses for Self-Affirmation*. Onitsha: Spiritan Publications, 2001.

Mbiti, John S. *African Religions and Philosophy*. New York: Frederick A. Praeger Publishers, 1969.

McBrien, P. Richard. "An Ecclesiological Analysis of Catholic Social Teachings." In *Catholic Social Thought and the New World Order: Building on One Hundred Years*. Ed. Oliver F. Williams and John W. Houck. Notre Dame: University of Notre Dame Press, 1993 (147-177).

McBrien, P. Richard *et al.* (Eds). "*Populorum Progressio.*" In *Harper Collins Encyclopedia of Catholicism.* San Francisco: Harper Collins Publishers, Inc., 1989 (1033).

McCarthy, M. David. "Procreation, the Development of Peoples, and the Final Destiny of Humanity." In *Communio: International Catholic Review.* 26, Winter 1999 (698-721).

____. "Love in Fundamental Moral Theology." In *Moral Theology: New Directions and Fundamental Issues, Festschrift for James P. Hanigan.* Ed. James Keating. New York/Mahwah, N.J.: Paulist Press, 2004 (181-206).

McKenna, Kevin E. *A Concise Guide to Catholic Social Teaching,* Notre Dame, Indiana: Ave Maria Press, 2002.

McKnight, Tom. (Gen.Ed.). *Graphica: The Complete Illustrated Atlas of the World.* New York: Barnes and Noble Books, 2004.

Merkle, Judith A. *From the Heart of the Church: The Catholic Social Tradition.* Collegeville, Minnesota: Liturgical Press, 2004.

Middleton, John. *Lugbara Religion: Ritual and Authority Among an East African People.* London: Oxford University Press, 1960.

____. *The Lugbara of Uganda.* New York: Holt, Rinehart and Winston, 1964.

Ministry of Finance, Planning and Economic Development. *Poverty Eradication Action Plan (2000-2003).* Volume 1, Kampala, February 2001.

Morsink, Johannes. *The Universal Declaratiuon of Human Rights: Origins, Drafting, and Intent.* Philadelphia: University of Pennsylvania Press, 1999.

Mother Teresa. "Planning Something Beautiful for God." In *Natural Family Planning: Nature's Way—God's Way.* Ed. Anthony Zimmerman et al. St. Cloud, Minnesota: De Rance, Inc., 1980 (2).

Mugaju, Justus. "The Historical Context." In *Uganda's Age of Reforms: A Critical Overview*. Ed. Justus Mugaju, Kampala: Fountain Publisher, 1999 (10-39).

Mugumya Levis. "Human Rights: An Insight into Uganda's Education Sector." In *Developing a Culture of Peace and Human Rights in Africa: African Peace Series*. Vol. One. Ed. Nkrunziza, R.K. Deusdedit and Mugumya Levis, Kampala, Uganda: Konrad Adeenauer Stiftung (KAS), 2003 (113-125).

Mugyeni, R. Mary. "Towards the Empowerment of Women: A Critique of NRM Policies and Programmes." In *Developing Uganda*. Ed. Holger Hansen Bernt and Michael Twaddle. Kampala: Fountain Publishers, 1998 (133-144).

Mulera, Muniini K. "Raise Teachers' Salaries." In *Daily Monitor*, Kampala, Uganda, Sunday April 30, 2006. Cfr. www.monitor.co.ug/news.

Munby, Denys. Ed. *World Development: Challenge to Churches*. Washington, DC and Cleveland, Ohio: Corpus Books, 1969.

Museveni, K. Yoweri. "The Relationship between Church and State." In *Church Contribution to Integral Development*. Ed. Joseph Therese Agbasiere and Boniface K. Zabajungu. Eldoret, Kenya: AMECEA Gaba Publications, 1989 (13-20).

Mutibwa, Phares. *Uganda Since Independence: A Story of Unfulfilled Hopes*. Kampala, Uganda: Fountain Puiblishers, 1992.

Nalugala, Reginald and Richard Mutua. "A Practical Approach to Empowerment of the Poor in Kenya." In *The Poor Discover Their Own Resources: A Practical Approach to Poverty Reduction in Urban and Rural Areas in Africa*. Nairobi: Pauline Publications, Africa, 2002, (9-27).

National Conference of Catholic Bishops. *The Challenge of Peace: God's Promise and Our Response*. Washington, D.C: United States Catholic Conference, May 3, 1983.

____. *Economic Justice for All: Pastoral Letter on Catholic Social Teaching and the U.S. Economy.* Washington, D.C, 1986.

The New Jerusalem Bible, New York: Doubleday, 1985.

The New International Webster's Quick Reference Our Nation Notebook: U.S. Presidents, U.S. States, Declaration of Independence, Constitution of the United States, Government of the United States, Executive Agencies, Magna Carta and Other Documents of Freedom. United States: Trident Press International, 2002.

Ngologoza, Paul. *Kigezi and its People.* Kampala: Fountain Publishers, 1998.

Niebuhr, Reinhold. *Moral Man and Immoral Society: A Study in Ethics and Politics.* (Introduction by Langdon B. Gilkey) Louisville, Kentucky: Westminister John Knox Press, 2001.

Nzita, Richard and Mbaga-Niwampa. *Peoples and Cultures of Uganda.* Kampala: Fountain Publishers, 1997.

Nkrunziza, R.K. Deusdedit. "The Role of Civil Society in Peace Building: The Case of Uganda." In *Developing a Culture of Peace and Human Rights in Africa: African Peace Series.* Vol. One. Ed. Nkrunziza, R.K. Deusdedit and Mugumya Levis, Kampala, Uganda: Konrad Adeenauer Stiftung (KAS), 2003 (23-33).

____. *Bantu Philosophy of Life in the Light of the Christian Message: A Basis for African Vitalistic Theology.* Frankfurt am Main: Peter Lang, 1989.

Novak, Michael. *Free Persons and the Common Good.* New York: Madison Books, 1989.

____. *Catholic Social Thought and Liberal Institutions: Freedom with Justice.* Second Edition. New Brunswick (U.S.A.) and Oxford (U.K.): Transaction Publishers, 1989.

____. "Human Dignity, Human Rights." In *First Things.* No. 97, New York: Institute on Religion and Public Life, November 1999 (39-42).

Novelli, Bruno. "Church and Development for Nomads." In *Church Contribution to Integral Development*. Ed. Joseph Therese Agbasiere and Boniface K. Zabajungu. Eldoret, Kenya: AMECEA Gaba Publications, 1989. (143-153).

O'Brien, David J. and Thomas A. Shannon. Ed. *Catholic Social Thought: The Documentary Heritage*. Maryknoll, New York: Orbis Books, 2001.

O'Collins, Gerald and Edward, G. Farugia. *A Concise Dictionary of Theology*. Revised and Expanded Edition. New York: Paulist Press, 2000.

O'Connell, Timothy E. *Principles for a Catholic Morality*. New York: Seabury Press, 1978.

Odama, John Baptist. *I Have Seen the Humiliation of My People and Heard their Cry (Ex.3:7)*. Gulu, Uganda, 29th June 2003.

Oketch, Martin Luther. "Uganda Is Not a Medium Income Country." *Daily Monitor*. Kampala, Uganda, Thursday, February 2, 2006 (22aa). Cfr. www.monitor.co.ug/news.

Okot, Oburu Vincent. "The Church's role in Promoting National Unity." In *Church Contribution to Integral Development*. Ed. Joseph Therese Agbasiere and Boniface K. Kabajungu. Eldoret, Kenya: AMECEA Gaba Publications, 1989. (97-112).

O'Neill, William. "Private Property." In *The New Dictionary of Catholic Social Thought*. Ed. Judith A. Dwyer. Collegeville, Minnesota: Liturgical Press, 1994 (785-790).

Onions, C.T. et al. *The Oxford Dictionary of English Etymology*. London; Oxford University Press, 1966.

Oxford World Encyclopedic World Atlas, 6th Edition, New York: Oxford University Press, Inc., 2002.

Paul VI, Pope. *Populorum Progressio: On the Development of Peoples*. Washington, D C: United States Catholic Conference, 1967.

____. *On the Regulation of Birth: Humanae Vitae*. Rome, July 25, 1968.

____. *Octogesima Adveniens: A Call to Action* (On the Eightieth Anniversary of *Rerum Novarum*). Washington, DC: United States Catholic Conference, 1971.

____. *Evangelii Nuntiandi: On Evangelization in the Modern World*. Boston: Pauline Books and Media, 1975.

Perry, Michael J. *The Idea of Human Rights: Four Inquiries*. Oxford: Oxford University Press, 1998.

Pfaff, Franz. "People's Participation in Development." In *Church Contribution to Integral Development*. Ed. Joseph Therese Agbasiere and Boniface K. Zabajungu. Eldoret, Kenya: AMECEA Gaba Publications, 1989 (154-166).

Pius XI. *Quadragesimo Anno: On Reconstructing the Social Order*, Forty Years Later, On the Fortieth Anniversary of *Rerum Novarum*. Chicago, Illinois: Outline Press, 1931.

Pontifical Council for Justice and Peace. (Libreria Editrice) Vaticana. *Compendium of the Social Doctrine of the Church*. Washington, D C: United States Conference of Catholic Bishops, 2005.

Rawls, John. *A Theory of Justice*. Revised Edition. Cambridge, Massachusetts: The Belknap Press of Harvard University Press, 1999.

Regan, Anthony J. "Decentralization Policy: Reshaping State and Society." In *Developing Uganda*. Ed. Holger Hansen Bernt and Michael Twaddle. Kampala: Fountain Publishers, 1998 (159-175).

Reichmann, James B. *Philosophy of the Human Person*. Chicago: Loyola University Press, 1985.

Rhaner, Karl and Herbert Vorgrimler. *Theological Dictionary*. Ed. Cornelius Ernst. Trans. Richard Strachan. New York: Herder and Herder, 1968.

Riga, Peter J. *The Church of the Poor: A Commentary on Paul VI's Encyclical On The Development of Peoples*. Techny, Illinois: Divine Word Publications, 1968.

Roberts, J. Deotis. *Bonhoeffer and King: Speaking Truth to Power*. Louisville, Kentucky: Westminister John Knox Press, 2005.

The Rome Statement on the International Conference on Population and Development. (ICPD): Religion Counts. January 1999.

Rousseau, Richard W. *Human Dignity and the Common Good: The Great Papal Social Encyclicals from Leo XIII to John Paul II*. Westport, Connecticut: Greenwood Press, 2002.

Royal, Robert. "*Populorum Progressio* (1967)." In *A Century of Catholic Social Thought: Essays on Rerum Novarum and Nine Other Key Documents*. Ed. George Wiegel and Royal Robert, Washington, DC: Ethics and Public Policy Center, 1991 (115-130).

Rychner, Rose-Marie. "The Context and Background of Ugandan Art." In *Uganda: The Cultural Landscape*. Ed. Richard Breitinger, Kampala: Fountain Publishers, 2000 (263-274).

Sandel, J. Michael. *Liberalism and the Limits of Justice*. Cambridge: Cambridge University Press (1982) 8.

Schafers, Michael. "*Rerum Novarum*: The Result of Christian Social Movements 'From Below.'" In *Concilium, Rerum Novarum: A Hundred Years of Catholic Social Teaching*. Ed. John Coleman and Gregory Baum. London: SCM Press, 1991(3-17).

Schall, James V., ed. *Out of Justice, Peace: Joint Letter of the West Germany Bishops*, (April 18, 1983) and *Winning the Peace: Joint Pastoral Letter of the French Bishops*, (November 8, 1983), San Francisco: Ignatius Press, 1984.

Schockenhoff, Eberhard. *Natural Law and Human Dignity: Universal Ethics in an Historical World*. Trans. Brian McNeil. Washington, DC: The Catholic University of America Press, 2003.

Servitje, Sendra Lorenzo. "Reevaluating Private Enterprise." In *Curing World Poverty: The New Role of Property*. (Ed.) John H. Miller, Social Justice Review: Saint Louis, Missouri, 1994 (75-92).

Shipley, Joseph T. *Dictionary of Word Origins*. New York: Dorset Press, 1995.

Sigmund, Paul E. "Catholicism and Liberal Democracy." In *Catholic Social Thought and the New World Order: Building on One Hundred Years*. Ed. Oliver F. Williams and John W. Houck. Notre Dame: University of Notre Dame Press, 1993 (51-72).

Sirico Robert A. and Maciej Zieba. *The Social Agenda: A Collection of Magisterial Texts*. Citta del Vaticano: Pontifical Council for Justice and Peace, 2000.

Skeat, Walter W. *A Concise Etymological Dictionary of English Language*. New York: Capricon Books, 1963.

Smith, Herbert F. "The Proliferation of Population Problems." In *Why Humanae Vitae was Right: A Reader*. Ed. Janet E. Smith, San Francisco: Ignatius Press, 1993 (385-403).

Soifer Paul, et al. *Cliffs Quick Review American Government*. Cleveland, Ohio: Hungry Minds, 2001.

Southhall, Aidan. "Isolation and Underdevelopment: Periphery and Centre." In *Developing Uganda*. Ed. Holger Hansen Bernt and Michael Twaddle. Kampala: Fountain Publishers, 1998 (254-260).

Ssekamwa, J.C. and S.M.E. Lugumba. *A History of Education in East Africa*. Kampala: Fountain Publishers, 2001.

Synod of Bishops. Second General Assembly. *Justitia in Mundo: Justice in the World*. Rome, Vatican City: Pontifical Commission for Justice and Peace, 1971.

Tempels, Placide. *Bantu Philosophy*. Trans. Rubbens A. *Paris: Presence Africaine*, 1959.

Thompson, Gardner. *Governing Uganda: British Colonial Rule and its Legacy*. Kampala: Fountain Publishers, 2003.

Thompson, J. Milburn. *Justice and Peace: A Christian Primer*. Maryknoll, New York: Orbis Books, 1997.

Tibor, Machan. *Private Rights and Public Illusions*. New Brunswick/London: Transaction Publishers, 1995.

Tripp, Mari Aili. "Local Women's Association and Politics in Contemporary Uganda." In *Developing Uganda*. Ed. Holger Hansen Bernt and Michael Twaddle. Kampala: Fountain Publishers, 1998 (120-132).

——. "The Politics of Women's Rights and Cultural Diversity in Uganda." In *Gender, Justice, Development, and Rights*. Ed. Maxine Molyneux and Shahra Razavi Oxford: Oxford University Press, 2002 (413-440).

Tuyizere, Alice. "Introduction of Peace Education in Secondary Schools: A Strategy for Promotion of Peace in Uganda." In *Developing a Culture of Peace and Human Rights in Africa: African Peace Series*. Volume One. Ed. R. K. Deusdedit Nkrunziza and Mugumya Levis. Kampala, Uganda: Konrad Adeenauer Stiftung (KAS), 2003 (73-92).

Twaddle, Michael and Bernt Hogler Hansen. "The Changing State of Uganda." In *Developing Uganda*. Ed. Holger Hansen Bernt and Michael Twaddle. Kampala: Fountain Publishers, 1998 (1-17).

The Uganda Episcopal Conference. *Education Policy 1997*. Kampala: Kisubi, 1997.

USAID, *Democracy and Governance Assessment: Republic of Uganda, 2005*. Burlington, Vermont (USA): ARD, Inc., November 2005.

Uzukwu E. Elochuku *A Listening Church: Autonomy and Communion in African Churches*. New York: Orbis Books, Maryknoll, 1996.

Vacek, Edward Collins. "Charity." In *The New Dictionary of Catholic Social Thought*. Ed. Judith A. Dwyer. Collegeville, Minnesota: Liturgical Press, 1994 (143-143).

Valadier, Paul. "The Person Who Lacks Dignity." Trans. John Bowden. In *The Discourse of Human Dignity, Concilium.* Ed. Regina Ammichht-Quinn et al. London: SCM Press, 2003/2 (49-56).

Verspieren, Patrick. "Dignity in Political and Bioethical Debates." Trans. John Bowden. In *The Discourse of Human Dignity, Concilium.* Ed. Regina Ammichht-Quinn et al. London: SCM Press, 2003/2 (13-22).

Vitillo, Robert J., and Donna Toliver Grimes. (Ed.) *Principles, Prophecy, and a Pastoral Response: An Overview of Modern Catholic Social Teaching, Catholic Campaign for Human Development.* Revised Edition. Washington, DC: United States Conference of Catholic Bishops, 2001.

Walsh, Michael and Brian Davies, Ed. *Proclaiming Justice and Peace: Papal Documents from Rerum Novarum through Centesimus Annus.* Revised and Expanded Edition. Mystic, Connecticut: Twenty Third Publications, 1994.

Waluya, Gerald. "Government to Raise Teachers' Pay to Shs 200,000." In *Daily Monitor*, Kampala, Uganda, April 19, 2006. Cfr. www.monitor.co.ug/news.

Walzer, Michael. "The Communitarian Critique of Liberalism." In *Political Theory: An International Journal of Political Philosophy.* Ed. Tracy B. Strong, et al. Newbury Park, California: Sage Publications, Inc. Vol.18, No.1, February 1990 (6-23).

Warwick, Montgomery, John. *Human Rights and Human Dignity.* Grand Rapids: Michigan: Zondervan Publishing House, 1986.

Webster's New Universal Unabridged Dictionary. Second Edition, New York: Simon and Schuster, 1979.

Wermter, Oskar. *Politics for Everyone and by Everyone: A Christian Approach.* Nairobi: Pauline Publications, Africa, 2003.

Whitmore Todd David. "Catholic Social Teaching: Starting with the Common Good." In *Living the Catholic Social Tradition: Cases and Commentary.*

Ed. Kathleen Maas Weighert and Alexia K. Kelly. Lanham: Rowman and Littlefield Publishers, Inc., 2005 (59-85).

Whyte, Reynolds Susan and Michael A. Whyte. "The Values of Development: Conceiving Growth and Progress in Bunyole." In *Developing Uganda*. Ed. Bernt, Holger Hansen and Michael Twaddle. Kampala: Fountain Publishers, 1998 (227-244).

Williams, D. Thomas. *Who is My Neighbor?: Personalism and the Foundations of Human Rights*. Washington, DC: The Catholic University of America Press, 2005.

Williams, F. Oliver. "Catholic Social Teaching: A Communitarian Democratic Capitalism for New World Order." In *Catholic Social Thought and the New World Order: Building on One Hundred Years*. Ed. Oliver F. Williams and John W. Houck. Notre Dame: University of Notre Dame Press, 1993 (5-28).

Wojtyla, Karol Cardinal (John Paul II). *The Acting Person*. Trans. Andrezej Potocki. Dordrecht: D. Reidel Publishing Company, 1979.

World Bank. *World Development Report, 2004: Making Services Work for the Poor*. Washington, D C: World Bank and Oxford University Press, 2003.

World Bank. *World Development Report, 2000/2001: Attacking Poverty*. Oxford: Oxford University Press, 2000/2001.

World Bank. *World Development Report, 1994: Infrastructure for Development*. Oxford: Oxford University Press, 1994.

World Bank. *World Development Report, 2005: A Better Investment Climate for Everyone*. Oxford: Oxford University Press, 2005.

Woznicki, N. Andrew. "The Christian Humanism of Cardinal Karol Wojtyla." In *The Human Person*. Vol. LIII. Ed. George F. McLean. Washington, DC: The American Catholic Philosophical Association, 1979 (28-35).

Zagrzebski, Linda. "The Uniqueness of Persons." In *Journal of Religious Ethics*, Vol. 29. No.3 Washington, D C: Journal of Religious Ethics, Inc., 2001 (401-423).

Zimmerman, Anthony (The Coodinator). "Large Families, Child-Spacing, and When to Start NFP." In *Natural Family Planning: Nature's Way—God's Way*. Ed. Anthony Zimmerman et al. St. Cloud, Minnesota: De Rance, Inc., 1980 (77-80).